75 Readings

Plus

Tenth Edition

Santi V. Buscemi
Middlesex County College

Charlotte Smith
SUNY Adirondack

Mc
Graw
Hill

Connect
Learn
Succeed™

Tranqu Illy - Calm

cartoon my a Friends

75 READINGS PLUS, TENTH EDITION

Published by McGraw-Hill, a business unit of The McGraw-Hill Companies, Inc., 1221 Avenue of the Americas, New York, NY 10020. Copyright © 2013 by The McGraw-Hill Companies, Inc. All rights reserved. Previous editions © 2010, 2007, and 2004. Printed in the United States of America. No part of this publication may be reproduced or distributed in any form or by any means, or stored in a database or retrieval system, without the prior written consent of The McGraw-Hill Companies, Inc., including, but not limited to, in any network or other electronic storage or transmission, or broadcast for distance learning.

phase - gap

example - Constants

Some ancillaries, including electronic and print components, may not be available to customers outside the United States.

Sanctuary - a place of safety

5 6 7 8 9 10 DOC 21 20 19 18 17 16

ISBN 978-0-07-742644-6
MHID 0-07-742644-4

Vice President & Editor-in-Chief: *Michael Ryan*
Vice President of Specialized Publishing: *Janice M. Roerig-Blong*
Publisher: *David Patterson*
Sponsoring Editor: *Debra B. Hash*
Marketing Manager: *Kevin Colleary*
Project Manager: *Melissa Leick*
Design Coordinator: *Margarite Reynolds*
Cover Designer: *Studio Montage, St. Louis, Missouri*
Cover Image Credit: *Tinke Hamming/Ingram Publishing*
Buyer: *Susan K. Culbertson*
Media Project Manager: *Sridevi Palani*
Compositor: *MPS Limited, a Macmillan Company*
Typeface: 10/12 *Palatino*
Printer: *R.R. Donnelley*

Library of Congress Cataloging-in-Publication Data

75 readings plus / [edited by] Santi V. Buscemi, Charlotte Smith. — 10th ed.
    p. cm.
Includes bibliographical references and index.
ISBN 978-0-07-742644-6 (acid-free paper)
1. College readers. 2. English language—Rhetoric—Problems, exercises, etc. 3. Report writing—Problems, exercises, etc. I. Buscemi, Santi V. II. Smith, Charlotte, 1957- III. Title: Seventy-five readings plus.

PE1417.A14 2013
808'.0427—dc23

                                                          2011037388

www.mhhe.com

About the Authors

SANTI BUSCEMI is a professor of English at Middlesex County College in Edison, New Jersey. He teaches developmental and first-year composition.

CHARLOTTE SMITH is a professor of English at SUNY Adirondack in Queensbury, New York, where she teaches technical writing and directs the Center for Reading and Writing.

Contents

THEMATIC CONTENTS

Rites of Passage

Aging

Learning and Education

Culture and Identity

Gender Politics

Science and Technology

Health and Medicine

Uses and Abuses of Language

CONTENTS GROUPED BY GENRE AND DISCIPLINE

Satire, Parody, Humor

Letters

Speeches

DISCIPLINES

Anthropology

Arts and Humanities

Gender Studies

Government/Public Policy

History

International Studies

Law

Linguistics/Communication

Natural Sciences

Preface

75 Readings Plus is an expanded version of *75 Readings*, the popular and inexpensive collection of essays for first-year composition that was first published in 1987 and is now in its twelfth edition. The tables of contents of the two texts are identical, but the presentation of instructional materials differs.

Questions for discussion, suggestions for writing, and other instructional apparatus for *75 Readings* are presented in an online manual from which professors may copy materials for students as needed. In *75 Readings Plus*, on the other hand, instructional materials appear in the text. Accompanying each selection are an author biography, a set of discussion questions on content and strategy, and three suggestions for sustained writing, the last of which calls for research. In addition, in order to help instructors exploit the connection among reading, writing, and critical thinking, *75 Readings Plus* again offers a set of prompts for short writing that are inspired by each essay selection and used as journal assignments or as warm-up exercises for projects such as those described in the Suggestions for Sustained Writing. In some cases, they can even be expanded into assignments for complete essays.

For instructors who like the selections but who do not organize their classes around rhetorical modes, we have included two alternate tables of contents, which arrange selections by themes and genres. As with previous editions, we have sought the advice of many colleagues across the nation to determine changes that would make this book even more effective and appealing as a learning tool for college readers and writers. Many of these professionals have put both the new and the old selections in this book to the ultimate test by using them in their classrooms. They have also provided helpful suggestions that have enabled us to fashion a new table of contents that makes *75 Readings Plus* both versatile and representative of contemporary American culture.

CHANGES IN THE TENTH EDITION

Based on reviewers' suggestions, we have included the following:

- More essays on contemporary technology; food production, distribution, and use; and cultural identity in America.

- New readings that add depth and diversity and that pique student interest:

Louise Erdrich: *Beneath My House*
Peter Elbow: *Desperation Writing*
Richard Rodriguez: *"Blaxicans" and Other Reinvented Americans*
Brandon Griggs: *12 Most Annoying Types of Facebookers*
Gary Soto: *Like Mexicans*
Maxine Hong Kingston: *Family Ghosts*
Carlo Petrini: *The Value and Price of Food*
Rebecca Brown: *Extreme Reading*
Janet Kornblum: *Tapping into Text Messaging*
Michael Rubinkam: *Texting in Class Is Rampant*
Jonathan Safran Foer: *Let Them Eat Dog*
Sherman Alexie: *Superman and Me*

As before, *75 Readings Plus* contains an eleventh chapter, which includes essays worth teaching because of the effective mix of rhetorical strategies 5 they use.

SUPPLEMENTS

75 Readings offers many additional resources to Students and Instructors at: www.mhhe.com/75readings.

ACKNOWLEDGMENTS

Special thanks are due to those instructors who reviewed and helped us shape this anthology with their suggestions, particularly: William Sheldon, Hutchinson Community College; Dr. Fran Rancourt, Granite State College; Aaron Reini, Hibbing Community College; Natasha Bauman, El Camino College, Cypress College; Alex Solis, East Los Angeles College; Portia Jeffries, Seattle Central Community College; Chris Gardner, Austin Community College; Judith Ramos, Moorpark College; Janice R. Showler, Ph.D., Holy Family University; Jane Honeycutt (nee Thorne), Austin Community College; Tim Skeen, California State University-Fresno; Bill Tigue, East Los Angeles College; and Janet Cobb, Austin Community College.

We also thank our friends at McGraw-Hill, who encouraged us and helped us continue these texts.

Santi Buscemi
Charlotte Smith

1

Narration

One of the things that defines us as human is the universal desire and ability to create narrative. "Tell me a story," the child implores, and we willingly oblige by reciting an old favorite passed down through the generations—or by making up one of our own.

We are naturally curious creatures, wanting to know what happened, when, and to whom—even if none of it is true. Perhaps that is why we feel compelled to create mythologies on the one hand and to report the news or write history on the other.

Some narratives contain long, evocative descriptions of setting. Others present fascinating characters whose predicaments rivet our attention or whose lives mirror our own. Still others seem more like plays, heavy with dialogue by which writers enable their characters to reveal themselves. Whatever combination of techniques authors use, all stories—from the briefest anecdotes to the longest novels—have a plot. They recount events in a more-or-less chronological order. They reveal what happened and, in most cases, allow readers or listeners to draw their own conclusions about the significance of those events.

This is perhaps the chief difference between what you will read in Chapter 1 and the essays in other parts of this text. While some types of writing are aimed at explaining or persuading, narration dramatizes important human concerns by presenting events that, when taken together, create a world the author wants the reader to share. Moving from beginning to end, recounting events in the order in which they occurred, narration generally relies on a more natural pattern of organization than other types of writing, but it is no less sophisticated or powerful a tool for explaining complex ideas or for changing readers' opinions than, say, analogy, classification, or formal argument. All storytellers, no matter how entertaining their tales, have something to say about human beings and the world they inhabit. If you have already read selections from the chapters that follow, you know that writers often couple narration with other techniques to develop ideas and support opinions that might otherwise have remained abstract, unclear, or unconvincing. A good story may reveal more about a person or a place than physical description, and it can sometimes help readers understand an important problem or issue beyond our most valiant attempts to explain it "logically."

The point is that writers of narrative are not compelled to underscore the connection between the events in a story and the point it makes. Readers can find their own "theses."

Many of the essays you will read in this chapter are autobiographical: Maya Angelou, Langston Hughes, and Malcolm X show how they confronted difficult situations and, in the process, gained significant insight into themselves, their families, and the human personality. The writing of essays like theirs often derives from a profound compulsion to find meaning in what once seemed devoid of it, a process that may define the act of narration itself.

Very different in content and purpose is the essay by Barbara Tuchman. It shows us how effective narration can be as a tool for transmitting history in a way that is both accurate and moving. The selections by George Orwell and Martin Gansberg might be placed in yet another category. They point beyond themselves to social and political issues that are universal and perennial.

However the pieces in this chapter seem to be related—and you will surely find connections of your own to talk about—remember that each has been included because it has a poignant story to tell. Read each selection carefully, and learn what you can about the techniques of narration. Here's hoping that at least a few will inspire you to narrate a personal vision of the world that will enrich both you and your readers.

Shooting an Elephant

George Orwell

George Orwell is the pseudonym of Eric Blair (1903–1950). Born in India, where his father served in the British colonial government, Orwell was educated at Eton. As a young man, he served as a British policeman in Burma, the setting for this selection. Later, he was wounded while fighting for the loyalists in the Spanish Civil War, about which he wrote in Homage to Catalonia. *Orwell despised the "Big Brother" mentalities of both the fascists and the communists, who backed opposing sides in that war. However, he also condemned the crass bureaucracy of the democratic governments of his time. In short, Orwell became an enemy of politics and politicians in general. He is remembered for* Animal Farm *(1946) and* 1984 *(1949), classics of political satire, and for his many essays.*

"Shooting an Elephant" is at once an indictment of colonialism, a discourse on the clash of cultures, and a brutal self-examination of individual conscience.

VOCABULARY

perplexing, supplant, *saecula saeculorum*, prostrate, *in terrorem*, "must," mahout, labyrinth, squalid, Dravidian, coolie, paddy, futility, dahs

In Moulmein, in Lower Burma, I was hated by large numbers of people— 1
the only time in my life that I have been important enough for this to
happen to me. I was sub-divisional police officer of the town, and in an
aimless, petty kind of way anti-European feeling was very bitter. No one
had the guts to raise a riot, but if a European woman went through the
bazaars alone somebody would probably spit betel juice over her dress.
As a police officer I was an obvious target and was baited whenever
it seemed safe to do so. When a nimble Burman tripped me up on the
football field and the referee (another Burman) looked the other way, the
crowd yelled with hideous laughter. This happened more than once. In
the end the sneering yellow faces of young men that met me everywhere,
the insults hooted after me when I was at a safe distance, got badly on
my nerves. The young Buddhist priests were the worst of all. There were
several thousands of them in the town and none of them seemed to have
anything to do except stand on street corners and jeer at Europeans.

All this was perplexing and upsetting. For at that time I had already 2
made up my mind that imperialism was an evil thing and the sooner I
chucked up my job and got out of it the better. Theoretically—and secretly,
of course—I was all for the Burmese and all against their oppressors, the
British. As for the job I was doing, I hated it more bitterly than I can perhaps make clear. In a job like that you see the dirty work of Empire at
close quarters. The wretched prisoners huddling in the stinking cages of
the lock-ups, the grey, cowed faces of the long-term convicts, the scarred
buttocks of the men who had been Bogged with bamboos—all these
oppressed me with an intolerable sense of guilt. But I could get nothing
into perspective. I was young and ill-educated and I had had to think out
my problems in the utter silence that is imposed on every Englishman in
the East. I did not even know that the British Empire is dying, still less
did I know that it is a great deal better than the younger empires that are
going to supplant it. All I knew was that I was stuck between my hatred of
the empire I served and my rage against the evil-spirited little beasts who
tried to make my job impossible. With one part of my mind I thought of
the British Raj as an unbreakable tyranny, as something clamped down, in
saecula saeculorum, upon the will of prostrate peoples; with another part I
thought that the greatest joy in the world would be to drive a bayonet into
a Buddhist priest's guts. Feelings like these are the normal by-products of
imperialism; ask any Anglo-Indian official, if you can catch him off duty.

One day something happened which in a roundabout way was 3
enlightening. It was a tiny incident in itself, but it gave me a better glimpse
than I had had before of the real nature of imperialism—the real motives
for which despotic governments act. Early one morning the subinspector
at a police station at the other end of the town rang me up on the phone
and said that an elephant was ravaging the bazaar. Would I please come
and do something about it? I did not know what I could do, but I wanted

to see what was happening and I got on to a pony and started out. I took my rifle, an old .44 Winchester and much too small to kill an elephant, but I thought the noise might be useful *in terrorem*. Various Burmans stopped me on the way and told me about the elephant's doings. It was not, of course, a wild elephant, but a tame one which had gone "must." It had been chained up, as tame elephants always are when their attack of "must" is due, but on the previous night it had broken its chain and escaped. Its mahout, the only person who could manage it when it was in that state, had set out in pursuit, but had taken the wrong direction and was now twelve hours' journey away, and in the morning the elephant had suddenly reappeared in the town. The Burmese population had no weapons and were quite helpless against it. It had already destroyed somebody's bamboo hut, killed a cow and raided some fruit-stalls and devoured the stock; also it had met the municipal rubbish van and, when the driver jumped out and took to his heels, had turned the van over and inflicted violences upon it.

4   The Burmese sub-inspector and some Indian constables were waiting for me in the quarter where the elephant had been seen. It was a very poor quarter, a labyrinth of squalid bamboo huts, thatched with palmleaf, winding all over a steep hillside. I remember that it was a cloudy, stuffy morning at the beginning of the rains. We began questioning the people as to where the elephant had gone and, as usual, failed to get any definite information. That is invariably the case in the East; a story always sounds clear enough at a distance, but the nearer you get to the scene of events the vaguer it becomes. Some of the people said that the elephant had gone in one direction, some said that he had gone in another, some professed not even to have heard of any elephant. I had almost made up my mind that the whole story was a pack of lies, when we heard yells a little distance away. There was a loud, scandalized cry of "Go away, child! Go away this instant!" and an old woman with a switch in her hand came round the corner of a hut, violently shooing away a crowd of naked children. Some more women followed, clicking their tongues and exclaiming; evidently there was something that the children ought not to have seen. I rounded the hut and saw a man's dead body sprawling in the mud. He was an Indian, a black Dravidian coolie, almost naked, and he could not have been dead many minutes. The people said that the elephant had come suddenly upon him round the corner of the hut, caught him with its trunk, put its foot on his back and ground him into the earth. This was the rainy season and the ground was soft, and his face had scored a trench a foot deep and a couple of yards long. He was lying on his belly with arms crucified and head sharply twisted to one side. His face was coated with mud, the eyes wide open, the teeth bared and grinning with an expression of unendurable agony. (Never tell me, by the way, that the dead look peaceful. Most of the corpses I have seen looked devilish.) The friction

of the great beast's foot had stripped the skin from his back as neatly as one skins a rabbit. As soon as I saw the dead man I sent an orderly to a friend's house nearby to borrow an elephant rifle. I had already sent back the pony, not wanting it to go mad with fright and throw me if it smelt the elephant.

The orderly came back in a few minutes with a rifle and five car- 5 tridges, and meanwhile some Burmans had arrived and told us that the elephant was in the paddy fields below, only a few hundred yards away. As I started forward practically the whole population of the quarter flocked out of the houses and followed me. They had seen the rifle and were all shouting excitedly that I was going to shoot the elephant. They had not shown much interest in the elephant when he was merely ravaging their homes, but it was different now that he was going to be shot. It was a bit of fun to them, as it would be to an English crowd; besides they wanted the meat. It made me vaguely uneasy. I had no intention of shooting the elephant—I had merely sent for the rifle to defend myself if necessary—and it is always unnerving to have a crowd following you. I marched down the hill, looking and feeling a fool, with the rifle over my shoulder and an ever-growing army of people jostling at my heels. At the bottom, when you got away from the huts, there was a metalled road and beyond that a miry waste of paddy fields a thousand yards across, not yet ploughed but soggy from the first rains and dotted with coarse grass. The elephant was standing eight yards from the road, his left side towards us. He took not the slightest notice of the crowd's approach. He was tearing up bunches of grass, beating them against his knees to clean them and stuffing them into his mouth.

I had halted on the road. As soon as I saw the elephant I knew with 6 perfect certainty that I ought not to shoot him. It is a serious matter to shoot a working elephant—it is comparable to destroying a huge and costly piece of machinery—and obviously one ought not to do it if it can possibly be avoided. And at that distance, peacefully eating, the elephant looked no more dangerous than a cow. I thought then and I think now that his attack of "must" was already passing off; in which case he would merely wander harmlessly about until the mahout came back and caught him. Moreover, I did not in the least want to shoot him. I decided that I would watch him for a little while to make sure that he did not turn savage again, and then go home.

But at that moment I glanced round at the crowd that had followed 7 me. It was an immense crowd, two thousand at the least and growing every minute. It blocked the road for a long distance on either side. I looked at the sea of yellow faces above the garish clothes—faces all happy and excited over this bit of fun, all certain that the elephant was going to be shot. They were watching me as they would watch a conjurer about to perform a trick. They did not like me, but with the magical rifle in my hands I was momentarily worth watching. And suddenly I realized that I should have to shoot the elephant after all. The people expected it of me and I had got to do it; I could feel their two thousand wills pressing me forward, irresistibly. And it was at this moment, as I stood there with the rifle in my hands, that I first grasped the hollowness, the futility of the white man's dominion in the East. Here was I, the white man with his gun, standing in front of the unarmed native crowd—seemingly the leading actor of the piece; but in reality I was only an absurd puppet pushed to and fro by the will of those yellow faces behind. I perceived in this moment that when the white man turns tyrant it is his own freedom that he destroys. He becomes a sort of hollow, posing dummy, the conventionalized figure of a sahib. For it is the condition of his rule that he shall spend his life in trying to impress the "natives," and so in every crisis he has got to do what the "natives" expect of him. He wears a mask, and his face grows to fit it. I had got to shoot the elephant. I had committed myself to doing it when I sent for the rifle. A sahib has got to act like a sahib; he has got to appear resolute, to know his own mind and do definite things. To come all that way, rifle in hand, with two thousand people marching at my heels, and then to trail feebly away, having done nothing—no, that was impossible. The crowd would laugh at me. And my whole life, every white man's life in the East, was one long struggle not to be laughed at.

8   But I did not want to shoot the elephant. I watched him beating his bunch of grass against his knees, with that preoccupied grandmotherly air that elephants have. It seemed to me that it would be murder to shoot him. At that age I was not squeamish about killing animals, but I had never shot an elephant and never wanted to. (Somehow it always seems worse to kill a *large* animal.) Besides, there was the beast's owner to be considered. Alive, the elephant was worth at least a hundred pounds; dead, he would only be worth the value of his tusks, five pounds, possibly. But I had got to act quickly. I turned to some experienced-looking Burmans who had been there when we arrived, and asked them how the elephant had been behaving. They all said the same thing: he took no notice of you if you left him alone, but he might charge if you went too close to him.

9   It was perfectly clear to me what I ought to do. I ought to walk up to within, say, twenty-five yards of the elephant and test his behavior. If he charged, I could shoot; if he took no notice of me, it would be safe to leave him until the mahout came back. But also I knew that I was going to do no such thing. I was a poor shot with a rifle and the ground was soft mud into which one would sink at every step. If the elephant charged and I missed him, I should have about as much chance as a toad under a steam-roller. But even then I was not thinking particularly of my own skin, only of the watchful yellow faces behind. For at that moment, with the crowd watching me, I was not afraid in the ordinary sense, as I would

have been if I had been alone. A white man mustn't be frightened in front of "natives"; and so, in general, he isn't frightened. The sole thought in my mind was that if anything went wrong those two thousand Burmans would see me pursued, caught, trampled on and reduced to a grinning corpse like that Indian up the hill. And if that happened it was quite probable that some of them would laugh. That would never do. There was only one alternative. I shoved the cartridges into the magazine and lay down on the road to get a better aim.

The crowd grew very still, and a deep, low, happy sigh, as of people 10 who see the theatre curtain go up at last, breathed from innumerable throats. They were going to have their bit of fun after all. The rifle was a beautiful German thing with cross-hair sights. I did not then know that in shooting an elephant one would shoot to cut an imaginary bar running from ear-hole to ear-hole. I ought, therefore as the elephant was sideways on, to have aimed straight at his ear-hole, actually I aimed several inches in front of this, thinking the brain would be further forward.

When I pulled the trigger I did not hear the bang or feel the kick— 11 one never does when a shot goes home—but I heard the devilish roar of glee that went up from the crowd. In that instant, in too short a time, one would have thought, even for the bullet to get there, a mysterious, terrible change had come over the elephant. He neither stirred nor fell, but every line of his body had altered. He looked suddenly stricken, shrunken, immensely old, as though the frightful impact of the bullet had paralysed him without knocking him down. At last, after what seemed a long time—it might have been five seconds, I dare say—he sagged flabbily to his knees. His mouth slobbered. An enormous senility seemed to have settled upon him. One could have imagined him thousands of years old. I fired again into the same spot. At the second shot he did not collapse but climbed with desperate slowness to his feet and stood weakly upright, with legs sagging and head drooping. I fired a third time. That was the shot that did it for him. You could see the agony of it jolt his whole body and knock the last remnant of strength from his legs. But in falling he seemed for a moment to rise, for as his hind legs collapsed beneath him he seemed to tower upward like a huge rock toppling, his trunk reaching skyward like a tree. He trumpeted, for the first and only time. And then down he came, his belly towards me, with a crash that seemed to shake the ground even where I lay.

I got up. The Burmans were already racing past me across the mud. 12 It was obvious that the elephant would never rise again, but he was not dead. He was breathing very rhythmically with long rattling gasps, his great mound of a side painfully rising and falling. His mouth was wide open—I could see far down into caverns of pale pink throat. I waited a long time for him to die, but his breathing did not weaken. Finally I fired my two remaining shots into the spot where I thought his heart must be.

The thick blood welled out of him like red velvet, but still he did not die. His body did not even jerk when the shots hit him, the tortured breathing continued without a pause. He was dying, very slowly and in great agony, but in some world remote from me where not even a bullet could damage him further. I felt that I had got to put an end to that dreadful noise. It seemed dreadful to see the great beast lying there, powerless to move and yet powerless to die, and not even to be able to finish him. I sent back for my small rifle and poured shot after shot into his heart and down his throat. They seemed to make no impression. The tortured gasps continued as steadily as the ticking of a clock.

13   In the end I could not stand it any longer and went away. I heard later that it took him half an hour to die. Burmans were bringing dahs and baskets even before I left, and I was told they had stripped his body almost to the bones by the afternoon.

14   Afterwards, of course, there were endless discussions about the shooting of the elephant. The owner was furious, but he was only an Indian and could do nothing. Besides, legally I had done the right thing, for a mad elephant has to be killed, like a mad dog, if its owner fails to control it. Among the Europeans opinion was divided. The older men said I was right, the younger men said it was a damn shame to shoot an elephant for killing a coolie, because an elephant was worth more than any damn Coringhee coolie. And afterwards I was very glad that the coolie had been killed; it put me legally in the right and it gave me a sufficient pretext for shooting the elephant. I often wondered whether any of the others grasped that I had done it solely to avoid looking a fool.

1936

QUESTIONS FOR DISCUSSION

Content

a. What is Orwell's opinion of the Burmese? Of the British Raj? What conflict in him do these attitudes create?
b. What historical/political developments might the author be prefiguring in paragraph 2?
c. What does Orwell's experience teach him about the nature of imperialism?
d. What reasons does he give for not wanting to kill the elephant?
e. Why do the Burmese want Orwell to kill the elephant? Explain their motives in terms of what Orwell says about them early in this essay.

f. What does Orwell mean when, in paragraph 7, he says that a tyrant "wears a mask, and his face grows to fit it"? How does this statement explain his reason for killing the elephant?
g. Why are Orwell's opinions of older and younger Europeans (paragraph 14) important?

Strategy and Style

h. What purpose does Orwell intend his narrative to serve?
i. How do the author's comments about the Burmese, the Europeans, and the British Raj (paragraphs 1 and 2) help him achieve that purpose?
j. Orwell spends more time discussing the sociology of the event than about the setting in which it occurs. Explain why doing so is appropriate to his purpose.
k. Why does the author spend so much time narrating the death of the elephant?

ENGAGING THE TEXT

a. In what way is this essay a study in self-deception? Make specific reference to the text to explain your answer.
b. After reading this text, how would you explain Orwell's definition of imperialism? What role does his view of the natives of Burma play in this definition?

SUGGESTIONS FOR SUSTAINED WRITING

a. Orwell communicates his opinions on several political, social, and humanitarian issues. Use narration to discuss an issue about which you hold strong opinions. Present your opinions by drawing on narrative techniques such as detailed description, the chronological sequencing of events, dialogue, and narrator commentary, to name a few. In short, embed your opinion in the framework of the story.
b. Orwell reveals much about himself by telling us how he reacted to emotional stress. Something similar occurs in Langston Hughes's "Salvation" and in Maya Angelou's "Grandmother's Victory," which also appear in this chapter. Write an essay that points out similarities and differences between the ways these three narratives communicate the presence of emotional stress to their readers. For example, you might explain that one uses setting and dialogue to accomplish this, whereas another relies on a detailed retelling of events, and yet another makes use of character development.

c. Find out more about the British presence in Burma (now Myanmar) by researching at least four academic sources in your college library or on the Internet. Then, write an essay in which you discuss the historical background that might explain Orwell's opposition to British colonial rule in that country. Make sure to cite information from these sources—whether directly quoted, paraphrased, or summarized—in the text of your paper and in an appropriate listing of sources. Ask your instructor about the required documentation format.

READ MORE

Orwell and His Works

Davison, Peter Hobley. *George Orwell: A Literary Life*. New York: St. Martin's Press, 1995.

"George Orwell: (1903–1950)" *Project Gutenberg Australia* (http://gutenberg.net.au/pages/orwell.html): *Gutenberg site on the works of Orwell, containing links to ebooks.*

British Colonialism, Myanmar (Burma)

Dirks, Nicholas B., ed. *Colonialism and Culture*. Ann Arbor: University of Michigan, 1992.

"Burma Guide to Rights and Democracy." *BurmaGuide.net* (http://www.burmaguide.net): *Site contains many links to information about the current state of Burma (Myanmar).*

Salvation

Langston Hughes

Among the chief figures of the Harlem Renaissance in the 1920s, Langston Hughes (1902–1967) is one of the best-known poets and playwrights in America. A native of Mississippi, Hughes also wrote numerous essays that detail life in the South during the early part of this century. His novels and his autobiography, I Wonder As I Wander, *are still read widely. In this selection, he captures the trauma and disillusionment he experienced during a childhood incident. The title and first line of this piece, though ironic, stand as models for the kinds of beginnings that never fail to pique the reader's interest. Although brief, this essay is an emotional tour de force in which the author assumes the persona of himself as an adolescent. What we read here is testament to the power of narration as a tool for analysis and persuasion.*

VOCABULARY

mourners' bench, dire, gnarled, rounder, deacons, knickerbocker

I was saved from sin when I was going on thirteen. But not really saved. 1
It happened like this. There was a big revival at my Auntie Reed's church.
Every night for weeks there had been much preaching, singing, praying, and shouting, and some very hardened sinners had been brought
to Christ, and the membership of the church had grown by leaps and
bounds. Then just before the revival ended, they held a special meeting
for children, "to bring the young lambs to the fold." My aunt spoke of it
for days ahead. That night I was escorted to the front row and placed on
the mourners' bench with all the other young sinners, who had not yet
been brought to Jesus.

My aunt told me that when you were saved you saw a light, and 2
something happened to you inside! And Jesus came into your life! And
God was with you from then on! She said you could see and hear and feel
Jesus in your soul. I believed her. I had heard a great many old people
say the same thing and it seemed to me they ought to know. So I sat there
calmly in the hot, crowded church, waiting for Jesus to come to me.

The preacher preached a wonderful rhythmical sermon, all moans and 3
shouts and lonely cries and dire pictures of hell, and then he sang a song
about the ninety and nine safe in the fold, but one little lamb was left out in
the cold. Then he said: "Won't you come? Won't you come to Jesus? Young
lambs, won't you come?" And he held out his arms to all us young sinners
there on the mourners' bench. And the little girls cried. And some of them
jumped up and went to Jesus right away. But most of us just sat there.

A great many old people came and knelt around us and prayed, old 4
women with jet-black faces and braided hair, old men with work-gnarled
hands. And the church sang a song about the lower lights are burning,
some poor sinners to be saved. And the whole building rocked with
prayer and song.

Still I kept waiting to *see* Jesus.   5

Finally all the young people had gone to the altar and were saved, 6
but one boy and me. He was a rounder's son named Westley. Westley
and I were surrounded by sisters and deacons praying. It was very hot in
the church, and getting late now. Finally Westley said to me in a whisper:
"God damn! I'm tired o' sitting here. Let's get up and be saved." So he got
up and was saved.

Then I was left all alone on the mourners' bench. My aunt came and 7
knelt at my knees and cried, while prayers and songs swirled all around me
in the little church. The whole congregation prayed for me alone, in a mighty
wail of moans and voices. And I kept waiting serenely for Jesus, waiting,

waiting—but he didn't come. I wanted to see him, but nothing happened to me. Nothing! I wanted something to happen to me, but nothing happened.

8   I heard the songs and the minister saying: "Why don't you come? My dear child, why don't you come to Jesus? Jesus is waiting for you. He wants you. Why don't you come? Sister Reed, what is this child's name?"

9   "Langston," my aunt sobbed.

10   "Langston, why don't you come? Why don't you come and be saved? Oh, Lamb of God! Why don't you come?"

11   Now it was really getting late. I began to be ashamed of myself, holding everything up so long. I began to wonder what God thought about Westley, who certainly hadn't seen Jesus either, but who was now sitting proudly on the platform, swinging his knickerbockered legs and grinning down at me, surrounded by deacons and old women on their knees praying. God had not struck Westley dead for taking his name in vain or for lying in the temple. So I decided that maybe to save further trouble, I'd better lie, too, and say that Jesus had come, and get up and be saved.

12   So I got up.

13   Suddenly the whole room broke into a sea of shouting, as they saw me rise. Waves of rejoicing swept the place. Women leaped in the air. My aunt threw her arms around me. The minister took me by the hand and led me to the platform.

14   When things quieted down, in a hushed silence, punctuated by a few ecstatic "Amens," all the new young lambs were blessed in the name of God. Then joyous singing filled the room.

15   That night, for the last time in my life but one—for I was a big boy twelve years old—I cried. I cried, in bed alone, and couldn't stop. I buried my head under the quilts, but my aunt heard me. She woke up and told my uncle I was crying because the Holy Ghost had come into my life, and because I had seen Jesus. But I was really crying because I couldn't bear to tell her that I had lied, that I had deceived everybody in the church, that I hadn't seen Jesus, and that now I didn't believe there was a Jesus any more, since he didn't come to help me.

1940

QUESTIONS FOR DISCUSSION

Content

a. What is Hughes's purpose in recalling this event?

b. The author's portrayal of the revival meeting is extremely realistic. What rhetorical techniques make it so?

c. What exactly is a religious revival?
d. What biblical metaphor is Hughes alluding to when he tells the reader that this was to be a special meeting "to bring the young lambs to the fold"?
e. Why does Hughes spend time talking about Westley? How is young Langston different from this boy?
f. What does the author's waiting so long before going up to be "saved" tell you about him?
g. Explain why Langston cries so much after coming home. Is there only one reason behind his tears? What does the last paragraph tell you about the young Langston?

Strategy and Style

h. The telling of this story is enhanced by the author's description of the church and the members of the congregation. In which paragraphs is Hughes's facility with description most evident?
i. What examples of metaphoric language do you find in this essay? How do such figures of speech help Hughes accomplish his purpose?
j. Hughes often makes use of a childlike perspective to relate the incident at his aunt's church. What details help him create that perspective? Does he use words like those a child might use?
k. What is Hughes's attitude or tone when recalling this incident?

ENGAGING THE TEXT

a. Write about one of your religious experiences, comparing or contrasting it to that of Hughes. Include specific references to his essay.
b. Write an imaginary interview (both your questions and his answers) with Hughes, asking him about his experiences at the revival meeting. Hughes's answers should be consistent with what he writes in the essay.

SUGGESTIONS FOR SUSTAINED WRITING

a. At one time or another, we all have been pressured into doing things we did not want to do. Recount such an incident from your experience; make sure to describe your feelings both during that experience and after it occurred. If appropriate, narrate the incident in a letter addressed to the individual or individuals who did the pressuring. In the process, however, make reference to Hughes's experience in "Salvation" and compare or contrast it to your own.
b. Read Ortiz Cofer's "A Partial Remembrance of a Puerto Rican Childhood" in Chapter 2. Then write an essay that draws similarities and differences between the kinds of families in which Hughes and

Ortiz Cofer grew up. In other words, from the reading, draw inferences that would compare and contrast the emotional lives these two authors experienced as children.

c. Describe a religious ceremony that has or used to have significance for you. As clearly and convincingly as you can, describe the emotional or spiritual benefits you derive or derived from that ceremony. Address your essay to someone who you know is skeptical about the value of religious or social ceremonies and observances. Support your position by including facts, ideas, and opinions about this ceremony or about religious or social ceremonies in general, which you research in at least three secondary sources found in your college library or on the Internet. (We list a few below to get you started.) Make sure to include and cite your research, using a format or style approved by your instructor.

READ MORE

Hughes and His Works

Gates, Henry Louis, and K. A. Appiah, eds. *Langston Hughes: Critical Perspectives Past and Present*. New York: Amistad Publishing, 1993.

"Langston Hughes" *Poets.org*. Academy of American Poets (http://www. poets.org/poet.php/prmPID/83): *Background on Hughes's life and work, along with biography and important links*.

Revival Meetings/Early Twentieth-Century African-American Culture and History

Cox, Sherman Haywood II. "Revival I" (http://www.theafricanameri-canlectionary.org/PopupCulturalAid.asp?LRID=162): *The African-American Lectionary Cultural Resources. Contains text to hymns and notes to further reading*.

Hurt, Douglas. *African-American Life in the Rural South: 1900–1950*. Columbia, MO: University of Missouri, 2003.

Raboteau, Albert J. *African-American Religion*. New York: Oxford University Press, 1999.

Grandmother's Victory

Maya Angelou

Born Marguerita Johnson in 1928, Maya Angelou spent most of her childhood in Stamps, Arkansas, where her family owned the general store that is the setting for this

selection. After a difficult youth, Angelou became a dancer, actress, and writer. She has performed all over the world, most notably in the U.S. State Department–sponsored production of Porgy and Bess, *in the television miniseries* Roots, *and in a production of Jean Genet's* The Blacks. *She has also taught dance in Rome and Tel Aviv. Active in the Civil Rights movement, Angelou was appointed northern director for the Southern Christian Leadership Conference by Martin Luther King, Jr., in the 1960s. In 1970, she published the first volume of her autobiography,* I Know Why the Caged Bird Sings, *of which this selection is the fifth chapter. Five other volumes have followed, with the sixth in the series,* A Song Flew up to Heaven, *being published in 2002. Angelou has also written several books of poetry, including* And Still I Rise *(1978) and* I Shall Not Be Moved *(1990). Recent works include three autobiographies:* The Heart of a Woman *(1981),* Shaker, Why Don't You Sing? *(1983), and* All God's Children Need Traveling Shoes *(1986).*

In the selection that follows, Angelou reveals much about the personality of the woman who raised her. Through amazing patience, self-control, and perseverance, Angelou's grandmother becomes for us an icon of spiritual stability, a bulwark against racism and stupidity, and proof that with strength of character we can rise above the world, no matter how vile and stupid it may sometimes be.

VOCABULARY

clabbered, impudent, appellations, gaggle, apparitions, servile, roustabout, paranoia

"Thou shall not be dirty" and "Thou shall not be impudent" were the two   1
commandments of Grandmother Henderson upon which hung our total salvation.

Each night in the bitterest winter we were forced to wash faces, arms,   2
necks, legs, and feet before going to bed. She used to add, with a smirk that unprofane people can't control when venturing into profanity, "and wash as far as possible, then wash possible."

We would go to the well and wash in the ice-cold, clear water, grease   3
our legs with the equally cold stiff Vaseline, then tiptoe into the house. We wiped the dust from our toes and settled down for schoolwork, cornbread, clabbered milk, prayers, and bed, always in that order. Momma was famous for pulling the quilts off after we had fallen asleep to examine our feet. If they weren't clean enough for her, she took the switch (she kept one behind the bedroom door for emergencies) and woke up the offender with a few aptly placed burning reminders.

The area around the well at night was dark and slick, and boys told   4
about how snakes love water, so that anyone who had to draw water at night and then stand there alone and wash knew that moccasins and rattlers, puff adders, and boa constrictors were winding their way to the well and would arrive just as the person washing got soap in her eyes.

But Momma convinced us that not only was cleanliness next to Godliness, dirtiness was the inventor of misery.

5   The impudent child was detested by God and a shame to its parents and could bring destruction to its house and line. All adults had to be addressed as Mister, Missus, Miss, Auntie, Cousin, Unk, Uncle, Buhbah, Sister, Brother, and a thousand other appellations indicating familial relationship and the lowliness of the addressor.

6   Everyone I knew respected these customary laws, except for the powhitetrash children.

7   Some families of powhitetrash lived on Momma's farmland behind the school. Sometimes a gaggle of them came to the Store, filling the whole room, chasing out the air, and even changing the well-known scents. The children crawled over the shelves and into the potato and onion bins, twanging all the time in their sharp voices like cigar-box guitars. They took liberties in my Store that I would never dare. Since Momma told us that the less you say to whitefolks (or even powhitetrash) the better, Bailey and I would stand, solemn, quiet, in the displaced air. But if one of the playful apparitions got close to us, I pinched it. Partly out of angry frustration and partly because I didn't believe in its flesh reality.

8   They called my uncle by his first name and ordered him around the Store. He, to my crying shame, obeyed them in his limping dip-straight-dip fashion.

9   My grandmother, too, followed their orders, except that she didn't seem to be servile because she anticipated their needs.

10   "Here's sugar, Miz Potter, and here's baking powder. You didn't buy soda last month, you'll probably be needing some."

11   Momma always directed her statements to the adults, but sometimes, Oh painful sometimes, the grimy, snotty-nosed girls would answer her.

12   "Naw, Annie. . ."—to Momma? Who owned the land they lived on? Who forgot more than they would ever learn? If there was any justice in the world, God should strike them dumb at once!—"Just give us some extra sody crackers, and some more mackerel."

13   At least they never looked in her face, or I never caught them doing so. Nobody with a smidgen of training, not even the worst roustabout, would look right in a grown person's face. It meant the person was trying to take the words out before they were formed. The dirty little children didn't do that, but they threw their orders around the Store like lashes from a cat-o'-nine-tails.

14   When I was around ten years old, those scruffy children caused me the most painful and confusing experience I had ever had with my grandmother.

15   One summer morning, after I had swept the dirt yard of leaves, spearmint-gum wrappers and Vienna-sausage labels, I raked the yellow-red dirt, and made half-moons carefully, so that the design stood out clearly

and mask-like. I put the rake behind the Store and came through the back of the house to find Grandmother on the front porch in her big, wide white apron. The apron was so stiff by virtue of the starch that it could have stood alone. Momma was admiring the yard, so I joined her. It truly looked like a flat redhead that had been raked with a big-toothed comb. Momma didn't say anything but I knew she liked it. She looked over toward the school principal's house and to the right at Mr. McElroy's. She was hoping one of those community pillars would see the design before the day's business wiped it out. Then she looked upward to the school. My head had swung with hers, so at just about the same time we saw a troop of powhitetrash kids marching over the hill and down by the side of the school.

I looked to Momma for direction. She did an excellent job of sagging from her waist down, but from the waist up she seemed to be pulling for the top of the oak tree across the road. Then she began to moan a hymn. Maybe not to moan, but the tune was so slow and the meter so strange that she could have been moaning. She didn't look at me again. When the children reached halfway down the hill, halfway to the Store, she said without turning, "Sister, go on inside." 16

I wanted to beg her, "Momma, don't wait for them. Come on inside with me. If they come in the Store, you go to the bedroom and let me wait on them. They only frighten me if you're around. Alone I know how to handle them." But of course I couldn't say anything, so I went in and stood behind the screen door. 17

Before the girls got to the porch I heard their laughter crackling and popping like pine logs in a cooking stove. I suppose my lifelong paranoia was born in those cold, molasses-slow minutes. They came finally to stand on the ground in front of Momma. At first they pretended seriousness. Then one of them wrapped her right arm in the crook of her left, pushed out her mouth and started to hum. I realized that she was aping my grandmother. Another said, "Naw, Helen, you ain't standing like her. This here's it." Then she lifted her chest, folded her arms and mocked that strange carriage that was Annie Henderson. Another laughed, "Naw, you can't do it. Your mouth ain't pooched out enough. It's like this." 18

I thought about the rifle behind the door, but I knew I'd never be able to hold it straight, and the .410, our sawed-off shotgun, which stayed loaded and was fired every New Year's night, was locked in the trunk and Uncle Willie had the key on his chain. Through the fly-specked screen door, I could see that the arms of Momma's apron jiggled from the vibrations of her humming. But her knees seemed to have locked as if they would never bend again. 19

She sang on. No louder than before, but no softer either. No slower or faster. 20

The dirt of the girls' cotton dresses continued on their legs, feet, arms, and faces to make them all of a piece. Their greasy uncolored hair 21 hung down, uncombed, with a grim finality. I knelt to see them better, to remember them for all time. The tears that had slipped down my dress left unsurprising dark spots, and made the front yard blurry and even more unreal. The world had taken a deep breath and was having doubts about continuing to revolve.

22   The girls had tired of mocking Momma and turned to other means of agitation. One crossed her eyes, stuck her thumbs in both sides of her mouth and said, "Look here, Annie." Grandmother hummed on and the apron strings trembled. I wanted to throw a handful of black pepper in their faces, to throw lye on them, to scream that they were dirty, scummy peckerwoods, but I knew I was as clearly imprisoned behind the scene as the actors outside were confined to their roles.

23   One of the smaller girls did a kind of puppet dance while her fellow clowns laughed at her. But the tall one, who was almost a woman, said something very quietly, which I couldn't hear. They all moved backward from the porch, still watching Momma. For an awful second I thought they were going to throw a rock at Momma, who seemed (except for the apron strings) to have turned into stone herself. But the big girl turned her back, bent down and put her hands flat on the ground—she didn't pick up anything. She simply shifted her weight and did a hand stand.

24   Her dirty bare feet and long legs went straight for the sky. Her dress fell down around her shoulders, and she had on no drawers. The slick pubic hair made a brown triangle where her legs came together. She hung in the vacuum of that lifeless morning for only a few seconds, then wavered and tumbled. The other girls clapped her on the back and slapped their hands.

25   Momma changed her song to "Bread of Heaven, Bread of Heaven, feed me till I want no more."

26   I found that I was praying too. How long could Momma hold out? What new indignity would they think of to subject her to? Would I be able to stay out of it? What would Momma really like me to do?

27   Then they were moving out of the yard, on their way to town. They bobbed their heads and shook their slack behinds and turned, one at a time:

28   "'Bye, Annie."

29   "'Bye, Annie."

30   "'Bye, Annie."

31   Momma never turned her head or unfolded her arms, but she stopped singing and said, "'Bye, Miz Helen, 'bye, Miz Ruth, 'bye, Miz Eloise."

32   I burst. A firecracker July-the-Fourth burst. How could Momma call them Miz? The mean nasty things. Why couldn't she have come inside the sweet, cool store when we saw them breasting the hill? What did she prove? And then if they were dirty, mean, and impudent, why did Momma have to call them Miz?

She stood another whole song through and then opened the screen 33
door to look down on me crying in rage. She looked until I looked up. Her
face was a brown moon that shone on me. She was beautiful. Something
had happened out there, which I couldn't completely understand, but I
could see that she was happy. Then she bent down and touched me as
mothers of the church "lay hands on the sick and afflicted" and I quieted.

"Go wash your face, Sister." And she went behind the candy counter 34
and hummed, "Glory, glory, hallelujah, when I lay my burden down."

I threw the well water on my face and used the weekday handker- 35
chief to blow my nose. Whatever the contest had been out front, I knew
Momma had won.

I took the rake back to the front yard. The smudged footprints were 36
easy to erase. I worked for a long time on my new design and laid the
rake behind the wash pot. When I came back in the Store, I took Momma's
hand and we both walked outside to look at the pattern.

It was a large heart with lots of hearts growing smaller inside, and 37
piercing from the outside rim to the smallest heart was an arrow. Momma
said, "Sister, that's right pretty." Then she turned back to the Store and
resumed, "Glory, glory, hallelujah, when I lay my burden down."

1970

QUESTIONS FOR DISCUSSION

Content

a. Is this simply a story about bad-mannered children and racism? Or is
   Angelou's intent more complex?
b. Why does the speaker bother to tell us that she made careful patterns
   when she raked the yard? Why did Momma admire these designs?
c. Angelou describes a number of outdated social observances such as
   never looking "right in a grown person's face." What other examples
   can you find in this selection? Why does she make it a point to include
   them in this recollection of her childhood?
d. Grandmother Henderson addresses each of the white girls as "Miz."
   Does her doing so have anything to do with her strange victory over
   these brats?
e. What details does Angelou use to create this obviously unflattering
   picture of "powhitetrash children"?
f. What does Angelou mean when she describes her uncle's limping in
   "dip-straight-dip fashion"?

Strategy and Style

g. In light of what she says early in the narrative, is it important for her
   to quote all three of the girls as they leave the store (paragraphs 28
   through 30)? In general, what effect does Angelou's extensive use of
   dialogue create?
h. This selection begins with two rather odd commandments, which both
   startle and amuse the reader. Why are they important to the rest of the
   essay?
i. Angelou's use of metaphor is brilliant. In paragraph 18, she tells us that
   her "paranoia was born in those cold, molasses-slow minutes." What
   other examples of figurative language can you find?
j. How would you describe the speaker's tone at the beginning of this
   essay? When, exactly, does this tone change?

ENGAGING THE TEXT

a. What does victory mean to Angelou's grandmother? Write a definition
   of victory as Angelou's grandmother would define it.
b. Write your own definition of victory. In other words, what does this
   concept mean to you personally? Compare your definition with that of
   Angelou's grandmother.

SUGGESTIONS FOR SUSTAINED WRITING

a. Relying on your own experiences, narrate an incident from the life of
   a relative, friend, or neighbor that illustrates the nobility of his or her
   character, much in the same way that Angelou illustrates the nobility
   of her grandmother's character. Through description, dialogue, and
   action, include details that provide the reader with a vivid picture of
   the person you are discussing. Address your essay to someone who has
   never met your subject and/or knows little about him or her.
b. Grandmother Henderson's triumph may well have resided in the fact
   that she had done a far better job of raising children than had many
   of her "powhitetrash" neighbors. Analyze Angelou's essay in order to
   explain this and other sources of Momma's victory. In short, discuss
   aspects of Momma's character that prompted Angelou to make her
   the centerpiece of this narrative. Make direct reference to the essay by
   quoting, paraphrasing, or summarizing it.
c. Two authors in this chapter write about the influence of their families on their lives. Langston Hughes and Maya Angelou write about
   incidents from their childhoods in which the action of an older relative
   so influenced them that, later in their lives, they felt compelled to share
   them with their readers. Obviously, these were significant events—

perhaps even turning points in the authors' lives. Write an essay in which you compare and contrast the two families in these essays. Also, explain what each author is telling us about the process of growing up.

READ MORE

Angelou and Her Works

"Maya Angelou." Academy of American Poets, (http://www.poets.org/ poet.php/prmPID/87): *An excellent introduction with a bibliography.* "Maya Angelou." *Voices from the Gap.* University of Minnesota, (http:// voices.cla.umn.edu/artistpages/angelouMaya.php): *Critical and biographical information about Angelou as well as a bibliography. Includes links to other sites.*

The African-American Family

Lilton, Deborah. *Resources for African American & Diaspora Studies.* Jean and Alexander Heard Library of Vanderbilt University (http://www. library.vanderbilt.edu/central/afam.html): *An excellent guide with links to essays, documents, and other resource centers and organizations.*

Littlejohn-Blake, Sheila, and Carol A. Darling. "Understanding the Strengths of African-American Families." *Journal of Black Studies* 23.4 (1993): 460–71.

Coming to an Awareness of Language

Malcolm X

Born Malcolm Little in Omaha, Nebraska, Malcolm X (1925–1965) was the son of a Baptist minister who espoused the cause of black nationalism. After moving to Lansing, Michigan, the Little family suffered the torching of their home and the murder of their father by white supremacists. In junior high school, Malcolm Little expressed a desire to study law, a dream one of his teachers called "no realistic goal for a nigger." Eventually, Malcolm settled in New York City and entered the Harlem underworld, where he became known as "Big Red." In 1946, he was convicted of burglary. While in prison, he took it upon himself to improve his education, as narrated in this selection, and he studied the writings of Elijah Muhammad, leader of the Nation of Islam. Paroled in 1952, he changed his surname to X to replace his lost African name (he considered Little a "slave name"). Working with Elijah Muhammad, Malcolm X established new mosques in Detroit and Harlem, increasing Nation of Islam membership from 500 to 30,000 from 1952 to 1963. In 1964, however, he severed his relationship with Elijah Muhammad, after learning that his spiritual mentor had committed adultery with six women and had fathered several illegitimate children. He then embarked on a pilgrimage to Mecca, Islam's holiest city, from which he returned embracing a more peaceful and tolerant form of Islam and abandoning his enmity for white people, whom he had once called "devils." After a speech in Harlem's Audubon Ballroom in February 1965, Malcolm X was murdered by three gunmen. All three men, members of the Nation of Islam, were convicted of first-degree murder. This selection is taken from the Autobiography of Malcolm X, *which he wrote with the help of Alex Haley, the author of* Roots.

VOCABULARY

hustling, hype, articulate, emulate, riffling

1 I've never been one for inaction. Everything I've ever felt strongly about, I've done something about. I guess that's why, unable to do anything else, I soon began writing to people I had known in the hustling world, such as Sammy the Pimp, John Hughes, the gambling house owner, the thief Jumpsteady, and several dope peddlers. I wrote them all about Allah and Islam and Mr. Elijah Muhammad. I had no idea where most of them lived. I addressed their letters in care of the Harlem or Roxbury bars and clubs where I'd known them.

2 I never got a single reply. The average hustler and criminal was too uneducated to write a letter. I have known many slick, sharp-looking hustlers, who would have you think they had an interest in Wall Street; privately, they would get someone else to read a letter if they received one. Besides, neither would I have replied to anyone writing me something as wild as "the white man is the devil."

3 What certainly went on the Harlem and Roxbury wires was that Detroit Red was going crazy in stir, or else he was trying some hype to shake up the warden's office.

4 During the years that I stayed in the Norfolk Prison Colony, never did any official directly say anything to me about those letters, although, of course, they all passed through the prison censorship. I'm sure, however, they monitored what I wrote to add to the files which every state and federal prison keeps on the conversion of Negro inmates by the teachings of Mr. Elijah Muhammad.

5 But at that time, I felt that the real reason was that the white man knew that he was the devil.

6 Later on, I even wrote to the Mayor of Boston, to the Governor of Massachusetts, and to Harry S. Truman. They never answered; they probably never even saw my letters. I handscratched to them how the white man's society was responsible for the black man's condition in this wilderness of North America.

7 It was because of my letters that I happened to stumble upon starting to acquire some kind of a homemade education.

I became increasingly frustrated at not being able to express what 8
I wanted to convey in letters that I wrote, especially those to Mr. Elijah
Muhammad. In the street, I had been the most articulate hustler out there—
I had commanded attention when I said something. But now, trying to write
simple English, I not only wasn't articulate, I wasn't even functional. How
would I sound writing in slang, the way I would *say* it, something such as,
"Look, daddy, let me pull your coat about a cat, Elijah Muhammad—"

Many who today hear me somewhere in person, or on television, or 9
those who read something I've said, will think I went to school far beyond
the eighth grade. This impression is due entirely to my prison studies.

It had really begun back in the Charlestown Prison, when Bimbi first 10
made me feel envy of his stock of knowledge. Bimbi had always taken
charge of any conversation he was in, and I had tried to emulate him.
But every book I picked up had few sentences which didn't contain anywhere from one to nearly all of the words that might as well have been
in Chinese. When I just skipped those words, of course, I really ended up
with little idea of what the book said. So I had come to the Norfolk Prison
Colony still going through only book-reading motions. Pretty soon, I
would have quit even these motions, unless I had received the motivation
that I did.

I saw that the best thing I could do was get hold of a dictionary—to 11
study, to learn some words. I was lucky enough to reason also that I
should try to improve my penmanship. It was sad. I couldn't even write
in a straight line. It was both ideas together that moved me to request a
dictionary along with some tablets and pencils from the Norfolk Prison
Colony school.

I spent two days just riffling uncertainly through the dictionary's 12
pages. I'd never realized so many words existed! I didn't know *which*
words I needed to learn. Finally, just to start some kind of action, I began
copying.

In my slow, painstaking, ragged handwriting, I copied into my tablet 13
everything printed on that first page, down to the punctuation marks.

I believe it took me a day. Then, aloud, I read back, to myself, every- 14
thing I'd written on the tablet. Over and over, aloud, to myself, I read my
own handwriting.

I woke up the next morning, thinking about those words—immensely 15
proud to realize that not only had I written so much at one time, but I'd
written words that I never knew were in the world. Moreover, with a
little effort, I also could remember what many of these words meant. I
reviewed the words whose meanings I didn't remember. Funny thing,
from the dictionary first page right now, that "aardvark" springs to my
mind. The dictionary had a picture of it, a long-tailed, long-eared, bur-
rowing African mammal, which lives off termites caught by sticking out
its tongue as an anteater does for ants.

16   I was so fascinated that I went on—I copied the dictionary's next page. And the same experience came when I studied that. With every succeeding page, I also learned of people and places and events from history. Actually the dictionary is like a miniature encyclopedia. Finally the dictionary's A section had filled a whole tablet—and I went on into the B's. That was the way I started copying what eventually became the entire dictionary. It went a lot faster after so much practice helped me to pick up handwriting speed. Between what I wrote in my tablet, and writing letters, during the rest of my time in prison I would guess I wrote a million words.

17   I suppose it was inevitable that as my word-base broadened, I could for the first time pick up a book and read and now begin to understand what the book was saying. Anyone who has read a great deal can imagine the new world that opened. Let me tell you something: from then until I left that prison, in every free moment I had, if I was not reading in the library, I was reading on my bunk. You couldn't have gotten me out of books with a wedge. Between Mr. Muhammad's teachings, my correspondence, my visitors … and my reading of books, months passed without my even thinking about being imprisoned. In fact, up to then, I never had been so truly free in my life.

1965

QUESTIONS FOR DISCUSSION

Content

a. Explain the process by which the author improved his reading and writing abilities.

b. What distinction does Malcolm X imply when, in paragraph 8, he says "I not only wasn't articulate, I wasn't even functional"?

c. What is it about Bimbi that makes the narrator wish to "emulate him" (paragraph 10)?

d. What distinction does Malcolm X draw between being articulate in the "hustling world" and being truly literate?

e. At first, Malcolm X wanted to improve his ability to communicate in the letters he wrote, "especially to Elijah Muhammad." Does this motivation change later on? Explain.

f. Is this essay about a conversion? If so, how do paragraphs 4 and 5 illuminate that conversion?

g. Define the kind of freedom that the author mentions in his conclusion.

Strategy and Style

h. What is the effect of the author's mentioning the names of hustlers such as Sammy the Pimp and of Elijah Muhammad in the same paragraph?
i. The author's letters contained statements such as "the white man is the devil." Do such comments affect his credibility? Why or why not?
j. What use does this selection make of dialogue? Why is this dialogue important?

ENGAGING THE TEXT

a. Analyze any two paragraphs in this selection. Evaluate the writer's command of the language and his believability.
b. Comment on the narrator's voice. How would you characterize the personality of the speaker? Play close attention to the street language that he weaves into the fabric of this narrative.

SUGGESTIONS FOR SUSTAINED WRITING

a. Like Malcolm X, tell the story of how you accomplished an important goal in your life. Use specific detail to convey how difficult the task was. Be as detailed when you explain how achieving this goal changed your life, your lifestyle, or your personality.
b. Read Richard Marius's "Writing Drafts," a selection in Chapter 3. What can Marius tell us about the process by which Malcolm came to "an awareness of language"? In what way does Malcolm's essay shed light on Marius?
c. Research the life of Malcolm X in greater depth in print sources and on the Internet. Then, write an essay that informs the reader of a limited aspect of that life. For example, explain how and why he accepted Islam, why and how he changed his opinion of white people, his rise to prominence in the Harlem community, or the events that led to his assassination. Another assignment you might choose is to explain the tenets of Islam that attracted Malcolm to this faith.

READ MORE

El-Beshti, Bashir M. "The Semiotics of Salvation: Malcolm X and the Autobiographical Self." *Journal of Negro History* 82.4 (1997): 359–67. *An analysis of Malcolm X's powerful ability to use language.*
"Malcolm X Project at Columbia University" (http://www.columbia.edu/cu/ccbh/mxp): *Site provides a good place to start research on the author.*

"Selected Resources on Malcolm X." John Henrik Clarke Africana Library of
Cornell University (http://www.library.cornell.edu/africana/guides/
malcolmx.html): *Site provides an extensive bibliography on the author.*

37 Who Saw Murder
Didn't Call the Police

Martin Gansberg

Martin Gansberg (1921–1995) worked for the New York Times *for 43 years. Born in
Brooklyn, New York, Gansberg took his bachelor's degree at St. John's University and
joined the* Times *as an office assistant in 1942. After becoming a reporter, he rose to
the position of news editor and was then transferred to Paris, France, where he served
as the editor of the newspaper's international edition. Gansberg is remembered chiefly as
the author of "37 Who Saw Murder Didn't Call the Police," which was published in the*
Times *in 1964. For it, Gansberg received an award from the Silurians, an association of
professional journalists, for the best news story of the year.*

*"37 Who Saw Murder Didn't Call the Police" is the story of the brutal killing of
Catherine ("Kitty") Genovese, a young woman living alone in the quiet, upper-middle-
class neighborhood of Kew Gardens, in Queens, New York. The crime was doubly terrifying because, as the story's title indicates, witnesses to the crime might very well have saved
Genovese's life if only they had had the courage and the compassion to get involved.*

VOCABULARY

deliberation, distraught, punctuated, recitation, Tudor

1 For more than half an hour 37 respectable, law-abiding citizens in Queens
watched a killer stalk and stab a woman in three separate attacks in Kew
Gardens.

2   Twice the sound of their voices and the sudden glow of their bedroom
lights interrupted him and frightened him off. Each time he returned,
sought her out and stabbed her again. Not one person telephoned the
police during the assault; one witness called after the woman was dead.

3   That was two weeks ago today. But Assistant Chief Inspector
Frederick M. Lussen, in charge of the borough's detectives and a veteran
of 25 years of homicide investigations, is still shocked.

4   He can give a matter-of-fact recitation of many murders. But the Kew
Gardens slaying baffles him—not because it is a murder, but because the
"good people" failed to call the police.

5   "As we have reconstructed the crime," he said, "the assailant had
three chances to kill this woman during a 35-minute period. He returned

twice to complete the job. If we had been called when he first attacked, the woman might not be dead now."

This is what the police say happened beginning at 3:20 A.M. in the 6 staid, middle-class, tree-lined Austin Street area:

Twenty-eight-year-old Catherine Genovese, who was called Kitty by 7 almost everyone in the neighborhood, was returning home from her job as manager of a bar in Hollis. She parked her red Fiat in a lot adjacent to the Kew Gardens Long Island Rail Road Station, facing Mowbray Place. Like many residents of the neighborhood, she had parked there day after day since her arrival from Connecticut a year ago, although the railroad frowns on the practice.

She turned off the lights to her car, locked the door and started to 8 walk the 100 feet to the entrance of her apartment at 82-70 Austin Street, which is in a Tudor building, with stores on the first floor and apartments on the second.

The entrance to the apartment is in the rear of the building because 9 the front is rented to retail stores. At night the quiet neighborhood is shrouded in the slumbering darkness that marks most residential areas.

Miss Genovese noticed a man at the far end of the lot, near a seven- 10 story apartment house at 82-40 Austin Street. She halted. Then, nervously, she headed up Austin Street toward Leffers Boulevard, where there is a call box to the 102d Police Precinct in nearby Richmond Hill.

She got as far as a street light in front of a bookstore before the man 11 grabbed her. She screamed. Lights went on in the 10-story apartment house at 82-67 Austin Street, which faces the bookstore. Windows slid open, and voices punctured the early-morning stillness.

Miss Genovese screamed: "Oh, my God, he stabbed me! Please help 12 me! Please help me!"

From one of the upper windows in the apartment house, a man called 13 down: "Let that girl alone!"

The assailant looked up at him, shrugged and walked down Austin 14 Street toward a white sedan parked a short distance away. Miss Genovese struggled to her feet.

Lights went out. The killer returned to Miss Genovese, now trying to 15 make her way around the side of the building by the parking lot to get to her apartment. The assailant stabbed her again.

"I'm dying!" she shrieked. "I'm dying!"   16

Windows were opened again, and lights went on in many apartments. 17 The assailant got into his car and drove away. Miss Genovese staggered to her feet. A city bus, Q-10, the Lefferts Boulevard line to Kennedy International Airport, passed. It was 3:35 A.M.

The assailant returned. By then, Miss Genovese had crawled to 18 the back of the building, where the freshly painted brown doors to the apartment house held out hope of safety. The killer tried the first door; she wasn't there. At the second door, 82-62 Austin Street, he saw her slumped on the floor at the foot of the stairs. He stabbed her a third time—fatally.

19   It was 3:50 by the time the police received their first call, from a man who was a neighbor of Miss Genovese. In two minutes they were at the scene. The neighbor, a 70-year-old woman and another woman were the only persons on the street. Nobody else came forward.

20   The man explained that he had called the police after much deliberation. He had phoned a friend in Nassau County for advice and then he had crossed the roof of the building to the apartment of the elderly woman to get her to make the call.

21   "I didn't want to get involved," he sheepishly told the police.

22   Six days later, the police arrested Winston Moseley, a 29-year-old business-machine operator, and charged him with the homicide. Moseley had no previous record. He is married, has two children and owns a home at 133-19 Sutter Avenue, South Ozone Park, Queens. On Wednesday, a court committed him to Kings County Hospital for psychiatric observation.

23   When questioned by the police, Moseley also said that he had slain Mrs. Annie Mae Johnson, 24, of 146-12 133d Avenue, Jamaica, on Feb. 29 and Barbara Kralik, 15, of 174-17 140th Avenue, Springfield Gardens, last July. In the Kralik case the police are holding Alvin L. Mitchell, who is said to have confessed to that slaying.

24   The police stressed how simple it would have been to have gotten in touch with them. "A phone call," said one of the detectives, "would have done it." The police may be reached by dialing "O" for operator or SPring 7-3100.

25   The question of whether the witnesses can be held legally responsible in any way for the failure to report the crime was put to the Police Department's legal bureau. There, a spokesman said:

26   "There is no legal responsibility, with few exceptions, for any citizen to report a crime."

27   Under the statutes of the city, he said, a witness to a suspicious or violent death must report it to the medical examiner. Under the state law, a witness cannot withhold information in a kidnapping.

28   Today witnesses from the neighborhood, which is made up of one-family homes in the $35,000 to $60,000 range with the exception of the two apartment houses near the railroad station, find it difficult to explain why they didn't call the police.

29   Lieut. Bernard Jacobs, who handled the investigation by the detectives, said:

30   "It is one of the better neighborhoods. There are few reports of crimes. You only get the usual complaints about boys playing or garbage cans being turned over."

31   The police said most persons had told them they had been afraid to call but had given meaningless answers when asked what they had feared.

"We can understand the reticence of people to become involved in 32 an area of violence," Lieutenant Jacobs said, "but when they are in their homes, near phones, why should they be afraid to call the police?"

He said his men were able to piece together what happened—and 33 capture the suspect—because the residents furnished all the information when detectives rang doorbells during the days following the slaying.

"But why didn't someone call us that night?" he asked unbelievingly. 34

Witnesses—some of them unable to believe what they had allowed to 35 happen—told a reporter why.

A housewife, knowingly if quite casual, said, "We thought it was 36 a lover's quarrel." A husband and wife both said, "Frankly, we were afraid." They seemed aware of the fact that events might have been different. A distraught woman, wiping her hands in her apron, said, "I didn't want my husband to get involved."

One couple, now willing to talk about that night, said they heard the 37 first screams. The husband looked thoughtfully at the bookstore where the killer first grabbed Miss Genovese.

"We went to the window to see what was happening," he said, "But 38 the light from our bedroom made it difficult to see the street." The wife, still apprehensive, added: "I put out the light, and we were able to see better."

Asked why they hadn't called the police, she shrugged and replied: "I 39 don't know."

A man peeked out from a slight opening in the doorway to his apart- 40 ment and rattled off an account of the killer's second attack. Why hadn't he called the police at the time? "I was tired," he said without emotion. "I went back to bed."

It was 4:25 A.M. when the ambulance arrived for the body of Miss 41 Genovese. It drove off. "Then," a solemn police detective said, "the people came out."

1964

QUESTIONS FOR DISCUSSION

Content

a. The essay's thesis might be stated as follows: "People seem to be losing their sense of community for fear of 'getting involved.'" Using details from Gansberg's story, explain this idea more fully. If you have another thesis in mind, state it and explain it by making specific reference to the text.

b. Catherine Genovese "was called Kitty by almost everyone in the neighborhood" (paragraph 7). What does this fact reveal about her relationship with her neighbors? How is it related to Gansberg's thesis?

c. What do Assistant Chief Inspector Lussen's comments (paragraphs 4 and 5) reveal that is important to understanding the significance of this narrative?

d. What should we make of the fact that the murder occurred in three separate attacks?

e. Gansberg describes the setting of this story well. In what kind of neighborhood does the murder take place?

Strategy and Style

f. What can we infer about the people who live in this neighborhood—not just about their standard of living, but about their characters?

g. As a reporter, Gansberg clearly remains objective in this piece, yet it is clear that he is indicting the witnesses for their failure to get involved. Explain how he does this.

h. The author keeps the story moving by mentioning the times at which various episodes in the attack took place. In which paragraphs does he mention these times?

i. What transitional words or expressions does Gansberg use to show the passage of time?

j. The story's verbs demonstrate the brutality and terror of the murder of Kitty Genovese. Identify a few of these verbs.

ENGAGING THE TEXT

a. If you had the opportunity, what questions might you ask any of the witnesses to this crime? Make a list of such questions. Then, speculate in writing about what the witnesses' answers might be.

b. Examine your own conscience and explain how you might have reacted if you were witnessing this murder? Then, think about an incident, circumstance, or context in which your "involvement" was needed or is still needed. How involved were or have you been? Note that this context does not have to involve violence or danger.

SUGGESTIONS FOR SUSTAINED WRITING

a. Of course, this narrative shows what can happen when people refuse to "get involved." Tell the story of an event you witnessed that relates to an individual's personal responsibility to his or her neighbors.

Perhaps you witnessed or were even the victim of a crime or of a natural disaster. What was the response of people to others in need? Did they, like the witnesses to Genovese's murder, refuse to do anything? Or were they more compassionate, more responsible people? Through your story, explain what the incident tells us about human nature.

b. In recent years, several accounts of the murder of Kitty Genovese have challenged Gansberg's version of the story. Two of them appear under Read More, below. Read the information on the two websites. Then, write an essay that contrasts Gansberg's account with at least one other account of the murder. Make sure to cite sources from which you have quoted, paraphrased, or summarized material.

c. Research another high-profile murder case. Here are some examples:

>   The murders of Nicole Brown Simpson and Ronald Goldman
>
>   The Scarsdale Diet Doctor murder
>
>   The Unabomber murders
>
>   The Lindbergh baby kidnapping
>
>   The Leopold and Loeb case
>
>   The disappearance and presumed murder of Jimmy Hoffa
>
>   The murder of Marilyn Shepherd
>
>   The Charles Manson murders
>
>   The Menendez brothers' murder of their parents

Research one of the cases in this list or a case in which you have a particular interest. Then, write a paper that discusses two opposing opinions about the cause of the murders, the guilt of those accused, the whereabouts of the body of the victim, or any other controversial issue associated with this case. Make sure to cite any information you take from secondary sources.

READ MORE

De May, J. "Kitty Genovese: What You Think You Know about the Case Might Not Be True." *A Picture History of Kew Gardens*, (http://wn.com/Kitty_Genovese).

Rosenthal, A. M. *Thirty-Eight Witnesses: The Kitty Genovese Case.* Berkeley: University of California Press, 1999.

The Plague

Barbara Tuchman

Barbara Tuchman (1912–1989) was born in New York City to a wealthy and prominent family. Her grandfather was President Wilson's ambassador to Turkey; her father was a very successful financier. After Tuchman graduated from Radcliffe College, she began working as a journalist for The Nation *magazine, for which she covered the Spanish Civil War, and then for the* New Statesman *in London. Her first book,* The Lost British Policy *(1938), concerns Britain's failed policies as they related to the Spanish Civil War (1936–1939). Her best-known works are* The Guns of August *(1964), which discusses the causes of World War I, and* Stillwell and the American Experience in China, 1911–45 *(1971), the biography of World War II General Joseph Stillwell. Each of these books earned a Pulitzer Prize. Her last work was* The First Salute *(1988), a study of the American Revolution.*

The selection that follows is excerpted from A Distant Mirror *(1978), which chronicles the horrendous events that made the fourteenth century in Europe one of the darkest and most dangerous eras in human history.*

VOCABULARY

pneumonic, malignity, pestilence, remissions, foiled, oblivion, atrophy, truncated, transept, calamity, loathsomeness, sextons, patricians, pastoral, dearth, innocuous, virulent, physiology, chronic, acute

1   In October 1347, two months after the fall of Calais, Genoese trading ships put into the harbor of Messina in Sicily with dead and dying men at the oars. The ships had come from the Black Sea port of Caffa (now Feodosiya) in the Crimea, where the Genoese maintained a trading post. The diseased sailors showed strange black swellings about the size of an egg or an apple in the armpits and groin. The swellings oozed blood and pus and were followed by spreading boils and black blotches on the skin from internal bleeding. The sick suffered severe pain and died quickly within five days of the first symptoms. As the disease spread, other symptoms of continuous fever and spitting of blood appeared instead of the swellings or buboes. These victims coughed and sweated heavily and died even more quickly, within three days or less, sometimes in 24 hours. In both types everything that issued from the body—breath, sweat, blood from the buboes and lungs, bloody urine, and blood-blackened excrement—smelled foul. Depression and despair accompanied the physical symptoms, and before the end "death is seen seated on the face."

2   The disease was bubonic plague, present in two forms: one that infected the bloodstream, causing the buboes and internal bleeding, and was spread by contact; and a second, more virulent pneumonic type that

infected the lungs and was spread by respiratory infection. The presence of both at once caused the high mortality and speed of contagion. So lethal was the disease that cases were known of persons going to bed well and dying before they woke, of doctors catching the illness at a bedside and dying before the patient. So rapidly did it spread from one to another that to a French physician, Simon de Covino, it seemed as if one sick person "could infect the whole world." The malignity of the pestilence appeared more terrible because its victims knew no prevention and no remedy.

The physical suffering of the disease and its aspect of evil mystery ₃ were expressed in a strange Welsh lament which saw "death coming into our midst like black smoke, a plague which cuts off the young, a rootless phantom which has no mercy for fair countenance. Woe is me of the shilling in the armpit! It is seething, terrible . . . a head that gives pain and causes a loud cry . . . a painful angry knob . . . Great is its seething like a burning cinder . . . a grievous thing of ashy color." Its eruption is ugly like the "seeds of black peas, broken fragments of brittle seacoal ... the early ornaments of black death, cinders of the peelings of the cockle weed, a mixed multitude, a black plague like halfpence, like berries . . .."

Rumors of a terrible plague supposedly arising in China and spread- ₄ ing through Tartary (Central Asia) to India and Persia, Mesopotamia, Syria, Egypt, and all of Asia Minor had reached Europe in 1346. They told of a death toll so devastating that all of India was said to be depopulated, whole territories covered by dead bodies, other areas with no one left alive. As added up by Pope Clement VI at Avignon, the total of reported dead reached 23,840,000. In the absence of a concept of contagion, no serious alarm was felt in Europe until the trading ships brought their black burden of pestilence into Messina while other infected ships from the Levant carried it to Genoa and Venice.

By January 1348 it penetrated France via Marseille, and North Africa ₅ via Tunis. Shipborne along coasts and navigable rivers, it spread westward from Marseille through the ports of Languedoc to Spain and northward up the Rhône to Avignon, where it arrived in March. It reached Narbonne, Montpellier, Carcassonne, and Toulouse between February and May, and at the same time in Italy spread to Rome and Florence and their hinterlands. Between June and August it reached Bordeaux, Lyon, and Paris, spread to Burgundy and Normandy, and crossed the Channel from Normandy into southern England. From Italy during the same summer it crossed the Alps into Switzerland and reached eastward to Hungary.

In a given area the plague accomplished its kill within four to six ₆ months and then faded, except in the larger cities, where, rooting into the close-quartered population, it abated during the winter, only to reappear in spring and rage for another six months.

In 1349 it resumed in Paris, spread to Picardy, Flanders, and the ₇ Low Countries, and from England to Scotland and Ireland as well as to Norway, where a ghost ship with a cargo of wool and a dead crew drifted offshore until it ran aground near Bergen. From there the plague passed into Sweden, Denmark, Prussia, Iceland, and as far as Greenland. Leaving a strange pocket of immunity in Bohemia, and Russia unattacked until 1351, it had passed from most of Europe by mid-1350. Although the mortality rate was erratic, ranging from one fifth in some places to nine tenths or almost total elimination in others, the overall estimate of modern demographers has settled—for the area extending from India to Iceland—around the same figure expressed in Froissart's casual words: "a third of the world died." His estimate, the common one at the time, was not an inspired guess but a borrowing of St. John's figure for mortality from plague in Revelation, the favorite guide to human affairs of the Middle Ages.

8   A third of Europe would have meant about 20 million deaths. No one knows in truth how many died. Contemporary reports were an awed impression, not an accurate count. In crowded Avignon, it was said, 400 died daily; 7,000 houses emptied by death were shut up; a single graveyard received 11,000 corpses in six weeks; half the city's inhabitants reportedly died, including 9 cardinals or one third of the total, and 70 lesser prelates. Watching the endlessly passing death carts, chroniclers let normal exaggeration take wings and put the Avignon death toll at 62,000 and even at 120,000, although the city's total population was probably less than 50,000.

9   When graveyards filled up, bodies at Avignon were thrown into the Rhône until mass burial pits were dug for dumping the corpses. In London, in such pits, corpses piled up in layers until they overflowed. Everywhere reports speak of the sick dying too fast for the living to bury. Corpses were dragged out of homes and left in front of doorways. Morning light revealed new piles of bodies. In Florence the dead were gathered up by the Compagnia della Misericordia—founded in 1244 to care for the sick—whose members wore red robes and hoods masking the face except for the eyes. When their efforts failed, the dead lay putrid in the streets for days at a time. When no coffins were to be had, the bodies were laid on boards, two or three at once, to be carried to graveyards or common pits. Families dumped their own relatives into the pits, or buried them so hastily and thinly "that dogs dragged them forth and devoured their bodies."

10   Amid accumulating death and fear of contagion, people died without last rites and were buried without prayers, a prospect that terrified the last hours of the stricken. A bishop in England gave permission to laymen to make confession to each other as was done by the Apostles, "or if no man is present then even to a woman," and if no priest could be found to administer extreme unction, "then faith must suffice." Clement VI found it necessary to grant remissions of sin to all who died of the plague

because so many were unattended by priests. "And no bells tolled," wrote a chronicler of Siena, "and nobody wept no matter what his loss because almost everyone expected death .... And people said and believed, 'This is the end of the world.'?"

In Paris, where the plague lasted through 1349, the reported death 11 rate was 800 a day, in Pisa 500, in Vienna 500 to 600. The total dead in Paris numbered 50,000 or half the population. Florence, weakened by the famine of 1347, lost three to four fifths of its citizens, Venice two thirds, Hamburg and Bremen, though smaller in size, about the same proportion. Cities, as centers of transportation, were more likely to be affected than villages, although once a village was infected, its death rate was equally high. At Givry, a prosperous village in Burgundy of 1,200 to 1,500 people, the parish register records 615 deaths in the space of fourteen weeks, compared to an average of thirty deaths a year in the previous decade. In three villages of Cambridgeshire, manorial records show a death rate of 47 percent, 57 percent, and in one case 70 percent. When the last survivors, too few to carry on, moved away, a deserted village sank back into the wilderness and disappeared from the map altogether, leaving only a grass-covered ghostly outline to show where mortals once had lived.

In enclosed places such as monasteries and prisons, the infection of 12 one person usually meant that of all, as happened in the Franciscan convents of Carcassonne and Marseille, where every inmate without exception died. Of the 140 Dominicans at Montpellier only seven survived. Petrarch's brother Gherardo, member of a Carthusian monastery, buried the prior and 34 fellow monks one by one, sometimes three a day, until he was left alone with his dog and fled to look for a place that would take him in. Watching every comrade die, men in such places could not but wonder whether the strange peril that filled the air had not been sent to exterminate the human race. In Kilkenny, Ireland, Brother John Clyn of the Friars Minor, another monk left alone among dead men, kept a record of what had happened lest "things which should be remembered perish with time and vanish from the memory of those who come after us." Sensing "the whole world, as it were, placed within the grasp of the Evil One," and waiting for death to visit him too, he wrote, "I leave parchment to continue this work, if perchance any man survive and any of the race of Adam escape this pestilence and carry on the work which I have begun." Brother John, as noted by another hand, died of the pestilence, but he foiled oblivion.

The largest cities of Europe, with populations of about 100,000, 13 were Paris and Florence, Venice and Genoa. At the next level, with more than 50,000, were Ghent and Bruges in Flanders, Milan, Bologna, Rome, Naples, and Palermo, and Cologne. London hovered below 50,000, the only city in England except York with more than 10,000. At the level of 20,000 to 50,000 were Bordeaux, Toulouse, Montpellier, Marseille, and

Lyon in France, Barcelona, Seville, and Toledo in Spain, Siena, Pisa, and other secondary cities in Italy, and the Hanseatic trading cities of the Empire. The plague raged through them all, killing anywhere from one third to two thirds of their inhabitants. Italy, with a total population of 10 to 11 million, probably suffered the heaviest toll. Following the Florentine bankruptcies, the crop failures and workers' riots of 1346–47, the revolt of Cola di Rienzi that plunged Rome into anarchy, the plague came as the peak of successive calamities. As if the world were indeed in the grasp of the Evil One, its first appearance on the European mainland in January 1348 coincided with a fearsome earthquake that carved a path of wreckage from Naples up to Venice. Houses collapsed, church towers toppled, villages were crushed, and the destruction reached as far as Germany and Greece. Emotional response, dulled by horrors, underwent a kind of atrophy epitomized by the chronicler who wrote, "And in these days was burying without sorrowe and wedding without friendschippe."

14   In Siena, where more than half the inhabitants died of the plague, work was abandoned on the great cathedral, planned to be the largest in the world, and never resumed, owing to loss of workers and master masons and "the melancholy and grief" of the survivors. The cathedral's truncated transept still stands in permanent witness to the sweep of death's scythe. Agnolo di Tura, a chronicler of Siena, recorded the fear of contagion that froze every other instinct. "Father abandoned child, wife husband, one brother another," he wrote, "for this plague seemed to strike through the breath and sight. And so they died. And no one could be found to bury the dead for money or friendship …. And I, Agnolo di Tura, called the Fat, buried my five children with my own hands, and so did many others likewise."

15   There were many to echo his account of inhumanity and few to balance it, for the plague was not the kind of calamity that inspired mutual help. Its loathsomeness and deadliness did not herd people together in mutual distress, but only prompted their desire to escape each other. "Magistrates and notaries refused to come and make the wills of the dying," reported a Franciscan friar of Piazza in Sicily; what was worse, "even the priests did not come to hear their confessions." A clerk of the Archbishop of Canterbury reported the same of English priests who "turned away from the care of their benefices from fear of death." Cases of parents deserting children and children their parents were reported across Europe from Scotland to Russia. The calamity chilled the hearts of men, wrote Boccaccio in his famous account of the plague in Florence that serves as introduction to the *Decameron*. "One man shunned another … kinsfolk held aloof, brother was forsaken by brother, oftentimes husband by wife; nay, what is more, and scarcely to be believed, fathers and mothers were found to abandon their own children to their fate, untended, unvisited as if they had been strangers." Exaggeration and literary pessimism were

common in the 14th century, but the Pope's physician, Guy de Chauliac, was a sober, careful observer who reported the same phenomenon: "A father did not visit his son, nor the son his father. Charity was dead."

Yet not entirely. In Paris, according to the chronicler Jean de Venette, [16] the nuns of the Hôtel Dieu or municipal hospital, "having no fear of death tended the sick with all sweetness and humility." New nuns repeatedly took the places of those who died, until the majority "many times renewed by death now rest in peace with Christ as we may piously believe."

When the plague entered northern France in July 1348, it settled first [17] in Normandy and, checked by winter, gave Picardy a deceptive interim until the next summer. Either in mourning or warning, black flags were flown from church towers of the worst-stricken villages of Normandy. "And in that time," wrote a monk of the abbey of Fourcarment, "the mortality was so great among the people of Normandy that those of Picardy mocked them." The same unneighborly reaction was reported of the Scots, separated by a winter's immunity from the English. Delighted to hear of the disease that was scourging the "southrons," they gathered forces for an invasion, "laughing at their enemies." Before they could move, the savage mortality fell upon them too, scattering some in death and the rest in panic to spread the infection as they fled.

In Picardy in the summer of 1349 the pestilence penetrated the castle [18] of Coucy to kill Enguerrand's mother, Catherine, and her new husband. Whether her nine-year-old son escaped by chance or was perhaps living elsewhere with one of his guardians is unrecorded. In nearby Amiens, tannery workers, responding quickly to losses in the labor force, combined to bargain for higher wages. In another place villagers were seen dancing to drums and trumpets, and on being asked the reason, answered that, seeing their neighbors die day by day while their village remained immune, they believed they could keep the plague from entering "by the jollity that is in us. That is why we dance." Further north in Tournai on the border of Flanders, Gilles li Muisis, Abbot of St. Martin's, kept one of the epidemic's most vivid accounts. The passing bells rang all day and all night, he recorded, because sextons were anxious to obtain their fees while they could. Filled with the sound of mourning, the city became oppressed by fear, so that the authorities forbade the tolling of bells and the wearing of black and restricted funeral services to two mourners. The silencing of funeral bells and of criers' announcements of deaths was ordained by most cities. Siena imposed a fine on the wearing of mourning clothes by all except widows.

Flight was the chief recourse of those who could afford it or arrange [19] it. The rich fled to their country places like Boccaccio's young patricians of Florence, who settled in a pastoral palace "removed on every side from the roads" with "wells of cool water and vaults of rare wines." The urban poor died in their burrows, "and only the stench of their bodies informed neighbors of their death." That the poor were more heavily afflicted than the rich was clearly remarked at the time, in the north as in the south. A Scottish chronicler, John of Fordun, stated flatly that the pest "attacked especially the meaner sort and common people—seldom the magnates." Simon de Covino of Montpellier made the same observation. He ascribed it to the misery and want and hard lives that made the poor more susceptible, which was half the truth. Close contact and lack of sanitation was the unrecognized other half. It was noticed too that the young died in greater proportion than the old; Simon de Covino compared the disappearance of youth to the withering of flowers in the fields.

20   In the countryside peasants dropped dead on the roads, in the fields, in their houses. Survivors in growing helplessness fell into apathy, leaving ripe wheat uncut and livestock untended. Oxen and asses, sheep and goats, pigs and chickens ran wild and they too, according to local reports, succumbed to the pest. English sheep, bearers of the precious wool, died throughout the country. The chronicler Henry Knighton, canon of Leicester Abbey, reported 5,000 dead in one field alone, "their bodies so corrupted by the plague that neither beast nor bird would touch them," and spreading an appalling stench. In the Austrian Alps wolves came down to prey upon sheep and then, "as if alarmed by some invisible warning, turned and fled back into the wilderness." In remote Dalmatia bolder wolves descended upon a plague-stricken city and attacked human survivors. For want of herdsmen, cattle strayed from place to place and died in hedgerows and ditches. Dogs and cats fell like the rest.

21   The dearth of labor held a fearful prospect because the 14th century lived close to the annual harvest both for food and for next year's seed. "So few servants and laborers were left," wrote Knighton, "that no one knew where to turn for help." The sense of a vanishing future created a kind of dementia of despair. A Bavarian chronicler of Neuberg on the Danube recorded that "Men and women . . . wandered around as if mad" and let their cattle stray "because no one had any inclination to concern themselves about the future." Fields went uncultivated, spring seed unsown. Second growth with nature's awful energy crept back over cleared land, dikes crumbled, salt water reinvaded and soured the lowlands. With so few hands remaining to restore the work of centuries, people felt, in Walsingham's words, that "the world could never again regain its former prosperity."

22   Though the death rate was higher among the anonymous poor, the known and the great died too. King Alfonso XI of Castile was the only reigning monarch killed by the pest, but his neighbor King Pedro of Aragon lost his wife, Queen Leonora, his daughter Marie, and a niece in the space of six months. John Cantacuzene, Emperor of Byzantium, lost his son. In France the lame Queen Jeanne and her daughter-in-law Bonne de Luxemburg, wife of the Dauphin, both died in 1349 in the same phase

that took the life of Enguerrand's mother. Jeanne, Queen of Navarre, daughter of Louis X, was another victim. Edward III's second daughter, Joanna, who was on her way to marry Pedro, the heir of Castile, died in Bordeaux. Women appear to have been more vulnerable than men, perhaps because, being more housebound, they were more exposed to fleas. Boccaccio's mistress Fiammetta, illegitimate daughter of the King of Naples, died, as did Laura, the beloved—whether real or fictional—of Petrarch. Reaching out to us in the future, Petrarch cried, "Oh happy posterity who will not experience such abysmal woe and will look upon our testimony as a fable."

In Florence Giovanni Villani, the great historian of his time, died at 68 in the midst of an unfinished sentence: ". . .*e dure questo pistolenza fino a* . . . (in the midst of this pestilence there came to an end . . .)." Siena's master painters, the brothers Ambrogio and Pietro Lorenzetti, whose names never appear after 1348, presumably perished in the plague, as did Andrea Pisano, architect and sculptor of Florence. William of Ockham and the English mystic Richard Rolle of Hampole both disappear from mention after 1349. Francisco Datini, merchant of Prato, lost both his parents and two siblings. Curious sweeps of mortality afflicted certain bodies of merchants in London. All eight wardens of the Company of Cutters, all six wardens of the Hatters, and four wardens of the Goldsmiths died before July 1350. Sir John Pulteney, master draper and four times Mayor of London, was a victim, likewise Sir John Montgomery, Governor of Calais.

Among the clergy and doctors the mortality was naturally high because of the nature of their professions. Out of 24 physicians in Venice, 20 were said to have lost their lives in the plague, although, according to another account, some were believed to have fled or to have shut themselves up in their houses. At Montpellier, site of the leading medieval medical school, the physician Simon de Covino reported that, despite the great number of doctors, "hardly one of them escaped." In Avignon, Guy de Chauliac confessed that he performed his medical visits only because he dared not stay away for fear of infamy, but "I was in continual fear." He claimed to have contracted the disease but to have cured himself by his own treatment; if so, he was one of the few who recovered.

Clerical mortality varied with rank. Although the one-third toll of cardinals reflects the same proportion as the whole, this was probably due to their concentration in Avignon. In England, in strange and almost sinister procession, the Archbishop of Canterbury, John Stratford, died in August 1348, his appointed successor died in May 1349, and the next appointee three months later, all three within a year. Despite such weird vagaries, prelates in general managed to sustain a higher survival rate than the lesser clergy. Among bishops the deaths have been estimated at about one in twenty. The loss of priests, even if many avoided their fearful duty of attending the dying, was about the same as among the population as a whole.

26   Government officials, whose loss contributed to the general chaos, found, on the whole, no special shelter. In Siena four of the nine members of the governing oligarchy died, in France one third of the royal notaries, in Bristol 15 out of the 52 members of the Town Council or almost one third. Tax collecting obviously suffered, with the result that Philip VI was unable to collect more than a fraction of the subsidy granted him by the Estates in the winter of 1347–48.

27   Lawlessness and debauchery accompanied the plague as they had during the great plague of Athens of 430 B.C., when according to Thucydides, men grew bold in the indulgence of pleasure: "For seeing how the rich died in a moment and those who had nothing immediately inherited their property, they reflected that life and riches were alike transitory and they resolved to enjoy themselves while they could." Human behavior is timeless. When St. John had his vision of plague in Revelation, he knew from some experience or race memory that those who survived "repented not of the work of their hands . . . . Neither repented they of their murders, nor of their sorceries, nor of their fornication, nor of their thefts."

28   Ignorance of the cause augmented the sense of horror. Of the real carriers, rats and fleas, the 14th century had no suspicion, perhaps because they were so familiar. Fleas, though a common household nuisance, are not once mentioned in contemporary plague writings, and rats only incidentally, although folklore commonly associated them with pestilence. The legend of the Pied Piper arose from an outbreak of 1284. The actual plague bacillus, *Pasturella pestis*, remained undiscovered for another 500 years. Living alternately in the stomach of the flea and the bloodstream of the rat who was the flea's host, the bacillus in its bubonic form was transferred to humans and animals by the bite of either rat or flea. It traveled by virtue of *Rattus rattus*, the small medieval black rat that lived on ships, as well as by the heavier brown or sewer rat. What precipitated the turn of the bacillus from innocuous to virulent form is unknown, but the occurrence is now believed to have taken place not in China but somewhere in central Asia and to have spread along the caravan routes. Chinese origin was a mistaken notion of the 14th century based on real but belated reports of huge death tolls in China from drought, famine, and pestilence, which have since been traced to the 1330s, too soon to be responsible for the plague that appeared in India in 1346.

29   The phantom enemy had no name. Called the Black Death only in later recurrences, it was known during the first epidemic simply as the Pestilence or Great Mortality. Reports from the East, swollen by fearful imaginings, told of strange tempests and "sheets of fire" mingled with huge hailstones that "slew almost all," or a "vast rain of fire" that burned

up men, beasts, stones, trees, villages, and cities. In another version, "foul blasts of wind" from the fires carried the infection to Europe "and now as some suspect it cometh round the seacoast." Accurate observation in this case could not make the mental jump to ships and rats because no idea of animal- or insect-borne contagion existed.

The earthquake was blamed for releasing sulfurous and foul fumes 30 from the earth's interior, or as evidence of a titanic struggle of planets and oceans causing waters to rise and vaporize until fish died in masses and corrupted the air. All these explanations had in common a factor of poisoned air, of miasmas and thick, stinking mists traced to every kind of natural or imagined agency from stagnant lakes to malign conjunc-tion of the planets, from the hand of the Evil One to the wrath of God. Medical thinking, trapped in the theory of astral influences, stressed air as the communicator of disease, ignoring sanitation or visible carriers. The existence of two carriers confused the trail, the more so because the flea could live and travel independently of the rat for as long as a month and, if infected by the particularly virulent septicemic form of the bacillus, could infect humans without reinfecting itself from the rat. The simulta-neous presence of the pneumonic form of the disease, which was indeed communicated through the air, blurred the problem further.

The mystery of the contagion was "the most terrible of all the terrors," 31 as an anonymous Flemish cleric in Avignon wrote to a correspondent in Bruges. Plagues had been known before, from the plague of Athens (believed to have been typhus) to the prolonged epidemic of the 6th century A.D., to the recurrence of sporadic outbreaks in the 12th and 13th centuries, but they had left no accumulated store of understanding. That the infection came from contact with the sick or with their houses, clothes, or corpses was quickly observed but not comprehended. Gentile da Foligno, renowned physician of Perugia and doctor of medicine at the universities of Bologna and Padua, came close to respiratory infec-tion when he surmised that poisonous material was "communicated by means of air breathed out and in." Having no idea of microscopic carri-ers, he had to assume that the air was corrupted by planetary influences. Planets, however, could not explain the ongoing contagion. The agonized search for an answer gave rise to such theories as transference by sight. People fell ill, wrote Guy de Chauliac, not only by remaining with the sick but "even by looking at them." Three hundred years later Joshua Barnes, the 17th century biographer of Edward III, could write that the power of infection had entered into beams of light and "darted death from the eyes."

Doctors struggling with the evidence could not break away from the 32 terms of astrology, to which they believed all human physiology was sub-ject. Medicine was the one aspect of medieval life, perhaps because of its links with the Arabs, not shaped by Christian doctrine. Clerics detested astrology, but could not dislodge its influence. Guy de Chauliac, physician to three popes in succession, practiced in obedience to the zodiac. While his *Cirurgia* was the major treatise on surgery of its time, while he understood the use of anesthesia made from the juice of opium, mandrake, or hemlock, he nevertheless prescribed bleeding and purgatives by the planets and divided chronic from acute diseases on the basis of one being under the rule of the sun and the other of the moon.

33   In October 1348 Philip VI asked the medical faculty of the University of Paris for a report on the affliction that seemed to threaten human survival. With careful thesis, antithesis, and proofs, the doctors ascribed it to a triple conjunction of Saturn, Jupiter, and Mars in the 40th degree of Aquarius said to have occurred on March 20, 1345. They acknowledged, however, effects "whose cause is hidden from even the most highly trained intellects." The verdict of the masters of Paris became the official version. Borrowed, copied by scribes, carried abroad, translated from Latin into various vernaculars, it was everywhere accepted, even by the Arab physicians of Cordova and Granada, as the scientific if not the popular answer. Because of the terrible interest of the subject, the translations of the plague tracts stimulated use of national languages. In that one respect, life came from death.

34   To the people at large there could be but one explanation—the wrath of God. Planets might satisfy the learned doctors, but God was closer to the average man. A scourge so sweeping and unsparing without any visible cause could only be seen as Divine punishment upon mankind for its sins. It might even be God's terminal disappointment in his creature. Matteo Villani compared the plague to the Flood in ultimate purpose and believed he was recording "the extermination of mankind." Efforts to appease Divine wrath took many forms, as when the city of Rouen ordered that everything that could anger God, such as gambling, cursing, and drinking, must be stopped. More general were the penitent processions authorized at first by the Pope, some lasting as long as three days, some attended by as many as 2,000, which everywhere accompanied the plague and helped to spread it.

35   Barefoot in sackcloth, sprinkled with ashes, weeping, praying, tearing their hair, carrying candles and relics, sometimes with ropes around their necks or beating themselves with whips, the penitents wound through the streets, imploring the mercy of the Virgin and saints at their shrines. In a vivid illustration for the *Très Riches Heures* of the Due de Berry, the Pope is shown in a penitent procession attended by four cardinals in scarlet from hat to hem. He raises both arms in supplication to the angel on top of the Castel Sant' Angelo, while white-robed priests bearing banners and relics in golden cases turn to look as one of their number, stricken by the plague, falls to the ground, his face contorted with anxiety. In the rear, a gray-clad monk falls beside another victim already on the ground as the

townspeople gaze in horror. (Nominally the illustration represents a 6th century plague in the time of Pope Gregory the Great, but as medieval artists made no distinction between past and present, the scene is shown as the artist would have seen it in the 14th century.) When it became evident that these processions were sources of infection, Clement VI had to prohibit them.

In Messina, where the plague first appeared, the people begged the 36 Archbishop of neighboring Catania to lend them the relics of St. Agatha. When the Catanians refused to let the relics go, the Archbishop dipped them in holy water and took the water himself to Messina, where he carried it in a procession with prayers and litanies through the streets. The demonic, which shared the medieval cosmos with God, appeared as "demons in the shape of dogs" to terrify the people. "A black dog with a drawn sword in his paws appeared among them, gnashing his teeth and rushing upon them and breaking all the silver vessels and lamps and candlesticks on the altars and casting them hither and thither . . . . So the people of Messina, terrified by this prodigious vision, were all strangely overcome by fear."

The apparent absence of earthly cause gave the plague a supernatural 37 and sinister quality. Scandinavians believed that a Pest Maiden emerged from the mouth of the dead in the form of a blue flame and flew through the air to infect the next house. In Lithuania the Maiden was said to wave a red scarf through the door or window to let in the pest. One brave man, according to legend, deliberately waited at his open window with drawn sword and, at the fluttering of the scarf, chopped off the hand. He died of his deed, but his village was spared and the scarf long preserved as a relic in the local church.

Beyond demons and superstition the final hand was God's. The Pope 38 acknowledged it in a Bull of September 1348, speaking of the "pestilence with which God is afflicting the Christian people." To the Emperor John Cantacuzene it was manifest that a malady of such horrors, stenches, and agonies, and especially one bringing the dismal despair that settled upon its victims before they died, was not a plague "natural" to mankind but "a chastisement from Heaven." To Piers Plowman "these pestilences were for pure sin."

The general acceptance of this view created an expanded sense of 39 guilt, for if the plague were punishment there had to be terrible sin to have occasioned it. What sins were on the 14th century conscience? Primarily greed, the sin of avarice, followed by usury, worldliness, adultery, blasphemy, falsehood, luxury, irreligion. Giovanni Villani, attempting to account for the cascade of calamity that had fallen upon Florence, concluded that it was retribution for the sins of avarice and usury that oppressed the poor. Pity and anger about the condition of the poor, especially victimization of the peasantry in war, was often expressed by writers of the time and was certainly on the conscience of the century. Beneath it all was the daily condition of medieval life, in which hardly an act or thought, sexual, mercantile, or military, did not contravene the dictates of the Church. Mere failure to fast or attend mass was sin. The result was an underground lake of guilt in the soul that the plague now tapped.

40   That the mortality was accepted as God's punishment may explain in part the vacuum of comment that followed the Black Death. An investigator has noticed that in the archives of Périgord references to the war are innumerable, to the plague few. Froissart mentions the great death but once, Chaucer gives it barely a glance. Divine anger so great that it contemplated the extermination of man did not bear close examination.

QUESTIONS FOR DISCUSSION

Content

a. Explain Tuchman's thesis and purpose in your own words.

b. What was it about the plague that made it even more frightening than a modern disease such as AIDS, for example?

c. Look up the following historical events and people on the Internet or in a reference book: Battle of Calais, 1347 (paragraph 1); Petrarch (paragraph 12); Cola di Rienzi (paragraph 13); Boccaccio (paragraph 15); and Engerrand de Coucy (paragraph 13).

d. Explain the scientific causes of the plague and its spread. Why were medieval physicians unable to identify the true cause?

e. How did people in the fourteenth century explain the coming of the plague? (Summarize the process used to explain how the plague spread.)

f. What were the plague's immediate effects on Europe's economy?

g. Explain some of the effects that the plague had on people's behavior and morals.

Strategy and Style

h. Reread Tuchman's introduction. What is it about this first paragraph that makes one want to read on?

i. Historians often use direct quotations from eyewitnesses, journalists, and other historians (Tuchman mentions chroniclers). Find a few places where Tuchman does so.

j. Tuchman also makes excellent use of statistics. What effect do such statistics produce in the reader? Pay special attention to paragraph 8.

k. Narration is often accompanied by vivid and moving description. However, Tuchman also explains causes and effects, defines, draws comparisons and contrasts, and uses examples. Identify paragraphs in which she does at least one of these things.

l. This essay argues that the plague attacked all classes and segments of society. Explain why Tuchman is effective in making this point. Why does she mention exceptions to this idea?

m.How does making references to the Bible help the author capture the tenor of the times?

n. Tuchman closes the essay with an explanation of how fourteenth century Europeans accounted for the plague and how they responded to its perceived causes. Why is this sort of conclusion both appropriate and effective?

ENGAGING THE TEXT

a. In paragraph 12, Tuchman discusses the terror that afflicted people during the plague. Reread this paragraph. Find other places where she discusses terror. Write a short paragraph that summarizes her ideas on this subject in paragraph 12 and elsewhere. Make direct and frequent reference to the text.

b. "The plague," claims the author, "was not the kind of calamity that inspired mutual help" (paragraph 15). Using examples taken from various paragraphs in this essay, explain what Tuchman means.

SUGGESTIONS FOR SUSTAINED WRITING

a. Write an essay in which you narrate an experience you or someone you know has had with a life-threatening illness or injury. The problem might be physical or emotional or both. Explain both the illness's/injury's causes (if appropriate) and its effects. If appropriate, talk about the physical suffering experienced by the patient, but also include information about his or her mental or emotional pain, as well as any mental or emotional distress experienced by family, friends, schoolmates, or coworkers. Discuss any treatment or therapy the patient had to undergo, and explain its results. If the patient is still suffering, end your essay by looking to the future and explaining what he or she might expect in the coming days, months, or years.

b. Paul Salopeck's "Shattered Sudan" (Chapter 8, Cause and Effect) is another essay that discusses human suffering. Read this essay, noting in the margins any similarities to or differences from Tuchman's essay in style, technique, or purpose. For example, both authors include description and explain causes and effects. Both also make use of quotations. However, their purposes differ, as do the ways they structure and develop paragraphs. The biggest difference, of course, is that they are writing about different periods and parts of the world. Using the marginal notes you have gathered, write an essay that points out similarities and differences in these essays. In the process, make frequent and specific reference to the text of each.

c. In paragraph 33, Tuchman says that "translations of plague tracts stimulated use of national languages." (Recall that in medieval Europe, the dominant language for government, scholarly, and scientific documents had been Latin.) Through both library and Internet research, explain at least one other positive effect of the plague. Then discuss a modern disease, such as AIDS, and consider what positive effects the arrival of this disease has produced.

READ MORE

Barbara Tuchman

Brody, Seymour. "Barbara Wertheim Tuchman (1912–1989)." *Jewish Virtual Library* (http://www.jewishvirtuallibrary.org/jsource/biography/tuchman.html).

"Barbara Tuchman." *The Pennsylvania Center for the Book.* Pennsylvania State University (http://pabook.libraries.psu.edu/palitmap/bios/Tuchman__Barbara.html): *A biography and bibliography of the author.*

Tuchman, Barbara. *The Guns of August.* New York: Random House, 2009. *An account of causes and beginnings of World War I.*

___. *The March of Folly: From Troy to Vietnam.* New York: Ballantine, 2002. *Essays on the greatest missteps in human history.*

The Plague

"The Black Death: Bubonic Plague" (http://www.themiddleages.net/plague.html): *This informative site contains several links to other important sources.*

Ziegler, Philip. *The Black Death.* New York: Torchbook, 1971.

2

Description

Description makes for diversity. The people, places, and things described in the six selections that follow vary as widely as the distinctive styles and perspectives of their authors. Nonetheless, each essay is a verbal picture sketched in details that are at once concrete, specific, and vivid.

Good description is never hurried; it is crafted with carefully chosen details that *show* the reader something. In "Beneath My House," for example, Louise Erdrich uses such details to describe a kitten she has chased and caught in the crawl space under her house: "Out it come with a squeak of terror, a series of panting comic hisses, and a whirl of claws and teeth, tiny needles it didn't yet know how to use."

Appealing to the senses is fundamental to the process of describing. Some writers rely almost solely upon vision and hearing as sources of descriptive detail, but the authors in this chapter teach us that we can use the other senses as well—taste, smell, and touch—to guide readers through our private worlds. Perhaps one of the best examples appears in E.B. White's "Once More to the Lake":

> ... I remembered clearest of all the early mornings, when the lake was cool and motionless, remembered how the bedroom smelled of the lumber it was made of and of the wet woods whose scent entered through the screen. The partitions in the camp were thin and did not extend clear to the top of the rooms, and as I was always the first up I would dress softly so as not to wake the others, and sneak out into the sweet outdoors and start out in the canoe, keeping close along the shore in the long shadows of the pines. I remembered being very careful never to rub my paddle against the gunwale for fear of disturbing the stillness of the cathedral.

Several essays in this chapter also show that writers of description exploit techniques often associated with narration, especially the use of verbs that are informative and evocative. We know that how a person behaves can tell us a great deal about his or her character. So it is with a place, for what happens there often reveals much about its character. In another passage from "Once More to the Lake," White combines narration and description to show us—in concrete terms—what this place means to him:

> We caught two bass, hauling them in briskly as if they were mackerel, pulling them over the side of the boat in a businesslike manner without

any landing net, and stunning them with a blow on the back of the head. When we got back for a swim before lunch, the lake was exactly where we had left it, the same number of inches from the dock, and there was only the merest suggestion of a breeze. This seemed an utterly enchanted sea, this lake you could leave to its own devices for a few house and come back to, and find that it had not stirred, this constant and trustworthy body of water. In the shallows the dark, water-soaked sticks and twigs, wet and old were undulating in clusters on the bottom against the clean ribbed sand, and the track of the mussel was plain. A school of minnows swam by, each minnow with its small individual shadow, doubling the attendance, so clear and sharp in the sunlight.

Another tool writers of description use to enliven and concretize their writing is figurative language—simile, metaphor, personification, just to name the three most common forms. Notice how figures of speech spark the readers' interest in the introduction to Erdrich's essay:

It was as if the house itself had given birth. One day the floor cried where I stepped on it, and I jumped back. I was near a heating vent, and when I bent and pried the cover off and thrust my hand in, I briefly grabbed a ball of fur that hissed and spat. I heard the kitten scrambling away, the tin resounding like a small thunder along the length of its flight.

Erdrich's description reminds us that invoking images from the knowledge we share with readers is a good way to show them something new. But flashes of brilliance appear throughout the chapter. Take James Baldwin's reminder that the residents of the ghetto "must struggle stolidly, incessantly, to keep [a] sense [of honor] alive in themselves in spite of the insults, the indifference, and the cruelty they are certain to encounter in their working day." Or read Michael Byers's description of the Vietnam Memorial:

This monument is public architecture at its finest: open, instructive, and moving. The ambivalent descent, deeper and deeper, along a sinister black wall, exactly mimics the national experience of the war: the early trickle of bad news, the growing sense of obligation, the gradual realization that we are in over our heads, and at its nadir, the dark hopelessness from which there seems no escaping.

These and many more passages in this chapter testify to the power and clarity with which writers of great description invest their writing.

While relying heavily on physical description, none of the essays collected here is a purely sensate record of its subject. More often than not, describing is a means to an end. It is hard to read a narrative, for example, without stumbling over details that reveal setting and character. Even writers of scientific prose use information that appeals to the senses as a way to discuss the lives of plants and animals or to explore the workings of machines and processes.

Like other writers in this chapter, Joan Didion reminds us that discussing the people who inhabit a place is a way to reveal its soul. So does Judith Ortiz Cofer, who, in "A Partial Remembrance of a Puerto Rican Childhood" tells us much about her grandmother and the other members of her family so as to describe the emotional space in which she was raised. Finally, Erdrich and White seem to be telling us about the landscape of their souls as well as the places in which their essays are set.

As always, you are invited to make your own comparisons and to draw conclusions as you see fit. What makes the selections in this chapter so enjoyable is that each reveals the strong and distinctive voice of its author. Enjoy the artists behind the subjects they describe. They will teach you that your personal commitment to a subject is worth sharing with others.

Fifth Avenue, Uptown

James Baldwin

James Baldwin (1924–1987) was born in Harlem. In 1927 his mother married David Baldwin, a minister who had moved to New York from New Orleans and who preached in a storefront church. With both of his parents working, James became the caretaker of his eight siblings and balanced his time between tending to them and going to school. His teachers at DeWitt Clinton High School encouraged his literary talent, and he began writing poems, stories, plays, and essays while editing the school's literary magazines. At 14 he had a religious awakening and began preaching, becoming increasingly popular while his stepfather's congregation decreased. But his religious calling was short-lived, and Baldwin, becoming disillusioned with Christianity, stopped preaching after three years. He moved to New Jersey in 1942 but returned to New York a year later when his father was dying. After his father's death, he moved to Greenwich Village to focus on his literary career; after five difficult years he published his first work in 1947, book reviews for The Nation *and the* New Leader. *In 1948 he received a fellowship and left the United States to live in France. There he wrote his most famous works,* Go Tell It on the Mountain *(1953), a novel about a boy's religious awakenings;* Giovanni's Room *(1956), a novel about a young homosexual man living in Paris; and* Notes of a Native Son *(1955), a nonfiction work about racism in American society. In 1957 he returned to the United States and became active in the Civil Rights movement, publishing* Another Country *(1962) and* The Fire Next Time *(1963). His other works include novels, nonfiction, essays, and plays. Disillusioned by the assassinations of Martin Luther King, Jr., and Malcolm X, he returned to France, where he lived the rest of his life.*

A classic of description, "Fifth Avenue, Uptown" is as much about the psychology of a place as it is about its physical characteristics. The title and the first paragraph, especially, portray a bitter irony that prepares us well for the Harlem Baldwin describes.

VOCABULARY

rehabilitated, proprietor, reparation, parlance, billy, fanatical, affiliation, animated, shrewd, fetid, instill, stolidly, incessantly, browbeat, prodigious, habitable, perpetually, paranoia

1 There is a housing project standing now where the house in which we grew up once stood, and one of those stunted city trees is snarling where our doorway used to be. This is on the rehabilitated side of the avenue. The other side of the avenue—for progress takes time—has not been rehabilitated yet and it looks exactly as it looked in the days when we sat with our noses pressed against the windowpane, longing to be allowed to go "across the street." The grocery store which gave us credit is still there, and there can be no doubt that it is still giving credit. The people in the project certainly need it—far more, indeed, than they ever needed the project. The last time I passed by, the Jewish proprietor was still standing among his shelves, looking sadder and heavier but scarcely any older. Farther down the block stands the shoe-repair store in which our shoes were repaired until reparation became impossible and in which, then, we bought all our "new" ones. The Negro proprietor is still in the window, head down, working at the leather.

2   These two, I imagine, could tell a long tale if they would (perhaps they would be glad to if they could), having watched so many, for so long, struggling in the fishhooks, the barbed wire, of this avenue.

3   The avenue is elsewhere the renowned and elegant Fifth. The area I am describing, which, in today's gang parlance, would be called "the turf," is bounded by Lenox Avenue on the west, the Harlem River on the east, 135th Street on the north, and 130th Street on the south. We never lived beyond these boundaries; this is where we grew up. Walking along 145th Street—for example—familiar as it is, and similar, does not have the same impact because I do not know any of the people on the block. But when I turn east on 131st Street and Lenox Avenue, there is first a soda-pop joint, then a shoeshine "parlor," then a grocery store, then a dry cleaners', then the houses. All along the street there are people who watched me grow up, people who grew up with me, people I watched grow up along with my brothers and sisters; and, sometimes in my arms, sometimes underfoot, sometimes at my shoulder—or on it—their children, a riot, a forest of children, who include my nieces and nephews.

4   When we reach the end of this long block, we find ourselves on wide, filthy, hostile Fifth Avenue, facing that project which hangs over the avenue like a monument to the folly, and the cowardice, of good intentions. All along the block, for anyone who knows it, are immense human gaps, like craters. These gaps are not created merely by those who have moved

away, inevitably into some other ghetto; or by those who have risen, almost always into a greater capacity for self-loathing and self-delusion; or yet by those who, by whatever means—World War II, the Korean war, a policeman's gun or billy, a gang war, a brawl, madness, an overdose of heroin, or, simply, unnatural exhaustion—are dead. I am talking about those who are left, and I am talking principally about the young. What are they doing? Well, some, a minority, are fanatical churchgoers, members of the more extreme of the Holy Roller sects. Many, many more are "moslems," by affiliation or sympathy, that is to say that they are united by nothing more—and nothing less—than a hatred of the white world and all its works. They are present, for example, at every Buy Black street-corner meeting—meetings in which the speaker urges his hearers to cease trading with white men and establish a separate economy. Neither the speaker nor his hearers can possibly do this, of course, since Negroes do not own General Motors or RCA or the A & P, nor, indeed, do they own more than a wholly insufficient fraction of anything else in Harlem (those who *do* own anything are more interested in their profits than in their fellows). But these meetings nevertheless keep alive in the participators a certain pride of bitterness without which, however futile this bitterness may be, they could scarcely remain alive at all. Many have given up. They stay home and watch the TV screen, living on the earnings of their parents, cousins, brothers, or uncles, and only leave the house to go to the movies or to the nearest bar. "How're you making it?" one may ask, running into them along the block, or in the bar. "Oh, I'm TV-ing it"; with the saddest, sweetest, most shamefaced of smiles, and from a great distance. This distance one is compelled to respect; anyone who has traveled so far will not easily be dragged again into the world. There are further retreats, of course, than the TV screen or the bar. There are those who are simply sitting on their stoops, "stoned," animated for a moment only, and hideously, by the approach of someone who may lend them the money for a "fix." Or by the approach of someone from whom they can purchase it, one of the shrewd ones, on the way to prison or just coming out.

And the others, who have avoided all of these deaths, get up in the 5 morning and go downtown to meet "the man." They work in the white man's world all day and come home in the evening to this fetid block. They struggle to instill in their children some private sense of honor or dignity which will help the child to survive. This means, of course, that they must struggle, stolidly, incessantly, to keep this sense alive in themselves, in spite of the insults, the indifference, and the cruelty they are certain to encounter in their working day. They patiently browbeat the landlord into fixing the heat, the plaster, the plumbing; this demands prodigious patience; nor is patience usually enough. In trying to make their hovels habitable, they are perpetually throwing good money after bad. Such frustration, so long endured, is driving many strong, admirable men and women whose only crime is color to the very gates of paranoia.

6   One remembers them from another time—playing handball in the playground, going to church, wondering if they were going to be promoted at school. One remembers them going off to war—gladly, to escape this block. One remembers their return. Perhaps one remembers their wedding day. And one sees where the girl is now—vainly looking for salvation from some other embittered, trussed, and struggling boy—and sees the all-but-abandoned children in the streets.

1948

QUESTIONS FOR DISCUSSION

Content

a. What is the image of Harlem that Baldwin creates in your mind? How does that image mesh with or conflict with other images you may have of Harlem?

b. What do the metaphors "fishhooks" and "barbed wire" in paragraph 2 mean? What other metaphors would make the same point?

c. How does Baldwin feel about Harlem? Where in the essay is this feeling revealed?

d. What are the main landmarks along the way? What does Baldwin see as significant about each one?

e. Why have many of the people in Harlem "given up"?

f. Why does Baldwin choose Fifth Avenue as the street to describe?

Strategy and Style

g. Besides the fishhooks and barbed wire metaphors in paragraph 2, what other metaphors does Baldwin use, and why?

h. This essay is from a book written in the 1950s. What do you find in the sentence style or word choice that recalls that time?

i. This is an excerpt from a longer work. From what this essay leads you to expect, what does Baldwin most likely describe immediately before and after the piece? What about this piece sets up those expectations?

j. How does Baldwin sequence this essay? In what order does he take us along this street in Harlem?

k. Baldwin uses a literary tone—calm, dispassionate, evenly paced. What sentences and words in particular create this tone?

ENGAGING THE TEXT

a. Rewrite a paragraph or short passage to create a different tone, such as one of excitement, anger, romance, or nostalgia. Keep a list of the words you remove from Baldwin and explain, in writing, why you changed those words.
b. Summarize "Fifth Avenue, Uptown."

SUGGESTIONS FOR SUSTAINED WRITING

a. Reread paragraph 5, where Baldwin reveals much about the struggles of the inhabitants of his former neighborhood. Then, using this paragraph as a point of reference, write an extended description that uses sensory details to explain the problems faced by people living in inner-city apartments. For example, you might use details associated with sight, sound, smell, and touch to expand upon Baldwin's statement, "In trying to make their hovels habitable, they are perpetually throwing good money after bad." Rely on what you have learned about poverty from the media or from your own observations to provide information. You might also read Jo Goodwin Parker's "What Is Poverty?" (Chapter 4) for additional information and insights.
b. Compare or contrast the picture of poverty in this essay with what you see in Parker's "What Is Poverty?" (Chapter 4). Make sure to consider the setting and the people the authors describe, but also comment on their use of narrative and especially tone.
c. Research Baldwin's life. (The brief biographical headnote provided here does not begin to describe the author's interesting life.) Write a biographical essay, focusing on the aspect of his life you find most significant. Include at least four secondary sources from your library or the Internet. (We list a few below to get you started.)

READ MORE

Gates Henry Louis, Jr. "The First Last Time." *The New Republic* 206.22 (1992): 37–44. *A profile of Baldwin by a renowned scholar of African-American history and culture.*

"James Baldwin: About the Author" (http://www.pbs.org/wnet/americanmasters/episodes/james-baldwin/about-the-author/59).

"James Baldwin" (http://www.biography.com/articles/James-Baldwin-9196635): *Comprehensive biography of the author.*

"James Baldwin." *BookFinder.com* (http://www.bookfinder.com/author/james-baldwin): *A list of books by Baldwin.*

Once More to the Lake

E. B. White

A regular contributor to The New Yorker *and* Harper's *magazines, E(lwyn) B(rooks) White (1899–1985) was one of the best-known American essayists of the twentieth century. He was born in Mt. Vernon, New York, but lived much of his life in Maine. After serving with the U.S. Army in World War I, White worked as a journalist for the United Press and the Seattle Times, then began writing for* The New Yorker. *In 1938, he launched "One Man's Meat" a regular column for* Harper's. *Among his friends were important writers such as Dorothy Parker, Stephen Leacock, and Robert Benchley. With his good friend James Thurber, White collaborated on a work with the intriguing title* Is Sex Necessary? *(1929). His most famous collections include* One Man's Meat *(1942),* The Points of My Compass *(1962), and* Poems and Sketches *(1981). Among his other works are several books for children, such as* Stuart Little *(1945),* Charlotte's Web *(1952), and* The Trumpet of the Swan *(1970). He was also responsible for revising the classic* Elements of Style, *written by William Strunk, one of his professors at Cornell University. White was the recipient of the Presidential Medal of Freedom and of a citation from the Pulitzer Prize Committee. In 1939, he took up permanent residence in Brookline, Maine, where he produced the bulk of his writings. "Once More to the Lake" recalls his many boyhood vacations in that state.*

"Once More to the Lake" captures an idyllic time in the life of the author. But it also presents a brilliant image of summer as a time of beauty, spiritual refreshment, and self-reflection.

VOCABULARY

incessant, placidity, haunts, primeval, helgramite, cultist, premonitory

AUGUST 1941

1 One summer, along about 1904, my father rented a camp on a lake in Maine and took us all there for the month of August. We all got ring-worm from some kittens and had to rub Pond's Extract on our arms and legs night and morning, and my father rolled over in a canoe with all his clothes on; but outside of that the vacation was a success and from then on none of us ever thought there was any place in the world like that lake in Maine. We returned summer after summer—always on August 1 for one month. I have since become a salt-water man, but sometimes in summer there are days when the restlessness of the tides and the fearful cold of the sea water and the incessant wind that blows across the afternoon and into the evening make me wish for the placidity of a lake in the woods. A few weeks ago this feeling got so strong I bought myself a couple of bass hooks and a spinner and returned to the lake where we used to go, for a week's fishing and to revisit old haunts.

2   I took along my son, who had never had any fresh water up his nose and who had seen lily pads only from train windows. On the journey over to the lake I began to wonder what it would be like. I wondered how time would have marred this unique, this holy spot—the coves and streams, the hills that the sun set behind, the camps and the paths behind the camps. I was sure that the tarred road would have found it out, and I wondered in what other ways it would be desolated. It is strange how much you can remember about places like that once you allow your mind to return into the grooves that lead back. You remember one thing, and that suddenly reminds you of another thing. I guess I remembered clearest of all the early mornings, when the lake was cool and motionless, remembered how the bedroom smelled of the lumber it was made of and of the wet woods whose scent entered through the screen. The partitions in the camp were thin and did not extend clear to the top of the rooms, and as I was always the first up I would dress softly so as not to wake the others, and sneak out into the sweet outdoors and start out in the canoe, keeping close along the shore in the long shadows of the pines. I remembered being very careful never to rub my paddle against the gunwale for fear of disturbing the stillness of the cathedral.

The lake had never been what you would call a wild lake. There   3 were cottages sprinkled around the shores, and it was in farming country although the shores of the lake were quite heavily wooded. Some of the cottages were owned by nearby farmers, and you would live at the shore and eat your meals at the farmhouse. That's what our family did. But although it wasn't wild, it was a fairly large and undisturbed lake and there were places in it that, to a child at least, seemed infinitely remote and primeval.

I was right about the tar: it led to within half a mile of the shore. But   4 when I got back there, with my boy, and we settled into a camp near a farmhouse and into the kind of summertime I had known, I could tell that it was going to be pretty much the same as it had been before—I knew it, lying in bed the first morning smelling the bedroom and hearing the boy sneak quietly out and go off along the shore in a boat. I began to sustain the illusion that he was I, and therefore, by simple transposition, that I was my father. This sensation persisted, kept cropping up all the time we were there. It was not an entirely new feeling, but in this setting it grew much stronger. I seemed to be living a dual existence. I would be in the middle of some simple act, I would be picking up a bait box or laying down a table fork, or I would be saying something and suddenly it would be not I but my father who was saying the words or making the gesture. It gave me a creepy sensation.

We went fishing the first morning. I felt the same damp moss cover-   5 ing the worms in the bait can, and saw the dragonfly alight on the tip of my rod as it hovered a few inches from the surface of the water. It was the arrival of this fly that convinced me beyond any doubt that everything was as it always had been, that the years were a mirage and that there had been no years. The small waves were the same, chucking the rowboat under the chin as we fished at anchor, and the boat was the same boat, the same color green and the ribs broken in the same places, and under the floorboards the same fresh water leavings and debris—the dead hellgrammite, the wisps of moss, the rusty discarded fishhook, the dried blood from yesterday's catch. We stared silently at the tips of our rods, at the dragonflies that came and went. I lowered the tip of mine into the water, tentatively, pensively dislodging the fly, which darted two feet away, poised, darted two feet back, and came to rest again a little farther up the rod. There had been no years between the ducking of this dragonfly and the other one—the one that was part of memory. I looked at the boy, who was silently watching his fly, and it was my hands that held his rod, my eyes watching. I felt dizzy and didn't know which rod I was at the end of.

6   We caught two bass, hauling them in briskly as though they were mackerel, pulling them over the side of the boat in a businesslike manner without any landing net, and stunning them with a blow on the back of the head. When we got back for a swim before lunch, the lake was exactly where we had left it, the same number of inches from the dock, and there was only the merest suggestion of a breeze. This seemed an utterly enchanted sea, this lake you could leave to its own devices for a few hours and come back to, and find that it had not stirred, this constant and trustworthy body of water. In the shallows, the dark, water-soaked sticks and twigs, smooth and old, were undulating in clusters on the bottom against the clean ribbed sand, and the track of the mussel was plain. A school of minnows swam by, each minnow with its small individual shadow, doubling the attendance, so clear and sharp in the sunlight. Some of the other campers were in swimming, along the shore, one of them with a cake of soap, and the water felt thin and clear and unsubstantial. Over the years there had been this person with the cake of soap, this cultist, and here he was. There had been no years.

7   Up to the farmhouse to dinner through the teeming dusty field, the road under our sneakers was only a two-track road. The middle track was missing, the one with the marks of the hooves and the splotches of dried, flaky manure. There had always been three tracks to choose from in choosing which track to walk in; now the choice was narrowed down to two. For a moment I missed terribly the middle alternative. But the way led past the tennis court, and something about the way it lay there in the sun reassured me; the tape had loosened along the backline, the alleys were green with plantains and other weeds, and the net (installed in June and removed in September) sagged in the dry noon, and the whole place steamed with midday heat and hunger and emptiness. There was a choice of pie for dessert, and one was blueberry and one was apple, and the waitresses were the same country girls, there having been no passage of time, only

the illusion of it as in a dropped curtain—the waitresses were still fifteen; their hair had been washed, that was the only difference—they had been to the movies and seen the pretty girls with the clean hair.

Summertime, oh, summertime, pattern of life indelible with fade- 8 proof lake, the wood unshatterable, the pasture with the sweetfern and the juniper forever and ever, summer without end; this was the background, and the life along the shore was the design, the cottages with their innocent and tranquil design, their tiny docks with the flagpole and the American flag floating against the white clouds in the blue sky, and little paths over the roots of the trees leading from camp to camp and the paths leading back to the outhouses and the can of lime for sprinkling, and at the souvenir counters at the store the miniature birch-bark canoes and the postcards that showed things looking a little better than they looked. This was the American family at play, escaping the city heat, wondering whether the newcomers in the camp at the head of the cove were "common" or "nice," wondering whether it was true that the people who drove up for Sunday dinner at the farmhouse were turned away because there wasn't enough chicken.

It seemed to me, as I kept remembering all this, that those times and 9 those summers had been infinitely precious and worth saving. There had been jollity and peace and goodness. The arriving (at the beginning of August) had been so big a business in itself, at the railway station the farm wagon drawn up, the first smell of the pine-laden air, the first glimpse of the smiling farmer, and the great importance of the trunks and your father's enormous authority in such matters, and the feel of the wagon under you for the long ten-mile haul, and at the top of the last long hill catching the first view of the lake after eleven months of not seeing this cherished body of water. The shouts and cries of the other campers when they saw you, and the trunks to be unpacked, to give up their rich burden. (Arriving was less exciting nowadays, when you sneaked up in your car and parked it under a tree near the camp and took out the bags and in five minutes it was all over, no fuss, no loud wonderful fuss about trunks.)

Peace and goodness and jollity. The only thing that was wrong now, 10 really, was the sound of the place, an unfamiliar nervous sound of the outboard motors. This was the note that jarred, the one thing that would sometimes break the illusion and set the years moving. In those other summertimes all motors were inboard; and when they were at a little distance, the noise they made was a sedative, an ingredient of summer sleep. They were one-cylinder and two-cylinder engines, and some were make-and-break and some were jump-spark, but they all made a sleepy sound across the lake. The one-lungers throbbed and fluttered, and the twin-cylinder ones purred and purred, and that was a quiet sound, too. But now the campers all had outboards. In the daytime, in the hot mornings, these motors made a petulant, irritable sound; at night in the still evening when the afterglow lit the water, they whined about one's ears like mosquitoes. My boy loved our rented outboard, and his great desire was to achieve single-handed mastery over it, and authority, and he soon learned the trick of choking it a little (but not too much), and the adjustment of the needle valve. Watching him I would remember the things you could do with the old one-cylinder engine with the heavy flywheel, how you could have it eating out of your hand if you got really close to it spiritually. Motorboats in those days didn't have clutches, and you would make a landing by shutting off the motor at the proper time and coasting in with a dead rudder. But there was a way of reversing them, if you learned the trick, by cutting the switch and putting it on again exactly on the final dying revolution of the flywheel, so that it would kick back against compression and begin reversing. Approaching a dock in a strong following breeze, it was difficult to slow up sufficiently by the ordinary coasting method, and if a boy felt he had complete mastery over his motor, he was tempted to keep it running beyond its time and then reverse it a few feet from the dock. It took a cool nerve, because if you threw the switch a twentieth of a second too soon you would catch the flywheel when it still had speed enough to go up past center, and the boat would leap ahead, charging bull-fashion at the dock.

11   We had a good week at the camp. The bass were biting well and the sun shone endlessly, day after day. We would be tired at night and lie down in the accumulated heat of the little bedrooms after the long hot day and the breeze would stir almost imperceptibly outside and the smell of the swamp drifted in through the rusty screens. Sleep would come easily and in the morning the red squirrel would be on the roof, tapping out his gay routine. I kept remembering everything, lying in bed in the mornings—the small steamboat that had a long rounded stern like the lip of a Ubangi, and how quietly she ran on the moonlight sails, when the older boys played their mandolins and the girls sang and we ate doughnuts dipped in sugar, and how sweet the music was on the water in the shining night, and what it had felt like to think about girls then. After breakfast we would go up to the store and the things were in the same place—the minnows in a bottle, the plugs and spinners disarranged and pawed over by the youngsters from the boys' camp, the Fig Newtons and the Beeman's gum. Outside, the road was tarred and cars stood in front of the store. Inside, all was just as it had always been, except there was more Coca-Cola and not so much Moxie and root beer and birch beer and sarsaparilla. We would walk out with a bottle of pop apiece and sometimes the pop would backfire up our noses and hurt. We explored the streams, quietly, where the turtles slid off the sunny logs and dug their way into the soft bottom; and we lay on the town wharf and fed worms to the tame bass. Everywhere we went I had trouble making out which was I, the one walking at my side, the one walking in my pants.

One afternoon while we were at that lake, a thunderstorm came up. 12
It was like the revival of an old melodrama that I had seen long ago with
childish awe. The second-act climax of the drama of the electrical distur-
bance over a lake in America had not changed in any important respect.
This was the big scene, still the big scene. The whole thing was so familiar,
the first feeling of oppression and heat and a general air around camp of
not wanting to go very far away. In mid-afternoon (it was all the same) a
curious darkening of the sky, and a lull in everything that had made life
tick; and then the way the boats suddenly swung the other way at their
moorings with the coming of a breeze out of the new quarter, and the
premonitory rumble. Then the kettle drum, then the snare, then the bass
drum and cymbals, then crackling light against the dark, and the gods
grinning and licking their chops in the hills. Afterward the calm, the rain
steadily rustling in the calm lake, the return of light and hope and spirits,
and the campers running out in joy and relief to go swimming in the rain,
their bright cries perpetuating the deathless joke about how they were
getting simply drenched, and the children screaming with delight at the
new sensation of bathing in the rain, and the joke about getting drenched
linking the generations in a strong indestructible chain. And the comedian who waded in carrying an umbrella.

When the others went swimming my son said he was going in, too. He 13
pulled his dripping trunks from the line where they had hung all through
the shower and wrung them out. Languidly, and with no thought of going
in, I watched him, his hard little body, skinny and bare, saw him wince
slightly as he pulled up around his vitals the small, soggy, icy garment. As
he buckled the swollen belt, suddenly my groin felt the chill of death.

1939

QUESTIONS FOR DISCUSSION

Content

a. In paragraph 6, White calls the lake "an enchanted sea . . . this constant
   and trustworthy body of water." What evidence does he provide in this
   and other paragraphs to support this view?
b. Given a quick, cursory reading, "Once More to the Lake" might suggest that change is not inevitable. Can you point to passages that indicate just the opposite?
c. Ostensibly, White returns to the lake to seek "the placidity of a lake in
   the woods." What else is he seeking? What else does he discover?
d. What is the significance of the line with which this essay ends?

Strategy and Style

e. Why does White mention some of the mishaps on his first visit to the lake in the first paragraph?

f. Early in the essay, the author creates a brilliant metaphor by comparing the lake to a cathedral. What other metaphors does he use? What do they help him achieve as he describes the lake and recalls his youth?

g. In what paragraphs does White make especially good use of sensory details?

h. In what paragraphs does he list concrete details in quick succession to create a kind of verbal photograph?

i. Read paragraphs 4 and 5 again. What function do they serve in the essay?

j. Although this essay is rich in description, it might also be used to teach students techniques relevant to comparison/contrast. Explain.

ENGAGING THE TEXT

a. Respond to the tone of White's essay, especially to the tone at the end. Why does the tone become darker at the end of the essay?

b. Compare White's experiences to your own on a family vacation, a reunion, or a return to an old haunt. How are your experiences similar to or different from those of White?

SUGGESTIONS FOR SUSTAINED WRITING

a. As you recall from the Questions for Discussion, White calls the lake an "enchanted sea . . . this constant and trustworthy body of water" (paragraph 6). Write a paper that begins with a paragraph or two supporting White's claim. Make frequent and direct reference to the text as you develop this part of your paper. Then, following White's lead, describe a favorite refuge of your own—a spot where you can relax, unwind, or even make important decisions without distraction. Like the author of "Once More to the Lake," use concrete, sensory details to explain what about this place draws you back to it time and again.

b. Is there a difference between White's perceptions of the lake as a child and as an adult? Why does he bother to give us both views? Write an essay in which you contrast your recollection of a spot you once frequented with the present reality of that place. Make your essay interesting by including as many specific, concrete, and vivid details as you can.

c. Write an essay about a place that might serve as the basis for a travel brochure. In other words, try to convince your readers that this is an interesting, enjoyable, or even important place to visit. Focus on a limited space, such as a particular government building or monument, a war memorial, a stretch of beach, a town or city center, or a museum. You might want to write about a place you have seen firsthand, but you can also write about a place you would like to visit. Either way, include researched material from at least three library and/or Internet sources.

READ MORE

"E. B. White." *Encyclopedia of World Biography*, (http:// www.notablebiographies.com/We-Z/White-E-B.html).

O'Loughlin, Amy. "E. B. White (1899–1985)" (http://www.suite101. com/content/eb-white-18991985-a191856): *Contains valuable information about the author and his works, as well as a helpful bibliography.*

White, E. B. *Essays of E.B. White.* New York, Perennial Classics, 1999.

Marrying Absurd

Joan Didion

Born in Sacramento, California, Didion (b. 1934) earned a B.A. from the University of California at Berkeley and went on to serve as an associate feature editor for Vogue *magazine, as a columnist for* The Saturday Evening Post, *and as a contributing editor to* The National Review. *Her essays are subtle portraits of the American experience, which she scrutinizes carefully and recreates with both incisiveness and irony. Her major works include novels:* Play It As It Lays *(1971),* A Book of Common Prayer *(1977),* Democracy *(1984), and* The Last Thing He Wanted *(1996); collections of essays:* Slouching Towards Bethlehem *(1968),* The White Album *(1979); and nonfiction:* Salvador *(1983),* Miami *(1987),* After Henry *(1992),* Political Fictions *(2001), and* The Year of Magical Thinking *(2005). She is the co-author of several screenplays, including* The Panic in Needle Park *(1971),* A Star Is Born *(1976), and* True Confessions *(1981). "Marrying Absurd" appears in* Slouching Towards Bethlehem.*

In "Marrying Absurd," Didion makes use of description as a tool of subtle irony. Although this piece shows us something about Las Vegas, it tells us even more about contemporary "expectations" concerning marriage and commitment. Obviously critical of this assembly-line approach, the essay echoes a soft note of sadness over something lost.

VOCABULARY

bouvardia, liaisons, en masse, venality, obliteration, implausibility, imperative, facsimile, peau de soie, nosegay

1   To be married in Las Vegas, Clark County, Nevada, a bride must swear that she is eighteen or has parental permission and a bridegroom that he is twenty-one or has parental permission. Someone must put up five dollars for the license. (On Sundays and holidays, fifteen dollars. The Clark County Courthouse issues marriage licenses at any time of the day or night except between noon and one in the afternoon, between eight and nine in the evening, and between four and five in the morning.) Nothing else is required. The State of Nevada, alone among these United States, demands neither a premarital blood test nor a waiting period before or after the issuance of a marriage license. Driving in across the Mojave from Los Angeles, one sees the signs way out on the desert, looming up from that moonscape of rattlesnakes and mesquite, even before the Las Vegas lights appear like a mirage on the horizon: "GETTING MARRIED? Free License Information First Strip Exit." Perhaps the Las Vegas wedding industry achieved its peak operational efficiency between 9:00 P.M. and midnight of August 26, 1965, an otherwise unremarkable Thursday which happened to be, by Presidential order, the last day on which anyone could improve his draft status merely by getting married. One hundred and seventy-one couples were pronounced man and wife in the name of Clark County and the State of Nevada that night, sixty-seven of them by a single justice of the peace, Mr. James A. Brennan. Mr. Brennan did one wedding at the Dunes and the other sixty-six in his office, and charged each couple eight dollars. One bride lent her veil to six others. "I got it down from five to three minutes," Mr. Brennan said later of his feat. "I could've married them *en masse*, but they're people, not cattle. People expect more when they get married."

2   What people who get married in Las Vegas actually do expect—what, in the largest sense, their "expectations" are—strikes one as a curious and self-contradictory business. Las Vegas is the most extreme and allegorical of American settlements, bizarre and beautiful in its venality and in its devotion to immediate gratification, a place the tone of which is set by mobsters and call girls and ladies' room attendants with amyl nitrite poppers in their uniform pockets. Almost everyone notes that there is no "time" in Las Vegas, no night and no day and no past and no future (no Las Vegas casino, however, has taken the obliteration of the ordinary time sense quite so far as Harold's Club in Reno, which for a while issued, at odd intervals in the day and night, mimeographed "bulletins" carrying news from the world outside); neither is there any logical sense of where one is. One is standing on a highway in the middle of a vast hostile desert looking at an eighty-foot sign which blinks "STARDUST" or "CAESAR'S PALACE." Yes, but what does that explain? This geographical implausibility reinforces the sense that what happens there has no connection with "real" life; Nevada cities like Reno and Carson City are ranch towns, Western towns, places behind which there is some historical imperative. But Las Vegas seems to exist only in the eye of the beholder. All of which makes it an extraordinarily

stimulating and interesting place, but an odd one in which to want to wear a candlelight satin Priscilla of Boston wedding dress with Chantilly lace insets, tapered sleeves and a detachable modified train.

And yet the Las Vegas wedding business seems to appeal to pre- 3 cisely that impulse. "Sincere and Dignified Since 1954," one wedding chapel advertises. There are nineteen such wedding chapels in Las Vegas, intensely competitive, each offering better, faster, and, by implication, more sincere services than the next: Our Photos Best Anywhere, Your Wedding on A Phonograph Record, Candlelight with Your Ceremony, Honeymoon Accommodations, Free Transportation from Your Motel to Courthouse to Chapel and Return to Motel, Religious or Civil Ceremonies, Dressing Rooms, Flowers, Rings, Announcements, Witnesses Available, and Ample Parking. All of these services, like most others in Las Vegas (sauna baths, payroll-check cashing, chinchilla coats for sale or rent) are offered twenty-four hours a day, seven days a week, presumably on the premise that marriage, like craps, is a game to be played when the table seems hot.

But what strikes one most about the Strip chapels, with their wishing 4 wells and stained-glass paper windows and their artificial bouvardia, is that so much of their business is by no means a matter of simple convenience, of late-night liaisons between show girls and baby Crosbys. Of course there is some of that. (One night about eleven o'clock in Las Vegas I watched a bride in an orange minidress and masses of flame-colored hair stumble from a Strip chapel on the arm of her bridegroom, who looked the part of the expendable nephew in the movies like *Miami Syndicate*. "I gotta get the kids," the bride whimpered. "I gotta pick up the sitter, I gotta get to the midnight show." "What you gotta get," the bridegroom said, opening the door of a Cadillac Coupe de Ville and watching her crumple on the seat, "is sober.") But Las Vegas seems to offer something other than "convenience"; it is merchandising "niceness," the facsimile of proper ritual, to children who do not know how else to find it, how to make the arrangements, how to do it "right." All day and evening long on the Strip, one sees actual wedding parties, waiting under the harsh lights at a crosswalk, standing uneasily in the parking lot of the Frontier while the photographer hired by The Little Church of the West ("Wedding Place of the Stars") certifies the occasion, takes the picture: the bride in a veil and white satin pumps, the bridegroom usually in a white dinner jacket, and even an attendant or two, a sister or a best friend in hot-pink *peau de soie*, a flirtation veil, a carnation nosegay. "When I Fall in Love It Will Be Forever," the organist plays, and then a few bars of Lohengrin. The mother cries; the stepfather, awkward in his role, invites the chapel hostess to join them for a drink at the Sands. The hostess declines with a professional smile; she has already transferred her interest to the group waiting outside. One bride out, another in, and again the sign goes up on the chapel door: "One moment please—Wedding."

5   I sat next to one such wedding party in a Strip restaurant the last time I was in Las Vegas. The marriage had just taken place; the bride still wore her dress, the mother her corsage. A bored waiter poured out a few swallows of pink champagne ("on the house") for everyone but the bride, who was too young to be served. "You'll need something with more kick than that," the bride's father said with heavy jocularity to his new son-in-law; the ritual jokes about the wedding night had a certain Panglossian character, since the bride was clearly several months pregnant. Another round of pink champagne, this time not on the house, and the bride began to cry. "It was just as nice," she sobbed, "as I hoped and dreamed it would be."

1967

QUESTIONS FOR DISCUSSION

Content

a. On the surface, Didion's purpose is to expose the "absurdity" of getting married in Las Vegas. What else is she trying to accomplish?
b. Didion calls what goes on in Las Vegas a "wedding business." How does she support this view?
c. What does Didion's description of setting contribute to her essay? What does she mean by the "geographical implausibility" of Las Vegas?
d. How do you interpret the first sentence of paragraph 2? How does Didion support this idea?
e. What does she mean by telling us that "Las Vegas seems to exist only in the eye of the beholder" (paragraph 2)?
f. In paragraph 4, the author mentions the "baby Crosbys." These were the sons of singer/actor Bing Crosby, who died in 1977. What other references to past people, events, and phenomena do you find in this essay? Do such references date the essay and thereby make it less effective?
g. Who or what is Lohengrin (paragraph 4)? Who or what is Pangloss (paragraph 5)? Look up the answers in a good all-purpose encyclopedia or other library reference text. How do these allusions help Didion advance her point?

Strategy and Style

h. How would you characterize the essay's tone?
i. The author's voice is fairly obvious in this essay? To what end has the author made her presence felt?
j. To what end were the direct quotations in this essay chosen?

k. Comment on the length of the essay's introduction. Is it appropriate? Why or why not?

l. What technique(s) does Didion use in her conclusion?

ENGAGING THE TEXT

a. Reread Didion's essay. List specific details she includes to describe the Las Vegas–style wedding. Explain why she sees the Las Vegas wedding as reflecting American culture.

b. Didion focuses on her personal reactions to what she witnesses. Reread the essay and make a list of her personal, subjective responses to Las Vegas and the Las Vegas wedding. Use the list to inspire a personal description of your own of a place you have visited.

SUGGESTIONS FOR SUSTAINED WRITING

a. Like Didion, describe a religious, social, academic, or community ritual or ceremony that you know well. When you write the first draft, pretend you are producing a multisensory documentary by describing what you have heard, seen, felt, tasted, and smelled. In other words, be as objective as possible; do not include personal responses to what you have experienced. As you develop subsequent drafts, however, be more subjective. Adopt a distinctive voice and add details that will reveal your attitude or attitudes about what you are describing.

b. Read another criticism of contemporary American life, such as Goodman's "The Company Man" (Chapter 4) or Lutz's "Doublespeak" (Chapter 5). Then write an essay in which you explain what Didion and the other author you have selected are saying about our culture. Are we a superficial, materialistic, dishonest, or deceptive people? Are we simply too interested in the here and now, too concerned with appearances rather than with things that really matter? End your paper by explaining, in detail, why you agree or disagree with each of these two authors. In the process, make direct reference to and quote from their essays.

c. Write a research essay in which you explain several of the traditions associated with a typical American wedding. For example, you might explain why the bride wears white; why her father "gives her away"; why the groom should not see the bride on their wedding day until she walks down the aisle; or why the bride carries "something old, something new, something borrowed, something blue." If this assignment does not interest you, describe the typical wedding of people from a culture very unlike our own. In either case, research your topic in the library and/or on the Internet. Rely on at least four secondary sources.

READ MORE

Didion, Joan. *A Book of Common Prayer.* New York: Vintage, 1995.

_____. *Slouching Towards Bethlehem.* New York: Farrar, 1990.

_____. *The White Album.* New York: Farrar, 1990.

The three books listed above are later editions of classic works by Didion.

Eggers, Dave. "The Salon Interview: Joan Didion" (http://www.salon.com/oct96/didion961028.html).

Grizzuti Harrison, Barbara. "Joan Didion: Only Disconnect." *Off Center: Essays by Barbara Grizzuti Harrison.* New York: Dell, 1980. *An essay by Grizzuti Harrison that, although critical of Didion's style, provides insights to be considered.*

A Partial Remembrance of a Puerto Rican Childhood

Judith Ortiz Cofer

Born in Puerto Rico in 1952, Judith Ortiz Cofer came to the United States in 1956, but her family maintained ties with relatives on the island. In fact, they moved between Puerto Rico and the mainland several times during her childhood and adolescence. After taking a B.A. from Augusta College and an M.A. from Florida Atlantic University, she studied at Oxford University. Currently professor of English and creative writing at the University of Georgia, she has been a visiting writer at Vanderbilt University, a visiting professor at the University of Michigan, and an instructor at Macon College. She writes fiction, nonfiction, and poetry. Her books include Woman in Front of the Sun: On Becoming a Writer *(2000),* The Latin Deli *(1993),* The Year of Our Revolution: Selected and New Prose and Poetry *(1998),* An Island Like You: Stories of the Barrio *(1998), and* Silent Dancing: A Partial Remembrance of a Puerto Rican Childhood *(1990), from which this selection is taken. More recently, Ortiz Cofer has written* The Meaning of Consuelo *and* Call Me Maria; *both novels were published in 2004. She has also written two collections of poetry:* Reaching for the Mainland *(1995) and* Love Story Beginning in Spanish *(2005).*

"A Partial Remembrance of a Puerto Rican Childhood" can be seen as a minidrama that illustrates the psychology of Ortiz Cofer's childhood. Though brief, it also delineates several key characters and allows them to convey the author's message both clearly and emphatically.

VOCABULARY

histrionic, conclave, auditor, impassively, ministrations, matriarchal, pueblo, haciendas, plait, grotesque, chameleons, epithet, denouement

At three or four o'clock in the afternoon, the hour of *café con leche*, the   1
women of my family gathered in Mamá's living room to speak of important things and retell familiar stories meant to be overheard by us young
girls, their daughters. In Mamá's house (everyone called my grandmother
Mamá) was a large parlor built by my grandfather to his wife's exact
specifications so that it was always cool, facing away from the sun. The
doorway was on the side of the house so no one could walk directly into
her living room. First they had to take a little stroll through and around
her beautiful garden where prize-winning orchids grew in the trunk of
an ancient tree she had hollowed out for that purpose. This room was
furnished with several mahogany rocking chairs, acquired at the births of
her children, and one intricately carved rocker that had passed down to
Mamá at the death of her own mother.

It was on these rockers that my mother, her sisters, and my grand-   2
mother sat on these afternoons of my childhood to tell their stories, teaching each other, and my cousin and me, what it was like to be a woman,
more specifically, a Puerto Rican woman. They talked about life on the
island, and life in *Los Nueva Yores*, their way of referring to the United
States from New York City to California: the other place, not home, all the
same. They told real-life stories though, as I later learned, always embel-
lishing them with a little or a lot of dramatic detail. And they told *cuentos*,
the morality and cautionary tales told by the women in our family for
generations: stories that became a part of my subconscious as I grew up
in two worlds, the tropical island and the cold city, and that would later
surface in my dreams and in my poetry.

One of these tales was about the woman who was left at the altar.   3
Mamá liked to tell that one with histrionic intensity. I remember the rise
and fall of her voice, the sighs, and her constantly gesturing hands, like
two birds swooping through her words. This particular story usually
would come up in a conversation as a result of someone mentioning a
forthcoming engagement or wedding. The first time I remember hearing
it, I was sitting on the floor at Mamá's feet, pretending to read a comic
book. I may have been eleven or twelve years old, at that difficult age
when a girl was no longer a child who could be ordered to leave the room
if the women wanted freedom to take their talk into forbidden zones, nor
really old enough to be considered a part of their conclave. I could only
sit quietly, pretending to be in another world, while absorbing it all in a
sort of unspoken agreement of my status as silent auditor. On this day,
Mamá had taken my long, tangled mane of hair into her ever-busy hands.
Without looking down at me and with no interruption of her flow of
words, she began braiding my hair, working at it with the quickness and
determination that characterized all her actions. My mother was watching
us impassively from her rocker across the room. On her lips played a little
ironic smile. I would never sit still for *her* ministrations, but even then,

I instinctively knew that she did not possess Mamá's matriarchal power to command and keep everyone's attention. This was never more evident than in the spell she cast when telling a story.

4   "It is not like it used to be when I was a girl," Mamá announced. "Then a man could leave a girl standing at the church altar with a bouquet of fresh flowers in her hands and disappear off the face of the earth. No way to track him down if he was from another town. He could be a married man, with maybe even two or three families all over the island. There was no way to know. And there were men who did this. Hombres with the devil in their flesh who would come to a pueblo, like this one, take a job at one of the haciendas, never meaning to stay, only to have a good time and to seduce the women."

5   The whole time she was speaking, Mamá would be weaving my hair into a flat plait that required pulling apart the two sections of hair with little jerks that made my eyes water; but knowing how grandmother detested whining and *boba* (sissy) tears, as she called them, I just sat up as straight and stiff as I did at La Escuela San José, where the nuns enforced good posture with a flexible plastic ruler they bounced off of slumped shoulders and heads. As Mamá's story progressed, I noticed how my young Aunt Laura lowered her eyes, refusing to meet Mamá's meaningful gaze. Laura was seventeen, in her last year of high school, and already engaged to a boy from another town who had staked his claim with a tiny diamond ring, then left for Los Nueva Yores to make his fortune. They were planning to get married in a year. Mamá had expressed serious doubts that the wedding would ever take place. In Mamá's eyes, a man set free without a legal contract was a man lost. She believed that marriage was not something men desired, but simply the price they had to pay for the privilege of children and, of course, for what no decent (synonymous with "smart") woman would give away for free.

6   "María La Loca was only seventeen when *it* happened to her." I listened closely at the mention of this name. María was a town character, a fat middle-aged woman who lived with her old mother on the outskirts of town. She was to be seen around the pueblo delivering the meat pies the two women made for a living. The most peculiar thing about María, in my eyes, was that she walked and moved like a little girl though she had the thick body and wrinkled face of an old woman. She would swing her hips in an exaggerated, clownish way, and sometimes even hop and skip up to someone's house. She spoke to no one. Even if you asked her a question, she would just look at you and smile, showing her yellow teeth. But I had heard that if you got close enough, you could hear her humming a tune without words. The kids yelled out nasty things to her, calling her *La Loca*, and the men who hung out at the bodega playing dominoes sometimes whistled mockingly as she passed by with her funny, outlandish walk.

But María seemed impervious to it all, carrying her basket of *pasteles* like a grotesque Little Red Riding Hood through the forest.

María La Loca interested me, as did all the eccentrics and crazies of 7 our pueblo. Their weirdness was a measuring stick I used in my serious quest for a definition of normal. As a Navy brat shuttling between New Jersey and the pueblo, I was constantly made to feel like an oddball by my peers, who made fun of my two-way accent: a Spanish accent when I spoke English, and when I spoke Spanish I was told that I sounded like a *Gringa*. Being the outsider had already turned my brother and me into cultural chameleons. We developed early on the ability to blend into a crowd, to sit and read quietly in a fifth story apartment building for days and days when it was too bitterly cold to play outside, or, set free, to run wild in Mamá's realm, where she took charge of our lives, releasing Mother for a while from the intense fear for our safety that our father's absences instilled in her. In order to keep us from harm when Father was away, Mother kept us under strict surveillance. She even walked us to and from Public School No. 11, which we attended during the months we lived in Paterson, New Jersey, our home base in the states. Mamá freed all three of us like pigeons from a cage. I saw her as my liberator and my model. Her stories were parables from which to glean the *Truth*.

"María La Loca was once a beautiful girl. Everyone thought she 8 would marry the Méndez boy." As everyone knew, Rogelio Méndez was the richest man in town. "But," Mamá continued, knitting my hair with the same intensity she was putting into her story, "this *macho* made a fool out of her and ruined her life." She paused for the effect of her use of the word *macho*, which at that time had not yet become a popular epithet for an unliberated man. This word had for us the crude and comical connotation of "male of the species," stud; a *macho* was what you put in a pen to increase your stock.

I peeked over my comic book at my mother. She too was under 9 Mamá's spell, smiling conspiratorially at this little swipe at men. She was safe from Mamá's contempt in this area. Married at an early age, an unspotted lamb, she had been accepted by a good family of strict Spaniards whose name was old and respected, though their fortune had been lost long before my birth. In a rocker Papá had painted sky blue sat Mamá's oldest child, Aunt Nena. Mother of three children, step-mother of two more, she was a quiet woman who liked books but had married an ignorant and abusive widower whose main interest in life was accumulating wealth. He too was in the mainland working on his dream of returning home rich and triumphant to buy the *finca* of his dreams. She was waiting for him to send for her. She would leave her children with Mamá for several years while the two of them slaved away in factories. He would one day be a rich man, and she a sadder woman. Even now her life-light was dimming. She spoke little, an aberration in Mamá's house, and she read avidly, as if storing up spiritual food for the long winters that awaited her in Los Nueva Yores without her family. But even Aunt Nena came alive to Mamá's words, rocking gently, her hands over a thick book in her lap.

10   Her daughter, my cousin Sara, played jacks by herself on the tile porch outside the room where we sat. She was a year older than I. We shared a bed and all our family's secrets. Collaborators in search of answers, Sara and I discussed everything we heard the women say, trying to fit it all together like a puzzle that, once assembled, would reveal life's mysteries to us. Though she and I still enjoyed taking part in boys' games—chase, volleyball and even *vaqueros*, the island version of cowboys and Indians involving capgun battles and violent shoot-outs under the mango tree in Mamá's backyard—we loved best the quiet hours in the afternoon when the men were still at work and the boys had gone to play serious baseball at the park. Then Mamá's house belonged only to us women. The aroma of coffee perking in the kitchen, the mesmerizing creaks and groans of the rockers, and the women telling their lives in *cuentos* are forever woven into the fabric of my imagination, braided like my hair that day I felt my grandmother's hands teaching me about strength, her voice convincing me of the power of storytelling.

11   That day Mamá told how the beautiful María had fallen prey to a man whose name was never the same in subsequent versions of the story; it was Juan one time, José, Rafael, Diego, another. We understood that neither the name nor any of the *facts* were important, only that a woman had allowed love to defeat her. Mamá put each of us in María's place by describing her wedding dress in loving detail: how she looked like a princess in her lace as she waited at the altar. Then, as Mamá approached the tragic denouement of her story, I was distracted by the sound of my Aunt Laura's violent rocking. She seemed on the verge of tears. She knew the fable was intended for her. That week she was going to have her wedding gown fitted, though no firm date had been set for the marriage. Mamá ignored Laura's obvious discomfort, digging out a ribbon from the sewing basket she kept by her rocker while describing María's long illness, "a fever that would not break for days." She spoke of a mother's despair: "that woman climbed the church steps on her knees every morning, wore only black as a *promesa* to the Holy Virgin in exchange for her daughter's health." By the time María returned from her honeymoon with death, she was ravished, no longer young or sane. "As you can see, she is almost as old as her mother already," Mamá lamented while tying the ribbon to the ends of my hair, pulling it back with such force that I just knew I would never be able to close my eyes completely again.

12   "That María is getting crazier every day." Mamá's voice would take a lighter tone now, expressing satisfaction, either for the perfection of my

braid, or for a story well told—it was hard to tell. "You know that tune María is always humming?" Carried away by her enthusiasm, I tried to nod, but Mamá still had me pinned between her knees.

"Well, that's the wedding march." Surprising us all, Mamá sang out, 13 "Da, da, dara. . .da, da, dara." Then lifting me off the floor by my skinny shoulders, she would lead me around the room in an impromptu waltz— another session ending with the laughter of women, all of us caught up in the infectious joke of our lives.

1990

QUESTIONS FOR DISCUSSION

Content

a. What is the purpose of Mamá's retelling of familiar stories, especially the "cuentos," during afternoon coffees?
b. What contrasts does the author draw between Mamá and her daughters? How would you describe the relationship between them?
c. Explain Mamá's views on men and marriage. In what ways do her views inform the discussion of what it meant to be a woman in Puerto Rico?
d. What meaning for the term "La Loca" can you infer from paragraph 7? Is the story of this woman true, or is La Loca a convenient object around which Mamá can spin a tale that conveys a lesson?
e. Mamá's message to her daughters and granddaughters is more practical than moral. Explain.
f. What does the author mean when, in her conclusion, she uses the phrase "caught up in the infectious joke of our lives"?

Strategy and Style

g. What is the effect of Mamá's braiding the narrator's hair as she tells the story of La Loca? Why does the narrator explain how hard Mamá pulled her hair as she was braiding it?
h. Why is the story of La Loca interrupted several times? Why doesn't the author convey it in one installment?
i. What is the purpose of the narrator's contrasting her life in New Jersey and her life in Puerto Rico?
j. Why is the dialogue in this essay reserved for Mamá alone?
k. Is the author making an analogy in her description of the setting? If so, to what?

ENGAGING THE TEXT

a. This is an essay describing the personality of a strong woman. What do you think of Mamá? Make specific reference to the text to support your conclusions.
b. This essay also discusses a particular view of womanhood. What is that view?

SUGGESTIONS FOR SUSTAINED WRITING

a. Ortiz Cofer creates a picture of her grandmother by explaining what occurred in a ritual or experience often repeated in that woman's household. Consider a ritual or experience often repeated by your family, and write an essay that explains what it revealed about one or more of the people who took part in it. As an alternative, you might explain what that ritual or experience revealed about your family's makeup, overall philosophy of life, or other important trait.
b. Like this selection, Kesaya E. Noda's "Growing Up Asian in America" (Chapter 5) discusses issues concerning a woman's place in society. Write an essay that compares (points out similarities) between the concerns expressed in these essays. In addition, however, explain the differences in the way these concerns are expressed and dramatized in each of these essays.
c. Using information found in print and Internet sources, write an essay that explains prevailing views on marriage or the place of women in a particular culture at a particular time. You may wish to discuss the culture in which you were raised, or you may choose one that is foreign to you. For example, a great deal has been written in recent years about the plight of Afghan women under the Taliban. You may even wish to delve into the past and discuss, for example, the role and rights of married women in first-century Rome or in ancient Egypt.

READ MORE

Cofer, Judith Ortiz. "Corazon's Café." *Calloloo* 17.3 (1994): 715–29. *Original short story.*

"Judith Ortiz Cofer." *Academy of American Poets,* (http://www.poets.org/ poet.php/prmPID/738): *Offers a good introduction to the author and her work.*

Ocasio, Rafael. "The Infinite Variety of Puerto Rican Reality: An Interview with Judith Ortiz Cofer." *Calloloo* 17.3 (1994): 730–42.

Monuments to Our Better Nature

Michael Byers

Michael Byers (b. 1969) is a professor of English at the University of Michigan. He earned an M.F.A. at the University of Michigan and was a Stegner Fellow at Stanford University. He is the author of Long for This World *(2003), a novel, and* The Coast of Good Intentions *(1998), a collection of short stories that won the Sue Kaufman Prize for First Fiction. Byers's work has appeared in* Prize Stories: The O'Henry Awards *and in* The Best American Short Stories.

"Monuments to Our Better Nature" was first published in Preservation *magazine (2003), then anthologized in* The Best American Travel Writing *(2004). Byers shows us that description can be put to many uses. Here, his discussion of several Washington, D.C. landmarks helps us begin to understand what it means to be part of that great political experiment called American democracy.*

VOCABULARY

cupidity, solace, dais, rotunda, cilia, patina, metatarsals, chauvinism, transcendent, aggregate, Doric, demagogic, benign, extemporaneous, Whitmanesque, admonitory obliquely, Pantheon, arcane, obelisk, demigod, impeccable, ambivalent, nadir, venerable

Growing up in the seventies in Bethesda, Maryland, a suburb of 1 Washington, D.C., I had the good fortune to be taken regularly to the National Mall by my mother. She was a scientist, and in the aftermath of the Vietnam War she found much to be disheartened by. The immense Smithsonian museums on the Mall acted, for her, as repositories of truth and exactitude in an age of cupidity, paranoia, and evasion; they were her solace.

In the National Museum of Natural History, the gargantuan blue 2 whale hanging above us with its great grooved throat was a *fact* about the world that could not be denied. The stuffed African elephant on its circular dais in the rotunda was composed of billions of skin cells and tiny cilia, and its ivory tusks wore an unfalsifiable brown patina of age. The chambered skull of the brontosaurus, the irrefutable chain of his vertebrae, his ponderous thighbones, and his sculpted metatarsals— each the size and heft of an anchor—had been painstakingly recovered from a stony Canadian grave, cleaned, and finally pieced together again, eons after the original owner had ceased to have any use for them.

Certain truths, the museums assured us, were undeniable. The mete- 3 orites upstairs had roamed the vacuum of space for billions of years until at last, following the Keplerian laws of orbit and velocity, they had collided with Earth, their nickel cores becoming polished by the final scalding plunge through the atmosphere. What a wonder it all was, and how true. And how could anyone not grasp that these truths were, in so many cases, utterly beautiful? This was the sort of thing my young mother wanted to be reassured of in those days, and it was an idea she wanted me to appreciate, too.

4   But my secret love was not the museums themselves but their grand exteriors and their placement among the other monuments and memorials. Looking ghostly in the distance, these stone structures spoke of a grandeur whose reach and glory had no measure. While for my mother these temples were tainted by chauvinism—in them she saw the young, rough-edged country trying to polish its image—for me they were transcendent. Even as a very young boy I knew they had the power to draw me across the grass, and they still do.

5   Washington, particularly the vast, open Mall, is the place where I first felt like a *citizen*. Standing in front of this monument or that memorial, I understood what it meant to belong to a country so populous as this one. This is the first purpose of these places, it seems to me: to inform citizens of the nation's collective character. They are massive, and beside them we are tiny. So it is politically. Alone, each of us is almost without value, but in the aggregate we are the point of the whole improbable enterprise. One is lost in the multitude, but the multitude itself is essential. It is no mistake that the White House—often the scene of great reputations made and lost—is on the back of the twenty-dollar bill, while Lincoln and his memorial find themselves on the penny. You are only a penny, the monuments tell us, but you are dearly counted.

6   And in life, while the White House may resemble an overbuilt embassy, the Lincoln Memorial is sublime. What American can approach Henry Bacon's temple to the humble son of Illinois and not feel his own soul beginning to rise eerily through the top of his head? What a glory to mount the broad stairs; what a thrilling incantation to count the thirty-six Doric columns, one for every state of the Union in 1864. And what a pleasure it is to call out the rank of states whose names, inscribed here above the entrance—VIRGINIA TENNESSEE GEORGIA—bring to mind not demagogic governors or backward pockets of creation science but ideal, benign subrepublics run by citizens much like ourselves. All around us, as we climb the stairs, fellow Americans are dressed in logo-covered T-shirts and careless blue jeans, and many are young, and loud. But there they are beside us anyhow, and at the top of the stairs we all stop and turn—we cannot help ourselves—to see where we have come from. And how far indeed it is that we, as a people, have traveled. Below us lie the steps where in Easter of 1939 the contralto Marian Anderson, black daughter of a coal dealer, sang "America" and "Nobody Knows the

Trouble I've Seen," as seventy-five thousand looked on in the April cold. On these steps, Martin Luther King, Jr., shrugged himself away from his prepared text and in that extemporaneous moment produced a supreme example of American oratory—his long Whitmanesque lines echoing with the names of the states carved high on the temple's walls behind him: "Let freedom ring from the snowcapped Rockies of Colorado! Let freedom ring from the curvaceous peaks of California! But not only that; let freedom ring from Stone Mountain of Georgia! Let freedom ring from Lookout Mountain of Tennessee! Let freedom ring from every hill and every molehill of Mississippi!"

What a glory it is to stand where Anderson sang and King spoke— 7 and what a glory to have been permitted to climb these steps unwatched, unquestioned, without a ticket of admission, and at last to arrive at the portico, where the simple Indiana limestone pillars are much larger than they appeared from below, and where the Tennessee pink marble floor is scuffed with millions of our footsteps, and where, as we pass inside, the Alabama marble ceiling—soaked in paraffin to make it translucent—casts a pale light. Hushed, we stop. There he is, Lincoln, on his throne, looking down at us all, while at the other end of the Mall the messy business of the Capitol goes on under his tireless, admonitory gaze.

Americans are not known for good behavior in public, but here we 8 become subdued, reflective. It is a long way to the ceiling, and our voices fade. Who is not moved by the sentences carved into the walls? "With malice toward none; with charity for all; with firmness in the right. . .Let us strive on to finish the work we are in; to bind up the nation's wounds. . . to do all which may achieve and cherish a just and lasting peace, among ourselves, and with all nations." At this, who does not feel grateful, and feel a lump in the throat? And even those few of us who are ignorant, or disdainful, who choose to snap gum or answer cell phones—well, we are Americans, and this is our monument, and whatever we do here is by definition permissible because it is ours.

Everyone goes to the Lincoln Memorial. Not everyone goes to the 9 Jefferson. You can drive there and park, but from the Lincoln Memorial you must walk along the Tidal Basin and cross a busy bridge. The monument faces the water, so you must approach it obliquely, or from the back. Jefferson stands, bronze, his coattails flared, his proud calves on display, his handsome head erect. Under the dome, pigeons flutter from place to place like thoughts moving in a great curved brain. The building, designed by John Russell Pope, is modeled after the Pantheon in Rome, but where is the dramatic soaring reach of the ceiling? Jefferson seems too large for his temple.

Disappointment may come from our feelings about Jefferson himself: 10 we appreciate the need for him, but still we do not much like him. Surely we take him too much for granted. He is remote, a rationalist. And what are we to make of the arcane inscriptions? "I am not an advocate for frequent changes in laws and constitution, but laws and institutions go hand in hand with the progress of the human mind. . . . We might as well require a man to wear the same coat that fitted him when he was a boy." All right, but where is the poetry? We have left it over there across the water, in the big rough hands of Lincoln.

11   We approach the third great presidential monument, Robert Mills's stark tribute to George Washington, without much excitement. It is the Mall's least lovely structure, and its most primitive. Thirty-seven years in the making, and what do we have? An obelisk, which seems to the eye not quite vertical as it rises above the city. But maybe it is fitting that this most distant figure of the American pantheon should have this least expressive tower built in his name: the first president as Zoroaster, a demigod whose name we have heard but whom we do not know personally. This monument seems Egyptian, and as such out of place here on the green among the more welcoming Greek and Roman temples. But this is fitting too. Washington, we know, was himself somewhat uncomfortable in civilian life, by turns noble, humble, and clumsy. Like some of the other lifelong military men who would later find themselves in the presidency, he was never quite sure where he stood. At the top of his monument, people shove their way to the windows. If we swoon at the drop and step back from the glass, our place is quickly taken.

12   There is no shoving at the Vietnam Veterans Memorial. Behavior here is impeccable, and we have its intuitive, minimalist design by Maya Lin to thank. This monument is public architecture at its finest: open, instructive, and moving. The ambivalent descent, deeper and deeper, along a sinister black wall, exactly mimics the national experience of the war: the early trickle of bad news, the growing sense of obligation, the gradual realization that we are in over our heads, and at its nadir, the dark hopelessness from which there seems no escaping. We catch our breath as we descend. We are silent, knowing that some of the visitors here will have lost a brother, son, father, friend.

13   Adults climb out of this hole sadder and wiser. But do the twelve-year-olds also behave well here only because of the crying man in the army fatigues? Or do they, like their parents, feel that something terrible has happened, and been preserved somehow in black marble? And will their children feel the same way, or will they need to learn the lessons of Vietnam again?

14   At the top of the ramp we are released again onto the green. We walk to the Korean War Veterans Memorial but leave with a bad taste. It tries too hard to move us, and it fails. And so we look suspiciously at the construction under way at the foot of the Reflecting Pool where the World War II Memorial is at last taking shape. We are willing to suspend judgment, but we are concerned about the loss of open space.

Because ultimately the defined space of the Mall is its greatest asset. 15
It is one of America's most venerable and trafficked pedestrian public
spaces, where you can fly a kite alone or stand among a hundred thousand and hear a speech being given half a mile away by a barely dis-
cernible figure. It is the *distance* between monuments that I find myself
appreciating every time I visit. The buildings appear on the horizon and
resolve, slowly, as you approach them on foot across the grass. In this way
the Mall itself functions like an enormous museum, and these imperfect
places are what we have so far in our national display case, laid out on
the green velvet of the enormous lawn.

As adults, we eventually learn that the brontosaurus is now called 16
apatosaurus, and half of its bones are informed reconstructions. We discover there were ten million African elephants in 1930, and that now there
are only thirty-five thousand. We see that government is bought and paid
for, no matter what party is in power. But still: Who can stand on the top
step of the Lincoln Memorial and not think, *I am a participant in a world
civilization, I have history entrusted to me, we are all in this together*—and feel
it, for a minute or two, as the simple, honest truth?

2003

QUESTIONS FOR DISCUSSION

Content

a. Reread Byers's conclusion. State his thesis in your own words.
b. What does Byers mean by "the messy business of the Capitol" in paragraph 7?
c. What is Byers's attitude toward Lincoln and the Lincoln Memorial?
How does it differ from his attitude toward the other presidents he
mentions and their monuments?
d. In what way does the Vietnam Veterans Memorial reflect our nation's
experience in the Vietnam War?
e. What does including Dr. Martin Luther King, Jr., and Marian Anderson
in paragraph 6 accomplish?
f. In paragraph 8, Byers engages in description that is clearly subjective.
How does this paragraph help him advance his thesis?

Strategy and Style

g. If this essay is about monuments, why does Byers begin it with a
description of exhibits in the National Museum of Natural History?

h. Why does Byers describe the visitors to the Lincoln Memorial?
i. Why does he tell us that the stone from the Lincoln Memorial comes from Indiana, Tennessee, and Alabama (paragraph 7)?
j. Where in this essay does Byers use contrast? Where does he explain causes and effects?

ENGAGING THE TEXT

a. Who is Kepler (paragraph 3)? What are his laws? Research these questions in an encyclopedia or on the Internet. Then write a paragraph or two that explains the significance of Kepler's laws to this essay.
b. In paragraph 5, Byers says that "It is no mistake that the White House—often the scene of great reputations made and lost—is on the back of the twenty-dollar bill, while Lincoln and his memorial find themselves on the penny." Explain what this sentence means in the context of the paragraph in which it is placed. Then, explain its significance to the essay as a whole.

SUGGESTIONS FOR SUSTAINED WRITING

a. Byers describes several important American monuments that make us feel that we have "history entrusted" to us. Describe a public place that commemorates or is associated with an important person or event. Explain what the design, layout, architecture, or appearance of the place is trying to tell us. As you do this, explain why you think it is (or is not) appropriate to the event or person it commemorates.
b. In what ways is "Monuments to Our Better Nature" like John (Fire) Lame Deer and Richard Erdoes's "Alone on a Hilltop"? Write an essay in which you point out similarities and differences in the purposes, content, and approaches seen in these two essays. As you develop your paper, make specific reference to each piece, quoting directly from or paraphrasing the text whenever it is appropriate to do so.
c. Research the history of one of the buildings that Byers mentions in his essay. Then, write a paper that explains why and how that monument was built. In addition, explain its significance to you personally and to the nation as a whole. Make sure to include information that is directly quoted, paraphrased, or summarized from the sources you researched. As always, give your sources credit by using internal citations and including a works-cited or references list.

READ MORE

Byers and His Works

Byers, Michael. *The Coast of Good Intentions*. New York: Houghton Mifflin, 2004.

Byers, Michael. *Long for This World*. New York: Houghton Mifflin, 2003.

Pandolfe, David. "Interview with Michael Byers." *Blackbird: An Online Journal of Literature and the Arts*. Virginia Commonwealth University (http://www.blackbird.vcu.edu/v3n2/features/byers_m_011705/byers_m_text.htm).

National Monuments

"The Virtual Wall: Vietnam Veterans Memorial" (http://www.virtualwall.org): *A site maintained by private citizens; it contains links to information about the wall and allows visitors to search the Memorial itself for names of the fallen.*

"Washington D.C.: A National Register of Historic Places Travel Itinerary." *National Parks Service: U.S. Department of the Interior* (http://www.nps.gov/nr/travel/wash): *Links to websites of many historical monuments in and around Washington, D.C.*

Beneath My House

Louise Erdrich

Louise Erdrich (1954), who is part Native American, grew up in North Dakota, where her mother and father taught at a school run by the Bureau of Indian Affairs. She took her B.A. at Dartmouth University and her M.A. in creative writing at Johns Hopkins University. Erdrich co-authored several early novels with her husband, Michael Dorris. The first of these, Love Machine *(1984), which was awarded the National Book Critics' Circle Award, is about a Native-American family living on a reservation in North Dakota. The novel features multiple narrators (Erdrich was influenced by the writing of Faulkner), a technique that she uses again in* The Beet Queen *(1986). She followed with several other novels set on reservations.*

After her divorce from Dorris in the late 1990s, Erdrich continued to write novels that used information and took inspiration from her multi-ethnic family background (she is part German and part French as well as Native American). In 2009, her novel The Plague of Doves *was a finalist for the Pulitzer Prize. In 2010, she published* Shadow Tag, *the story of two Native Americans who find themselves in a loveless and violent marriage from which they are unable to extricate themselves.*

Erdrich has also published poetry, short stories, and essays. "Beneath My House" is an excerpt from "Foxglove," an essay published in the Georgia Review *in 1992. Parts of this essay also appear in* The Blue Jay's Dance: A Birthyear *(1995), which chronicles a period during which the author was pregnant and gave birth. "Beneath My House" describes a not uncommon place: the crawl cellar under an old house. But it is unique because Erdrich uses description not only to picture a place but also to capture deep emotions about pregnancy, birth, and death.*

VOCABULARY

resounding, piteous, silken, husk

1 It was as if the house itself had given birth. One day the floor cried where I stepped on it, and I jumped back. I was near a heating vent, and when I bent and pried the cover off and thrust my hand in, I briefly grabbed a ball of fur that hissed and spat. I heard the kitten scrambling away, the tin resounding like small thunder along the length of its flight.

2 I went down to the basement, looking for it with a flashlight, but, of course, at my step the untamed creature fled from the concrete-floored area and off into the earthen crawl space—draped with spiderwebs as thick as cotton, a place of unpeeled log beams, the underside of the house. I put out milk in a saucer. I crouched on the other side of the furnace, and I waited until I fell half-asleep. But the kitten was too young to drink from a dish and never came. Instead, she set up, from just beyond where I could catch her, a piteous crying that I could hardly stand to hear.

3 I went after her. The earth was moldy, a dense clay. No sun had fallen here for over two centuries. I climbed over the brick retaining wall and crawled toward the sound of the kitten. As I neared, as it sensed my presence was too large to be its mother, it went silent and scrabbled away from the reach of my hand. I brushed fur, though, and that slight warmth filled me with what must have been a mad calm because when the creature squeezed into a bearing wall of piled stones, I inched forward on my stomach. My back was now scraping along the beams that bore the weight of the whole house above me. Tons and tons of plaster, boards, appliances, and furniture, this was no crawl space anymore. I could hardly raise my shoulders to creep forward, could move only by shifting my hips up and down. On the edge of panic—I had never before been in a space so tight— one thought pressed in: if I heard the house creak, if it settled very suddenly upon my back, my last crushed words would be, "Shit! I don't even like cats." Because I don't like cats, just find their silken ways irresistible.

4 Its face popped out right in front of me, and vanished. How far back did the piled rock go? If I moved a rock, would the whole house fall on me? I reached for the kitten, missed, reached again, missed. I tried to breathe,

to be patient. Then, after a time, the kitten backed toward me, away from a clump of dirt I managed to throw at the far wall. Its tail flicked through a space in the rocks, and I snatched it. Held it, drew it toward me. Out it came with a squeak of terror, a series of panting comic hisses, and a whirl of claws and teeth, tiny needles it didn't yet know how to use.

She is a pretty cat, a calico marbled evenly with orange and black. 5 Rocky. She sits near as I write, leaps into the warmth of my chair when I leave, and is jealous of the baby.

The night after I pulled her from the house, the darkness pressed 6 down on me until I woke. I'd swum weightlessly into a smaller and smaller space. What the body remembers of birth it anticipates as death. In the house of my dreams the basement is the most fearful: the awful place filled with water, the place of both comfort and death. I fear in particular the small space, the earth closing in on me, the house like a mother settling its cracked bones and plumbing.

That afternoon, from underneath, I had heard the house all around 7 me like an old familiar body. I hadn't told anybody else that I was going after the kitten, so nobody knew I was below. The normal sounds of my family's daily life were magnified. Their steps trailed and traveled around me, boomed in my ears. Their voices jolted me, their words loud but meaningless, warped by their travel through the walls and beams. Water flowed through invisible pipes around me, hitched and gurgled. It was like being dead, or unborn. I hadn't thought about it then, but now I could clearly see part of me, the husk of myself, still buried against the east wall: a person sacrificed to ensure the good luck of a temple, a kind of house god, a woman lying down there, still, an empty double.

QUESTIONS FOR DISCUSSION

Content

a. What does Erdrich mean in paragraph 3 when she says that she finds cats' "silken ways irresistible"?
b. Was the author pregnant when she went after the kitten? How can we tell?
c. What analogy does Erdrich make between being in a crawl space and being born? What does the house stand for in this analogy?
d. What analogy does Erdrich make between being in a crawl space and dying? What might the house stand for in this case?
e. How do the analogies mentioned in items *c* and *d* explain what Erdrich means when she writes: "What the body remembers of birth, it anticipates as death" (paragraph 6)?
f. State the central idea (thesis) of this essay in your own words.

Strategy and Style

g. The author includes explanations of how she relives the experience in the crawl space. Why does she tell about these recollections?
h. This essay is more about the author herself than about the crawl cellar of an old house. What does the crawl space symbolize for Erdrich? What does the kitten symbolize?
i. Find details in this essay that appeal to the physical senses.
j. Explain what Erdrich does to personify the house. What other examples of figurative language appear in this work?
k. The essay begins with a reference to birth and ends with a reference to death. Are the introduction and conclusion effective? Why or why not?
l. What elements or techniques usually found in a narrative appear here?

ENGAGING THE TEXT

a. In the last paragraph, Erdrich tells us that she sees the "husk" of herself "lying down there, still, an empty double." What emotions has crawling under the house raised in Erdrich? Is she anxious, fearful, resigned? And what is she anxious, fearful, or resigned about? Answer these questions in a paragraph or two, making specific reference to the text. Then, in another paragraph or two, explain how you might have reacted had you been in that crawl space instead of Erdrich.
b. Analyze paragraphs 3 and 7 in order to explain how Erdrich communicates the fear and panic she felt. Then write one or more paragraphs about a fairly recent personal experience involving intense fear or panic. What caused the emotion? What went through your mind during the incident? What did you do in reaction to what was happening?

SUGGESTIONS FOR SUSTAINED WRITING

a. In item *b* under Engaging the Text, you were asked to write about an incident that caused you intense fear or panic. Expand this into an essay whose purpose is to reveal something significant about your personality or character. In other words, while narrating an event, focus on details that reveal something important about your emotional make-up. Include details about what happened but, more important, discuss how you reacted to what happened.
b. "Beneath My House" is a short essay, but it is so packed with detail that it succeeds in telling us a great deal about a person as well as a place. Another essay in this chapter that accomplishes this is James Baldwin's "Fifth Avenue: Uptown." Write an essay that begins by comparing the purpose of Erdrich's essay with that of Baldwin's. Then point out

contrasts in terms of style (sentence structure and word usage) as well as tone (an author's attitude toward his or her subject).

c. The emotions that accompany being pregnant and giving birth certainly provided some inspiration for Erdrich's essay. Using research (library and/or Internet, as your professor requires), write an essay that describes the emotions or the emotional problems occasioned by a significant event or change in a person's life. You need not discuss pregnancy. You might write about what someone goes through while preparing for surgery or after having been in a serious automobile accident. Other possibilities include discussing the range of emotions one feels after losing a spouse or being laid off from a job he or she has held for a long time. In short, pick a life-altering event that you or someone you know has experienced. Follow your instructor's directions when choosing a documentation style (MLA, APA, or other).

READ MORE

About Erdrich and Her Work

Beidler, Peter G., and Gay Barton. *A Reader's Guide to the Novels of Louise Erdrich.* Columbia, MO: University of Missouri, 2006.

"Louise Erdrich" (http://www.answers.com/topic/louise-erdrich): *A compilation of websites that discuss Erdrich's life and writings. It also contains a useful bibliography of the author's work.*

Spellman, Robert. "The Creative Instinct" (http://www.salon.com/weekly/interview960506.html): *A Salon.com interview with the author.*

Stookey, Lorena. *Louise Erdrich: A Critical Companion.* Westport, CT: Greenwook, 1999.

About Pregnancy

"Emotions During Pregnancy." *UI Maternity Center.* University of Iowa Hospitals and Clinics (http://www.uihealthcare.com/depts/maternitycenter/pregnancy/emotions.html).

Harms, Roger W. *The Mayo Clinic Guide to a Healthy Pregnancy.* New York: HarperCollins, 2004. *A practical guide to maintaining physical and emotional health during pregnancy and childbirth.*

Process Analysis

Often thought of as a way to develop scientific papers, process analysis can be used with a variety of topics and in combination with many of the other methods of development illustrated in this text. It is the type of writing used to convey instructions—how to change a tire, take someone's temperature, or write the draft of a college essay. Process analysis can also explain how something happens or happened—the birth of a planet, the way you convinced your boss to give you a raise, or even how light and sound are transmitted to our eyes and ears.

Like narratives, essays on such topics generally follow chronological order, with each step in the process likened to events in a well-developed plot. Much is made of transitional words and phrases to keep the reader on the right track. "When you have said everything you can say in this [first] draft," Richard Marius tells us, "print it out. . . ." And like any good storyteller, the writer of process analysis usually begins at the beginning and follows through to the end, sometimes listing steps by number but always providing sufficient detail to help the reader picture the activity accurately and concretely.

Sometimes writers of process analysis infuse their work with vivid, if not unnerving, description like the kind we find in Gretel Ehrlich's "Chronicles of Ice," which traces the process by which the world's ice flows are deteriorating. Note that this essay also comments on the causes of the problem in language that is both moving and persuasive.

Nonetheless, the purpose of process analysis is instructive in the most practical sense: narration and description may show *what* happens, causal analysis may explain *why* it happens, but process analysis always focuses on *how* it happens. The most important aspect of any process essay, therefore, is clarity. Readers will not follow unless your explanations are complete, your language is familiar, and your organization is simple. Take your lead from Richard Marius, who lists important advice and information about writing in easy-to-follow steps. And whenever you give instructions, pay your readers the courtesy of preparing them for the task by mentioning required tools, materials, and expectations. Note that John (Fire) Lame Deer and Richard Erdoes mention the quilt, the peace pipe, and the gourd used during Lame Deer's first "vision-seeking."

Of course, explaining a process does not give you license to produce prose that is dull. Indeed, there is no rule that process papers can't be colorful and engaging, that they can't contain figures of speech and analogies. Take the opening paragraph from Peter Elbow's "Desperation Writing":

> I know I am not alone in my recurring twinges of panic that I won't be able to write something when I need to, I won't be able to produce coherent speech or thought. And that lingering doubt is a great hindrance to writing. It's a constant fog or static that clouds the mind. I never got out of its clutches till I discovered that it was possible to write something— not something great or pleasing but at least something usable, workable —when my mind is out of commission. The trick is that you have to do all your cooking out on the table: your mind is incapable of doing any inside. It means using symbols and pieces of paper not as a crutch but as a wheel chair.

Like selections in other parts of this text, those that appear here represent a variety of subjects, approaches, and styles. But there is a common denominator. As you might expect, the selections that follow are models of clarity, but their authors never seem cold and detached, even when explaining what might first seem recondite or abstract. The committed, sometimes impassioned, voice of the writer always comes through. That is probably why we read these sometimes "technical" pieces with alacrity. Each selection has something important to teach us, but the lesson has relatively little to do with the process its author describes. What we learn here is a need to respect the reader, to understand our attitude toward the subject, and to believe that what we have to say is important.

Why Leaves Turn Color in the Fall

Diane Ackerman

Diane Ackerman (b. 1948) was born in Waukegan, Illinois, and was educated at Pennsylvania State University and Cornell University. A versatile writer and student of nature, Ackerman is probably best known for A Natural History of the Senses *(1990), from which this selection is taken. Her prose works include* The Rarest of the Rare *(1995),* A Natural History of Love *(1994), and* On Extended Wings *(1985). She has also published several volumes of poetry, among which are* Origami Bridges *(2002),* I Praise My Destroyer *(2000), and* Jaguar of Sweet Laughter *(1991). Ackerman's books for young people include* The Senses of Animals *(2001),* Bats: Shadows in the Night *(1997), and* Monk Seal Hideaway *(1995). Her latest work is* One Hundred Names for Love *(2011) (2004). Ackerman is a recipient of the John Burroughs Nature Award (1997), the Lavan Poetry Award (1985), and the Art of Fact Award for Creative Nonfiction (2000). She has even had a molecule named after her: dianeackerone. Ackerman has been a staff writer for* The New Yorker *magazine and has been a visiting professor at Cornell and at the University of Richmond. She has also directed Washington University's Writing Program. In 2008, Ackerman won Orion magazine's Orion Book Award for* The Zookeeper's Wife, *the story of a Polish couple's heroic activities in saving many who would otherwise have fallen victim to the Nazis. "Why Leaves Turn Color in the Fall" shows that scientific writing, although clear, accurate, and objective, can also be quite engaging.*

VOCABULARY

stealth, macabre, solstice, petioles, xylem, vexing, predisposed, dupe, sublime, confetti, humus

1   The stealth of autumn catches one unaware. Was that a goldfinch perching in the early September woods, or just the first turning leaf? A red-winged blackbird or a sugar maple closing up shop for the winter? Keen-eyed as leopards, we stand still and squint hard, looking for signs of movement. Early morning frost sits heavily on the grass, and turns barbed wire into a string of stars. On a distant hill, a small square of yellow appears to be a lighted stage. At last the truth dawns on us: Fall is staggering in, right on schedule, with its baggage of chilly nights, macabre holidays, and spectacular, heart-stoppingly beautiful leaves. Soon the leaves will start cringing on the trees, and roll up in clenched fists before they actually fall off. Dry seedpods will rattle like tiny gourds. But first there will be weeks of gushing color so bright, so pastel, so confettilike, that people will travel up and down the East Coast just to stare at it—a whole season of leaves.

2   Where do the colors come from? Sunlight rules most living things with its golden edicts. When the days begin to shorten, soon after the summer solstice on June 21, a tree reconsiders its leaves. All summer it feeds them so they can process sunlight, but in the dog days of summer the tree begins pulling nutrients back into its trunk and roots, pares down, and gradually chokes off its leaves. A corky layer of cells forms at the leaves' slender petioles, then scars over. Undernourished, the leaves stop producing the pigment chlorophyll, and photosynthesis ceases. Animals can migrate, hibernate, or store food to prepare for winter. But where can a tree go? It survives by dropping its leaves, and by the end of autumn only a few fragile threads of fluid-carrying xylem hold leaves to their stems.

3   A turning leaf stays partly green at first, then reveals splotches of yellow and red as the chlorophyll gradually breaks down. Dark green seems to stay longest in the veins, outlining and defining them. During the summer, chlorophyll dissolves in the heat and light, but it is also being steadily replaced. In the fall, on the other hand, no new pigment is produced, and so we notice the other colors that were always there, right in the leaf, although chlorophyll's shocking green hid them from view. With

their camouflage gone, we see these colors for the first time all year, and marvel, but they were always there, hidden like a vivid secret beneath the hot glowing greens of summer.

The most spectacular range of fall foliage occurs in the northeastern 4 United States and in eastern China, where the leaves are robustly colored, thanks in part to a rich climate. European maples don't achieve the same flaming reds as their American relatives, which thrive on cold nights and sunny days. In Europe, the warm, humid weather turns the leaves brown or mildly yellow. Anthocyanin, the pigment that gives apples their red and turns leaves red or red-violet, is produced by sugars that remain in the leaf after the supply of nutrients dwindles. Unlike the carotenoids, which color carrots, squash, and corn, and turn leaves orange and yellow, anthocyanin varies from year to year, depending on the temperature and amount of sunlight. The fiercest colors occur in years when the fall sunlight is strongest and the nights are cool and dry (a state of grace scientists find vexing to forecast). This is also why leaves appear dizzyingly bright and clear on a sunny fall day: The anthocyanin flashes like a marquee.

Not all leaves turn the same colors. Elms, weeping willows, and the 5 ancient ginkgo all grow radiant yellow, along with hickories, aspens, bottlebrush buckeyes, cottonweeds, and tall, keening poplars. Basswood turns bronze, birches bright gold. Water-loving maples put on a symphonic display of scarlets. Sumacs turn red, too, as do flowering dogwoods, black gums, and sweet gums. Though some oaks yellow, most turn a pinkish brown. The farmlands also change color, as tepees of cornstalks and bales of shredded-wheat-textured hay stand drying in the fields. In some spots, one slope of a hill may be green and the other already in bright color, because the hillside facing south gets more sun and heat than the northern one.

An odd feature of the colors is that they don't seem to have any spe- 6 cial purpose. We are predisposed to respond to their beauty, of course. They shimmer with the colors of sunset, spring flowers, the tawny buff of a colt's pretty rump, the shuddering pink of a blush. Animals and flowers color for a reason—adaptation to their environment—but there is no adaptive reason for leaves to color so beautifully in the fall any more than there is for the sky or ocean to be blue. It's just one of the haphazard marvels the planet bestows every year. We find the sizzling colors thrilling, and in a sense they dupe us. Colored like living things, they signal death and disintegration. In time, they will become fragile and, like the body, return to dust. They are as we hope our own fate will be when we die: Not to vanish, just to sublime from one beautiful state into another. Though leaves lose their green life, they bloom with urgent colors, as the woods grow mummified day by day, and Nature becomes more carnal, mute, and radiant.

We call the season "fall," from the Old English *feallan*, to fall, which 7 leads back through time to the Indo-European *phol*, which also means to fall. So the word and the idea are both extremely ancient, and haven't really changed since the first of our kind needed a name for fall's leafy abundance. As we say the word, we're reminded of that other Fall, in the garden of Eden, when fig leaves never withered and scales fell from our eyes. Fall is the time when leaves fall from the trees, just as spring is when flowers spring up, summer is when we simmer, and winter is when we whine from the cold.

8   Children love to play in piles of leaves, hurling them into the air like confetti, leaping into soft unruly mattresses of them. For children, leaf fall is just one of the odder figments of Nature, like hailstones or snowflakes. Walk down a lane overhung with trees in the never-never land of autumn, and you will forget about time and death, lost in the sheer delicious spill of color. Adam and Eve concealed their nakedness with leaves, remember? Leaves have always hidden our awkward secrets.

9   But how do the colored leaves fall? As a leaf ages, the growth hormone, auxin, fades, and cells at the base of the petiole divide. Two or three rows of small cells, lying at right angles to the axis of the petiole, react with water, then come apart, leaving the petioles hanging on by only a few threads of xylem. A light breeze, and the leaves are airborne. They glide and swoop, rocking in invisible cradles. They are all wing and may flutter from yard to yard on small whirlwinds or updrafts, swiveling as they go. Firmly tethered to earth, we love to see things rise up and fly— soap bubbles, balloons, birds, fall leaves. They remind us that the end of a season is capricious, as is the end of life. We especially like the way leaves rock, careen, and swoop as they fall. Everyone knows the motion. Pilots sometimes do a maneuver called a "falling leaf," in which the plane loses altitude quickly and on purpose, by slipping first to the right, then to the left. The machine weighs a ton or more, but in one pilot's mind it is a weightless thing, a falling leaf. She has seen the motion before, in the Vermont woods where she played as a child. Below her the trees radiate gold, copper, and red. Leaves are falling, although she can't see them fall, as she falls, swooping down for a closer view.

10   At last the leaves leave. But first they turn color and thrill us for weeks on end. Then they crunch and crackle underfoot. They *shush*, as children drag their small feet through leaves heaped along the curb. Dark, slimy mats of leaves cling to one's heels after a rain. A damp, stuccolike mortar of semidecayed leaves protects the tender shoots with a roof until spring, and makes a rich humus. An occasional bulge or ripple in the leafy mounds signals a shrew or a field mouse tunneling out of sight. Sometimes one finds in fossil stones the imprint of a leaf, long since disintegrated whose outlines remind us how detailed, vibrant, and alive are the things of this earth that perish.

1990

QUESTIONS FOR DISCUSSION

Content

a. Besides the obvious as indicated in the title, what is the purpose of this selection?
b. Summarize the process by which leaves change color as explained in paragraphs 2–6.
c. Why does the most "spectacular range" of colors occur in the northeastern United States and in eastern China?
d. What is Ackerman alluding to when she mentions "a state of grace" in paragraph 4?
e. What explains the fact that in the fall, one side of a mountain can be green while another is in full color?
f. The author says that the colors we see in the fall have been there all through the spring and summer. Explain.
g. "Leaves have always hidden our awkward secrets," says Ackerman (paragraph 8). What is she getting at?

Strategy and Style

h. Explain the effect of including so many figures of speech in this essay.
i. How do Ackerman's comments in paragraph 7, especially about the "other Fall," help her achieve her purpose in this essay?

ENGAGING THE TEXT

a. Explain how the author's purpose is served by what we read in paragraphs 9 and 10. Pay special attention to the last line of this selection.
b. Analyze this essay to demonstrate both the scientific acumen and the writing abilities of the author. In other words, explain why this essay is so convincing and so interesting.

SUGGESTIONS FOR SUSTAINED WRITING

a. Write an explanation of a natural phenomenon related to one of the seasons of the year. You need not base your essay on scientific research. You can rely on common knowledge and your own observations and experiences for information. For example, if you have lived through a long summer drought, tell what happens to crops in the field, explain how wild animals react, or describe the effects on natural vegetation. You might also relate the steps local municipalities have had to take to conserve water, or even discuss the physical and emotional toll on human beings during times of drought.

b. Read Ehrlich's "Chronicles of Ice" in this chapter. Then, write an essay that both compares and contrasts it to Ackerman's. Consider purpose, tone, and language—literal and figurative. Also, make sure to explain how each of these authors views the natural world.

c. Using both library and Internet research, write an essay that explains how a specific natural phenomenon occurs. For example, explain the eruption of a volcano, the changing of the tides, the way food is digested, the development of a butterfly, or the production of sun spots. If that doesn't interest you, consider explaining a "natural" phenomenon one might encounter in science fiction. For example, explain the theory of time travel, the way androids developed, or the process by which computers may someday evolve into the dominant species. If you choose the latter course, try to be as convincing as possible by referencing as much legitimate scientific knowledge and theory as you can.

READ MORE

Ackerman, Diane. "The Morse Code of the Heart: Poems Foster Self-Discovery." *New York Times*, June 3, 2002: E1. *Ackerman talks about her writing of poetry and her new book*, Origami Bridges: Poems of Psychoanalysis and Fire.

"Diane Ackerman: Books" (http://www.dianeackerman.com/works. htm): *Site contains annotated bibliography of her work. Invites readers' emails.*

"Tea, Sympathy and Superheroes." *U.S. News & World Report*, February 10, 1997, 70. *An interview with the author.*

Writing Drafts

Richard Marius

A native of Tennessee, Richard Marius (1933–1999) took his bachelor's degree in journalism at the University of Tennessee and his master's and doctorate in history at Yale University. He also held a B.D. from Southern Baptist Theological Seminary. Marius was the author of several historical studies and has received wide acclaim for his full-length biographies of Martin Luther and Thomas More. He also wrote three novels, including The Coming of Rain *(1969) and* Bound for the Promised Land *(1976). A director of the Expository Writing Program at Harvard University, Marius published several books on writing, including* The McGraw-Hill College Handbook, *which he coauthored with Harvey Wiener, and* A Short Guide to Writing about History *(1987). "Writing Drafts" first appeared in* The Writer's Companion *(1985), his splendid guide for both novice and experienced writers.*

Although interesting and effective as a model of process analysis, this selection also serves as a practical guide for beginning writers who are committed to seeing writing itself as a process. In addition, Marius's style is light, accessible, and always engaging.

VOCABULARY

digress, compelling, harried, demean

Finally the moment comes when you sit down to begin your first draft. 1
It is always a good idea at the start to list the points you want to cover. A
list is not as elaborate as a formal outline. In writing your first list, don't
bother to set items down in the order of importance. List your main points
and trust your mind to organize them. You will probably make one list,
study it, make another, study it, and perhaps make another. You can organize each list more completely than the last. This preliminary process may
save you hours of starting and stopping.

Write with your list outline in front of you. Once you begin to write, 2
commit yourself to the task at hand. Do not get up until you have written
for an hour. Write your thoughts quickly. Let one sentence give you an idea
to develop in the next. Organization, grammar, spelling, and even clarity
of sentences are not nearly as important as getting the first draft together.
No matter how desperate you feel, keep going.

Always keep your mind open to new ideas that pop into your head 3
as you write. Let your list outline help you, but don't become a slave to it.
Writers often start an essay with one topic in mind only to discover that
another pushes the first one aside as they work. Ideas you had not even
thought of before you began to write may pile onto your paper, and five
or six pages into your first draft you may realize that you are going to
write about something you did not imagine when you started.

If such a revelation comes, be grateful and accept it. But don't imme- 4
diately tear up or erase your draft and start all over again. Make yourself
keep on writing, developing these new ideas as they come. If you suddenly start all over again, you may break the train of thought that has
given you the new topic. Let your thoughts follow your new thesis, sailing on that tack until the wind changes.

When you have said everything you can say in this draft, print it out 5
if you are working on a computer. Get up from your desk and go sit in a
chair somewhere else to read it without correcting anything. Then put it
aside, preferably overnight. If possible, read your rough draft just before
you go to sleep. Many psychological tests have shown that our minds
organize and create while we sleep if we pack them full before bedtime.
Study a draft just before sleep, and you may discover new ideas in the
morning.

6   Be willing to make radical changes in your second draft. If your thesis changed while you were writing your first draft, you will base your
second draft on this new subject. Even if your thesis has not changed, you
may need to shift paragraphs around, eliminate paragraphs, or add new
ones. Inexperienced writers often suppose that revising a paper means
changing only a word or two or adding a sentence or two. This kind of
editing is part of the writing process, but it is not the most important part.
The most important part of rewriting is a willingness to turn the paper
upside down, to shake out of it those ideas that interest you most, to set
them in a form where they will interest the reader, too.

7   I mentioned earlier that some writers cut up their first drafts with
a pair of scissors. They toss some paragraphs into the trash; others they
paste up with rubber cement in the order that seems most logical and
coherent. Afterward they type the whole thing through again, smoothing
out the transitions, adding new material, getting new ideas as they work.
The translation of the first draft into the second nearly always involves
radical cutting and shifting around. Now and then you may firmly fix the
order of your thoughts in your first draft, but I find that the order of my
essays is seldom established until the second draft.

8   With the advent of computers the shifting around of parts of the
essays has become easy. We can cut and paste electronically with a few
strokes of the keyboard. We can also make back-up copies of our earlier
drafts so we can go back to them if we wish. But as I said earlier, computers do not remove from us the necessity to think hard about revising.

9   Always be firm enough with yourself to cut out thoughts or stories
that have nothing to do with your thesis, even if they are interesting.
Cutting is the supreme test of a writer. You may create a smashing paragraph or sentence only to discover later that it does not help you make
your point. You may develop six or seven examples to illustrate a point
and discover you need only one.

10   Now and then you may digress a little. If you digress too often or too
far, readers will not follow you unless your facts, your thoughts, and your
style are so compelling that they are somehow driven to follow you. Not
many writers can pull such digressions off, and most editors will cut out
the digressions even when they are interesting. In our hurried and harried time, most readers get impatient with the rambling scenic route. They
want to take the most direct way to their destination. To appeal to most of
them, you must cut things that do not apply to your main argument.

11   In your third draft, you can sharpen sentences, add information here
and there, cut some things, and attend to other details to heighten the
force of your writing. In the third draft, writing becomes a lot of fun (for
most of us). By then you have usually decided what you want to say. You
can now play a bit, finding just the right word, choosing just the right
sentence form, compressing here, expanding there.

I find it helpful to put a printed draft down beside my keyboard and   12
type the whole thing through again as a final draft, letting all the words
run through my mind and fingers one more time rather than merely delet-
ing and inserting on the computer screen. I wrote four drafts of the first
edition of this book; I have preserved the final draft of that edition on
computer diskettes. But I am writing this draft by propping the first edition up here beside me and typing it all over again. By comparing the first
draft and the second draft, one can see how many changes I have made,
most of them unforeseen until I sat down here to work.

I have outlined here my own writing process. It works for me. You   13
must find the process that works for you. It may be different from mine.
A friend tells me that his writing process consists of writing a sentence,
agonizing over it, walking around the room, thinking, sitting down, and
writing the next sentence. He does not revise very much. I think it unnecessarily painful to bleed out prose that way, but he bleeds out enough to
write what he needs to write. Several of my friends tell me they cannot
compose at a typewriter; they must first write with a pencil on a yellow
pad. These are the people most likely to cut up their drafts with scissors
and paste them together in a different form. They also tend to be older.
Most young writers are learning to compose at a keyboard, and they cannot imagine another way to write. Neither can I—though on occasion yet
I go back to my pencil for pages at a time.

The main thing is to keep at it. B. F. Skinner has pointed out that if   14
you write only fifty words a night, you will produce a good-sized book
every two or three years. That's not a bad record for any writer. William
Faulkner outlined the plot of his Nobel Prize–winning novel *A Fable* on a
wall inside his house near Oxford, Mississippi. You can see it there to this
day. Once he got the outline on the wall, he sat down with his typewriter
and wrote, following the outline to the end. If writing an outline on a
kitchen wall does the trick for you, do it. You can always repaint the wall
if you must.

Think of writing as a process making its way toward a product—   15
sometimes painfully. Don't imagine you must know everything you are
going to say before you begin. Don't demean yourself and insult your
readers by letting your first draft be your final draft. Don't imagine that
writing is easy or that you can do it without spending time on it. And
don't let anything stand in your way of doing it. Let your house get
messy. Leave your magazines unread and your mail unanswered. Put off
getting up for a drink of water or a cup of tea. (Never mix alcohol with
your writing; true, lots of writers have become alcoholics, but it has not
helped their writing.) Don't make a telephone call. Don't straighten up
your desk. Sit down and write. And write, and write, and write.

1988

QUESTIONS FOR DISCUSSION

Content

a. Marius advises using a list outline, but he cautions us not to follow it slavishly. Why not?

b. "Cutting is the supreme test of a writer," the author tells us in paragraph 9. What does he mean?

c. How is rewriting different from simple editing?

d. In what way is writing the second draft different from writing the first? In what way is writing the third draft different from writing the second?

e. How does Marius's suggested process compare with the way you usually write a paper? Which of his suggestions have you tried with success? Which without success? Which suggestions might you try for your next paper?

f. Are there any suggestions in "Writing Drafts" that you disagree with? What is the basis of your disagreement?

Strategy and Style

g. The author's personal voice can be heard clearly and distinctly throughout this selection. Is this subjective approach appropriate to writing that instructs?

h. If the writing process Marius follows may not work for you, why does he explain that process in careful detail?

i. Marius draws on several metaphors to help him describe the drafting process. One is the sailing metaphor at the end of paragraph 4: "Let your thoughts follow your new thesis, sailing on that tack until the wind changes." What connection does he want us to see between writing and sailing? What other metaphors can you find in the essay?

j. How does including personal experience, as in paragraph 13, help the author achieve his purposes? Why does he make reference to the experiences of well-known writers such as B. F. Skinner and William Faulkner?

k. Marius writes directly to you, the student. What was your reaction to this technique when you first read the essay? Why did he choose this technique?

ENGAGING THE TEXT

a. Quickly, and without looking back at Marius's essay, list the steps he suggests in writing drafts. Check what you have written against Marius's essay.

b. What piece of advice in "Writing Drafts" did you find most helpful? In what way do you think it will help you improve your writing?

SUGGESTIONS FOR SUSTAINED WRITING

a. Outline your own writing process. You may want to use as an example the last academic paper you wrote. Then, roughly following Marius's essay as a model, describe your ideal process for writing papers. As you complete this assignment, keep in mind techniques and practices you might try out with your next academic paper.
b. Write an essay similar to Marius's in which you put forth a set of sequenced suggestions for doing something other than writing drafts for an academic paper. The task you explain could be another kind of writing—poetry or short stories, for instance—or it might be any activity that people often find intimidating. Either way, make the activity seem both unintimidating and fruitfully challenging.
c. Marius explains how to draft an essay. But what about other parts of the writing process? Research the process of writing by reading further in Marius's *The Writer's Companion* or in the other works mentioned in the short biography preceding "Writing Drafts." However, focus on a stage in the writing process other than drafting. For example, read about how to gather information, to revise, or to edit/proofread. Then do some more research by consulting the works of composition experts such as Peter Elbow, William Zinsser, and Donald Murray. You can also find information on the websites of college and university writing centers. Turn your notes into instructions that will help a fellow student learn how to complete the stage of the writing process you are explaining.

READ MORE

Marius and His Works

"Richard Marius" (http://www.bookfinder.com/author/richard-marius): *List of Marius's books.*
"Richard Marius, Former Director of Expository Writing Program, Dies" (http://www.news.harvard.edu/gazette/1999/11.11/Marius.html): *Provides insight into the life and works of the author.*

The Writing Process

Marius, Richard. *The Writer's Companion.* New York: McGraw-Hill, 1994.
Zinsser, William. *On Writing Well.* New York: Harper & Row, 1976.

Alone on the Hilltop

John (Fire) Lame Deer and Richard Erdoes

Richard Erdoes (b. 1912) writes extensively on the American West. Born in Germany, Erdoes immigrated to the United States, where he first made his living as a photographer and illustrator. Among his many books are The Sun Dance People: The Plains Indians *(1972),* The Rain Dance People: The Pueblo Indians *(1976),* Tales of the American West *(1998), and* Thunderwoman: A Mythic Novel of the Pueblos *(1999). In 1967, Erdoes met John (Fire) Lame Deer (1903–1976) while both were participating in a march led by Dr. Martin Luther King, Jr. A Lakota Sioux, Lame Deer was born in South Dakota, but he traveled around the country, working as a rodeo clown, a tribal police officer, a sign painter, a bootlegger, and a sheepherder. At age 16, he had a spiritual experience as part of his training as a* wicasa wakan, *or Sioux holy man. However, it was only after he had left the U.S. Army, which he joined in 1942, that Lame Deer began to pursue his training more vigorously in a lifelong quest to find his Sioux identity. One of his major goals was to preserve as much as he could of his native culture, but Lame Deer had had little formal education. Therefore, he persuaded Erdoes to coauthor a book on the culture of the Lakota Sioux. That book was to become* Lame Deer: Seeker of Visions *(1971), from which "Alone on the Hilltop" is taken.*

This essay leads us through the process that a young Lakotan would undertake during his hanblechia, *or vision-seeking, a physical and spiritual trial essential to his training as a "healer, carrying on the ancient ways of the Sioux nation."*

VOCABULARY

There is no vocabulary for this essay.

1   I was all alone on the hilltop. I sat there in the vision pit, a hole dug into the hill, my arms hugging my knees as I watched old man Chest, the medicine man who had brought me there, disappear far down in the valley. He was just a moving black dot among the pines, and soon he was gone altogether.

2   Now I was all by myself, left on the hilltop for four days and nights without food or water until he came back for me. You know, we Indians are not like some white folks—a man and a wife, two children, and one baby sitter who watches the TV set while the parents are out visiting somewhere.

3   Indian children are never alone. They are always surrounded by grandparents, uncles, cousins, relatives of all kinds, who fondle the kids, sing to them, tell them stories. If the parents go someplace, the kids go along.

4   But here I was, crouched in my vision pit, left alone by myself for the first time in my life. I was sixteen then, still had my boy's name and, let

me tell you, I was scared. I was shivering and not only from the cold. The nearest human being was many miles away, and four days and nights is a long, long time. Of course, when it was all over, I would no longer be a boy, but a man. I would have had my vision. I would be given a man's name.

Sioux men are not afraid to endure hunger, thirst and loneliness, 5 and I was only ninety-six hours away from being a man. The thought was comforting. Comforting, too, was the warmth of the star blanket which old man Chest had wrapped around me to cover my nakedness. My grandmother had made it especially for this, my first *hanblechia*, my first vision-seeking. It was a beautifully designed quilt, white with a large morning star made of many pieces of brightly colored cloth. That star was so big it covered most of the blanket. If Waken Tanka, the Great Spirit, would give me the vision and the power, I would become a medicine man and perform many ceremonies wrapped in that quilt. I am an old man now and many times a grandfather, but I still have that star blanket my grandmother made for me. I treasure it; some day I shall be buried in it.

The medicine man had also left a peace pipe with me, together with 6 a bag of *kinnickinnick*—our kind of tobacco made of red willow bark. This pipe was even more of a friend to me than my star blanket. To us the pipe is like an open Bible. White people need a church house, a preacher and a pipe organ to get into a praying mood. There are so many things to distract you: who else is in the church, whether the other people notice that you have come, the pictures on the wall, the sermon, how much money you should give and did you bring it with you. We think you can't have a vision that way.

For us Indians there is just the pipe, the earth we sit on and the open 7 sky. The spirit is everywhere. Sometimes it shows itself through an animal, a bird or some trees and hills. Sometimes it speaks from the Badlands, a stone, or even from the water. That smoke from the peace pipe, it goes straight up to the spirit world. But this is a two-way thing. Power flows down to us through that smoke, through the pipe stem. You feel that power as you hold your pipe; it moves from the pipe right into your body. It makes your hair stand up. That pipe is not just a thing; it is alive. Smoking this pipe would make me feel good and help me to get rid of my fears.

As I ran my fingers along its bowl of smooth red pipestone, red like 8 the blood of my people, I no longer felt scared. That pipe had belonged to my father and to his father before him. It would someday pass to my son and, through him, to my grandchildren. As long as we had the pipe there would be a Sioux nation. As I fingered the pipe, touched it, felt its smoothness that came from long use, I sensed that my forefathers who had once smoked this pipe were with me on the hill, right in the vision pit. I was no longer alone.

Besides the pipe the medicine man had also given me a gourd. In it 9 were forty small squares of flesh which my grandmother had cut from her arm with a razor blade. I had seen her do it. Blood had been streaming down from her shoulder to her elbow as she carefully put down each piece of skin on a handkerchief, anxious not to lose a single one. It would have made those anthropologists mad. Imagine, performing such an ancient ceremony with a razor blade instead of a flint knife! To me it did not matter. Someone dear to me had undergone pain, given me something of herself, part of her body, to help me pray and make me stronghearted. How could I be afraid with so many people—living and dead— helping me?

10   One thing still worried me. I wanted to become a medicine man, a *yuwipi*, a healer carrying on the ancient ways of the Sioux nation. But you cannot learn to be a medicine man like a white man going to medical school. An old holy man can teach you about herbs and the right ways to perform a ceremony where everything must be in its proper place, where every move, every word has its own, special meaning. These things you can learn—like spelling, like training a horse. But by themselves these things mean nothing. Without the vision and the power this learning will do no good. It would not make me a medicine man.

11   What if I failed, if I had no vision? Or if I dreamed of the Thunder Beings, or lightning struck the hill? That would make me at once into a *heyoka*, a contrarywise, an upside-down man, a clown. "You'll know it, if you get the power," my Uncle Chest had told me. "If you are not given it, you won't lie about it, you won't pretend. That would kill you, or kill somebody close to you, somebody you love."

12   Night was coming on. I was still lightheaded and dizzy from my first sweat bath in which I had purified myself before going up the hill. I had never been in a sweat lodge before. I had sat in the little beehive-shaped hut made of bent willow branches and covered with blankets to keep the heat in. Old Chest and three other medicine men had been in the lodge with me. I had my back against the wall, edging as far away as I could from the red-hot stones glowing in the center. As Chest poured water over the rocks, hissing white steam enveloped me and filled my lungs. I thought the heat would kill me, burn the eyelids off my face! But right in the middle of all this swirling steam I heard Chest singing. So it couldn't be all that bad. I did not cry out "All my relatives!"—which would have made him open the flap of the sweat lodge to let in some cool air—and I was proud of this. I heard him praying for me: "Oh, holy rocks, we receive your white breath, the steam. It is the breath of life. Let this young boy inhale it. Make him strong."

13   The sweat bath had prepared me for my vision-seeking. Even now, an hour later, my skin still tingled. But it seemed to have made my brains empty. Maybe that was good, plenty of room for new insights.

14   Darkness had fallen upon the hill. I knew that *hanhepiwi* had risen, the night sun, which is what we call the moon. Huddled in my narrow cave,

I did not see it. Blackness was wrapped around me like a velvet cloth. It seemed to cut me off from the outside world, even from my own body. It made me listen to the voices within me. I thought of my forefathers who had crouched on this hill before me, because the medicine men in my family had chosen this spot for a place of meditation and vision-seeking ever since the day they had crossed the Missouri to hunt for buffalo in the White River country some two hundred years ago. I thought that I could sense their presence right through the earth I was leaning against. I could feel them entering my body, feel them stirring in my mind and heart.

Sounds came to me through the darkness: the cries of the wind, the whisper of the trees, the voices of nature, animal sounds, the hooting of an owl. Suddenly I felt an overwhelming presence. Down there with me in my cramped hole was a big bird. The pit was only as wide as myself, and I was a skinny boy, but that huge bird was flying around me as if he had the whole sky to himself. I could hear his cries, sometimes near and sometimes far, far away. I felt feathers or a wing touching my back and head. This feeling was so overwhelming that it was just too much for me. I trembled and my bones turned to ice. I grasped the rattle with the forty pieces of my grandmother's flesh. It also had many little stones in it, tiny fossils picked up from an ant heap. Ants collect them. Nobody knows why. These little stones are supposed to have a power in them. I shook the rattle and it made a soothing sound, like rain falling on rock. It was talking to me, but it did not calm my fears. I took the sacred pipe in my other hand and began to sing and pray: "Tunkashila, grandfather spirit, help me." But this did not help. I don't know what got into me, but I was no longer myself. I started to cry. Crying, even my voice was different. I sounded like an older man, I couldn't even recognize this strange voice. I used long-ago words in my prayer, words no longer used nowadays. I tried to wipe away my tears, but they wouldn't stop. In the end I just pulled that quilt over me, rolled myself up in it. Still I felt the bird wings touching me.

Slowly I perceived that a voice was trying to tell me something. It was 16 a bird cry, but I tell you, I began to understand some of it. That happens sometimes. I know a lady who had a butterfly sitting on her shoulder. That butterfly told her things. This made her become a great medicine woman.

I heard a human voice too, strange and high-pitched, a voice which 17 could not come from an ordinary, living being. All at once I was way up there with the birds. The hill with the vision pit was way above everything. I could look down even on the stars, and the moon was close to my left side. It seemed as though the earth and the stars were moving below me. A voice said, "You are sacrificing yourself here to be a medicine man. In time you will be one. You will teach other medicine men. We are the fowl people, the winged ones, the eagles and the owls. We are a nation and you shall be our brother. You will never kill or harm any one of us. You are going to understand us whenever you come to seek a vision here on this hill. You will learn about herbs and roots, and you will heal people. You will ask them for nothing in return. A man's life is short. Make yours a worthy one."

18   I felt that these voices were good, and slowly my fear left me. I had lost all sense of time. I did not know whether it was day or night. I was asleep, yet wide awake. Then I saw a shape before me. It rose from the darkness and the swirling fog which penetrated my earth hole. I saw that this was my great-grandfather, Tahca Ushte, Lame Deer, old man chief of the Minneconjou. I could see the blood dripping from my great-grandfather's chest where a white soldier had shot him. I understood that my great-grandfather wished me to take his name. This made me glad beyond words.

19   We Sioux believe that there is something within us that controls us, something like a second person almost. We call it *nagi*, what other people might call soul, spirit or essence. One can't see it, feel it or taste it, but that time on the hill—and only that once—I knew it was there inside of me. Then I felt the power surge through me like a flood. I cannot describe it, but it filled all of me. Now I knew for sure that I would become a *wicasa wakan*, a medicine man. Again I wept, this time with happiness.

20   I didn't know how long I had been up there on that hill—one minute or a lifetime. I felt a hand on my shoulder gently shaking me. It was old man Chest, who had come for me. He told me that I had been in the vision pit four days and four nights and that it was time to come down. He would give me something to eat and water to drink and then I was to tell him everything that had happened to me during my *hanblechia*. He would interpret my visions for me. He told me that the vision pit had changed me in a way that I would not be able to understand at that time. He told me also that I was no longer a boy, that I was a man now. I was Lame Deer.

1972

QUESTIONS FOR DISCUSSION

Content

a. At the end of the trial, the narrator tells us that his name has become "Lame Deer." What is the purpose of the ordeal he has just gone through?

b. Why does the narrator describe the blanket and the peace pipe that the medicine man leaves him? What function do they serve in the ceremony?

c. What does Lame Deer mean when, in paragraph 8, he says, "As long as we had the pipe there would be a Sioux nation"?

d. What comparison is being made between Native American spirituality and white spirituality in paragraph 6? Is this comparison valid?

e. What does the gourd contain, and why is this instrument important to the trial the boy undergoes?

f. In what ways does the sweat bath prepare the boy for his vision-seeking?

g. If this selection is intended to help keep alive elements of the ancient Sioux culture, what roles do Lame Deer's great-grandfather and his grandmother play in achieving that goal?

Strategy and Style

h. Why do the authors include Sioux words in this essay? Why don't they simply use their English equivalents?

i. Although this is clearly a piece of process analysis, it is unlike most pieces of scientific writing that we read. For one thing, it uses a great many figures of speech. Identify a few of these.

j. Besides process and contrast, what other methods of development does this essay employ?

k. Judging from the lack of unfamiliar vocabulary, the style of this essay is simple and direct. What accounts for that? Consider the interaction of Lame Deer and Erdoes as they planned and wrote *Lame Deer: Seeker of Visions*.

ENGAGING THE TEXT

a. Write a summary of the "steps" that we are told about in this initiation ceremony.

b. At various points in the text, Lame Deer tells us about the emotions running through him as he went through his trial. Find these points and explain what they tell us about Lame Deer the boy and Lame Deer the man.

SUGGESTIONS FOR SUSTAINED WRITING

a. Lame Deer explains a Lakota coming-of-age ritual. However, many cultures have such rituals. Think of a trial, a ceremony, or a ritual that you or someone you know went through to mark a transition from childhood to adulthood. Explain the process you or your subject went through step-by-step. Like the authors of "Alone on the Hilltop," record your emotional reactions and explain the significance of important aspects of the experience to your culture.

b. Recall what you wrote in response to the items under Engaging the Text, especially item *b*. Then, write an essay in which you analyze the character of the speaker in "Alone on the Hilltop." Quote from and make specific reference to the text to support your analysis.

c. Write a research paper in which you contrast what a child of one culture must go through to be considered an adult with what a child in another culture must go through to achieve the same goal. (Of course, one of these cultures might be your own.) To focus your essay, consider concentrating on a particular process, such as the training one must go through to become self-sufficient or the ritual involved in finding a mate. If appropriate, point out similarities as well.

READ MORE

The Authors and Their Works

Erdoes, Richard. *The Sun Dance People: The Plains Indians, Their Past and Present*. New York: Random House, 1972.

Erdoes, Richard, and Alfonso Ortiz, eds., *American Indian Myths and Legends*. New York: Pantheon, 1984.

Lame Deer, John (Fire), and Richard Erdoes. *Lame Deer: Seeker of Visions*. New York: Washington Square Press, 1972.

"Lame Deer, Seeker of Visions." *Colonial and Postcolonial Dialogues*. University of Western Michigan (http://www.wmich.edu/dialogues/texts/lamedeer.html): *Provides an overview of the book and links to several important sites on Native American culture.*

On Native American Culture

Forbes, Jack D. "Indigenous Americans: Spirituality and Ecos." *American Academy of Arts and Sciences* (http://www.amacad.org/publications/fall2001/forbes.aspx): *A valuable essay that mentions important scholarly sources.*

"Native American Sites." *American Indian Library Association* (http://www.nativeculturelinks.com/indians.html): *Home page of the American Indian Library Association with links to many valuable resources.*

"Native American Spirituality." *Religious Tolerance.org*. Ontario Consultants on Religious Tolerance (http://www.religioustolerance.org/nataspir.htm).

Chronicles of Ice

Gretel Ehrlich

Born on a ranch near Santa Barbara, California, Gretel Ehrlich (1946–) studied at Bennington College and the University of California, later working as a maker of documentary films. Her last film project (1978) was on a Wyoming sheep farm, where she stayed and took up ranching as her day job, devoting the evenings to her new writing career.

A great deal of Ehrlich's work shows a reverence for nature, as is the case with the essay that follows. However, her interests are varied. Her first published work is The Solace of Open Spaces *(1984), a book of essays centered on her Wyoming experience. In 1987 she published a novel,* Heart Mountain, *about a Japanese internment camp during World War II. A second book of essays,* Islands, the Universe, and Home *appeared in 1991. In 1994 she wrote* A Match to the Heart, *which discusses the effects of having been struck by lighting, an event that hospitalized her.*

Ehrlich is an avid traveler, having made trips to the Himalayas, which inspired her to write Questions of Heaven *(1994), and to Greenland, about which she wrote* This Cold Heaven: Seven Seasons in Greenland *(2002). "Chronicles of Ice" is from* The Future of Ice: A Journey into Cold *(2004). This essay is about a trip to a glacier at the southern end of Argentina, quite near the South Pole. It reflects her concern for the natural world and her fear that human activity is doing it irreversible harm.*

VOCABULARY

timpani, accretes, cacophony, ablation, archivist, incarnate, denigration

A trapped turbulence—as if wind had solidified. Then noise: timpani and 1
a hard crack, the glacier's internal heat spilling out as an ice stream far below. I've come on a bus from El Calafate, Argentina, to visit the World Heritage glacier Perito Moreno, to see its bowls, lips, wombs, fenders, gravelly elbows, ponds, and ice streams, and to learn whatever lessons a glacier has to teach.

Some glaciers retreat, some surge, some do both, advancing and 2
retreating even as the climate warms. Perito Moreno is 257 square kilometers across. It advances two meters a day at the center. From where I'm standing, I can look directly down on the glacier's snout. Two spires tilt forward, their lips touching. They meet head to head, but their bodies are hollow. Sun scours them as they twist toward light.

I walk down stairs to a platform that gives me a more intimate view. 3
A row of ice teeth is bent sideways, indicating basal movement. Out of the corner of my eye I see something fall. A spectator gasps. An icy cheekbone crumbles. People come here to see only the falling and failings, not the power it takes for the glacier to stay unified.

4   A glacier is not static. Snow falls, accretes, and settles until finally its own weight presses it down. The flakes become deformed. They lose coherence and pattern, become something crystalline called *firn* which then turns to ice. As an ice mountain grows, its weight displaces its bulk and it spreads outward, filling whole valleys, hanging off mountains, running toward seas.

5   There are warm glaciers and cold glaciers, depending on latitude and altitude. Cold glaciers don't slide easily; they're fixed and frozen to rock. They move like men on stilts—all awkwardness, broken bones of sheared rock. Internal deformation affects flow patterns; melting occurs faster at the margins than in the center. Warm glaciers have internal melt-streams at every level and torrents of water flow out from under the ice at the glacier's foot. The "sole" of the glacier is close to the melting point and slides easily over rock. Friction creates heat, heat increases sole-melt, slipperiness, and speed. The quasi-liquid surface that results is a disordered layer, a complicated boundary where heat and cold, melting and freezing, play off each other and are inextricably bound, the way madness and sanity, cacophony and stillness, are.

6   Because ice melts as it moves and moves as it melts, a glacier is always undermining itself. It lives by giving itself away.

7   A glacier balances its gains and losses like a banker. Accumulation has to exceed ablation for a glacier to grow. At the top, snow stacks up and does not melt. Midway down, the area of "mass balance" is where the profits and losses of snow can go either way. Surface melting can mean that water percolates down, refreezes, melts, and freezes again, creating a lens of ice. Below this region of equilibrium, ablation occurs. Profits are lost when the rate of melting exceeds the rate of accumulation. But a glacier will still advance if enough snow falls at the top and stays. . . .

8   A glacier is an archivist and historian. It registers every fluctuation of weather. It saves everything no matter how small or big, including pollen, dust, heavy metals, bugs, and minerals. As snow becomes firn and then ice, oxygen bubbles are trapped in the glacier, providing samples of ancient atmosphere: carbon dioxide and methane. Records of temperatures and levels of atmospheric gases from before industrialization can be compared with those after—a mere 150 years. We can now see that the steady gains in greenhouse gases and air and water temperatures have occurred only since the rise of our smokestack and tailpipe society.

9   A glacier is time incarnate. When we lose a glacier—and we are losing most of them—we lose history, an eye into the past; we lose stories of how living beings evolved, how weather vacillated, why plants and animals died. The retreat and disappearance of glaciers—there are only 160,000 left—means we're burning libraries and damaging the planet, possibly beyond repair. Bit by bit glacier by glacier, rib by rib, we're living the Fall. . . .

Twenty thousand years ago temperatures plummeted and ice grew 10 from the top of the world like vines and ground covers. Glaciers sprouted and surged, covering 10 million square miles—more than thirteen times what they cover now. As a result of their worldwide retreat and a global decrease in winter snow cover, the albedo effect—the ability of ice and snow to deflect heat back into space—is quickly diminishing. Snow and ice are the Earth's built-in air conditioner—crucial to the health of the planet. Without winter's white mantle, Earth will become a heat sponge. As heat escalates, all our sources of fresh water will disappear.

Already, warmer temperatures are causing meltwater to stream into 11 oceans, changing temperature and salinity; sea ice and permafrost are thawing, pulsing methane into the air; seawater is expanding, causing floods and intrusions. Islands are disappearing, and vast human populations in places like Bangladesh are in grave danger. The high-mountain peoples of Peru, Chile, and Bolivia who depend on meltwater from snowpack are at risk; the Inuit cultures in Alaska, Arctic Canada, Siberia, and Greenland that depend on ice for transportation, and live on a diet of marine mammals, could disappear.

In temperate climates everywhere, the early onset of spring and the 12 late arrival of winter are creating ecosystem pandemonium. It is not unreasonable to think that a whole season can become extinct, at least for a time. Winter might last only one day—minor punctuation in a long sentence of heat. Mirages rising from shimmering heat waves would be the only storms. . . .

The bus takes me back to town. I get out near a grove of trees where 13 loose horses wander. It's good to be in a place where there are such freedoms. All over the world the life of rocks, ice, mountains, snow, oceans, islands, albatross, sooty gulls, whales, crabs, limpets, and guanaco once flowed up into the bodies of the people who lived in small hunting groups and villages, and out came killer-whale prayers, condor chants, crab feasts, and guanaco songs. Life went where there was food. Food occurred in places of great beauty, and the act of living directly fueled people's movements, thoughts, and lives.

Everything spoke. Everything made a sound—birds, ghosts, ani- 14 mals, oceans, bogs, rocks, humans, trees, flowers, and rivers—and when they passed each other a third sound occurred. That's why weather, mountains, and each passing season were so noisy. Song and dance, sex and gratitude, were the season-sensitive ceremonies linking the human psyche to the larger, wild, weather-ridden world.

Now, the enterprise we human beings in the "developed world" have 15 engaged in is almost too darkly insane to contemplate. Our bent has been to "improve" on nature and local culture, which has meant that we've reduced the parallel worlds of spirit, imagination, and daily life to a single secularized pile. The process of empire-building is a kind of denigration.

Nothing that's not nuts and bolts and money-making is allowed in. Our can-do optimism and our head-in-the-sand approach to economics—one that takes only profit, and not the biological health of our planet, into account—has left us one-sided.

16   When did we begin thinking that weather was something to be rescued from? Why did we trade in our ceremonial lives for the workplace? Is this a natural progression or a hiccup in human civilization that we'll soon renounce?

17   I eat at a rustic bar with other travelers. It's late when night comes, maybe 10:30. In the darkness, Perito Moreno is still calving and moving, grabbing snowflakes, stirring weather, spitting out ice water, and it makes me smile.

QUESTIONS FOR DISCUSSION

Content

a. What is the stated purpose of the author's trip to the Perito Moreno glacier?
b. In paragraph 5, Ehrlich contrasts two types of glaciers. Summarize the differences in your own words.
c. Explain what Ehrlich is saying in paragraph 6.
d. Why does she label the glacier an "archivist" (paragraph 8)? What does she mean by saying that it is "time incarnate" (paragraph 9)?
e. Write a sentence that might serve as this essay's thesis.

Strategy and Style

f. Why is the word Fall capitalized in paragraph 9?
g. In what ways is this essay typical of process analysis essays? In what ways is it not?
h. Find evidence that Ehrlich personifies the glacier. Pick out examples of similes and metaphors. What does Ehrlich's use of this kind of language tell you about her audience?
i. Where in this essay does the author explain causes and effects? Where does she define terms or concepts?
j. Is the essay's conclusion appropriate? Why or why not? What does it tell us about the author's attitude toward her subject?

ENGAGING THE TEXT

a. In paragraphs 11–16, Ehrlich makes some startling claims. How might you respond to those claims? Are they convincing, or should Ehrlich have developed them in greater detail, perhaps through documented research?

b. What is the author driving at in paragraphs 13 and 14? In what way is paragraph 15 a logical follow-up to those ideas?

SUGGESTIONS FOR SUSTAINED WRITING

a. Write an essay that explains the process by which an environmental problem evolved. You need not write about a global problem as Ehrlich did. Instead pick a "local" problem, one that you know a great deal about. Explain how the lake in a nearby park became polluted; trace the deterioration of a public place where people have littered or drawn graffiti; or write about the destruction wrought by a forest fire due to human negligence.

b. Read Petrini's "The Value and Price of Food" (Chapter 8) or Lame Deer and Erdoes's "Alone on the Hilltop" (this chapter). Both of these essays, like "Chronicles of Ice," appeal to the reader's respect for the natural world. Write an essay that explains how and to what extent the essay you read delivers a message similar or at least related to the message of Ehrlich's essay.

c. Reread your response to Engaging the Text (item *a*). (If you have not responded to that prompt, do so now.) Make sure you fully understand what Ehrlich is saying. Then, using library and/or Internet research (check with your instructor to determine appropriate sources of research), write an essay that addresses her opinion. You might disagree, agree, or do some of both.

READ MORE

Gretel Ehrlich and Her Works

Welch, Dave. "Gretel Ehrlich" (http://www.powells.com/authors/ehrlich.html): *Interview with the author*, "Gretel Ehrlich," (http://gretel-ehrlich.com).

Global Warming

"Climate Change." *U.S. Environmental Protection Agency* (http://www.epa.gov/climatechange).

"Global Warming: Early Warning Signs." *Intergovernmental Panel on Climate Change* (http://www.climatehotmap.org): *Offers links to other valuable sources.*

Desperation Writing

Peter Elbow

Peter Elbow (1935) graduated from Williams College in 1957 and took a second bachelor's and a master's degree at Exeter College, Oxford University. He then went to Brandeis University, where he earned a doctorate. While at Brandeis, Elbow developed his now-famous process of writing, which begins with freewriting, the technique that he explains in "Desperation Writing." Elbow has taught at the Massachusetts Institute of Technology, Franconia College, and the University of Massachusetts at Amherst.

His first book on writing was Writing Without Teachers *(1976), which introduced the practice of dividing writing classes into groups and allowing students to brainstorm and critique each other's work. Among his other books are* Writing with Power *(1991);* A Community of Writers *(1989) and* Sharing and Responding *(1999), which he co-authored with Pat Belanoff; and* Everyone Can Write *(2000).*

"Desperation Writing," which has been excerpted from "The Process of Writing: Cooking," a chapter in Writing Without Teachers, *describes a practice that Elbow developed to perfect his own writing skills while pursuing his doctorate. Something he once said may serve to inspire all students, especially those who find writing difficult: "I got interested in writing because of my own difficulties with it." We might compare Elbow to the Clerk in Chaucer's* Canterbury Tales, *who would "gladly learn and gladly teach."*

VOCABULARY

recurring, assertion, comatose, mulling, passive, intuition, subsidiary, configuration, randomness

1   I know I am not alone in my recurring twinges of panic that I won't be able to write something when I need to, I won't be able to produce coherent speech or thought. And that lingering doubt is a great hindrance to writing. It's a constant fog or static that clouds the mind. I never got out of its clutches till I discovered that it was possible to write something—not something great or pleasing but at least something usable, workable—when my mind is out of commission. The trick is that you have to do all your cooking out on the table: your mind is incapable of doing any inside. It means using symbols and pieces of paper not as a crutch but as a wheelchair.

2   The first thing is to admit your condition: because of some mood or event or whatever, your mind is incapable of anything that could be called thought. It can put out a babbling kind of speech utterance, it can put a simple feeling, perception or sort-of-thought into understandable (though terrible) words. But it is incapable of considering anything in relation to anything else. The moment you try to hold that thought or feeling up against some other to see the relationship, you simply lose the picture—you get nothing but buzzing lines or waving colors.

So admit this. Avoid anything more than one feeling, perception, or ₃ thought. Simply write as much as possible. Try simply to steer your mind in the direction or general vicinity of the thing you are trying to write about and start writing and keep writing.

Just write and keep writing. (Probably best to write on only one side ₄ of the paper in case you should want to cut parts out with scissors–but you probably won't.) Just write and keep writing. It will probably come in waves. After a flurry, stop and take a brief rest. But don't stop too long. Don't think about what you are writing or what you have written or else you will overload the circuit again. Keep writing as though you are drugged or drunk. Keep doing this till you feel you have a lot of material that might be useful; or, if necessary, till you can't stand it any more–even if you doubt that there's anything useful there.

Then take a pad of little pieces of paper-or perhaps 3 x 5 cards-and sim- ₅ ply start at the beginning of what you were writing, and as you read over what you wrote, every time you come to any thought, feeling, perception, or image that could be gathered up into one sentence or one assertion, do so and write it by itself on a little sheet of paper. In short, you are trying to turn, say, ten or twenty pages of wandering mush into twenty or thirty hard little crab apples. Sometimes there won't be many on a page. But if it seems to you that there are none on a page, you are making a serious error–the same, foolish, worthless ideas for no ideas at all. Your job is not to pick out good ideas but to pick out ideas. As long as you were conscious, your words will be full of things that could be called feelings, utterances, ideas–things that can be squeezed into one simple sentence. This is your job. Don't ask for too much.

After you have done this, take those little slips or cards, read ₆ through them a number of times–not struggling with them, simply wandering and mulling through them; perhaps shifting them around and looking through them in various sequences. In a sense these are cards you are playing solitaire with, and the rules of this particular game permit shuffling the unused pile.

The goal of this procedure with the cards is to get them to distribute ₇ themselves in two or three or ten or fifteen different piles on your desk. You can get them to do this almost by themselves if you simply keep reading through them in different orders; certain cards will begin to feel like they go with other cards. I emphasize this passive, thoughtless mode because I want to talk about desperation writing in its pure state. In practice, almost invariably at some point in the procedure, your sanity begins to return. It is often at this point. You actually are moved to have thoughts or–and the difference between active and passive is crucial here–to *exert* thought; to hold two cards together and *build* or *assert* a relationship. It is a matter of bringing energy to bear.

8   So you may start to be able to do something active with these cards, and begin actually to think. But if not, just allow the cards to find their own piles with each other by feel, by drift, by intuition, by mindlessness.

9   You have now engaged in the two main activities that will permit you to get something cooked out on the table rather than in your brain: writing out into messy words, summing up into a single assertions, and even sensing relationships between assertions. You can simply continue to deploy these two activities.

10   If, for example, after the first round of writing, assertion-making, and pile-making, your piles feel as though they are useful and satisfactory for what you are writing–paragraphs or sections or trains of thought–then you can carry on from there. See if you can gather each pile up into a single assertion. When you can, then put the subsidiary assertions of that pile into their best order to fit with that single unifying one. If you *can't* get the pile into one assertion, then take the pile as the basis for doing some more writing out into words. In the course of this writing, you may produce for yourself the single unifying assertion you were looking for; or you may have to go through the cycle of turning the writing into assertions and piles and so forth. Perhaps more than once. The pile may turn out to want to be two or more piles itself; or it may want to become part of a pile you already have. This is natural. This kind of meshing into one configuration, then coming apart, then coming together and meshing into a different configuration–this is growing and cooking. It makes a terrible mess, but if you can't do it in your head, you have to put up with a cluttered desk and a lot of confusion.

11   If, on the other hand, all that writing didn't have useful material in it, it means that your writing wasn't loose, drifting, quirky, jerky, associative enough. This time try especially to let things simply remind you of things that are seemingly crazy or unrelated. Follow these old associations. Make as many metaphors as you can–be as nutty as possible–and explore the metaphors themselves–open them out. You may have all your energy tied up in some area of your experience that you are leaving out. Don't refrain from writing about whatever else is on your mind: how you feel at the moment, what you are losing your mind over, randomness that intrudes itself on your consciousness, the pattern on the wallpaper, what those people you see out the window have on their minds–though keep coming back to the wateveritis you are supposed to be writing about. Treat it, in short, like ten-minute writing exercises. Your best perceptions and thoughts are always going to be tied up in whatever is really occupying you, and that is also where your energy is. You may end up writing a love poem–or a hate poem–in one of those little piles while the other piles will finally turn into a lab report on data processing or whatever you have to write about. But you couldn't, in your present state of having your head

shot off, have written that report without also writing the poem. And the report will have some of the juice of the poem in it and vice versa.

QUESTIONS FOR DISCUSSION

Content

a. State Elbow's thesis in your own words.
b. In paragraph 1, the author uses an analogy to "cooking" as well as one that refers to a "wheel chair." Explain these analogies.
c. Where else in this essay does he use analogy? Find two or three other analogies and explain what they mean.
d. What, according to Elbow, constitutes "a great hindrance to writing? What light does this statement shed on Elbow's purpose?
e. Explain the contrast in paragraph 5 that is crucial to understanding Elbow's notion of "desperation writing"?
f. Often when explaining how to do something, writers have to provide alternate steps or instructions just in case the first ones they recommend don't work. Find places where Elbow does this.
g. Why does Elbow tell us not to "refrain from writing about whatever else is on your mind" (paragraph 11) if we get stuck? What purpose does doing this serve?

Strategy and Style

h. Elbow addresses the reader directly by using the second-person pronoun "you." Defend his adopting this practice.
i. How would you describe the audience for this essay? Make specific reference to the text to support your answer.
j. Comment on Elbow's style: his choice of words, his analogies, and his sentence structure. Focusing on one paragraph, explain why this style is appropriate to his audience.
k. Is Elbow's conclusion effective? How does it relate to his introduction?

ENGAGING THE TEXT

a. In paragraph 2, Elbow describes a state of mind that might lead to "desperation writing." Paraphrase this paragraph. Then, explain how it relates to an experience you have had with writing or with some other activity.
b. In paragraph 7, we read that "almost invariably at some point in the process, your sanity begins to return." Making close reference to the text, explain how this happens in your own words.

SUGGESTIONS FOR SUSTAINED WRITING

a. We can draw an analogy between the emotional/mental state of a writer, which Elbow describes in his introduction, with what athletes feel when they are in a slump, what artists experience when they have lost inspiration, or what scientists go through when they can't seem to make a breakthrough on a research project. Write an essay addressed to another athlete, to another artist, or to any other person passionately pursuing the same activity that you pursue. Based on your own experiences, explain how he or she might get out of that slump or regain inspiration so as to excel once again in what he or she loves to do.

b. This is an essay about how to overcome a problem common to writers, especially beginning college writers. Write an essay in which you provide a plan for overcoming another problem common to beginning college students. For example, you might explain how to outline a chapter in a textbook, how to overcome math phobia, how to take and organize notes for a research paper, how to budget one's time or money. Address your remarks to first-year college students.

  If this assignment doesn't interest you, read or re-read Marius's "Writing Drafts," which also appears in this chapter. Then, write an essay that draws similarities and/or differences between what Elbow says about writing and what Marius says.

c. In paragraph 2, Elbow tells us that the first thing we have to do is to "admit [our] condition." While this essay is about trying to overcome a mental block to writing, "admitting your condition" is the kind of advice many psychologists and addiction counselors give their patients as a way to start them on the road to recovery. Write a research paper in which you explain <u>how</u> someone might learn to admit his or her condition as the first step in a process toward recovering from an addiction to alcohol, drugs, sex, gambling, shopping, food or from any other form of dependence.

  Use relevant personal observations and experiences in this essay. However, also include information you have researched in the library, on electronic databases, and on the Internet per your professor's instructions. Use a documentation format stipulated by your teacher.

READ MORE

Elbow and His Works

Elbow, Peter. *Everyone Can Write: Essays Toward a Hopeful Theory of Teaching Writing*. New York: Oxford, 2000.
Elbow, Peter. *Witting with Power*. New York: Oxford, 1998.

"Selected Works of Peter Elbow" (http://works.bepress.com/peter_elbow): *Site includes links to several essays published by Elbow in scholarly journals as well as draft chapters from a book in progress.*

On Writing

"Getting Started: Freewrite." *Guide to Grammar and Writing.* Capital Community College Foundation (http://grammar.ccc.commnet.edu/grammar/composition/brainstorm_freewrite.htm): *Contains advice on and examples of freewriting.* Krystle, C. et al. "How to Freewrite." *WikiHow* (http://www.wikihow.com/Freewrite).

"Writing Prompts" (http://www.writersdigest.com/WritingPrompts): *Includes dozens of interesting writing prompts and allows writer to post responses on the Web.*

4

Definition

Generally speaking, definitions fall into three broad categories: lexical, stipulative, and extended. The dictionary is of course the best place to begin familiarizing yourself with new concepts, but lexical definitions tend to be abstract, for they sometimes explain terms without reference to particular contexts. And stipulative definitions, while practical, are by their very nature limited to special purposes. Say you were writing a paper on the advantages and disadvantages of being a part-time student. You might stipulate that, for the purposes of your essay, "a part-timer is someone enrolled for less than 12 credits." Thus, while both lexical and stipulative definitions have their uses, extended definitions are the type used most often to explain complex topics such as those discussed in this chapter.

The many practical uses to which extended definition can be applied make it a powerful tool for exposition. In the hands of writers like Richard Rodriguez and Gloria Naylor, it becomes a systematic way to grapple with social, economic, or moral questions. It can correct common, sometimes dangerous, misconceptions, as in Joseph Epstein's "The Green Eyed Monster" or Jo Goodwin Parker's "What Is Poverty?" But it can also be used to explain deep but abstract ideas that are important to the human condition. Take Dagoberto Gilb's "Pride," for example.

Like process essays, extended definitions are developed by using a number of methods. Among the most common are analogy and comparison/contrast. Rodriguez, for example, contrasts his appraisal of the word "Hispanic," which he calls a "contrivance," with its commonly accepted meaning.

As a matter of fact, many techniques can be used to develop extended definitions. The examples and anecdotes (brief, illustrative stories) Jo Goodwin Parker uses to define poverty are powerful and incisive tools for correcting social myopia. Tom Haines uses a wide variety of methods including narration, description, and cause/effect to explain the terror that haunts a people fighting famine. Epstein relies on lexical and etymological information to introduce or clarify specific points in a larger context. Approaches to the process of defining, then, are as varied as the authors who use them.

You can learn a great deal more about techniques for writing extended definitions by considering the Questions for Discussion, the items under Engaging the Text, and the Suggestions for Sustained Writing that follow each selection in this chapter. Another good way to learn the skills of definition is to read each of the essays in this chapter twice. On your first pass, simply make sure you understand each selection thoroughly and accurately. The second time around, ask yourself how you might define the term being explained, whether you agree with the author's perception, or if you can add information to make the definition even more credible. The method described above might require more time than you had planned to spend on this chapter, but it is a kind of mental exercise that will strengthen your analytical muscles and help you use definition as a powerful tool whenever you need to explain complex ideas.

What Is Poverty?

Jo Goodwin Parker

Although more than three decades old, "What Is Poverty?" holds as much meaning for us today as it did when it was first written. Parker's use of description and anecdote makes this definition essay both moving and incisive. In some ways, however, Parker seems to verge on argument. This becomes especially clear as we realize that, by anticipating reader objections, Parker has framed a dialogue that keeps us engaged and fascinated.

VOCABULARY

chronic, anemia, oleo, antihistamines, repossessed

You ask me what is poverty? Listen to me. Here I am, dirty, smelly, and   1
with no "proper" underwear on and with the stench of my rotting teeth near you. I will tell you. Listen to me. Listen without pity. I cannot use your pity. Listen with understanding. Put yourself in my dirty, worn out, ill-fitting shoes, and hear me.

Poverty is getting up every morning from a dirt- and illness-stained   2
mattress. The sheets have long since been used for diapers. Poverty is living in a smell that never leaves. This is a smell of urine, sour milk, and spoiling food sometimes joined with the strong smell of long-cooked onions. Onions are cheap. If you have smelled this smell, you did not know how it came. It is the smell of the outdoor privy. It is the smell of young children who cannot walk the long dark way in the night. It is the smell of the mattresses where years of "accidents" have happened. It is

the smell of the milk which has gone sour because the refrigerator long has not worked, and it costs money to get it fixed. It is the smell of rotting garbage. I could bury it, but where is the shovel? Shovels cost money.

3   Poverty is being tired. I have always been tired. They told me at the hospital when the last baby came that I had chronic anemia caused from poor diet, a bad case of worms, and that I needed a corrective operation. I listened politely—the poor are always polite. The poor always listen. They don't say that there is no money for iron pills, or better food, or worm medicine. The idea of an operation is frightening and costs so much that, if I had dared, I would have laughed. Who takes care of my children? Recovery from an operation takes a long time. I have three children. When I left them with "Granny" the last time I had a job, I came home to find the baby covered with fly specks, and a diaper that had not been changed since I left. When the dried diaper came off, bits of my baby's flesh came with it. My other child was playing with a sharp bit of broken glass, and my oldest was playing alone at the edge of a lake. I made twenty-two dollars a week, and a good nursery school costs twenty dollars a week for three children. I quit my job.

4   Poverty is dirt. You can say in your clean clothes coming from your clean house, "Anybody can be clean." Let me explain about housekeeping with no money. For breakfast I give my children grits with no oleo or cornbread without eggs and oleo. This does not use up many dishes. What dishes there are, I wash in cold water and with no soap. Even the cheapest soap has to be saved for the baby's diapers. Look at my hands, so cracked and red. Once I saved for two months to buy a jar of Vaseline for my hands and the baby's diaper rash. When I had saved enough, I went to buy it and the price had gone up two cents. The baby and I suffered on. I have to decide every day if I can bear to put my cracked sore hands into the cold water and strong soap. But you ask, why not hot water? Fuel costs money. If you have a wood fire it costs money. If you burn electricity, it costs money. Hot water is a luxury. I do not have luxuries. I know you will be surprised when I tell you how young I am. I look so much older. My back has been bent over the wash tubs every day for so long. I cannot remember when I ever did anything else. Every night I wash every stitch my school age child has on and just hope her clothes will be dry by morning.

5   Poverty is staying up all night on cold nights to watch the fire knowing one spark on the newspaper covering the walls means your sleeping child dies in flames. In summer, poverty is watching gnats and flies devour your baby's tears when he cries. The screens are torn and you pay so little rent you know they will never be fixed. Poverty means insects in your food, in your nose, in your eyes, and crawling over you when you sleep. Poverty is hoping it never rains because diapers won't dry when it rains and soon you are using newspapers. Poverty is seeing your children

forever with runny noses. Paper handkerchiefs cost money and all your rags you need for other things. Even more costly are antihistamines. Poverty is cooking without food and cleaning without soap.

Poverty is asking for help. Have you ever had to ask for help, know- 6 ing your children will suffer unless you get it? Think about asking for a loan from a relative, if this is the only way you can imagine asking for help. I will tell you how it feels. You find out where the office is that you are supposed to visit. You circle that block four or five times. Thinking of your children, you go in. Everyone is very busy. Finally, someone comes out and you tell her that you need help. That never is the person you need to see. You go see another person, and after spilling the whole shame of your poverty all over the desk between you, you find that this isn't the right office after all—you must repeat the whole process, and it never is any easier at the next place.

You have asked for help, and after all it has a cost. You are again told 7 to wait. You are told why, but you don't really hear because of the red cloud of shame and the rising cloud of despair.

Poverty is remembering. It is remembering quitting school in junior 8 high because "nice" children had been so cruel about my clothes and my smell. The attendance officer came. My mother told him I was pregnant. I wasn't, but she thought that I could get a job and help out. I had jobs off and on, but never long enough to learn anything. Mostly I remember being married. I was so young then. I am still young. For a time, we had all the things you have. There was a little house in another town, with hot water and everything. Then my husband lost his job. There was unemployment insurance for a while and what few jobs I could get. Soon, all our nice things were repossessed and we moved back here. I was pregnant then. This house didn't look so bad when we first moved in. Every week it gets worse. Nothing is ever fixed. We now had no money. There were a few odd jobs for my husband, but everything went for food then, as it does now. I don't know how we lived through three years and three babies, but we did. I'll tell you something, after the last baby I destroyed my marriage. It had been a good one, but could you keep on bringing children in this dirt? Did you ever think how much it costs for any kind of birth control? I knew my husband was leaving the day he left, but there were no goodbyes between us. I hope he has been able to climb out of this mess somewhere. He never could hope with us to drag him down.

That's when I asked for help. When I got it, you know how much it 9 was? It was, and is, seventy-eight dollars a month for the four of us; that is all I ever can get. Now you know why there is no soap, no needles and thread, no hot water, no aspirin, no worm medicine, no hand cream, no shampoo. None of these things forever and ever and ever. So that you can see clearly, I pay twenty dollars a month rent, and most of the rest goes for food. For grits and cornmeal, and rice and milk and beans. I try my best to use only the minimum electricity. If I use more, there is that much less for food.

10   Poverty is looking into a black future. Your children won't play with my boys. They will turn to other boys who steal to get what they want. I can already see them behind the bars of their prison instead of behind the bars of my poverty. Or they will turn to the freedom of alcohol or drugs, and find themselves enslaved. And my daughter? At best, there is for her a life like mine.

11   But you say to me, there are schools. Yes, there are schools. My children have no extra books, no magazines, no extra pencils, or crayons, or paper and most important of all, they do not have health. They have worms, they have infections, they have pinkeye all summer. They do not sleep well on the floor, or with me in my one bed. They do not suffer from hunger, my seventy-eight dollars keeps us alive, but they do suffer from malnutrition. Oh yes, I do remember what I was taught about health in school. It doesn't do much good. In some places there is a surplus commodities program. Not here. The county said it costs too much. There is a school lunch program. But I have two children who will already be damaged by the time they get to school.

12   But, you say to me, there are health clinics. Yes, there are health clinics and they are in the towns. I live out here eight miles from town. I can walk that far (even if it is sixteen miles both ways), but can my little children? My neighbor will take me when he goes; but he expects to get paid, *one way or another*. I bet you know my neighbor. He is that large man who spends his time at the gas station, the barbershop, and the corner store complaining about the government spending money on the immoral mothers of illegitimate children.

13   Poverty is an acid that drips on pride until all pride is worn away. Poverty is a chisel that chips on honor until honor is worn away. Some of you say that you would do *something* in my situation, and maybe you would, for the first week or the first month, but for year after year after year?

14   Even the poor can dream. A dream of a time when there is money. Money for the right kinds of food, for worm medicine, for iron pills, for toothbrushes, for hand cream, for a hammer and nails and a bit of screening, for a shovel, for a bit of paint, for some sheeting, for needles and thread. Money to pay *in money* for a trip to town. And, oh, money for hot water and money for soap. A dream of when asking for help does not eat away the last bit of pride. When the office you visit is as nice as the offices of other governmental agencies, when there are enough workers to help you quickly, when workers do not quit in defeat and despair. When you have to tell your story to only one person, and that person can send you for other help and you don't have to prove your poverty over and over and over again.

I have come out of my despair to tell you this. Remember I did not 15 come from another place or another time. Others like me are all around you. Look at us with an angry heart, anger that will help you help me. Anger that will let you tell of me. The poor are always silent. Can you be silent too?

1971

QUESTIONS FOR DISCUSSION

Content

a. How would you define the author's purpose? Besides paragraph 15, in what parts of the essay is that purpose most apparent?

b. Why does the speaker address her audience directly, especially in paragraphs 4 and 10? How would you describe that audience?

c. What is the speaker's attitude toward her estranged husband? Do you find it curious? What does it tell you about her? What does it tell you about Parker's purpose?

d. In paragraph 8, the speaker seems to describe a cycle of poverty into which the poor are born and in which they remain. Explain. In what other sections of the essay does she allude to this cycle?

e. How does she account for her inability to keep her family clean? Why is it futile for her to seek a job?

f. What is the distinction between "hunger" and "malnutrition" that she makes in paragraph 11? Why does she deny the usefulness of school lunch programs?

g. The speaker relates incidents in which she has had to endure both public and private humiliation in order to obtain help for her family. What is the source of such humiliation? How does Parker's inclusion of these incidents help her define "poverty"?

Strategy and Style

h. Often, the speaker makes sure to anticipate and to discuss opposing arguments. What is the effect of her doing so? How does this practice help illuminate her character?

i. Parker has organized the essay by having her speaker enunciate a series of characteristics that define poverty. What is the effect of her beginning several paragraphs with "Poverty is . . ."?

j. Comment on the author's use of illustrations. To what physical senses does she appeal most often? What use does she make of metaphor?

k. Parker has created a "persona" or speaker who tells her story by using the first-person pronoun ("I"). How would you describe this persona?

l. What is the purpose of paragraph 15 besides concluding the essay? How would you describe the speaker's tone in this paragraph? Does it differ from the tone she uses in other parts of the essay?

ENGAGING THE TEXT

a. Write a dictionary definition of poverty without using a dictionary. Then look up the word and compare your definition with the dictionary's. How specific were you or the dictionary able to get? Compare your definition to Parker's.

b. Describe your emotional response to Parker's essay as you read it.

SUGGESTIONS FOR SUSTAINED WRITING

a. The speaker tells us about material poverty. Are there other kinds of poverty that are less frequently talked about—intellectual, spiritual, or moral poverty, for instance? Try to define one of these less commonly discussed types of poverty by using concrete details and illustrations as Parker does in this selection. If this assignment doesn't interest you, think about another abstract term that describes a human reality with which you are thoroughly familiar: power, personal ambition, example, explain what that term means to you. Use your own personal experiences as concrete illustrations.

b. In this essay we read that Parker had a difficult time trying to get help from the government and the community. The frustration, anger, and hopelessness that she felt on account of these experiences come across quite clearly. Write an essay in which you have felt hopeless, angry, or frustrated over the way you were treated when you asked for help from people at a government, school, community, or private agency or office. Your purpose here is to define governmental or bureaucratic irresponsibility or unresponsiveness.

c. Parker creates a definition of poverty in 1971. Is this picture still accurate, or do people have more opportunities to lift themselves out of poverty than they did before? Using library or Internet research, focus on the plight of single mothers in America today. Explain the major economic and social problems they face. Is their situation materially different from what Parker's was? If it isn't, in what ways is it similar? If it is, discuss the kinds of opportunities, including public and private assistance, available today that would have improved Parker's life.

READ MORE

Almanac of Policy Issues: Poverty (http://www.policyalmanac.org/social_
welfare/poverty.shtml): *Sponsored by a private, nonpartisan group, con-
tains links to articles and sites on poverty and other related social issues.*
Pressman, Steven. *Poverty in America: An Annotated Bibliography*. Lanham,
MD: Scarecrow, 1994.
Rahmanou, Hedieh, and Amy LeMar. *Marriage and Poverty: An Annotated
Bibliography*. Institute for Women's Policy Research (http://www.iwpr
.org/publications/resources/manuals-guides).

The Company Man

Ellen Goodman

*Ellen Goodman was born in Newton, Massachusetts, in 1941. She took a B.A. from
Radcliffe College in 1963 and attended Harvard University on a Nieman Fellowship.
Goodman began her journalistic career with* Newsweek, *where she was a researcher and
reporter. She then moved to the* Detroit Free Press *as a feature writer. In 1967, she joined
the* Boston Globe *as a feature writer and columnist. Her syndicated column, "At Large,"
appears in more than 200 newspapers across the country. Her first book,* Turning Points
*(1979), was based on interviews she conducted about current changes in society. She has
won several awards for her commentary, including a Pulitzer Prize in 1980. Many of her
columns have been collected in* Close to Home *(1979), in which "The Company Man"
appeared. Other collections include* At Large *(1981),* Keeping in Touch *(1985),* Making
Sense *(1989), and* Value Judgments *(1993). Her most recent books are* I Know Just
What You Mean: The Power of Friendship in Women's Lives *(2000) and* Paper
Trail: Common Sense in Uncommon Times *(2004).*

*"The Company Man" indicts corporate America for fostering the development of
individuals who, apparently, have little in the way of souls. Goodman paints a bleak and
pronounced portrait of people who have lost touch with their families, with their values,
and even with themselves.*

VOCABULARY

thrombosis, Type A

He worked himself to death, finally and precisely, at 3:00 A.M. Sunday   1
morning.
    The obituary didn't say that, of course. It said that he died of a   2
coronary thrombosis—I think that was it—but everyone among his
friends and acquaintances knew it instantly. He was a perfect Type A, a

workaholic, a classic, they said to each other and shook their heads—and thought for five or ten minutes about the way they lived.

3   This man who worked himself to death finally and precisely at 3:00 A.M. Sunday morning—on his day off—was fifty-one years old and a vice-president. He was, however, one of six vice-presidents, and one of three who might conceivably—if the president died or retired soon enough—have moved to the top spot. Phil knew that.

4   He worked six days a week, five of them until eight or nine at night, during a time when his own company had begun the four-day week for everyone but the executives. He worked like the Important People. He had no outside "extracurricular interests," unless, of course, you think about a monthly golf game that way. To Phil, it was work. He always ate egg salad sandwiches at his desk. He was, of course, overweight, by 20 or 25 pounds. He thought it was okay, though, because he didn't smoke.

5   On Saturdays, Phil wore a sports jacket to the office instead of a suit, because it was the weekend.

6   He had a lot of people working for him, maybe sixty, and most of them liked him most of the time. Three of them will be seriously considered for his job. The obituary didn't mention that.

7   But it did list his "survivors" quite accurately. He is survived by his wife, Helen, forty-eight years old, a good woman of no particular marketable skills, who worked in an office before marrying and mothering. She had, according to her daughter, given up trying to compete with his work years ago, when the children were small. A company friend said, "I know how much you will miss him." And she answered, "I already have."

8   "Missing him all these years," she must have given up part of herself which had cared too much for the man. She would be "well taken care of."

9   His "dearly beloved" eldest of the "dearly beloved" children is a hard-working executive in a manufacturing firm down South. In the day and a half before the funeral, he went around the neighborhood researching his father, asking the neighbors what he was like. They were embarrassed.

10   His second child is a girl, who is twenty-four and newly married. She lives near her mother and they are close, but whenever she was alone with her father, in a car driving somewhere, they had nothing to say to each other.

11   The youngest is twenty, a boy, a high-school graduate who has spent the last couple of years, like a lot of his friends, doing enough odd jobs to stay in grass and food. He was the one who tried to grab at his father, and tried to mean enough to him to keep the man at home. He was his father's favorite. Over the last two years, Phil stayed up nights worrying about the boy.

12   The boy once said, "My father and I only board here." At the funeral, the sixty-year-old company president told the forty-eight-year-old widow that

the fifty-one-year-old deceased had meant much to the company and would be missed and would be hard to replace. The widow didn't look him in the eye. She was afraid he would read her bitterness and, after all, she would need him to straighten out the finances—the stock options and all that.

Phil was overweight and nervous and worked too hard. If he wasn't 13 at the office, he was worried about it. Phil was a Type A, a heart-attack natural. You could have picked him out in a minute from a lineup.

So when he finally worked himself to death, at precisely 3:00 A.M. 14 Sunday morning, no one was really surprised.

By 5:00 P.M. the afternoon of the funeral, the company president had 15 begun, discreetly of course, with care and taste, to make inquiries about his replacement. One of three men. He asked around: "Who's been working the hardest?"

1981

QUESTIONS FOR DISCUSSION

Content

a. One of the characteristics of the "company man" is that he is a "workaholic." What are the others?
b. Explain the relationship of Phil and his younger son. How did this relationship differ from his relationship with his other children? Why does Goodman bother to make the distinction?
c. What does Goodman's telling us about Phil's wife and children add to the definition of the "company man"?
d. In what ways is this essay an indictment of corporate America?
e. What is the irony in Goodman's saying that "You could have picked [Phil] out in a minute from a lineup" (paragraph 13)?
f. What do you infer from the author's telling us that her subject "worked like the 'Important People'"?
g. Why does Goodman emphasize the fact that Phil died at 3 A.M. on Sunday?

Strategy and Style

h. Discuss Goodman's voice in this essay. Is it ironic, acerbic, sarcastic, neutral?
i. What does the author think of Phil? Is her tone appropriate?
j. There are several players in this short drama. Does Goodman develop each of them in enough detail?

k. How has the author prepared us for the conclusion to this piece? Does her preparation make it more effective, more biting?

ENGAGING THE TEXT

a. Write a short dialogue in which Phil's older son interviews a neighbor to find out more about his father.
b. Using what Goodman has told you about the company man, write a list of characteristics that might define the contemporary company woman.

SUGGESTIONS FOR SUSTAINED WRITING

a. Do you know someone who fits Goodman's definition of a company man or who fits the definition of a company woman according to the list of characteristics you prepared in response to Engaging the Text (item *b*)? If so, write an essay that uses this individual as a model for your own definition of a company man/woman. If this assignment doesn't interest you, write about a person you know who illustrates another lifestyle or personality label. For example, define a "gossip," a "snob," a "do-gooder," or an "egotist."
b. Goodman has put her finger on one of the great absurdities of contemporary American life: the willingness to sacrifice oneself on the altar of success. There are other essays in this book that discuss absurdities of modern life. Take, for example, Didion's "Marrying Absurd" in Chapter 2. Relying on such pieces for inspiration, write an essay that explains a human phenomenon, convention, or activity you believe is absurd. If appropriate, draw information and/or direct quotations from other essays in this text.
c. Although corporate America is often portrayed in a bad light, large American companies and their employees often do a great deal of good for others. For example, Microsoft is a generous contributor of money and equipment to education. General Electric fosters mentoring programs for young people. And Johnson & Johnson supports numerous community projects related to public health care and education. Using print and Internet sources, write an essay in which you argue against the notion that all of corporate America should be condemned. Focus on one large company and explain what it does to better the lives of people in its community.

READ MORE

Archive of Stories by Ellen Goodman (http://www.boston.com/bostonglobe/ editorial_opinion/ellen_goodman): *Links to Goodman's writings for* The Boston Globe.

"Ellen Goodman." *Utne Reader,* Jan./Feb. 1999: 102—03. *An interview with the author.*

"Ellen Goodman." *The Washington Post Writers Group* (http://www.post-writersgroup.com/goodman.htm): *Brief life of Goodman with links to her writings for* The Washington Post.

Meanings of a Word

Gloria Naylor

Born in New York City in 1950, Gloria Naylor has lived in the Bronx, Chicago, North Carolina, and Florida. She attended Medgar Evers College and Brooklyn College, from which she took a B.A. in 1981. During that time, she read Toni Morrison's The Bluest Eye, *the first novel written by a black woman she had ever encountered. Taking inspiration from Morrison's work as well as from her association with Marcia Gillespie of* Essence *magazine, Naylor went on to earn an M.A. in African American studies at Yale University (1983) and to launch her writing career. In 1983, she published her first novel,* The Women of Brewster Place, *which was made into a television film and for which she received the National Book Award. She then published the following novels:* Linden Hills *(1985),* Mama Day *(1988),* Bailey's Café *(1992), and* The Men of Brewster Place *(1998). She has been writer-in-residence at Cummington Community of the Arts and at George Washington University, is the recipient of a National Endowment for the Arts fellowship and a Guggenheim fellowship, and was a cultural exchange lecturer in India for the United States Information Agency. She has also been a scholar-in-residence at the University of Pennsylvania and a visiting professor at New York University, Princeton University, Brandeis University, and Boston University. "Meanings of a Word" was first published in the* New York Times *in 1986. It discusses both the complexity of language and its malleability when used in different social contexts. More important, this essay is a powerful explanation of the effects of a particularly volatile word on the human psyche.*

Please note: the author (Gloria Naylor) wants it understood that the use of the word 'nigger' is reprehensible in today's society. This essay speaks to a specific time and place when that word was utilized to empower African-Americans; today it is used to degrade them even if spoken from their own mouths.

VOCABULARY

intermittent, reprieve, innocuous, consensus, nymphomaniac, necrophiliac, mecca, inflections, stratum, internalization, degradation, impotent

Language is the subject. It is the written form with which I've managed   1
to keep the wolf away from the door and, in diaries, to keep my sanity. In
spite of this, I consider the written word inferior to the spoken, and much
of the frustration experienced by novelists is the awareness that whatever
we manage to capture in even the most transcendent passages falls far

short of the richness of life. Dialogue achieves its power in the dynamics of a fleeting moment of sight, sound, smell and touch.

2   I'm not going to enter the debate here about whether it is language that shapes reality or vice versa. That battle is doomed to be waged whenever we seek intermittent reprieve from the chicken and egg dispute. I will simply take the position that the spoken word, like the written word, amounts to a nonsensical arrangement of sounds or letters without a consensus that assigns "meaning." And building from the meanings of what we hear, we order reality. Words themselves are innocuous; it is the consensus that gives them true power.

3   I remember the first time I heard the word nigger. In my third-grade class, our math tests were being passed down the rows, and as I handed the papers to a little boy in back of me, I remarked that once again he had received a much lower mark than I did. He snatched his test from me and spit out that word. Had he called me a nymphomaniac or a necrophiliac, I couldn't have been more puzzled. I didn't know what a nigger was, but I knew that whatever it meant, it was something he shouldn't have called me. This was verified when I raised my hand, and in a loud voice repeated what he had said and watched the teacher scold him for using a "bad" word. I was later to go home and ask the inevitable question that every black parent must face—"Mommy, what does 'nigger' mean?"

4   And what exactly did it mean? Thinking back, I realize that this could not have been the first time the word was used in my presence. I was part of a large extended family that had migrated from the rural South after World War II and formed a close-knit network that gravitated around my maternal grandparents. Their ground-floor apartment in one of the buildings they owned in Harlem was a weekend mecca for my immediate family, along with countless aunts, uncles and cousins who brought along assorted friends. It was a bustling and open house with assorted neighbors and tenants popping in and out to exchange bits of gossip, pick up an old quarrel or referee the ongoing checkers game in which my grandmother cheated shamelessly. They were all there to let down their hair and put up their feet after a week of labor in the factories, laundries and shipyards of New York.

5   Amid the clamor, which could reach deafening proportions—two or three conversations going on simultaneously, punctuated by the sound of a baby's crying somewhere in the back rooms or out on the street—there was still a rigid set of rules about what was said and how. Older children were sent out of the living room when it was time to get into the juicy details about "you-know-who" up on the third floor who had gone and gotten herself "p-r-e-g-n-a-n-t!" But my parents, knowing that I could spell well beyond my years, always demanded that I follow the others out to play. Beyond sexual misconduct and death, everything else was considered harmless for our young ears. And so among the anecdotes of the triumphs and disappointments in the various workings of their lives,

the word nigger was used in my presence, but it was set within contexts and inflections that caused it to register in my mind as something else.

In the singular, the word was always applied to a man who had dis- 6 tinguished himself in some situation that brought their approval for his strength, intelligence or drive:

"Did Johnny really do that?"   7

"I'm telling you, that nigger pulled in $6,000 of overtime last year. 8 Said he got enough for a down payment on a house."

When used with a possessive adjective by a woman—"my nigger"— 9 it became a term of endearment for husband or boyfriend. But it could be more than just a term applied to a man. In their mouths it became the pure essence of manhood—a disembodied force that channeled their past history of struggle and present survival against the odds into a victorious statement of being: "Yeah, that old foreman found out quick enough— you don't mess with a nigger."

In the plural, it became a description of some group within the com- 10 munity that had overstepped the bounds of decency as my family defined it: Parents who neglected their children, a drunken couple who fought in public, people who simply refused to look for work, those with exces- sively dirty mouths or unkempt households were all "trifling niggers." This particular circle could forgive hard times, unemployment, the occasional bout of depression—they had gone through all of that them- selves—but the unforgivable sin was lack of self-respect.

A woman could never be a "nigger" in the singular, with its connota- 11 tion of confirming worth. The noun "girl" was its closest equivalent in that sense, but only when used in direct address and regardless of the gender doing the addressing. "Girl" was a token of respect for a woman. The one-syllable word was drawn out to sound like three in recognition of the extra ounce of wit, nerve or daring that the woman had shown in the situation under discussion.

"G-i-r-l, stop. You mean you said that to his face?"   12

But if the word was used in a third-person reference or shortened so 13 that it almost snapped out of the mouth, it always involved some element of communal disapproval. And age became an important factor in these exchanges. It was only between individuals of the same generation, or from an older person to a younger (but never the other way around), that "girl" would be considered a compliment.

I don't agree with the argument that use of the word nigger at this 14 social stratum of the black community was an internalization of racism. The dynamics were the exact opposite: the people in my grandmother's living room took a word that whites used to signify worthlessness or degradation and rendered it impotent. Gathering there together, they transformed "nigger" to signify the varied and complex human beings they knew themselves to be. If the word was to disappear totally from the mouths of even the most racist of white society, no one in that room was naïve enough to believe it would disappear from white minds. Meeting the word head on, they proved it had absolutely nothing to do with the way they were determined to live their lives.

15   So there must have been dozens of times that the word "nigger" was spoken in front of me before I reached the third grade. But I didn't "hear" it until it was said by a small pair of lips that had already learned it could be a way to humiliate me. That was the word I went home and asked my mother about. And since she knew that I had to grow up in America, she took me in her lap and explained.

1986

QUESTIONS FOR DISCUSSION

Content

a. What is Naylor's thesis? What does she mean by "consensus" as applied here?

b. In what way was the author's grandparents' apartment a "mecca"?

c. What are the various definitions of the word *nigger* as explained in this essay?

d. What does the author mean when she says that the "people in [her] grandmother's living room … rendered the word 'nigger' impotent"?

e. To what end did Naylor's family use this word? Make reference to paragraph 14.

f. What does the author mean when she claims that, although the word had been uttered in her presence several times before, she did not "hear" it until it was used by a classmate?

Strategy and Style

g. Why does Naylor explain the meaning and use of the word *girl* in her family?

h. In what way is this definition essay also a contrast essay? Go beyond the obvious contrast between the uses of "nigger" in the white and African American communities.

i. The introduction to this essay is different in tone, content, and perhaps even purpose from the body of the essay. What accounts for these differences?

j. Comment upon Naylor's use of dialogue. In what way does this dialogue support the claim made at the end of paragraph 14?

k. How does Naylor's contrasting the spoken and the written word make for an appropriate introduction to this selection?

ENGAGING THE TEXT

a. Naylor's conclusion invites us to imagine a conversation between her and her mother. Making use of information and insights gleaned from this selection, write a dialogue between mother and daughter that would capture this conversation and extend the essay.
b. Explain what the author is saying in the first few sentences of paragraph 14. In what ways does this part of the essay reveal her thinking about her family and the community in which she grew up?

SUGGESTIONS FOR SUSTAINED WRITING

a. In paragraph 10, Naylor distinguishes between the plural and singular forms of nigger and, in so doing, leads us to the conclusion that in her community "the unforgivable sin was lack of self-respect." Explain what she means. Then apply this statement—and the thinking behind it—to any person or group of people you know.
b. In some ways, Naylor uses an analysis of spoken language to comment on the sociology of her family and her community. Langston Hughes comments on the sociology of his family and community in "Salvation," a selection in Chapter 1. Compare Naylor's essay and another essay in this text in terms of what they tell us about the communities that the authors are analyzing. Focus on purpose, tone, organization, and vision.
c. Choose another common racial, ethnic, religious, or sexual slur. Research the origins of this term in print or electronic sources. Then define its current use or uses, clearly distinguishing between any differences by using appropriate examples or dialogue. Make sure to explain how people who are the object of such language react to it.

READ MORE

Fowler, Virginia. *Gloria Naylor: In Search of Sanctuary*. New York: Twayne, 1996.
"Gloria Naylor." *African American Literature Book Club*, (http://aalbc.com/authors/gloria.htm): A brief biography and listing of her books.
Whitt, Margaret. *Understanding Gloria Naylor*. Columbia: University of South Carolina, 1999.

The Green-Eyed Monster: Envy Is Nothing to Be Jealous Of

Joseph Epstein

Born in Chicago in 1937, Epstein is the author of numerous essays and books. Among the latter are Divorced in America: Marriage in the Age of Possibility *(1974),* Fabulous Small Jews: A Collection of Stories *(2003),* Snobbery: The American Version *(2003), and* Envy *(2004), from which this essay was excerpted in* Washington Monthly *magazine. More recently, Epstein published* Alexis de Tocqueville: Democracy's Guide *(2006) and* Fred Astaire *(2008). From 1974 to 2002, Epstein taught English at Northwestern University. He has also served as an editor at the American Scholar and has published in* The New York Times, Harper's, *and* The Atlantic Monthly.

In "The Green-Eyed Monster," Epstein defines envy by using both lexical and extended definitions. In the process, he clarifies many modern misconceptions of the word. Envy, as Epstein mentions, is one of the seven deadly sins, a medieval religious construct. (The other deadly sins are pride, avarice, anger, lust, gluttony, and sloth.)

VOCABULARY

entails, recompense, insidious, endemic, lacerating, rancorous, disposition, stigmata, implicit, malignant, enmity, mortification, malevolence, emulation, pedantic, pejorative, parlance, *ipso facto*, rendering, inept, malice, impotent, stiletto

1   Of the seven deadly sins, only envy is no fun at all. Sloth may not seem that enjoyable, nor anger either, but giving way to deep laziness has its pleasures, and the expression of anger entails a release that is not without its small delights. In recompense, envy may be the subtlest—perhaps I should say the most insidious—of the seven deadly sins. Surely it is the one that people are least likely to want to own up to, for to do so is to admit that one is probably ungenerous, mean, small-hearted. It may also be the most endemic. Apart from Socrates, Jesus, Marcus Aurelius, Saint Francis, Mother Teresa, and only a few others, at one time or another, we have all felt flashes of envy, even if in varying intensities, from its minor pricks to its deep, soul-destroying, lacerating stabs. So widespread is it—a word for envy, I have read, exists in all known languages—that one is ready to believe it is the sin for which the best argument can be made that it is part of human nature.

2   In politics, envy, or at any rate the hope of eliminating it, is said to be the reigning principle of socialism, as greed is said to be that of capitalism (though modern capitalist advertising is about few things more than the regular stimulation of envy). On the international scene, many if not

most wars have been fought because of one nation's envy of another's territory and all they derive from it, or out of jealously guarded riches that a nation feels are endangered by those less rich who are likely to be envious of their superior position. In this connection, it is difficult not to feel that, at least in part, much of the anti-American feeling that arose after September 11, 2001, had envy, some of it fairly rancorous, at its heart. In the magazine *Granta*, the Indian writer Ramachandra Guha wrote that "historically, anti-Americanism in India was shaped by an aesthetic distaste for America's greatest gift—the making of money." But can "aesthetic distaste" here be any more than a not-very-well-disguised code word for envy?

Is envy a "feeling," an "emotion," a "sin," a "temperamental disposi- 3 tion," or a "world-view"? Might it also be a Rorschach test: Tell what you envy, and you reveal a great deal about yourself. It can be all of these things—and more. No one would doubt that, whatever else it is, envy is certainly a charged, indeed a supercharged, word: One of the few words left in the English language that retains the power to scandalize. Most of us could still sleep decently if accused of any of the other six deadly sins; but to be accused of envy would be seriously distressing, so clearly does such an accusation go directly to character. The other deadly sins, though all have the disapproval of religion, do not so thoroughly, so deeply demean, diminish, and disqualify a person. Not the least of its stigmata is the pettiness implicit in envy.

The *Webster's* definition of the word won't quite do: "(1) *Obs.* malice; 4 (2) painful or resentful awareness of the advantage enjoyed by another joined with a desire to possess the same advantage." The *Oxford English Dictionary* is rather better: It defines envy first as "malignant or hostile feeling; ill-will, malice, enmity," and then as "active evil, harm, mischief," both definitions accounted *Obscure*. But the great *OED* only gets down to serious business in its third definition, where it defines envy as "the feeling of mortification and ill-will occasioned by the contemplation of superior advantages possessed by another," in which usage the word envy first pops up around 1500. It adds a fourth definition, one in which the word is used without "notions of malevolence," and has to do with the (a) "desire to equal another in achievement, or excellence; emula- tion," and (b) speaks to "a longing for the advantages enjoyed by another person." Aristotle, in *The Rhetoric*, writes of emulation as good envy, or envy ending in admiration and thus in the attempt to imitate the qualities one began by envying. Yet it must be added that envy doesn't generally work this way. Little is good about envy, except shaking it off, which, as any of us who have felt it deeply knows, is not so easily done.

Both the *OED* and *Webster's* definitions are inattentive to the crucial 5 distinction between envy and jealousy. Most people, failing to pick up the useful distinction, mistakenly use the two words interchangeably.

I suspect people did not always do so. H. W. Fowler, in his splendid *Modern English Usage* of 1926, carries no entry on either word, suggesting that formerly there was no confusion. Bryan A. Garner, in his 1998 *Dictionary of Modern American Usage*, says that "the careful writer distinguishes between these terms," but does not himself do so sufficiently. He writes that *"jealousy* is properly restricted to contexts involving affairs of the heart, *envy* is used more broadly of resentful contemplation of a more fortunate person."

6   With the deep pedantic delight one takes in trumping a recognized usage expert, it pleases me to say, "Not quite so." The real distinction is that *one is jealous of what one has, envious of what other people have.* Jealousy is not always pejorative; one can after all be jealous of one's dignity, civil rights, honor. Envy, except when used in the emulative sense mentioned by Aristotle, is always pejorative. If jealousy is, in cliché parlance, spoken of as the "green-eyed monster," envy is cross-, squinty-, and blearily red-eyed. Never, to put it very gently, a handsome or good thing, envy. Although between jealousy and envy, jealousy is often the more intensely felt of the two, it can also be the more realistic: One is, after all, sometimes correct to feel jealousy. And not all jealousy plays the familiar role of sexual jealousy. One may be jealous—again, rightly—of one's reputation, integrity, and other good things. One is almost never right to feel envy: To be envious is to be, *ipso facto*, wrong.

7   Apart from emulative envy, the only aspect of envy that does not seem to me pejorative is a form of envy I have myself felt, as I suspect have others who are reading this article: the envy that I think of as faith envy. This is the envy one feels for those who have the true and deep and intelligent religious faith that sees them through the darkest of crises, death among them. If one is oneself without faith and wishes to feel this emotion, I cannot recommend a better place to find it than in the letters of Flannery O'Connor. There one will discover a woman still in her thirties, who, after coming into her radiant talent, knows she is going to die well before her time and, fortified by her Catholicism, faces her end without voicing complaint or fear. I not long ago heard, in Vienna, what seemed to me a perfect rendering of Beethoven's *Ninth Symphony*, and was hugely moved by it, but how much more would I have been moved, I could not help wonder, if I were in a state of full religious belief, since the *Ninth Symphony* seems to me in many ways a religious work. Faith envy is envy, alas, about which one can do nothing but quietly harbor it.

8   Envy must also be distinguished from general yearning. One sees people at great social ease and wishes to be more like them; or feels keenly how good it would be once more to be young; or longs to be wealthier; or pines to be taller, thinner, more muscular, less awkward, more beautiful generally. All this is yearning. Envy is never general, but always very particular—at least envy of the kind one feels strongly.

The envious tend to be injustice collectors. "Envy, among other ingre- 9 dients, has a love of justice in it," William Hazlitt wrote. "We are more angry at undeserved than at deserved good fortune." Something to it, but, my sense is, not all that much. Much more often than not, envy expresses feelings more personal than the love of justice. In another useful distinction, Kierkegaard in *The Sickness Unto Death* wrote that "admiration is happy self-surrender; envy is unhappy self-satisfaction." Envy asks one leading question: What about me? Why does he or she have beauty, talent, wealth, power, the world's love, and other gifts, or at any rate a larger share of them than I? Why not me? Dorothy Sayers, in a little book on the seven deadly sins, writes: "Envy is the great leveler: if it cannot level things up, it will level them down.... At its best, envy is a climber and a snob; at its worst it is a destroyer—rather than have anyone happier than itself, it will see us all miserable together." A self-poisoning of the mind, envy is usually less about what one lacks than about what other people have. A strong element of the begrudging resides in envy, thus making the envious, as Immanuel Kant remarked in *The Metaphysics of Morals*, "intent on the destruction of the happiness of others."

One might call someone or something—another's family life, health, 10 good fortune—"enviable" without intending rancor. In the same way, one might say, "I envy you your two-month holiday in the south of France," without, in one's mind, plotting how to do the person out of it. Or one might say, "I don't envy him the responsibilities of his job," by which one merely means that one is pleased not to have another's worries. There probably ought to be a word falling between envy and admiration, as there ought to be a word that falls between talent and genius. Yet there isn't. The language is inept. Nor ought envy to be confused with open conflict. Someone has something that one feels one wants—customers, a high ranking or rating, government office, a position of power—and one contends for it, more or less aggressively, but out in the open. The openness changes the nature of the game. Envy is almost never out in the open; it is secretive, plotting, behind the scenes. Helmut Schoeck, who in *Envy: A Theory of Social Behavior* has written the most comprehensive book on the subject, notes that it "is a silent, secretive process and not always verifiable." Envy, to qualify as envy, has to have a strong touch—sometimes more than a touch—of malice behind it. Malice that cannot speak its name, cold-blooded but secret hostility, impotent desire, hidden rancor, and spite all cluster at the center of envy. La Rochefoucauld opened the subject of envy nicely with a silver stiletto, when he wrote: "In the misfortune of our best friends, we always find something that is not displeasing to us." Yes, really not displeasing at all. Dear old envy.

2003

QUESTIONS FOR DISCUSSION

Content

a. Why, according to Epstein, is envy "the most insidious" of the seven deadly sins?

b. Why does he believe that envy is "one of the few words left in the English language that retains the power to scandalize" (paragraph 3)?

c. Epstein believes that all envy, save "faith envy," is wrong (paragraph 7). Explain this distinction.

d. How does he distinguish between yearning and envy? Between jealousy and envy?

e. What do you make of the quotation from La Rochefoucauld in Epstein's conclusion? What does this quotation add to his definition of envy? Does it make for an appropriate conclusion?

f. What does the author mean when, in paragraph 10, he claims that "the language is inept." What is the purpose of this paragraph other than serving as a conclusion?

Strategy and Style

g. Why does Epstein begin by commenting on the seven deadly sins? Why does he discuss the political ramifications of envy?

h. Read the beginning of paragraph 6 again. In what way is the first sentence ironic? Is Epstein having fun here? Are we?

i. Analyze the author's tone. Where does it shift, and why?

j. It is clear that this definition essay uses contrast. But where does Epstein use examples?

ENGAGING THE TEXT

a. Paragraph 9 contains quotations from famous writers and philosophers: Hazlitt, Kierkegaard, Sayers, and Kant. Summarize what this material tells us about envy, and explain why Epstein includes it.

b. Reread paragraph 4 and, in a paragraph or two, explain the distinctions among the various definitions of envy given by the Oxford English Dictionary.

SUGGESTIONS FOR SUSTAINED WRITING

a. Using a personal perspective, define envy or any of the other seven deadly sins that Epstein mentions. Use details from your own experiences or from those of people you know well.

b. Write an essay in which you contrast your view of a particular sin, misdeed, or evil with the view of it held by someone you know or by someone whose work you have read. As an alternative, write an essay in which you contrast what you think is sinful or inappropriate behavior with the way in which that behavior is portrayed by the media. You might consider two or three movies or television programs you have seen recently, discuss a popular novel, or survey current trends in advertising.

c. Write an essay defining one of the other seven deadly sins from a historical perspective. Research your subject in the library or on the Internet. As you write your paper, point out similarities and differences between how we view this sin today and how it was viewed in the Middle Ages. Let's say you choose to write about gluttony, for example. Do we still see excessive overeating and drinking as a sin that can be controlled by applying a little willpower? Or do we account for such behavior in other ways? As with any research paper, make sure to include internal citations and a works-cited or references list.

READ MORE

Epstein and His Works

Birnbaum, Robert. "An Interview with Joseph Epstein" (http://www. identitytheory.com/interviews/birnbaum122.php).

Epstein, Joseph. "In a Snob-Free Zone" (http://www.washingtonmonthly. com/features/2001/0206.epstein.html).

Epstein, Joseph. "The Perpetual Adolescent" (http://www.weeklystandard. com/Content/Public/Articles/000/000/003/825grtdi.asp).

The Seven Deadly Sins

O'Neil, Arthur Charles. "Sin." *The Catholic Encyclopedia* (http://www. newadvent.org/cathen/14004b.htm).

"Seven Deadly Sins as Cultural Constructions During the Middle Ages." *NEH Summer Seminar 2004.* Trinity University, (http://www.trinity. edu/rnewhaus/outline.html).

Pride

Dagoberto Gilb

Dagoberto Gilb's name signals his heritage: His mother was Mexican, his father German American. Gilb was born in Los Angeles in 1950. After studying at a number of two-year colleges, he enrolled in UCLA at Santa Barbara as a religion and philosophy major. After earning both a B.A. and an M.A., he worked in California's construction industry, eventually earning credentials as a journeyman carpenter. Today, however, Gilb holds a tenured professorship in creative writing at Texas State University in San Marcos.

His first published work was Winners on the Pass Lane *(1985). This was followed by* The Magic of Blood *(1993), which won the 1994 PEN/Hemingway Award. This important book turned Gilb into a hero of the working class as well as of the Chicano community.* Woodcuts of Women *(2001), a collection of short stories about men who have an obsession with women, illustrates that some male authors can portray the psychology of women in a fair and convincing manner. In 1994, Gilb published a novel,* The Last Known Residence of Mickey Acuna. *In 2006, he became the editor of* Hecho en Tejas: An Anthology of Texas Mexican Literature. *"Pride" is taken from* Gritos: Essays by Dagoberto Gilb *(2003).*

VOCABULARY

Agave

1   It's almost time to close at the northwest corner of Altura and Copia in El Paso. That means it is so dark that it is as restful as the deepest un-remembering sleep, dark as the empty space around this spinning planet, as a black star. Headlights that beam a little cross-eyed from a fatso American car are feeling around the asphalt road up the hill toward the Good Time Store, its yellow plastic smiley face bright like a sugary suck candy. The loose muffler holds only half the misfires, and, dry springs squeaking, the automobile curves slowly into the establishment's lot, swerving to avoid the new self-serve gas pump island. Behind it, across the street, a Texas flag—out too late this and all the nights—pops and slaps in a summer wind that finally is cool.

2   A good man, gray on the edges, an assistant manager in a brown starched and ironed uniform, is washing the glass windows of the store, lit up by as many watts as Venus, with a roll of paper towels and the blue liquid from a spray bottle. Good night, m'ijo! he tells a young boy coming out after playing the video game, a Grande Guzzler the size of a wastebasket balanced in one hand, an open bag of Flaming Hot Cheetos, its red dye already smearing his mouth and the hand not carrying the weight of the soda, his white T-shirt, its short sleeves reaching halfway down his wrists, the whole XXL of it billowing and puffing in the outdoor gust.

3   A plump young woman steps out of that car. She's wearing a party dress, wide scoops out of the top, front, and back, its hemline way above the knees.

4   Did you get a water pump? the assistant manager asks her. Are you going to make it to Horizon City? He's still washing the glass of the storefront, his hand sweeping in small hard circles.

The young woman is patient and calm like a loving mother. I don't know yet, she tells him as she stops close to him, thinking. I guess I should make a call, she says, and her thick-soled shoes, the latest fashion, slap against her heels to one of the pay phones at the front of the store.

Pride is working a job like it's as important as art or war, is the happiness of a new high score on a video arcade game, of a pretty new black dress and shoes. Pride is the deaf and blind confidence of the good people who are too poor but don't notice.

A son is a long time sitting on the front porch where he played all those years with the squirmy dog who still licks his face, both puppies then, even before he played on the winning teams of Little League baseball and City League basketball. They sprint down the sidewalk and across streets, side by side, until they stop to rest on the park grass, where a red ant, or a spider, bites the son's calf. It swells, but he no longer thinks to complain to his mom about it—he's too old now—when he comes home. He gets ready, putting on the shirt and pants his mom would have ironed but he wanted to iron himself. He takes the ride with his best friend since first grade. The hundreds of moms and dads, abuelos y abuelitas, the tios and primos, baby brothers and older married sisters, all are at the Special Events Center for the son's high school graduation. His dad is a man bigger than most, and when he walks in his dress eel-skin boots down the cement stairs to get as close to the hardwood basketball-court floor and ceremony to see—m'ijo!—he feels an embarrassing sob bursting from his eyes and mouth. He holds it back, and with his hands, hides the tears that do escape, wipes them with his fingers, because the chavalitos in his aisle are playing and laughing and they are so small and he is so big next to them. And when his son walks to the stage to get his high school diploma and his dad wants to scream his name, he hears how many others, from the floor in caps and gowns and from around the arena, are already screaming it—could be any name, it could be any son's or daughter's: Alex! Vanessa! Carlos! Veronica! Ricky! Tony! Estella! Isa!—and sees his boy waving back to all of them.

Pride hears gritty dirt blowing against an agave whose stiff fertile stalk, so tall, will not bend—the love of land, rugged like the people who live on it. Pride sees the sunlight on the Franklin Mountains in the first light of morning and listens to a neighbor's gallo—the love of culture and history. Pride smells a sweet, musky drizzle of rain and eats huevos con chile in corn tortillas heated on a cast-iron pan—the love of heritage.

Pride is the fearless reaction to disrespect and disregard. It is knowing the future will prove that wrong.

10   Seeing the beauty: Look out there from a height of the mountain and on the north and south of the Rio Grande, to the far away and close, the so many miles more of fuzz on the wide horizon, knowing how many years the people have passed and have stayed, the ancestors, the ones who have medaled, limped back on crutches or died or were heroes from wars in the Pacific or Europe or Korea or Vietnam or the Persian Gulf, the ones who have raised the fist and dared to defy, the ones who wash the clothes and cook and serve the meals, who stitch the factory shoes and the factory slacks, who assemble and sort, the ones who laugh and the ones who weep, the ones who care, the ones who want more, the ones who try, the ones who love, those ones with shameless courage and hardened wisdom, and the old ones still so alive, holding their grandchildren, and the young ones in their glowing prime, strong and gorgeous, holding each other, the ones who will be born from them. The desert land is rock-dry and ungreen. It is brown. Brown like the skin is brown. Beautiful brown.

QUESTIONS FOR DISCUSSION

Content

a. There seem to be several ideas associated with the way Gilb defines pride. What does the assistant manager tell us about pride?

b. How about m'ijo ("my son"), who walks out of the Good Time Store (paragraph 2), or the young woman in the "pretty new black dress" (paragraph 6)? How do they help Gilb define pride?

c. Who is the "son" mentioned in paragraph 7? Is it Gilb himself? Is it a generic "son," who represents all of the young men of Gilb's community? Is it all Chicanos?

d. Is there any significance to the high school graduation's not being held in the school's auditorium or on one of its athletic fields?

e. Is this about personal pride? What other type or types of pride might it discuss?

f. Write a thesis statement for this essay in your own words.

Strategy and Style

g. This essay uses an interesting organizational structure. For example, Gilb follows what occurs at the Good Time Store with a paragraph that defines pride in terms relevant to what we see in that episode. Explain the repetition of this pattern later in the essay.

h. What does Gilb accomplish in paragraph 10? Is this an appropriate conclusion?

j. This essay obviously makes use of examples from Gilb's own experiences and observation. Identify places where it uses description and figurative language, especially personification.

ENGAGING THE TEXT

a. Write a paragraph in which you summarize as many of the personal attributes and qualities that Gilb includes here in order to define pride.
b. As you probably have deduced, Gilb is discussing several types of pride: personal, familial, and communal. Write a paragraph or two that define this term by pointing out aspects of yourself, your family, and/ or your community that make you proud.

SUGGESTIONS FOR SUSTAINED WRITING

a. Read the response you made to item *b* under Engaging the Text. Use this material as prewriting that will help you launch a full-length essay providing your definition of personal, familial, communal, or any other kind of pride. Like Gilb, use illustrations (anecdotes work well here) from your own experience. Note that you need not be the central figure in this essay. You might provide illustrations of pride that focus on the lives of people you know well.
b. Read two other essays in this chapter: Parker's "What Is Poverty?" and Epstein's "The Green-Eyed Monster: Envy Is Nothing to Be Jealous Of." Is Gilb's essay more like Parker's or more like Epstein's? Write an essay that answers this question by pointing out similarities and differences in organization, vocabulary, methods of development, and any other areas of discussion you want.
c. Gilb writes an essay that contains much evidence of his pride in his Chicano roots. Are you proud of your heritage? If so, write an essay that shows it. Begin by using examples taken from your own experiences with and observations of other members of your family and, if appropriate, of your community. Then, complete library and/or Internet research (check with your instructor for the best approach) to gather information about your particular ethnic, national, or racial heritage. Use this information to support your essay's thesis.

READ MORE

Birnbaum, Robert. "Interview with Dagoberto Gilb" (http://www. identitytheory.com/interviews/birnbaum180.php).
Smith, Clay. "The Art of Being Dagoberto Gilb" (http://www. austinchronicle.com/books/2001-03-23/81167).

"Blaxicans" and Other Reinvented Americans

Richard Rodriguez

The son of immigrant Mexican parents in San Francisco, Richard Rodriguez (b. 1944) grew up in a Mexican American section of Sacramento. He was educated in Catholic grammar and high schools, and he attended Stanford and Columbia universities, where he took a bachelor's and a master's degree, as well as the Warburg Institute in Great Britain. He is the winner of a Fulbright Fellowship, a National Endowment for the Arts Fellowship, and a Peabody Award, which recognizes outstanding work in the electronic media.

Rodriguez achieved recognition in 1981, when he published Hunger of Memory: The Education of Richard Rodriguez. *The book includes a criticism of both affirmative action and bilingual education on the grounds that they tend to separate rather than unite people. He is also the author of* Days of Obligation: An Argument with my Mexican Father *(1992) and of* Brown: The Last Discovery of America *(2002). He is currently working on a book about Christianity, Judaism, and Islam. Rodriguez has written numerous essays, which have appeared in* Harper's *Magazine,* American Scholar, Time, Mother Jones, Forum, *and* Nuestro.

The essay that follows was first published in the Chronicle of Higher Education, *a publication for college professors and administrators. In it Rodriguez argues that the old racial classifications—black, white, Hispanic, and so on—should be abandoned, for they misrepresent the cultural and ethnic realities of today's America.*

VOCABULARY

incomprehensibly, mythic, rind, aforementioned, perpetual, dilute, ineffable, mulatto, fallacious, archetypal, demythologizing

1 There is something unsettling about immigrants because ... well, because they chatter incomprehensibly, and they get in everyone's way. Immigrants seem to be bent on undoing America. Just when Americans think we know who we are—we are Protestants, culled from Western Europe, are we not? —then new immigrants appear from Southern Europe or from Eastern Europe. We—we who are already here—we don't know exactly what the latest comers will mean to our community. How will they fit in with us? Thus we—we who were here first—we begin to question our own identity.

2   After a generation or two, the grandchildren or the great-grandchildren of immigrants to the United States and the grandchildren of those who tried to keep immigrants out of the United States will romanticize the immigrant, will begin to see the immigrant as the figure who teaches us most about what it means to be an American. The immigrant, in

mythic terms, travels from the outermost rind of America to the very center of American mythology. None of this, of course, can we admit to the Vietnamese immigrant who served us our breakfast at the hotel this morning. In another 40 years, we will be prepared to say to the Vietnamese immigrant that he, with his breakfast tray, with his intuition for travel, with his memory of tragedy, with his recognition of peerless freedoms, he fulfills the meaning of America.

In 1997, Gallup conducted a survey on race relations in America, but ₃ the poll was concerned only with white and black Americans. No question was put to the aforementioned Vietnamese man. There was certainly no question for the Chinese grocer, none for the Guatemalan barber, none for the tribe of Mexican Indians who reroofed your neighbor's house.

The American conversation about race has always been a black-and- ₄ white conversation, but the conversation has become as bloodless as badminton.

I have listened to the black-and-white conversation for most of my ₅ life. I was supposed to attach myself to one side or the other, without asking the obvious questions: What is this perpetual dialectic between Europe and Africa? Why does it admit so little reference to anyone else?

I am speaking to you in American English that was taught me by Irish ₆ nuns—immigrant women. I wear an Indian face; I answer to a Spanish surname as well as this California first name, Richard. You might wonder about the complexity of historical factors, the collision of centuries, that creates Richard Rodriguez. My brownness is the illustration of that collision, or the bland memorial of it. I stand before you as an Impure-American, an Ambiguous-American.

In the 19th century, Texans used to say that the reason Mexicans ₇ were so easily defeated in battle was because we were so dilute, being neither pure Indian nor pure Spaniard. Yet, at the same time, Mexicans used to say that Mexico, the country of my ancestry, joined two worlds, two competing armies. José Vasconcelos, the Mexican educator and philosopher, famously described Mexicans as *la raza cósmica,* the cosmic race. In Mexico what one finds as early as the 18th century is a predominant population of mixed-race people. Also, once the slave had been freed in Mexico, the incidence of marriage between Indian and African people there was greater than in any other country in the Americas and has not been equaled since.

Race mixture has not been a point of pride in America. Americans ₈ speak more easily about "diversity" than we do about the fact that I might marry your daughter; you might become we; we might become us. America has so readily adopted the Canadian notion of multiculturalism because it preserves our preference for thinking ourselves separate—our elbows need not touch, thank you. I would prefer that table. I can remain Mexican, whatever that means, in the United States of America.

9   I would propose that instead of adopting the Canadian model of multiculturalism, America might begin to imagine the Mexican alternative—that of a mestizaje society.

10   Because of colonial Mexico, I am mestizo. But I was reinvented by President Richard Nixon. In the early 1970s, Nixon instructed the Office of Management and Budget to identify the major racial and ethnic groups in the United States. OMB came up with five major ethnic or racial groups. The groups are white, black, Asian/Pacific Islander, American Indian/ Eskimo, and Hispanic.

11   It's what I learned to do when I was in college: to call myself a Hispanic. At my university we even had separate cafeteria tables and "theme houses," where the children of Nixon could gather —of a feather. Native Americans united. African Americans. Casa Hispanic.

12   The interesting thing about Hispanics is that you will never meet us in Latin America. You may meet Chileans and Peruvians and Mexicans. You will not meet Hispanics. If you inquire in Lima or Bogotá about Hispanics, you will be referred to Dallas. For "Hispanic" is a gringo contrivance, a definition of the world according to European patterns of colonization. Such a definition suggests I have more in common with Argentine Italians than with American Indians; that there is an ineffable union between the white Cuban and the mulatto Puerto Rican because of Spain. Nixon's conclusion has become the basis for the way we now organize and understand American society.

13   The Census Bureau foretold that by the year 2003, Hispanics would outnumber blacks to become the largest minority in the United States. And, indeed, the year 2003 has arrived and the proclamation of Hispanic ascendancy has been published far and wide. While I admit a competition has existed—does exist—in America between Hispanic and black people, I insist that the comparison of Hispanics with blacks will lead, ultimately, to complete nonsense. For there is no such thing as a Hispanic race. In Latin America, one sees every race of the world. One sees white Hispanics, one sees black Hispanics, one sees brown Hispanics who are Indians, many of whom do not speak Spanish because they resist Spain. One sees Asian-Hispanics. To compare blacks and Hispanics, therefore, is to construct a fallacious equation.

14   Some Hispanics have accepted the fiction. Some Hispanics have too easily accustomed themselves to impersonating a third race, a great new third race in America. But Hispanic is an ethnic term. It is a term denoting culture. So when the Census Bureau says by the year 2060 one-third of all Americans will identify themselves as Hispanic, the Census Bureau is not speculating in pigment or quantifying according to actual historical narratives, but rather is predicting how by the year 2060 one-third of all Americans will identify themselves culturally. For a country that traditionally has taken its understandings of community from blood and

color, the new circumstance of so large a group of Americans identifying themselves by virtue of language or fashion or cuisine or literature is an extraordinary change, and a revolutionary one.

People ask me all the time if I envision another Quebec forming in the 15 United States because of the large immigrant movement from the south. Do I see a Quebec forming in the Southwest, for example? No, I don't see that at all. But I do notice the Latin American immigrant population is as much as 10 years younger than the U.S. national population. I notice the Latin American immigrant population is more fertile than the U.S. national population. I see the movement of the immigrants from south to north as a movement of youth—like approaching spring! —into a country that is growing middle-aged. I notice immigrants are the archetypal Americans at a time when we—U.S. citizens—have become post-Americans, most concerned with subsidized medications.

I was at a small Apostolic Assembly in East Palo Alto a few years 16 ago—a mainly Spanish-speaking congregation in an area along the freeway, near the heart of the Silicon Valley. This area used to be black East Palo Alto, but it is quickly becoming an Asian and Hispanic Palo Alto neighborhood. There was a moment in the service when newcomers to the congregation were introduced. Newcomers brought letters of introduction from sister evangelical churches in Latin America. The minister read out the various letters and pronounced the names and places of origin to the community. The congregation applauded. And I thought to myself: It's over. The border is over. These people were not being asked whether they had green cards. They were not being asked whether they arrived here legally or illegally. They were being welcomed within a new community for reasons of culture. There is now a north-south line that is theological, a line that cannot be circumvented by the U.S. Border Patrol.

I was on a British Broadcasting Corporation interview show, and a 17 woman introduced me as being "in favor" of assimilation. I am not in favor of assimilation any more than I am in favor of the Pacific Ocean or clement weather. If I had a bumper sticker on the subject, it might read something like ASSIMILATION HAPPENS. One doesn't get up in the morning, as an immigrant child in America, and think to oneself, "How much of an American shall I become today?" One doesn't walk down the street and decide to be 40 percent Mexican and 60 percent American. Culture is fluid. Culture is smoke. You breathe it. You eat it. You can't help hearing it —Elvis Presley goes in your ear, and you cannot get Elvis Presley out of your mind.

I am in favor of assimilation. I am not in favor of assimilation. I rec- 18 ognize assimilation. A few years ago, I was in Merced, Calif. —a town of about 75,000 people in the Central Valley where the two largest immigrant groups at that time (California is so fluid, I believe this is no longer the case) were Laotian Hmong and Mexicans. Laotians have never in the history of the world, as far as I know, lived next to Mexicans. But there they were in Merced, and living next to Mexicans. They don't like each other. I was talking to the Laotian kids about why they don't like the Mexican kids. They were telling me that the Mexicans do this and the Mexicans don't do that, when I suddenly realized that they were speaking English with a Spanish accent.

19   On his interview show, Bill Moyers once asked me how I thought of myself. As an American? Or Hispanic? I answered that I am Chinese, and that is because I live in a Chinese city and because I want to be Chinese. Well, why not? Some Chinese American people in the Richmond and Sunset districts of San Francisco sometimes paint their houses (so many qualifiers!) in colors I would once have described as garish: lime greens, rose reds, pumpkin. But I have lived in a Chinese city for so long that my eye has taken on that palette, has come to prefer lime greens and rose reds and all the inventions of this Chinese Mediterranean. I see photographs in magazines or documentary footage of China, especially rural China, and I see what I recognize as home. Isn't that odd?

20   I do think distinctions exist. I'm not talking about an America tomorrow in which we're going to find that black and white are no longer the distinguishing marks of separateness. But many young people I meet tell me they feel like Victorians when they identify themselves as black or white. They don't think of themselves in those terms. And they're already moving into a world in which tattoo or ornament or movement or commune or sexuality or drug or rave or electronic bombast are the organizing principles of their identity. The notion that they are white or black simply doesn't occur.

21   And increasingly, of course, one meets children who really don't know how to say what they are. They simply are too many things. I met a young girl in San Diego at a convention of mixed-race children, among whom the common habit is to define one parent over the other—black over white, for example. But this girl said that her mother was Mexican and her father was African. The girl said "Blaxican." By reinventing language, she is reinventing America.

22   America does not have a vocabulary like the vocabulary the Spanish empire evolved to describe the multiplicity of racial possibilities in the New World. The conversation, the interior monologue of America cannot rely on the old vocabulary—black, white. We are no longer a black-white nation.

23   So, what myth do we tell ourselves? The person who got closest to it was Karl Marx. Marx predicted that the discovery of gold in California would be a more central event to the Americas than the discovery of the Americas by Columbus—which was only the meeting of two tribes, essentially, the European and the Indian. But when gold was discovered in California in the 1840s, the entire world met. For the first time in human history, all of the known world gathered. The Malaysian stood in

the gold fields alongside the African, alongside the Chinese, alongside the Australian, alongside the Yankee.

24   That was an event without parallel in world history and the beginning of modern California—why California today provides the mythological structure for understanding how we might talk about the American experience: not as biracial, but as the re-creation of the known world in the New World.

25   Sometimes truly revolutionary things happen without regard. I mean, we may wake up one morning and there is no black race. There is no white race either. There are mythologies, and—as I am in the business, insofar as I am in any business at all, of demythologizing such identities as black and white—I come to you as a man of many cultures. I come to you as Chinese. Unless you understand that I am Chinese, then you have not understood anything I have said.

QUESTIONS FOR DISCUSSION

Content

a. In your own words, state Rodriguez's thesis.
b. In paragraph 2, the author says we cannot admit certain things to "the Vietnamese immigrant who served us our breakfast." What are those things? Why does Rodriguez say we can't admit them?
c. What is meant by the term "Ambiguous-American" (paragraph 6)? What is *la raza cósmica* (paragraph 7)?
d. Explain what the author means by "the Canadian notion of multiculturalism" (paragraph 8)? What model does he want us to follow?
e. What does Rodriguez mean when he says that he was "reinvented" by President Nixon (paragraph 10)?
f. Why does the author object to being called "Hispanic"? Why does he object to comparing blacks and Hispanics?
g. Explain the reference to Quebec in paragraph 15. If necessary, research this question on the Internet.
h. Paragraph 16 ends with a curious sentence. Re-read that paragraph and explain what that sentence means.
i. On what grounds does the author claim to be Chinese?
j. What does he mean in paragraph 24 when he says: "California … provides the mythical structure for understanding how we might talk about the American experience"?

Strategy and Style

k. What is Rodriguez's purpose? Does it go beyond pure definition?
l. How does paragraph 2 set the tone for the rest of the essay?

m. How would you evaluate Rodriguez's introduction? What methods does he use to capture our attention?

n. As you learned in the introduction, this essay first appeared in a publication for college teachers and administrators. What in Rodriguez's style indicates that he is writing to such an audience?

o. Often, writers define things by explaining what they're not. Where does Rodriguez do this?

p. Where does the author use anecdotes? Where does he use contrast?

q. What function, other than ending the essay, does the conclusion serve?

ENGAGING THE TEXT

a. In paragraph 15, Rodriguez claims that immigrants are "archetypal Americans" while citizens are "post-Americans, most concerned with subsidized medications." What does he mean? Is he being fair and accurate? Explain why or why not.

b. In paragraph 20, the author asserts that today's young people use categories other than those of race to identify themselves. Paraphrase that paragraph. Then, write a paragraph or two in which you support or deny that assertion.

SUGGESTIONS FOR SUSTAINED WRITING

a. Rodriguez tells Bill Moyers that he's Chinese. Have you ever wished to be a member of an ethnic, cultural, or religious group other than your own? If so, which one, and why? Write an essay in which you define that group by discussing its most interesting or attractive characteristics, and customs.

b. In paragraph 24, the author states that in California the "known world" has been re-created in the "New World." His point is that a multitude of people from different countries reside in this state. Can you say the same about your campus, your state, your city, or your community? If so, write an essay that defines this locale as a gathering point for many diverse cultures.

If this assignment does not interest you, write an essay that begins by explaining how, in "Blaxicans," Rodriguez views the attitudes of American citizens towards immigrants. Continue the essay by discussing your own opinions on this issue.

c. Paragraph 23 of Rodriguez's essay mentions that Karl Marx believed that the California Gold Rush was "a more central event to the Americas" than Columbus's discovery. Write an essay that uses scholarly research to support or deny this claim.

As an alternative, you might write about another historical event that you consider central to the development of the United States. Possible topics include the Boston Tea Party, the adoption of the U.S. Constitution, the Battle of Gettysburg, the assassination of Abraham Lincoln, the Mexican American War, the bombing of Pearl Harbor, the assassination of President Kennedy, the passing of the Civil Rights Act of 1964, the assassination of Dr. Martin Luther King, or the terrorist attacks of September 11, 2001. You can also look into the distant future and predict ways in which an event like the election of the first African American president will change the United States.

READ MORE

About and by the Author

London, Scott. "A View from the Melting Pot: An Interview with Richard Rodriguez." *scottlondon.com* (http://www.scottlondon.com/interviews/rodriguez.html): *Adapted from a broadcast of the radio program Insight & Outlook, this interview first appeared in print as "Crossing Borders" in* The Sun *magazine of August 1997.*
Rodriguez, Richard. *Days of Obligation: An Argument with My Mexican Father.* New York: Viking, 1992.
Rodriguez, Richard. "Essays" (http://www.pbs.org/newshour/essays/richard_rodriguez.html): *Provides access to dozens of essays by Rodriquez online.*
Rodriguez, Richard. *Hunger of Memory: The Education of Richard Rodriguez.* Boston: Godine, 1981.

Rodriguez's Autobiography

Woods, Richard D. "Richard Rodriguez" *Dictionary of Literary Biography.* Thomson Gale (http://www.bookrags.com/biography/richard-rodriguez-dlb).

On Race and Racial Classification

Hacking, Ian. "Why Race Still Matters." *Daedalus* 134:1 (2005):102–16.
"OMB Standards for Data on Race and Ethnicity." *The Office of Minority Health. US Department of Health and Human Services* (http://minorityhealth.hhs.gov/templates/browse.aspx?lvl=2&lvlID=172): *Includes links to important definitions and legislation.*
Prewitt, Kenneth. "Racial Classification in America: Where Do We Go from Here?" *Daedalus* 134:1 (2005): 5–17.

5

Division and Classification

Division and classification are attempts to explain the nature and connections between bits of information that may, at first, seem unrelated and confusing. Writers often find it useful to identify like qualities or characteristics among various facts, ideas, people, or things so as to create related categories or classes by which the material can be divided logically and discussed systematically.

If you are a people watcher, you know that public places—a bus station, a sports stadium, or even a college library—offer a variety of subjects. Let's say that two days before a math midterm, you resolve to study hard in the library. As you walk into the main reading room, you hear the giggles of young lovers seated in a corner. A few yards beyond, you spot one of the college's maintenance workers who is spending her lunch hour noisily turning the pages of a large newspaper. To your right, you begin to eavesdrop on a few students discussing a fraternity party, and you realize that their chatter is annoying a woman trying to take notes for a term paper. In a less crowded part of the room, two of your friends kill time by browsing through a few magazines they found lying about. After a while, you decide that the reading room offers too many distractions, so you find a corner in the basement where you can hide. It is no coincidence that other members of your math class had the same idea, so you sit down quietly and begin studying.

The decision to join your classmates and not stay in the reading room resulted from dividing the group of people you found at the library into three smaller categories: fun-seekers, browsers, and serious students! Your analysis may have been quick and informal, but it was effective. What's more, it revealed something important about the nature and function of classification: You began by observing similarities among individuals; you created categories based on those similarities and placed each individual you observed into one of them; and you made a decision—to study in one place and not another—based upon what your classification revealed.

Classification is a versatile tool. It can be used to explain various stages in human development as in Gail Sheehy's "Predictable Crises of Adulthood" or to discuss the manipulation of language in business and

148

politics as in William Lutz's "Doublespeak." In "Growing Up Asian in America," Kesaya E. Noda uses classification as a tool for self-analysis as she explores various aspects—ethnic, cultural, and sexual—of her identity. As we read her work, we cannot help but think that she may be shedding light on aspects of our own personalities.

The success of a classification paper depends upon how logically an author divides the material and how thoroughly and concretely he or she develops each category. Among the most effective methods to develop such an essay is illustration. Examples like those in Judith's Viorst's "The Truth about Lying" and in Brandon Griggs' "The 12 Most Annoying Types of Facebookers" are often essential to the writer's purpose. Without them, an essay might remain a list of ill-defined labels and abstractions. The essay by Lutz, though different in style and approach, also contains examples to support important points. But good writers use a variety of techniques to keep readers interested. For example, Sheehy makes excellent use of definition; Noda relies on definition, contrast, and anecdote. Griggs includes interesting, entertaining comparisons. Finally, Luc Sante, in "What Secrets Tell," makes good use of illustration, but he also includes effective figures of speech, and he often entertains the reader with his sarcasm.

As you read the selections that follow, remember that almost any conglomeration of seemingly unrelated information can be classified to reveal patterns of meaning readers will find valuable and interesting. The perspectives from which you view a subject and the choices you make to impose order on the material should be determined only by your purpose. Read the items under Engaging the Text and the Suggestions for Sustained Writing after each selection. They describe activities that will help you use classification to accomplish a well-defined purpose. But even if you approach a writing assignment without a clear notion of purpose—something not uncommon even among experienced writers—you may still want to use classification in the early stages of your project to review the raw information you have collected, to group facts, ideas, and insights logically, and, ultimately, to improve your understanding both of the material and of your purpose

Predictable Crises of Adulthood

Gail Sheehy

Born in New York City and educated at the University of Vermont and Columbia University, Gail Sheehy (b. 1937) has been a contributing editor for New York *Magazine and has written for* Paris Match, *the* London Sunday Telegraph, The New York

Purpose - Depending on your age and gender you go through different aspects of life

Times Magazine, Cosmopolitan, *and* Glamour. *Sheehy's first sustained work was* Lovesounds *(1970). This novel was followed by several pieces of nonfiction, including* Hustling: Prostitution in Our Wide Open Society *(1973);* Character: America's Search for Leadership *(1988); and* Gorbachev: The Man Who Changed the World *(1990). In 1986, Sheehy published* Spirit of Survival, *the story of a Cambodian girl she found and later adopted as a result of a journalistic assignment on refugee children in Southeast Asia. Her latest work is* Middletown America: One Town's Passage from Trauma to Hope *(2003), which concerns the effects of the 9/11 terrorist attacks on four Middletown, New Jersey, widows.* Passages *(1976), from which "Predictable Crises of Adulthood" is taken, discusses several natural crises through which everyone must pass and which, if understood and handled properly, can lay the foundation for a stable and fulfilling life. Her key works are* Understanding Men's Passages *(1998),* H. Llary's Choice *(1999), and* Passages in Caregiving: Turning Chaos into Confidence *(2010).*

Life, like writing, says Sheehy, is a process. Developing oneself through that process is far more important than fully accomplishing a stated set of goals at each stage. This is an essay that advises us not simply to accept change but to manage and relish it as we move toward and into middle age.

VOCABULARY

crustacean, sloughed, yeasty, embryonic, tranquility, autonomy, listless-ness, plausible, dynamic, sanctuary, diverge, transient, wunderkind, mutuality, reintegration, disassembling, qualms, pro bono, chagrin, crucible

1   We are not unlike a particularly hardy crustacean. The lobster grows by developing and shedding a series of hard, protective shells. Each time it expands from within, the confining shell must be sloughed off. It is left exposed and vulnerable until, in time, a new covering grows to replace the old.

2   With each passage from one stage of human growth to the next we, too, must shed a protective structure. We are left exposed and vulner-able—but also yeasty and embryonic again, capable of stretching in ways we hadn't known before. These sheddings may take several years or more. Coming out of each passage, though, we enter a longer and more stable period in which we can expect relative tranquility and a sense of equilibrium regained. . . .

3   As we shall see, each person engages the steps of development in his or her own characteristic *step-style*. Some people never complete the whole sequence. And none of us "solves" with one step—by jumping out of the parental home into a job or marriage, for example—the problems in separating from the caregivers of childhood. Nor do we "achieve" autonomy once and for all by converting our dreams into concrete goals, even when we attain those goals. The central issues or tasks of one period

are never fully completed, tied up, and cast aside. But when they lose their primacy and the current life structure has served its purpose, we are ready to move on to the next period.

Can one catch up? What might look to others like listlessness, con- 4 trariness, a maddening refusal to face up to an obvious task may be a person's own unique detour that will bring him out later on the other side. Developmental gains won can later be lost—and rewon. It's plausible, though it can't be proven, that the mastery of one set of tasks fortifies us for the next period and the next set of challenges. But it's important not to think too mechanistically. Machines work by units. The bureaucracy (supposedly) works step by step. Human beings, thank God, have an individual inner dynamic that can never be precisely coded.

Although I have indicated the ages when Americans are likely to go 5 through each stage, and the differences between men and women where they are striking, do not take the ages too seriously. The stages are the thing, and most particularly the sequence.

Here is the briefest outline of the developmental ladder.   6

PULLING UP ROOTS

"Freedom"

Before 18, the motto is loud and clear: "I have to get away from my par- 7 ents." But the words are seldom connected to action. Generally still safely part of our families, even if away at school, we feel our autonomy to be subject to erosion from moment to moment.

After 18, we begin Pulling Up Roots in earnest. College, military 8 service, and short-term travels are all customary vehicles our society provides for the first round-trips between family and a base of one's own. In the attempt to separate our view of the world from our family's view, despite vigorous protestations to the contrary—"I know exactly what I want!"—we cast about for any beliefs we can call our own. And in the process of testing those beliefs we are often drawn to fads, preferably those most mysterious and inaccessible to our parents.

Whatever tentative memberships we try out in the world, the fear 9 haunts us that we are really kids who cannot take care of ourselves. We cover that fear with acts of defiance and mimicked confidence. For allies to replace our parents, we turn to our contemporaries. They become conspirators. So long as their perspective meshes with our own, they are able to substitute for the sanctuary of the family. But that doesn't last very long. And the instant they diverge from the shaky ideals of "our group," they are seen as betrayers. Rebounds to the family are common between the ages of 18 and 22.

The tasks of this passage are to locate ourselves in a peer group role, 10 a sex role, an anticipated occupation, an ideology or world view. As a result, we gather the impetus to leave home physically and the identity to *begin* leaving home emotionally.

11   Even as one part of us seeks to be an individual, another part longs to restore the safety and comfort of merging with another. Thus one of the most popular myths of this passage is: We can piggyback our development by attaching to a Stronger One. But people who marry during this time often prolong financial and emotional ties to the family and relatives that impede them from becoming self-sufficient.

12   A stormy passage through the Pulling Up Roots years will probably facilitate the normal progression of the adult life cycle. If one doesn't have an identity crisis at this point, it will erupt during a later transition, when the penalties may be harder to bear.

THE TRYING TWENTIES

13   The Trying Twenties confront us with the question of how to take hold in the adult world. Our focus shifts from the interior turmoils of late adolescence—"Who am I?" "What is truth?"—and we become almost totally preoccupied with working out the externals. "How do I put my aspirations into effect?" "What is the best way to start?" "Where do I go?" "Who can help me?" "How did you do it?"

14   In this period, which is longer and more stable compared with the passage that leads to it, the tasks are as enormous as they are exhilarating: To shape a Dream, that vision of ourselves which will generate energy, aliveness, and hope. To prepare for a lifework. To find a mentor if possible. And to form the capacity for intimacy without losing in the process whatever consistency of self we have thus far mustered. The first test structure must be erected around the life we choose to try.

15   Doing what we "should" is the most pervasive theme of the twenties. The "shoulds" are largely defined by family models, the press of the culture, or the prejudices of our peers. If the prevailing cultural instructions are that one should get married and settle down behind one's own door, a nuclear family is born. If instead the peers insist that one should do one's own thing, the 25-year-old is likely to harness himself onto a Harley-Davidson and burn up Route 66 in the commitment to have no commitments.

16   One of the terrifying aspects of the twenties is the inner conviction that the choices we make are irrevocable. It is largely a false fear. Change is quite possible, and some alteration of our original choices is probably inevitable.

17   Two impulses, as always, are at work. One is to build a firm, safe structure for the future by making strong commitments, to "be set." Yet people who slip into a readymade form without much self-examination are likely to find themselves *locked* in.

The other urge is to explore and experiment, keeping any structure 18
tentative and therefore easily reversible. Taken to the extreme, these are
people who skip from one trial job and one limited personal encounter to
another, spending their twenties in the *transient* state.

Although the choices of our twenties are not irrevocable, they do set 19
in motion a Life Pattern. Some of us follow the lock-in pattern, others
the transient pattern; the wunderkind pattern, the caregiver pattern, and
there are a number of others. Such patterns strongly influence the particular questions raised for each person during each passage. . . .

Buoyed by powerful illusions and belief in the power of the will, we 20
commonly insist in our twenties that what we have chosen to do is the
one true course in life. Our backs go up at the merest hint that we are like
our parents, that two decades of parental training might be reflected in
our current actions and attitudes.

"Not me," is the motto, "I'm different." 21

CATCH-30 Establishing yourself, making your name

Impatient with devoting ourselves to the "shoulds," a new vitality 22
springs from within as we approach 30. Men and women alike speak of
feeling too narrow and restricted. They blame all sorts of things, but what
the restrictions boil down to are the outgrowth of career and personal
choices of the twenties. They may have been choices perfectly suited to
that stage. But now the fit feels different. Some inner aspect that was left
out is striving to be taken into account. Important new choices must be
made, and commitments altered or deepened. The work involves great
change, turmoil, and often crisis—a simultaneous feeling of rock bottom
and the urge to bust out.

One common response is the tearing up of the life we spent most of 23
our twenties putting together. It may mean striking out on a secondary
road toward a new vision or converting a dream of "running for president" into a more realistic goal. The single person feels a push to find a
partner. The woman who was previously content at home with children
chafes to venture into the world. The childless couple reconsiders children. And almost everyone who is married, especially those married for
seven years, feels a discontent.

If the discontent doesn't lead to a divorce, it will, or should, call for a 24
serious review of the marriage and of each partner's aspirations in their
Catch-30 condition. The gist of that condition was expressed by a 29-year-
old associate with a Wall Street law firm:

"I'm considering leaving the firm. I've been there four years now; 25
I'm getting good feedback, but I have no clients of my own. I feel weak.
If I wait much longer, it will be too late, too close to that fateful time of

decision on whether or not to become a partner. I'm success-oriented. But the concept of being 55 years old and stuck in a monotonous job drives me wild. It drives me crazy now, just a little bit. I'd say that 85 percent of the time I thoroughly enjoy my work. But when I get a screwball case, I come away from court saying, 'What am I doing here?' It's a *visceral* reaction that I'm wasting my time. I'm trying to find some way to make a social contribution or a slot in city government. I keep saying, 'There's something more.'"

26   Besides the push to broaden himself professionally, there is a wish to expand his personal life. He wants two or three more children. "The concept of a home has become very meaningful to me, a place to get away from troubles and relax. I love my son in a way I could not have anticipated. I never could live alone."

27   Consumed with the work of making his own critical life-steering decisions, he demonstrates the essential shift at this age: An absolute requirement to be more self-concerned. The self has new value now that his competency has been proved.

28   His wife is struggling with her own age-30 priorities. She wants to go to law school, but he wants more children. If she is going to stay home, she wants him to make more time for the family instead of taking on even wider professional commitments. His view of the bind, of what he would most like from his wife, is this:

29   "I'd like not to be bothered. It sounds cruel, but I'd like not to have to worry about what she's going to do next week. Which is why I've told her several times that I think she should do something. Go back to school and get a degree in social work or geography or whatever. Hopefully that would fulfill her, and then I wouldn't have to worry about her line of problems. I want her to be decisive about herself."

30   The trouble with his advice to his wife is that it comes out of concern with *his* convenience, rather than with *her* development. She quickly picks up on this lack of goodwill: He is trying to dispose of her. At the same time, he refuses her the same latitude to be "selfish" in making an independent decision to broaden her horizons. Both perceive a lack of mutuality. And that is what Catch-30 is all about for the couple.

ROOTING AND EXTENDING

31   Life becomes less provisional, more rational and orderly in the early thirties. We begin to settle down in the full sense. Most of us begin putting down roots and sending out new shoots. People buy houses and become very earnest about climbing career ladders. Men in particular concern themselves with "making it." Satisfaction with marriage generally goes downhill in the thirties (for those who have remained together) compared

with the highly valued, vision-supporting marriage of the twenties. This coincides with the couple's reduced social life outside the family and the inturned focus on raising their children.

THE DEADLINE DECADE   *Deciding on what you going to do for the rest of your life*

In the middle of the thirties we come upon a crossroads. We have reached   32
the halfway mark. Yet even as we are reaching our prime, we begin to see
there is a place where it finishes. Time starts to squeeze.

The loss of youth, the faltering of physical powers we have always   33
taken for granted, the fading purpose of stereotyped roles by which we
have thus far identified ourselves, the spiritual dilemma of having no
absolute answers—any or all of these shocks can give this passage the
character of crisis. Such thoughts usher in a decade between 35 and 45
that can be called the Deadline Decade. It is a time of both danger and
opportunity. All of us have the chance to rework the narrow identity
by which we defined ourselves in the first half of life. And those of us
who make the most of the opportunity will have a full-out authenticity
crisis.

To come through this authenticity crisis, we must reexamine our pur-   34
poses and reevaluate how to spend our resources from now on. "Why am
I doing all this? What do I really believe in?" No matter what we have
been doing, there will be parts of ourselves that have been suppressed
and now need to find expression. "Bad" feelings will demand acknowl-
edgment along with the good.

It is frightening to step off onto the treacherous footbridge leading to   35
the second half of life. We can't take everything with us on this journey
through uncertainty. Along the way, we discover that we are alone. We
no longer have to ask permission because we are the providers of our
own safety. We must learn to give ourselves permission. We stumble
upon feminine or masculine aspects of our natures that up to this time
have usually been masked. There is grieving to be done because an old
self is dying. By taking in our suppressed and even our unwanted parts,
we prepare at the gut level for the reintegration of an identity that is
ours and ours alone—not some artificial form put together to please the
culture or our mates. It is a dark passage at the beginning. But by disassembling ourselves, we can glimpse the light and gather our parts into
a renewal.

Women sense this inner crossroads earlier than men do. The time   36
pinch often prompts a woman to stop and take an all-points survey at
age 35. Whatever options she has already played out, she feels a "my
last chance" urgency to review those options she has set aside and those
that aging and biology will close off in the now *foreseeable* future. For all

her qualms and confusion about where to start looking for a new future, she usually enjoys an exhilaration of release. Assertiveness begins rising. There are so many firsts ahead.

37   Men, too, feel the time push in the mid-thirties. Most men respond by pressing down harder on the career accelerator. It's "my last chance" to pull away from the pack. It is no longer enough to be the loyal junior executive, the promising young novelist, the lawyer who does a little *pro bono* work on the side. He wants now to become part of top management, to be recognized as an established writer, or an active politician with his own legislative program. With some chagrin, he discovers that he has been too anxious to please and too vulnerable to criticism. He wants to put together his own ship.

38   During this period of intense concentration on external advancement, it is common for men to be unaware of the more difficult, gut issues that are propelling them forward. The survey that was neglected at 35 becomes a crucible at 40. Whatever rung of achievement he has reached, the man of 40 usually feels stale, restless, burdened, and unappreciated. He worries about his health. He wonders, "Is this all there is?" He may make a series of departures from well-established lifelong base lines, including marriage. More and more men are seeking second careers in midlife. Some become self-destructive. And many men in their forties experience a major shift of emphasis away from pouring all their energies into their own advancement. A more tender, feeling side comes into play. They become interested in developing an ethical self.

RENEWAL OR RESIGNATION

39   Somewhere in the mid-forties, equilibrium is regained. A new stability is achieved, which may be more or less satisfying.

40   If one has refused to budge through the midlife transition, the sense of staleness will calcify into resignation. One by one, the safety and supports will be withdrawn from the person who is standing still. Parents will become children; children will become strangers; a mate will grow away or go away; the career will become just a job—and each of these events will be felt as an abandonment. The crisis will probably emerge again around 50. And although its wallop will be greater, the jolt may be just what is needed to prod the resigned middle-ager toward seeking revitalization.

41   On the other hand...

42   If we have confronted ourselves in the middle passage and found a renewal of purpose around which we are eager to build a more authentic life structure, these may well be the best years. Personal happiness takes a sharp turn upward for partners who can now accept the fact: "I cannot

expect *anyone* to fully understand me." (Parents can be forgiven for the
burdens of our childhood.) Children can be let go without leaving us in
collapsed silence. At 50, there is a new warmth and mellowing. Friends
become more important than ever, but so does privacy. Since it is so often
proclaimed by people past midlife, the motto of this stage might be "No
more bullshit.") - *moving on, like finally growing up.*

1976

QUESTIONS FOR DISCUSSION

Content

a. The author explains that each of us has our own "step-style." What
   does she mean? *All it's our steps of deli*
b. Do any people you know—your parents, for example—fit neatly into
   Sheehy's ladder? Explain.
c. What qualifications does the author include in her introductory paragraphs to allow her to generalize?
d. Why should we not think "too mechanistically" (paragraph 4) when it
   comes to understanding how people move through life stages?
e. Why are "rebounds to the family" common between the ages of 18 and
   21? *It's harder to be on your own, yet people want to move*
f. What, according to Sheehy, is the common response to approaching
   age 30? *You want change, feel stuck*
g. How is establishing identity during the Deadline Decade different
   from establishing it during earlier years? What does Sheehy mean by
   "disassembling ourselves" (paragraph 35)? *Deciding what deciding without*
h. In what way might reaching age 50 bring renewal? In what way might
   it bring resignation? *Forgiving and moving on into retirement*

Strategy and Style

i. Is the analogy in the introduction appropriate? Does it help prepare us
   for what is to follow?
j. Sheehy's approach is, for the most part, objective, even detached. At
   times, however, she does express her personal reaction to the material.
   Find places in which the author's personal voice can be heard.
k. Why are explanations of the steps on the developmental ladder written in fairly generalized terms? Would it have been possible to be more
   specific? What are some of the strategies Sheehy uses to make these
   explanations seem specific?

Main idea: step ladder there are six stage that people go through to life. depending on age and gender

ENGAGING THE TEXT

a. Sheehy begins this essay with an analogy linking humans to lobsters. Explain why her analogy is an apt one. What other animals could you use in an analogy to describe human development? Make a list of two or three, and explain the analogy you see.
b. Briefly explain to what extent your chosen "course in life" is different from that of your parents or of other members of your family. Refer to Sheehy's essay in your response.

SUGGESTIONS FOR SUSTAINED WRITING

a. Where are you on Sheehy's developmental ladder? Write a narrative essay, using specific examples from your life, to discuss how your life fits Sheehy's categories or how it does not. This essay can be extended to include other members of your family. If this assignment doesn't interest you, write an essay in which you discuss someone who has gone through the "middle passage" Sheehy discusses in paragraphs 39–42. Briefly tell the story of this passage and explain whether this individual experienced "renewal" or "resignation."
b. Read Sanders's "The Men We Carry in Our Minds" in Chapter 6 or Noda's "Growing Up Asian in America" in this chapter. Then write an essay that explains how what Sheehy says about life's passages might apply to either or both of the speakers in those essays.
c. For a research essay, find other theories of adult development using library and Internet sources. (We list a few below to get you started.) Categorize each of them by applying age groups as Sheehy has done. Then compare and contrast the theories, speculating on which most accurately describes adult development. Use your own experiences and your observations of your family and friends to form criteria for judging the theories.

READ MORE

Sheehy, Gail. "Racing toward Midlife." *Men's Health*. May 1998: 148–54.

Essay adapted from Men's Passages: Discovering the New Map of Men's Lives.

___. "Readers' Guide." *New York* 19, April 1993: 73–74. *Presents selections from Sheehy's book* Catch-30 and Other Predictable Crises of Growing Up Adult.

___. "The Victorious Personality." *New York Times Magazine* 20, April 1986: 24–34. *Adaptation from the book* Spirit of Survival, *in which she argues that facing and overcoming adversity, even in childhood, can produce a strong and healthy personality.*

Growing Up Asian in America

Kesaya E. Noda

Born in a Japanese community in California, Kesaya E. Noda (b. 1950) was raised in New England. She studied Japanese after graduating from high school and lived in Japan for a year and a half. Noda is the author of Yamoto Colony *(1981), a history of the California community where her grandparents settled after immigrating to America. She earned a Master of Divinity degree from Harvard University in 1987. "Growing Up Asian in America" first appeared in a collection of essays entitled* Making Waves *(1989), which was published by Asian Women United in California.*

Most classification pieces focus on things, activities, social or moral conventions, and the like. Noda's essay is unique: It classifies Noda.

VOCABULARY

perpetuated, allusions, abounded, context, ineligible, Shinto, immaculate, samisens, savoring, ajar, harried, ravaged, backbiting, gait, pluralism, harangued, affirmation

Sometimes when I was growing up, my identity seemed to hurtle toward   1
me and paste itself right to my face. I felt that way, encountering the stereotypes of my race perpetuated by non-Japanese people (primarily white)
who may or may not have had contact with other Japanese in America.
"You don't like cheese, do you?" someone would ask. "I know your
people don't like cheese." Sometimes questions came making allusions to
history. That was another aspect of the identity. Events that had happened
quite apart from the me who stood silent in that moment connected my
face with an incomprehensible past. "Your parents were in California?
Were they in those camps during the war?" And sometimes there were
phrases or nicknames: "Lotus Blossom." I was sometimes addressed or
referred to as racially Japanese, sometimes as Japanese-American, and
sometimes as an Asian woman. Confusions and distortions abounded.

How is one to know and define oneself? From the inside—within a   2
context that is self-defined, from a grounding in community and a connection with culture and history that are comfortably accepted? Or from

the outside—within terms or messages received from the media and people who are often ignorant? Even as an adult I can still see two sides of my face and past. I can see from the inside out, in freedom. And I can see from the outside in, driven by the old voices of childhood and lost in anger and fear.

I AM RACIALLY JAPANESE

3   A voice from my childhood says: "You are other. You are less than. You are unalterably alien." This voice has its own history. We have indeed been seen as other and alien since the early years of our arrival in the United States. The very first immigrants were welcomed and sought as laborers to replace the dwindling numbers of Chinese, whose influx had been cut off by the Chinese Exclusion Act of 1882. The Japanese fell natural heir to the same anti-Asian prejudice that had arisen against the Chinese. As soon as they began striking for better wages, they were no longer welcomed.

4   I can see myself today as a person historically defined by law and custom as being forever alien. Being neither "free white," nor "African," our people in California were deemed "aliens, ineligible for citizenship," no matter how long they intended to stay here. Aliens ineligible for citizenship were prohibited from owning, buying, or leasing land. They did not and could not belong here. The voice in me remembers that I am always a *Japanese*-American in the eyes of many. A third-generation German-American is an American. A third-generation Japanese-American is a Japanese-American. Being Japanese means being a danger to the country during the war and knowing how to use chopsticks. I wear this history on my face.

5   I move to the other side. I see a different light and claim a different context. My race is a line that stretches across ocean and time to link me to the shrine where my grandmother was raised. Two high, white banners lift in the wind at the top of the stone steps leading to the shrine. It is time for the summer festival. Black characters are written against the sky as boldly as the clouds, as lightly as kites, as sharply as the big black crows I used to see above the fields in New Hampshire. At festival time there is liquor and food, ritual, discipline, and abandonment. There is music and drunkenness and invocation. There is hope. Another season has come. Another season has gone.

6   I am racially Japanese. I have a certain claim to this crazy place where the prayers intoned by a neighboring Shinto priest (standing in for my grandmother's nephew who is sick) are drowned out by the rehearsals for the pop singing contest in which most of the villagers will compete later that night. The village elders, the priest, and I stand respectfully upon the immaculate, shining wooden floor of the outer shrine, bowing our heads

before the hidden powers. During the patchy intervals when I can hear him, I notice the priest has a stutter. His voice flutters up to my ears only occasionally because two men and a woman are singing gustily into a microphone in the compound, testing the sound system. A pre-recorded tape of guitars, samisens, and drums accompanies them. Rock music and Shinto prayers. That night, to loud applause and cheers, a young man is given the award for the most *netsuretsu*—passionate, burning—rendition of a song. We roar our approval of the reward. Never mind that his voice had wandered and slid, now slightly above, now slightly below the given line of the melody. Netsuretsu. Netsuretsu.

In the morning, my grandmother's sister kneels at the foot of the 7 stone stairs to offer her morning prayers. She is too crippled to climb the stairs, so each morning she kneels here upon the path. She shuts her eyes for a few seconds, her motions as matter of fact as when she washes rice. I linger longer than she does, so reluctant to leave, savoring the connection I feel with my grandmother in America, the past, and the power that lives and shines in the morning sun.

Our family has served this shrine for generations. The family's need 8 to protect this claim to identity and place outweighs any individual claim to any individual hope. I am Japanese.

I AM A JAPANESE-AMERICAN

"Weak." I hear the voice from my childhood years. "Passive," I hear. Our 9 parents and grandparents were the ones who were put into those camps. They went without resistance; they offered cooperation as proof of loyalty to America. "Victim," I hear. And, "Silent."

Our parents are painted as hard workers who were socially uncom- 10 fortable and had difficulty expressing even the smallest opinion. Clean, quiet, motivated, and determined to match the American way; that is us, and that is the story of our time here.

"Why did you go into those camps?" I raged at my parents, fright- 11 ened by my own inner silence and timidity. "Why didn't you do anything to resist? Why didn't you name it the injustice it was?" Couldn't our parents even think? Couldn't they? Why were we so passive?

I shift my vision and my stance. I am in California. My uncle is in 12 the midst of the sweet potato harvest. He is pressed, trying to get the harvesting crews onto the field as quickly as possible, worried about the flow of equipment and people. His big pickup is pulled off to the side, motor running, door ajar. I see two tractors in the yard in front of an old shed; the flatbed harvesting platform on which the workers will stand has already been brought over from the other field. It's early morning. The workers stand loosely grouped and at ease, but my uncle looks as harried and tense as a police officer trying to unsnarl a New York City traffic jam. Driving toward the shed, I pull my car off the road to make way for an approaching tractor. The front wheels of the car sink luxuriously into the soft, white sand by the roadside and the car slides to a dreamy halt, tail still on the road. I try to move forward. I try to move back. The front bites contentedly into the sand, the back lifts itself at a jaunty angle. My uncle sees me and storms down the road, running. He is shouting before he is even near me.

13   "What's the matter with you?" he screams. "What the hell are you doing?" In his frenzy, he grabs his hat off his head and slashes it through the air across his knee. He is beside himself. "Don't you know how to drive in sand? What's the matter with you? You've blocked the whole roadway. How am I supposed to get my tractors out of here? Can't you use your head? You've cut off the whole roadway, and we've got to get out of here."

14   I stand on the road before him helplessly thinking. "No, I don't know how to drive in sand. I've never driven in sand."

15   "I'm sorry, uncle," I say, burying a smile beneath a look of sincere apology. I notice my deep amusement and my affection for him with great curiosity. I am usually devastated by anger. Not this time.

16   During the several years that follow I learn about the people and the place, and much more about what has happened in this California village where my parents grew up. The issei, our grandparents, made this settlement in the desert. Their first crops were eaten by rabbits and ravaged by insects. The land was so barren that men walking from house to house sometimes got lost. Women came here too. They bore children in 114-degree heat, then carried the babies with them into the fields to nurse when they reached the end of each row of grapes or other truck-farm crops.

17   I had had no idea what it meant to buy this kind of land and make it grow green. Or how, when the war came, there was no space at all for the subtlety of being who we were—Japanese-Americans. Either/or was the way. I hadn't understood that people were literally afraid for their lives then, that their money had been frozen in banks; that there was a five-mile travel limit; that when the early evening curfew came and they were inside their houses, some of them watched helplessly as people they knew went into their barns to steal their belongings. The police were patrolling the road, interested only in violators of curfew. There was no help for them in the face of thievery. I had not been able to imagine before what it must have felt like to be an American—to know absolutely that one is an American—and yet to have almost everyone else deny it. Not only deny it, but challenge that identity with machine guns and troops of white American soldiers. In those circumstances it was difficult to say, "I'm a Japanese-American." "American" had to do.

18   But now I can say that I am a Japanese-American. It means I have a place here in this country, too. I have a place here on the East Coast,

where our neighbor is so much a part of our family that my mother never passes her house at night without glancing at the lights to see if she is home and safe; where my parents have hauled hundreds of pounds of rocks from fields and arduously planted Christmas trees and blueberries, lilacs, asparagus, and crab apples; where my father still dreams of angling a stream to a new bed so that he can dig a pond in the field and fill it with water and fish. "The neighbors already came for their Christmas tree?" he asks in December. "Did they like it? Did they like it?"

I have a place on the West Coast where my relatives still farm, where 19 I heard the stories of feuds and backbiting, and where I saw that people survived and flourished because fundamentally they trusted and relied upon one another. A death in the family is not just a death in a family; it is a death in the community. I saw people help each other with money, materials, labor, attention, and time. I saw men gather once a year, without fail, to clean the grounds of a ninety-year-old woman who had helped the community before, during, and after the war. I saw her remembering them with birthday cards sent to each of their children.

I come from a people with a long memory and a distinctive grace. We 20 live our thanks. And we are Americans. Japanese-Americans.

I AM A JAPANESE-AMERICAN WOMAN

Woman. The last piece of my identity. It has been easier by far for me to 21 know myself in Japan and to see my place in America than it has been to accept my line of connection with my own mother. She was my dark self, a figure in whom I thought I saw all that I feared most in myself. Growing into womanhood and looking for some model of strength, I turned away from her. Of course, I could not find what I sought. I was looking for a black feminist or a white feminist. My mother is neither white nor black.

My mother is a woman who speaks with her life as much as with her 22 tongue. I think of her with her own mother. Grandmother had Parkinson's disease and it had frozen her gait and set her fingers, tongue, and feet jerking and trembling in a terrible dance. My aunts and uncles wanted her to be able to live in her own home. They fed her, bathed her, dressed her, awoke at midnight to take her for one last trip to the bathroom. My aunts (her daughters-in-law) did most of the care, but my mother went from New Hampshire to California each summer to spend a month living with Grandmother, because she wanted to and because she wanted to give my aunts at least a small rest. During those hot summer days, mother lay on the couch watching the television or reading, cooking foods that Grandmother liked, and speaking little. Grandmother thrived under her care.

The time finally came when it was too dangerous for Grandmother to 23 live alone. My relatives kept finding her on the floor beside her bed when they went to wake her in the mornings. My mother flew to California to help clean the house and make arrangements for Grandmother to enter a local nursing home. On her last day at home, while Grandmother was sitting in her big, overstuffed armchair, hair combed and wearing a green summer dress, my mother went to her and knelt at her feet. "Here, Mamma," she said. "I've polished your shoes." She lifted Grandmother's legs and helped her into the shiny black shoes. My Grandmother looked down and smiled slightly. She left her house walking, supported by her children, carrying her pocketbook, and wearing her polished black shoes. "Look, Mamma," my mom had said, kneeling. "I've polished your shoes."

24   Just the other day, my mother came to Boston to visit. She had recently lost a lot of weight and was pleased with her new shape and her feeling of good health. "Look at me, Kes," she exclaimed, turning toward me, front and back, as naked as the day she was born. I saw her small breasts and the wide, brown scar, belly button to pubic hair, that marked her because my brother and I were both born by Caesarean section. Her hips were small. I was not a large baby, but there was so little room for me in her that when she was carrying me she could not even begin to bend over toward the floor. She hated it, she said.

25   "Don't I look good? Don't you think I look good?"

26   I looked at my mother, smiling and as happy as she, thinking of all the times I have seen her naked. I have seen both my parents naked throughout my life, as they have seen me. From childhood through adulthood we've had our naked moments, sharing baths, idle conversations picked up as we moved between showers and closets, hurried moments at the beginning of days, quiet moments at the end of days.

27   I know this to be Japanese, this ease with the physical, and it makes me think of an old Japanese folk song. A young nursemaid, a fifteen-year-old girl, is singing a lullaby to a baby who is strapped to her back. The nursemaid has been sent as a servant to a place far from her own home. "We're the beggars," she says, "and they are the nice people. Nice people wear fine sashes. Nice clothes."

> If I should drop dead,
> bury me by the roadside!
> I'll give a flower to
> everyone who passes.

> What kind of flower?
> The cam-cam-camellia [tsun-tsun-tsubaki]
> watered by Heaven:
> alms water.

28   The nursemaid is the intersection of heaven and earth, the intersection of the human, the natural world, the body, and the soul. In this

song, with clear eyes, she looks steadily at life, which is sometimes so very terrible and sad. I think of her while looking at my mother, who is standing on the red and purple carpet before me, laughing, without any clothes.

I am my mother's daughter. And I am myself.   29
I am a Japanese-American woman.   30

EPILOGUE

I recently heard a man from West Africa share some memories of his   31
childhood. He was raised Muslim, but when he was a young man, he found himself deeply drawn to Christianity. He struggled against his inner impulse for years, trying to avoid the church yet feeling pushed to return to it again and again. "I would have done anything to avoid the change," he said. At last, he became Christian. Afterwards he was afraid to go home, fearing that he would not be accepted. The fear was ground-less, he discovered, when at last he returned—he had separated himself, but his family and friends (all Muslim) had not separated themselves from him.

The man, who is now a professor of religion, said that in the Africa he   32
knew as a child and a young man, pluralism was embraced rather than feared. There was "a kind of tolerance that did not deny your particular-ity," he said. He alluded to zestful, spontaneous debates that would some-times loudly erupt between Muslims and Christians in the village's public spaces. His memories of an atheist who harangued the villagers when he came to visit them once a week moved me deeply. Perhaps the man was an agricultural advisor or inspector. He harassed the women. He would say: "Don't go to the fields! Don't even bother to go to the fields. Let God take care of you. He'll send you the food. If you believe in God, why do you need to work? You don't need to work! Let God put the seeds in the ground. Stay home."

The professor said, "The women laughed, you know? They just   33
laughed. Their attitude was, 'Here is a child of God. When will he come home?'"

The storyteller, the professor of religion, smiled a most fantastic ten-   34
der smile as he told this story. "In my country, there is a deep affirmation of the oneness of God," he said. "The atheist and the women were having quite different experiences in their encounter, though the atheist did not know this. He saw himself as quite separate from the women. But the women did not see themselves as being separate from him. 'Here is a child of God,' they said. 'When will he come home?'"

1989

QUESTIONS FOR DISCUSSION

Content

a. What function is served by the questions Noda asks in paragraph 2?
b. What is the distinction Noda draws between Japanese Americans and other Americans (paragraph 4)?
c. What are the implications of the author's seeing herself "as a person historically defined by law and custom as being forever alien" (paragraph 4)?
d. Discuss this essay as an exercise in self-definition. In what way is classification appropriate to this exercise?
e. Summarize each of the three subsections of this piece by explaining the three ways in which Noda sees herself: as racially Japanese, as a Japanese American, and as a Japanese American woman.
f. What was Noda's reaction to learning about the internment of Japanese Americans during World War II? Why does she describe this reaction?
g. How does the story of the author's getting her car stuck in sand help define her as a Japanese American? As an individual?
h. Explain what Noda sees when she looks at her mother. What role does the story of the nursemaid play in her defining herself as a Japanese American woman?

Strategy and Style

i. Is Noda's introduction (paragraph 1) appropriate to this classification essay? Explain.
j. In what ways are paragraphs 5, 12, and 24 alike? What function do they serve? What function do paragraphs 8, 20, and 29/30 serve?
k. What light does the story of a West African Muslim in the epilogue shed on Noda's essay?
l. What role does narration play in this classification piece?
m. Noda divides her essay into three major sections and an epilogue. Describe the pattern she uses to organize her three major sections. What is the effect of her organizing all three sections the same way?

ENGAGING THE TEXT

a. In paragraph 4, Noda says, "A third-generation German American is an American. A third-generation Japanese American is a Japanese American." What can you infer from this statement about Noda's opinion of the "melting pot" concept? Can you name other ethnic groups who, after three or more generations, are still seen as "hyphenated Americans"?

b. Summarize each of the three subsections of this piece by explaining the three ways in which Noda sees herself: as racially Japanese, as a Japanese American, and as a Japanese American woman.

SUGGESTIONS FOR SUSTAINED WRITING

a. There is a great deal of talk these days about cultural diversity. Unfortunately, some people are all too happy to define others as members of a particular group rather than as individuals. Yet members of ethnic, religious, economic, gender, or other groups can be very different from one another. Using classification as a method of organization, discuss various types of people you have encountered in a group to which you belong. In the process, explain how you are different from other members of your group. In essence, then, use your essay to define your group and yourself.

b. Noda defines herself by using ethnic categories. Yet we can define ourselves by using categories based on various principles. For example, you might define yourself by grouping your daily activities or responsibilities under various headings: "I am a student," "I am a bank teller," or "I am a parent." Then again, you might discuss various aspects of your emotional makeup: "I am a romantic," "I am an extrovert," or "I am family-oriented." Using the above as examples, discuss three or four categories that would help define your emotional makeup, lifestyle, value system, career aspirations, and so forth.

c. Define a particular religion, occupation, species of domestic animal, or other topic that lends itself to classification. After gathering information about your topic in the library or on the Internet, write an essay in which you explain various divisions of your subject to define it. For example, you might define the term Muslim by discussing Shiite Muslims, Sunni Muslims, and African American Muslims. Or you might even limit your discussion to the term Shiite by discussing each of this Islamic branch's major sects, such as the Druses, Fatimids, Ismailis, Assassins, and Karmathians.

READ MORE

"Denshō: The Japanese American Legacy Project" (http://www.densho. org): *Website of the Japanese American Legacy Project. Contains writings and images important to understanding the Japanese American experience.*

"Hirasaki National Resource Center Resources" (http://www.janm.org/ nrc): *List of links sponsored by this Japanese American National Museum Resource Center.*

Niiya, Biran, ed. *Japanese-American History: An A-to-Z Reference from 1868 to the Present. Facts on File.* New York, 1993.

The Truth about Lying

Judith Viorst

A contributing editor at Redbook *magazine, Judith Viorst (b. 1931) began her career as a poet in 1965 when she published* The Village Square. *This book of verse was followed by several other volumes of prose and poetry with intriguing titles. Among them are* It's Hard to Be Hip over Thirty and Other Tragedies of Married Life *(1968),* People and Other Aggravations *(1971),* Yes, Married: A Saga of Love and Complaint *(1972), and* When Did I Stop Being Twenty and Other Injustices *(1987). Viorst has also published several works of children's fiction and nonfiction, including* Alexander and the Terrible, Horrible, No Good, Very Bad Day *(1972), as well as a musical drama,* Birthday and Other Humiliations. *"The Truth about Lying" first appeared in* Redbook *in 1981.*

Not simply an examination of contemporary social mores, Viorst's essay asks us to examine our own consciences. Her skillful use of anecdote, coupled with an interest grabbing refrain at the end of each section, allows us to apply what she is saying in an assessment of our own ability to tell the truth.

VOCABULARY

compulsively, assailing, evasion, rationalized, supersede, dissemble, triangulation, concede, adamant

1 I've been wanting to write on a subject that intrigues and challenges me: The subject of lying. I've found it very difficult to do. Everyone I've talked to has a quite intense and personal but often rather intolerant point of view about what we can—and can never *never*—tell lies about. I've finally reached the conclusion that I can't present any ultimate conclusions, for too many people would promptly disagree. Instead, I'd like to present a series of moral puzzles, all concerned with lying. I'll tell you what I think about them. Do you agree?

SOCIAL LIES

2 Most of the people I've talked with say that they find social lying acceptable and necessary. They think it's the civilized way for folks to behave.

Without these little white lies, they say, our relationships would be short and brutish and nasty. It's arrogant, they say, to insist on being so incorruptible and so brave that you cause other people unnecessary embarrassment or pain by compulsively assailing them with your honesty. I basically agree. What about you?

Will you say to people, when it simply isn't true, "I like your new 3
hairdo," "You're looking much better," "It's so nice to see you," "I had a wonderful time"?

Will you praise hideous presents and homely kids?   4

Will you decline invitations with "We're busy that night—so sorry we 5
can't come," when the truth is you'd rather stay home than dine with the So-and-sos?

And even though, as I do, you may prefer the polite evasion of "You 6
really cooked up a storm" instead of "The soup"—which tastes like warmed-over coffee—"is wonderful," will you, if you must, proclaim it wonderful?

There's one man I know who absolutely refuses to tell social lies. 7
"I can't play that game," he says; "I'm simply not made that way." And his answer to the argument that saying nice things to someone doesn't cost anything is, "Yes, it does—it destroys your credibility." Now, he won't, unsolicited, offer his views on the painting you just bought, but you don't ask his frank opinion unless you want *frank*, and his silence at those moments when the rest of us liars are muttering, "Isn't it lovely?" is, for the most part, eloquent enough. My friend does not indulge in what he calls "flattery, false praise and mellifluous comments." When others tell fibs he will not go along. He says that social lying is lying, that little white lies are still lies. And he feels that telling lies is morally wrong. What about you?

PEACE-KEEPING LIES

Many people tell peace-keeping lies; lies designed to avoid irritation or 8
argument; lies designed to shelter the liar from possible blame or pain; lies (or so it is rationalized) designed to keep trouble at bay without hurting anyone.

I tell these lies at times, and yet I always feel they're wrong. I under- 9
stand why we tell them, but still they feel wrong. And whenever I lie so that someone won't disapprove of me or think less of me or holler at me, I feel I'm a bit of a coward, I feel I'm dodging responsibility, I feel ... guilty. What about you?

Do you, when you're late for a date because you overslept, say that 10
you're late because you got caught in a traffic jam?

Do you, when you forget to call a friend, say that you called several 11
times but the line was busy?

12   Do you, when you didn't remember that it was your father's birthday, say that his present must be delayed in the mail?

13   And when you're planning a weekend in New York City and you're not in the mood to visit your mother, who lives there, do you conceal— with a lie, if you must—the fact that you'll be in New York? Or do you have the courage—or is it the cruelty?—to say, "I'll be in New York, but sorry—I don't plan on seeing you"?

14   (Dave and his wife Elaine have two quite different points of view on this very subject. He calls her a coward. She says she's being wise. He says she must assert her right to visit New York sometimes and not see her mother. To which she always patiently replies: "Why should we have useless fights? My mother's too old to change. We get along much better when I lie to her.")

15   Finally, do you keep the peace by telling your husband lies on the subject of money? Do you reduce what you really paid for your shoes? And in general do you find yourself ready, willing and able to lie to him when you make absurd mistakes or lose or break things?

16   "I used to have a romantic idea that part of intimacy was confessing every dumb thing that you did to your husband. But after a couple of years of that," says Laura, "have I changed my mind!"

17   And having changed her mind, she finds herself telling peace-keeping lies. And yes, I tell them too. What about you?

PROTECTIVE LIES

18   Protective lies are lies folks tell—often quite serious lies—because they're convinced that the truth would be too damaging. They lie because they feel there are certain human values that supersede the wrong of having lied. They lie, not for personal gain, but because they believe it's for the good of the person they're lying to. They lie to those they love, to those who trust them most of all, on the grounds that breaking this trust is justified.

19   They may lie to their children on money or marital matters.

20   They may lie to the dying about the state of their health.

21   They may lie about adultery, and not—or so they insist—to save their own hide, but to save the heart and the pride of the men they are married to.

22   They may lie to their closest friend because the truth about her talents or son or psyche would be—or so they insist—utterly devastating.

23   I sometimes tell such lies, but I'm aware that it's quite presumptuous to claim I know what's best for others to know. That's called playing God. That's called manipulation and control. And we never can be sure, once we start to juggle lies, just where they'll land, exactly where they'll roll.

24   And furthermore, we may find ourselves lying in order to back up the lies that are backing up the lie we initially told.

And furthermore—let's be honest—if conditions were reversed, we 25 certainly wouldn't want anyone lying to us.

Yet, having said all that, I still believe that there are times when pro- 26 tective lies must nonetheless be told. What about you?

If your Dad had a very bad heart and you had to tell him some bad 27 family news, which would you choose: To tell him the truth or to lie?

If your former husband failed to send his monthly child support 28 check and in other ways behaved like a total rat, would you allow your children—who believed he was simply wonderful—to continue to believe that he was wonderful?

If your dearly beloved brother selected a wife whom you deeply dis- 29 liked, would you reveal your feelings or would you fake it?

And if you were asked, after making love, "And how was that for 30 you?" would you reply, if it wasn't too good, "Not too good"?

Now, some would call a sex lie unimportant, little more than social 31 lying, a simple act of courtesy that makes all human intercourse run smoothly. And some would say all sex lies are bad news and unacceptably protective. Because, says Ruth, "a man with an ego that fragile doesn't need your lies—he needs a psychiatrist." Still others feel that sex lies are indeed protective lies, more serious than simple social lying, and yet at times they tell them on the grounds that when it comes to matters sexual, everybody's ego is somewhat fragile.

"If most of the time things go well in sex," says Sue, "I think you're 32 allowed to dissemble when they don't. I can't believe it's good to say, 'Last night was four stars, darling, but tonight's performance rates only a half.'"

I'm inclined to agree with Sue. What about you?   33

TRUST-KEEPING LIES

Another group of lies are trust-keeping lies, lies that involve triangula- 34 tion, with *A* (that's you) telling lies to *B* on behalf of *C* (whose trust you'd promised to keep). Most people concede that once you've agreed not to betray a friend's confidence, you can't betray it, even if you must lie. But I've talked with people who don't want you telling them anything that they might be called on to lie about.

"I don't tell lies for myself," says Fran, "and I don't want to have 35 to tell them for other people." Which means, she agrees, that if her best friend is having an affair, she absolutely doesn't want to know about it.

"Are you saying," her best friend asks, "that if I went off with a lover 36 and I asked you to tell my husband I'd been with you, that you wouldn't lie for me, that you'd betray me?"

Fran is very pained but very adamant. "I wouldn't want to betray 37 you, so … don't ask me."

38   Fran's best friend is shocked. What about you?

39   Do you believe you can have close friends if you're not prepared to receive their deepest secrets?

40   Do you believe you must always lie for your friends?

41   Do you believe, if your friend tells a secret that turns out to be quite immoral or illegal, that once you've promised to keep it, you must keep it?

42   And what if your friend were your boss—if you were perhaps one of the President's men—would you betray or lie for him over, say, Watergate?

43   As you can see, these issues get terribly sticky.

44   It's my belief that once we've promised to keep a trust, we must tell lies to keep it. I also believe that we can't tell Watergate lies. And if these two statements strike you as quite contradictory, you're right—they're quite contradictory. But for now they're the best I can do. What about you?

45   Some say that truth will out and thus you might as well tell the truth. Some say you can't regain the trust that lies lose. Some say that even though the truth may never be revealed, our lies pervert and damage our relationships. Some say...well, here's what some of them have to say.

46   "I'm a coward," says Grace, "about telling close people important, difficult truths. I find that I'm unable to carry it off. And so if something is bothering me, it keeps building up inside till I end up just not seeing them any more."

47   "I lie to my husband on sexual things, but I'm furious," says Joyce, "that he's too insensitive to know I'm lying."

48   "I suffer most from the misconception that children can't take the truth," says Emily. "But I'm starting to see that what's harder and more damaging for them is being told lies, is *not* being told the truth."

49   "I'm afraid," says Joan, "that we often wind up feeling a bit of contempt for the people we lie to."

50   And then there are those who have no talent for lying.

51   "Over the years, I tried to lie," a friend of mine explained, "but I always got found out and I always got punished. I guess I gave myself away because I feel guilty about any kind of lying. It looks as if I'm stuck with telling the truth."

52   For those of us, however, who are good at telling lies, for those of us who lie and don't get caught, the question of whether or not to lie can be a hard and serious moral problem. I liked the remark of a friend of mine who said, "I'm willing to lie. But just as a last resort—the truth's always better."

53   "Because," he explained, "though others may completely accept the lie I'm telling, I don't."

54   I tend to feel that way too.

55   What about you?

1981

QUESTIONS FOR DISCUSSION

Content

a. Is the essay's thesis explicit? What is it?

b. What arguments does the author offer to defend social lying? What arguments does she offer against social lying?

c. Why does Viorst believe that telling protective lies is a form of manipulation?

d. What else does she find objectionable or dangerous about protective lies?

e. Under what conditions does the author believe that telling protective lies is appropriate?

f. In what way is her position on trust-keeping lies contradictory? How does she respond to that contradiction?

Strategy and Style

g. What is the introduction to this essay designed to do? Does it succeed?

h. To what end does Viorst address the reader directly?

i. What is the effect of her asking "What about you?" at the end of each section?

j. Where and to what end does Viorst use contrast? How is her creating contrast related to her thesis?

k. Viorst uses examples throughout this essay. What form do these examples take? Are they convincing?

l. Where in the essay does the author engage in definition?

m. Does Viorst's quoting her friends make an effective way to develop this essay? Why or why not?

n. What point does the author make in the conclusion? Does it bring closure to the essay, or is it simply another of the "moral puzzles" she mentions in her introduction?

ENGAGING THE TEXT

a. Respond to Viorst by explaining how you react to what she says about one of the four kinds of lies she discusses. In other words, respond to the question with which she closes each section of this essay: "What about you?"

b. List examples of representative social, peace-keeping, protective, and trust-keeping lies that you tell or are told by others. Compare your examples to the examples in Viorst's essay.

SUGGESTIONS FOR SUSTAINED WRITING

a. Write a letter to Viorst explaining why you tell lies like those discussed in her essay or why you refuse to tell such lies. If this doesn't interest you, think of another type of lie, one that Viorst does not discuss. Write an essay that explains that category. Like Viorst, include examples and direct quotations from others to develop your point.

b. Write a classification essay in which you develop three or four major categories related to a type of human behavior or activity about which you have mixed feelings. For example, you might discuss "the truth about dieting," "the truth about gambling," "the truth about exercising," "the truth about being assertive," or "the truth about gossiping." For further inspiration, consult the essay by Lutz, which follows in this chapter.

c. Using each of the categories Viorst presents, and following the format she uses, write an essay in which you use your own examples of lies and liars. To gather information, read up on lies told by prominent historical or contemporary figures in politics, entertainment, the media, sports, and other high-profile professions. Incorporate this library or Internet research into your paper.

READ MORE

"Judith Viorst: 1998." *Friends of the OSU Library* , (http://www.library. okstate.edu/friends/cobb/viorst.htm): *Profiles Viorst upon her being chosen for the 1998 H. Louise Cobb Distinguished Author Award.*

"Judith Viorst." *Poets.org.* Academy of American Poets (http://www. poets.org/poet.php/prmPID/61): *Short biography.*

"Judith Viorst" (http://www.poemhunter.com/judith-viorst): *Links to fifteen of Viorst's poems.*

Viorst, Judith. *Suddenly Sixty: And Other Shocks of Later Life.* New York: Simon & Schuster, 2000. *A collection of short stories and essays by Viorst.*

Doublespeak
William Lutz

A professor of English at Rutgers University in New Jersey and a member of the Pennsylvania Bar, William Lutz (b. 1941) is America's premier critic of "doublespeak," the use of evasive, unnecessarily complex, and misleading language used to manipulate or even deceive the reader. Doublespeak, Lutz believes, is most often encountered in U.S. government publications and announcements, followed by those of big business as a close second. Lutz edited the National Council of Teachers of English Quarterly Review of Doublespeak for 14 years, and he chaired the Committee on Public Doublespeak for 15 years. He has been a guest on television's C-SPAN, Larry King Live, The Today Show, The MacNeil-Lehrer NewsHour, *and* The CBS Evening News. *His many books include* Doublespeak: From Revenue Enhancement to Terminal Living *(1989),* The New Doublespeak: Why No One Knows What Anyone's Saying Anymore *(1996), and* A Dictionary of Doublespeak *(1999). Lutz also collaborated on* A Plain English Handbook: How to Create Clear SEC Disclosure Documents, *published by the Securities and Exchange Commission.*

VOCABULARY

purported, deprivation, sanctioned, variance, incontinent, ordnance, pretentious, esoteric, profundity, calibration

There are no potholes in the streets of Tucson, Arizona, just "pavement deficiencies." The Reagan Administration didn't propose any new taxes, just "revenue enhancement" through new "user's fees." Those aren't bums on the street, just "non-goal-oriented members of society." There are no more poor people, just "fiscal underachievers." There was no robbery of an automatic teller machine, just an "unauthorized withdrawal." The patient didn't die because of medical malpractice, it was just a "diagnostic misadventure of a high magnitude." The U.S. Army doesn't kill the enemy anymore, it just "services the target." And the doublespeak goes on.   1

Doublespeak is language that pretends to communicate but really doesn't. It is language that makes the bad seem good, the negative appear positive, the unpleasant appear attractive or at least tolerable. Doublespeak is language that avoids or shifts responsibility, language that is at variance with its real or purported meaning. It is language that conceals or prevents thought; rather than extending thought, doublespeak limits it....   2

HOW TO SPOT DOUBLESPEAK

How can you spot doublespeak? Most of the time you will recognize doublespeak when you see or hear it. But, if you have any doubts, you can identify doublespeak just by answering these questions: Who is saying what to whom, under what conditions and circumstances, with what intent, and with what results? Answering these questions will usually   3 help you identify as doublespeak language that appears to be legitimate or that at first glance doesn't even appear to be doublespeak.

First Kind of Doublespeak

4   There are at least four kinds of doublespeak. The first is the euphemism, an inoffensive or positive word or phrase used to avoid a harsh, unpleasant, or distasteful reality. But a euphemism can also be a tactful word or phrase which avoids directly mentioning a painful reality, or it can be an expression used out of concern for the feelings of someone else, or to avoid directly discussing a topic subject to a social or cultural taboo.

5   When you use a euphemism because of your sensitivity for someone's feelings or out of concern for a recognized social or cultural taboo, it is not doublespeak. For example, you express your condolences that someone has "passed away" because you do not want to say to a grieving person, "I'm sorry your father is dead." When you use the euphemism "passed away," no one is misled. Moreover, the euphemism functions here not just to protect the feelings of another person, but to communicate also your concern for that person's feelings during a period of mourning. When you excuse yourself to go to the "restroom," or you mention that someone is "sleeping with" or "involved with" someone else, you do not mislead anyone about your meaning, but you do respect the social taboos about discussing bodily functions and sex in direct terms. You also indicate your sensitivity to the feelings of your audience, which is usually considered a mark of courtesy and good manners.

6   However, when a euphemism is used to mislead or deceive, it becomes doublespeak. For example, in 1984 the U.S. State Department announced that it would no longer use the word "killing" in its annual report on the status of human rights in countries around the world. Instead, it would use the phrase "unlawful or arbitrary deprivation of life," which the department claimed was more accurate. Its real purpose for using this phrase was simply to avoid discussing the embarrassing situation of government-sanctioned killings in countries that are supported by the United States and have been certified by the United States as respecting the human rights of their citizens. This use of a euphemism constitutes doublespeak, since it is designed to mislead, to cover up the unpleasant. Its real intent is at variance with its apparent intent. It is language designed to alter our perception of reality.

7   The Pentagon, too, avoids discussing unpleasant realities when it refers to bombs and artillery shells that fall on civilian targets as "incontinent ordnance." And in 1977 the Pentagon tried to slip funding for the neutron bomb unnoticed into an appropriations bill by calling it a "radiation enhancement device."

Second Kind of Doublespeak

A second kind of doublespeak is jargon, the specialized language of a   8
trade, profession, or similar group, such as that used by doctors, lawyers,
engineers, educators, or car mechanics. Jargon can serve an important
and useful function. Within a group, jargon functions as a kind of verbal
shorthand that allows members of the group to communicate with each
other clearly, efficiently, and quickly. Indeed, it is a mark of membership
in the group to be able to use and understand the group's jargon.

But jargon, like the euphemism, can also be doublespeak. It can be—   9
and often is—pretentious, obscure, and esoteric terminology used to
give an air of profundity, authority, and prestige to speakers and their
subject matter. Jargon as doublespeak often makes the simple appear
complex, the ordinary profound, the obvious insightful. In this sense it is
used not to express but impress. With such doublespeak, the act of smelling something becomes "organoleptic analysis," glass becomes "fused
silicate," a crack in a metal support beam becomes a "discontinuity,"
conservative economic policies become "distributionally conservative
notions."

Lawyers, for example, speak of an "involuntary conversion" of   10
property when discussing the loss or destruction of property through
theft, accident, or condemnation. If your house burns down or if your
car is stolen, you have suffered an involuntary conversion of your
property. When used by lawyers in a legal situation, such jargon is a
legitimate use of language, since lawyers can be expected to understand
the term.

However, when a member of a specialized group uses its jargon to   11
communicate with a person outside the group, and uses it knowing that
the nonmember does not understand such language, then there is doublespeak. For example, on May 9, 1978, a National Airlines 727 airplane
crashed while attempting to land at the Pensacola, Florida, airport. Three
of the fifty-two passengers aboard the airplane were killed. As a result of
the crash, National made an after-tax insurance benefit of $1.7 million, or
an extra 18¢ a share dividend for its stock-holders. Now National Airlines
had two problems: It did not want to talk about one of its airplanes crashing, and it had to account for the $1.7 million when it issued its annual
report to its stockholders. National solved the problem by inserting a
footnote in its annual report which explained that the $1.7 million income
was due to "the involuntary conversion of a 727." National thus acknowledged the crash of its airplane and the subsequent profit it made from
the crash, without once mentioning the accident or the deaths. However,
because airline officials knew that most stockholders in the company, and
indeed most of the general public, were not familiar with legal jargon, the
use of such jargon constituted doublespeak.

Third Kind of Doublespeak

12 A third kind of doublespeak is gobbledygook or bureaucratese. Basically, such doublespeak is simply a matter of piling on words, of overwhelming the audience with words, the bigger the words and the longer the sentences the better. Alan Greenspan, then chair of President Nixon's Council of Economic Advisors, was quoted in *The Philadelphia Inquirer* in 1974 as having testified before a Senate committee that "It is a tricky problem to find the particular calibration in timing that would be appropriate to stem the acceleration in risk premiums created by falling incomes without prematurely aborting the decline in the inflation-generated risk premiums."

13   Nor has Mr. Greenspan's language changed since then. Speaking to the meeting of the Economic Club of New York in 1988, Mr. Greenspan, now Federal Reserve chair, said, "I guess I should warn you, if I turn out to be particularly clear, you've probably misunderstood what I've said." Mr. Greenspan's doublespeak doesn't seem to have held back his career.

14   Sometimes gobbledygook may sound impressive, but when the quote is later examined in print it doesn't even make sense. During the 1988 presidential campaign, vice-presidential candidate Senator Dan Quayle explained the need for a strategic defense initiative by saying, "Why wouldn't an enhanced deterrent, a more stable peace, a better prospect to denying the ones who enter conflict in the first place to have a reduction of offensive systems and an introduction to defense capability? I believe this is the route the country will eventually go."

15   The investigation into the *Challenger* disaster in 1986 revealed the doublespeak of gobbledygook and bureaucratese used by too many involved in the shuttle program. When Jesse Moore, NASA's associate administrator, was asked if the performance of the shuttle program had improved with each launch or if it had remained the same, he answered, "I think our performance in terms of the liftoff performance and in terms of the orbital performance, we knew more about the envelope we were operating under, and we have been pretty accurately staying in that. And so I would say the performance has not by design drastically improved. I think we have been able to characterize the performance more as a function of our launch experience as opposed to it improving as a function of time." While this language may appear to be jargon, a close look will reveal that it is really just gobbledygook laced with jargon. But you really have to wonder if Mr. Moore had any idea what he was saying.

Fourth Kind of Doublespeak

16 The fourth kind of doublespeak is inflated language that is designed to make the ordinary seem extraordinary; to make everyday things seem

impressive; to give an air of importance to people, situations, or things that would not normally be considered important; to make the simple seem complex. Often this kind of doublespeak isn't hard to spot, and it is usually pretty funny. While car mechanics may be called "automotive internists," elevator operators members of the "vertical transportation corps," used cars "pre-owned" or "experienced cars," and black-and-white television sets described as having "nonmulticolor capability," you really aren't misled all that much by such language.

However, you may have trouble figuring out that, when Chrysler 17 "initiates a career alternative enhancement program," it is really laying off five thousand workers; or that "negative patient care outcome" means the patient died; or that "rapid oxidation" means a fire in a nuclear power plant.

The doublespeak of inflated language can have serious consequences. 18 In Pentagon doublespeak, "pre-emptive counterattack" means that American forces attacked first; "engaged the enemy on all sides" means American troops were ambushed; "backloading of augmentation personnel" means a retreat by American troops. In the doublespeak of the military, the 1983 invasion of Grenada was conducted not by the U.S. Army, Navy, Air Force, and Marines, but by the "Caribbean Peace Keeping Forces." But then, according to the Pentagon, it wasn't an invasion, it was a "predawn vertical insertion."…

THE DANGERS OF DOUBLESPEAK

These … examples of doublespeak should make it clear that doublespeak 19 is not the product of carelessness or sloppy thinking. Indeed, most doublespeak is the product of clear thinking and is carefully designed and constructed to appear to communicate when in fact it doesn't. It is language designed not to lead but mislead. It is language designed to distort reality and corrupt thought…. When a fire in a nuclear reactor building is called "rapid oxidation," an explosion in a nuclear power plant is called an "energetic disassembly," the illegal overthrow of a legitimate government is termed "destabilizing a government," and lies are seen as "inoperative statements," we are hearing doublespeak that attempts to avoid responsibility and make the bad seem good, the negative appear positive, something unpleasant appear attractive; and which seems to communicate but doesn't. It is language designed to alter our perception of reality and corrupt our thinking. Such language does not provide us with the tools we need to develop, advance, and preserve our culture and our civilization. Such language breeds suspicion, cynicism, distrust, and, ultimately, hostility.

1989

QUESTIONS FOR DISCUSSION

Content

a. Summarize Lutz's general definition of doublespeak.
b. How does the author advise those who would wish to identify double-speak?
c. According to Lutz, is it ever advisable to use euphemisms? When? When is it not?
d. The author claims that jargon can serve useful purposes. Explain.
e. When does jargon become doublespeak?
f. What does Lutz mean by "gobbledygook"? By "inflated language"? Why are they dangerous?
g. In what way does this essay's conclusion clarify Lutz's purpose?

Strategy and Style

h. The organization of this classification essay is logical and easy to follow. Lutz simply labels and discusses four categories. Why does he also label his conclusion?
i. In what parts of this essay does Lutz use contrast, examples, and definition to support his thesis?
j. How would you characterize the tone of this essay? Does Lutz ever vary his tone? If so, to what end?
k. Lutz's writing style makes the essay easy to follow and appealing. Analyze one or two paragraphs to explain this statement.
l. How would you describe the intended audience for this piece?

ENGAGING THE TEXT

a. Is higher education guilty of doublespeak? Summarize Lutz's definition of doublespeak and apply that definition to one, two, or three examples that you have noticed at your school.
b. Summarize the definition of each of the four types of doublespeak that Lutz includes. Then find or create at least one additional example for each of those four types.

SUGGESTIONS FOR SUSTAINED WRITING

a. Write an essay in which you expose examples of doublespeak put forth by members of a particular industry or of several industries in an attempt to consciously deceive the public. For example, you might discuss several examples of doublespeak taken from the entertainment industry, or you might discuss one from that industry and one from the news media, one from the tobacco industry, and one from automobile manufacturers.

b. Lutz explains ways in which language is manipulated to deceive readers. Write an essay explaining other types of manipulation. For example, in what ways do movies, television sitcoms and commercials, highway billboards, musical recordings, music videos, and so on try to manipulate us? Focus on one source of this manipulation, discuss its purpose, and explain how it works.

c. This selection is more than twenty years old. List and discuss examples of doublespeak used today, especially by people in government, big business, advertising, the news media, the entertainment industry, or another source of public information. You might also analyze doublespeak put forth by groups interested in advancing a particular political or social ideology. To gather information on this topic, rely on your own observations and reading, but consult library and Internet sources as well.

READ MORE

Lutz and His Works

Lutz, William. "Professor Lutz Assigns Your Homework: A Summer Reading List on Doublespeak." *Curriculum Review* 34.9 (1995): 3. *Discussion of several classic books on the abuse of language.*

___. "Rules for Writing Plain English." *Plain Language Association International* (http://www.plainlanguagenetwork.org/Resources/lutz.htm).

"William Lutz Talks about How Doublespeak Has Taken over the Business World." *Business News New Jersey*, January 26, 1998: 13.

Use and Abuse of Language

"The 1999 Doublespeak Awards." ETC: *A Review of General Semantics* 56.4 (1999–2000): 483–85.

Orwell, George. "Politics and the English Language" *George Orwell: 1903–1950* (http://www.classicshorts.com/stories/patel.html): *Classic essay on language published in 1946.*

What Secrets Tell

Luc Sante

Born in Belgium in 1954, Sante came to the United States as a child and grew up in a suburb of New York City, a place that figures in much of his work. He attended Columbia University and then launched a career as a professional writer. He now teaches at Bard

College. Sante's books include Low Life: Lures and Snares of Old New York *(1991);* The Factory of Facts *(1998), a memoir of his university days;* Walker Evans *(1999); and* Kill All Your Darlings *(2007), a collection of essays that he had already published in several prestigious American magazines. "What Secrets Tell" is part of a longer essay first published in the* New York Times Magazine *on December 3, 2000.*

VOCABULARY

black holes, mantle, motley, susceptibilities, gamut, regime, chaff, peccadilloes, *fait accompli*, ostensibly, *qua*, carny barker, bruited, gulls, imponderable, prurient, constituency, banal, esoteric, acrylic, descends, pretensions, votaries, tome, scrupulously, stratum, esoterica, oxymoron, protocol, mystics, ken, corollary, destabilization

1   Secrets are a permanent feature of the human condition. We need secrets the way we need black holes, for their mystery; the way we need landspeed records, for their enlargement of scale; the way we need sexy models in advertisements, for their seductively false promises; the way we need lotteries, for their vague possibility. We also need them the way we need bank vaults and sock drawers and glove compartments. Anybody who doesn't carry around one or two secrets probably has all the depth of a place mat.

2   But then the word *secret* conceals under its mantle a teeming and motley population of types. Secrets cater to the entire range of human susceptibilities, from the laughably trivial to the terrifyingly fundamental. Principal landmarks along the way include:

3   **Personal Secrets**   In other words, those secrets that are chiefly of interest to the persons who carry them around. You know the sort: You pick your nose when no one's looking; your real first name is Eustace; you wear a truss for nonmedical reasons. If such things were revealed, your ego might take a beating and your intimates could gain a weapon for use in squabbles or extortions, but the foundations of your house would not be shaken.

4   **Romantic Secrets**   They run the gamut. That interval of passion you once shared with your dentist when the two of you were stuck in an elevator with a bottle of Cherry Kijafa may remain swathed in gauze for all eternity, although your partner might eventually demand to know the identity of this "Shirley" whose name you utter in your sleep. That you enjoy above all the erotic sensation of being pinched with tweezers until you bleed might not matter a whole lot to anyone, unless you decide to run for office, and then you will find yourself sending discreet sums of money to people you haven't thought of in years. Couples often tacitly erect a whole edifice of secrets, based on real or imagined causes for jealousy. This can be relatively harmless, or it can be a symptom of the relationship's becoming a regime.

Secrets in Gossip   That is, the wheat left over when gossip's chaff 5
is sifted out. Secrets that surface as gossip are usually of the mildest sort,
personal eccentricities and romantic peccadilloes not of much interest
outside a closed circle. (It is understood that there is a direct correlation
between the degree of triviality of the secret transmitted as gossip and
the rank of the gossip's subject within that circle.) Gossip, though, demonstrates how secrets can become currency, as the teller invests the hearer
with power in exchange for esteem. The possession of a secret concerning
another is, like all forms of power, something of a burden, a weight pressing one's lips together, which can be relieved only by telling someone else.
This, added to a hunger for knowledge on the part of all within the gossip
circle, keeps the wheel of the secret-fueled gossip economy turning.

Trade Secrets   The monetary economy, meanwhile, revolves around 6
a wide and diverse range of secrets. A business strategy is a secret until it
becomes a fait accompli. The details of the financial health of a company
are kept as secret as the law allows. Anyone with a degree of power in
the market is continually keeping secrets—from competitors, from the
press, from anyone who is an outsider, including friends and family, but
sometimes from colleagues and office mates. The reasons are obvious:
Everyone is naked in a cutthroat world, and secrets are clothing. It goes
without saying that secrets protect innovations and that they also hide
various extralegal undertakings—the ostensibly respectable bank that
takes in laundry on the side, for example. Business also employs secrets
strategically, as secrets qua secrets, usually painting the word *secret* in
letters ten stories tall. Naturally the new car model will differ little from
the previous year's, but a bit of cloak-and-dagger about it will increase
public interest. The "secret recipe" is on a par with "new and improved"
as a carny barker's hook. The cake mix or soft drink or laundry soap may,
of course, actually include a secret ingredient, known only to staff chem-
ists and highly placed executives, but very often a "secret ingredient" is
rumored or bruited about primarily as a lure to the gulls of the public.

Secret Formulas   The public hunger for secrets is primordial. It is 7
first and foremost a matter of curiosity, but it also springs from a painful awareness of rank and a belief that things are different upstairs, with
a more or less fanciful idea of the specifics. These days, with fortune-
building running at a pitch not seen since the 1920s, there is widespread
demand for financial folklore. You can make a lot of money catering to the
suspicion that there exist shortcuts known only to a few. That some people are richer, thinner, more charismatic or whiter of teeth may be a result
of a variety of imponderable factors, but for everyone who in moments of
desperation has imagined that there must be some simple trick, some formula or high sign or investment routine or hidden spa, there is an author
with a book aimed at the exact combination of vulnerability and prurient imagination. Such publications run along the entire span of implied

legitimacy based upon demographics, from the crudities aimed at the supermarket-tabloid constituency (diets centered on junk food named in the Bible, for instance) to the overpriced hardcover pamphlets catering to the anxieties of the managerial class by dressing up received ideas with slogans and numbered lists. For centuries, the secret has been a sure-fire sales gimmick. All you have to do is combine the banal and the esoteric.

8   **Secret Societies**   There are probably a lot fewer than there once were, but somewhere in America, no doubt, insurance adjusters and trophy engravers still gather once a month in acrylic gowns and button-flap underwear to exchange phrases in pseudobiblical double Dutch and then get down to the business of drinking beer. It helps them feel special to be the only ones in town who know the three-finger handshake. The setup descends from the heresies of the Middle Ages by the way of the pecking order of the playground. We can laugh at them, now that they are so enfeebled, but there was a time not long ago when they dominated the social life of male middle-class America, and in many ways their pretensions are not so far removed from those of the Mafia or the CIA.

9   **Mystical Secrets**   The secret is bait. The secret leads votaries by the nose through a maze of connected chambers, in each of which they must ante up. Only when they have finally tumbled to there being no secret (and they have run through the better part of their inheritances) can they truly be counted as initiates. But few have the stamina to get that far, and most instead spend their spare afternoons consuming one tome after another promoting the secrets of, variously, the pyramids, the Templars, the ascended masters, the elders of Mu, the Essene scrolls, and so on through greater and lesser degrees of perceived legitimacy, all of which flutter around the edges of the secret, none of which make so bold as to suggest what it might consist of.

10   **State Secrets**   "Our laws are not generally known; they are kept secret by the small group of nobles who rule us," wrote Kafka in one of his miniature stories. "We are convinced that these ancient laws are scrupulously administered; nevertheless it is an extremely painful thing to be ruled by laws that one does not know." This is the essence of state secrets. A government does not have to be totalitarian, particularly, to possess a stratum of laws whose existence cannot be generally known because they describe the limits of the knowable. It is forbidden for unauthorized persons to possess certain kinds of information. What kinds of information? Well, that's the trouble; if you knew that, you would already know too much. State secrets range all the way from banal prohibitions on photographing customs booths and power plants to the highest levels of technical esoterica.

11   **Atomic Secrets**   "Stop me if you've heard this atomic secret," cracked William Burroughs in *Naked Lunch*. Atomic secrets may be the world's most famous class of secret, an oxymoron, surely, but for the fact

that few enough people would recognize or understand an atomic secret if it landed in their mailboxes. The workaday state secret may be a matter of mere protocol or protection of resources, not unlike industries safeguarding the peculiarities of their production methods. The atomic secret, however, ascends to the level of the sacred because it manifests in concrete form the terror that mystics can only suggest: the end of the world. The secret of life may be an empty proposition, but the secret of death is actually legible to those who possess the language and the tools. . . .

People need secrets because they need the assurance that there is 12 something left to discover, that they have not exhausted the limits of their environment, that a prize might lie in wait like money in the pocket of an old jacket, that the existence of things beyond their ken might propose as a corollary that their own minds contain unsuspected corridors. People need uncertainty and destabilization the way they need comfort and security. It's not that secrets make them feel small but that they make the world seem bigger—a major necessity these days, when sensations need to be extreme to register at all. Secrets reawaken that feeling from childhood that the ways of the world were infinitely mysterious, unpredictable and densely packed, and that someday you might come to know and master them. Secrets purvey affordable glamour, suggest danger without presenting an actual threat. If there were no more secrets, an important motor of life would be stopped, and the days would merge into a continuous blur. Secrets hold out the promise, false but necessary, that death will be deferred until their unveiling.

QUESTIONS FOR DISCUSSION

Content

a. Reread paragraphs 1 and 2. In your own words, state Sante's thesis. Then reread paragraph 12. Now, revise the version of Sante's thesis that you just wrote.
b. What is Sante's purpose?
c. What does he mean, in paragraph 2, when he says that we need secrets for "their enlargement of scale"?
d. What is the author saying about romantic secrets at the end of paragraph 4?
e. In paragraph 6, he refers to a bank's taking in "laundry on the side." What illegal practice is he referring to?
f. Look up the Templars, the ascended masters, the elders of Mu, and the Essene scrolls (paragraph 9) in the library or on the Internet. How does Sante's mention of them help explain "mystical secrets"?
g. Who are Franz Kafka (paragraph 10) and William Burroughs (paragraph 11)? Explain why Sante chose to cite these writers to explain "state secrets" and "atomic secrets."

Strategy and Style

h. In his introduction, Sante says that "Secrets cater to the entire range of human susceptibilities. . . . Principal landmarks along the way include. . . ." Is this an appropriate lead-in to what follows? Explain why or why not.

i. Sante's essay first appeared in the *New York Times Magazine*, which is included in the Sunday edition. What does the author's style (his vocabulary, sentence structure, choice of allusions, and use of irony or sarcasm, for example) tell us about his audience? Also why would the *Times* not have published this piece in a weekday edition?

j. Identify examples of figurative language in this essay; metaphor, simile, and hyperbole are the most obvious. How does Sante's use of such language reflect his tone (his attitude toward his subject) and his purpose?

k. Sante uses sarcasm in paragraph 7 when he mentions "diets centered on junk food mentioned in the Bible." Find other places in which he becomes sarcastic.

l. In paragraph 12, Sante concludes by making reference to his introduction. But he goes beyond a simple restatement of his introduction. Explain what the conclusion adds to this essay. Would you have ended "What Secrets Tell" with a different conclusion? Explain.

m. Sante's style is generally esoteric and sophisticated. Identify places in which he lapses into a more familiar and relaxed style.

n. This is a classification essay, but what other methods of development does Sante use to support his thesis? Look especially for cause/effect, definition, and illustration.

ENGAGING THE TEXT

a. Write a one-sentence summary of each of Sante's categories.

b. Choose any one of Sante's categories and continue his discussion of it by adding your own information. Especially useful here are illustrations.

SUGGESTIONS FOR SUSTAINED WRITING

a. In paragraph 3, Sante talks about personal secrets. Using his definition of such secrets, write an essay in which you take the discussion a step further: classify three or four types of personal secrets of your own choosing. Use your own experiences and observations as sources of information. In the process, explain why people tend to keep each of the types of personal secrets you are writing about. Also explain the repercussions that keeping such secrets might eventually have on the secret keeper, as well as on other people. If this assignment doesn't interest you, write a classification essay that, unlike Sante's, takes a more serious approach. List and explain various types of secrets that need to be kept for the good of the secret holder and for the benefit of others. Then, again, you might write about types of secrets that, if held too long, could cause real damage—emotional or otherwise—to yourself or to others.

b. Compare and contrast Sante's essay with Viorst's "The Truth about Lying" or Lutz's "Doublespeak," both in this chapter. Discuss similarities and differences in tone, style, methods of development, use of figurative language, the appeal to a particular audience, and other rhetorical considerations.

c. Write a classification paper in which you explain why some people cheat on their taxes, shoplift, ignore traffic laws, overeat, or engage in any other negative or harmful behavior. Base your paper in part on your own experiences with and observations of others. (Of course, you may draw information from your own behavior as well.) But also be sure to research your topic on the Internet (first seek your instructor's approval to use this research tool) and/or in the library.

READ MORE

"Luc Sante" (http://www.pbs.org/wnet/newyork/series/interview/sante_frame.html): *PBS interview with the author.*

Sante, Luc. *The Factory of Facts.* New York: Pantheon, 1998. *A memoir concerning what the author found out about himself when he visited relatives in Belgium.*

___."French without Tears" (http://www.threepennyreview.com/samples/sante_su04.html).

___. *Low Life: Lures and Snares of Old New York.* Farrar, Strauss, and Giroux, 2003. *History of the dark side of New York City during the nineteenth and early twentieth centuries.*

The 12 Most Annoying Types of Facebookers

Brandon Griggs

Brandon Griggs (1960) is the producer of the Tech Section of CNN.com, for which he writes and edits articles and produces multimedia presentations on various subjects including those relating to computer technology and electronic communication. However, his blogs also comment on other technical and scientific subjects such as global warming and the environment. Griggs graduated from Tufts University in 1982.

His essay, entitled "The 12 Most Annoying Types of Facebookers," was posted on August 20, 2009. It is a satiric look, not only at Facebookers, but at twelve personality types we encounter in our daily lives, whether in person or in cyberspace.

VOCABULARY

navel-gazing, mundane, unsolicited, schmoozers, wannabees, innuendo, unabashedly, anglers, manipulative, voyeurs, curmudgeons, leering

1   Facebook, for better or worse, is like being at a big party with all your friends, family, acquaintances and co-workers.

2   There are lots of fun, interesting people you're happy to talk to when they stroll up. Then there are the other people, the ones who make you cringe when you see them coming. This article is about those people.

3   Sure, Facebook can be a great tool for keeping up with folks who are important to you. Take the status update, the 160-character message that users post in response to the question, "What's on your mind?" An artful, witty or newsy status update is a pleasure—a real-time, tiny window into a friend's life.

4   But far more posts read like navel-gazing diary entries, or worse, spam. A recent study categorized 40 percent of Twitter tweets as "pointless babble," and it wouldn't be surprising if updates on Facebook, still a fast-growing social network, break down in a similar way. Combine dull status updates with shameless self-promoters, "friend-padders" and that friend of a friend who sends you quizzes every day, and Facebook becomes a daily reminder of why some people can get on your nerves.

5   Here are 12 of the most annoying types of Facebook users:

6   **The Let-Me-Tell-You-Every-Detail-of-My-Day Bore.** "I'm waking up." "I had Wheaties for breakfast." "I'm bored at work." "I'm stuck in traffic." You're kidding! How fascinating! No moment is too mundane for some people to broadcast unsolicited to the world. Just because you have 432 Facebook friends doesn't mean we all want to know when you're waiting for the bus.

7   **The Self-Promoter.** OK, so we've probably all posted at least once about some achievement. And sure, maybe your friends really do want to read the fascinating article you wrote about beet farming. But when almost EVERY update is a link to your blog, your poetry reading, your 10k results or your art show, you sound like a bragger or a self-centered careerist.

8   **The Friend-Padder.** The average Facebook user has 120 friends on the site. Schmoozers and social butterflies—you know, the ones who make

lifelong pals on the subway—might reasonably have 300 or 400. But 1,000 "friends?" Unless you're George Clooney or just won the lottery, no one has that many. That's just showing off.

The Town Crier. "Michael Jackson is dead!!!" You heard it from me 9 first! Me, and the 213,000 other people who all saw it on TMZ. These Matt Drudge wannabes are the reason many of us learn of breaking news not from TV or news sites but from online social networks. In their rush to trumpet the news, these people also spread rumors, half-truths and innuendo. No, Jeff Goldblum did not plunge to his death from a New Zealand cliff.

The TMIer. "Brad is heading to Walgreens to buy something for these 10 pesky hemorrhoids." Boundaries of privacy and decorum don't seem to exist for these too-much-information updaters, who unabashedly offer up details about their sex lives, marital troubles and bodily functions. Thanks for sharing.

The Bad Grammarian. "So sad about Fara Fauset but Im so gladd its 11 friday yippe." Yes, I know the punctuation rules are different in the digital world. And, no, no one likes a spelling-Nazi schoolmarm. But you sound like a moron.

The Sympathy-Baiter. "Barbara is feeling sad today." "Man, am I 12 glad that's over." "Jim could really use some good news about now." Like anglers hunting for fish, these sad sacks cast out their hooks—baited with vague tales of woe—in the hopes of landing concerned responses. Genuine bad news is one thing, but these manipulative posts are just pleas for attention.

The Lurker. The Peeping Toms of Facebook, these voyeurs are too 13 cautious, or maybe too lazy, to update their status or write on your wall. But once in a while, you'll be talking to them and they'll mention something you posted, so you know they're on your page, hiding in the shadows. It's just a little creepy.

The Crank. These curmudgeons, like the trolls who spew hate in blog 14 comments, never met something they couldn't complain about. "Carl isn't really that impressed with idiots who don't realize how idiotic they are." [Actual status update.] Keep spreading the love.

The Paparazzo. Ever visit your Facebook page and discover that 15 someone's posted a photo of you from last weekend's party—a photo you didn't authorize and haven't even seen? You'd really rather not have to explain to your mom why you were leering like a drunken hyena and French-kissing a bottle of Jagermeister.

The Obscurist. "If not now then when?" "You'll see…" "Grist for 16 the mill." "John is, small world." "Dave thought he was immune, but no. No, he is not." [Actual status updates, all.] Sorry, but you're not being mysterious—just nonsensical.

The Chronic Inviter. "Support my cause. Sign my petition. Play Mafia 17 Wars with me. Which 'Star Trek' character are you? Here are the 'Top 5 cars I have personally owned.' Here are '25 Things About Me.' Here's a drink. What drink are you? We're related! I took the 'What President Are You?' quiz and found out I'm Millard Fillmore! What president are you?"

18   You probably mean well, but stop. Just stop. I don't care what president I am—can't we simply be friends? Now excuse me while I go post the link to this story on my Facebook page.

QUESTIONS FOR DISCUSSION

Content

a. What is Griggs's thesis?
b. What does the author mean by "a spelling-Nazi schoolmarm"? (paragraph 11)
c. Besides annoyance, what other negatives does Griggs associate with the Facebookers classified here?
d. Explain the analogy Griggs makes in the first two paragraphs. How does this analogy advance his purpose?
e. What, in your opinion, are some of the most annoying aspects of Facebookers, as mentioned in this essay? Can you think of any more?

Strategy and Style

f. This article appears on a CNN website. What about its style and structure tells us that it was intended for electronic publication?
g. Should this essay have covered fewer than twelve types? Would it have been as effective if it had discussed six types, for example?
h. In paragraph 8, the author uses irony to compare Facebook users and people "who make lifelong pals in the subway." What other examples of irony appear in this essay?
i. How does Griggs's use of irony affect his style?
j. Who are Matt Drudge and Jeff Goldblum (paragraph 9)? Why are they mentioned?
k. Griggs does not define "Jagermeister" (paragraph 15)? What does his choosing not to do so tell you about his audience?
l. Is the conclusion of this essay in keeping with the tone of what precedes it? What is the effect of Griggs's making fun of himself?

ENGAGING THE TEXT

a. Though effective, Griggs's conclusion is short. Write an alternative conclusion to this essay. You might try explaining how to avoid annoying Facebookers or making a prediction about what social networking tools like Facebook might look like in five or ten years.

b. We meet annoying people every day in person, not just in real life. Using two or three of the categories in Griggs's essay, write as many paragraphs that provide detailed examples of people you know who fall into these categories.

SUGGESTIONS FOR SUSTAINED WRITING

a. In item *b* of Engaging the Text, you were asked to provide examples of people you know personally—not simply from Facebook or some other social networking site—who fit under two or three of Griggs's categories. Expand this work into a full-length essay. Add at least six other categories to the two or three you have already started writing about. Make sure that each category is fully developed with concrete details and direct quotations like those Griggs uses.

b. Griggs classifies annoying Facebookers, but there are certainly other types of annoying people. For example, you could classify annoying neighbors, cell phone users, restaurant patrons, students, teachers, drivers, or roommates, for example. Write an essay that discusses another type of annoying person by type. You might use some of Griggs's categories to get you started, but invent some of your own as well.

If this assignment doesn't interest you, write an essay that uses an adjective other than "annoying" in its title. For example, instead of writing about the most annoying drivers, write about the most dangerous drivers.

A third choice is to write not about people, but about things, such as annoying types of commercials, mindless reality shows, or unrealistic romance or war movies.

c. This essay touches on the notion that social networking sites have affected the way in which we interact with others. Write a research paper that focuses on such sites and explains their effects on ways in which people in your generation are interacting. What are the positive and negative effects of networking via the Internet? Does prolonged use of the computer to communicate with others have an effect on the users' personalities and lifestyles? Per your professor's instructions, use library, scholarly database, and Internet sources to gather information to develop this essay. Use the documentation system your instructor requires.

READ MORE

By the Author

Griggs, Brandon. "SciTechBlog" (http://scitech.blogs.cnn.com/tag/brandon-griggs): *Various postings on numerous subjects by Griggs.*

About Social Networking Sites

Hernandez, Vittorio. "British Psychiatrist Warns about Dangers of Social Networking Websites" (http://www.dbune.com/news/tech/4918-number-of-underage-social-networking-site-users-increasing.html).

"Social Networking Websites Review" (http://social-networking-websites-review.toptenreviews.com): *Rates the top-ten social networking sites for security, help/support, and other important features.*

Meredith, Leslie. "Facebook Etiquette." (http://social-networking-websites-review.toptenreviews.com/facebook-etiquette.html): *A useful article for anyone who uses Facebook regularly.*

6

Comparison and Contrast

The human tendency to measure one thing against another is so persuasive that it is only natural that it be used as a way to explore and explain complex ideas in writing. Comparison reveals similarities, and contrast points up differences. Both allow the writer to explain and explore new ideas by making reference to what the reader already knows. One way to begin describing a microwave oven to someone who has never seen one is to liken it to the oven in the conventional kitchen stove with which he or she is familiar. Both use energy to heat and cook food. Both are relatively easy to use, and both are no fun to clean! But there the similarities end. A microwave is quicker and more economical. And whoever heard of making popcorn in a conventional oven? Spend enough time explaining similarities and differences, and you are sure to give your reader at least a rudimentary acquaintance with this appliance.

As with all writing, the key to composing effective comparison/ contrast papers is to collect important information—and plenty of it— before you begin. Look at your subjects long and hard, take careful notes, and gather the kinds of details that will help you reveal differences and similarities of the most telling kind.

You can use a variety of techniques to develop a comparison or contrast. As suits his purpose, Mark Twain relies heavily on description in "Two Views of the Mississippi," whereas Suzanne Britt includes examples and a plethora of specific details to create a humorous comparison of personality types. Narration informs Bruce Catton's brilliant study of Grant and Lee, Scott Russell Sanders's "The Men We Carry in Our Minds," and Bharati Mukherjee's discussion of the problems and choices that immigrants face. It is also the foundation upon which Gary Soto builds his comparison of Mexican and Japanese families in the United States. Finally, in "China's Biggest Gamble: Can It Have Capitalism without Democracy? A Prediction," Henry Blodget uses description as well as the cause/effect method to contrast two views of modern China's social and economic future.

193

One of the major advantages of using comparison/contrast to explain ideas is that it can lend itself quite naturally to two easy-to-arrange and easy-to-follow patterns of organization. In the point-by-point method, writers address a series of characteristics or features shared by the two subjects; they compare or contrast the two subjects on one point, and then move on to the next point. This is how the selection by Henry Blodget is arranged. In the subject-by-subject method, one subject is thoroughly discussed before the writer moves on to the second. You can see a good example of the subject-by-subject method in the essay by Mark Twain. For example, Twain first describes the beautiful and poetic Mississippi before going on to the dangerous Mississippi.

But do not be misled. No writer represented in this chapter is content to follow a predetermined schema. Each author has a specific purpose in mind, and each draws on other organizational patterns to shape the essay. Indeed, Catton shifts from the point-by-point to the subject-by-subject arrangement so deftly that the reader hardly notices.

The selections in this chapter present a variety of subjects and purposes—from analyzing psychological motivations behind the way men and women communicate to assessing the virtues of solitude. Carefully consider the Questions for Discussion, the items under Engaging the Text, and the Suggestions for Sustained Writing that follow each essay. They will lead you to many more insights about using comparison/contrast as a way to explore new ideas and to make your writing more powerful, no matter what your topic or purpose.

Grant and Lee: A Study in Contrasts

Bruce Catton

Born in Michigan, Bruce Catton (1899–1978) has come to be regarded as one of the most important historians of the American Civil War. Catton received the Pulitzer Prize and the National Book Award for A Stillness at Appomattox *(1953). Among his other works are* This Hallowed Ground *(1956),* Mr. Lincoln's Army *(1951), and* Gettysburg: The Final Fury *(1974). The piece on Grant and Lee is one of the most frequently anthologized short selections on the subject of the Civil War. Though brief, this selection succeeds in capturing the essence of both great generals through portraits drawn from carefully chosen details.*

VOCABULARY

tidewater, age of chivalry, leisure class, sinewy, obeisance, static, diametrically, burgeoning, tenacity

When Ulysses S. Grant and Robert E. Lee met in the parlor of a mod- 1
est house at Appomattox Court House, Virginia, on April 9, 1865, to work
out the terms for the surrender of Lee's Army of Northern Virginia, a great
chapter in American life came to a close, and a great new chapter began.

These men were bringing the Civil War to its virtual finish. To be 2
sure, other armies had yet to surrender, and for a few days the fugitive
Confederate government would struggle desperately and vainly, trying
to find some way to go on living now that its chief support was gone. But
in effect it was all over when Grant and Lee signed the papers. And the
little room where they wrote out the terms was the scene of one of the
poignant, dramatic contrasts in American history.

They were two strong men, these oddly different generals, and they 3
represented the strengths of two conflicting currents that, through them,
had come into final collision.

Back of Robert E. Lee was the notion that the old aristocratic concept 4
might somehow survive and be dominant in American life.

Lee was tidewater Virginia, and in his background were family, 5
culture, and tradition...the age of chivalry transplanted to a New World
which was making its own legends and its own myths. He embodied a
way of life that had come down through the age of knighthood and the
English country squire. America was a land that was beginning all over
again, dedicated to nothing much more complicated than the rather hazy
belief that all men had equal rights, and should have an equal chance in
the world. In such a land Lee stood for the feeling that it was somehow
of advantage to human society to have a pronounced inequality in the
social structure. There should be a leisure class, backed by ownership of
land; in turn, society itself should be keyed to the land as the chief source
of wealth and influence. It would bring forth (according to this ideal) a
class of men with a strong sense of obligation to the community; men
who lived not to gain advantage for themselves, but to meet the solemn
obligations which had been laid on them by the very fact that they were
privileged. From them the country would get its leadership; to them it
could look for the higher values—of thought, of conduct, of personal
deportment—to give it strength and virtue.

Lee embodied the noblest elements of this aristocratic ideal. Through 6
him, the landed nobility justified itself. For four years, the Southern states
had fought a desperate war to uphold the ideals for which Lee stood. In
the end, it almost seemed as if the Confederacy fought for Lee; as if he
himself was the Confederacy . . . the best thing that the way of life for
which the Confederacy stood could ever have to offer. He had passed into
legend before Appomattox. Thousands of tired, underfed, poorly clothed
Confederate soldiers, long-since past the simple enthusiasm of the early
days of the struggle, somehow considered Lee the symbol of everything
for which they had been willing to die. But they could not quite put this

feeling into words. If the Lost Cause, sanctified by so much heroism and so many deaths, had a living justification, its justification was General Lee.

7   Grant, the son of a tanner on the Western frontier, was everything Lee was not. He had come up the hard way, and embodied nothing in particular except the eternal toughness and sinewy fiber of the men who grew up beyond the mountains. He was one of a body of men who owed reverence and obeisance to no one, who were self-reliant to a fault, who cared hardly anything for the past but who had a sharp eye for the future.

8   These frontier men were the precise opposites of the tidewater aristocrats. Back of them, in the great surge that had taken people over the Alleghenies and into the opening Westerncountry, there was a deep, implicit dissatisfaction with a past that had settled into grooves. They stood for democracy, not from any reasoned conclusion about the proper ordering of human society, but simply because they had grown up in the middle of democracy and knew how it worked. Their society might have privileges, but they would be privileges each man had won for himself. Forms and patterns meant nothing. No man was born to anything, except perhaps to a chance to show how far he could rise. Life was competition.

9   Yet along with this feeling had come a deep sense of belonging to a national community. The Westerner who developed a farm, opened a shop or set up in business as a trader, could hope to prosper only as his own community prospered—and his community ran from the Atlantic to the Pacific and from Canada down to Mexico. If the land was settled, with towns and highways and accessible markets, he could better himself. He saw his fate in terms of the nation's own destiny. As its horizons expanded, so did his. He had, in other words, an acute dollars-and-cents stake in the continued growth and development of his country.

10   And that, perhaps, is where the contrast between Grant and Lee becomes most striking. The Virginia aristocrat, inevitably, saw himself in relation to his own region. He lived in a static society which could endure almost anything except change. Instinctively, his first loyalty would go to the locality in which that society existed. He would fight to the limit of endurance to defend it, because in defending it he was defending everything that gave his own life its deepest meaning.

11   The Westerner, on the other hand, would fight with an equal tenacity for the broader concept of society. He fought so because everything he lived by was tied to growth, expansion, and a constantly widening horizon. What he lived by would survive or fall with the nation itself. He could not possibly stand by unmoved in the face of an attempt to destroy the Union. He would combat it with everything he had, because he could only see it as an effort to cut the ground out from under his feet.

12   So Grant and Lee were in complete contrast, representing two diametrically opposed elements in American life. Grant was the modern man emerging; beyond him, ready to come on the stage, was the great

age of steel and machinery, of crowded cities and a restless, burgeoning vitality. Lee might have ridden down from the old age of chivalry, lance in hand, silken banner fluttering over his head. Each man was the perfect champion of his cause, drawing both his strengths and his weaknesses from the people he led.

Yet it was not all contrast, after all. Different as they were—in back- 13 ground, in personality, in underlying aspiration—these two great soldiers had much in common. Under everything else, they were marvelous fighters. Furthermore, their fighting qualities were really very much alike.

Each man had, to begin with, the great virtue of utter tenacity and 14 fidelity. Grant fought his way down the Mississippi Valley in spite of acute personal discouragement and profound military handicaps. Lee hung on in the trenches at Petersburg after hope itself had died. In each man there was an indomitable quality . . . the born fighter's refusal to give up as long as he can still remain on his feet and lift his two fists.

Daring and resourcefulness they had, too; the ability to think faster 15 and move faster than the enemy. These were the qualities which gave Lee the dazzling campaigns of Second Manassas and Chancellorsville and won Vicksburg for Grant.

Lastly, and perhaps greatest of all, there was the ability, at the end, to 16 turn quickly from war to peace once the fighting was over. Out of the way these two men behaved at Appomattox came the possibility of a peace of reconciliation. It was a possibility not wholly realized, in the years to come, but which did, in the end, help the two sections to become one nation again . . . after a war whose bitterness might have seemed to make such a reunion wholly impossible. No part of either man's life became him more than the part he played in their brief meeting in the McLean house at Appomattox. Their behavior there put all succeeding genera-tions of Americans in their debt. Two great Americans, Grant and Lee— very different, yet under everything very much alike. Their encounter at Appomattox was one of the great moments of American history.

1958

QUESTIONS FOR DISCUSSION

Content

a. What does Catton mean in paragraph 5 when he says, "[Lee] embodied a way of life that had come down through the age of knighthood and the English country squire"?

b. Catton groups Grant with men who believed: "Forms and patterns meant nothing. No man was born to anything, except perhaps to a chance to show how far he could rise" (paragraph 8). Explain what he means by that.

c. Catton's thesis is stated rather early in the essay. What is it? How does it signal the pattern of organization to follow?

d. If this selection is "A Study in Contrasts," why does Catton spend the last four paragraphs discussing the similarities between Grant and Lee?

e. What are some of these similarities?

f. How would you explain the Westerner's "deep sense of belonging to a national community," which Catton mentions in paragraph 9? How does this idea differ from what tidewater aristocrats like Lee felt?

g. Discuss the other characteristics that Catton attributes to frontier men.

Strategy and Style

h. What function do paragraphs 10 and 11 play in the structure of this essay?

i. Catton organizes his prose by alternating the discussion from point to point rather than completing his discussion of one figure before moving on to the next. Is this method effective?

ENGAGING THE TEXT

a. Describe what you consider to be the ideal general for today. In your opinion, do generals today share the same qualities as those in Grant and Lee's time?

b. Describe the meeting that might have occurred between Grant and Lee if the Confederacy had won the war.

SUGGESTIONS FOR SUSTAINED WRITING

a. Choose two individuals with whom you have the same kind of relationship, such as two grandfathers, two aunts, or two close friends. How do these individuals differ? List the major differences in their personalities or their outlooks on life. Is one a pessimist, the other an optimist? Is one an introvert, the other an extrovert? If you don't want to write about people you know personally, choose two figures from the world of politics, art, science, or business about whom you know a great deal. Write a well-developed essay that makes the contrast clear.

b. Catton characterized Lee as a "living justification" of the "Lost Cause." Do you see yourself as such an idealist? Do you espouse "lost causes" simply because you think they are right? Or are you more pragmatic and realistic in your approach to life? Whatever your answer, explain it in an essay; cite sufficient examples to be convincing and clear.

c. Select two rival candidates in an upcoming or recent political election (local, state, or national). Isolate and explain the major differences in their ideologies. Make sure to include information you have found through research in newspapers, magazines, and journals or on the Internet.

READ MORE

Catton and His Works

"Bruce Catton, Historian 1899–1978" (http://clevelandartsprize.org/awardees/bruce_catton.html).

Catton, Bruce. *Prefaces to History.* New York: Doubleday, 1970. *An anthology of essays and prefaces written by Catton.*

The Civil War

Civil War Information Available on the Internet. U.S. Civil War Center., (http://www.civilwarhome.com/indexcivilwarinfo.htm): *The home page of the U.S. Civil War Center, with many links to resources and information arranged alphabetically according to subject.*

Hoemann, George (http://sunsite.utk.edu/civil-war): *The American Civil War Homepage. Contains 10,000 links to memoirs, essays, histories, and other information relating to the Civil War.*

Two Views of the Mississippi

Mark Twain

Mark Twain (1835–1910) was, of course, the pen name of Samuel Langhorne Clemens, the Missourian who learned to pilot Mississippi riverboats and who grew to become one of America's leading humorists, social critics, and men of letters. Twain recorded his experiences in numerous newspaper features and columns and in several books, including Life on the Mississippi *(1883),* The Adventures of Tom Sawyer *(1876), and his masterpiece,* The Adventures of Huckleberry Finn *(1885). Indeed, for some literary historians, the true American novel has its beginnings in the work of Twain. In the selection that follows, Twain contrasts his views of the Mississippi, first as a novice and then as an experienced river pilot.*

VOCABULARY

conspicuous, opal, ruddy, radiating, bluff, shoal, compassing, rapture, unwholesome

1 Now when I had mastered the language of this water, and had come to know every trifling feature that bordered the great river as familiarly as I knew the letters of the alphabet, I had made a valuable acquisition. But I had lost something, too. I had lost something which could never be restored to me while I lived. All the grace, the beauty, the poetry, had gone out of the majestic river! I still keep in mind a certain wonderful sunset which I witnessed when steamboating was new to me. A broad expanse of the river was turned to blood; in the middle distance the red hue brightened into gold, through which a solitary log came floating black and conspicuous; in one place a long, slanting mark lay sparkling upon the water; in another the surface was broken by boiling, tumbling rings, that were as many-tinted as an opal; where the ruddy flush was faintest, was a smooth spot that was covered with graceful circles and radiating lines, ever so delicately traced; the shore on our left was densely wooded, and the somber shadow that fell from this forest was broken in one place by a long, ruffled trail that shone like silver; and high above the forest wall a cleanstemmed dead tree waved a single leafy bough that glowed like a flame in the unobstructed splendor that was flowing from the sun. There were graceful curves, reflected images, woody heights, soft distances; and over the whole scene, far and near, the dissolving lights drifted steadily, enriching it every passing moment with new marvels of coloring.

2   I stood like one bewitched. I drank it in, in a speechless rapture. The world was new to me, and I had never seen anything like this at home. But as I have said, a day came when I began to cease from noting the glories and the charms which the moon and the sun and the twilight wrought upon the river's face; another day came when I ceased altogether to note them. Then, if that sunset scene had been repeated, I should have looked upon it without rapture, and should have commented upon it, inwardly, after this fashion: "This sun means that we are going to have wind tomorrow; that floating log means that the river is rising, small thanks to it; that slanting mark on the water refers to a bluff reef which is going to kill somebody's steamboat one of these nights, if it keeps on stretching out like that; those tumbling 'boils' show a dissolving bar and a changing channel there; the lines and circles in the slick water over yonder are a warning that that troublesome place is shoaling up dangerously; that silver streak in the shadow of the forest is the 'break' from a new snag, and he has located himself in the very best place he could have found to fish for steamboats; that tall dead tree, with a single living branch, is not

going to last long, and then how is a body ever going to get through this blind place at night without the friendly old landmark?"

No, the romance and beauty were all gone from the river. All the value 3 any feature of it had for me now was the amount of usefulness it could furnish toward compassing the safe piloting of a steamboat. Since those days, I have pitied doctors from my heart. What does the lovely flush in a beauty's cheek mean to a doctor but a "break" that ripples above some deadly disease? Are not all her visible charms sown thick with what are to him the signs and symbols of hidden decay? Does he ever see her beauty at all, or doesn't he simply view her professionally, and comment upon her unwholesome condition all to himself? And doesn't he sometimes wonder whether he has gained most or lost most by learning his trade?

1883

QUESTIONS FOR DISCUSSION

Content

a. Why does Twain pity doctors?
b. What purpose does paragraph 3 serve? Why does Twain compare the work of a steamboat pilot to that of a doctor? In what way is the conduct of their work similar?
c. Twain fully describes his view of the river when he was a novice and then goes on to talk about his perception of it after he became a trained steamboat pilot. Does this pattern serve him better than discussing various aspects of the river point by point?
d. What details does Twain offer to prove that at one time in his life the river held grace, beauty, and poetry for him?

Strategy and Style

e. Twain's thesis, which appears in paragraph 1, is presented in an obvious and straightforward manner. How does it help determine the organization of the rest of the piece?
f. The first paragraph is filled with descriptive language that captures a subjective, almost rhapsodic, view of the river. How would you characterize the language found in paragraph 2?
g. What use does paragraph 2 make of the details Twain has already introduced in paragraph 1?

ENGAGING THE TEXT

a. Brainstorm a list of metaphors and similes that Twain might have used to describe the Mississippi River. For example, "the Mississippi River is a _____," or "the Mississippi River is like a _____."
b. Summarize Twain's essay by dividing his comments about the Mississippi River into two columns, one column for each way the river can be viewed. Add your own items to the lists. Can the river be viewed only in two ways? In what other ways can it be seen?

SUGGESTIONS FOR SUSTAINED WRITING

a. Twain's training as a pilot seems to have had a negative effect in that it took the romance out of his view of the river. However, learning more about a subject may enhance one's appreciation of it. Can you relate an instance from your own experience to illustrate this notion? For example, mastering the fundamentals of swimming may have given you the confidence you needed to try skin diving. Tuning your first engine may have motivated you to learn more about auto mechanics in general.
b. Scan the topics and titles of the essays in Chapter 10, "Argument and Persuasion." Look for an essay that takes a position with which you disagree. After you have read that selection carefully, write an essay in which you explain whether and to what extent the argument you just read changed or modified your original opinion. If what you read changed your opinion only slightly or not at all, write an essay in which you explain why you continue to hold your original position.
c. As children, we become excited, enraptured, and even mystified by the rituals and customs associated with important religious or national holidays: Christmas, Yom Kippur, Ramadan, Thanksgiving, Halloween, the Fourth of July. Think about the holiday you found most exciting as a child. Has your view of it changed? Write an essay in which you define that holiday and explain why and how your vision of that holiday has or has not changed. To lend authority to your essay, include facts, ideas, and opinions from secondary sources found in your library or on the Internet.

READ MORE

"Mark Twain (1835–1910)." *Perspectives in American Literature.* California State University (http://www.csustan.edu/english/reuben/pal/chap5/twain.html): *Offers an extended bibliography of critical and biographical works about Twain, as well as links to original works.*

"Mark Twain and His Circle Series." *University of Missouri* (http://press.umsystem.edu/twainser.htm): *List of texts containing Mark Twain scholarship.*

"Mark Twain and His Times" *Department of English University of Virginia,* (http://etext.lib.virginia.edu/railton/index2.html): *Site contains links to texts of Twain's works and to information about his life.*

Twain, Mark. *The Autobiography of Mark Twain.* Ed. Charles Neider. New York: HarperCollins, 1990.

The Men We Carry in Our Minds

Scott Russell Sanders

Scott Russell Sanders (b. 1945) was born in Tennessee and is now a full professor of English at Indiana University. Among his favorite subjects are nature and the American wilderness, about which he has written several books, including Wilderness Plots: Tales about the Settlement of the American Land *(1983),* Audubon's Early Years *(1984), and* In Limestone Country *(1985). His most recent works include* Staying Put: Making a Home in a Restless World *(1993) and* Writing from the Center *(1995). In 2006, he published* A Private History of Awe, *a memoir. Sanders first published "The Men We Carry in Our Minds" in a periodical called the* Milkweed Chronicle *in 1984. It also has been anthologized in Sanders's* Paradise of Bombs, *a collection of essays on violence, which was published in 1987.*

Though relatively brief, "The Men We Carry in Our Minds" is a complex series of insights woven together into a brilliant and beautiful tapestry that helps shed light on the images of men in today's society and on the way men and women view each other.

VOCABULARY

sodden, acrid, boll-weevil, overseers, emblem, bafflement, fretted, iron-clad, expansiveness

The first men, besides my father, I remember seeing were black convicts 1 and white guards, in the cottonfield across the road from our farm on the outskirts of Memphis. I must have been three or four. The prisoners wore dingy gray-and-black zebra suits, heavy as canvas, sodden with sweat. Hatless, stooped, they chopped weeds in the fierce heat, row after row, breathing the acrid dust of boll-weevil poison. The overseers wore dazzling white shirts and broad shadowy hats. The oiled barrels of their shotguns flashed in the sunlight. Their faces in memory are utterly blank. Of course those men, white and black, have become for me an emblem of racial hatred. But they have also come to stand for the twin poles of my early vision of manhood—the brute toiling animal and the boss.

2   When I was a boy, the men I knew labored with their bodies. They were marginal farmers, just scraping by, or welders, steel workers, carpenters; they swept floors, dug ditches, mined coal, or drove trucks, their forearms ropy with muscle; they trained horses, stoked furnaces, built tires, stood on assembly lines wrestling parts onto cars and refrigerators. They got up before light, worked all day long whatever the weather, and when they came home at night they looked as though somebody had been whipping them. In the evenings and on weekends they worked on their own places, tilling gardens that were lumpy with clay, fixing broken-down cars, hammering on houses that were always too drafty, too leaky, too small.

3   The bodies of the men I knew were twisted and maimed in ways visible and invisible. The nails of their hands were black and split, the hands tattooed with scars. Some had lost fingers. Heavy lifting had given many of them finicky backs and guts weak from hernias. Racing against conveyor belts had given them ulcers. Their ankles and knees ached from years of standing on concrete. Anyone who had worked for long around machines was hard of hearing. They squinted, and the skin of their faces was creased like the leather of old work gloves. There were times, studying them, when I dreaded growing up. Most of them coughed, from dust or cigarettes, and most of them drank cheap wine or whiskey, so their eyes looked bloodshot and bruised. The fathers of my friends always seemed older than the mothers. Men wore out sooner. Only women lived into old age.

4   As a boy I also knew another sort of men, who did not sweat and break down like mules. They were soldiers, and so far as I could tell they scarcely worked at all. During my early school years we lived on a military base, an arsenal in Ohio, and every day I saw GIs in the guard-shacks, on the stoops of barracks, at the wheels of olive drab Chevrolets. The chief fact of their lives was boredom. Long after I left the Arsenal I came to recognize the sour smell the soldiers gave off as that of souls in limbo. They were all waiting—for wars, for transfers, for leaves, for promotions, for the end of their hitch—like so many braves waiting for the hunt to begin. Unlike the warriors of older tribes, however, they would have no say about when the battle would start or how it would be waged. Their waiting was broken only when they practiced for war. They fired guns at targets, drove tanks across the churned-up fields of the military reservation, set off bombs in the wrecks of old fighter planes. I knew this was all play. But I also felt certain that when the hour for killing arrived, they would kill. When the real shooting started, many of them would die. This was what soldiers were *for*, just as a hammer was for driving nails.

Warriors and toilers: those seemed, in my boyhood vision, to be the 5 chief destinies for men. They weren't the only destinies, as I learned from having a few male teachers, from reading books, and from watching television. But the men on television—the politicians, the astronauts, the generals, the savvy lawyers, the philosophical doctors, the bosses who gave orders to bothsoldiers and laborers—seemed as remote and unreal to me as the figures in tapestries. I could no more imagine growing up to become one of these cool, potent creatures than I could imagine becoming a prince.

A nearer and more hopeful example was that of my father, who had 6 escaped from a red-dirt farm to a tire factory, and from the assembly line to the front office. Eventually he dressed in a white shirt and tie. He carried himself as if he had been born to work with his mind. But his body, remembering the earlier years of slogging work, began to give out on him in his fifties, and it quit on him entirely before he turned sixty-five. Even such partial escape from man's fate as he had accomplished did not seem possible for most of the boys I knew. They joined the Army, stood in line for jobs in the smoky plants, helped build highways. They were bound to work as their fathers had worked, killing themselves or preparing to kill others.

A scholarship enabled me not only to attend college, a rare enough 7 feat in my circle, but even to study in a university meant for the children of the rich. Here I met for the first time young men who had assumed from birth that they would lead lives of comfort and power. And for the first time I met women who told me that men were guilty of having kept all the joys and privileges of the earth for themselves. I was baffled. What privileges? What joys? I thought about the maimed, dismal lives of most of the men back home. What had they stolen from their wives and daughters? The right to go five days a week, twelve months a year, for thirty or forty years to a steel mill or a coal mine? The right to drop bombs and die in war? The right to feel every leak in the roof, every gap in the fence, every cough in the engine, as a wound they must mend? The right to feel, when the layoff comes or the plant shuts down, not only afraid but ashamed?

I was slow to understand the deep grievances of women. This was 8 because, as a boy, I had envied them. Before college, the only people I had ever known who were interested in art or music or literature, the only ones who read books, the only ones who ever seemed to enjoy a sense of ease and grace were the mothers and daughters. Like the menfolk, they fretted about money, they scrimped and made-do. But, when the pay stopped coming in, they were not the ones who had failed. Nor did they have to go to war, and that seemed to me a blessed fact. By comparison with the narrow, ironclad days of fathers, there was an expansiveness, I thought, in the days of mothers. They went to see neighbors, to shop in town, to run errands at school, at the library, at church. No doubt, had I looked harder at their lives, I would have envied them less. It was not my fate to become a woman, so it was easier for me to see the graces. Few of them held jobs outside the home, and those who did filled thankless roles as clerks and waitresses. I didn't see, then, what a prison a house could be, since houses seemed to me brighter, handsomer places than any factory. I did not realize—because such things were never spoken of—how often women suffered from men's bullying. I did learn about the wretchedness of abandoned wives, single mothers, widows; but I also learned about the wretchedness of lone men. Even then I could see how exhausting it was for a mother to cater all day to the needs of young children. But if I had been asked, as a boy, to choose between tending a baby and tending a machine, I think I would have chosen the baby. (Having now tended both, I know I would choose the baby.)

9   So I was baffled when the women at college accused me and my sex of having cornered the world's pleasures. I think something like my baf- flement has been felt by other boys (and by girls as well) who grew up in dirt-poor farm country, in mining country, in black ghettos, in Hispanic barrios, in the shadows of factories, in Third World nations—any place where the fate of men is as grim and bleak as the fate of women. Toilers and warriors. I realize now how ancient these identities are, how deep the tug they exert on men, the undertow of a thousand generations. The miseries I saw, as a boy, in the lives of nearly all men I continue to see in the lives of many—the body-breaking toil, the tedium, the call to be tough, the humiliating powerlessness, the battle for a living and for territory.

10   When the women I met at college thought about the joys and privi- leges of men, they did not carry in their minds the sort of men I had known in my childhood. They thought of their fathers, who were bankers, physicians, architects, stockbrokers, the big wheels of the big cities. These fathers rode the train to work or drove cars that cost more than any of my childhood houses. They were attended from morning to night by female helpers, wives and nurses and secretaries. They were never laid off, never short of cash at month's end, never lined up for welfare. These fathers made decisions that mattered. They ran the world.

11   The daughters of such men wanted to share in this power, this glory. So did I. They yearned for a say over their future, for jobs worthy of their abilities, for the right to live at peace, unmolested, whole. Yes, I thought, yes yes. The difference between me and these daughters was that they saw me, because of my sex, as destined from birth to become like their fathers, and therefore as an enemy to their desires. But I knew better. I wasn't an enemy, in fact or in feeling. I was an ally. If I had known, then, how to tell them so, would they have believed me? Would they now?

1984

QUESTIONS FOR DISCUSSION

Content

a. In what ways did the soldiers Sanders observed in his youth resemble the laborers he knew? In what ways were they different?
b. Consider the essay's title. What other people does Sanders contrast in this essay?
c. How did Sanders's view of women change after he went to college? Why did it change?
d. Why was the author "slow to understand the deep grievances of women" (paragraph 8)?
e. What was the vision of men carried by the women the author met at college?
f. In what way or ways was the author like these women?
g. What are the purpose and thesis of this essay?

Strategy and Style

h. How would you describe this essay's tone and its audience?
i. Where in this selection does the author use description? Classification?
j. The essay is enriched by Sanders's use of figurative language. Find examples of metaphor, simile, or other figures of speech, and explain how they help the author make or develop a point.
k. Why does the author begin this piece with an image of "racial hatred"? Is his introduction effective? Why or why not?
l. Why does Sanders end this essay with a question? Does this question provide a logical conclusion to what has come before, or does it open up a new topic of discussion?

ENGAGING THE TEXT

a. What is the first image of men or women that you held in your mind? Explain one way in which that image changed as you matured. Refer to Sanders's essay in your response.
b. Sanders says that the "bodies of the men [he] knew were twisted and maimed in ways visible and invisible" (paragraph 3), and he provides examples of the "visible" ways. What might some of the "invisible" ways be?

SUGGESTIONS FOR SUSTAINED WRITING

a. Have you ever misjudged a person and then realized your error after getting to know him or her better? List details or freewrite for

10 minutes to gather information that you then turn into an essay contrasting your two perceptions of this individual. As an alternative, write an essay in which you contrast the way in which you now perceive or interact with members of the opposite sex with the way you perceived or interacted with them when you were an adolescent.

b. Attending college should teach us more than the facts, ideas, and skills contained within our academic coursework. It should change our vision of and attitudes toward other people. Explain a major change in how you perceive, work with, or interact with others. For additional insight, read the essay by Brent Staples in Chapter 7.

c. In paragraph 2, Sanders mentions men who worked at various types of physical labor. Do some research in the library or on the Internet about an occupation that requires or required hard physical labor in difficult conditions, whether in this country or abroad. For example, focus on contemporary coal miners, truck drivers, construction workers, or oil drillers. You might also discuss the immigrant dressmaker who worked in America's sweatshop factories in the 1920s or the "Third World" child who, at the dawn of the twenty-first century, still toils 12 hours a day in horrible conditions for less than a living wage. Write an essay that explains how hard these people work(ed) and/or the living standards they enjoy(ed) or endure(d).

READ MORE

Sanders, Scott Russell. *A Conservationist Manifesto*. Bloomington: Indiana University Press, 2009. *An acclaimed and beautifully written defense of conservation.*

Sanders, Scott Russell. *A Private History of Awe*. New York: North Point Press, 2006. *A personal memoir of Russell's early years that has received critical acclaim.*

"Scott Russell Sanders" (http://www.scottrussellsanders.com): *Sanders's official website.*

Neat People vs. Sloppy People
Suzanne Britt

Suzanne Britt teaches English at Meredith College in North Carolina. Her works have appeared in Newsweek, *the* Boston Globe, *and the* New York Times. *Currently she writes a column for* North Carolina Gardens and Homes *and for the* Dickens Dispatch, *a newsletter for fans of Charles Dickens. In addition to two composition texts, she has published two collections of essays,* Skinny People Are Dull and Crunchy Like Carrots *(1982) and* Show and Tell *(1983), from which this selection is taken.*

In "Neat People vs. Sloppy People," Britt makes excellent use of contrast to define and examine two types of compulsive behavior. Often indulging in hyperbole, she creates an animated vision, which entertains and provides interesting glimpses into the human character.

VOCABULARY

stupendous, Never-Never Land, métier, meticulously

I've finally figured out the difference between neat people and sloppy 1
people. The distinction is, as always, moral. Neat people are lazier and
meaner than sloppy people.

Sloppy people, you see, are not really sloppy. Their sloppiness is merely 2
the unfortunate consequence of their extreme moral rectitude. Sloppy
people carry in their mind's eye a heavenly vision, a precise plan, that is so
stupendous, so perfect, it can't be achieved in this world or the next.

Sloppy people live in Never-Never Land. Someday is their métier. 3
Someday they are planning to alphabetize all their books and set up home
catalogs. Someday they will go through their wardrobes and mark certain
items for tentative mending and certain items for passing on to relatives
of similar shape and size. Someday sloppy people will make family scrap-
books into which they will put newspaper clippings, postcards, locks of
hair, and the dried corsage from their senior prom. Someday they will file
everything on the surface of their desks, including the cash receipts from
coffee purchases at the snack shop. Someday they will sit down and read
all the back issues of the *New Yorker*.

For all these noble reasons and more, sloppy people never get neat. 4
They aim too high and wide. They save everything, planning someday
to file, order, and straighten out the world. But while these ambitious
plans take clearer and clearer shape in their heads, the books spill from
the shelves onto the floor, the clothes pile up in the hamper and closet,
the family mementos accumulate in every drawer, the surface of the desk
is buried under mounds of paper and the unread magazines threaten to
reach the ceiling.

Sloppy people can't bear to part with anything. They give loving 5
attention to every detail. When sloppy people say they're going to tackle
the surface of the desk, they really mean it. Not a paper will go unturned;
not a rubber band will go unboxed. Four hours or two weeks into the
excavation, the desk looks exactly the same, primarily because the sloppy
person is meticulously creating new piles of papers with new headings

and scrupulously stopping to read all the old book catalogs before he throws them away. A neat person would just bulldoze the desk.

6   Neat people are bums and clods at heart. They have cavalier attitudes toward possessions, including family heirlooms. Everything is just another dustcatcher to them. If anything collects dust, it's got to go and that's that. Neat people will toy with the idea of throwing the children out of the house just to cut down on the clutter.

7   Neat people don't care about process. They like results. What they want to do is get the whole thing over with so they can sit down and watch the rasslin' on TV. Neat people operate on two unvarying principles: Never handle any item twice, and throw everything away.

8   The only thing messy in a neat person's house is the trash can. The minute something comes to a neat person's hand, he will look at it, try to decide if it has immediate use and, finding none, throw it in the trash.

9   Neat people are especially vicious with mail. They never go through their mail unless they are standing directly over a trash can. If the trash can is beside the mailbox, even better. All ads, catalogs, pleas for charitable contributions, church bulletins and money-saving coupons go straight into the trash can without being opened. All letters from home, postcards from Europe, bills and paychecks are opened, immediately responded to, then dropped in the trash can. Neat people keep their receipts only for tax purposes. That's it. No sentimental salvaging of birthday cards or the last letter a dying relative ever wrote. Into the trash it goes.

10   Neat people place neatness above everything, even economics. They are incredibly wasteful. Neat people throw away several toys every time they walk through the den. I knew a neat person once who threw away a perfectly good dish drainer because it had mold on it. The drainer was too much trouble to wash. And neat people sell their furniture when they move. They will sell a La-Z-Boy recliner while you are reclining in it.

11   Neat people are no good to borrow from. Neat people buy everything in expensive little single portions. They get their flour and sugar in two-pound bags. They wouldn't consider clipping a coupon, saving a leftover, reusing plastic nondairy whipped cream containers or rinsing off tin foil and draping it over the unmoldy dish drainer. You can never borrow a neat person's newspaper to see what's playing at the movies. Neat people have the paper all wadded up and in the trash by 7:05 A.M.

12   Neat people cut a clean swath through the organic as well as the inorganic world. People, animals, and things are all one to them. They are so insensitive. After they've finished with the pantry, the medicine cabinet, and the attic, they will throw out the red geranium (too many leaves), sell the dog (too many fleas), and send the children off to boarding school (too many scuffmarks on the hardwood floors).

1983

QUESTIONS FOR DISCUSSION

Content

a. What does Britt mean by the moral distinction between neat and sloppy people? How is this a moral distinction? Why, according to Britt's implication, are neat people immoral?

b. Do you agree that "sloppiness is merely the unfortunate consequence of . . . extreme moral rectitude" (paragraph 2)? Where is this idea repeated?

c. What kind of neatness and sloppiness is the author actually talking about? She focuses on clutter, but does she imply other kinds of neatness and sloppiness?

d. Is Britt a neat or a sloppy person? How can you tell from the clues she gives in the essay?

e. On the surface, this essay might seem frivolous. Are there serious implications to it?

f. Does the author ever prove that neat people are lazy and mean and that sloppy people are less so?

Strategy and Style

g. Analyze the vocabulary Britt uses to discuss sloppy people. How would you describe Britt's tone in this part of the essay? What tone does she use to discuss neat people?

h. Comment on her use of generalizations. Why does she make statements such as "Neat people place neatness above everything, even economics" (paragraph 10)?

i. Britt calls neat people "bums and clods at heart" (paragraph 6). Is she being harsh? If so, does her attitude destroy her credibility, or does it serve another purpose?

j. Where does Britt use irony especially well? How does the irony establish the tone of the piece?

ENGAGING THE TEXT

a. Define yourself as neat or sloppy. Write a short description of your bedroom, your closet, or the inside of your car; talk about your grooming habits and your clothing; or discuss the way you go about completing a common task such as preparing a meal, painting a bedroom, or packing a suitcase.

b. Britt attributes various character traits to neat and sloppy people. In paragraph 7, for example, she says that "Neat people don't care about process." Challenge one such assertion by using personal experience as a source of information.

SUGGESTIONS FOR SUSTAINED WRITING

a. Turn the tables on Britt and write an essay in which you argue that sloppy people are immoral, neat people moral. Begin by trying to answer each of Britt's assertions about neat people. Then explain what is immoral about sloppiness. You might find inspiration and information for this assignment in your responses to the second item under Engaging the Text.

b. Select two other oppositions into which people, animals, or objects can be divided, and write an essay in which you compare and contrast them. Depending on your topic, consider using the subject-by-subject pattern, seen in Britt's essay, to organize your work.

c. Write an essay in which you contrast two types of people, behaviors, or personalities. For example, contrast the introverted college student with his or her extroverted classmate; a leader and a follower; or an emotional giver and an emotional taker. If this assignment doesn't interest you, try contrasting two types of personalities or people that are often confused, such as a sociopath and a psychopath, a neurotic and a psychotic, a gourmet and a gourmand, an egoist and an egotist, or an atheist and an agnostic.

READ MORE

Laskin, David. "Neatness Counts" (http://www.dadmag.com/dadskills/neatness_counts.php): *Essay in which a father talks about neatness with his teenagers.*

Trunk, Penelope. "Neatness Counts: A Messy Desk Can Hurt Your Career" (http://blog.penelopetrunk.com/2003/01/06/neatness-counts-a-messy-desk-can-hurt-your-career): *Penelope Trunk's Brazen Careerist.*

Two Ways to Belong in America

Bharati Mukherjee

Born in Calcutta, India, in 1940, Bharati Mukherjee took a bachelor's and a master's degree from the University of Calcutta. Her family moved to Britain in 1947, and she immigrated to the United States in 1961 to attend the University of Iowa, where she took a master's in fine arts in 1968 and a doctorate in English and comparative literature in 1969. Now a U.S. citizen, she teaches at the University of California, Berkeley. Mukherjee has published several novels that have earned her international acclaim. They include Jasmine *(1989),* The Holder of the World *(1993),* Leave It to Me *(1997),* Desirable Daughters *(2002), and* The Tree Bride *(2004). In 1988, she won the National Book Critics Award for her collection of short stories* The Middleman and Other Stories.

One of Mukherjee's major concerns has to do with the often confusing roles Indian women are expected to play and the cultural challenges they face after relocating in the United States. In addition, she focuses on questions having to do with immigration and with immigration policies in the United States. "Two Ways to Belong in America," which was first published in the New York Times *in 1996, was written in response to proposed changes in legislation governing immigration and resident aliens. One of these changes would have resulted in denying legal aliens Social Security benefits. However, the essay clearly evolved beyond that into an exploration and contrast of identities, those of her sister and herself.*

VOCABULARY

case-observant, erasure, mythic, scapegoating, discretion, curtailing, expatriate, hysteria, divergence, trauma

This is a tale of two sisters from Calcutta, Mira and Bharati, who have 1 lived in the United States for some 35 years, but who find themselves on different sides in the current debate over the status of immigrants. I am an American citizen and she is not. I am moved that thousands of long-term residents are finally taking the oath of citizenship. She is not.

Mira arrived in Detroit in 1960 to study child psychology and pre- 2 school education. I followed her a year later to study creative writing at the University of Iowa. When we left India, we were almost identical in appearance and attitude. We dressed alike, in saris; we expressed identical views on politics, social issues, love and marriage in the same Calcutta convent-school accent. We would endure our two years in America, secure our degrees, then return to India to marry the grooms of our father's choosing.

Instead, Mira married an Indian student in 1962 who was getting 3 his business administration degree at Wayne State University. They soon acquired the labor certifications necessary for the green card of hassle-free residence and employment.

Mira still lives in Detroit, works in the Southfield, Mich., school sys- 4 tem, and has become nationally recognized for her contributions in the fields of pre-school education and parent-teacher relationships. After 36 years as a legal immigrant in this country, she clings passionately to her Indian citizenship and hopes to go home to India when she retires.

In Iowa City in 1963, I married a fellow student, an American of 5 Canadian parentage. Because of the accident of his North Dakota birth, I bypassed labor-certification requirements and the race-related "quota" system that favored the applicant's country of origin over his or her merit. I was prepared for (and even welcomed) the emotional strain that came with marrying outside my ethnic community. In 33 years of marriage, we have lived in every part of North America. By choosing a husband who was not my father's selection, I was opting for fluidity, self-invention, blue jeans and T-shirts, and renouncing 3000 years (at least) of caste-observant, "pure culture" marriage in the Mukherjee family. My books have often been read as unapologetic (and in some quarters overenthusiastic) texts for cultural and psychological "mongrelization." It's a word I celebrate.

6   Mira and I have stayed sisterly close by phone. In our regular Sunday morning conversations, we are unguardedly affectionate. I am her only blood relative on this continent. We expect to see each other through the looming crises of aging and ill health without being asked. Long before Vice President Gore's "Citizenship U.S.A." drive, we'd had our polite arguments over the ethics of retaining an overseas citizenship while expecting the permanent protection and economic benefits that come with living and working in America.

7   Like well-raised sisters, we never said what was really on our minds, but we probably pitied one another. She, for the lack of structure in my life, the erasure of Indianness, the absence of an unvarying daily core. I, for the narrowness of her perspective, her uninvolvement with the mythic depths or the superficial pop culture of this society. But, now, with the scapegoating of "aliens" (documented or illegal) on the increase, and the targeting of long-term legal immigrants like Mira for new scrutiny and new self-consciousness, she and I find ourselves unable to maintain the same polite discretion. We were always unacknowledged adversaries, and we are now, more than ever, sisters.

8   "I feel used," Mira raged on the phone the other night. "I feel manipulated and discarded. This is such an unfair way to treat a person who was invited to stay and work here because of her talent. My employer went to the I.N.S. and petitioned for the labor certification. For over 30 years, I've invested my creativity and professional skills into the improvement of *this* country's pre-school system. I've obeyed all the rules, I've paid my taxes, I love my work, I love my students, I love the friends I've made. How dare America now change its rules in midstream? If America wants to make new rules curtailing benefits of legal immigrants, they should apply only to immigrants who arrive after those rules are already in place."

9   To my ears, it sounded like the description of a long-enduring, comfortable yet loveless marriage, without risk or recklessness. Have we the right to demand, and to expect, that we be loved? (That, to me, is the subtext of the arguments by immigration advocates.) My sister is an expatriate, professionally generous and creative, socially courteous and gracious, and that's as far as her Americanization can go. She is here to maintain an identity, not to transform it.

I asked her if she would follow the example of others who have 10
decided to become citizens because of the anti-immigration bills in
Congress. And here, she surprised me. "If America wants to play the
manipulative game, I'll play it too," she snapped. "I'll become a U.S. citizen for now, then change back to Indian when I'm ready to go home. I feel
some kind of irrational attachment to India that I don't to America. Until
all this hysteria against legal immigrants, I was totally happy. Having my
green card meant I could visit any place in the world I wanted to and then
come back to a job that's satisfying and that I do very well."

In one family, from two sisters alike as peas in a pod, there could not 11
be a wider divergence of immigrant experience. America spoke to me—I
married it—I embraced the demotion from expatriate aristocrat to immigrant nobody, surrendering those thousands of years of "pure culture,"
the saris, the delightfully accented English. She retained them all. Which
of us is the freak?

Mira's voice, I realize, is the voice not just of the immigrant South 12
Asian community but of an immigrant community of the millions who
have stayed rooted in one job, one city, one house, one ancestral culture,
one cuisine, for the entirety of their productive years. She speaks for
greater numbers than I possibly can. Only the fluency of her English
and the anger, rather than fear, born of confidence from her education,
differentiate her from the seamstresses, the domestics, the technicians,
the shop owners, the millions of hard-working but effectively silenced
documented immigrants as well as their less fortunate "illegal" brothers
and sisters.

Nearly 20 years ago, when I was living in my husband's ancestral 13
homeland of Canada, I was always well-employed but never allowed to
feel part of the local Quebec or larger Canadian society. Then, through
a Green Paper that invited a national referendum on the unwanted side
effects of "nontraditional" immigration, the Government officially turned
against its immigrant communities, particularly those from South Asia.

I felt then the same sense of betrayal that Mira feels now. I will never 14
forget the pain of that sudden turning, and the casual racist outbursts
the Green Paper elicited. That sense of betrayal had its desired effect and
drove me, and thousands like me, from the country.

Mira and I differ, however, in the ways in which we hope to interact 15
with the country that we have chosen to live in. She is happier to live
in America as expatriate Indian than as an immigrant American. I need
to feel like a part of the community I have adopted (as I tried to feel in
Canada as well). I need to put roots down, to vote and make the difference
that I can. The price that the immigrant willingly pays, and that the exile
avoids, is the trauma of self-transformation.

1996

QUESTIONS FOR DISCUSSION

Content

a. What is Mukherjee's thesis?
b. This piece was originally written to address various changes in immigration laws. Where in the essay does the author discuss such concerns?
c. What reasons does the author's sister give for not wanting to become a citizen of the United States?
d. In paragraph 5, the author explains that she celebrates the word *mongrelization*. What does she mean by this word, and why does she celebrate it?
e. How does Mukherjee respond to her sister's claim that she feels "manipulated" (see paragraphs 8–12)?
f. This essay is not all contrast. On what points do the two sisters agree?

Strategy and Style

g. What is the predominant method of organization in this essay: subject-by-subject or point-by-point? Why is this method appropriate to the essay?
h. Why does the author talk about her experiences in Canada?
i. What is the effect of Mukherjee's using her sister's own words to present her feelings as an immigrant in America?

ENGAGING THE TEXT

a. Summarize Mukherjee's arguments for becoming a citizen. Summarize her sister's arguments against opting for citizenship.
b. If you had the opportunity to speak with either Mukherjee or her sister on questions concerning immigration policy, what might you say to each of them? What questions might you ask each?

SUGGESTIONS FOR SUSTAINED WRITING

a. Focusing on an important question or issue about which you disagree with a sibling or other close relative, write a contrast essay that presents both sides as fairly and objectively as you can. For example, you might write about gay marriage, illegal immigration, America's war on terror, premarital sex, embryonic stem-cell research, late-term abortion, or any other major issue often in the news. Then again, you might write about your opinions concerning something far more personal—such as the kinds of people with whom you choose to associate, the kinds of music and movies you like, or your opinions of one or more of your relatives.

b. Write an essay in which you contrast the roles of men and women in your family. Does your family have different expectations for members of each sex? Do they treat the young men differently from the way they treat women? Are men supposed to act in certain ways and women in others? Are members of one sex admired for doing things that members of the other might be condemned for? One way to get inspiration for this essay is to read the essay by Scott Russell Sanders that also appears in this chapter.

c. Using library and Internet sources, write an essay in which you contrast two views on an issue concerning immigration to the United States. For example, you might choose to write about the notion that there should be a moratorium on all immigration—legal and illegal. Or you might contrast two ways of dealing with illegal immigration. Then again, you might research opinions on whether children born in the United States to undocumented parents should be granted citizenship or whether undocumented immigrants should be issued driver's licenses or be granted government benefits such as free schooling, health care, and Social Security.

READ MORE

Mukherjee and Her Works

Mukherjee, Bharati. *The Middleman and Other Stories*. New York: Grove Press, 1988. *A collection of stories, each one of which is about a different individual who finds him/herself in a new cultural and spiritual environment.*

Weich, Dave. "Bharati Mukherjee Runs the West Coast Offense." (http:// www.powells.com/authors/mukherjee.html): *Powell's Books interview with the author.*

Soderberg, Erin. "Bharati Mukherjee" (http://voices.cla.umn.edu/artist-pages/mukherjee_bharati.php): *Voices from the Gaps, University of Minnesota. A detailed essay discussing the author's life and works. Several useful links are included.*

Immigration

"South Asian Diaspora" (http://www.lib.berkeley.edu/SSEAL/SouthAsia/diaspora.html): *Online center maintained by the University of California, Berkeley, South/Southeast Asia Library, with information on Mukherjee and other South Asian writers.*

American Immigration Council Homepage. American Immigration Council, (http://www.americanimmigrationcouncil.org): *The mission of this organization (formerly the American Immigration Law Foundation) is to "strengthen America by honoring our immigrant history and shaping how Americans think and act towards immigration now and in the future."*

Federation for American Immigration Reform Homepage (http://www.fairus.org/site/PageServer): *This organization is "a national, nonprofit, public-interest, membership organization of concerned citizens who share a common belief that our nation's immigration policies must be reformed to serve the national interest."*

China's Biggest Gamble: Can It Have Capitalism without Democracy? A Prediction

Henry Blodget

Henry Blodget (b. 1966) took a bachelor's degree at Yale University and later completed a financial training course sponsored by Prudential Securities. By 2000, Blodget had become a star on Wall Street. He was named the Street's best Internet securities analyst both by Institutional Investor *and by* The Street.com, *an Internet site catering to the investment community.*

After some financial setbacks, Blodget started Cherry Hill Research, a financial consulting firm that he now heads. He is also the co-founder and editor of Silicon Valley Insider, an Internet site that covers the world of finance, and the editor of Internet Outsider, a financial blog devoted to the high-tech sector. Blodget has contributed to several major newspapers and magazines, including Newsweek, the New York Times, Fortune, Forbes Online, *and the* Financial Times. *He is also the author of* The Wall Street Self-Defense Manual: A Consumer's Guide to Investing *(2007). This essay was posted on Slate.com, an Internet magazine, in April 2005.*

VOCABULARY

choreographed, Cultural-Revolution, destabilizing, allocation, ravaged, repercussions, buttressing, penchant, oligarchs

1   On my last evening in Beijing, I walked west on the long blocks of the city's main drag toward Tiananmen Square. The sun was setting when I arrived, and, on the north side of the road, beneath the portrait of

Chairman Mao on the Gate of Heavenly Peace, crowds of tourists were streaming out of the Forbidden City. On the south side, in Tiananmen Square itself, kites and flags were flying, and entrepreneurs posing as "students" were cruising around entreating foreigners to visit a nearby art "exhibit" in which their works were purportedly displayed. The students' story was clever and well-choreographed, but I'd already fallen for it once that day (enduring a guided tour of machine-made paintings being sold to fund a "trip to America"). So, I just wandered around the square and watched the sun set over the Chinese flag.

The story of what happened in Tiananmen in June of 1989 is different   2 in China than the one we tell in the United States. In America, we remember the student protests as a plea for democracy, for *our* form of government (who has forgotten the students' mock-up of the Statue of Liberty?). But in China, people describe the students' goals as not *democracy*, per se, but as the end to corruption, the ability to air grievances, and the right to more control over their lives (or, as one person put it, the right to refuse to be shipped off to some dumpy factory for 40 years—a fate that would drive anyone into the streets). Although these ideals were closer to our form of government than China's was in 1989, they were not the "one man, one vote" system we hold so dear, the one that, in America, we herald the Tiananmen students as having died for. And, by local estimation, Chinese have gotten much of what the students were really hoping for 16 years ago.

In Beijing, as in Shanghai, the businesspeople I spoke to seemed more   3 concerned about preserving their ability to make money than about gaining the ability to vote leaders out of office or to express themselves however they pleased. One expects businesspeople to tend toward this end of the idealism scale, but in the U.S., democracy and freedom of speech are so fundamental to our sense of ourselves and our country that even our businesspeople can't imagine life (or economic success) without them. So, it is interesting to see China succeeding—on the surface, anyway—without them.

The question remains: Can the Chinese model—capitalism without   4 elections or free expression—succeed forever? The common Western theory is that the more China's wealth grows, the more the pressure will build, until one day, the Communist Party's chokehold on power will break and American-style freedom of speech and democracy will follow (or, alternatively, that, in a desperate attempt to preserve itself, the party will revert to Cultural Revolution–style oppression and stop the economy cold). Both theories presume that free speech and elections are high on the average Chinese citizen's agenda, but, for now, a strong economy seems to take priority. ("The average guy wants to buy a car, eat vitamins, and get his kids into Berkeley," said one Beijing entrepreneur. "As long as the government doesn't screw that up, he's willing to play along.")

The Western theories also presume that the transition from socialism to capitalism inevitably includes a transition from one-party rule to elected, multi-party democracy, but perhaps this isn't so. Especially when the leaders of the one party know exactly what keeps them in power—fat consumer wallets—and are willing to go to extraordinary lengths to control the spread of potentially destabilizing ideas.

5   For China's economy to continue to thrive—and for its companies to grow strong enough to compete globally on something other than price—the government will have to continue to reduce corruption, strengthen property and legal rights, and develop a more efficient capital allocation system (including a securities market in which government connections are not a prerequisite for raising cash). In a democracy with a free press, the pressure that forces such changes often comes from decision-makers' fear of being ravaged in the media and/or voted out of office. In China, the repercussions may not be so immediate and direct, but based on the government's actions over the last decade, it knows well that continued economic reform and success are not only good for the country but key to its survival. The pressure is there, in other words, with or without the media, and the government continues to make progress in reducing corruption and buttressing legal and property rights.

6   The government also seems to be deciding that, at least in the realm of business and finance, greater press freedom helps advance its economic goals and lessen its regulatory burden. Business journalism keeps companies honest and makes customers and investors comfortable that they at least have a forum in which to complain. Such freedom is not all good—in the media's eagerness to advance its own economic agenda, it often manufactures scandals where there are none and spins normal free-market processes into institutional or regulatory failures. But just as a free market is more effective than central planning at, say, managing crop production and pricing, a free press enhances the regulatory abilities of a government and creates the information flow that capitalism requires.

7   But the Chinese government will probably continue to stifle the press's freedom to criticize it. As demonstrated by the government's subtle, sophisticated control of all forms of media and its ongoing penchant for firing, beating up, jailing, and perhaps even killing journalists who cross vaguely defined lines, we won't see a Michael Moore of China anytime soon...But I doubt this will hinder the ongoing development of China's vibrant economy.

8   The key test of China's version of capitalism, of course, will be during the bust that inevitably will follow the current boom (some day). If elections were held today, many in China suggest, the current leaders would win the popular vote. On the whole, thanks to the economy, people feel they have done a good job. During the bust, the pressure for change will increase, with or without the press. If the government is to

maintain control in such an environment, it will probably have to engage in a practice that has long been a fixture of oligarchies and democracies alike: blame. As long as the countrywide pain can be laid at the feet of an individual or group, instead of the system—and as long as the scapegoats can be tossed out on their respective rears—the public pressure for revolutionary change can probably be controlled. If China can survive that inevitable economic crisis without a political uprising, we will probably be able to conclude that a dynamic free-market economy need not, in fact, go hand in hand with democracy.

QUESTIONS FOR DISCUSSION

Content

a. In your own words, state Blodget's thesis. Before you do this, you might want to reread paragraph 8.
b. Look up Chairman Mao, the Forbidden City, and Tiananmen Square on the Internet or in the library. Make sure you understand their significance to this essay.
c. Why does China's government want to continue "to make progress in reducing corruption and buttressing legal and property rights" (paragraph 6)?
d. Explain the difference between American perceptions and Chinese perceptions about what happened in Tiananmen Square.
e. What does Blodget mean by the "idealism scale" in paragraph 3?
f. Why does the author claim that it is interesting to see China succeeding without "democracy and freedom of speech" (paragraph 3)? In what sense is it succeeding? What two points is the author contrasting in paragraph 5?
g. What two points is he contrasting in paragraphs 6 and 7?
h. Who is Michael Moore, and why won't we "see a Michael Moore of China anytime soon" (paragraph 7)?
i. What, according to the author, might prevent the rise of democracy and the end of one-party rule in a China that is economically prosperous?
j. What assumption or assumptions about the relationship between capitalism and democracy does the author call into question?

Strategy and Style

k. Why does the essay begin with the author's taking a walk around Tiananmen Square? What happened there that is related to the rise of limited free enterprise in China?
l. In paragraph 4, Blodget asks an important question. How is this question related to the rest of the essay?

m. Why does the author quote the Beijing entrepreneur in paragraph 4?

n. Blodget's conclusion claims that as long as the Chinese government can lay the blame for "the bust that inevitably will follow" on a specific person or group "instead of the system," it will stay in power. Why does this paragraph make an appropriate conclusion to the essay?

o. Comment on Blodget's style. Then read a few more essays posted on Slate.com to determine what kind of reader this Internet magazine targets. Is Blodget's style appropriate to Slate's intended audience?

ENGAGING THE TEXT

a. Is this essay organized subject-by-subject or point-by-point? Write a short, informal outline of the essay to support your answer.

b. Paragraph 4 uses the cause that may effect method to predict two possible outcomes resulting from current economic and political developments in China. Explain both outcomes.

SUGGESTIONS FOR SUSTAINED WRITING

a. Write an essay in which you contrast the ways in which two people accomplish the same task. For example, you might consider the management styles of two bosses you have worked for, the teaching techniques of two of your mathematics instructors, the ways in which two sets of parents raise their children, or the approaches used by two athletic coaches to inspire their teams. Rely on your own experiences and observations for information. If necessary, however, gather quotations from other people who know or have known your subjects. For example, use quotations from a classmate who studied under one or both of the instructors you are discussing. Depending on the paper's length, you might want to organize it using the subject-by-subject method.

b. In paragraph 4, a Beijing entrepreneur claims that as long as the Chinese government keeps the economy strong, the average Chinese "is willing to play along"—that is, willing to tolerate an oppressive regime. Do you know anyone (or any group) who has sacrificed his or her (its) pride, self-esteem, freedom, or moral values for financial or material gain? Explain how this came about, making sure to discuss the pressures this person or group had to face. Also explain the nature and extent of the loss suffered by your subject.

c. Blodget's essay was written several years ago. Discuss the economic and social changes China has undergone since the writing of the essay. Make sure to limit your research to sources published since 2005.

Note: Some of these might be Internet sources; make sure that all online sources are accurate, reliable, and unbiased.

If this prompt does not interest you, discuss the change in the social and economic environment of any ex-communist country (Hungary, Poland, Ukraine, or Russia, for example) since the collapse of the Soviet Union.

READ MORE

"The Chinese Economy" (http://www.asianinfo.org/asianinfo/china/ pro-economy.htm): *Links to articles on China's economy.*

Lu, Kevin. "What Is the China Model?" (http://voices.washingtonpost. com/davos-diary/2011/01/what_is_the_china_model.html): *An essay written by a reporter attending the World Economic Forum in Davos, Switzerland, in 2011.*

Like Mexicans

Gary Soto

Gary Soto (1952) was born and raised in the Mexican American community in Fresno, California. Members of the Soto family worked in the San Joaquin Valley, picking fruits and vegetables. When Soto was five years old, his father was killed in a farming accident and, when he and his two siblings got older, they too worked in the fields and factories near their hometown. Today, Soto is a spokesperson for the United Farm Workers Union, the largest agricultural-workers union in the United States.

Soto took a B.A. at Fresno State College in 1974. He started to write when he was in college, taking inspiration from contemporary poets and novelists such as James Wright, Pablo Neruda, Elmore Leonard, and Gabriel Garcia Marquez, among many others. Considering himself primarily a poet, Soto has written over 50 books for children, adolescents, and adults. His primary subject is the Mexican American experience, but he prides himself on being able to relate to the "feelings and experiences of most American kids."

Soto is the recipient of a National Endowment of the Arts fellowship, a Guggenheim fellowship, and an American Book Award. He has taught at UCLA Berkeley and UCLA Riverside. One of Soto's most acclaimed short story collections is Petty Crimes *(1998). Among his most notable novels are* Buried Onions *(1997),* The Afterlife *(2003), and* Accidental Love *(2006).*

"Like Mexicans" first appeared in Soto's Small Faces *(1986). Although it recalls a personal experience, it communicates something universal. Soto tells us about the anxiety he experienced when he made the most important decision a young person—of any race or nationality—will make: the choice of a spouse. What makes the essay even more meaningful, however, is that the woman with whom Soto fell in love was not Mexican, a fact that*

allows the author to explore a second and even more universal emotion. It is one that all young people feel as they leave their native communities in search of their place in a wider and stranger world.

VOCABULARY

meager

1 My grandmother gave me bad advice and good advice when I was in my early teens. For the bad advice, she said that I should become a barber because they made good money and listened to the radio all day. "Honey, they don't work *como buros*," she would say every time I visited her. She made the sound of donkeys braying: "Like that, honey!" For the good advice, she said that I should marry a Mexican girl. "No Okies, hijo"— she would say—. "Look my son. He marry one and they fight every day about I don't know what and I don't know what." For her, everyone who wasn't Mexican, black, or Asian were Okies. The French were Okies, the Italians in suits were Okies. When I asked about Jews, whom I had read about, she asked for a picture. I rode home on my bicycle and returned with a calendar depicting the important races of the world. *"Pues si, son Okies tambien!"* she said, nodding her head. She waved the calendar away and we went to the living room where she lectured me on the virtues of the Mexican girl: first, she could cook and, second, she acted like a woman, not a man, in her husband's home. She said she would tell me about a third when I got a little older.

2 I asked my mother about it—becoming a barber and marrying Mexican. She was in the kitchen. Steam curled from a pot of boiling beans, the radio was on, looking as squat as a loaf of bread. "Well, if you want to be a barber—they say they make good money." She slapped a round steak with a knife, her glasses slipping down with each strike. She stopped and looked up. "If you find a good Mexican girl, marry her of course." She returned to slapping the meat and I went to the backyard where my brother and David King were sitting on the lawn feeling the inside of their cheeks.

3 "This is what girls feel like," my brother said, rubbing the inside of his cheek. David put three fingers inside his mouth and scratched. I ignored them and climbed the back fence to see my best fiend, Scott, a second-generation Okie. I called him and his mother pointed to the side of the house where his bedroom was a small aluminum trailer, the kind you gawk at when they're flipped over on the freeway, wheels spinning in the air. I went around to find Scott pitching horseshoes.

4 I picked up a set of rusty ones and joined him. While we played, we talked about school and friends and record albums. The horseshoes

scuffed up dirt, sometimes ringing the iron that threw out a meager shadow like a sundial. After three argued-over games, we pulled two oranges a piece from his tree and started down the alley still talking school and friends and record albums. We pulled more oranges from the alley and talked about who we would marry. "No offense, Scott," I said with an orange slice in my mouth, "but I would never marry an Okie." We walked in step, almost touching, with a sled of shadows dragging behind us. "No, offense, Gary," Scott said, " but I would never marry a Mexican." I looked at him: a fang of orange slice showed from his munching mouth. I didn't think anything of it. He had his girl and I had mine. But our seventh-grade vision was the same: to marry, get jobs, buy cars and maybe a house if we had money left over.

We talked about our future lives until, to our surprise, we were on 5 the downtown mall, two miles from home. We bought a bag of popcorn at Penneys and sat down on a bench near the fountain watching Mexican and Okie girls pass. "That one's mine," I pointed with my chin when a girl with eyebrows arched into black rainbows ambled by. "She's cute," Scott said about a girl with yellow hair and a mouthful of gum. We dreamed aloud, our chins busy pointing out girls. We agreed that we couldn't wait to become men and lift them onto our laps.

But the woman I married was not Mexican but Japanese. It was a 6 surprise to me. For years, I went about wide-eyed in my search for the brown girl in a white dress at a dance. I searched the playground at the baseball diamond. When the girls raced for grounders, their hair bounced like something that couldn't be caught. When they sat together in the lunchroom, heads pressed together, I knew they were talking about us Mexican guys. I saw them and dreamed them. I threw my face into my pillow, making up sentences that were good as in the movies.

But when I was twenty, I fell in love with this other girl who wor- 7 ried my mother, who had my grandmother asking once again to see the calendar of the Important Races of the World. I told her I had thrown it away years before. I took a much-glanced-at snapshot from my wallet. We looked at it together, in silence. Then grandma reclined in her chair, lit a cigarette, and said, "Es pretty." She blew and asked with all her worry pushed up to her forehead: "Chinese?"

I was in love and there was no looking back. She was the one. I told 8 my mother who was slapping hamburger into patties. "Well, sure if you want to marry her," she said. But the more I talked, the more concerned she became. Later I began to worry. Was it all a mistake? "Marry a Mexican girl," I heard my mother say in my mind. I heard it a breakfast. I heard it over math problems, between Western Civilization and cultural geography. But then one afternoon while I was hitchhiking home from school, it struck me like a baseball in the back: my mother wanted me to marry someone of my own social class—a poor girl. I considered my fiancée, Carolyn, and she didn't look poor, though I knew she came from a family of farm workers and pull-yourself-up-by-your-bootstraps ranchers. I asked my brother, who was marrying Mexican poor that fall, if I should marry a poor girl. He screamed "Yeah" above his terrible guitar playing in his bedroom. I considered my sister who had married Mexican. Cousins were dating Mexican. Uncles were remarrying poor women. I asked Scott, who was still my best friend, and he said, "She's too good for you, so you better not."

9   I worried about it until Carolyn took me home to meet her parents. We drove in her Plymouth until the houses gave way to farms and ranches and finally her house fifty feet from the highway. When we pulled into the drive, I panicked and begged Carolyn to make a U-turn and go back so we could talk about it over a soda. She pinched my cheek, calling me a "silly boy." I felt better, though, when I got out of the car and saw the house: the chipped paint, a cracked window, boards for a walk to the back door. There were rusting cars near the barn. A tractor with a net of spider webs under a mulberry. A field. A bale of barbed wire like children's scribbling leaning against an empty chicken coop. Carolyn took my hand and pulled me to my future mother-in-law who was coming out to greet us.

10   We had lunch: sandwiches, potato chips, and iced tea. Carolyn and her mother talked mostly about neighbors and the congregation at the Japanese Methodist Church in West Fresno. Her father, who was in khaki work clothes, excused himself with a wave that was almost a salute and went outside. I heard a truck start, a dog bark, and the truck rattle away.

11   Carolyn's mother offered another sandwich, but I declined with a shake of my head and a smile. I looked around when I could, when I was not saying over and over that I was a college student, hinting that I could take care of her daughter. I shifted my chair. I saw newspapers piled in corners, dusty cereal boxes and vinegar bottles in corners. The wallpaper was bubbled from rain that had come in from a bad roof. Dust. Dust lay on lamp shades and window sills. These people are just like Mexicans, I thought. Poor people.

12   Carolyn's mother asked me through Carolyn if I would like a sushi. A plate of black and white things were held in front of me. I took one, wide-eyed, and turned it over like a foreign coin. I was biting into one when I saw a kitten crawl up the window screen over the sink. I chewed and the kitten opened its mouth of terror as she crawled higher, wanting in to paw the leftovers from our plates. I looked at Carolyn who said that the cat was just showing off. I looked up in time to see it fall. It crawled up, then fell again.

13   We talked for an hour and had apple pie and coffee, slowly. Finally, we got up with Carolyn taking my hand. Slightly embarrassed, I tried to pull away but her grip held me. I let her have her way as she led me down the hallway with her mother right behind me. When I opened the door, I

was startled by a kitten clinging to the screen door, its mouth screaming "cat food, dog biscuits, sushi…." I opened the door and the kitten, still holding on, whined in the language of hungry animals. When I got into Carolyn's car, I looked back: the cat was still clinging. I asked Carolyn if it were possibly hungry, but she said the cat was being silly. She started the car, waved to her mother, and bounced us over the rain-poked drive, patting my thigh for being her lover baby. Carolyn waved again. I looked back, waving, then gawking at a window screen where there were now three kittens clawing and screaming to get in. Like Mexicans, I thought. I remembered the Molinas and how the cats clung to their screens—cats they shot down with squirt guns. On the highway, I felt happy, pleased by it all. I patted Carolyn's thigh. Her people were like Mexicans, only different.

QUESTIONS FOR DISCUSSION

Content

a. In your own words, write a sentence that might serve as this essay's thesis.

b. What might *"Pues si, son Okies tambien!"* (paragraph 1) mean?

c. What is the bedroom of Soto's best friend Scott like? Why does the author tell us about it?

d. What can we conclude about the purpose of this essay from Soto's claiming that he and Scott shared a "vision" (paragraph 4)? What was that vision?

e. What important fact does Soto reveal about the kind of woman his mother wants him to marry? How does this revelation relate to his thesis?

f. What gave the young Soto the confidence to follow through with his visit to Carolyn's parents (paragraph 9)?

g. What did he learn from this visit?

h. Does Soto draw a connection between his mother and his future mother-in-law? What is that connection?

Strategy and Style

i. What is Soto driving at when he says that his grandmother would tell him about a third virtue possessed by a Mexican girl when he grew up (paragraph 1)? What does this tell us about Soto's tone, his attitude toward his subject?

j. How would you describe Soto's style? Analyze his word choice, phrasing, and sentence structure. Are they appropriate to his purpose?

k. Why does the author tell us so much about the kittens in his conclusion? Is this conclusion effective? Why or why not?

l. The author begins comparing his own family and that of Carolyn in paragraph 7. What purpose, then, do the first six paragraphs serve in this comparison?

ENGAGING THE TEXT

a. In the introduction to this piece, you read that the experiences and feelings Soto discusses relate not only to Mexican American but to all American youngsters. In paragraph 6, for example, he tells us that at night he practiced lines that he might use to impress girls, something common among young men of any ethnic group. Make a list of other experiences and emotions in this essay similar to ones you or someone you know may have had or felt. Makes specific reference to the text by quoting or paraphrasing.

b. Make a list of the details Soto uses to show that Carolyn's home and family are much like his own (paragraphs 9–11). Then, write a paragraph that explains similarities between your family and a family you know from another ethnic group. Focus on common values, concerns, problems, dreams, hopes, and/or goals. For example, in what ways is your Italian American family like the O'Briens, who live three blocks away? In what ways is your Cuban American family like your Hindu American neighbors, the Patels?

SUGGESTIONS FOR SUSTAINED WRITING

a. In item *b* under Engaging the Text, you were asked to write a paragraph in which you began comparing your family's values, concerns, problems, dreams, hopes and/or goals with those of another family from a different ethnic group. Expand this cultural analysis into a full-length essay. Begin with a thesis that identifies the common denominator or basis for your comparison. In Soto's essay, for example, it was social class. Then get as detailed as Soto does to support that thesis.

b. Read or re-read Bharati Mukherjee's "Two Ways to Belong in America," an essay that also appears in this chapter. Then, using insights and information from both Soto and Mukherjee, write an essay that explains what you think are the most significant problems facing people from various ethnic groups—whether native born or immigrants—as they try to find their place in American culture and achieve the American dream.

c. Compare and/or contrast the way in which two cultures—your own and one you would like to learn more about—mark personal milestones. For example, you might compare/contrast the way these cultures celebrate weddings, births, college graduations, or the purchase of a home. On the other hand, you could explain the rituals associated with courtship or with a young person's coming of age. You might even compare/contrast funeral customs. Whatever your topic, use your own experience and knowledge as sources of information about your own culture. In addition, complete library or Internet research, per your professor's instructions, to gather information about the other culture. Make sure to cite your sources, using a documentation style specified by your instructor.

READ MORE

About Soto and His Work

"Gary Soto" http://www.answers.com/topic/gary-soto): *Includes a useful bibliography of Soto's many writings.*

"Gary Soto." *Encyclopedia of World Biography* (http://www.notablebiographies.com/news/Sh-Z/Soto-Gary.html): *A detailed biography and critical analysis of his work, which includes a bibliography with several useful Web links.*

"Gary Soto." *Poets.org.* Academy of American Poets, (http://www.poets.org/poet.php/prmPID/230): *A shorter biography of the author.*

Soto, Gary. "How Things Work." *Modern and Contemporary American Poetry.* University of Pennsylvania (http://writing.upenn.edu/~afilreis/88/soto-how-things-work.html): *A short poem by Soto published in 1985.*

About Cross-Cultural Romances

Arnold, Harold L. "Ten Tips for Protecting Your Cross-Cultural Marriage from Outside Influences." *Marriage and Relationships. Focus on the Family* (http://www.focusonthefamily.com/marriage/strengthening_your_marriage/defending_your_marriage_from_external_stressors/ten_tips_for_protecting_your_cross_cultural_marriage.aspx).

Benlafquich, Christine. "Cross-Cultural Marriage: Tips for Successful Relationships" (http://www.suite101.com/content/cross-cultural-marriage-a48838).

Jankowiak, William R., and Edward F. Fischer. "A Cross-Cultural Perspective on Romantic Love." *Ethnology* 31.2 (1992): 149–55.

Yang, Wesley. "Paper Tigers: What Happens to All the Asian-American Overachievers When the Test-Taking Ends?" *New York*, 16 May 2011: 22–95.

Example and Illustration

Illustration is a natural habit of mind. How often have we offered a "for example" or "for instance" when, as we try to make a point, our listeners respond quizzically or simply shake their heads in disbelief? "What's so unhealthy about my diet?" demands a good friend whose eating habits you have just impugned. "For starters," you respond, "you are a frenchfry fanatic, stuffing your face with the greasy, salt-laden sticks at nearly every meal. You eat so much red meat, butter, ice cream, and candy that the *New England Journal of Medicine* ought to report your intake of cholesterol, calories, and fat. And you probably don't even remember what fruits and vegetables look like."

The three examples that explain what you meant by *unhealthy* are products of a powerful and effective technique common to all types of expository or persuasive prose. Good writers are rarely content to tell their readers what they mean; they want to show it. One way to do this is to fill your work with relevant, well-developed illustrations—concrete representations of abstract ideas.

Effective illustrations make possible the explanation of ideas that might otherwise remain vague; they enable the reader to grasp particular realities behind the abstraction, to see specific and pertinent instances of the generality. "My Aunt Tillie is the most unselfish person in town," you may exclaim. But consider how much more convincing your claim would become if you recalled the times she opened her home to people who had no place to live, donated her savings to the hospital building fund, and took time off from work to help sick friends and relatives.

The clarity and strength that illustration brings to your writing depend not on the number of examples you include—although sheer volume can be convincing—but on the degree to which each example is clear, well developed, and appropriate to your thesis. In "Black Men and Public Space," Brent Staples recalls only four brief anecdotes to explain the care with which young black men must conduct themselves in public. Each situation is narrated in such detail, however, that readers can picture themselves in his place, and they share his frustration, indignation, and sadness.

Depending on your purpose, you can choose from several kinds of examples to give your writing variety and power. Maxine Hong Kingston relates several short ghost stories to illustrate the use of such stories in her Chinese families. William Zinsser uses numerous and specific words that constitute "clutter" in public speaking and writing, Richard Wiseman tells numerous jokes to illustrate his theories about humor, and Bailey White lists, verbatim, a number of signs that forbid errant behavior.

Like most other methods of development, illustration is rarely used to the exclusion of other rhetorical techniques. In the selection by Robertson Davies, for instance, well-chosen examples develop categories (classification) through which the author sheds new and interesting light on the subject. Brent Staples makes excellent use of narration, Bailey White draws on her powers of description, and Richard Wiseman uses a convivial voice to analyze jokes.

Enjoy the selections in this chapter. They vary significantly in purpose, tone, and subject. Each is effective, however, because it explains an abstract idea in terms that enable the reader to experience the concrete realities for which that abstraction stands. Each shows us ways to grapple with even the most unwieldy notions in language that is clear, powerful, and convincing.

A Few Kind Words for Superstition

Robertson Davies

One of Canada's best-known satirists, novelists, and playwrights, Robertson Davies (1913–1995) was educated at Upper Canada College in Toronto, at Queen's University in Kingston, and at Oxford University in England. He began his career as a London actor and then worked as an editor for Saturday Night *in Toronto and for the* Examiner *in Petersborough, Ontario. He taught English at the University of Toronto and at Massey College and served as governor of the Stratford Shakespearean Festival in Stratford, Ontario. He was a fellow of the Royal Society of Canada and was a recipient of the Stephen Leacock Medal for Humor. He was also the first Canadian to become an honorary member of the American Academy and Institute of Arts and Letters. Davies published numerous plays and critical studies on drama and stagecraft and is known throughout Canada for the delightful satires he wrote under the pseudonym "Samuel Marchbanks." However, his reputation rests chiefly on his novels. The Salterton Trilogy—which includes* Tempest-Tost *(1951),* Leaven of Malice *(1954), and* A Mixture of Frailties *(1958)—is a study of a fictional university town in Canada and of its middle-class inhabitants. The Deptford Trilogy, which is made up of* Fifth Business *(1970),* The Manticore *(1972), and* World of Wonders *(1976), affirms the important part that the irrational plays in an individual's search for spiritual identity. Other popular books by Davies are* What's Bred in the Bone *(1985),* The Papers of Samuel Marchbanks *(1986), and* The Lyre of Orpheus *(1989).*

In "A Few Kind Words for Superstition," Davies attempts to explain why, in our scientific times, superstitions are still so strongly believed, even by the most educated people.

1 In grave discussions of "the renaissance of the irrational" in our time, superstition does not figure largely as a serious challenge to reason or science. Parapsychology, UFOs, miracle cures, transcendental meditation and all the paths to instant enlightenment are condemned, but superstition is merely deplored. Is it because it has an unacknowledged hold on so many of us?

2 Few people will admit to being superstitious; it implies naïveté or ignorance. But I live in the middle of a large university, and I see superstition in its four manifestations, alive and flourishing among people who are indisputably rational and learned.

3 You did not know that superstition takes four forms? Theologians assure us that it does. First is what they call Vain Observances, such as not walking under a ladder, and that kind of thing. Yet I saw a deeply learned professor of anthropology, who had spilled some salt, throwing a pinch of it over his left shoulder; when I asked him why, he replied, with a wink, that it was "to hit the Devil in the eye." I did not question him further about his belief in the Devil: but I noticed that he did not smile until I asked him what he was doing.

4 The second form is Divination, or consulting oracles. Another learned professor I know, who would scorn to settle a problem by tossing a coin (which is a humble appeal to Fate to declare itself), told me quite seriously that he had resolved a matter related to university affairs by consulting the I Ching. And why not? There are thousands of people on this continent who appeal to the I Ching, and their general level of education seems to absolve them of superstition. Almost, but not quite. The I Ching, to the embarrassment of rationalists, often gives excellent advice.

5 The third form is Idolatry, and universities can show plenty of that. If you have ever supervised a large examination room, you know how many jujus, lucky coins and other bringers of luck are placed on the desks of the candidates. Modest idolatry, but what else can you call it?

6 The fourth form is Improper Worship of the True God. A while ago, I learned that every day, for several days, a $2 bill (in Canada we have $2 bills, regarded by some people as unlucky) had been tucked under a candlestick on the altar of a college chapel. Investigation revealed that an engineering student, worried about a girl, thought that bribery of the Deity might help. When I talked with him, he did not think he was pricing God cheap, because he could afford no more. A reasonable argument, but perhaps God was proud that week, for the scientific oracle went against him.

7 Superstition seems to run, a submerged river of crude religion, below the surface of human consciousness. It has done so for as long as we have any chronicle of human behavior, and although I cannot prove it, I doubt if it is more prevalent today than it has always been. Superstition, the theologians tell us, comes from the Latin *supersisto*, meaning to stand in

terror of the Deity. Most people keep their terror within bounds, but they cannot root it out, nor do they seem to want to do so.

The more the teaching of formal religion declines, or takes a sociological 8 form, the less God appears to great numbers of people as a God of Love, resuming his older form of a watchful, minatory power, to be placated and cajoled. Superstition makes its appearance, apparently unbidden, very early in life, when children fear that stepping on cracks in the sidewalk will bring ill fortune. It may persist even among the greatly learned and devout, as in the case of Dr. Samuel Johnson, who felt it necessary to touch posts that he passed in the street. The psychoanalysts have their explanation, but calling a superstition a compulsion neurosis does not banish it.

Many superstitions are so widespread and so old that they must 9 have risen from a depth of the human mind that is indifferent to race or creed. Orthodox Jews place a charm on their door-posts; so do (or did) the Chinese. Some peoples of Middle Europe believe that when a man sneezes, his soul, for that moment, is absent from his body, and they hasten to bless him, lest the soul be seized by the Devil. How did the Melanesians come by the same idea? Superstition seems to have a link with some body of belief that far antedates the religions we know—religions which have no place for such comforting little ceremonies and charities.

People who like disagreeable historical comparisons recall that when 10 Rome was in decline, superstition proliferated wildly, and that something of the same sort is happening in our Western world today. They point to the popularity of astrology, and it is true that sober newspapers that would scorn to deal in love philters carry astrology columns and the fashion magazines count them among their most popular features. But when has astrology not been popular? No use saying science discredits it. When has the heart of man given a damn for science?

Superstition in general is linked to man's yearning to know his fate, 11 and to have some hand in deciding it. When my mother was a child, she innocently joined her Roman Catholic friends in killing spiders on July 11, until she learned that this was done to ensure heavy rain the day following, the anniversary of the Battle of Boyne, when the Orangemen would hold their parade. I knew an Italian, a good scientist, who watched every morning before leaving his house, so that the first person he met would not be a priest or a nun, as this would certainly bring bad luck.

I am not one to stand aloof from the rest of humanity in this matter, 12 for when I was a university student, a gypsy woman with a child in her arms used to appear every year at examination time, and ask a shilling of anyone who touched the Lucky Baby; that swarthy infant cost me four shillings altogether, and I never failed an examination. Of course, I did it merely for the joke—or so I thought then. Now, I am humbler.

1978

QUESTIONS FOR DISCUSSION

Content

a. What is Davies's thesis? Which paragraphs supply examples supporting this thesis?

b. Davies asserts in paragraph 11 that "superstition in general is linked to man's yearning to know his fate, and to have some hand in deciding it." Do you agree with this assertion? Is this a generalization?

c. What examples of superstitions does Davies include? What were his probable reasons for including them?

d. Are the examples of superstitions used as persuasive devices? If so, what are the readers being persuaded to do?

e. To what does the phrase "'the renaissance of the irrational'" in the first sentence refer? What examples does Davies use? What examples can you add to the list?

f. What is Davies's answer to the last question in the first paragraph? How do you know? Why might Davies have used a question rather than a statement?

g. What are the four kinds of superstitions? Do you agree with Davies that these types of superstitions are still prevalent today?

h. According to Davies, what is the relationship between superstition and religion? Between superstition and science? Between superstition and history?

Strategy and Style

i. Why might Davies have first listed the four forms of superstitions and then gone on to a discussion of superstition in general? How do the four forms of superstitions establish expectations for the rest of the essay?

j. The author traces the word *superstition* to its Latin origin, *"supersisto"* (paragraph 7). Look up the origin of the words *divination, idolatry,* or any of the superstitions he lists. How do the origins of these words and superstitions help illustrate his thesis?

k. What is Davies's attitude toward superstition? How is his attitude revealed through the tone of the piece?

ENGAGING THE TEXT

a. Describe the superstitions to which you or someone you know adheres. Into which of Davies's categories do they fall?

b. Are the several questions Davies asks merely rhetorical? Try writing an answer to one or more of them.

SUGGESTIONS FOR SUSTAINED WRITING

a. Write a few unkind words for superstition. In what ways does belief in superstition harm society? Why should people try to divest themselves of superstitious beliefs?

b. Compare Davies's essay with "Family Ghosts" by Maxine Hong Kingston in this chapter. What do the essays say about human behavior and cultural beliefs?

c. Interview friends and fellow students, asking them what superstitions they have and how strongly they believe in them. Using these examples as the raw material for your essay, analyze these superstitions, putting forth your theory of why people believe in them.

READ MORE

Davies and His Works

Grant, Judith Skelton. *Robertson Davies: Man of Myth*. Toronto: Viking, 1994.

"Robertson Davies" (http://www.fantasticfiction.co.uk/d/robertson-davies/): *Brief background on Davies's life and work, along with selected texts online and links to other sites.*

Superstition

Opie, Iona Archibald, and Moira Tatem. *A Dictionary of Superstitions.* New York: Oxford UP, 1989.

"Superstitions from Europe" (http://www.pitt.edu/~dash/folktexts2. html): *Definitions of superstitions and links to other sites on superstitions and folklore in general, on the University of Pittsburgh site.*

Black Men and Public Space

Brent Staples

Brent Staples (b. 1951), the oldest of nine children, was born in Chester, Pennsylvania. His father was a truck driver who lost his job along with 40,000 other workers in the 1960s because of plant closings in the area. The family was reduced to poverty. Staples had never considered college until a college professor took an interest in him and encouraged him to apply to a program that recruited black students. He enrolled at Widener University (B.A. 1973), where he excelled and received a Danforth Fellowship for graduate study. He took a Ph.D. in behaviorial psychology at the University of Chicago in 1977. From 1977 to 1981 he taught psychology at several colleges in Pennsylvania and Illinois, but a job as a reporter for the Chicago Sun-Times *in 1982 and 1983 began his shift to journalism. He began writing for the* New York Times *in 1983 and has served on the editorial board of that newspaper, for which he writes opinion pieces on race, social problems, politics, and contemporary culture.*

In 1994, Staples published the autobiographical Parallel Time: Growing Up in Black and White, *which won the Anisfield Wolff Book Award and in which "Black Men and Public Space" appears. The term public space is just 30 years old, and definitions vary. One definition states that public spaces "protect the rights of user groups. They are accessible to all groups and provide for freedom of action but also for temporary claim and ownership. A public space can be a place to act more freely" (Steven Carr, quoted in "The Death of Public Space?" at http://www.columbia.edu/~gs228/writing/histps.htm).*

1   My first victim was a woman—white, well dressed, probably in her late twenties. I came upon her late one evening on a deserted street in Hyde Park, a relatively affluent neighborhood in an otherwise mean, impoverished section of Chicago. As I swung onto the avenue behind her, there seemed to be a discreet, uninflammatory distance between us. Not so. She cast back a worried glance. To her, the youngish black man—a broad six feet two inches with a beard and billowing hair, both hands shoved into the pockets of a bulky military jacket—seemed menacingly close. After a few more quick glimpses, she picked up her pace and was soon running in earnest. Within seconds, she disappeared into a cross street.

2   That was more than a decade ago. I was twenty-two years old, a graduate student newly arrived at the University of Chicago. It was in the echo of that terrified woman's footfalls that I first began to know the unwieldy inheritance I'd come into—the ability to alter public space in ugly ways. It was clear that she thought herself the quarry of a mugger, a rapist, or worse. Suffering a bout of insomnia, however, I was stalking sleep, not defenseless wayfarers. As a softy who is scarcely able to take a knife to a raw chicken—let alone hold one to a person's throat—I was surprised, embarrassed, and dismayed all at once. Her flight made me feel like an accomplice in tyranny. It also made it clear that I was indistinguishable from the muggers who occasionally seeped into the area from the surrounding ghetto. That first encounter, and those that followed, signified that a vast, unnerving gulf lay between nighttime pedestrians—particularly women—and me. And I soon gathered that being perceived as dangerous is a hazard in itself. I only needed to turn a corner into a dicey situation, or crowd some frightened, armed person in a foyer somewhere, or make an errant move after being pulled over by a policeman. Where fear and weapons meet—and they often do in urban America—there is always the possibility of death.

3   In that first year, my first away from my hometown, I was to become thoroughly familiar with the language of fear. At dark, shadowy

intersections, I could cross in front of a car stopped at a traffic light and elicit the *thunk*, thunk, thunk, thunk of the driver—black, white, male, or female—hammering down the door locks. On less traveled streets after dark, I grew accustomed to but never comfortable with people crossing to the other side of the street rather than pass me. Then there were the standard unpleasantries with policemen, doormen, bouncers, cabdrivers, and others whose business it is to screen out troublesome individuals *before* there is any nastiness.

I moved to New York nearly two years ago and I have remained an 4 avid night walker. In central Manhattan, the near-constant crowd cover minimizes tense one-on-one street encounters. Elsewhere—in SoHo, for example, where sidewalks are narrow and tightly spaced buildings shut out the sky—things can get very taut indeed.

After dark, on the warrenlike streets of Brooklyn where I live, I often 5 see women who fear the worst from me. They seem to have set their faces on neutral, and with their purse straps strung across their chests bandolier-style, they forge ahead as though bracing themselves against being tackled. I understand, of course, that the danger they perceive is not a hallucination. Women are particularly vulnerable to street violence, and young black males are drastically overrepresented among the per-petrators of that violence. Yet these truths are no solace against the kind of alienation that comes of being ever the suspect, a fearsome entity with whom pedestrians avoid making eye contact.

It is not altogether clear to me how I reached the ripe old age of 6 twenty-two without being conscious of the lethality nighttime pedestri-ans attributed to me. Perhaps it was because in Chester, Pennsylvania, the small, angry industrial town where I came of age in the 1960s, I was scarcely noticeable against a backdrop of gang warfare, street knifings, and murders. I grew up one of the good boys, had perhaps a half-dozen fistfights. In retrospect, my shyness of combat has clear sources.

As a boy, I saw countless tough guys locked away; I have since bur- 7 ied several, too. They were babies, really—a teenage cousin, a brother of twenty-two, a childhood friend in his mid-twenties—all gone down in episodes of bravado played out in the streets. I came to doubt the virtues of intimidation early on. I chose, perhaps unconsciously, to remain a shadow—timid, but a survivor.

The fearsomeness mistakenly attributed to me in public places often 8 has a perilous flavor. The most frightening of these confusions occurred in the late 1970s and early 1980s, when I worked as a journalist in Chicago. One day, rushing into the office of a magazine I was writing for with a dead-line story in hand, I was mistaken for a burglar. The office manager called security and, with an ad hoc posse, pursued me through the labyrinthine halls, nearly to my editor's door. I had no way of proving who I was. I could only move briskly toward the company of someone who knew me.

9   Another time I was on assignment for a local paper and killing time before an interview. I entered a jewelry store on the city's affluent Near North Side. The proprietor excused herself and returned with an enormous red Doberman pinscher straining at the end of a leash. She stood, the dog extended toward me, silent to my questions, her eyes bulging nearly out of her head. I took a cursory look around, nodded, and bade her good night.

10   Relatively speaking, however, I never fared as badly as another black male journalist. He went to nearby Waukegan, Illinois, a couple of summers ago to work on a story about a murderer who was born there. Mistaking the reporter for the killer, police officers hauled him from his car at gunpoint and but for his press credentials would probably have tried to book him. Such episodes are not uncommon. Black men trade tales like this all the time.

11   Over the years, I learned to smother the rage I felt at so often being taken for a criminal. Not to do so would surely have led to madness. I now take precautions to make myself less threatening. I move about with care, particularly late in the evening. I give a wide berth to nervous people on subway platforms during the wee hours, particularly when I have exchanged business clothes for jeans. If I happen to be entering a building behind some people who appear skittish, I may walk by, letting them clear the lobby before I return, so as not to seem to be following them. I have been calm and extremely congenial on those rare occasions when I've been pulled over by the police.

12   And on late-evening constitutionals I employ what has proved to be an excellent tension-reducing measure: I whistle melodies from Beethoven and Vivaldi and the more popular classical composers. Even steely New Yorkers hunching toward nighttime destinations seem to relax, and occasionally they even join in the tune. Virtually everybody seems to sense that a mugger wouldn't be warbling bright, sunny selections from Vivaldi's *Four Seasons*. It is my equivalent of the cowbell that hikers wear when they know they are in bear country.

1986

QUESTIONS FOR DISCUSSION

Content

a. What does Staples mean in paragraph 2 by "the ability to alter public space"?
b. What does he learn from the encounter with a white woman as recalled in paragraphs 1 and 2?

c. What other anecdotes does Staples use to illustrate the problem of "black men and public space"?

d. What is the essay's thesis?

e. What "truths" does the author describe in paragraph 5, and how does this paragraph help him advance his thesis?

f. In paragraph 10, the author claims that "Black men trade tales like this all the time." To what kinds of tales is he referring? How does including that sentence help him accomplish his purpose?

g. Why has he forced himself "to smother the rage [he] felt at so often being taken for a criminal" (paragraph 11)?

h. Who are Beethoven and Vivaldi? Why does Staples whistle their music?

Strategy and Style

i. Besides illustration, what methods of development does this essay employ?

j. Staples begins with an anecdote. Discuss the effectiveness of this story as an introductory device.

k. The thesis of the essay is implied. Would the essay have been more effective had it been explicit?

l. Staples's tone is remarkably subdued. Discuss the reason(s) behind his adopting such a tone. Should he have expressed more emotion?

ENGAGING THE TEXT

a. Reread paragraphs 8, 9, and 10. Then try to remember being wrongly accused of something. Write a paragraph or two briefly narrating this incident and explaining how you tried to establish your innocence or to resolve the misunderstanding. Compare your response to Staples's essay.

b. Have you ever acted like the white women in paragraphs 1 and 2, like the office manager in paragraph 8, or like the jewelry-store proprietor in paragraph 9 by seriously misjudging someone's motives or intent? Can you justify your behavior? If so, on what grounds? If not, have you attempted to understand your behavior and amend your thinking? How have you done that? Compare your response to Staples's essay.

SUGGESTIONS FOR SUSTAINED WRITING

a. Read what you wrote in response to item *a* under Engaging the Text. Expand this material by discussing two or three more incidents of a similar nature. In the process, explain what these experiences taught you about human nature and what your reactions to them taught you about yourself and your ability to solve problems, to deal with others, and/or to cope with stress.

b. Write an essay in which you explain the reaction of a particular race or group of people to an "outsider" or "outsiders" who might accidentally enter its "space." Use your own experiences, observations, and reading as sources of information. For example, how might a black community react to seeing a Pakistani family move in? How might a white suburban neighborhood react upon seeing a group of black teenage girls walking along its streets at dusk? Compare your essay to the ideas in Bharati Mukherjee's "Two Ways to Belong in America" (Chapter 6), Richard Rodriguez's "Blaxicans and Other Reinvented Americans" (Chapter 4), or Gary Soto's "Like Mexicans" (Chapter 6).

c. At the end of paragraph 2, Staples remarks, "Where fear and weapons meet—and they often do in urban America—there is always the possibility of death." Using the Internet or materials in your college library, find information about recent events reported by the media that have a bearing on Staples's idea. Then, turn your notes into a short research paper that explains how extensive and/or serious this problem is. There are several ways to approach this topic. One is to discuss incidents involving police shootings of armed and/or unarmed residents of the inner city; another is to discuss accidental shootings of innocent citizens by other innocent citizens; still another is to write about the shootings of children who got caught in the crossfire of gang warfare. Choose your own topic; just be sure to limit and focus it.

READ MORE

Staples and His Works

"Brent Staples" (http://www.pbs.org/blackpress/modern_journalist/index.html): *Biographical information about Staples, including a video of Staples speaking about racial identity.*

"Brent Staples" (http://topics.nytimes.com/top/reference/timestopics/people/s/brent_staples/index.html): List of and links to *New York Times* articles by Staples.

Racial Identity and Urban Studies

Lamont, Michèle. *The Cultural Territories of Race: Black and White Boundaries.* Chicago: U of Chicago P, 1999.

"H-Urban" (http://www.h-net.org/~urban/): *Links to online sources and scholarly articles on the topics of urban history and planning.*

Clutter

William Zinsser

William Zinsser (b. 1922) took his B.A. at Princeton University. After serving in the United States Army during World War II, he began his journalistic career by writing for and becoming an editor at the New York Herald Tribune. *He later became a freelance writer, being published in* The New Yorker, the Atlantic, and LIFE *magazines. Zinsser, who has taught at Yale University and the New School for Social Research, is the author of over 20 books. Among his most recent works are* Writing about Your Life: A Journey into the Past *(2004) and* Going in Faith: Writing as a Spiritual Quest *(1999). In 2010, Zinsser began a blog called "Zinsser on Fridays," which is posted weekly on* The American Scholar. *Besides writing and teaching, he also composes music and plays jazz piano at various New York clubs.*

However, Zinsser's most famous work is On Writing Well: The Classic Guide to Writing Nonfiction, *first published in 1976. For Zinsser, writing is a craft—more than an art—that has to be practiced regularly and intently. In the following essay from that book, the author discusses ways to streamline and, thereby, strengthen your writing. This version of "Clutter" is from the 2006 edition of* On Writing Well.

Fighting clutter is like fighting weeds—the writer is always slightly 1 behind. New varieties sprout overnight, and by noon they are part of American speech. Consider what President Nixon's aide John Dean accomplished in just one day of testimony on television during the Watergate hearings. The next day everyone in America was saying "at this point in time" instead of "now."

Consider all the prepositions that are draped onto verbs that don't 2 need any help. We no longer head committees. We head them up. We don't face problems anymore. We face up to them when we can free up a few minutes. A small detail, you may say—not worth bothering about. It *is* worth bothering about. Writing improves in direct ratio to the number of things we can keep out of it that shouldn't be there. "Up" in "free up" shouldn't be there. Examine every word you put on paper. You'll find a surprising number that don't serve any purpose.

Take the adjective "personal," as in "a personal friend of mine," "his 3 personal feeling" or "her personal physician." It's typical of hundreds of words that can be eliminated. The personal friend has come into the language to distinguish him or her from the business friend, thereby debasing both language and friendship. Someone's feeling *is* that person's personal feeling—that's what "his" means. As for the personal physician, that's the man or woman summoned to the dressing room of a stricken actress so she won't have to be treated by the impersonal physician assigned to the theater. Someday I'd like to see that person identified as "her doctor." Physicians are physicians, friends are friends. The rest is clutter.

4   Clutter is the laborious phrase that has pushed out the short word that means the same thing. Even before John Dean, people and businesses had stopped saying "now." They were saying "currently" ("all our operators are currently assisting other customers"), or "at the present time," or "presently" (which means "soon"). Yet the idea can always be expressed by "now" to mean the immediate moment ("Now I can see him"), or by "today" to mean the historical present ("Today prices are high"), or simply by the verb "to be" ("It is raining"). There's no need to say, "At the present time we are experiencing precipitation."

5   "Experiencing" is one of the worst clutterers. Even your dentist will ask if you are experiencing any pain. If he had his own kid in the chair he would say, "Does it hurt?" He would, in short, be himself. By using a more pompous phrase in his professional role he not only sounds more important, he blunts the painful edge of truth. It's the language of the flight attendant demonstrating the oxygen mask that will drop down if the plane should run out of air. "In the unlikely possibility that the aircraft should experience such an eventuality," she begins—a phrase so oxygen-depriving in itself that we are prepared for any disaster.

6   Clutter is the ponderous euphemism that turns a slum into a depressed socioeconomic area, garbage collectors into waste-disposal personnel and the town dump into the volume reduction unit. I think of Bill Mauldin's cartoon of two hoboes riding a freight car. One of them says, "I started as a simple bum, but now I'm hard-core unemployed." Clutter is political correctness gone amok. I saw an ad for a boys' camp designed to provide "individual attention for the minimally exceptional."

7   Clutter is the official language used by corporations to hide their mistakes. When the Digital Equipment Corporation eliminated 3,000 jobs its statement didn't mention layoffs; those were "involuntary methodologies." When an Air Force missile crashed, it "impacted with the ground prematurely." When General Motors had a plant shutdown, that was a "volume-related production-schedule adjustment." Companies that go belly-up have "a negative cash-flow position."

8   Clutter is the language of the Pentagon calling an invasion a "reinforced protective reaction strike" and justifying its vast budgets on the need for "counterforce deterrence." As George Orwell pointed out in "Politics and the English Language," an essay written in 1946 but often cited during the wars in Cambodia, Vietnam and Iraq, "political speech and writing are largely the defense of the indefensible. . . . Thus political language has to consist largely of euphemism, question-begging and sheer cloudy vagueness." Orwell's warning that clutter is not just a nuisance but a deadly tool has come true in the recent decades of American military adventurism. It was during George W. Bush's presidency that "civilian casualties" in Iraq became "collateral damage."

Verbal camouflage reached new heights during General Alexander 9
Haig's tenure as President Reagan's secretary of state. Before Haig
nobody had thought of saying "at this juncture of maturization" to mean
"now." He told the American people that terrorism could be fought with
"meaningful sanctionary teeth" and that intermediate nuclear missiles
were "at the vortex of cruciality." As for any worries that the public might
harbor, his message was "leave it to Al," though what he actually said
was: "We must push this to a lower decibel of public fixation. I don't think
there's much of a learning curve to be achieved in this area of content."

I could go on quoting examples from various fields—every profession 10
has its growing arsenal of jargon to throw dust in the eyes of the populace.
But the list would be tedious. The point of raising it now is to serve notice
that clutter is the enemy. Beware, then, of the long word that's no better
than the short word: "assistance" (help), "numerous" (many), "facilitate"
(ease), "individual" (man or woman), "remainder" (rest), "initial" (first),
"implement" (do), "sufficient" (enough), "attempt" (try), "referred to as"
(called) and hundreds more. Beware of all the slippery new fad words:
paradigm and parameter, prioritize and potentialize. They are all weeds
that will smother what you write. Don't dialogue with someone you can
talk to. Don't interface with anybody.

Just as insidious are all the word clusters with which we explain 11
how we propose to go about our explaining: "I might add," "It should be
pointed out," "It is interesting to note." If you might add, add it. If it should
be pointed out, point it out. If it is interesting to note, *make* it interesting; are
we not all stupefied by what follows when someone says, "This will interest
you"? Don't inflate what needs no inflating: "with the possible exception
of" (except), "due to the fact that" (because), "he totally lacked the ability
to" (he couldn't), "until such time as" (until), "for the purpose of" (for).

Is there any way to recognize clutter at a glance? Here's a device 12
my students at Yale found helpful. I would put brackets around every
component in a piece of writing that wasn't doing useful work. Often
just one word got bracketed: the unnecessary preposition appended to
a verb ("order up"), or the adverb that carries the same meaning as the
verb ("smile happily"), or the adjective that states a known fact ("tall
skyscraper"). Often my brackets surrounded the little qualifiers that
weaken any sentence they inhabit ("a bit," "sort of"), or phrases like "in a
sense," which don't mean anything. Sometimes my brackets surrounded
an entire sentence—the one that essentially repeats what the previous
sentence said, or that says something readers don't need to know or can
figure out for themselves. Most first drafts can be cut by 50 percent without losing any information or losing the author's voice.

My reason for bracketing the students' superfluous words, instead 13
of crossing them out, was to avoid violating their sacred prose. I wanted
to leave the sentence intact for them to analyze. I was saying, "I may be

wrong, but I think this can be deleted and the meaning won't be affected. But *you* decide. Read the sentence without the bracketed material and see if it works." In the early weeks of the term I handed back papers that were festooned with brackets. Entire paragraphs were bracketed. But soon the students learned to put mental brackets around their own clutter, and by the end of the term their papers were almost clean. Today many of those students are professional writers, and they tell me, "I still see your brackets—they're following me through life."

14   You can develop the same eye. Look for the clutter in your writing and prune it ruthlessly. Be grateful for everything you can throw away. Reexamine each sentence you put on paper. Is every word doing new work? Can any thought be expressed with more economy? Is anything pompous or pretentious or faddish? Are you hanging on to something useless just because you think it's beautiful?

15   Simplify, simplify.

2006

QUESTIONS FOR DISCUSSION

Content

a. Zinsser begins with an analogy. What does that analogy mean? Could this analogy contain his thesis?
b. What is the distinction between "presently" and "currently" in paragraph 4?
c. Why does Zinsser believe that the phrase "experiencing any pain" is pompous (paragraph 5)? Why do people use such phrases?
d. What is the purpose behind the government's and business's use of clutter (paragraphs 6 through 7)?
e. Why is clutter bad for the reader? Why is it bad for the writer?
f. Explain how Zinsser helped his Yale students eliminate clutter.
g. What do you make of Zinsser's advice in his conclusion? How does this advice illustrate his thesis?

Strategy and Style

h. Other than the analogy that begins this essay, identify as many figures of speech as you can.
i. Where in this essay does Zinsser use sarcasm to create humor?
j. Why does he quote from General Alexander Haig and Digital Equipment Corporation? What would have been the effect of leaving out paragraphs 7 and 9?

ENGAGING THE TEXT

a. Look up John Dean (paragraphs 1 and 4), Bill Mauldin (paragraph 6), and George Orwell (paragraph 8) on the Internet or in some other source. Who are they, and how does mentioning them help Zinsser advance his thesis?
b. In paragraph 10 Zinsser mentions new fad words that arose in the mid-1980s. Make a list of today's fad words. Then make a list of simpler alternatives.

SUGGESTIONS FOR SUSTAINED WRITING

a. Zinsser writes about one way in which people can improve their writing. Write an essay in which you explain ways in which people can improve their ability to complete an activity or task that you know how to do well. Like Zinsser, who focuses on ways to identify and eliminate wordiness, limit your paper to one aspect of the activity. For example, if you want to help people lose weight, focus your paper on the kinds of diet one might follow or the kinds of exercises one might do, but don't try to cover both.
b. Read William Lutz's "Doublespeak" (Chapter 5). Then, write an essay in which you list and explain the points on which Lutz and Zinsser would agree. As you do this, try to add examples of verbal "clutter" and "doublespeak" that you have encountered lately in your reading, through the media, or in conversation.
c. Using Internet sites, printed or televised advertisements, or articles in newspapers and magazines, write an essay that analyzes the language used by these sources. Does it contain the kind of language that Zinsser is talking about? To what purpose is such language put? Of course, you will have to make specific and repeated reference to the texts you are using in order to make your essay clear and convincing.

READ MORE

Zinsser and His Works

Zinsser, William. "Beauty and the Book" (http://www.globalprovince.com/zindart-zinsser.htm): *Interesting essay on the physical appearance of books.*
"On Memoir, Truth and 'Writing Well'" (http://www.npr.org/templates/story/story.php?storyId=5340618): Audio interview with Zinsser on National Public Radio.
"Zinsser on Friday" (http://www.theamericanscholar.org/zinsser): *Zinsser's weekly blog.*

Being Concise

"Conciseness: Methods of Eliminating Wordiness" (http://owl.english. purdue.edu/handouts/general/gl_concise.htm): *Purdue University Online Writing lab advice on becoming concise.*

"Language Exercises (Being Concise)" (http://www.writing.engr.psu. edu/exercises/language4.html): *Penn State University guide with a series of exercises to make your writing less wordy.*

Forbidden Things

Bailey White

Bailey White (b. 1950) is best known for her National Public Radio commentary on All Things Considered, *which she has done since 1990. She lives in Thomasville, Georgia, in the house in which she grew up. After receiving a B.A. from Florida State University in 1973, White worked as a first-grade teacher in Thomasville, but she soon began writing full-time. Although some of her writing is fiction, such as her novel* Quite a Year for Plums *(1998), most of her writing is nonfiction.* Mama Makes Up Her Mind: And Other Dangers of Southern Living *(1993) and* Sleeping at the Starlight Motel: And Other Adventures on the Way Back Home *(1995) are collections of humorous essays. Her radio commentaries have been collected in several audio books, such as* An Interesting Life *(1992),* Native Air *(1994),* Among the Mushrooms *(2002),* Summer Afternoon and Other Stories *(2004), and* Nothing with Strings: NPR's Beloved Holiday Stories *(2008). "Forbidden Things" is from* Sleeping at the Starlight Motel.*

"Forbidden Things" could be considered a satire, a rant, or a revenge fantasy—or all three. As you read, consider whether or why it is necessary to have rules that control behavior.

1   I was leaning over the little railing, looking down into the Devil's Millhopper, an interesting geological formation and the focal point of a Florida state park. Waterfalls plunge 120 feet down into a bowl-shaped sinkhole; maidenhair ferns and moss grow in little crevices along the steep, sloping sides of the gorge; and a beautiful mist rises up.

2   I stood there, gazing down, and feeling a reverence for these spectacles of the natural world. I felt the slow sweep of geologic time. I felt the remnants of the spiritual significance this place had had for the Indians who lived here for thousands of years. I felt the wonder and awe of the first European explorers of Florida looking down into this chasm for the first time.

3   Then another feeling crept over me, a deep, almost atavistic longing. It was the urge to throw something down into the Devil's Millhopper. I looked around. A stone or a stick would do, but what I really wanted was a piece of food, the nibbled end of a hotdog bun or a wedge of chocolate

cake without the icing. Then I noticed the sign, one of those tastefully unobtrusive state park signs:

DO NOT THROW FOOD OR TRASH IN GORGE

It was 4:00 A.M. I was at the Los Angeles, California, bus station, my ₄ next-to-last stop on a dreary transcontinental bus trip—three days and three nights on a Greyhound bus. My back ached, my knees ached, my head ached. Ever since El Paso, Texas, my seatmate had been an old man who chain-smoked Marlboro cigarettes and sucked and slobbered over a perpetual ham sandwich that kept oozing out of a greasy crumple of waxed paper.

I longed for a bath in my own bathtub, and then a deep sleep in my ₅ own bed, stretched out full-length between clean sheets. But, I thought, pushing open the door of the bus station bathroom, if I just wash my feet and my hair I will be all right. I lined up my soap, my washrag, and my little bottle of shampoo on the back of the sink and took off my shoes and socks. Ahh, I thought. Then I saw the sign on the mirror:

DO NOT WASH HAIR OR FEET IN SINK

A few weeks ago I went into our little downtown restaurant and ₆ saw that it had replaced its tired old salad bar with a gorgeous saltwater aquarium with sea anemones, chunks of living coral, and big slow-moving colorful fish with faces I could almost recognize. I spent my whole lunchtime staring into that tank, mesmerized by the fish as they gracefully looped and glided, sending the tentacles of the sea anemones into slow twirls and fanning out the tall grasses.

When I finished my sandwich I noticed that there were a couple of ₇ crumbs left on my plate, just the size to pinch between thumb and finger. Oh, I thought, to pinch up those crumbs and dip my fingers down into the water, breaking through the smooth surface into the coolness and silence of that peaceful world. One of the fish would make a looping turn, his odd exophthalmic eyes would rotate slowly in their sockets and fix upon the crumbs in my fingers. Then he would angle up, and I would feel for just one exquisite instant those thorny fish lips rasping across my fingertips. With rising delight and anticipation, I pinched up a crumb, two crumbs. I scrabbled across the plastic top of the tank, found the little door, lifted it open—and then I saw the sign:

DO NOT FEED THE FISH
WE PROHIBIT CLIMBING IN ANY MANNER FROM OR ALONG THE CANYON RIM
DO NOT PICK FLOWERS
NO SMOKING EATING OR DRINKING
NO SWINGING FROM VINES IN TREES
NO PEDESTRIAN TRAFFIC IN WOODS

No FISHING

No SWIMMING

No TRESPASSING

8   Don't get me wrong; I approve of these prohibitions. Imagine the nasty mess in the bottom of the Devil's Millhopper if every self-indulgent tourist threw a piece of food into the sinkhole. Imagine the puddles on the floor and the plumbing complications in the Los Angeles bus station if every weary transcontinental traveler washed her hair and feet in the sink. Imagine the deadly scum of grease on the surface of that saltwater aquarium if every fish-dazed diner fed the catalufa his last mayonnaise-coated crumbs.

9   But sometimes I wonder: Who makes up these necessary and useful rules, and how does he know so well the deep and touching urges of human beings to pick flowers, walk in the woods, climb canyon walls, swing from vines, and feed already well-nourished animals? I imagine with distaste a mean, sour, silent little man skulking around in public places, watching us furtively with squinny eyes while scribbling notes on his pad with a gnawed pencil. In national parks he disguises himself as a tourist in reflective sunglasses and plaid Bermuda shorts. "Bryce Canyon," he notes with a smirk, "Urinating on hoodoos and off cliffs." In zoos he wears khaki and lurks in the shadows, hiding behind a bag of peanuts. "Touching giraffe's tongue through fence wire. . . . Feeling camel's hump," he scribbles.

10   At night he goes home, and in his stark white workshop, illuminated with fluorescent lights, he makes those signs. Rounded letters routed out of cypress boards for the parks: "We Prohibit. . . , No . . ., No . . . , and No . . ." Spiky green on white for zoos: "Do Not . . . , . . . Not Allowed, . . . Is Prohibited." *And-we-meanit* black and white for commercial establishments: "Absolutely NO . . . , . . . Are Required, We Forbid . . ."

11   I imagine, one night, as he works late stacking and bundling signs for the next day's delivery, the tendril of a grapevine creeps in at his window. When his back is turned, its pale nose will gently nudge itself around him.

12   "No Touching!" he will admonish.

13   But with a clutch and a snatch the vine will retract, and he will find himself yanked through the night sky above a central Florida state park.

14   "Do Not Swing from Vines!" he will shriek.

15   And with that, the vine will untwine and drop him into the vortex of a limpid spring.

16   "No Swimming!" he will sputter as the dark, icy water closes over his head. As he sinks, strange, pale-colored fish will swim up and cock their eyes at him. "Do Not Feed the Fish," he will squeak. But, slowly and precisely, the fish will angle up, move in, and then, all over, he will feel the pick pick pick of those prickly lips.

1995

QUESTIONS FOR DISCUSSION

Content

a. What is White's thesis? Is she saying that such signs are not necessary?
b. Have you ever felt as White does about "No . . ." signs? Or, conversely, have you felt glad that such signs exist? To what extent do you sympathize with White?
c. Why are signs that forbid things more common than signs that encourage things? What does White imply?
d. What are the "No . . ." signs primarily meant to do? Are they there to curtail pleasures, to protect people, to protect the environment?

Strategy and Style

e. Describe the narrator of this essay. What has White done to create a particular picture of herself as speaker?
f. What does White do to draw on the senses in this essay? Point to places in the text where the senses are engaged.
g. What examples does White use to illustrate her negative reaction to "NO . . ." signs?
h. What is the purpose of the fantasy that ends this essay?
i. Why might White have made the fantasy rather mean-spirited toward the sign maker?

ENGAGING THE TEXT

a. Write your own "No . . ." signs that would be appropriate for your own safety and success—real or wishful—in life.
b. Why might White have ended her examples with what the signs forbid her to do? Do you think she obeyed the signs? Speculate about her possible actions, based on clues from the text.

SUGGESTIONS FOR SUSTAINED WRITING

a. Describe a world in which there are no signs at all directing our behavior. This can be done as a short story or as an essay. If the latter, discuss what you have seen of human nature that would either (1) suggest that humans do not need such signs in order to be civilized, or (2) suggest that civilization is impossible without such signs.
b. Write an essay in which you discuss the purposes of rules. Why are rules useful? Consider the rules described in the following essays:

Brent Staples's "Black Men and Public Space" or William Zinsser's "Clutter" in this chapter, Philip Meyer's "If Hitler Asked You . . ." in Chapter 8, and Alan M. Dershowitz's "Shouting 'Fire!'" in Chapter 10.

c. Research rules of social behavior for your culture or region that govern one type of social situation, such as a college classroom, a dinner party, a family reunion. What are the rules that govern behavior in this situation? What happens when rules are broken? Illustrate your essay with examples and statistics from articles in the field of social psychology.

As an alternative topic for the truly curious and perseverant, research how signs are created for national or provincial parks. Who decides when and where they are needed? Who writes them? What are the rules that curtail the signs?

READ MORE

White and Her Works

"Bailey White" (http://www.baileywhite.com/index.shtml): *Links to audio versions of White's NPR essays.*

"National Public Radio" (http://www.npr.org): *NPR's home page.*

Signage

"1988 National Park Service Sign Manual" (http://www.alternatewars .com/BBOW/Sources/NPS_sign_manual_1988.pdf): *The official manual for signage in national parks.*

Silk Parachute

John McPhee

John McPhee (b. 1931) graduated from Princeton University and then studied for a year at Cambridge University, where he read literature and played basketball. He started work at The New Yorker *in 1965 and has been a staff writer there ever since. He has also been with the same publisher—Farrar, Straus & Giroux—since his first book,* A Sense of Where You Are, *was published in 1965. McPhee mainly writes nonfiction, seeking to explain natural phenomena; through his use of narrative detail, his books are as riveting as novels. Among his many publications are* Oranges *(1967);* The Pine Barrens *(1968);* The Crofter and the Laird *(1969);* Encounters with the Archdruid *(1972); In*

Suspect Terrain *(1983);* The Control of Nature *(1989);* Annals of the Former World *(1998), which received a Pulitzer Prize; and* Uncommon Carriers *(2006).*

Although he is usually known for his lengthy and detailed expository articles, this short piece, written for The New Yorker's *Talk of the Town column for Mother's Day 1997, shows McPhee's humorous and personal side.*

When your mother is ninety-nine years old, you have so many memories ₁ of her that they tend to overlap, intermingle, and blur. It is extremely difficult to single out one or two, impossible to remember any that exemplify the whole.

It has been alleged that when I was in college she heard that I had ₂ stayed up all night playing poker and wrote me a letter that used the word "shame" forty-two times. I do not recall this.

I do not recall being pulled out of my college room and into the ₃ church next door.

It has been alleged that on December 24, 1936, when I was five years ₄ old, she sent me to my room at or close to 7 P.M. for using four-letter words while trimming the Christmas tree. I do not recall that.

The assertion is absolutely false that when I came home from high ₅ school with an A-minus she demanded an explanation for the minus.

It has been alleged that she spoiled me with protectionism, because I ₆ was the youngest child and therefore the most vulnerable to attack from overhead—an assertion that I cannot confirm or confute, except to say that facts don't lie.

We lived only a few blocks from the elementary school and routinely ₇ ate lunch at home. It is reported that the following dialogue and ensuing action occurred on January 22, 1941:

"Eat your sandwich."   ₈

"I don't want to eat my sandwich."   ₉

"I made that sandwich, and you are going to eat it, Mister Man. You ₁₀ filled yourself up on penny candy on the way home, and now you're not hungry."

"I'm late. I have to go. I'll eat the sandwich on the way back to school." ₁₁

"Promise?"   ₁₂

"Promise."   ₁₃

Allegedly, I went up the street with the sandwich in my hand and ₁₄ buried it in a snowbank in front of Dr. Wright's house. My mother, holding back the curtain in the window of the side door, was watching. She came out in the bitter cold, wearing only a light dress, ran to the snowbank, dug out the sandwich, chased me up Nassau Street, and rammed the sandwich down my throat, snow and all. I do not recall any detail of that story. I believe it to be a total fabrication.

There was the case of the missing Cracker Jack at Lindel's corner ₁₅ store. Flimsy evidence pointed to Mrs. McPhee's smallest child. It has been averred that she laid the guilt on with the following words: "'Like mother like son' is a saying so true, the world will judge largely of mother by you." It has been asserted that she immediately repeated that proverb three times, and also recited it on other occasions too numerous to count. I have absolutely no recollection of her saying that about the Cracker Jack or any other controlled substance.

16   We have now covered everything even faintly unsavory that has been reported about this person in ninety-nine years, and even those items are a collection of rumors, half-truths, prevarications, false allegations, inaccuracies, innuendos, and canards.

17   This is the mother who—when Alfred Knopf wrote her twenty-two-year-old son a letter saying, "The readers' reports in the case of your manuscript would not be very helpful, and I think might discourage you completely"—said, "Don't listen to Alfred Knopf. Who does Alfred Knopf think he is, anyway? Someone should go in there and k-nock his block off." To the best of my recollection, that is what she said.

18   I also recall her taking me, on or about March 8th, my birthday, to the theatre in New York every year, beginning in childhood. I remember those journeys as if they were today. I remember "A Connecticut Yankee." Wednesday, March 8, 1944. Evidently, my father had written for the tickets, because she and I sat in the last row of the second balcony. Mother knew what to do about that. She gave me for my birthday an elegant spyglass, sufficient in power to bring the Connecticut Yankee back from Vermont. I sat there watching the play through my telescope, drawing as many guffaws from the surrounding audience as the comedy on the stage.

19   On one of those theatre days—when I was eleven or twelve—I asked her if we could start for the city early and go out to LaGuardia Field to see the comings and goings of airplanes. The temperature was well below the freeze point and the March winds were so blustery that the wind-chill factor was forty below zero. Or seemed to be. My mother figured out how to take the subway to a stop in Jackson Heights and a bus from there—a feat I am unable to duplicate to this day. At LaGuardia, she accompanied me to the observation deck and stood there in the icy wind for at least an hour, maybe two, while I, spellbound, watched the DC-3s coming in on final, their wings flapping in the gusts. When we at last left the observation deck, we went downstairs into the terminal, where she bought me what appeared to be a black rubber ball but on closer inspection was a pair of hollow hemispheres hinged on one side and folded together. They contained a silk parachute. Opposite the hinge, each hemisphere had a small nib. A piece of string wrapped round and round the two nibs kept the ball closed. If you threw it high into the air, the string unwound and the parachute blossomed. If you sent it up with a tennis racquet, you could put it into the clouds. Not until the development of the ten-megabyte

hard disk would the world ever know such a fabulous toy. Folded just so, the parachute never failed. Always, it floated back to you—silkily, beautifully—to start over and float back again. Even if you abused it, whacked it really hard—gracefully, lightly, it floated back to you.

1997

QUESTIONS FOR DISCUSSION

Content

a. What is the image of his mother created by McPhee? How is his mother the Ideal Mother?
b. What is the significance of the silk parachute? How is the silk parachute like McPhee's mother?
c. How does McPhee feel about his mother? How do you know?
d. What are McPhee's boyhood "crimes"? What makes them crimes?

Strategy and Style

e. What are the examples that McPhee lists in this essay? What do they exemplify?
f. McPhee repeatedly uses *alleged* and *allegedly*. What does this word do for the tone of the essay?
g. What other words does McPhee use to make an analogy between childhood behavior and the criminal world?
h. This essay was written for Mother's Day. How is it like a Mother's Day gift?

ENGAGING THE TEXT

a. List the examples used to cite the negative and the positive traits of McPhee as a boy, and note the differences in the style used to describe each type.
d. Imagine you are McPhee's mother and briefly write, in her words, how you would respond to this essay.

SUGGESTIONS FOR SUSTAINED WRITING

a. Using McPhee's structure of listing his negative and positive attributes, write an essay about your mother or father. If you desire, write this essay as a gift to her or him.

b. Relate McPhee's essay to other essays written about one's parents, such as Maya Angelou's "Grandmother's Victory" (Chapter 1), Scott Russell Sanders's "The Men We Carry in Our Minds" (Chapter 6), Amy Tan's "Mother Tongue" (Chapter 11), and Sandra Cisneros's "Only Daughter" (Chapter 11). Explain what these writers have in common in their relationships with their parents, and where they differ.

c. Read one of McPhee's essays on nature and construct a research project from it. A currently relevant essay is "Atchefalaya," an article about attempts to control the Mississippi River and prevent flooding in New Orleans; other essays can be found on *The New Yorker* website. For your project, choose one segment in McPhee's work that you would like to know more about, read more about that topic, and report to your classmates.

READ MORE

Mcphee and His Works

"John McPhee Home Page" (http://www.johnmcphee.com): *McPhee's personal website.*

"John McPhee's Fish Tales" (http://theconnection.wbur.org/2002/11/22/john-mcphees-fish-tales): *Audio of an interview broadcast on Boston's public radio station, WBUR, in 2002.*

The New Yorker archives (http://www.newyorker.com/search/query?query=john+mcphee&queryType=nonparsed): *The magazine's list of full-text articles by John McPhee.*

Mother/Son Relationships

"Mothers and Sons" (http://menstuff.org/books/byissue/motherssons.html): *List of and links to books about mothers and sons.*

The Search for the World's Funniest Joke

Richard Wiseman

Richard Wiseman (b. 1966) earned a degree in psychology from University College London and a Ph.D. in psychology from the University of Edinburgh. He is now a professor of public understanding of psychology at the University of Hertfordshire. His articles have appeared in numerous magazines and academic journals, and he is often a guest speaker in Britain and the United States. For his work, Wiseman received a CSICOP Public Education in Science Award in 2000, a Joseph Lister Award for Social Science in 2002, and a NESTA DreamTime Fellowship in 2004. He started out as a magician and now appears regularly on British television programs to show how magic tricks work and to expose other forms of public deception. As a member of the Committee for Skeptical Inquiry (CSI), he investigates reports of paranormal occurrences. The books he has written for the general public include Deception and Self-deception: Investigating Psychics *(1997),* Laughlab: The Scientific Search for the World's Funniest Joke *(2002),* The Luck Factor: Changing Your Luck, Changing Your Life *(2003), and* Quirkology: The Curious Science of Everyday Lives *(2007), which, as Wiseman puts it, "examines the curious psychology of everyday life, including laughter, lying, and love." He has recently focused on exposing self-help books while publishing his own:* 59 Seconds: Change Your Life in Under a Minute *(2009).*

"The Search for the World's Funniest Joke" is an excerpt from Quirkology. *In 2001, Wiseman began a quest to find the world's funniest joke by applying rigorous scientific methods. In the following article, he intersperses a discussion of his results with theories about the purposes of telling jokes.*

In the 1970s, Monty Python's Flying Circus created a sketch that revolved 1 entirely around the idea of finding the world's funniest joke. In this sketch, which is set in the 1940s, a man named Ernest Scribbler thinks of the joke, writes it down, and promptly dies laughing. The joke turns out to be so funny that it kills anyone who reads it and is turned into a weapon of war.

In 2001 I started to think about the possibility of really searching for 2 the world's funniest joke. I knew that there would be a firm scientific underpinning for the project, because some of the world's greatest thinkers, including Freud, Plato and Aristotle, had written extensively about humour.

I got the green light from the British Association for the Advancement 3 of Science (BAAS) for my plan for an international Internet-based project called "LaughLab." I would set up a website that had two sections. In one part, people could input their favourite joke. In the second section, people could answer a few simple questions about themselves (such as their sex, age and nationality), and then rate how funny they found various jokes randomly selected from the archive. During the course of the year, we would be able to discover scientifically what makes different groups of people laugh, and which joke made the whole world smile.

The success of the project hinged on being able to persuade thousands 4 of people worldwide to participate. To help spread the word, we launched LaughLab with an eye-catching photograph based on perhaps the most famous (and, as we would go on to prove scientifically, least funny) joke in the world: "Why did the chicken cross the road? To get to the other side."

5   Within a few hours of opening the website, we received more than 500 jokes and 10,000 ratings. Then we hit a major problem. Many of the jokes were rude; absolutely filthy, in fact. Other jokes cropped up again and again ("What is brown and sticky?" "A stick" was submitted more than 300 times).

6   Participants were asked to rate each joke on a five-point scale ranging from "not very funny" to "very funny." Initially most of the material was pretty poor . . . so [it] tended to obtain low percentages. Around 25–35% of participants found the following jokes funny, and at that point they came towards the top of the list:

> Did you hear about the man who was proud when he completed a jigsaw within 30 minutes, because it said 'five to six years' on the box?

and

> Texan: Where are you from?
> Harvard graduate: I come from a place where we do not end our sentences with prepositions.
> Texan: OK—where are you from, jackass?

7   The top jokes had one thing in common—they create a sense of superiority in the reader. The feeling arises because the person in the joke appears stupid (like the man with the jigsaw), or pricks the pomposity of another (like the Texan answering the Harvard graduate).

8   We were not the first to notice that people laugh when they feel superior. The theory was described by Plato in *The Republic*. Plato was not a fan of laughter. He thought it was wrong to laugh at the misfortune of others, and that hearty laughter involved a loss of control that resulted in people appearing to be less than fully human. In the middle ages, dwarves and hunchbacks caused much merriment. In Victorian times, people laughed at the mentally ill in psychiatric institutions.

9   Very early in LaughLab, we could see the superiority theory appearing in the age-old battle of the sexes. This joke was rated as being funny by 25% of women, but just 10% of men:

> A husband stepped onto one of those penny scales that tell you your fortune and weight, and dropped in a coin.
> 'Listen to this,' he said to his wife, showing her a small white card.
> 'It says I'm energetic, bright, resourceful and a great person.'
> 'Yeah,' his wife nodded, 'and it has your weight wrong, too.'

10   One obvious possibility for the difference in ratings between the sexes is that the butt of the joke is a man, and so appeals more to women. Or it could be that women generally find jokes funnier than men. A year-long study of 1200 examples of laughing in everyday conversation revealed that 71% of women laugh when a man tells a joke, but only 39% of men laugh when a woman tells a joke. To help try to tease apart these

competing interpretations, we studied the LaughLab archive to find jokes that put down women, such as:

> A man driving on a highway is pulled over by a police officer. The officer asks: 'Did you know your wife and children fell out of your car a mile back?' A smile creeps onto the man's face and he exclaims: 'Thank God! I thought I was going deaf!'

On average, 15% of women rated as funny jokes putting down 11 women, compared with 50% of men.

Research suggests that men tell a lot more jokes than women. People 12 with high social status tend to tell more jokes than those lower down the pecking order. Traditionally, women have had a lower social status than men, and thus may have learned to laugh at jokes, rather than tell them. Interestingly, the only exception to this status/joke-telling relationship concerns self-disparaging humour, with people who have low social status telling more self-disparaging jokes than those with high status. Researchers examining self-disparaging humour produced by male and female professional comedians found that 12% of male scripts contained self-disparaging humour, compared with 63% of female scripts.

Quite quickly we downloaded 10,000 jokes, and the ratings from 13 100,000 people. The top joke at that early stage had been rated as funny by 46% of participants. It involved the famous fictional detective Sherlock Holmes and his long-suffering sidekick Dr. Watson:

> Sherlock Holmes and Dr. Watson were going camping. They pitched their tent under the stars and went to sleep. Sometime in the middle of the night Holmes woke Watson up and said: 'Watson, look up at the stars, and tell me what you see.'
> Watson replied: 'I see millions and millions of stars.'
> Holmes said: 'And what do you deduce from that?'
> Watson replied: 'Well, if there are millions of stars, and if even a few of those have planets, it's quite likely there are some planets like earth out there. And if there are a few planets like earth out there, there might also be life.'
> And Holmes said: 'Watson, you idiot, it means that somebody stole our tent.'

It is a classic example of two-tiered superiority theory. We laugh at 14 Watson for missing the absence of the tent, and also at the pompous way in which Holmes delivered the news to Watson.

According to Freud, jokes act as a kind of psychological release valve 15 that helps prevent the pressure of repression from becoming too great. Many of the jokes submitted to LaughLab supported Freud's ideas. Time and again, we would get jokes about the stresses and strains of loveless marriage, inadequate sexual performance and, of course, death:

> I've been in love with the same woman for 40 years. If my wife finds out, she'll kill me.

> A patient says to his psychiatrist: 'Last night I made a Freudian slip. I was having dinner with my mother-in-law and wanted to say: "Could you please pass the butter." But instead I said: "You silly cow, you've completely ruined my life."'

16   We also examined another source of humour—computers. LaughLab attracted lots of jokes about this topic ("The software said it needed Windows 98 or better, so I bought a Mac."). However, it also contained a few jokes actually written by a computer.

17   We were keen to discover whether computers were funnier than humans, . . . so [we] entered into LaughLab several of the computer-composed jokes. The majority of them received some of the lowest ratings in the archive. One example of computer comedy, however, was surprisingly successful, and beat about 250 human jokes:

> What kind of murderer has fibre? A cereal killer.

18   The results from another mini-experiment we conducted during LaughLab supported the widely held theory that some words and sounds are funnier than others, notably the mysterious comedy potential of the letter "K." Early on in the experiment, we received the following submission:

> There were two cows in a field. One said: 'Moo.' The other one said: 'I was going to say that!'

19   We decided to use the joke to test the words/sounds theory. We re-entered the joke into the archive several times, using a different animal and noise: two tigers going "Gruurrr," two birds going "Cheep," two mice going "Eeek," two dogs going "Woof" and so on. At the end of the study, we examined what effect the different animals had on how funny people found the joke. In third place came the original cow joke, second were two cats going "Meow," but the winning animal-noise joke was:

> Two ducks were sitting in a pond. One of the ducks said: 'Quack.' The other duck said: 'I was going to say that!'

20   By the end of the project we had received 40,000 jokes, and had them rated by more than 350,000 people from 70 countries. We identified our top joke. It had been rated as funny by 55% of the people who had taken part in the experiment:

> Two hunters are out in the woods when one of them collapses. He doesn't seem to be breathing and his eyes are glazed. The other guy whips out his phone and calls the emergency services.
> He gasps, 'My friend is dead! What can I do?'
> The operator says, 'Calm down. I can help. First, let's make sure he's dead.'
> There is silence, then a shot is heard. Back on the phone, the guy says, 'OK, now what?'

The year-long search for the world's funniest joke concluded. Did 21
we really manage to find it? In fact, I don't believe such a thing exists. If
our research into humour tells us anything, it is that people find different
things funny. Women laugh at jokes in which men look stupid. The elderly
laugh at jokes involving memory loss and hearing difficulties. Those who
are powerless laugh at those in power. There is no one joke that will make
everyone guffaw. Perhaps we uncovered the world's blandest joke—the
gag that makes everyone smile but very few laugh out loud.

Five years after the study, I received a telephone call from a friend. 22
He explained that he had just seen a television documentary film about
Spike Milligan, comedian and co-founder of the Goons, and that the pro-
gramme contained a very early version of our winning joke. The docu-
mentary contained a brief clip from a 1951 BBC programme called *London
Entertains* with the following early Goon sketch:

> Michael Bentine: I just came in and found him lying on the carpet there.
> Peter Sellers: Oh, is he dead?
> Michael Bentine: I think so.
> Peter Sellers: Hadn't you better make sure?
> Michael Bentine: All right. Just a minute.
> (Sound of two gunshots.)
> Michael Bentine: He's dead.

Spike Milligan died in 2002, but with the help of the documentary- 23
makers, I contacted his daughter Sile, and she confirmed that it was highly
likely that her father would have written the material. We announced that
we believed we had identified the author of the world's funniest joke.

I am often asked what was my favourite joke from the thousands that 24
flooded in through the year. I always give the same reply:

> A dog goes into a telegraph office, takes a blank form and writes: 'Woof,
> Woof, Woof, Woof, Woof, Woof, Woof, Woof, Woof.'
>   The clerk examines the paper and politely tells the dog: 'There are
> only nine words here. You could send another "Woof" for the same price.'
>   The dog looks confused and replies, 'But that would make no sense
> at all.'

2007

QUESTIONS FOR DISCUSSION

Content

a. Which of the jokes that Wiseman includes do you find the funniest, and
why? Are you in agreement or disagreement with Wiseman's study?

b. What were Wiseman's criteria for a joke to be considered the funniest? What does the winning joke have that makes it funnier than other jokes? Can a joke be considered the funniest if only 55 percent of people think it is funny?

c. What theories does Wiseman use to explain why people think jokes are funny?

d. What does it mean to say that jokes are a "release valve" for the "pressure of repression" (paragraph 15)? How do the jokes that follow illustrate Freud's theory?

e. Why might computers not be able to generate truly funny jokes?

f. Might what is funny change over time? How does Wiseman account for this?

g. In your opinion, did Wiseman overlook any category of joke that should have been included in his study?

Strategy and Style

h. What evidence does Wiseman use to back up his claims?

i. Besides example and illustration, what methods of development does Wiseman use and for what purpose?

j. How effective are Wiseman's examples? Do you find the jokes as funny as he says they are?

k. How would you describe Wiseman's tone? How does his tone vary from what you would expect of a scientist?

l. In studying humor, a scientist might have a difficult time making the research seem serious. How does Wiseman make his research come across as serious?

ENGAGING THE TEXT

a. Rate your own response to the jokes that Wiseman quotes, and explain your ranking.

b. Write a new joke using any one of the jokes in Wiseman's essay as a structural model. Reflect on why it was easy (or difficult) to write a joke.

SUGGESTIONS FOR SUSTAINED WRITING

a. Reread Wiseman's essay and identify the criteria—as much as you can make out—for choosing the world's funniest joke. Use these criteria to analyze one of your favorite jokes, explaining where your joke would rank in Wiseman's study.

b. Why do you tell jokes? Citing Wiseman and using examples from your own joke repertoire to illustrate, explain your motivation for telling jokes and describe the effect your jokes have on others.

c. Take one of the points Wiseman makes about joke telling, such as that "men tell a lot more jokes than women" (paragraph 12), and find out whether the point is supported by other researchers. Report on what you find, agreeing or disagreeing with Wiseman.

READ MORE

Wiseman and His Works

"Richard Wiseman" (http://www.richardwiseman.com): *Wiseman's personal website.*

"Laughlab" (http://www.laughlab.co.uk): *The official site of Wiseman's project.*

Humor Theory

"The International Society for Humor Studies" (http://www.hnu.edu/ishs/index.htm): *Scholarly website dedicated to humor research, hosted by the Holy Names University in Oakland, California.*

"Humor" (http://www.iep.utm.edu/h/humor.htm): *Definitions of the main theories of humor on The Internet Encyclopedia of Philosophy, based on the University of Tennessee–Martin website.*

Family Ghosts

Maxine Hong Kingston

Born in 1940 to recently arrived immigrants from China, Maxine Hong Kingston grew up having to negotiate between two very different cultures. Her gender in a culture that valued males over females created further difficulties. These two issues are the main themes that inform much of Hong Kingston's work, most notably The Woman Warrior: Memoirs of a Girlhood among Ghosts *(1975), a collection of autobiographical narrative essays though which she seeks to understand her female ancestors and the ways they helped to form her own identity. "Family Ghosts" is an excerpt from one of the essays in this collection. The most well known of her other books are* China Men *(1980), a collection of character sketches from real and legendary sources;* Tripmaster Monkey: His Fake Book *(1989), a novel; and* The Fifth Book of Peace *(2003). She has received numerous awards for her books, including a National Book Critics Circle Award for* The Woman Warrior, *a National Book Award for* China Men, *and a PEN West Award in Fiction for* Tripmaster Monkey. *She has also received the National Humanities Medal (1997) and a National Book Foundation Medal for Distinguished Contribution to American Letters*

(2008), among many other awards, fellowships, and honorary degrees. She currently teaches creative writing at The University of California at Berkeley.

"Family Ghosts" is the editors' title for an excerpt from the chapter titled "Shaman" in The Woman Warrior. *"Shaman" is a series of related sections that tells the story of Hong Kingston's mother, who had trained as a doctor in China before emigrating to the United States. Ghosts and healing traditions are thematic threads stitching the tales together.*

1 When the thermometer in our laundry reached one hundred and eleven degrees on summer afternoons, either my mother or my father would say that it was time to tell another ghost story so that we could get some good chills up our backs. My parents, my brothers, sisters, great-uncle, and "Third Aunt," who wasn't really our aunt but a fellow villager, someone else's third aunt, kept the presses crashing and hissing and shouted out the stories. Those were our successful days, when so much laundry came in, my mother did not have to pick tomatoes. For breaks we changed from pressing to sorting.

2 "One twilight," my mother began, and already the chills travelled my back and crossed my shoulders; the air rose at the nape and the back of the legs, "I was walking home after doctoring a sick family. To get home I had to cross a footbridge. In China the bridges are nothing like the ones in Brooklyn and San Francisco. This one was made from rope, laced and knotted as if my magpies. Actually it had been built by men who had returned after harvesting sea swallow nests in Malaya. They had had to swing over the faces of the Malayan cliffs in baskets they had woven themselves. Though this bridge pitched and swayed in the updraft, no one had ever fallen into the river, which looked like a bright scratch at the bottom of the canyon, as if the Queen of Heaven had swept her great silver hairpin across the earth as well as the sky."

3 One twilight, just as my mother stepped on the bridge, two smoky columns spiraled up taller than she. Their swaying tops hovered over her head like white cobras, one at either handrail. From stillness came a wind rushing between the smoke spindles. A high sound entered her temple bones. Through the twin whirlwinds she could see the sun and the river, the river twisting in circles, the trees upside down. The bridge moved like a ship, sickening. The earth dipped. She collapsed to the wooden slates, a ladder up the sky, her fingers so weak she could not grip the rungs. The wind dragged her hair behind her, then whipped it forward across her face. Suddenly the smoke spindles disappeared. The world righted itself, and she crossed to the other side. She looked back, but there was nothing there. She used the bridge often, but she did not encounter those ghosts again.

4 "They were Sit Dom Kuei," said Great-Uncle. "Sit Dom Kuei."

5 "Yes, of course," said my mother. "Sit Dom Kuei."

I keep looking in dictionaries under those syllables. "Kuei" means 6
"ghost," but I don't find any other words that make sense. I only hear
my great-uncle's river-pirate voice, the voice of a big man who had killed
someone in New York or Cuba, make the sounds—"Sit Dom Kuei." How
do they translate?

When the Communists issued their papers on techniques for com- 7
bating ghosts, I looked for "Sit Dom Kuei." I have not found them
described anywhere, although now I see that my mother won in ghost
battle because she can eat anything—quick, pluck out the carp's eyes, one
for Mother and one for Father. All heroes are bold toward food. In the
research against ghost fear published by the Chinese Academy of Science
is the story of a magistrate's servant, Kao Chung, a capable eater who in
1683 ate five cooked chickens and drank ten bottles of wine that belonged
to the sea monster with branching teeth. The monster had arranged its
food around a fire on the beach and started to feed when Kao Chung
attacked. The swan-feather sword he wrested from this monster can be
seen in the Wentung County Armory in Shantung today.

Another big eater was Chou Yi-han of Changchow, who fried a ghost. 8
It was a meaty stick when he cut it up and cooked it. But before that it had
been a woman out at night.

Chen Luan-feng, during the Yuan Ho era of the T'ang dynasty (A.D. 9
806-820), ate yellow croaker and pork together, which the thunder god
had forbidden. But Chen wanted to incur thunderbolts during drought.
The first time he ate, the thunder god jumped out of the sky, its legs
like old trees. Chen chopped off the left one. The thunder god fell to the
earth, and the villagers could see that it was a blue pig or bear with horns
and fleshy wings. Chen leapt on it, prepared to chop its neck and bite
its throat, but the villagers stopped him. After that, Chen lived apart as
a rainmaker, neither relatives nor the monks willing to bring lightning
upon themselves. He lived in a cave, and for years whenever there was
drought the villagers asked him to eat yellow croaker and pork together,
and he did.

The most fantastic eater of them all was Wei Pang, a scholar-hunter 10
of the Ta Li era of the T'ang dynasty (A.D. 766-779). He shot and cooked
rabbits and birds, but he could also eat scorpions, snakes, cockroaches,
worms, slugs, beetles, and crickets. Once he spent the night in a house
that had been abandoned because its inhabitants feared contamination
from the dead man next door. A shining, twinkling sphere came flying
through the darkness at Wei. He felled it with three true arrows—the first;
making the thing crackle and flame; the second dimming it; and the third
putting out its lights, sputter. When his servant came running in with a
lamp, Wei saw his arrows sticking in a ball of flesh entirely covered with
eyes, some rolled back to show the dulling whites. He and the servant pulled
out the arrows and cut up the ball into little pieces. The servant cooked the

morsels in sesame oil, and the wonderful aroma made Wei laugh. They ate half, saving half to show the household, which would return now.

11   Big eaters win. When other passers-by stepped around the bundle wrapped in white silk, the anonymous scholar of Hanchow took it home. Inside were three silver ingots and a froglike evil, which sat on the ingots. The scholar laughed at it and chased it off. That night two frogs the size of year-old babies appeared in his room. He clubbed them to death cooked them, and ate them with white wine. The next night a dozen frogs, together the size of a pair of year-old babies, jumped from the ceiling. He ate all twelve for dinner. The third night thirty small frogs were sitting on his mat and starting at him with their frog eyes. He ate them too. Every night for a month smaller but more numerous frogs came so that he always had the same amount to eat. Soon his floor was like the healthy banks of a pond in spring when the tadpoles, having just turned, sprang in the wet grass. "Get a hedgehog to help eat," cried him family. "I'm as good as a hedgehog," the scholar said, laughing. And at the end of the month the frogs stopped coming, leaving the scholar with the white silk and the silver ingots.

QUESTIONS FOR DISCUSSION

Content

a. How do the ghosts in Hong Kingston's parents' stories differ from the ones you are familiar with from stories?

b. How is Hong Kingston's mother a "warrior"? What are her battles?

c. From what you can see in the examples of ghosts in this essay, what role do ghost fighters have in their communities?

d. What attitudes toward women, children, and animals are reflected in these examples?

e. Why might eating the ghost be the best way to vanquish it?

f. Why might the young Hong Kingston not be able to translate "Sit Dom Kuei" (paragraph 6)?

g. What points is Hong Kingston making about family?

Strategy and Style

h. As examples, how well do these ghost stories illustrate Hong Kingston's points about family traditions?

i. Where does Hong Kingston use humor? What is the effect of the humor on you?

j. Hong Kingston starts her mother's story as a direct quote (paragraph 2), but then switches to telling the story herself (paragraph 3). Why might she have done this?

k. What is the effect of the occasional use of dialogue?

l. Hong Kingston frequently shifts her voice or point of view. Where does she do this, and why might she have done this?

m. As ghost stories, what do the stories told by the family lack in structure? What might be expected of listeners to fill in the gaps?

ENGAGING THE TEXT

a. Reread the essay and note the connections Hong Kingston makes between ghosts and food. Describe the function of food in protecting humans and vanquishing ghosts.

b. List the examples of the ghost stories gold by Hong Kingston's parents. What are the recurring themes? What lessons are being taught to the children?

SUGGESTIONS FOR SUSTAINED WRITING

a. Retell one of the ghost stories from your childhood, a story told by your family or by your friends. Describe the context for the story—the environment, the storyteller and the audience, and the reasons for telling the story. Discuss what made this story memorable.

b. "Family Ghosts" is one short section of a much longer essay, "Shaman," from The Woman Warrior. Read the entire essay and discuss how "Family Ghosts" fits into the piece as a whole. Who is the "shaman" in the story? What other ghosts and visions are recounted? What do you learn about Hong Kingston's mother or about storytelling?

c. Research the Chinese Ghost Festival and compare that tradition to the celebration of Halloween, Day of the Dead, or All Soul's Day.

READ MORE

Hong Kingston and Her Works

"Maxine Hong Kingston" (http://www.nationalbook.org/amerletters_2008_kingston.html): *A page devoted to the author on the National Book Foundation website, which includes links to videos, interviews, and in-depth articles about the author.*

"Maxine Hong Kingston (b. 1948)" (http://voices.cla.umn.edu/artistpages/kingstonMaxine.php): *Voices from the Gap website, which provides critical and biographical information as well as a selected bibliography and links to other sites.*

Outka, Paul. "Publish or Perish: Food, Hunger, and Self-Construction in Maxine Hong Kingston's *The Woman Warrior*. *Contemporary Literature* 38(3), 1997: 447-482.

Storytelling Traditions

"The International Storytelling Center" (http://www.storytellingcenter .net/): *Information about storytelling around the globe, storytelling festivals, and the Center itself in Jonesborough, Tennessee.*

"Eth-Noh-Tec Kinetic Story Theater" (http://www.ethnohtec.org/): *Website of a dance and theater group based in San Francisco that draws on Asian-American stories and myths.*

"The Hungry Ghost Festival" (http://www.chinese-culture.net/html/ hungry_ghost_festival.html): Information about the tradition of hungry ghosts on the Chinese Culture Website.

"The Chinese-American Experience: An Introduction" (http://immigrants. harpweek.com/ChineseAmericans/1Introduction/BillWeiIntro.htm): *Overview of the Chinese-American experience with reference to the family.*

"How to Tell a Ghost Story" (http://www.guardian.co.uk/lifeandstyle/ 2009/oct/31/how-to-tell-ghost-story): *A thoughtful and detailed feature article by a veteran teller of ghost stories written for the British newspaper* The Guardian.

Cause and Effect

If you read Chapter 3, you know that explaining causes and effects is similar to analyzing a process. Whereas the latter explains *how* something happens, the former seeks to reveal *why* it happens. Causal analysis is often used to explore questions in science, history, economics, and the social sciences. If you have taken courses in these subjects, you may have written papers or essay exams that discuss the major causes of World War I, explain changes in the U.S. banking system brought on by the Great Depression, or predict the environmental consequences of uncontrolled pollution.

Causal analysis is so natural an activity that it appears in the earliest of stages of mental awareness. It is a tool by which we reflect upon and learn from our past: The child who burns a hand knows why to stay away from the stove. But causal analysis is also a common way to anticipate the future. Peering into metaphorical crystal balls, we create elaborate plans, theorize about the consequences of our actions, and make appropriate changes in the way we live. "If I graduate in four years and get a fellowship to law school," dreams the ambitious first-year college student, "I might land a job with Biddle and Biddle and even run for city council by the time I'm 30. But first, I'd better improve my grades, which will mean studying harder and spending less time socializing."

The student's thinking illustrates an important point about the connection between causes and effects: It is often more complex than we imagine. For example, in "If Hitler Asked You to Electrocute a Stranger, Would You? Probably," Philip Meyer cannot theorize about people's willingness to obey authorities until he thoroughly explains Stanley Milgram's experiment and discusses Milgram's conclusions.

Keep this example in mind as you begin to use causal analysis as a way to develop ideas. More often than not, each cause and effect you discuss will require a thorough explanation using details that are carefully chosen and appropriate to your purpose. Remember, too, that you can call on a variety of skills and techniques to help you develop your analysis.

Anytime you use cause and effect, an important question is where to place your emphasis. Will you discuss what caused a particular phenomenon or will you focus on its effects? Both Shelby Steele and K. C. Cole focus on effects: Steele discusses the relationship between "black power" and "white guilt" and the effects these two forces have had on American attitudes and political policy, and Cole describes the effects of entropy that she sees in daily life. Paul Salopek, on the other hand, focuses on explaining the causes of Sudan's recent civil war. Of course, you may decide to strike a balance, as does Carlo Petrini. Petrini discusses how commodification of food has come about, while at the same time warning that this commodification has serious and negative effects on society.

As with the other kinds of writing in this text, purpose determines content and strategy. You read earlier that causal analysis is used frequently to explain historical or scientific phenomena. Such writing is often objective and dispassionate, but causal analysis has many applications. Because it is an especially powerful tool for persuasion, you might want to use it to speak with a strong voice on issues to which you are firmly committed, such as expressing concern over the state of the family, as Barbara Dafoe Whitehead does in "Where Have All the Parents Gone?" You might even want to analyze your reactions to social, political, or other types of problems to see what they tell you about yourself.

White Guilt

Shelby Steele

Shelby Steele (b. 1946) is a social critic who teaches literature and writing at San Jose State University. As an undergraduate at Coe College, he led a student civil rights group called SCOPE, which was philosophically linked to Martin Luther King, Jr.'s Southern Christian Leadership Conference. Later, however, influenced by Malcolm X, he shifted his energies to the black power movement. While studying for his M.A. in sociology at Southern Illinois University, he taught African-American literature in an experimental program designed to provide college credit to blacks who could not afford tuition. He earned a Ph.D. in English in 1974 from the University of Utah. His experiences as an activist and educator provide a foundation for his sometimes controversial writings. Since 1994, Steele has been a research fellow for Stanford University's Hoover Institution, specializing in race relations. Besides writing for the Hoover Institution, he also writes for the New York Times, The Wall Street Journal, *and* Harper's. *His books include* The Content of Our Character: A New Vision of Race in America *(1990), which won the National Book Critics Circle Award;* A Dream Deferred: The Second Betrayal of Black Freedom in America *(1998); and* White Guilt: How the End of White Supremacy Has Failed to Empower Blacks in America *(2006). Steele also helped create* Seven Days in Bensonhurst, *a film documentary about the racial unrest following the murder of a black teenager in a white New York City neighborhood in 1989. Steele received an Emmy, a Writer's Guild Award, and a San Francisco Film Festival Award for his work on this film, and in 2004 he received a National Humanities Medal.*

In a 1990 New York Times *profile, Steele said, "Some people say I shine a harsh light on difficult problems. But I never shine a light on anything I haven't experienced or write about fear I don't see in myself first." "White Guilt" was first published in* The American Scholar *in 1990.*

I don't remember hearing the phrase "white guilt" very much before the   1
mid-1960s. Growing up black in the 1950s, I never had the impression that whites were much disturbed by guilt when it came to blacks. When I would stray into the wrong restaurant in pursuit of a hamburger, it didn't occur to me that the waitress was unduly troubled by guilt when she asked me to leave. I can see now that possibly she was, but then all I saw was her irritability at having to carry out so unpleasant a task. If there was guilt, it was mine for having made an imposition of myself. I can remember feeling a certain sympathy for such people, as if I was victimizing them by drawing them out of an innocent anonymity into the unasked-for role of racial policemen. Occasionally they came right out and asked me to feel sorry for them. A caddymaster at a country club told my brother and me that he was doing us a favor by not letting us caddy at this white club and that we should try to understand his position, "put yourselves in my shoes." Our color had brought this man anguish and, if a part of that anguish was guilt, it was not as immediate to me as my own guilt. I smiled at the man to let him know he shouldn't feel bad and then began my long walk home. Certainly I also judge him a coward, but in that era his cowardice was something I had to absorb.

In the 1960s, particularly the black-is-beautiful late 1960s, this absorp-   2
tion of another's cowardice was no longer necessary. The lines of moral power, like plates in the Earth, had shifted. White guilt became so palpable you could see it on people. At the time what it looked like to my eyes was a remarkable loss of authority. And what whites lost in authority, blacks gained. You cannot feel guilty about anyone without giving away power to them. Suddenly, this huge vulnerability had opened up in whites and, as a black, you had the power to step right into it. In fact, black power all but demanded that you do so. What shocked me in the late 1960s, after the helplessness I had felt in the fifties, was that guilt had changed the nature of the white man's burden from the administration of inferiors to the uplift of equals—from the obligations of dominance to the urgencies of repentance.

I think what made the difference between the fifties and sixties, at   3
least as far as white guilt was concerned, was that whites underwent an archetypal Fall. Because of the immense turmoil of the civil rights movement, and later the black-power movement, whites were confronted for more than a decade with their willingness to participate in, or comply with, the oppression of blacks, their indifference to human suffering and denigration, their capacity to abide evil for their own benefit and in the

defiance of their own sacred principles. The 1964 Civil Rights Bill that bestowed equality under the law on blacks was also, in a certain sense, an admission of white guilt. Had white society not been wrong, there would have been no need for such a bill. In this bill the nation acknowledged its fallenness, its lack of racial innocence, and confronted the incriminating self-knowledge that it had rationalized for many years a flagrant injustice. Denial is a common way of handling guilt, but in the 1960s there was little will left for denial except in the most recalcitrant whites. With this defense lost there was really only one road back to innocence—through actions and policies that would bring redemption.

4   In the 1960s the need for white redemption from racial guilt became the most powerful, yet unspoken, element in America's social-policy-making process, first giving rise to the Great Society and then to a series of programs, policies, and laws that sought to make black equality and restitution a national mission. Once America could no longer deny its guilt, it went after redemption, or at least the look of redemption, and did so with a vengeance. Yet today, some twenty years later, study after study tells us that by many measures the gap between blacks and whites is widening rather than narrowing. A University of Chicago study indicates that segregation is more entrenched in American cities today than ever imagined. A National Research Council study notes the "status of blacks relative to whites (in housing and education) has stagnated or regressed since the early seventies." A follow-up to the famous Kerner Commission Report warns that blacks are as much at risk today of becoming a "nation within a nation" as we were twenty years ago, when the original report was made.

5   I think the white need for redemption has contributed to this tragic situation by shaping our policies regarding blacks in ways that may deliver the look of innocence to society and its institutions but that do very little actually to uplift blacks. The specific effect of this hidden need has been to bend social policy more toward reparation for black oppression than toward the much harder and more mundane work of black uplift and development. Rather than facilitate the development of blacks to achieve parity with whites, these programs and policies—affirmative action is a good example—have tended to give blacks special entitlements that in many cases are of no use because blacks lack the development that would put us in a position to take advantage of them. I think the reason there has been more entitlement than development is (along with black power) the unacknowledged white need for redemption—not true redemption, which would have concentrated policy on black development, but the appearance of redemption, which requires only that society, in the name of development, seems to be paying back its former victims with preferences. One of the effects of entitlements, I believe, has been to encourage in blacks a dependency both on entitlements and on the white

guilt that generates them. Even when it serves ideal justice, bounty from another man's guilt weakens. While this is not the only factor in black "stagnation" and "regression," I believe it is one very potent factor.

It is easy enough to say that white guilt too often has the effect of 6 bending social policies in the wrong direction. But what exactly is this guilt, and how does it work in American life?

I think white guilt, in its broad sense, springs from a knowledge of ill- 7 gotten advantage. More precisely, it comes from the juxtaposition of this knowledge with the inevitable gratitude one feels for being white rather than black in America. Given the moral instincts of human beings, it is all but impossible to enjoy an ill-gotten advantage, much less to feel at least secretly grateful for it, without consciously or unconsciously experiencing guilt. If, as Kierkegaard writes, "innocence is ignorance," then guilt must always involve knowledge. White Americans *know* that their historical advantage comes from the subjugation of an entire people. So, even for whites today for whom racism is anathema, there is no escape from the knowledge that makes for guilt. Racial guilt simply accompanies the condition of being white in America.

I do not believe that this guilt is a crushing anguish for most whites, 8 but I do believe it constitutes a continuing racial vulnerability—an openness to racial culpability—that is a thread in white life, sometimes felt, sometimes not, but ever present as a potential feeling. In the late 1960s almost any black could charge this vulnerability with enough current for a white person to feel it. I had a friend who had developed this activity into a sort of specialty. I don't think he meant to be mean, though certainly he was mean. I think he was, in that hyperbolic era, exhilarated by the discovery that his race, which had long been a liability, now gave him a certain edge—that white guilt was the true force behind black power. To feel this power he would sometimes set up what he called "race experiments." Once I watched him stop a white businessman in the men's room of a large hotel and convince him to increase his tip to the black attendant from one to twenty dollars.

My friend's tactic was very simple, even corny. Out of the attendant's 9 earshot he asked the man simply to look at the attendant, a frail, elderly, and very dark man in a starched white smock that made the skin on his neck and face look as leathery as a turtle's. He sat listlessly, pathetically, on a straight-backed chair next to a small table on which sat a stack of hand towels and a silver plate for tips. Since the attendant offered no service whatever beyond the handing out of towels, one could only conclude the hotel management offered his lowly presence as flattery to their patrons, as an opportunity for that easy noblesse oblige that could reassure even the harried and weary traveling salesman of his superior station. My friend was quick to make this point to the businessman and to say that no white man would do this job. But when the businessman put the single back in his wallet and took out a five, my friend only sneered. Did he understand the tragedy of a life spent this way, of what it must be like to earn one's paltry living as a symbol of inferiority? And did he realize that his privilege as an affluent white businessman (ironically he had just spent the day trying to sell a printing press to the Black Muslims for their newspaper *Mohammed Speaks*) was connected to the deprivation of this man and others like him?

10   But then my friend made a mistake that ended the game. In the heat of argument, which until then had only been playfully challenging, he inadvertently mentioned his father. This stopped the victim cold and his eyes turned inward. "What about your father?" the businessman asked. My friend replied, "He had a hard life, that's all." "How did he have a hard life?" the businessman asked. Now my friend was on the defensive. I knew he did not get along with his father, a bitter man who worked nights in a factory and demanded that the house be dark and silent all day. My friend blamed his father's bitterness on racism, but I knew he had not meant to exploit his own pain in this silly "experiment." Things had gotten too close to home, but he didn't know how to get out of the situation without losing face. Now, caught in his own trap, he did what he least wanted to do. He gave forth the rage he truly felt to a white stranger in a public men's room. "My father never had a chance," he said with the kind of anger that could easily turn to tears. "He never had a freakin' chance. Your father had all the goddamn chances, and you know he did. You sell printing presses to black people and make thousands and your father probably lives down in Fat City, Florida, all because you're white." On and on he went in this vein, using—against all that was honorable in him—his own profound racial pain to extract a flash of guilt from a white man he didn't even know.

11   He got more than a flash. The businessman was touched. His eyes became mournful, and finally he simply said, "You're right. Your people got a raw deal." He took a twenty dollar bill from his wallet and walked over and dropped it in the old man's tip plate. When he was gone my friend and I could not look at the old man, nor could we look at each other.

12   It is obvious that this was a rather shameful encounter for all concerned—my friend and I, as his silent accomplice, trading on our racial pain, tampering with a stranger for no reason, and the stranger then buying his way out of the situation for twenty dollars, a sum that was generous by one count and cheap by another. It was not an encounter of people but of historical grudges and guilts. Yet, when I think about it now twenty years later, I see that it had all the elements of a paradigm that I believe has been very much at the heart of racial policy-making in America since the 1960s.

13   My friend did two things that made this businessman vulnerable to his guilt—that brought his guilt into the situation as a force. First he put

this man in touch with his own knowledge of his ill-gotten advantage as a white. The effect of this was to disallow the man any pretense of racial innocence, to let him know that, even if he was not the sort of white who used the word *nigger* around the dinner table, he still had reason to feel racial guilt. But, as disarming as this might have been, it was too abstract to do much more than crack open this man's vulnerability, to expose him to the logic of white guilt. This was the five-dollar, intellectual sort of guilt. The twenty dollars required something more visceral. In achieving this, the second thing my friend did was something he had not intended to do, something that ultimately brought him as much shame as he was doling out: He made a display of his own racial pain and anger. (What brought him shame was not the pain and anger, but his trading on them for what turned out to be a mere twenty bucks.) The effect of this display was to reinforce the man's knowledge of ill-gotten advantage, to give credibility and solidity to it by putting a face on it. Here was human testimony, a young black beside himself at the thought of his father's racially constricted life. The pain of one man evidenced the knowledge of the other. When the businessman listened to my friend's pain, his racial guilt—normally only one source of guilt lying dormant among others— was called out like a neglected debt he would finally have to settle. An ill-gotten advantage is not hard to bear—it can be marked up to fate—until it touches the genuine human pain it has brought into the world. This is the pain that hardens guilty knowledge.

Such knowledge is a powerful influence when it becomes conscious. 14 What makes it so powerful is the element of fear that guilt always carries, the fear of what the guilty knowledge says about us. Guilt makes us afraid for ourselves, and thus generates as much self-preoccupation as concern for others. The nature of this preoccupation is always the redemption of innocence, the reestablishment of good feeling about oneself.

In this sense, the fear for the self that is buried in all guilt is a pres- 15 sure toward selfishness. It can lead us to put our own need for innocence above our concern for the problem that made us feel guilt in the first place. But this fear for the self does not only inspire selfishness; it also becomes a pressure to *escape* the guilt-inducing situation. When selfishness and escapism are at work, we are no longer interested in the source of our guilt and, therefore, no longer concerned with an authentic redemption from it. Then we only want the look of redemption, the gesture of concern that will give us the appearance of innocence and escape from the situation. Obviously the businessman did not put twenty dollars in the tip plate because he thought it would uplift black Americans. He did it selfishly for the appearance of concern and for the escape it afforded him.

This is not to say that guilt is never the right motive for doing good 16 works or showing concern, only that it is a very dangerous one because of its tendency to draw us into self-preoccupation and escapism. Guilt is a civilizing emotion when the fear for the self that it carries is contained—a containment that allows guilt to be more selfless and that makes genuine concern possible. I think this was the kind of guilt that, along with the other forces, made the 1964 Civil Rights Bill possible. But since then I believe too many of our social policies related to race have been shaped by the fearful underside of guilt.

17   Black power evoked white guilt and made it a force in American institutions, very much in the same way as my friend brought it to life in the businessman. Few people volunteer for guilt. Usually others make us feel it. It was the expression of black anger and pain that hardened the guilty knowledge of white ill-gotten advantage. And black power—whether from militant fringe groups, the civil rights establishment, or big city political campaigns—knew exactly the kind of white guilt it was after. It wanted to trigger the kind of white guilt in which whites fear for their own decency and innocence; it wanted the guilt of white self-preoccupation and escapism. Always at the heart of black power, in whatever form, has been a profound anger at what was done to blacks and an equally profound feeling that there should be reparations. But a sober white guilt (in which fear for the self is still contained) seeks a strict fairness—the 1964 Civil Rights Bill that guaranteed equality under the law. It is of little value when one is after more than fairness. So black power made its mission to have whites fear for their innocence, to feel a visceral guilt from which they would have to seek a more profound redemption. In such redemption was the possibility of black reparation. Black power upped the ante on white guilt.

18   With black power, all of the elements of the hidden paradigm that shape America's race-related social policy were in place. Knowledge of ill-gotten advantage could now be shown and deepened by black power into the sort of guilt from which institutions could only redeem themselves by offering more than fairness—by offering forms of reparation and compensation for past injustice. I believe this bent our policies toward racial entitlements at the expense of racial development. In 1964, one of the assurances Senator Hubert Humphrey and others had to give Congress to get the landmark Civil Rights Bill passed was that the bill would not in any way require employers to use racial preferences to rectify racial imbalances. But this was before the explosion of black power in the late 1960s, before the hidden paradigm was set in motion. After black power, racial preferences became the order of the day.

19   If this paradigm brought blacks entitlements, it also brought the continuation of the most profound problem in American society, the invisibility of blacks as a people. The white guilt that this paradigm elicits is the kind of guilt that preoccupies whites with their own innocence and pressures them toward escapism—twenty dollars in the plate and out the door. With this guilt, as opposed to the contained guilt of genuine concern, whites tend to see only their own need for quick redemption.

Blacks then become a means to this redemption and, as such, they must be seen as generally "less than" others. Their needs are "special," "unique," "different." They are seen exclusively along the dimension of their victimization, so that they become "different" people with whom whites can negotiate entitlements but never fully see as people like themselves. Guilt that preoccupies people with their own innocence blinds them to those who make them feel guilty. This, of course, is not racism, and yet it has the same effect as racism since it makes blacks something of a separate species for whom normal standards and values do not automatically apply.

Nowhere is this more evident today than in American universities. 20 At some of America's most elite universities administrators have granted concessions in response to black student demands (black power) that all but sanction racial separatism on campus—black "theme" dorms, black student unions, black yearbooks, homecoming dances, and so forth. I don't believe administrators sincerely believe in these separatist concessions. Most of them are liberals who see racial separatism as wrong. But black student demands pull administrators into the paradigm of self-preoccupied white guilt, whereby they seek a quick redemption by offering special entitlements that go beyond fairness. As a result, black students become all but invisible to them. Though blacks have the lowest grade point average of any racial group in American universities, administrators never sit down with them and "demand" in kind that black students bring their grades up to par. The paradigm of white guilt makes the real problems of black students secondary to the need for white redemption. It also cuts administrators off from their own values, which would most certainly discourage racial separatism and encourage higher academic performance for black students. Lastly, it makes for escapist policies. There is no difference between giving black students a separate lounge and leaving twenty dollars in the tip plate on the way out the door.

1990

QUESTIONS FOR DISCUSSION

Content

a. According to Steele, what has caused white guilt? Trace the causal links he describes.
b. At the end of paragraph 6, Steele asks, "But what exactly is this guilt, and how does it work in American life?" How does he answer his question?

c. What does he mean when he says that "white guilt was the true force behind black power" (paragraph 8)?

d. What happened in the men's room between Steele's friend and the white businessman (paragraphs 8–13)? What was Steele's friend's "racial experiment"? What went "wrong" and why?

e. Why does the businessman put the $20 bill in the tip plate?

f. How does Steele define guilt? What is the difference between the general term *guilt* and the specific term *white guilt*?

g. According to Steele, what effects does white guilt have on society? What are both its positive and its negative effects?

h. What is the relationship between black power and white guilt?

i. According to Steele, what did the Civil Rights Act of 1964 cause?

Strategy and Style

j. Look up *visceral*, a key word in paragraphs 13 and 17. What does this word mean in the context of these paragraphs? What other words does Steele use in these paragraphs to help define the word? Why was being visceral a problem?

k. What is the effect on you of the example of the "racial experiment"? Is it more of a "visceral" effect or an intellectual effect? What effect might Steele have intended with this example?

l. Look up *paradigm* (paragraph 20). What does the word mean by itself? What does it mean in the phrase "paradigm of white guilt"?

m. How would you characterize the tone of this essay? Does Steele sound calm, angry, impassioned, or what?

ENGAGING THE TEXT

a. In paragraph 2 Steele writes, "You cannot feel guilty about anyone without giving away power to them." Describe an event or two from your own life that illustrates this statement.

b. Summarize this essay in the form of a letter to your parents telling them about the reading you are doing for this class. Besides your summary, mention the one or two things that strike you as most important about the essay.

SUGGESTIONS FOR SUSTAINED WRITING

a. By the end of the essay Steele begins to suggest ways to solve the problem of racial separatism; however, he does not elaborate on his suggestions. Write an essay in which you pick up on the points raised in paragraph 20 and present a detailed solution to the problem.

b. Compare Steele's essay to "Black Men and Public Space" by Brent Staples in Chapter 7, to "Coming to an Awareness of Language" by Malcolm X in Chapter 1, or to "Meanings of a Word" by Gloria Naylor in Chapter 4. What does each essay say about stereotypes, anger, and racism?

c. Do some research into a particular period or event mentioned by Steele—the black power movement of the late 1960s or the 1964 Civil Rights Act, for example. Do not merely summarize your research, but use it to come to an understanding of Steele's essay. You may wish to write the paper as a comparison of how you understood the essay on a first reading to how you understand it after your research.

READ MORE

Steele and His Works

"The New Betrayal of Black Freedom in America" (http://www .independent.org/events/transcript.asp?eventID=47): *Transcript of a speech by Steele to the Independent Institute.*

"Shelby Steele" (http://www.hoover.org/fellows/10347): *A brief biography of Steele on the Hoover Institution website.*

"Under the Skin: Shelby Steele on Race in America" (http://www.hoover .org/publications/hoover-digest/article/6285): *Transcript of an interview with Steele.*

Race Relations

"How Race Is Lived in America" (http://www.nytimes.com/library/ national/race/): *Links to articles and web resources.*

"U.S. Commission on Civil Rights" (http://www.usccr.gov): *The federal government's website devoted to civil rights.*

"Voices of Civil Rights" (http://www.voicesofcivilrights.org): *A collection of personal stories related to civil rights, compiled by the AARP, the Leadership Council on Civil Rights, and the Library of Congress.*

Where Have All the Parents Gone?

Barbara Dafoe Whitehead

Barbara Dafoe Whitehead (b. 1944) was born in Rochester, Minnesota. She received a B.A. in 1966 from the University of Wisconsin and an M.A. in 1972 and a Ph.D. in 1976 from the University of Chicago. Dafoe Whitehead is a social historian who co-directed the National Marriage Project from 1997 to 2009. She is currently the Director of the John Templeton Center for Thrift and Generosity at the Institute for American Values. She became an overnight celebrity for her article "Dan Quayle Was Right" (published in Atlantic Monthly, *1993) supporting Quayle's criticism of the television show* Murphy Brown, *which had broadcast an episode applauding single-parent families. Since then, Dafoe Whitehead has been interested in how American culture allows such a high rate of divorce, an interest that formed the basis for her book* The Divorce Culture *(1997). On a related topic, she has also written* Why There Are No Good Men Left: The Romantic Plight of the New Single Woman *(2003). She has written many articles about family issues—including* "Where Have All the Parents Gone?"—*which originally appeared in* New Perspectives Quarterly *in 1990.*

In an interview, Dafoe Whitehead touches on the causes of the breakdown of American families; one cause was the "sustained economic expansion for the American middle class" following World War II. She says, "This sense of economic affluence in turn bred a sense of psychological affluence. People felt that they could take risks and make changes in their personal and family lives that would improve their individual sense of well-being."

1   "Invest in kids," George Bush mused during his 1988 presidential campaign, "I like it." Apparently so do others. A growing number of corporate CEOs and educators, elected officials and child-welfare advocates have embraced the same language. "Invest in kids" is the bumper sticker for an important new cause, aptly tagged the *kids as capital* argument. It runs as follows:

2   America's human capital comes in two forms: The active work force and the prospective work force. The bulk of tomorrow's workers are today's children, of course. So children make up much of the stockpile of America's potential human capital.

3   If we look at them as tomorrow's workers, we begin to appreciate our stake in today's children. They will determine when we can retire, how well we can live in retirement, how generous our health insurance will be, how strong our social safety net, how orderly our society. What's more, today's children will determine how successfully we compete in the global economy. They will be going head-to-head against Japanese, Korean, and West German children.

4   Unfortunately, American children aren't prepared to run the race, let alone win it. Many are illiterate, undernourished, impaired, unskilled, poor. Consider the children who started first grade in 1986: 14 percent were illegitimate; 15 percent were physically or emotionally handicapped; 15 percent spoke another language other than English; 28 percent were poor; and fully 40 percent could be expected to live in a single-parent home before they reached eighteen. Given falling birth rates, this future work force is small—all the more reason to worry about its poor quality. So "invest in kids" is not the cry of the soft-hearted altruist but the call of the hardheaded realist.

5   *Kids as capital* has caught on because it responds to a broad set of national concerns. Whether one is worried about the rise of the underclass,

the decline of the family, our standing in the global economy, the nation's level of educational performance, or intergenerational conflict, kids as capital seems to offer an answer.

Further, *kids as capital* offers the rationale for a new coalition for child 6 welfare programs. The argument reaches beyond the community of traditional children's advocates and draws business into the child-saving fold. American corporations clearly have a stake in tomorrow's work force as they don't have in today's children. *Kids as capital* gives the tough-minded, fifty-five-year-old CEO a reason to "care" about the eight-year-old, Hispanic school girl.

Nevertheless, the argument left unchallenged could easily become 7 yet another "feel-good" formula that doesn't work. Worse, it could end up betraying those it seeks to save—the nation's children.

First, *kids as capital* departs from a classic American vision of the 8 future. Most often, our history has been popularly viewed as progressive, with each generation breaking with and improving on the past. As an immigrant nation, we have always measured our progress through the progress of our children; they have been the bearers of the dream.

Kids as capital turns this optimistic view on its head. It conjures up 9 a picture of a dark and disorderly future. Essentially, kids as capital is dystopic—closer to the spirit of *Blade Runner* and *Black Rain* than *Wizard of Oz* or *It's a Wonderful Life*. Children, in this view, do not bear the dream. They carry the seeds of our destruction. In short, *kids as capital* plays on our fears, rather than our hopes. It holds out the vision of a troubled future in order to secure a safer and more orderly present.

There is something troubling, too, in such an instrumental view of 10 children. To define them narrowly as tomorrow's wonders is to strip them of their full status as humans, as children: Kids can't be kids; they can only be embryonic workers. And treating *kids as capital* makes it easier to measure them solely through IQ tests, class standing, SAT scores, drop-out ratios, physical fitness tests. This leaves no place in the society for the slow starter, the handicapped, the quirky, and the nonconforming.

Yet *kids as capital* has an even more serious flaw. It evades the central 11 fact of life for American children: They have parents.

As we all know, virtually every child in America grows up in a family 12 with one or more parents. Parents house children. Parents feed children. Parents clothe children. Parents nurture and protect children. Parents instruct children in everything from using a fork to driving a car. To be sure, there have been vast changes in family life, and, increasingly, parents must depend on teachers, doctors, day-care workers, and technology to help care for and educate their children. Even so, these changes haven't altered one fundamental fact: In American society, parents still bear the primary responsibility for the material and spiritual welfare of children. As our teachers and counselors and politicians keep reminding us, everything begins at home. So, if today's children are in trouble, it's because today's parents are in trouble.

13   As recently as a dozen years ago, it was the central argument of an ambitious report by the Carnegie Council on Children. The Council put it plainly: "The best way to help children tomorrow is to support parents today." Yet, that view has been lost. The *kids as capital* argument suppresses the connection between parents and children. It imagines that we can improve the standing of children without improving the standing of the parents. In the new rhetoric, it is hard even to find the word "parent." Increasingly, kids are portrayed as standing alone out there somewhere, cosmically parent-free.

14   As a result, *kids as capital* ignores rather than addresses one of the most important changes in American life: The decline in the power and standing of the nation's parents.

15   Only a generation ago, parents stood at the center of society. First of all, there were so many of them—fully half the nation's households in 1960 were parent households with one or more children under eighteen. Moreover, parents looked alike—Dad worked and Mom stayed at home. And parents marched through the stages of childbearing and child rearing in virtual lockstep: Most couples who married in the 1940s and 1950s finished having their 3.2 children by the time they were in their late twenties.

16   Their demographic dominance meant two things: First, it made for broad common ground in child rearing. Parents could do a great deal to support each other in raising the new generation. They could, and did, create a culture hospitable to children. Secondly, it made for political clout. When so many adults were parents and so many parents were part of an expanding consumer economy, private and public interests converged. The concerns of parents—housing, health, education—easily found their way into the national agenda. Locally, too, parents were dominant. In some postwar suburbs like Levittown, Pennsylvania, three-quarters of all residents were either parents or children under ten. Not surprisingly, there was little dissent when it came to building a new junior high or establishing a summer recreation program or installing a new playground. What's more, parents and kids drove the consumer economy. Every time they bought a pair of sneakers or a new bike, they were acting in the nation's best interest.

17   Behind this, of course, lurked a powerful pronatal ideology. Parenthood was the definitive credential of adulthood. More than being married, more than getting a job, it was having a child that baptized you as an adult in postwar America. In survey after survey, postwar parents rated children above marriage itself as the greatest reward of private life. For a generation forced to make personal sacrifices during the Depression and the war, having children and pursuing a private life represented a new kind of freedom.

By the 1970s, parents no longer enjoyed so central a place in the   18
society. To baby boom children, postwar family life seemed suffocating
and narrow. Women, in particular, wanted room to breathe. The rights
movements of the sixties and seventies overturned the pronatal ideology,
replacing it with an ideology of choice. Adults were free to choose among
many options: Single, married, or divorced; career-primary or career-
secondary; parent, stepparent, or child-free.

Thus, parenthood lost its singular status. It no longer served as the   19
definitive credential of maturity and adult achievement. In fact, as careers
and personal fulfillment beckoned, parenthood seemed just the opposite:
A serious limitation on personal growth and success. As Gloria Steinem
put it, "I either gave birth to someone else or I gave birth to myself."

As the pronatal ideology vanished, so did the close connection   20
between private families and the public interest. Raising children was no
longer viewed as a valuable contribution to the society, an activity that
boosted the economy, built citizen participation, and increased the nation's
confidence in the future. Instead, it became one option among many. No
longer a moral imperative, child rearing was just another "lifestyle choice."

Viewed this way, raising children looked like an economic disaster.   21
Starting out, parents had to shell out $3,000 for basic prenatal care and
maternity costs; $3,000–$5,000 per child for day care; and $2,500 for the
basic baby basket of goods and services. Crib-to-college costs for middle-
class Americans could run as high as $135,000 per child. And, increasingly,
the period of economic dependency for children stretched well beyond
age eighteen. College tuitions and start-up subsidies for the new college
graduate became part of the economic burden of parenthood. In an ad
campaign, Manufacturers Hanover Trust gave prospective parents fair
warning: "If you want a bundle of joy; you'll need a bundle of money."

Hard-pressed younger Americans responded to these new realities in   22
several ways. Some simply chose not to have children. Others decided to
have one or two, but only after they had a good job and solid prospects.
Gradually, the number of parent households in the nation declined from
one-half to one-third, and America faced a birth dearth.

For those who chose the parent option, there was only one way to   23
face up to the new economic pressures of child rearing: Work longer
and harder outside the home. For all but the extremely well-off, a second income became essential. But in struggling to pay the bills, parents
seemed to be short-changing their children in another way. They weren't
taking their moral responsibilities seriously enough. They weren't spending enough time with their kids. They weren't reading to the children or
playing with the kids or supervising homework. And, most important,
they weren't teaching good values.

This emerging critique marked a dramatic change in the way society   24
viewed parents. In the postwar period, the stereotypical parent was

self-sacrificing, responsible, caring, attentive—an impossible standard, to be sure, but one that lent enormous popular support and approval to adults engaged in the messy and difficult work of raising children. Cruel, abusive, self-absorbed parents might exist, but the popular culture failed to acknowledge them. It was not until parents began to lose their central place in the society that this flattering image faded. Then, quite rapidly, the dominant image of The Good Parent gave way to a new and equally powerful image—the image of The Bad Parent.

25   The shift occurred in two stages. The first-stage critique emerged in the seventies and focused on an important new figure: The working mother. Working mothers were destroying their children and the family, conservative critics charged. They weren't feeding kids wholesome meals, they weren't taking the kids to church, they weren't serving as moral exemplars. Liberals sided with working mothers, but conceded that they were struggling with some new and difficult issues: Was day care as good as mother care? Was quality time good enough? Were the rewards of twelve-hour workdays great enough to make up for the loss of sleep and leisure-time? Where did the mother of a feverish child belong—at the crib or at her desk?

26   On the whole, the first-stage critique was a sympathetic critique. In its view, parents might be affected by stress and guilt, but they weren't yet afflicted by serious pathology. After all, in the seventies, the nation's most suspect drug was laetrile, not crack or ice. Divorce was still viewed as a healthy alternative to an unhappy family life. But as the eighties began, a darker image of parents appeared. In the second-stage critique, . . . parents became toxic.

27   Day after day, throughout the eighties, Americans confronted an ugly new reality. Parents were hurting and murdering their children. Day after day, the newspapers brought yet another story of a child abandoned or battered. Day after day, the local news told of a child sexually abused by a father or a stepfather or a mother's boyfriend. Week by week, the national media brought us into courtrooms where photographs of battered children were held up to the camera. The sheer volume of stories suggested an epidemic of historic proportion. In even the most staid publications, the news was sensational. *The New York Times* carried bizarre stories usually found only in tabloids: A father who tortured his children for years; a mother who left her baby in a suitcase in a building she then set on fire; parents who abandoned babies dead or alive, in toilets, dumpsters, and alleyways.

28   Drug use among parents was one clear cause of abuse. And, increasingly, child abuse and drug abuse were linked in the most direct way possible. Pregnant women were battering their children in the womb, delivering drugs through their umbilical cords. Nightly images of crack-addicted babies in neonatal units destroyed any lingering public

sympathy for mothers of the underclass. And as the highly publicized Joel Steinberg case made clear, middle-class parents, too, took drugs and killed babies. Even those parents who occasionally indulged were causing their children harm. The Partnership for Drug-Free America ran ads asking: "With millions of parents doing drugs, is it any wonder their kids are too?"

More than drugs, it was divorce that lay at the heart of middle-class 29 parental failure. It wasn't the crackhouse but the courthouse that was the scene of their collapse. Parents engaged in bitter custody battles. Parents kidnapped their own children. Parents used children as weapons against each other or simply walked away from their responsibilities. In an important new study on the long-term effects of divorce, Judith Wallerstein challenged the earlier notion that divorce is healthy for kids. She studied middle-class families for fifteen years after divorce and came up with some startling findings: Almost half of the children in the study entered adulthood as worried, underachieving, self-deprecating, and sometimes angry young men and women; one in four experienced a severe and enduring drop in their standard of living; three in five felt rejected by at least one parent. Her study concluded: "Divorce is almost always more devastating for children than for their parents. . . . [W]hile divorce can rescue a parent from an intolerable situation, it can fail to rescue the children."

As a group, today's parents have been portrayed as selfish and uncaring: Yuppie parents abandon the children to the au pair; working parents turn their kids over to the mall and the video arcade; single parents hang a key around their kids' necks and a list of emergency numbers on the refrigerator. Even in the healthiest families, parents fail to put their children first.

The indictment of parents is pervasive. In a survey by the Carnegie 31 Foundation, 90 percent of a national sample of public school teachers say a lack of parental support is a problem in their classrooms. Librarians gathered at a national convention to draft a new policy to deal with the problem of parents who send unattended children to the library after school. Daycare workers complain to Ann Landers that all too often parents hand over children with empty stomachs and full diapers. Everywhere, parents are flunking the most basic tests.

Declining demographically, hard-pressed economically, and disar- 32 rayed politically, parents have become part of the problem. For proponents of the *kids as capital* argument, the logic is clear: Why try to help parents—an increasingly marginal and unsympathetic bunch—when you can rescue their children?

To blame parents for larger social changes is nothing new. In the past, 33 child-saving movements have depended on building a public consensus that certain parents have failed. Child reformers in the Progressive Era, for example, were able to expand the scope of public sector responsibility for the welfare of children by exploiting mainstream fears about immigrant parents and their child-rearing practices. But what is new is the sense that the majority of parents—up and down the social ladder—are failing. Even middle-class parents, once solid, dependable caretakers of the next generation, don't seem to be up to the job.

34   By leaving parents out of the picture, *kids as capital* conjures up the image of our little workers struggling against the little workers of Germany and the little workers of Japan. But this picture is obviously false. For the little workers of Germany and Japan have parents too. The difference is that their parents are strongly valued and supported by the society for their contributions *as parents*. We won't be facing up to reality until we are ready to pit our parents against their parents, and thus our family policy against theirs.

1990

QUESTIONS FOR DISCUSSION

Content

a. What is the "kids as capital" argument (paragraphs 2–6)?
b. What is Dafoe Whitehead's initial response to this argument (paragraphs 7–14)?
c. Though this essay is in part a cause/effect analysis, it is also an argument. What is Dafoe Whitehead arguing?
d. What is the main cause/effect relationship on which this argument is based?
e. Paraphrase and elaborate on paragraph 9. What is Dafoe Whitehead's point in this paragraph? Do you agree with her?
f. In paragraph 17, the author refers to a "pronatal ideology." What does she mean?
g. What are the stages in the shift from the rosy view of parenthood in the 1950s to the dark view of parenthood now? What has happened at each stage to further harm the image of parents?

Strategy and Style

h. Writers who use the cause/effect approach often use particular words or phrases to signal the cause/effect relationships. Some of these words and phrases that Dafoe Whitehead uses are "as a result," "thus," "behind this," "then," "gave way to," and "lay at the heart of." Find these and other clues in this essay, and explain what the cause/effect relationships are.

i. Dafoe Whitehead begins her essay with several paragraphs (2–6) that present the other side of the argument; she then presents her own argument (paragraphs 7–14). What might have been her reasons for giving the other side so much attention?

j. Paragraph 7 is a transition between the two arguments. How does it link the two arguments? What are the key words that link the "kids as capital" argument with Dafoe Whitehead's argument?

k. Look at the transition words and phrases that frequently begin paragraphs (for example, "unfortunately" in paragraph 4, "further" in paragraph 6, "nevertheless" in paragraph 7, and "as we all know" in paragraph 12). What job do these words and phrases perform?

ENGAGING THE TEXT

a. List the points of the "kids as capital" argument (paragraphs 2–6) that Dafoe Whitehead summarizes before she presents her own argument. Then list the points of her own argument (paragraphs 7–14). Write a brief comparison of the two arguments. Which seems stronger?

b. Look up the Joel Steinberg case (mentioned in paragraph 28) in *The New York Times Index* and/or in a periodicals database. Find and summarize one or two articles about the case.

SUGGESTIONS FOR SUSTAINED WRITING

a. Write a counterargument to Dafoe Whitehead's argument. Before you begin drafting your paper, outline her essay so that you can clearly see its logic and main points. Then brainstorm a list of points that you could make against her points. Also mark places in your argument where facts and statistics would strengthen it.

b. Dafoe Whitehead does not provide a plan for solving the problem she has described because her intention in this essay is merely to convince us what the real problem is. She does, however, imply in her conclusion that we must find a way to value parents and to create stability in parenting. Write an essay in which you present a specific plan to achieve this. Bring in ideas from one or more of the following essays: Gail Sheehy's "Predictable Crises of Adulthood" (Chapter 5), Scott Russell Sanders's "The Men We Carry in Our Minds" (Chapter 6), and Sandra Cisneros's "Only Daughter" (Chapter 11).

c. Conversely, agree with Dafoe Whitehead's argument and write an essay that expands upon it. Look up in the library the surveys and studies she cites. Use at least one of these studies as the basis for your essay.

READ MORE

Whitehead and Her Works

"Institute of American Values" (http://www.americanvalues.org/) and "Center for Thrift and Generosity" (http://www.newthrift.org/index. php): *Linked websites for the organization that Dafoe Whitehead directs.*

"Let's Get Married" (http://www.pbs.org/wgbh/pages/frontline/ shows/marriage): Frontline *video, interview transcript with Whitehead and others, and links to readings about marriage.*

Marriage and Parenting

"The National Marriage Project" (http://marriage.rutgers.edu/): *Links to online articles and statistical information on marriage.*

"Family First" (http://www.familyfirst.net): *Advice on a range of topics concerning parenting.*

Hackstaff, Karla B. *Marriage in a Culture of Divorce.* Philadelphia: Temple UP, 1999.

If Hitler Asked You to Electrocute a Stranger, Would You? Probably

Philip Meyer

Philip Meyer (b. 1930) earned a B.S. in 1952 from Kansas State University, earned an M.A. in 1963 from the University of North Carolina, and did graduate work at Harvard University during 1966 and 1967. While attending college, he worked as the assistant state editor of the Topeka Daily Capital *and as a reporter for the* Miami Herald. *From 1962 to 1978 he was the Washington, D.C., correspondent for Knight-Ridder Newspapers, and from 1978 to 1982 he was Knight-Ridder's director of news and circulation research in Miami. Since then, he has taught journalism at the University of North Carolina at Chapel Hill, holding the Knight Chair in Journalism from 1993 to 2008. In 1968, he shared a Pulitzer Prize with the staff of the* Detroit Free Press *for covering the Detroit riots in 1967. His research interests include public/civic journalism and computer-assisted reporting; several of his articles on these subjects can be found on his web page (see* Read More *at the end of this selection). He has written several books about journalism, including* Precision Journalism, *which was first published in 1973 and has reappeared in subsequent editions;* To Keep the Republic, *written in collaboration with David Olson in 1975;* Editors, Publishers, and Newspaper Ethics *(1983); and* The Vanishing

Newspaper: Saving Journalism in the Information Age *(2005). He also contributes regularly to* Public Opinion Quarterly *and* Esquire. *"If Hitler Asked You . . ." was first published in* Esquire *in 1970.*

In a paper about public journalism, Meyer discusses objectivity in reporting, writing that objectivity is often defined by reporters too rigidly as "standing so far from the community that you see all events and all viewpoints as equally distant and important—or unimportant. . . . The result is a laying out of facts in a sterile, noncommittal manner, and then standing back to 'let the reader decide' which view is true. This, in effect, is objectivity of result, defining objectivity not by the way we go about our business of gathering and interpreting the news, but by what we put in the paper." A better way to report, Meyer writes, is by "objectivity of method," for which reports would follow the "objective scientific standard of replicability," include "theories about the underlying causes of events," and document the "paper trail that any other investigator could find and follow and come out with the same results." As you read the following essay, consider what rules Meyer followed for objective reporting.

In the beginning, Stanley Milgram was worried about the Nazi problem.   1
He doesn't worry much about the Nazis anymore. He worries about you and me, and, perhaps, himself a little bit too.

Stanley Milgram is a social psychologist, and when he began his   2
career at Yale University in 1960 he had a plan to prove, scientifically, that Germans are different. The Germans-are-different hypothesis has been used by historians, such as William L. Shirer, to explain the systematic destruction of the Jews by the Third Reich.

The appealing thing about this theory is that it makes those of us   3
who are not Germans feel better about the whole business. Obviously, you and I are not Hitler, and it seems equally obvious that we would never do Hitler's dirty work for him. But now, because of Stanley Milgram, we are compelled to wonder. Milgram developed a laboratory experiment which provided a systematic way to measure obedience. His plan was to try it out in New Haven on Americans and then go to Germany and try it out on Germans. He was strongly motivated by scientific curiosity, but there was also some moral content in his decision to pursue this line of research, which was, in turn, colored by his own Jewish background. If he could show that Germans are more obedient than Americans, he could then vary the conditions of the experiment and try to find out just what it is that makes some people more obedient than others. With this understanding, the world might, conceivably, be just a little bit better.

But he never took his experiment to Germany. He never took it any   4
farther than Bridgeport. The first finding, also the most unexpected and disturbing finding, was that we Americans are an obedient people: Not blindly obedient, and not blissfully obedient, just obedient. "I found so much obedience," says Milgram softly, a little sadly, "I hardly saw the need for taking the experiment to Germany."

5   There is something of the theatre director in Milgram, and his technique, which he learned from one of the old masters in experimental psychology, Solomon Asch, is to stage a play with every line rehearsed, every prop carefully selected, and everybody an actor except one person. That one person is the subject of the experiment. The subject, of course, does not know he is in a play. He thinks he is in real life.

6   The experiment worked like this: If you were an innocent subject in Milgram's melodrama, you read an ad in the newspaper or received one in the mail asking for volunteers for an educational experiment. The job would take about an hour and pay $4.50. So you make an appointment and go to an old Romanesque stone structure on High Street with the imposing name of The Yale Interaction Laboratory. It looks something like a broadcasting studio. Inside, you meet a young, crew-cut man in a laboratory coat who says he is Jack Williams, the experimenter. There is another citizen, fiftyish, Irish face, an accountant, a little overweight, and very mild and harmless-looking. This other citizen seems nervous and plays with his hat while the two of you sit in chairs side by side and are told that the $4.50 checks are yours no matter what happens. Then you listen to Jack Williams explain the experiment.

7   It is about learning, says Jack Williams in a quiet, knowledgeable way. Science does not know much about the conditions under which people learn and this experiment is to find out about negative reinforcement. Negative reinforcement is getting punished when you do something wrong, as opposed to positive reinforcement which is getting rewarded when you do something right. The negative reinforcement in this case is electric shock.

8   Then Jack Williams takes two pieces of paper, puts them in a hat, and shakes them up. One piece of paper is supposed to say, "Teacher" and the other, "Learner." Draw one and you will see which you will be. The mild-looking accountant draws one, holds it close to his vest like a poker player, looks at it, and says, "Learner." You look at yours. It says; "Teacher." You do not know that the drawing is rigged, and both slips say "Teacher." The experimenter beckons to the mild-mannered "learner."

9   "Want to step right in here and have a seat, please?" he says. "You can leave your coat on the back of that chair . . . roll up your right sleeve, please. Now what I want to do is strap down your arms to avoid excessive movement on your part during the experiment. This electrode is connected to the shock generator in the next room.

10   "And this electrode paste," he says, squeezing some stuff out of a plastic bottle and putting it on the man's arm, "is to provide a good contact and to avoid a blister or burn. Are there any questions now before we go into the next room?"

11   You don't have any, but the strapped-in "learner" does.

12   "I do think I should say this," says the learner. "About two years ago, I was at the veterans' hospital . . . they detected a heart condition. Nothing

serious, but as long as I'm having these shocks, how strong are they—how dangerous are they?"

Williams, the experimenter, shakes his head casually. "Oh, no," he says. 13 "Although they may be painful, they're not dangerous. Anything else?"

Nothing else. And so you play the game. The game is for you to read 14 a series of word pairs: For example, blue-girl, nice-day, fat-neck. When you finish the list, you read just the first word in each pair and then a multiple-choice list of four other words, including the second word of the pair. The learner, from his remote, strapped-in position, pushes one of four switches to indicate which of the four answers he thinks is the right one. If he gets it right, nothing happens and you go on to the next one. If he gets it wrong, you push a switch that buzzes and gives him an electric shock. And then you go to the next word. You start with 15 volts and increase the number of volts by 15 for each wrong answer. The control board goes from 15 volts on one end to 450 volts on the other. So that you know what you are doing, you get a test shock yourself, at 45 volts. It hurts. To further keep you aware of what you are doing to that man in there, the board has verbal descriptions of the shock levels, ranging from "Slight Shock" at the left-hand side, through "Intense Shock" in the middle, to "Danger: Severe Shock" toward the far right. Finally, at the very end, under 435- and 450-volt switches, there are three ambiguous X's. If, at any point, you hesitate, Mr. Williams calmly tells you to go on. If you still hesitate, he tells you again.

Except for some terrifying details, which will be explained in a 15 moment, this is the experiment. The object is to find the shock level at which you disobey the experimenter and refuse to pull the switch.

When Stanley Milgram first wrote this script, he took it to fourteen 16 Yale psychology majors and asked them what they thought would happen. He put it this way: Out of one hundred persons in the teacher's predicament, how would their breakoff points be distributed along the 15-to-450-volt scale? They thought a few would break off very early, most would quit someplace in the middle and a few would go all the way to the end. The highest estimate of the number out of one hundred who would go all the way to the end was three. Milgram then informally polled some of his fellow scholars in the psychology department. They agreed that very few would go to the end. Milgram thought so too.

"I'll tell you quite frankly," he says, "before I began this experiment, 17 before any shock generator was built, I thought that most people would break off at 'Strong Shock' or 'Very Strong Shock.' You would get only a very, very small proportion of people going out to the end of the shock generator, and they would constitute a pathological fringe."

In his pilot experiments, Milgram used Yale students as subjects. Each 18 of them pushed the shock switches, one by one, all the way to the end of the board.

19   So he rewrote the script to include some protests from the learner. At first, they were mild, gentlemanly, Yalie protests, but, "it didn't seem to have as much effect as I thought it would or should," Milgram recalls. "So we had more violent protestation on the part of the person getting the shock. All of the time, of course, what we were trying to do was not to create a macabre situation, but simply to generate disobedience. And that was one of the first findings. This was not only a technical deficiency of the experiment, that we didn't get disobedience. It really was the first finding: That obedience would be much greater than we had assumed it would be and disobedience would be much more difficult than we had assumed."

20   As it turned out, the situation did become rather macabre. The only meaningful way to generate disobedience was to have the victim protest with great anguish, noise, and vehemence. The protests were tape-recorded so that all the teachers ordinarily would hear the same sounds and nuances, and they started with a grunt at 75 volts, proceeded through a "Hey, that really hurts," at 125 volts, got desperate with, "I can't stand the pain, don't do that," at 180 volts, reached complaints of heart trouble at 195, an agonized scream at 285, a refusal to answer at 315, and only heartrending, ominous silence after that.

21   Still, sixty-five percent of the subjects, twenty- to fifty-year-old American males, everyday, ordinary people, like you and me, obediently kept pushing those levers in the belief that they were shocking the mild-mannered learner, whose name was Mr. Wallace, and who was chosen for the role because of his innocent appearance, all the way up to 450 volts.

22   Milgram was now getting enough disobedience so that he had something he could measure. The next step was to vary the circumstances to see what would encourage or discourage obedience.

23   He put the learner in the same room with the teacher. He stopped strapping the learner's hand down. He rewrote the script so that at 150 volts the learner took his hand off the shock plate and declared that he wanted out of the experiment. He rewrote the script some more so that the experimenter then told the teacher to grasp the learner's hand and physically force it down on the plate to give Mr. Wallace his unwanted electric shock.

24   "I had the feeling that very few people would go on at that point, if any," Milgram says. "I thought that would be the limit of obedience that you would find in the laboratory."

25   It wasn't.

26   Although seven years have now gone by, Milgram still remembers the first person to walk into the laboratory in the newly rewritten script. He was a construction worker, a very short man. "He was so small," says Milgram, "that when he sat on the chair in front of the shock generator, his feet didn't reach the floor. When the experimenter told him to push the

victim's hand down and give the shock, he turned to the experimenter, and he turned to the victim, his elbow went up, he fell down on the hand of the victim, his feet kind of tugged to one side, and he said, 'Like this, boss?' Zzumph!"

The experiment was played out to its bitter end. Milgram tried it with 27 forty different subjects. And thirty percent of them obeyed the experimenter and kept on obeying.

"The protests of the victim were strong and vehement, he was 28 screaming his guts out, he refused to participate, and you had to physically struggle with him in order to get his hand down on the shock generator," Milgram remembers. But twelve out of forty did it.

Milgram took his experiment out of New Haven. Not to Germany, 29 just twenty miles down the road to Bridgeport. Maybe, he reasoned, the people obeyed because of the prestigious setting of Yale University.

The new setting was a suite of three rooms in a run-down office 30 building in Bridgeport. The only identification was a sign with a fictitious name: "Research Associates of Bridgeport." Questions about professional connections got only vague answers about "research for industry."

Obedience was less in Bridgeport. Forty-eight percent of the subjects 31 stayed for the maximum shock, compared to sixty-five percent at Yale. But this was enough to prove that far more than Yale's prestige was behind the obedient behavior.

For more than seven years now, Stanley Milgram has been trying to 32 figure out what makes ordinary American citizens so obedient. The most obvious answer—that people are mean, nasty, brutish and sadistic—won't do. The subjects who gave the shocks to Mr. Wallace to the end of the board did not enjoy it. They groaned, protested, fidgeted, argued, and in some cases, were seized by fits of nervous, agitated giggling.

"They even try to get out of it," says Milgram, "but they are some- 33 how engaged in something from which they cannot liberate themselves. They are locked into a structure, and they do not have the skills or inner resources to disengage themselves."

Milgram's theory assumes that people behave in two different operat- 34 ing modes as different as ice and water. He does not rely on Freud or sex or toilet-training hang-ups for this theory. All he says is that ordinarily we operate in a state of autonomy, which means we pretty much have and assert control over what we do. But in certain circumstances, we operate under what Milgram calls a state of agency (after agent, *n* . . . one who acts for or in the place of another by authority from him; a substitute; a deputy—*Webster's Collegiate Dictionary*). A state of agency, to Milgram, is nothing more than a frame of mind.

"There's nothing bad about it, there's nothing good about it," he 35 says. "It's a natural circumstance of living with other people. . . . I think of a state of agency as a real transformation of a person; if a person has different properties when he's in that state, just as water can turn to ice under certain conditions of temperature, a person can move to the state of mind that I call agency . . . the critical thing is that you see yourself as the instrument of the execution of another person's wishes. You do not see yourself as acting on your own. And there's a real transformation, a real change of properties of the person."

36   So, for most subjects in Milgram's laboratory experiments, the act of giving Mr. Wallace his painful shock was necessary, even though unpleasant, and besides they were doing it on behalf of somebody else and it was for science.

37   Stanley Milgram has his problems, too. He believes that in the laboratory situation, he would not have shocked Mr. Wallace. His professional critics reply that in his real-life situation he has done the equivalent. He has placed innocent and naïve subjects under great emotional strain and pressure in selfish obedience to his quest for knowledge. When you raise this issue with Milgram, he has an answer ready. There is, he explains patiently, a critical difference between his naïve subjects and the man in the electric chair. The man in the electric chair (in the mind of the naïve subject) is helpless, strapped in. But the naïve subject is free to go at any time.

38   Immediately after he offers this distinction, Milgram anticipates the objection.

39   "It's quite true," he says, "that this is almost a philosophic position, because we have learned that some people are psychologically incapable of disengaging themselves. But that doesn't relieve them of the moral responsibility."

40   The parallel is exquisite. "The tension problem was unexpected," says Milgram in his defense. But he went on anyway. The naïve subjects didn't expect the screaming protests from the strapped-in learner. But they went on.

41   "I had to make a judgment," says Milgram. "I had to ask myself, was this harming the person or not? My judgment is that it was not. Even in the extreme cases, I wouldn't say that permanent damage results."

42   Sound familiar? "The shocks may be painful," the experimenter kept saying, "but they're not dangerous."

43   After the series of experiments was completed, Milgram sent a report of the results to his subjects and a questionnaire, asking whether they were glad or sorry to have been in the experiment. Eighty-three and seven-tenths percent said they were glad and only 1.3 percent were sorry; 15 percent were neither sorry nor glad. However, Milgram could not be sure at the time of the experiment that only 1.3 percent would be sorry.

44   Kurt Vonnegut Jr. put one paragraph in the preface to *Mother Night,* in 1966, which pretty much says it for the people with their fingers on the shock-generator switches, for you and me, and maybe even for Milgram.

"If I'd been born in Germany," Vonnegut said, "I suppose I would have *been* a Nazi, bopping Jews and gypsies and Poles around, leaving boots sticking out of snow banks, warming myself with my sweetly virtuous insides. So it goes."

Just so. One thing that happened to Milgram back in New Haven 45 during the days of the experiment was that he kept running into people he'd watched from behind the one-way glass. It gave him a funny feeling, seeing those people going about their everyday business in New Haven and knowing what they would do to Mr. Wallace if ordered to. Now that his research results are in and you've thought about it, you can get this funny feeling too. You don't need one-way glass. A glance in your own mirror may serve just as well.

1970

QUESTIONS FOR DISCUSSION

Content

a. Originally, what did Stanley Milgram intend his experiments to test? What unexpected turns did the experiment take?

b. Why did Milgram change the location and the details of the situation after the first experiment?

c. What are the probable reasons why the "teachers" in Milgram's experiments continued to administer shocks to the "learners"? List reasons Milgram gives plus any other reasons you think are likely.

d. What does Milgram conclude about people's willingness to obey?

e. In your opinion, what other changes to the experiment would have made the results different? What might have been these other results?

Strategy and Style

f. The use of *you*, starting in paragraph 6, puts you directly into the action, into the role of the "teacher." What effect does this have on you? What is your reaction to the experimenter's requests?

g. What does the startling title and bluntly worded first paragraph make you think the article will be about? Are your expectations met? Are the title and opening effective?

h. What techniques does Meyer use to make this nonfiction article read like a fictional story?

i. Meyer wrote this article for *Esquire*, a magazine aimed primarily at college-educated, fashion-conscious men. How would the effect of the article change if it were written for radically different audiences, such as scholars, psychiatrists, or young children?

j. How does the reference to Kurt Vonnegut's novel *Mother Night* (paragraph 44) interpret Milgram's experiment? What is Meyer's opinion, as expressed in paragraphs 44 and 45? Do you agree with his take on Milgram's findings?

ENGAGING THE TEXT

a. Describe what you would have done as a "teacher" in the experiment. Try to be as truthful as you can.

b. Do you think that Milgram's experiment was ethical? In other words, was it right of him to put his subjects in such a situation? Write a paragraph to explain your opinion about this.

SUGGESTIONS FOR SUSTAINED WRITING

a. Continue the response you wrote for item *b* in Engaging the Text. Write an expanded definition of *ethical* in which you reflect on the meaning of this word in your own life.

b. Do you agree with Meyer's and Vonnegut's opinions that if you had been born in Germany, you would have become a Nazi (paragraphs 44 and 45)? Write an argumentative essay in which you expand that basic opinion, explaining why you agree or disagree with their opinion and defending your answer against possible counterarguments. Read any set of essays in the Argument section of Chapter 10 to see how counterarguments can be written.

c. Do you think that continual exposure to violence (on television, on the news, in movies) desensitizes viewers to violence, even makes viewers violent themselves? Write a cause/effect essay in which you argue that, yes, exposure to violence has a direct relationship to increased violent crimes, or no, exposure to violence does not lead to violent behavior. You will need to do research to support your opinion.

READ MORE

Meyer and His Works

"Philip Meyer" (http://www.unc.edu/~pmeyer): *Philip Meyer's home page at the University of North Carolina.*

"Phil Meyer, Raising the Ante Again" (http://www.niemanwatchdog .org/index.cfm?fuseaction=showcase.view&showcaseid=0076): *Text of a speech by Meyer about journalism.*

Obedience to Authority

Blass, Thomas. *Obedience to Authority: Current Perspectives on the Milgram Paradigm.* Mahwah, NJ: Lawrence Erlbaum, 2000.

Blass, Thomas. *The Man Who Shocked the World: The Life and Legacy of Stanley Milgram.* New York: Basic Books, 2004.

A search through .edu and .org websites for "social psychology and obedience" will bring you to a selection of online scholarly articles about Stanley Milgram's experiment.

The Arrow of Time

K. C. Cole

A noted science writer who has written many works appealing to the lay or general reader, K. C. Cole (b. 1946) grew up in Rio de Janeiro, Brazil, in Port Washington, New York, and in Shaker Heights, Ohio. She is a graduate of Barnard College in political science and is currently a professor at the University of Southern California Annenberg's School of Journalism. Her writing career began after she published a piece on the Soviet invasion of Czechoslovakia for the New York Times. *Subsequently, she wrote pieces for* Saturday Review, *the* Washington Post, *and* Newsday, *where she became an editor. She published her first book,* What Only a Mother Can Tell You About Having a Baby, *in 1982;* Between the Lines, *the first of several collections of essays, followed in 1984. In 1994, she began writing a column, "Mind over Matter," for the* Los Angeles Times. *Today, she devotes most of her literary energy to writing about science, primarily for the* Los Angeles Times *and* Discover. *Her essays have been published in several collections, including* Sympathetic Vibrations *(1985),* The Universe and the Teacup *(1998),* First You Build a Cloud *(1999), and* The Hole in the Universe *(2001). Something Incredibly Wonderful Happens (2009) is a memoir and biography of her mentor, Frank Oppenheimer.*

"The Arrow of Time" first appeared as a "Hers" article in the New York Times. *In it, she explains disorder and decay as the natural order of events. Although she writes that entropy is "depressing," her tone is anything but depressing; indeed, her tone is engaging, even cheerful.*

It was about two months ago when I realized that entropy was getting the better of me. On the same day my car broke down (again), my refrigerator conked out and I learned that I needed root canal work in my right rear tooth. The windows in the bedroom were still leaking every time it rained and my son's baby sitter was still failing to show up every time I really needed her. My hair was turning gray and my typewriter was wearing out. The house needed paint and I needed glasses. My son's sneakers were developing holes and I was developing a deep sense of futility.

2   After all, what was the point of spending half of Saturday at the Laundromat if the clothes were dirty all over again the following Friday?

3   Disorder, alas, is the natural order of things in the universe. There is even a precise measure of the amount of disorder, called entropy. Unlike almost every other physical property (motion, gravity, energy), entropy does not work both ways. It can only increase. Once it's created it can never be destroyed. The road to disorder is a one-way street.

4   Because of its unnerving irreversibility, entropy has been called the arrow of time. We all understand this instinctively. Children's rooms, left on their own, tend to get messy, not neat. Wood rots, metal rusts, people wrinkle and flowers wither. Even mountains wear down; even the nuclei of atoms decay. In the city we see entropy in the rundown subways and worn-out sidewalks and torn-down buildings, in the increasing disorder of our lives. We know, without asking, what is old. If we were suddenly to see the paint jump back on an old building, we would know that something was wrong. If we saw an egg unscramble itself and jump back into its shell, we would laugh in the same way we laugh at a movie run backward.

5   Entropy is no laughing matter, however, because with every increase in entropy energy is wasted and opportunity is lost. Water flowing down a mountainside can be made to do some useful work on its way. But once all the water is at the same level it can work no more. That is entropy. When my refrigerator was working, it kept all the cold air ordered in one part of the kitchen and warmer air in another. Once it broke down the warm and cold mixed into a lukewarm mess that allowed my butter to melt, my milk to rot and my frozen vegetables to decay.

6   Of course the energy is not really lost, but it has diffused and dissipated into a chaotic caldron of randomness that can do us no possible good. Entropy is chaos. It is loss of purpose.

7   People are often upset by the entropy they seem to see in the haphazardness of their own lives. Buffeted about like so many molecules in my tepid kitchen, they feel that they have lost their sense of direction, that they are wasting youth and opportunity at every turn. It is easy to see entropy in marriages, when the partners are too preoccupied to patch small things up, almost guaranteeing that they will fall apart. There is much entropy in the state of our country, in the relationships between nations—lost opportunities to stop the avalanche of disorders that seems ready to swallow us all.

8   Entropy is not inevitable everywhere, however. Crystals and snowflakes and galaxies are islands of incredibly ordered beauty in the midst of random events. If it was not for exceptions to entropy, the sky would be black and we would be able to see where the stars spend their days; it is only because air molecules in the atmosphere cluster in ordered groups that the sky is blue.

9   The most profound exception to entropy is the creation of life. A seed soaks up some soil and some carbon and some sunshine and some water

and arranges it into a rose. A seed in the womb takes some oxygen and pizza and milk and transforms it into a baby.

The catch is that it takes a lot of energy to produce a baby. It also takes 10 energy to make a tree. The road to disorder is all downhill but the road to creation takes work. Though combating entropy is possible, it also has its price. That's why it seems so hard to get ourselves together, so easy to let ourselves fall apart.

Worse, creating order in one corner of the universe always creates 11 more disorder somewhere else. We create ordered energy from oil and coal at the price of the entropy of smog.

I recently took up playing the flute again after an absence of several 12 months. As the uneven vibrations screeched through the house, my son covered his ears and said, "Mom, what's wrong with your flute?" Nothing was wrong with my flute, of course. It was my ability to play it that had atrophied, or entropied, as the case may be. The only way to stop that process was to practice every day, and sure enough my tone improved, though only at the price of constant work. Like anything else, abilities deteriorate when we stop applying our energies to them.

That's why entropy is depressing. It seems as if just breaking even is 13 an uphill fight. There's a good reason that this should be so. The mechanics of entropy are a matter of chance. Take any ice cold air molecule milling around my kitchen. The chances that it will wander in the direction of my refrigerator at any point are exactly 50-50. The chances that it will wander away from my refrigerator are also 50-50. But take billions of warm and cold molecules mixed together, and the chances that all the cold ones will wander toward the refrigerator and all the warm ones will wander away from it are virtually nil.

Entropy wins not because order is impossible but because there are 14 always so many more paths toward disorder than toward order. There are so many more different ways to do a sloppy job than a good one, so many more ways to make a mess than to clean it up. The obstacles and accidents in our lives almost guarantee that constant collisions will bounce us on to random paths, get us off the track. Disorder is the path of least resistance, the easy but not the inevitable road.

Like so many others, I am distressed by the entropy I see around me 15 today. I am afraid of the randomness of international events, of the lack of common purpose in the world; I am terrified that it will lead into the ultimate entropy of nuclear war. I am upset that I could not in the city where I live send my child to a public school; that people are unemployed and inflation is out of control; that tensions between sexes and races seem to be increasing again; that relationships everywhere seem to be falling apart.

Social institutions—like atoms and stars—decay if energy is not 16 added to keep them ordered. Friendships and families and economies all fall apart unless we constantly make an effort to keep them working and well oiled. And far too few people, it seems to me, are willing to contribute consistently to those efforts.

17   Of course, the more complex things are, the harder it is. If there were only a dozen or so air molecules in my kitchen, it would be likely—if I waited a year or so—that at some point the six coldest ones would congregate inside the freezer. But the more factors in the equation—the more players in the game—the less likely it is that their paths will coincide in an orderly way. The more pieces in the puzzle, the harder it is to put back together once order is disturbed. "Irreversibility," said a physicist, "is the price we pay for complexity."

1982

QUESTIONS FOR DISCUSSION

Content

a. What is entropy? What *isn't* it? For instance, is "haphazardness" (paragraph 7) entropy?
b. Why might entropy by termed "the arrow of time" (paragraph 4)?
c. Why might entropy be a "loss of purpose" (paragraph 6)?
d. Why is it so difficult to counteract entropy? Why does entropy win?
e. What do the exceptions to the law of entropy, mentioned in paragraphs 9–12, have in common?
f. How would you characterize Cole's view of the effects of entropy on people, particularly as she describes them in paragraph 7?

Strategy and Style

g. Cole seems intent upon defining entropy, but is that her only purpose? In what way is this a cause/effect essay?
h. Where in this essay does Cole use illustration? What other methods of development do you see here?
i. Scientific writing normally is objective and concrete. Is Cole's choice of vocabulary appropriate to a scientific subject?
j. Is Cole's use of subjective words and phrases such as "a deep sense of futility," "unnerving," and "depressing" appropriate to her purpose and audience? Who is her audience?
k. What do you make of her including statements such as "a seed in the womb takes some oxygen and pizza and milk and transforms it into a baby" (paragraph 9)?
l. What makes the introduction to this essay enticing?

ENGAGING THE TEXT

a. Explain the likening of entropy to "the arrow of time." Why is this metaphor appropriate?

b. Describe what exceptions to the law of entropy, in addition to those Cole mentions, you can identify from your own experience.

SUGGESTIONS FOR SUSTAINED WRITING

a. Do you find evidence of entropy in your own life? Consider one aspect of your life: your college studies, your family, your workplace, a club or other organization you belong to, or a romantic relationship. Then, explain how Cole's definition of entropy might be illustrated by that aspect of your life.

b. Read or reread the selections by Dafoe Whitehead and Meyer in this chapter. Write an essay that applies Cole's definition of entropy to what you read in these two pieces. What parts of Cole's theory apply in each case? What examples of entropy might Cole have found in the work of these other authors?

c. Using cause/effect analysis as your principal method of development, write an essay that explains a scientific principle, law, or phenomenon. Your audience should be a person without scientific training. Possible topics: fusion, fission, Ohm's law, the principle of specific gravity, the Doppler effect, the aurora borealis, relativity, or chaos theory. You might also want to explain entropy in more depth than Cole does, discussing entropy in thermodynamics or entropy in information.

READ MORE

Cole and Her Works

"K. C. Cole" (http://annenberg.usc.edu/Faculty/Communication%20 and%20Journalism/ColeK.aspx): *Cole's faculty web page at the University of Southern California.*

"Categorically Not!" (http://www.kccole.net/): *Cole's website.*

"Science Writer K.C. Cole Tries Her Hand at Experimental Physics" (http://www.fnal.gov/pub/ferminews/ferminews03-12-01/p2.html): *An article about Cole's work as a scientist.*

Entropy

Parker, Sybil P. *McGraw-Hill Dictionary of Astronomy*. New York: McGraw-Hill, 1997.
There are countless sites for the search term "entropy"; for a more manageable selection, search for both "entropy" and "arrow of time" together.

Shattered Sudan

Paul Salopek

Paul Salopek (b. 1962) was born in California but grew up in Central Mexico. He studied at the University of California at Santa Barbara, where he received a degree in environmental biology in 1984. Now a well known journalist, he did not start out to be one—when his motorcycle broke down in New Mexico in 1985, he took a job reporting for a local paper to earn enough money to repair the machine. Since then, Salopek has been a bureau chief in Mexico City, a reporter for the El Paso Times, a reporter for National Geographic, and from 1996 to 2002 a foreign correspondent for The Chicago Tribune. *In 1998, he won a Pulitzer Prize for Explanatory Reporting for his two articles on the Human Genome Diversity Project. In 2001, he won another Pulitzer for International Reporting for his coverage of the civil war in the Congo, and in 2009, he received the George Polk Award for international reporting and for his three-story series "Waging War and Peace in Africa." In 2006, Salopek was detained in Sudan while working on an article for National Geographic. Salopek, his driver, and his translator were charged with espionage, but they were released the day before the trial, thanks to pressure from several U.S. Congress members and the international community.*

In this essay, originally written for National Geographic (with photographs by Randy Olson), Salopek combines historical background with interviews and personal experience to explain a situation that is confusing not only for outsiders, but for Sudanese as well.

1 The oldest civil war in the world is being fought, on one side, by men who wander like demented hospital orderlies across the primordial wastes of Africa.

2   I follow them one hot morning as they flee a government ambush in the oil fields of southern Sudan. One of their comrades has just been shot dead, his body abandoned on a parched savanna that hides nearly 20 billion dollars' worth of low-sulfur crude. We retreat for hours under a scalding sun, crossing in the process a vast, cauterized plain of cracked mud. I pause a moment to watch them: an ant-like column of rebels dressed in bizarre homemade uniforms of green cotton smocks and white plastic slippers, limping into the heat waves of distance. Five casualties bounce in stretchers. They suffer their bullet wounds in silence. A boy marching in front balances

a car battery on his head. He is the radio operator's assistant. Every few hundred yards he puts the battery down and empties blood out of a shoe.

3   When we finally reach a tree line, the fighters strip off their clothes and jump into a bog. The water stinks. It is infested with larvae of guinea worms, which, once ingested, burrow painfully through the body to the legs, and are extracted by making a small incision; you reel the worm out slowly, day after day, by winding it on a small stick. All around us, half-naked people move feebly through the thorn forest: ethnic Dinka herders displaced from the contested oil fields by fighting between rebels and the central government based in the faraway capital, Khartoum. Their children, stunted and ginger-haired from malnutrition, clamber in the trees. They are collecting leaves to eat. This awful place, I learn, is called Biem—a safe haven, such as it is, of the 40,000-strong Sudan People's Liberation Army.

"You cannot reclaim what is lost," the sweating rebel commander 4 says, squatting in the shade of an acacia, "so you just keep fighting for what little you have left."

He is trying to console himself. But I see little solace for the epic trag- 5 edy of Sudan. It is April 2002, and Africa's largest country is lurching into its 19th uninterrupted year of warfare—the latest round of strife that has brutalized Sudan, off and on, for most of the past half century. More than two million Sudanese are dead. We just left the latest fatality sprawling back in the yellow grasses, a bullet through his brain. And thousands of scarecrow civilians stagger through the scrub, starving atop a lucrative sea of petroleum.

Numbly, I crawl inside an empty grass hut to be alone. Lying flat on 6 my back—depressed, exhausted, stewing in my own helplessness—I try to remind myself why I have returned to Sudan: Because peace is in the air. Because oil, newly tapped by the government, is shaking up the wretched status quo in Africa's most fractured nation. Because the long nightmare of Biem—and a thousand other places like it in Sudan—may soon be over.

Bulging like a gigantic hornet's nest against the shores of the Red Sea, 7 Sudan has rarely known stability. Civil war erupted even before the nation gained independence from Britain in 1956. (A frail peace lasted between 1972 and 1983.) The roots of the violence have never changed: British-ruled Sudan wasn't a country; it was two. The south is tropical, underdeveloped, and populated by Dinkas, Nuers, Azandes, and some hundred other ethnic groups of African descent. The north, by contrast, is drier, and wealthier—a Saharan world with strong links to the Muslim Middle East. Shackled together by lunatic colonial borders, these two groups—northern Arabs and southern blacks—have been at odds since the 19th century, when northern slave raiders preyed on the tribes of the south.

At present, the rebel Sudan People's Liberation Army, or SPLA, controls 8 much of the southern third of Sudan. Its insurgents sometimes carry spears as well as Kalashnikovs and are fighting for greater autonomy. The northern government in Khartoum, now dominated by Islamic fundamentalists, drops bombs on them from old Russian-made cargo planes and employs famines and modern-day slavery as crude weapons of mass destruction. So far the death toll—mostly among southern civilians—exceeds that of many of the world's recent conflicts combined, including Rwanda, the Persian Gulf war, the Balkans, and Chechnya. Four million Sudanese have been displaced by violence and starvation. Yet the calamity of Sudan unfolds largely without witnesses—an apocalypse in a vacuum. Until now.

9   Two factors are bringing new hope to Sudan. Neither has anything to do with the suffering of millions of Sudanese. Both involve the self-interest of outsiders.

10   First, the U.S. war on terrorism appears to be pressuring reforms in the northern Islamist regime. When a military coup backed by the radical National Islamic Front toppled Sudan's last democratically elected government in 1989, the country plunged into a new dark age. Independent newspapers were banned. Labor unions suppressed. The north's moderate Islamic parties were hounded into exile. The civil war escalated to the drumbeat of jihad—holy struggle against indigenous religions and Christianity in the south. Outlaws ranging from Osama bin Laden to Carlos the Jackal settled into mansions in Khartoum's sandy outskirts. And the fundamentalists' secret police, the feared *mukhabarat*, added a new word to the lexicon of political repression—the "ghost house," or unmarked detention center.

11   Recently, however, Khartoum's extremists have begun mellowing. Chafing under U.S. economic sanctions, they have begun cooperating with the global war on terror. Desperate to shed their pariah status, they have bowed to Western pressure to enter peace negotiations in the civil war. In October 2002 the government and the SPLA signed a fragile cease-fire.

12   The second—and perhaps more profound—force of change in Sudan is less noble. It is about something the whole world wants. It is about oil.

13   In May 1999 engineers in Khartoum opened the tap on a new thousand-mile-long pipeline that connects the Muglad Basin, a huge, petroleum-rich lowland in the south, to a gleaming new tanker terminal on the shores of the Red Sea. The Muglad Basin, a prehistoric lake bed, is said to hold some three billion barrels of crude—nearly half the amount of recoverable oil that lies under the Arctic National Wildlife Refuge in Alaska. This bonanza, pessimists say, is just one more prize for the warring parties to fight over. But oil also has fueled renewed international interest in Sudan. And diplomats are more optimistic.

14   "It's a no-brainer," says a U.S. expert familiar with Sudan's many woes. "The rebels control much of the oil country. The government has access to the sea. They need each other to get rich."

15   A Canadian geologist who is mapping the Muglad Basin agrees: "Every Sudanese won't be driving a Mercedes tomorrow—we're not

talking about another Saudi Arabia here," he tells me, "but the reserves are big enough to transform Sudan forever."

There are good reasons for skepticism. Sudan's grievances are very 16 old and complex. They confound even the Sudanese. For many, the north-south war is rooted in the old toxic relationship between Arab master and African servant. For the religious, it is a contest between northern Islam and southern indigenous religions and Christianity. For the impoverished herdsmen on the front lines, it is a local skirmish over a water hole or favorite pastureland: Violent disputes among Sudan's hundreds of ethnic groups have been inflamed—and manipulated—by the main warring parties. Yet oil cuts, literally, across all of Sudan's overlapping wars. Better than any road, or river, or political theory, the shining new pipeline leads the way through a labyrinth of misery in the Horn of Africa that defies easy interpretation.

I have traveled before to Sudan. Like many journalists, I was sent 17 there to chronicle a freak show of human suffering: endless civil war, recurrent droughts, mass starvation, slaving raids, and epidemics of kill-ing diseases. Today, however, I am on a different mission. I will follow the flow of Sudan's oil wealth from the implacable war zones of the south to an ultramodern export terminal on the Red Sea; to the country's future.

This will not be an easy journey. I will be forced to complete it in 18 disjointed segments, side-stepping battlefronts, accommodating roadless deserts, avoiding suspicious bureaucrats—an erratic process that mirrors life in Sudan.

I pressed my ear against the pipeline once: The Nile Blend crude ooz- 19 ing inside emitted a faint liquid sigh. I listened hard, sweating under a tropical sun, trying to discern some hidden message—a clue as to whether 33 million Sudanese will stop killing each other anytime soon.

We are sneaking into Unity State, the start of Sudan's pipeline, some 450 20 miles northwest of the Kenyan border.

Flying into rebel-held southern Sudan from Kenya, you must be 21 prepared for certain compromises. First, the flight is illegal. The central government in Khartoum disapproves of independent visits to its unseen war. Then there is the question of facilities. They simply don't exist. For almost four hours we drone over a landscape of impressive emptiness—a sea of grass that is burned and reburned by wildfires into a mottling of purplish grays, as if the muscles of the earth itself lay exposed. Later, a huge bruise darkens the western horizon: the famous Sudd, an enormous swamp clogging the flow of the White Nile. When the chartered Cessna finally touches down at a rebel airstrip, the pilot anxiously dumps my bags in the dust and leaves immediately for Nairobi. This is natural. His shiny airplane, a target for government bombers, stands out dangerously in the bleakest liberated zone in the world.

22   I have come to see George Athor Deng. Deng is a Dinka fighter, an SPLA commander of note. And he has promised, via shortwave radio, to show me what oil is doing to his people. He smiles sourly when I tell him what the diplomats say, that oil can bring all the Sudanese together.

23   "When has the north ever shared anything with the south?" he says of the government oil fields a two-day's walk across the front lines. "In the near future we will shut them down. Shut the oil down completely."

24   I meet Deng where he spends most of his days, issuing orders from a folding chair under a shady acacia. His headquarters, Biem, is like an engraving from another era—from the journals of Stanley and Livingstone. Stockades of elephant grass surround his crude huts. Food is precarious. His soldiers scavenge off the land and, when possible, skim UN rations dropped from airplanes for starving civilians. (His troops' canteens are empty plastic jugs marked "Canada-Aid Soy Milk.") There are at least 25,000 displaced people jammed into Deng's territory, virtually all of them Dinka herders fleeing the fighting in the nearby oil fields, and whenever groups of famished refugees trudge through Biem, begging for food, the commander dispatches a marksman to shoot a hippo.

25   According to Deng—and he is broadly backed up by human rights groups—oil has sparked some of the ugliest fighting Sudan has seen in years. Deng and other SPLA commanders mortar oil rigs or shoot at oil company planes. And the Khartoum regime responds by striking back ferociously against local civilians. Government helicopters bought with new oil revenues strafe Dinka and Nuer villages. Sorghum crops are torched. And the dreaded *murahilin*, Muslim raiders armed by the Sudanese Army, sweep through porous rebel lines on horseback, sowing terror and taking slaves. Khartoum denies that it is targeting noncombatants, just as it has long rejected responsibility for slavery in Sudan; it calls these raids tribal abductions, and says they are beyond its control.

26   "It is simple," Deng declares. "The government is depopulating the area to make way for foreign oil companies."

27   Deng's outrage would inspire more sympathy if his own forces weren't so morally tainted. Traditionally, the SPLA has mistreated as much as defended Sudan's long marginalized southern peoples. Until the south's oil wealth helped forge a common cause, various rebel factions—especially the Dinka-dominated SPLA and a variety of ethnic Nuer militias—killed each other mercilessly, often with the encouragement of government bribes. Some commanders have kept civilians malnourished in order to "farm" UN aid. And the movement's political agenda has never really solidified. The SPLA's leader, an Iowa State University doctorate named John Garang, claims he is fighting for a secular, unified Sudan (as opposed to the north's theocracy), yet almost every field commander, Deng included, is gunning for full southern independence.

Knowing what I do about the SPLA, I am prepared to dislike Deng. 28 Compact, scar-faced, blinded in one eye, he promenades around the refugee lean-tos of Biem with a lackey in tow, carrying his chair. Yet there is also an ineffable sadness about him. His entire family—a wife, child, and four brothers—have been wiped out in the current phase of the civil war, which erupted in 1983. Such stupefying losses pervade life in the south. They surface all the time in small, melancholy gestures.

Like the way Deng announces the name of his soldier who is killed, 29 shot down and abandoned, on the ill-fated patrol that I attempt to accompany into the oil fields. "Mayak Arop," he sighs, waving a gnarled hand over a map of the expanding government oil roads, as if wishing to wipe them away.

Or, in the way a bowl-bellied Dinka girl stamps out a pretty little 30 dance on a dusty path in Biem, oblivious to the thousands of haunted figures camped in the bush around her.

Or, in the answers to a simple question.   31

What color is oil?   32

"It's like cow urine," says Chan Akuei, an old herder at Biem with a 33 belly wrinkled like elephant skin. Government troops have shot his cows, an incomprehensible crime in the Dinka universe. The Dinka adore their cattle. They rarely kill them for meat, and compose songs about their favorite animals. Akuei cannot stop talking about his murdered livestock.

"It is as clear as water," says a boy in Koch, a nearby frontline vil- 34 lage. He is a member of an ethnic Nuer militia. The last I see of him, he is marching off at dawn to attack an oil road along with hundreds of other rebels—many of them children.

Nyanayule Arop Deng (the name Deng is common among the Dinka) 35 doesn't know the color of oil. She sits by her skeletal husband, who is dying of kala-azar, a wasting disease that has killed tens of thousands in the oil zone. "All I know is the lights," she says dully. "They appear at night. We don't go near them."

The tower lights of Roll'n wildcat rig number 15 click on at dusk—an 36 unexpectedly pretty sight as the sun drops behind the iron silhouettes of the thorn trees. The quest for oil is tireless, urgent, expensive. It is like a physical thirst—an around-the-clock obsession. Before the evening shift comes on, Terry Hoffman, a sweat-soaked driller from British Columbia, runs one last stand of pipe down into the skin of Sudan.

"Killer bees, cobras, and acid-spewing bugs that give you blisters!" 37 Hoffman hollers over the rig's noisy generator, ticking off the dangers of roughnecking in Sudan. "Boredom's the worst, though. You can't even walk around this place."

Hoffman is a prisoner of his rig. He and his crew must eat their barbe- 38 cued chicken and cherry pies, read their e-mail, and lift weights inside a

Sudanese version of Fort Apache: a 15-foot-high berm has been bulldozed around the floodlit work site. Heavily armed government troops patrol the perimeter against the likes of George Athor Deng. Deng is doubtless out there tonight, plotting under his tree.

39   The idea behind rig 15—a small component in a billion-dollar complex of drilling equipment, dormitories, pumping stations, new roads, and prefabricated office buildings at Heglig, Sudan's torrid version of the North Slope—is visionary in its way.

40   At present, none of the Western energy majors dares to drill in Sudan. Chevron suspended its exploration in 1984 after three of its employees were shot dead by rebels, and pulled out of the country altogether in 1990. (All American companies abandoned Sudan once the U.S. listed it as a supporter of terrorism and imposed sanctions in the 1990s.) Yet today an improbable mix of engineers from communist China, authoritarian Malaysia, democratic Canada, and Islamist Khartoum have cobbled together an experiment in globalization on the baleful plains of the Sahel. The Greater Nile Petroleum Operating Company, as it is called, pumps 240,000 barrels of crude a day out of a war zone. Two years from now that output is projected to nearly double. It may surge even higher should lasting peace return to Sudan, and the rebels allow French, Swedish, and Austrian companies to explore their concessions in the south.

41   "All these stories about us pushing out local people to pump for oil? A total lie," says Bill, a rig supervisor with Talisman Energy, the Canadian partner in the Heglig project.

42   Bill wears cowboy boots and doesn't share his surname. Like everyone else I meet in Heglig, he seems aggrieved. Talisman has come under fire from human rights groups for allegedly turning a blind eye to government atrocities in the oil patch. (Partly because of this bad publicity, Talisman will later sell its Sudan operation to an Indian oil company.) In response to the criticism, a wary company official in Khartoum lectures me on the value of free markets in reforming oppressive regimes. Supervisors drive me around Heglig in a pickup truck, pointing out unmolested villagers in the savanna. Few of these people are southerners. Most are Baggaras, northern Muslim pastoralists who vie with the Dinkas for grazing lands, and who have come to the oil fields to hack down trees for charcoal.

43   "TV at home shows these incredible stories—famines and war in Sudan," says Bill. "Well, let me tell you, I've been in a 200-mile radius of this place, and I haven't seen that."

44   Bill may be willfully blind. But then so are his faraway customers. The only difference is, Bill must walk past a rebel bullet hole in his trailer wall every day and not see it. This is a difficult feat. But a common one in Sudan.

45   There is no fixed front line between SPLA territory and government-controlled Sudan. No walls. No razor wire fences. No permanent Thorn

Curtain. The war is fluid. One army cedes power invisibly to another, and what changes across the no-man's-land are things far subtler and more profound than claims of political control. The round grass huts of Africa give way, slowly, to the square mud houses of desert dwellers. The hot blue dome of the tropical sky recedes behind a veil of white Saharan dust. As I travel north, the 21st century begins to reappear—roads are graded by machines, and human beings once more begin to congregate into towns. Some of these towns have sidewalks. The sight—concrete poured on the ground merely to ease walking—is mesmerizing; a surreal extravagance after the utter desolation of the south.

The oil pipeline rockets north from Heglig and crosses the eerie rock 46
piles of the Nuba Mountains. The Nuba people, allied with the SPLA, have been fighting their own war of autonomy against Khartoum for years. A U.S.-brokered cease-fire is in place when I drive through. I see government trucks rolling up into the hills, loaded with satellite dishes. The equipment is meant for "peace clubs" designed to lure the stubborn Nubas down from their mountain strongholds and into areas of government control. "Many of them have never seen television before," a grinning official explains in the garrison town of Kadugli. "We give them 22 channels, including CNN. Their leaders are very irritated by this."

The pipeline burrows onward under a mound of raw earth—a monu- 47
mental tribal scar creasing the barren landscape. Construction began in 1998 and was finished in 14 months by 2,000 Chinese laborers sweating through double shifts. Workers who died in Sudan were cremated on the spot, and their ashes shipped back to China.

I chase the 28-inch-wide steel tube on bad roads. Dilling. El Obeid. 48
Rabak. The northern towns swell, turning into ramshackle mud cities. Two days north of Heglig, the pipeline disappears into slums. A cratered highway leads me into an enormous traffic jam that backs up for miles. Buses nudge through herds of sheep. Donkey carts jockey with taxis so battered they look like the products of junkyard crushing machines. Pedestrians step unhurriedly among the stalled vehicles. Yet no one is angry or abusive. There are no honking horns, insults, threats, or curses. Silently, patiently, the drivers creep forward. They advance, inch by inch, into a city of waiting.

This is Khartoum. 49

"Please put your notebook away," advises Asim el Moghraby. "We don't 50
want any problems."

El Moghraby and I are perched in a borrowed motorboat, bobbing 51
in the middle of the Nile. I have joined el Moghraby expressly to avoid problems—to admire an overlooked natural wonder of Africa: the meeting of the Blue Nile and White Nile. The two majestic streams, tributaries of the world's longest river, swirl together in a mile-wide dance of

light—one the hue of an evening sky and the other the color of a milky sunrise. Yet Sudan's troubles are insistent. El Moghraby, a retired University of Khartoum biologist and my unofficial guide in the city, is nervous. Western visitors are relatively rare in the city. And he worries that I will draw the attention of secret police. We are too close to shoreline government ministries. "The regime is loosening up," he says apologetically as we chug back to the marina, "but nobody knows how much."

52   Change is coming to Sudan, but few know if it is deep or real. The thinking of the small cabal of generals and fundamentalists who run the country is largely opaque. Nevertheless, the virulence of their Islamic revolution began fading even before 1998, when the Clinton Administration launched cruise missiles at a pharmaceutical plant in Khartoum in retaliation for al Qaeda's terrorist bombings of two U.S. embassies in Africa. Eager to put those years behind them, Sudan's secretive rulers claim they have expelled some 3,000 foreigners linked with terror groups (bin Laden and Carlos included) and that they have released most political prisoners. Opposition parties have been invited back in from the cold, though they often remain marginalized.

53   Driving around Khartoum with el Moghraby—a lean, balding scholar who reminds me of a patient turtle, with his wrinkled neck and watchful eyes that dart behind wire-rimmed glasses—I see a crumbling metropolis of seven million that seems to be fluttering its dusty eyelids after a long slumber beneath the sands. Young couples hold hands on the banks of the Nile, unmolested by the morality police. Flashes of oil money glint off fleets of new Korean-made cars. And freshly painted Coke signs and a new BMW dealership have popped up in the city's shabby downtown.

54   Still, it is staggering to think that this insular, puritanical city—with its turbaned Arab rulers, domed mosques, and tea shops blaring pop music—is the capital of the bleeding African south. Yet the war is here too. On a blazing afternoon I visit Wad el Bashir, one of the miserable camps where some of the nearly two million southerners are sweating away their lives in and around Khartoum. Nubas and Dinkas accost me in the maze of dirt lanes. "They are taking our children!" they whisper, describing how their young men are being yanked off sidewalks and buses to fight for the Sudanese Army against their own people in the south. Behind their mud huts I spot my old companion, the pipeline. Its inert presence now seems malevolent.

55   Popular discontent—and profound war-weariness—is only slightly less palpable among northerners in Khartoum. University students complain about the loss of jobs and political freedoms under the Islamists. Arab businessmen bemoan Sudan's ruinous isolation. ("Please tell the world we are not all terrorists and bullyboys," pleads one wealthy trader.) And several middle-class men openly boast of evading the draft—they aren't buying jihad's promise of a direct ticket to heaven.

"What you are seeing is the northern front in Sudan's civil war," 56
explains a human rights advocate named Osman Hummaida, when I
share my surprise at the cynicism I find on Khartoum's streets. "Sudan is
not just divided north-south. There is a broader struggle. It is the center
against the periphery—a tiny Khartoum clique against everyone else,
including fellow Arabs."

My tour guide, el Moghraby, is a casualty of this subtler northern 57
war. Bullying his Land Rover through Khartoum's downtown one day,
he points to a drab building and says, "That one's mine"—meaning the
old ghost house where he was detained in 1992, along with his politically
active lawyer. In 1995 he was arrested with his wife for producing a documentary film critical of Sudan's environmental record. He was imprisoned yet again, in 1999, for publicly questioning the country's oil projects.

Like many disillusioned northern intellectuals, el Moghraby has with- 58
drawn from public life. He has retreated into private enthusiasms—into the
past. He takes me one day to see a weathered colonial monument honoring
the charge of the 21st Lancers, a once famous skirmish in the British conquest
of Sudan in 1898. Wistfully, el Moghraby talks of an older, more cosmopolitan Khartoum of electric trams, midnight cafés, and clean-swept streets. This
nostalgia is sad, especially given Britain's divisive legacy in Sudan.

As a young soldier, Winston Churchill participated in the charge of 59
the 21st Lancers outside Khartoum. British horsemen slammed into the
ranks of defending Sudanese troops with such force, he wrote, that "for
perhaps ten wonderful seconds" all sides simply staggered about in a
daze. The beleaguered citizens of Sudan's capital know this feeling well.
They have endured it for the better part of 50 years. It is not wonderful.

Where is undemocratic, underdeveloped, and oil-rich Sudan headed? For 60
answers I must leave the periphery. I go to the center.

Sudan's president, Lt. Gen. Omar al-Bashir, almost never grants inter- 61
views. Hassan al-Turabi, the intellectual father of Sudan's Islamist movement, is also not available, having been put under house arrest by rivals
in the government. (He has since been locked up in Kober Prison.) So the
task of explaining the policies of the secretive National Islamic Front that
rules Sudan falls to Hasan Makki, an Islamic academic and one of the
regime's leading ideologues.

Makki greets me in a dazzling white djellaba, or Arab robe, in his spa- 62
cious home. He is a member of the elite "riverine" Arab tribes who have
monopolized power in Sudan for years. Like most of Sudan's political
inner circle, he is friendly, smart, and chooses his words carefully.

On the war: "It is effectively over, my friend. The south already has 63
lost. Millions of their people have moved up to join us in the north."
Ignoring the detail that the refugees have not come by choice, he calls
Khartoum "an American-style melting pot."

64   On Arab-black hostility: "How can there be racism? Look at my skin. No northern Sudanese is a pure Arab. For centuries our blood has mixed with Africans. We are brothers!"

65   On oil: "It is a blessing. It will hold Sudan together. Before oil, we northerners were tired of the south. Why lose our children there? Why fight for a wasteland? Oil has changed all that. Now our economic survival depends on it."

66   Regarding the unpopularity of the regime, Makki has little to say. He politely pours me another cup of tea and suggests that I go look at stones.

67 We have flown, walked, and driven more than 600 miles through Sudan.

68   The pipeline leads on—tireless and unerring, far more sure of itself in the turmoil of Sudan than I ever will be. Its oil is kept at 95 degrees Fahrenheit, the temperature required for it to be thin enough to flow freely. It tunnels through Khartoum's bleak refugee camps, then slips beneath the Nile. Emerging from the other side, it disappears north into an ocean of light: the Nubian Desert.

69   There, baking under the sun, are Makki's stones. They are the silent remains of ancient cities and temples.

70   At a city called Naga, a ruin of great beauty and stillness that juts from the eroding hills east of the Nile, I see a relief carved into an imposing temple wall. It depicts a queen grasping a handful of small, doomed captives. The queen is recognizably Nubian: Chiseled in pharaonic splendor, she is a mix of Egyptian elegance and full-hipped African beauty. Her prisoners too strike me as dead ringers. They look like the far-flung citizens of Sudan's modern fringe: fierce Beja nomads from the Red Sea Hills—or even Negroid Dinkas or Nubas from the south. Blinking sweat from my eyes, I stare in amazement at this antique blueprint for governance in Sudan—a 2,000-year-old political poster advertising the power of Nile-based elites over the weak periphery.

71   "Some things never change," says Dietrich Wildung, head of the Egyptian Museum and Papyrus Collection in Berlin and one of the sunburned archaeologists working at Naga. "The north always thinks itself supreme— Egypt over Sudan, Berlin over Munich, New York over Alabama."

72   Wildung, an almost dauntingly effusive man, pads briskly around his digs in a flimsy pair of sneakers, pointing out details on a half-excavated temple that make him exclaim with pure delight. According to archaeologists, Sudan's northern deserts hide one of the great civilizations not only of Africa but the world. These Sudanic realms—variously known as Nubia, Kush, or Meroë—were no mere appendages of neighboring Egypt, as was sometimes thought. Their intelligentsia created an Egyptian-derived writing system, Meroitic, for a still unintelligible language. And the "black pharaohs" of Sudan and their notorious archers eventually gained such power that they briefly ruled all of Egypt some 2,700 years ago.

Proudly, Wildung shows me his latest discovery: an altar excavated 73 from beneath a fallen wall. Nile gods painted on its plaster-covered pedestal indicate Egyptian influence, and the floral designs are pure Africa— all exuberance, singing colors. Ancient Greece reveals itself too in the classical flourishes on a figurine of the Egyptian goddess Isis. Crouched over a hole in the earth, we behold the unexpected beauty of Sudan's fractured nature, the art of a continental crossroads.

Can oil dilute the age-old divisiveness of Sudan? The pipeline is my 74 guide. But it is no oracle.

North of the city of Atbara, the steel artery is patrolled by wild- 75 looking men in vehicles mounted with heavy machine guns: *mujahidin,* or holy warriors, guarding the pipeline from being blown up, as it was nearby in 1999. (That act of sabotage was carried out by northern opposition forces in alliance with the SPLA.) The oil squirts across the Red Sea Hills at the pace of a fast walk. Then it races 3,000 feet down to the devastatingly hot Sudanese coast. To the Bashair Marine Terminal. To the end of the line. When I visit the high-tech export facility, a Singapore-flagged tanker is preparing to gulp a million barrels of crude.

"You are looking at our gateway to the world," a jumpsuited techni- 76 cian tells me grandly in the sleek control room, some 950 miles from the oil wells pocking the savannas of Africa.

I hope he is right. I hope oil helps create a new era of stability 77 in Sudan. I hope it prods international efforts, such as those of U.S. peacemaker John Danforth, to end the terrible civil war. I hope it bribes Sudan's cruel and insulated elites into abandoning selfish power struggles that have wreaked hell on millions of ordinary people. I hope it somehow lubricates relations with Egypt, the regional superpower, which exercises powerful interests in Sudan: Egypt strongly opposes southern independence, fearing that such a development will threaten its access to the vital middle reaches of the Nile. Most of all, I hope Sudan's new oil revenues—more than two million dollars a day—do not end up stoking what one analyst calls a "perfect war," a conflict waged, at tolerable cost, indefinitely. Hope: a commodity Sudan could use more of, even, than oil.

Near the end of my journey, I camp for a few days in the parched wilder- 78 ness of the Red Sea Hills. My host is Abu Fatna, an old Beja, a Muslim nomad whose ancestors have roamed the eastern wastes of Sudan for the past 5,000 years. His tent is pegged only 40 miles west of the pipeline, yet his life is as detached from its power and wealth as those of the southern Dinkas dying at the opposite end of the oil trail. Drought has forced Fatna to sell his camels. Saudi hunters have slaughtered all the local wild antelope. He is skinny and poor, and he has only two teeth left in his head. But he still knows which desert stars to travel by. He can still handle a tribal broadsword.

79   When I leave, Fatna offers me a gift: He dances good-bye in the dust. The flapping of his scrawny arms, the dry snatches of song—these are meant as an honor, though they seem more like a lament. Driving back to the pipeline, I wonder if this sadness, too, somehow gets pumped out of Sudan. Along with commander Deng's bitter hand-waving over a crude map. Or el Moghraby's demoralized retreat from the world. Or the terrible absences of so many dead.

80   So much heartbreak, it seems, gets burned up in Sudan's oil.

2003

QUESTIONS FOR DISCUSSION

Content

a. What are the main images that you take away from this essay? In what ways do these images alter—or reinforce—what you assumed about Sudan?

b. The Sudanese are described as "thousands of scarecrow civilians stagger[ing] through the scrub, starving atop a lucrative sea of petroleum" (paragraph 5). What comment does Salopek make about the Sudanese government with this descriptive sentence?

c. How does Salopek define *globalization* in paragraph 40?

d. What does Salopek see as the central tragedy of the situation?

e. Salopek writes that the "U.S. war on terrorism appears to be pressuring reforms" (paragraph 10). Several years later, do you think that this "war on terrorism" is having its intended effects?

Strategy and Style

f. Salopek occasionally uses similes and metaphors to explain concepts, such as describing the shape of Sudan as "like a gigantic hornet's nest" (paragraph 7) or calling the oil region an "oil patch" (paragraph 42). What other metaphorical language does he use in the essay? What might have been his reasons for using these phrases?

g. Besides cause/effect, what other rhetorical strategies does Salopek use, and to what effect?

h. Before he gets to the narrative portion of the essay, Salopek provides a long historical introduction. Why is this introduction necessary? What do its length and detail say about Salopek's readers?

i. How does Salopek highlight the difference between the pipeline and the people who live near it?

j. What is Salopek's stance toward the situation and toward the people he interviews? Does he remain objective?

ENGAGING THE TEXT

a. Explain what Salopek sees as the causes of the civil war in Sudan.
b. Based on what Salopek tells you, write a brief comparison of the two halves of the country, northern Sudan and southern Sudan.

SUGGESTIONS FOR SUSTAINED WRITING

a. With the starting point of paragraph 9, in which Salopek writes that there are two factors that might alleviate Sudan's problems, write an essay in which you reflect on these two factors, discussing the merits of each. Suggest further solutions to the problem as you see it.
b. Write an essay in which you compare Salopek's essay to another one in this book that uses precise description of a place to discuss a specific culture or historical event. Find examples of how each writer uses the senses to create a clear picture, and discuss how description helps each writer to make his or her case. Possible essays for comparison include "37 Who Saw Murder Didn't Call the Police" (Chapter 1) and "The Plague" (Chapter 1).
c. This article describes the situation in Sudan in 2002. Research the current situation, discussing whether the situation has become more peaceful or more violent. Explain what changes the oil pipeline has affected.

READ MORE

Salopek and His Works

"U.S. Wages Shadow War in Africa" (http://www.chicagotribune.com/news/nationworld/chi-africa-shadow-war,0,2738005.storygallery): *Full text of the series of three stories for which Salopek won the George Polk Award.*

"Shattered Sudan at National Geographic" (http://ngm.nationalgeographic.com/ngm/0302/feature2): *Salopek's article, some of the photographs that accompanied the article, the photographer's field notes, and a multimedia presentation on Sudan.*

"Sudanese Government Drops Spy Charges, Releases American Journalist" (http://www.pbs.org/newshour/bb/africa/july-dec06/salopek_10-09.html): *Interview with Salopek about his detention in Sudan, plus links to background and history of the conflict in Darfur.*

Sudan

"Sudan Page" (http://www.africa.upenn.edu/Country_Specific/Sudan. html): *Background information about the country and its current political events.*

"Sudan Information Gateway" (http://www.unsudanig.org): *The United Nations page on Sudan.*

Our Oceans Are Turning into Plastic . . . Are We?

Susan Casey

A native of Toronto, Susan Casey (b. 1962) was the editor in chief at Sports Illustrated Women *and the creative director of* Outside *magazine, before serving as development editor at* Time, Inc. *until 2006. At* Outside, *she helped develop the stories behind the books* Into Thin Air *and* The Perfect Storm *and the film* Blue Crush. *As a freelance journalist, she has had articles published in* Esquire, Time, Fortune, Sports Illustrated, *and* National Geographic, *and she has published two books,* Devil's Teeth: A True Story of Obsession and Survival among America's Great White Sharks *(2005) and* The Wave: In Pursuit of the Rogues, Freaks and Giants of the Ocean *(2010). An avid swimmer, she is on the board of directors of the Trident Swim Foundation, which was formed in 2007 to promote a Swimmer Scholar Program in New York City. She is currently editor-in-chief of* O, The Oprah Magazine.*

"Our Oceans Are Turning into Plastic . . . Are We?" was written for Best Life Magazine *and published in 2007; it was also selected for the anthology* Best American Magazine Writing 2007. *Although Casey uses cause/effect as her main organizing strategy, she also uses description and definition to report on "plastic pollution."*

1   A vast swath of the Pacific, twice the size of Texas, is full of a plastic stew that is entering the food chain. Scientists say these toxins are causing obesity, infertility . . . and worse.

2   Fate can take strange forms, and so perhaps it does not seem unusual that Captain Charles Moore found his life's purpose in a nightmare. Unfortunately, he was awake at the time, and 800 miles north of Hawaii in the Pacific Ocean.

3   It happened on August 3, 1997, a lovely day, at least in the beginning: Sunny. Little wind. Water the color of sapphires. Moore and the crew of Alguita, his 50-foot aluminum-hulled catamaran, sliced through the sea.

4   Returning to Southern California from Hawaii after a sailing race, Moore had altered Alguita's course, veering slightly north. He had the

time and the curiosity to try a new route, one that would lead the vessel through the eastern corner of a 10-million-square-mile oval known as the North Pacific subtropical gyre. This was an odd stretch of ocean, a place most boats purposely avoided. For one thing, it was becalmed. "The doldrums," sailors called it, and they steered clear. So did the ocean's top predators: the tuna, sharks, and other large fish that required livelier waters, flush with prey. The gyre was more like a desert—a slow, deep, clockwise-swirling vortex of air and water caused by a mountain of high-pressure air that lingered above it.

The area's reputation didn't deter Moore. He had grown up in Long 5 Beach, 40 miles south of L.A., with the Pacific literally in his front yard, and he possessed an impressive aquatic résumé: deckhand, able seaman, sailor, scuba diver, surfer, and finally captain. Moore had spent countless hours in the ocean, fascinated by its vast trove of secrets and terrors. He'd seen a lot of things out there, things that were glorious and grand; things that were ferocious and humbling. But he had never seen anything nearly as chilling as what lay ahead of him in the gyre.

It began with a line of plastic bags ghosting the surface, followed 6 by an ugly tangle of junk: nets and ropes and bottles, motor-oil jugs and cracked bath toys, a mangled tarp. Tires. A traffic cone. Moore could not believe his eyes. Out here in this desolate place, the water was a stew of plastic crap. It was as though someone had taken the pristine seascape of his youth and swapped it for a landfill.

How did all the plastic end up here? How did this trash tsunami 7 begin? What did it mean? If the questions seemed overwhelming, Moore would soon learn that the answers were even more so, and that his discovery had dire implications for human—and planetary—health. As Alguita glided through the area that scientists now refer to as the "Eastern Garbage Patch," Moore realized that the trail of plastic went on for hundreds of miles. Depressed and stunned, he sailed for a week through bobbing, toxic debris trapped in a purgatory of circling currents. To his horror, he had stumbled across the 21st-century Leviathan. It had no head, no tail. Just an endless body.

"Everybody's plastic, but I love plastic. I want to be plastic." This 8 Andy Warhol quote is emblazoned on a six-foot-long magenta and yellow banner that hangs—with extreme irony—in the solar-powered workshop in Moore's Long Beach home. The workshop is surrounded by a crazy Eden of trees, bushes, flowers, fruits, and vegetables, ranging from the prosaic (tomatoes) to the exotic (cherimoyas, guavas, chocolate persimmons, white figs the size of baseballs). This is the house in which Moore, 59, was raised, and it has a kind of open-air earthiness that reflects his '60s-activist roots, which included a stint in a Berkeley commune. Composting and organic gardening are serious business here—you can practically smell the humus—but there is also a kidney-shaped hot tub surrounded by palm trees. Two wet suits hang drying on a clothesline above it.

9   This afternoon, Moore strides the grounds. "How about a nice, fresh boysenberry?" he asks, and plucks one off a bush. He's a striking man wearing no-nonsense black trousers and a shirt with official-looking epaulettes. A thick brush of salt-and-pepper hair frames his intense blue eyes and serious face. But the first thing you notice about Moore is his voice, a deep, bemused drawl that becomes animated and sardonic when the subject turns to plastic pollution. This problem is Moore's calling, a passion he inherited from his father, an industrial chemist who studied waste management as a hobby. On family vacations, Moore recalls, part of the agenda would be to see what the locals threw out. "We could be in paradise, but we would go to the dump," he says with a shrug. "That's what we wanted to see."

10   Since his first encounter with the Garbage Patch nine years ago, Moore has been on a mission to learn exactly what's going on out there. Leaving behind a 25-year career running a furniture-restoration business, he has created the Algalita Marine Research Foundation to spread the word of his findings. He has resumed his science studies, which he'd set aside when his attention swerved from pursuing a university degree to protesting the Vietnam War. His tireless effort has placed him on the front lines of this new, more abstract battle. After enlisting scientists such as Steven B. Weisberg, Ph.D. (executive director of the Southern California Coastal Water Research Project and an expert in marine environmental monitoring), to develop methods for analyzing the gyre's contents, Moore has sailed Alguita back to the Garbage Patch several times. On each trip, the volume of plastic has grown alarmingly. The area in which it accumulates is now twice the size of Texas.

11   At the same time, all over the globe, there are signs that plastic pollution is doing more than blighting the scenery; it is also making its way into the food chain. Some of the most obvious victims are the dead seabirds that have been washing ashore in startling numbers, their bodies packed with plastic: things like bottle caps, cigarette lighters, tampon applicators, and colored scraps that, to a foraging bird, resemble baitfish. (One animal dissected by Dutch researchers contained 1603 pieces of plastic.) And the birds aren't alone. All sea creatures are threatened by floating plastic, from whales down to zooplankton. There's a basic moral horror in seeing the pictures: a sea turtle with a plastic band strangling its shell into an hourglass shape; a humpback towing plastic nets that cut into its flesh and make it impossible for the animal to hunt. More than a million seabirds, 100,000 marine mammals, and countless fish die in the North Pacific each year, either from mistakenly eating this junk or from being ensnared in it and drowning.

12   Bad enough. But Moore soon learned that the big, tentacled balls of trash were only the most visible signs of the problem; others were far less

obvious, and far more evil. Dragging a fine-meshed net known as a manta trawl, he discovered minuscule pieces of plastic, some barely visible to the eye, swirling like fish food throughout the water. He and his researchers parsed, measured, and sorted their samples and arrived at the following conclusion: By weight, this swath of sea contains six times as much plastic as it does plankton.

This statistic is grim—for marine animals, of course, but even more 13 so for humans. The more invisible and ubiquitous the pollution, the more likely it will end up inside us. And there's growing—and disturbing— proof that we're ingesting plastic toxins constantly, and that even slight doses of these substances can severely disrupt gene activity. "Every one of us has this huge body burden," Moore says. "You could take your serum to a lab now, and they'd find at least 100 industrial chemicals that weren't around in 1950." The fact that these toxins don't cause violent and immediate reactions does not mean they're benign: Scientists are just beginning to research the long-term ways in which the chemicals used to make plastic interact with our own biochemistry.

In simple terms, plastic is a petroleum-based mix of monomers that 14 become polymers, to which additional chemicals are added for suppleness, inflammability, and other qualities. When it comes to these substances, even the syllables are scary. For instance, if you're thinking that perfluorooctanoic acid (PFOA) isn't something you want to sprinkle on your microwave popcorn, you're right. Recently, the Science Advisory Board of the Environmental Protection Agency (EPA) upped its classification of PFOA to a likely carcinogen. Yet it's a common ingredient in packaging that needs to be oil- and heat-resistant. So while there may be no PFOA in the popcorn itself, if PFOA is used to treat the bag, enough of it can leach into the popcorn oil when your butter deluxe meets your superheated microwave oven that a single serving spikes the amount of the chemical in your blood.

Other nasty chemical additives are the flame retardants known as 15 poly-brominated diphenyl ethers (PBDEs). These chemicals have been shown to cause liver and thyroid toxicity, reproductive problems, and memory loss in preliminary animal studies. In vehicle interiors, PBDEs— used in moldings and floor coverings, among other things—combine with another group called phthalates to create that much-vaunted "new-car smell." Leave your new wheels in the hot sun for a few hours, and these substances can "off-gas" at an accelerated rate, releasing noxious by-products.

It's not fair, however, to single out fast food and new cars. PBDEs, 16 to take just one example, are used in many products, incuding computers, carpeting, and paint. As for phthalates, we deploy about a billion pounds of them a year worldwide despite the fact that California recently listed them as a chemical known to be toxic to our reproductive systems.

Used to make plastic soft and pliable, phthalates leach easily from millions of products—packaged food, cosmetics, varnishes, the coatings of timed-release pharmaceuticals—into our blood, urine, saliva, seminal fluid, breast milk, and amniotic fluid. In food containers and some plastic bottles, phthalates are now found with another compound called bisphenol A (BPA), which scientists are discovering can wreak stunning havoc in the body. We produce 6 billion pounds of that each year, and it shows: BPA has been found in nearly every human who has been tested in the United States. We're eating these plasticizing additives, drinking them, breathing them, and absorbing them through our skin every single day. Most alarming, these chemicals may disrupt the endocrine system—the delicately balanced set of hormones and glands that affect virtually every organ and cell—by mimicking the female hormone estrogen. In marine environments, excess estrogen has led to Twilight Zone–esque discoveries of male fish and seagulls that have sprouted female sex organs.

17   On land, things are equally gruesome. "Fertility rates have been declining for quite some time now, and exposure to synthetic estrogen—especially from the chemicals found in plastic products—can have an adverse effect," says Marc Goldstein, M.D., director of the Cornell Institute for Reproductive Medicine. Dr. Goldstein also notes that pregnant women are particularly vulnerable: "Prenatal exposure, even in very low doses, can cause irreversible damage in an unborn baby's reproductive organs." And after the baby is born, he or she is hardly out of the woods. Frederick vom Saal, Ph.D., a professor at the University of Missouri at Columbia who specifically studies estrogenic chemicals in plastics, warns parents to "steer clear of polycarbonate baby bottles. They're particularly dangerous for newborns, whose brains, immune systems, and gonads are still developing." Dr. vom Saal's research spurred him to throw out every polycarbonate plastic item in his house, and to stop buying plastic-wrapped food and canned goods (cans are plastic-lined) at the grocery store. "We now know that BPA causes prostate cancer in mice and rats, and abnormalities in the prostate's stem cell, which is the cell implicated in human prostate cancer," he says. "That's enough to scare the hell out of me." At Tufts University, Ana M. Soto, M.D., a professor of anatomy and cellular biology, has also found connections between these chemicals and breast cancer.

18   As if the potential for cancer and mutation weren't enough, Dr. vom Saal states in one of his studies that "prenatal exposure to very low doses of BPA increases the rate of postnatal growth in mice and rats." In other words, BPA made rodents fat. Their insulin output surged wildly and then crashed into a state of resistance—the virtual definition of diabetes. They produced bigger fat cells, and more of them. A recent scientific paper Dr. vom Saal coauthored contains this chilling sentence: "These findings suggest that developmental exposure to BPA is contributing to

the obesity epidemic that has occurred during the last two decades in the developed world, associated with the dramatic increase in the amount of plastic being produced each year." Given this, it is perhaps not entirely coincidental that America's staggering rise in diabetes—a 735 percent increase since 1935—follows the same arc.

This news is depressing enough to make a person reach for the bottle. 19 Glass, at least, is easily recyclable. You can take one tequila bottle, melt it down, and make another tequila bottle. With plastic, recycling is more complicated. Unfortunately, that promising-looking triangle of arrows that appears on products doesn't always signify endless reuse; it merely identifies which type of plastic the item is made from. And of the seven different plastics in common use, only two of them—PET (labeled with #1 inside the triangle and used in soda bottles) and HDPE (labeled with #2 inside the triangle and used in milk jugs)—have much of an aftermarket. So no matter how virtuously you toss your chip bags and shampoo bottles into your blue bin, few of them will escape the landfill—only 3 to 5 percent of plastics are recycled in any way.

"There's no legal way to recycle a milk container into another milk 20 container without adding a new virgin layer of plastic," Moore says, pointing out that, because plastic melts at low temperatures, it retains pollutants and the tainted residue of its former contents. Turn up the heat to sear these off, and some plastics release deadly vapors. So the reclaimed stuff is mostly used to make entirely different products, things that don't go anywhere near our mouths, such as fleece jackets and carpeting. Therefore, unlike recycling glass, metal, or paper, recycling plastic doesn't always result in less use of virgin material. It also doesn't help that fresh-made plastic is far cheaper.

Moore routinely finds half-melted blobs of plastic in the ocean, as 21 though the person doing the burning realized partway through the process that this was a bad idea, and stopped (or passed out from the fumes). "That's a concern as plastic proliferates worldwide, and people run out of room for trash and start burning plastic—you're producing some of the most toxic gases known," he says. The color-coded bin system may work in Marin County, but it is somewhat less effective in subequatorial Africa or rural Peru.

"Except for the small amount that's been incinerated—and it's a very 22 small amount—every bit of plastic ever made still exists," Moore says, describing how the material's molecular structure resists biodegradation. Instead, plastic crumbles into ever-tinier fragments as it's exposed to sunlight and the elements. And none of these untold gazillions of fragments is disappearing any time soon: Even when plastic is broken down to a single molecule, it remains too tough for biodegradation.

Truth is, no one knows how long it will take for plastic to biodegrade, 23 or return to its carbon and hydrogen elements. We only invented the stuff

144 years ago, and science's best guess is that its natural disappearance will take several more centuries. Meanwhile, every year, we churn out about 60 billion tons of it, much of which becomes disposable products meant only for a single use. Set aside the question of why we're creating ketchup bottles and six-pack rings that last for half a millennium, and consider the implications of it: Plastic never really goes away.

24   Ask a group of people to name an overwhelming global problem, and you'll hear about climate change, the Middle East, or AIDS. No one, it is guaranteed, will cite the sloppy transport of nurdles as a concern. And yet nurdles, lentil-size pellets of plastic in its rawest form, are especially effective couriers of waste chemicals called persistent organic pollutants, or POPs, which include known carcinogens such as DDT and PCBs.

25   The United States banned these poisons in the 1970s, but they remain stubbornly at large in the environment, where they latch on to plastic because of its molecular tendency to attract oils.

26   The word itself—nurdles—sounds cuddly and harmless, like a cartoon character or a pasta for kids, but what it refers to is most certainly not. Absorbing up to a million times the level of POP pollution in their surrounding waters, nurdles become supersaturated poison pills. They're light enough to blow around like dust, to spill out of shipping containers, and to wash into harbors, storm drains, and creeks. In the ocean, nurdles are easily mistaken for fish eggs by creatures that would very much like to have such a snack. And once inside the body of a bigeye tuna or a king salmon, these tenacious chemicals are headed directly to your dinner table. One study estimated that nurdles now account for 10 percent of plastic ocean debris. And once they're scattered in the environment, they're diabolically hard to clean up (think wayward confetti). At places as remote as Rarotonga, in the Cook Islands, 2100 miles northeast of New Zealand and a 12-hour flight from L.A., they're commonly found mixed with beach sand. In 2004, Moore received a $500,000 grant from the state of California to investigate the myriad ways in which nurdles go astray during the plastic manufacturing process. On a visit to a polyvinyl chloride (PVC) pipe factory, as he walked through an area where railcars unloaded ground-up nurdles, he noticed that his pant cuffs were filled with a fine plastic dust. Turning a corner, he saw windblown drifts of nurdles piled against a fence. Talking about the experience, Moore's voice becomes strained and his words pour out in an urgent tumble: "It's not the big trash on the beach. It's the fact that the whole biosphere is becoming mixed with these plastic particles. What are they doing to us? We're breathing them, the fish are eating them, they're in our hair, they're in our skin."

27   Though marine dumping is part of the problem, escaped nurdles and other plastic litter migrate to the gyre largely from land. That polystyrene cup you saw floating in the creek, if it doesn't get picked up

and specifically taken to a landfill, will eventually be washed out to sea. Once there, it will have plenty of places to go: The North Pacific gyre is only one of five such high-pressure zones in the oceans. There are similar areas in the South Pacific, the North and South Atlantic, and the Indian Ocean. Each of these gyres has its own version of the Garbage Patch, as plastic gathers in the currents. Together, these areas cover 40 percent of the sea. "That corresponds to a quarter of the earth's surface," Moore says. "So 25 percent of our planet is a toilet that never flushes."

It wasn't supposed to be this way. In 1865, a few years after Alexander 28 Parkes unveiled a precursor to man-made plastic called Parkesine, a scientist named John W. Hyatt set out to make a synthetic replacement for ivory billiard balls. He had the best of intentions: Save the elephants! After some tinkering, he created celluloid. From then on, each year brought a miraculous recipe: rayon in 1891, Teflon in 1938, polypropylene in 1954. Durable, cheap, versatile—plastic seemed like a revelation. And in many ways, it was. Plastic has given us bulletproof vests, credit cards, slinky spandex pants. It has led to breakthroughs in medicine, aerospace engineering, and computer science. And who among us doesn't own a Frisbee?

Plastic has its benefits; no one would deny that. Few of us, however, 29 are as enthusiastic as the American Plastics Council. One of its recent press releases, titled "Plastic Bags—A Family's Trusted Companion," reads: "Very few people remember what life was like before plastic bags became an icon of convenience and practicality—and now art. Remember the 'beautiful' [sic] swirling, floating bag in *American Beauty*?"

Alas, the same ethereal quality that allows bags to dance gracefully 30 across the big screen also lands them in many less desirable places. Twenty-three countries, including Germany, South Africa, and Australia, have banned, taxed, or restricted the use of plastic bags because they clog sewers and lodge in the throats of livestock. Like pernicious Kleenex, these flimsy sacks end up snagged in trees and snarled in fences, becoming eyesores and worse: They also trap rainwater, creating perfect little breeding grounds for disease-carrying mosquitoes.

In the face of public outrage over pictures of dolphins choking on "a 31 family's trusted companion," the American Plastics Council takes a defensive stance, sounding not unlike the NRA: Plastics don't pollute, people do.

It has a point. Each of us tosses about 185 pounds of plastic per year. 32 We could certainly reduce that. And yet—do our products have to be quite so lethal? Must a discarded flip-flop remain with us until the end of time? Aren't disposable razors and foam packing peanuts a poor consolation prize for the destruction of the world's oceans, not to mention our own bodies and the health of future generations? "If 'more is better' and that's the only mantra we have, we're doomed," Moore says, summing it up.

Oceanographer Curtis Ebbesmeyer, Ph.D., an expert on marine debris, 33 agrees. "If you could fast-forward 10,000 years and do an archaeological dig . . . you'd find a little line of plastic," he told the *Seattle Times* last April. "What happened to those people? Well, they ate their own plastic and disrupted their genetic structure and weren't able to reproduce. They didn't last very long because they killed themselves."

34   Our oceans are turning into plastic . . . are we? Wrist-slittingly depressing, yes, but there are glimmers of hope on the horizon. Green architect and designer William McDonough has become an influential voice, not only in environmental circles but among Fortune 500 CEOs. McDonough proposes a standard known as "cradle to cradle" in which all manufactured things must be reusable, poison-free, and beneficial over the long haul. His outrage is obvious when he holds up a rubber ducky, a common child's bath toy. The duck is made of phthalate-laden PVC, which has been linked to cancer and reproductive harm. "What kind of people are we that we would design like this?" McDonough asks. In the United States, it's commonly accepted that children's teething rings, cosmetics, food wrappers, cars, and textiles will be made from toxic materials. Other countries—and many individual companies—seem to be reconsidering. Currently, McDonough is working with the Chinese government to build seven cities using "the building materials of the future," including a fabric that is safe enough to eat and a new, nontoxic polystyrene.

35   Thanks to people like Moore and McDonough, and media hits such as Al Gore's *An Inconvenient Truth*, awareness of just how hard we've bitch-slapped the planet is skyrocketing. After all, unless we're planning to colonize Mars soon, this is where we live, and none of us would choose to live in a toxic wasteland or to spend our days getting pumped full of drugs to deal with our haywire endocrine systems and runaway cancer.

36   None of plastic's problems can be fixed overnight, but the more we learn, the more likely that, eventually, wisdom will trump convenience and cheap disposability. In the meantime, let the cleanup begin: The National Oceanographic & Atmospheric Administration (NOAA) is aggressively using satellites to identify and remove "ghost nets," abandoned plastic fishing gear that never stops killing. (A single net recently hauled up off the Florida coast contained more than 1000 dead fish, sharks, and one loggerhead turtle.) New biodegradable starch- and corn-based plastics have arrived, and Wal-Mart has signed on as a customer. A consumer rebellion against dumb and excessive packaging is afoot. And in August 2006, Moore was invited to speak about "marine debris and hormone disruption" at a meeting in Sicily convened by the science advisor to the Vatican. This annual gathering, called the International Seminars on Planetary Emergencies, brings scientists together to discuss mankind's worst threats. Past topics have included nuclear holocaust and terrorism.

37   The gray plastic kayak floats next to Moore's catamaran, *Alguita*, which lives in a slip across from his house. It is not a lovely kayak; in fact,

it looks pretty rough. But it's floating, a sturdy, eight-foot-long two-seater. Moore stands on Alguita's deck, hands on hips, staring down at it. On the sailboat next to him, his neighbor, Cass Bastain, does the same. He has just informed Moore that he came across the abandoned craft yesterday, floating just offshore. The two men shake their heads in bewilderment.

"That's probably a $600 kayak," Moore says, adding, "I don't even 38 shop anymore. Anything I need will just float by." (In his opinion, the movie *Cast Away* was a joke—Tom Hanks could've built a village with the crap that would've washed ashore during a storm.)

Watching the kayak bobbing disconsolately, it is hard not to wonder 39 what will become of it. The world is full of cooler, sexier kayaks. It is also full of cheap plastic kayaks that come in more attractive colors than battleship gray. The ownerless kayak is a lummox of a boat, 50 pounds of nurdles extruded into an object that nobody wants, but that'll be around for centuries longer than we will.

And as Moore stands on deck looking into the water, it is easy to 40 imagine him doing the same thing 800 miles west, in the gyre. You can see his silhouette in the silvering light, caught between ocean and sky. You can see the mercurial surface of the most majestic body of water on earth. And then below, you can see the half-submerged madhouse of forgotten and discarded things. As Moore looks over the side of the boat, you can see the seabirds sweeping overhead, dipping and skimming the water. One of the journeying birds, sleek as a fighter plane, carries a scrap of something yellow in its beak. The bird dives low and then boomerangs over the horizon. Gone.

2007

QUESTIONS FOR DISCUSSION

Content

a. What is "plastic pollution" and how does it get into the environment?
b. How do plastics get into the ocean? According to Casey, how much plastic is in the ocean, and where is it concentrated?
c. What are nurdles and why are they bad for us?
d. What solutions does Casey mention? How practical are these solutions?
e. What health problems are caused by the increasing amount of plastic in the environment?
f. Why is the Andy Warhol quotation in paragraph 8 ironic?

Strategy and Style

g. What might have been Casey's reason for describing Charles Moore and his home in such detail? How is this description of his personal life related to his professional life?

h. Why is it necessary to define what plastic is (paragraph 14)?

i. Casey uses many technical terms, such as *phthalates*, and acronyms, such as POP, HDPE, and PBDE, yet the article is fairly easy to read. What does Casey do to make her essay understandable to lay readers?

j. Casey describes the dire health effects of plastic pollution in frightening terms, particularly in paragraphs 14–19. To what extent is this an effective strategy?

k. Casey adds a hopeful note toward the end of her essay, suggesting that there are solutions to the problem. What might have been her motive for doing this?

ENGAGING THE TEXT

a. In paragraph 29, Casey tells us how plastic was invented as an alternative to ivory. Reflect on how inventions based on good intentions often end up creating new problems.

b. In paragraph 22, Casey quotes Moore as saying that "every bit of plastic ever made still exists." Imagine your home after one year if you did not throw away any of the plastic you used in that year, and write a description of that image.

SUGGESTIONS FOR SUSTAINED WRITING

a. It is natural that plastic pollution would concern environmentalists, but what about this topic would concern people typically considered anti-environmentalist, such as developers and industrialists? Write an essay in which you explain what the stakes are for everyone, and suggest ways for people to become involved in solving the problem. Use examples from your own community as a way to include specific examples.

b. Compare Casey's article to other essays about humankind's relationship to the environment. You can use selections from this book, such as Mark Twain's "Two Views of the Mississippi" (Chapter 6), Annie Dillard's "Living Like Weasels" (Chapter 9), Andrew C. Revkin's "Global Warming Is Eroding Glacial Ice" (Chapter 10), or Philip Stott's "Global Warming Is Not a Threat to Polar Ice" (Chapter 10), or find other essays outside of the book. Discuss how each writer you choose uses narration, description, and definition to explain the effects that humans and the environment have on each other.

c. Using the National Oceanographic Atmospheric Administration's "Marine Debris Program" website (http://marinedebris.noaa.gov) as one source for information, write a researched report about one aspect of marine debris. Consider whether the solutions briefly mentioned by Casey might be practical.

READ MORE

Casey and Her Works

"Author Interview: Susan Casey" (http://www.bookbrowse.com/author_interviews/full/index.cfm?author_number=1177): *Transcript of an interview with the author about her book* The Devil's Teeth.

Plastics

"Plastic" (http://www.mindfully.org/Plastic/plastic.htm): *Links to many articles about plastics in the environment.*

"Algalita Marine Research Foundation" (http://www.algalita.org): *Marine conservation and education website.*

"Plastics Division" (http://www.americanchemistry.com/plastics): *The website for the American Plastics Council cited in Casey's article.*

NOAA Marine Debris Program (http://marinedebris.noaa.gov): *The website for the National Oceanographic Atmospheric Administration's program cited in Casey's article.*

The Value and Price of Food

Carlo Petrini

Carlo Petrini (b. 1949), the founder of the Slow Food movement, was born in the Italian city of Bra. He began his career as a writer by contributing essays on food and gastronomy to several radical Italian newspapers including Il manifesto. *Today, Petrini spends his time writing weekly columns for* La Stampa, *one of Italy's most important newspapers, editing books and periodicals for Slow Food Editore, the publishing arm of the movement, and organizing and speaking at meetings and seminars that advance the cause of Slow Food around the world.*

The Slow Food movement is a reaction to what its adherents refer to as the artificiality and unhealthiness of much of day's mass-produced food, which is raised on large corporate farms, where pesticides and chemical fertilizers are used liberally in order to get the most product—whatever the quality—out of the smallest amount of land and in the cheapest way. Petrini first came to the attention of the international community when he helped lead a protest against the building of a MacDonald's restaurant near the Spanish Steps in the heart of the Italian capital. For Petrini, the attempt to produce abundant food at the lowest price has resulted in lowering the quality of food, destroying the quality of the soil, and impoverishing the family farmer and others who have a direct connection with and a love for the land.

Among the most important objectives of the Slow Food movement are promoting the diversity of domestic plants and animals, limiting waste in the processing and consumption of food, emphasizing the importance of consuming locally grown products, maintaining the health of the soil, outlawing the use of pesticides and artificial fertilizers, encouraging people to develop their own gardens and producing their own food, and informing the public about the harmful effects of food production by large agra-conglomerates.

Petrini explains much of the philosophy of the Slow Food movement in his Terra Madre (Mother Earth) *from which "The Value and Price of Food" is taken.*

1   The triumph of consumerism has seen the triumph of another prejudice-cum-cliché: the idea that the price and value of food has to be low—as low as possible, in fact.

2   It's natural, in a market, for us to opt for the product that costs least. But we should do so when quality is equal, or at least when we have the opportunity of choosing a standard of quality suitable for our needs. This is no longer possible in the case of food; it has to be cheap, period. Vegetables or pasta only have to go up by a few cents and the papers spew indignant reactions. Yet people don't protest the same way if their bank account or telephone bills cost more, if a professional fleeces them for his services, or if a television-repair call costs the equivalent of a dinner for two at a restaurant.

3   But food's a different matter; it isn't to be meddled with. The widely held opinion is: "With a great deal of effort we managed to beat hunger years ago. We are a rich, opulent society; food has to be available everywhere and, if possible, cost a trifle. If it's expensive, let's leave it to gluttons and guzzlers with plenty of money to spend." This is what comes of having transformed food into a consumer commodity, stripping it of all its spiritual, cultural, and material values: the system built around it or of which it is part has replaced value with price. Money has supplanted other values to become the secret of happiness.

4   Food is thus no longer produced to be eaten, but to be sold. Price becomes the principal, if not the only, choice criterion. In the global agro-industry food system, foodstuffs have become commodities just like all the others—no more, no less; just like oil, timber, or other tradable goods whose prices are established by international stock exchanges. Grain, corn, coffee, and cocoa are commodities like metals or energy, hence subject to the laws of supply and demand, distributed on the

market without differentiations in quality and without a care about who produces them.

Subjecting food to these laws leads to a standardization of food pro- 5 duction that tends to reduce biodiversity and increase "eco-unfriendly" monocultures. And it also causes a huge amount of injustice. Especially in the South of the world, and often on account of their colonialist or neo colonialist heritage, whole countries have become specialized in given agricultural products and promptly suffer huge upheavals when their prices plummet.

Mostly in countries that are experiencing rapid urbanization, the fact 6 that food is becoming something to buy and not to produce is creating poverty, hence hunger and malnutrition. A peasant farmer in a poor country who decides to abandon the hard life of the countryside for a move to the city stops producing the meager amount of food that allowed his family to get by, albeit in poor conditions. But if he doesn't find a job with a decent wage in the city, he won't be able to buy enough food for himself and his family. In a short space of time, he will descend from poverty to nothing—to hunger and downright squalor.

Total commodification is the price we pay for the degeneration in the 7 value of food in both the North and the South of the world. Yet practices exist that may not be viable in monetary terms—think of home jam making, which certainly costs less than buying jam in a store—but which enables us to earn value in terms of conviviality, personal gratification, community service, environmental protection, and, in a word, well-being.

We have perpetrated the most appalling disasters, all for the sake of 8 Mammon. Destitute of authenticity, food ultimately eats us. Deprived of cultural, social, and environmental values, it stops being an object of attention, care, and pride—as a true resource should be—morphing into a monster that devastates the countryside socially and ecologically, causing injustice everywhere. We may think we can nonchalantly throw away food, but we can't.

FOOD IS EATING THE ENVIRONMENT

Industrialization, as intense in the agri-food sector as it is in others, rele- 9 gates quality to the back seat. The drivers are quantity, productivity, standardization, and homogenization. Nature, characterized by complexity, indeterminateness, diversity, and multi-functionality, is something else.

Industrial agriculture (what an oxymoron!), the industrial processing 10 of food, the distribution over five continents of food-stuffs that could be cultivated in loco, low prices, and the laws of the free market—all these factors have combined to make the food sector one of the most unsustainable spheres of human activity.

11   Over the last hundred years, biodiversity has disappeared at an alarming rate: the need for vast monocultures to supply industry with large amounts of cheap food has limited people's choices to the few varieties suited to this production model—to the detriment of others. As a result, in the United States alone—the world leader in industrial agriculture—80.6 percent of all tomato varieties became extinct between 1903 and 1983, as did 92.8 percent of salad varieties, 86.2 percent of apple varieties, 90.8 percent of corn varieties, and 96.1 percent of sweet corn varieties. Of the 5,000 existing potato varieties, only 4 constitute the majority of those cultivated for commercial purposes in the United States. Only 2 varieties account for 96 percent of all cultivated American peas, and 6 varieties for 71 percent of the total of all cultivated corn. These have been the results wherever the industrialization of food has had the upper hand: a triumph for standardization and homogenization, and a serious peril for two of the cornerstones of life on earth—biological diversity and the ability of species to adapt.

12   The damage that has been done has achieved biblical proportions. In just one century, we have allowed the fruits of thousands of years of evolution to vanish. Luckily, many countries that have yet to experience the agro-industry boom still enjoy a decent level of biodiversity. But if their ambition is to emulate the example of the West, the disaster will become universal. Unfortunately, we are already seeing worrying signals of how, in countries such as Mexico, India, Brazil, and China—among those boasting the most edible vegetable varieties and animal breeds, but also with galloping industrial growth rates—the phenomenon of the destruction of biodiversity is repeating itself with unprecedented intensity.

13   Furthermore, even the land is being "eaten" by food on account of production being carried out on an industrial scale. Over the last few years, the use of chemical fertilizers and pesticides has increased exponentially. The same amount of synthetic chemicals has been applied to the world's soils and introduced into its natural systems in the last ten years as was used in the whole of the preceding century. The products in question are, of course, foreign to the natural cycle, and it is no secret that they will jeopardize soil fertility in the long term. The soil is a living thing, and we are murdering it. Industrial agriculture has embraced the idea of farming without farmers, but at this rate one day we'll be forced to farm without land.

14   Damage to the environment caused by the industrial global food system is so widespread and severe that the problem is now the first item on the ecological agenda. News about what is going on has leaked from the "alternative" world of organics and environmentalism and now entered the public domain. It's no longer possible to deny the facts.

15   The countryside used to be an oasis for town dwellers keen to escape from pollution. Today many areas of the planet have become dangerous

for our health, especially places where fertilizer is spread and pesticides are sprayed. Agriculture used to be—ought to be—an alliance between man and nature, but it has gradually become a war. It's no coincidence that the technologies used to produce pesticides all originate in the armaments industry. Industrial agriculture is de facto a declaration of war on the earth.

To date, environmental devastation has never been calculated as an 16 item in food economics, even though it does represent an increasingly onerous cost.

I believe that we pay a low market price for food, but that we also 17 pay a high—and hidden—price, not only in economic terms, but also in terms of the earth's capacity to produce food in the future, and in terms of the quality of our own life and health and of those of future generations, to whom we cannot deny the sacred right to enjoy well-being and happiness. The low cost of food not only devalues food itself, but also hides all the evil we are doing to the earth.

Sooner or later, someone will have to pay for all this, and ultimately it 18 will be "consumers," even if they are convinced they are getting a bargain when they spend small sums of money on eating.

QUESTIONS FOR DISCUSSION

Content

a. According to Petrini, what accounts for our demand that food has to be cheap?
b. In paragraph 8, the author claims that "food ultimately eats us." How might this statement serve as his thesis?
c. On what does Petrini place the blame for the decrease in the biodiversity of food?
d. How does he defend the claim that "the land is being 'eaten' by food"?
e. What is meant by the charge that "food is eating farmers"?
f. What accounts for the discrepancy between the fact that over one billion people in one part of the world are starving while those in another part of the world waste food at a rate that "leave[s] us speechless" (paragraph 25)?
g. What does the author suggest we do to overcome the problems that arise from the way we produce and consume food (paragraphs 29, 32, 33)?

Strategy and Style

h. Where in this essay does Petrini use contrast? To what end?
i. Where does he use statistics? What effect do they have on the reader?

j. What other methods does the author use to bolster the credibility of his argument?

k. What is the effect of Petrini's claiming that "technologies to produce pesticides all originate in the armaments industry" (paragraph 15)?

l. Paragraph 30 includes a long quotation from the novelist Italo Calvino. How does this material help develop this essay's thesis?

m.In addition to explaining causes and effects, what is the purpose of this essay?

ENGAGING THE TEXT

a. Summarize the short- and long-term effects of our demand for cheap food as expressed in this essay.

b. In paragraph 3, the author says that we have stripped food "of all its spiritual, cultural, and material values. . . ." After reading this essay, do you agree? Making close reference to the text, explain why or why not.

SUGGESTIONS FOR SUSTAINED WRITING

a. Write an essay in which you explain how you, your family, or your community is contributing to the problems that Petrini discusses. If that doesn't interest you, explain what you, your family, or your community is doing or might do to ameliorate or help solve these problems.

b. Petrini claims that industrial agriculture is a "de facto declaration of war on the earth" (paragraph 15). Can you think of other examples of industry's assault on the environment? Make a list of these examples. Then, read or re-read Susan Casey's "Our Oceans Are Turning to Plastic . . . Are We?" which also appears in this chapter. If Casey and Petrini were to discuss the causes and effects of modern industrialization and commerce on the environment, what might they agree on? Write an essay that summarizes such a discussion.

c. Are all of the effects of our demand for cheap food negative? Are there any positive effects? In response to Petrini, write an essay that identifies a few of the latter. If this assignment doesn't interest you, write an essay in which you point out the effects of what Petrini calls "the triumph of consumerism" (paragraph 1). Focus on one type of industry or commercial enterprise (for example, the auto industry, the cinema, television, the computer/electronics industry, the physical fitness business, the diet industry) and explain its role in your daily life or the lives of people you know. One way to proceed is to explain how this enterprise has changed the lives of people in a particular age group (adolescents or people in their twenties, for instance) from what their lives might have been like had they lived 20 or 30 years ago.

Whichever option you choose, make certain to include library and/or Internet research per your instructor's directions.

READ MORE

Petrini and His Work

"Carlo Petrini: The Slow Food Tsar." *The Independent.* 10 Dec. 2006. Web. 29 Jan 2011. *In-depth discussion of Petrini and Slow Foods.*

Hesser, Amanda. "Endangered Species: Slow Food—An Interview with Carlo Petrini." *Mindfully.org.* 26 July 2003. Web. 29 Jan. 2011. *An interview that provides insights into Petrini's philosophy. The Mindfully.org homepage accesses numerous links to natural foods and other environmental issues.*

Petrini, Carlo: *Terre Madre: Forging a New Global Network of Sustainable Food Communities.* White River Junction, VT: Chelsea Green, 2009. Print.

Petrini, Carlo, Ben Watson, and Deborah Madison. *Slow Food.* White River Junction, VT: Chelsea Green, 2001. Print.

Petrini, Carlo, Jonathan Hunt, and Alice Waters. *Slow Food Nation: Why Our Food Needs to Be Good, Clean, and Fair.* New York: Rizzoli, 2007. Print.

About Slow Food and Other Sustainable Food Communities

Slow Food. Slowfood.com. n.d. Web. 29 Jan. 2011. *The website for Slow Food Worldwide, the organization Petrini founded.*

Stevenson, Tim. "Feeding Ourselves." *Brattleboro Reformer.* 24 Jan. 2011. Web. 29 Jan. 2011. *The author is the co-founder of Post Oil Solutions, whose mission "to learn about and develop sustainable practices in our homes, neighborhoods, and larger communities, so as to begin creating the infrastructure in our region necessary for a post oil society."*

Terra Madre. TerraMadre.com. n.d. Web. 29 Jan. 2011. *The homepage of Terre Madre, an organization founded by Slow Food as a forum for "small-scale farmers, breeders, fishers and food artisans around the world whose approach to food production protects the environment and communities."*

Analogy

Have you ever taken a test that requires you to evaluate relationships between pairs of items or ideas? A typical question might go something like this: Truck is to driver as horse is to _____.

When used to develop ideas in writing, analogies take the form of well-developed comparisons that reveal particular similarities between members of the same or of different classes. Like other forms of comparison, analogy introduces new subjects or ideas by referencing and drawing parallels to information with which the reader is already familiar. Writers often use analogy to create unexpected and quite startling comparisons between items from very different classes. Consider Loren Eiseley's discussion of our earthly environment as a kind of cosmic prison and his startling revelation that our perspective on this planet may be as limited as that of a white blood cell traveling through the body of a cat. Nonetheless, the beauty of analogy is that it can be used effectively to shed new light, even on items from the same class.

Analogies, then, bring to light important relationships that can help define a term, describe a person, a place, or an object, or even argue an important point. Scientific writers rely on analogy to make their descriptions of complex mechanisms or obscure phenomena both interesting and accessible to lay readers. Analogy can also be used to emphasize the significance of particular personal issues, as in Rebecca Brown's "Extreme Reading."

Philosophical concepts, by their very nature abstract, also benefit from explanation through analogy. Plato's "The Myth of the Cave" illuminates humans' struggle to differentiate between images and reality; Annie Dillard explains her idea of how humans should live by describing the tenacious weasel. Analogy is indeed a versatile tool. Consider the brilliant social commentary of Horace Miner in "Body Ritual among the Nacirema."

The items under Engaging the Text and Suggestions for Sustained Writing that follow each selection should help you create and develop interesting analogies of your own. But the essays themselves are so provocative they might even help you come to grips with problems, issues, or concerns that play a significant role in your daily life. Can you compare your current social environment to a prison? Does the way modern college students date resemble courtship rituals among "primitive" peoples (real or fictitious)? If questions like these pop into your mind as you read this chapter, write them down and show them to your instructor; they might make good topics for an essay. At the very least, they will help you to begin using analogy as a tool for thinking and for writing.

The Myth of the Cave

Plato

The great Athenian philosopher Plato (c. 428 B.C.–c. 347 B.C.) was the student of Socrates, whom he made the principal speaker in his dialogues. He studied with Socrates and, after the execution of Socrates in 399 B.C., Plato traveled to Greece, Egypt, and Italy. In 387 B.C., he founded The Academy in Athens.

"The Myth of the Cave" appears in book VII of The Republic. In it, Socrates addresses a series of questions to Glaucon in an attempt to explain that the world in which we live is a world of illusions and shadows—a mere reflection of the "real world" of the intellect. He explains that the "idea of the good" is the "universal author of all things beautiful and right, the parent of light . . . in this visible world, and the immediate source of reason and truth in the intellectual."

And now, I said, let me show in a figure how far our nature is enlightened 1
or unenlightened:—Behold! human beings living in an underground den, which has a mouth open toward the light and reaching all along the den; here they have been from their childhood, and have their legs and necks chained so that they cannot move, and can only see before them, being prevented by the chains from turning round their heads. Above and behind them a fire is blazing at a distance, and between the fire and the prisoners there is a raised way; and you will see, if you look, a low wall built along the way, like the screen which marionette players have in front of them, over which they show the puppets.

I see.   2

And do you see, I said, men passing along the wall carrying all sorts 3
of vessels, and statues and figures of animals made of wood and stone and various materials, which appear over the wall? Some of them are talking, others silent.

You have shown me a strange image, and they are strange prisoners. 4

Like ourselves, I replied; and they see only their own shadows, or 5
the shadows of one another, which the fire throws on the opposite wall of the cave?

True, he said; how could they see anything but the shadows if they 6
were never allowed to move their heads?

And of the objects which are being carried in like manner they would 7
only see the shadows?

8   Yes, he said.

9   And if they were able to converse with one another, would they not suppose that they were naming what was actually before them?

10   Very true.

11   And suppose further that the prison had an echo which came from the other side, would they not be sure to fancy when one of the passers-by spoke that the voice which they heard came from the passing shadow?

12   No question, he replied.

13   To them, I said, the truth would be literally nothing but the shadows of the images.

14   That is certain.

15   And now look again, and see what will naturally follow if the prisoners are released and disabused of their error. At first, when any of them is liberated and compelled suddenly to stand up and turn his neck round and walk and look toward the light, he will suffer sharp pains; the glare will distress him, and he will be unable to see the realities of which in his former state he had seen the shadows; and then conceive someone saying to him, that what he saw before was an illusion, but that now, when he is approaching nearer to being and his eye is turned toward more real existence, he has a clearer vision—what will be his reply? And you may further imagine that his instructor is pointing to the objects as they pass and requiring him to name them—will he not be perplexed? Will he not fancy that the shadows which he formerly saw are truer than the objects which are now shown to him?

16   Far truer.

17   And if he is compelled to look straight at the light, will he not have a pain in his eyes which will make him turn away to take refuge in the objects of vision which he can see, and which he will conceive to be in reality clearer than the things which are now being shown to him?

18   True, he said.

19   And suppose once more, that he is reluctantly dragged up a steep and rugged ascent, and held fast until he is forced into the presence of the sun himself, is he not likely to be pained and irritated? When he approaches the light his eyes will be dazzled, and he will not be able to see anything at all of what are now called realities.

20   Not all in a moment, he said.

21   He will require to grow accustomed to the sight of the upper world. And first he will see the shadows best, next the reflections of men and other objects in the water, and then the objects themselves; then he will gaze upon the light of the moon and the stars and the spangled heaven; and he will see the sky and the stars by night better than the sun or the light of the sun by day?

22   Certainly.

23   Last of all he will be able to see the sun, and not mere reflections of him in the water, but he will see him in his own proper place, and not in another; and he will contemplate him as he is.

Certainly.   24

He will then proceed to argue that this is he who gives the season and   25
the years, and is the guardian of all that is in the visible world, and in a
certain way the cause of all things which he and his fellows have been
accustomed to behold?

Clearly, he said, he would first see the sun and then reason about him.   26

And when he remembered his old habitation, and the wisdom of the   27
den and his fellow-prisoners, do you not suppose that he would felicitate
himself on the change, and pity them?

Certainly, he would.   28

And if they were in the habit of conferring honors among themselves   29
on those who were quickest to observe the passing shadows and to
remark which of them went before, and which followed after, and which
were together; and who were therefore best able to draw conclusions as to
the future, do you think that he would care for such honors and glories, or
envy the possessors of them? Would he not say with Homer,

> Better to be the poor servant of a poor master,

and to endure anything, rather than think as they do and live after their
manner?

Yes, he said, I think that he would rather suffer anything than enter-   30
tain these false notions and live in this miserable manner.

Imagine once more, I said, such a one coming suddenly out of the sun   31
to be replaced in his old situation; would he not be certain to have his eyes
full of darkness?

To be sure, he said.   32

And if there were a contest, and he had to compete in measuring the   33
shadows with the prisoners who had never moved out of the den, while
his sight was still weak, and before his eyes had become steady (and the
time which would be needed to acquire this new habit of sight might be
very considerable), would he not be ridiculous? Men would say of him
that up he went and down he came without his eyes; and that it was better
not even to think of ascending and if anyone tried to loose another and
lead him up to the light, let them only catch the offender, and they would
put him to death.

No question, he said.   34

This entire allegory, I said, you may now append, dear Glaucon, to   35
the previous argument; the prison-house is the world of sight, the light of
the fire is the sun, and you will not misapprehend me if you interpret the
journey upwards to be the ascent of the soul into the intellectual world
according to my poor belief, which, at your desire, I have expressed—
whether rightly or wrongly God knows. But, whether true or false, my
opinion is that in the world of knowledge the idea of good appears last of
all, and is seen only with an effort; and, when seen, is also inferred to be
the universal author of all things beautiful and right, parent of light and of

the lord of light in this visible world, and the immediate source of reason and truth in the intellectual; and that this is the power upon which he who would act rationally either in public or private life must have his eye fixed.

36   I agree, he said, as far as I am able to understand you.

37   Moreover, I said, you must not wonder that those who attain to this beatific vision are unwilling to descend to human affairs; for their souls are ever hastening into the upper world where they desire to dwell; which desire of theirs is very natural, if our allegory may be trusted.

38   Yes, very natural.

39   And is there anything surprising in one who passes from divine contemplations to the evil state of man, misbehaving himself in a ridiculous manner; if, while his eyes are blinking and before he has become accustomed to the surrounding darkness, he is compelled to fight in courts of law, or in other places, about the images or the shadows of images of justice, and is endeavoring to meet the conceptions of those who have never yet seen absolute justice?

40   Anything but surprising, he replied.

41   Anyone who has common sense will remember that the bewilderments of the eyes are of two kinds, and arise from two causes, either from coming out of the light or from going into the light, which is true of the mind's eye, quite as much as of the bodily eye; and he who remembers this when he sees anyone whose vision is perplexed and weak, will not be too ready to laugh; he will first ask whether that soul of man has come out of the brighter life, and is unable to see because unaccustomed to the dark, or having turned from darkness to the day is dazzled by excess of light. And he will count the one happy in his condition and state of being, and he will pity the other; or, if he have a mind to laugh at the soul which comes from below into the light, there will be more reason in this than in the laugh which greets him who returns from above out of the light into the den.

42   That, he said, is a very just distinction.

c. 373 B.C.

QUESTIONS FOR DISCUSSION

Content

a. Why does Plato refer to "the world of sight" as a "prison-house"?

b. Does the fact that Plato has cast this extended analogy into a dialogue make it more effective than if he had written in conventional essay form?

c. What does the sun represent in Plato's analogy?

d. Consult an unabridged dictionary, encyclopedia, or reference book on ancient literature or civilization. Who was Homer? Why does Plato allude to him?

e. What is the "beatific" vision that Socrates describes to Glaucon? Why is it important that one "who would act rationally" experience this vision?

f. How does Plato account for the fact that honorable people, who are able to see the truth and relate it to others, often experience scorn and ridicule?

g. What has Glaucon learned by the end of the dialogue?

Strategy and Style

h. How effective is the dialogue form used in this selection? What is the function of Glaucon's brief responses? Of Socrates's questions?

i. How do Socrates' questions help determine the organization?

j. What is Plato's role in this selection? Is he invisible, a mere transcriber of the dialogue, or is his voice heard in some way?

ENGAGING THE TEXT

a. Write a short dialogue between yourself and Plato or between yourself and one of the dwellers in the cave.

b. This is an especially difficult selection. Try to capture the essence of Plato's ideas in a summary of one or two paragraphs.

SUGGESTIONS FOR SUSTAINED WRITING

a. Describe the human condition using another analogy besides the cave.

b. Do you believe that whatever is spiritual in a person can prevail? Write an essay in which you illustrate (from your own experiences, from those of people you know well, or from those you have read about) that people will deny themselves physical or material gratification in order to preserve the ethical principles or moral codes they believe in. Compare your ideas with the ideas in Maya Angelou's "Grandmother's Victory" (Chapter 1), Ellen Goodman's "The Company Man" (Chapter 4), or Carlo Petrini's "The Value and Price of Food" (Chapter 8).

c. Do you believe that we are prisoners of the material world as Plato suggests? If so, write an essay based on research in which you illustrate how people let their appetites (for food, money, sex, or material possessions, for example) determine the course of their lives.

READ MORE

"Plato and His Dialogues" (http://plato-dialogues.org/plato.htm): *Links to many texts, maps, and other sites.*

"Plato: *The Republic*" (http://www.ilt.columbia.edu/publications/plato_republic.htm): *Electronic text of* The Republic.

Body Ritual among the Nacirema

Horace Miner

Horace Miner (1912–1993) was a social anthropologist who studied at the University of Kentucky and the University of Chicago, where he earned a doctorate in 1937. He began his teaching career in 1945 at Wayne State University and then taught at the University of Michigan, with which he was connected until his death. In 1953, Miner wrote The Primitive City *of Timbuctoo, a seminal study of primitive urban culture. His expertise in African culture was well known, and he received several awards for his scholarship in this field.*

In "Body Ritual among the Nacirema," Miner departs from his serious scholarly style to write a parody that throws an interesting light on certain rituals practiced by a certain contemporary society. This essay first appeared as a "serious" article in 1956 in a professional journal, the American Anthropologist. *It was and continues to be one of the most popular satires of American society.*

1   The anthropologist has become so familiar with the diversity of ways in which different peoples behave in similar situations that he is not apt to be surprised by even the most exotic customs. In fact, if all of the logically possible combinations of behavior have not been found somewhere in the world, he is apt to suspect that they must be present in some yet undescribed tribe. This point has, in fact, been expressed with respect to clan organization by Murdock.[1] In this light, the magical beliefs and practices of the Nacirema present such unusual aspects that it seems desirable to describe them as an example of the extremes to which human behavior can go.

2   Professor Linton first brought the ritual of the Nacirema to the attention of anthropologists twenty years ago, but the culture of this people is still very poorly understood. They are a North American group living in the territory between the Canadian Cree, the Yaqui and Tarahumare of Mexico, and the Carib and Arawak of the Antilles.[2] Little is known of their origin, although tradition states that they came from the east. . . .

[1]American anthropologist George Peter Murdock, authority on primitive cultures.
[2]Native American tribes formerly inhabiting the Saskatchewan region of Canada, the Sonora region of Mexico, and the West Indies.

Nacirema culture is characterized by a highly developed market 3
economy which has evolved in a rich natural habitat. While much of the
people's time is devoted to economic pursuits, a large part of the fruits
of these labors and a considerable portion of the day are spent in ritual
activity. The focus of this activity is the human body, the appearance and
health of which loom as a dominant concern in the ethos of the people.
While such a concern is certainly not unusual, its ceremonial aspects and
associated philosophy are unique.

The fundamental belief underlying the whole system appears to be 4
that the human body is ugly and that its natural tendency is to debility
and disease. Incarcerated in such a body, man's only hope is to avert these
characteristics through the use of the powerful influences of ritual and
ceremony. Every household has one or more shrines devoted to this purpose. The more powerful individuals in the society have several shrines
in their houses and, in fact, the opulence of a house is often referred to in
terms of the number of such ritual centers it possesses. Most houses are of
wattle and daub construction, but the shrine rooms of the more wealthy
are walled with stone. Poorer families imitate the rich by applying pottery
plaques to their shrine walls.

While each family has at least one such shrine, the rituals associated 5
with it are not family ceremonies but are private and secret. The rites are
normally only discussed with children, and then only during the period
when they are being initiated into these mysteries. I was able, however, to
establish sufficient rapport with the natives to examine these shrines and
to have the rituals described to me.

The focal point of the shrine is a box or chest which is built into the 6
wall. In this chest are kept the many charms and magical potions without
which no native believes he could live. These preparations are secured
from a variety of specialized practitioners. The most powerful of these are
the medicine men, whose assistance must be rewarded with substantial
gifts. However, the medicine men do not provide the curative potions for
their clients, but decide what the ingredients should be and then write
them down in an ancient and secret language. This writing is understood
only by the medicine men and by the herbalists who, for another gift,
provide the required charm.

The charm is not disposed of after it has served its purpose, but is 7
placed in the charm-box of the household shrine. As these magical materials are specific for certain ills, and the real or imagined maladies of the
people are many, the charm-box is usually full to overflowing. The magical packets are so numerous that people forget what their purposes were
and fear to use them again. While the natives are very vague on this point,
we can only assume that the idea in retaining all the old magical materials
is that their presence in the charm-box, before which the body rituals are
conducted, will in some way protect the worshipper.

8   Beneath the charm-box is a small font. Each day every member of the family, in succession, enters the shrine room, bows his head before the charm-box, mingles different sorts of holy water in the font, and proceeds with a brief rite of ablution. The holy waters are secured from the Water Temple of the community, where the priests conduct elaborate ceremonies to make the liquid ritually pure.

9   In the hierarchy of magical practitioners, and below the medicine men in prestige, are specialists whose designation is best translated "holy-mouth-men." The Nacirema have an almost pathological horror of and fascination with the mouth, the condition of which is believed to have a supernatural influence on all social relationships. Were it not for the rituals of the mouth, they believe that their teeth would fall out, their gums bleed, their jaws shrink, their friends desert them, and their lovers reject them. They also believe that a strong relationship exists between oral and moral characteristics. For example, there is a ritual ablution of the mouth for children which is supposed to improve their moral fiber.

10   The daily body ritual performed by everyone includes a mouth-rite. Despite the fact that these people are so punctilious about care of the mouth, this rite involves a practice which strikes the uninitiated stranger as revolting. It was reported to me that the ritual consists of inserting a small bundle of hog hairs into the mouth, along with certain magical powders, and then moving the bundle in a highly formalized series of gestures.

11   In addition to the private mouth-rite, the people seek out a holy-mouth-man once or twice a year. These practitioners have an impressive set of paraphernalia, consisting of a variety of augers, awls, probes, and prods. The use of these objects in the exorcism of the evils of the mouth involves almost unbelievable ritual torture of the client. The holy-mouth-man opens the client's mouth and, using the above mentioned tools, enlarges any holes which decay may have created in the teeth. Magical materials are put into these holes. If there are not naturally occurring holes in the teeth, large sections of one or more teeth are gouged out so that the supernatural substance can be applied. In the client's view, the purpose of these ministrations is to arrest decay and to draw friends. The extremely sacred and traditional character of the rite is evident in the fact that the natives return to the holy-mouth-men year after year, despite the fact that their teeth continue to decay.

12   It is to be hoped that, when a thorough study of the Nacirema is made, there will be careful inquiry into the personality structure of these people. One has but to watch the gleam in the eye of a holy-mouth-man, as he jabs an awl into an exposed nerve, to suspect that a certain amount of sadism is involved. If this can be established, a very interesting pattern emerges, for most of the population shows definite masochistic tendencies. It was to these that Professor Linton referred in discussing a distinctive part of the daily body ritual which is performed only by men. This part of the

rite involves scraping and lacerating the surface of the face with a sharp instrument. Special women's rites are performed only four times during each lunar month, but what they lack in frequency is made up in barbarity. As part of this ceremony, women bake their heads in small ovens for about an hour. The theoretically interesting point is that what seems to be a preponderantly masochistic people have developed sadistic specialists.

The medicine men have an imposing temple, or latipso, in every community of any size. The more elaborate ceremonies required to treat very sick patients can only be performed at this temple. These ceremonies involve not only the thaumaturge but a permanent group of vestal maidens who move sedately about the temple chambers in distinctive costume and headdress. 13

The latipso ceremonies are so harsh that it is phenomenal that a fair proportion of the really sick natives who enter the temple even recover. Small children whose indoctrination is still incomplete have been known to resist attempts to take them to the temple because "that is where you go to die." Despite this fact, sick adults are not only willing but eager to undergo the protracted ritual purification, if they can afford to do so. No matter how ill the supplicant or how grave the emergency, the guardians of many temples will not admit a client if he cannot give a rich gift to the custodian. Even after one has gained admission and survived the ceremonies, the guardians will not permit the neophyte to leave until he makes still another gift. 14

The supplicant entering the temple is first stripped of all his or her clothes. In everyday life the Nacirema avoids exposure of his body and its natural functions. Bathing and excretory acts are performed only in the secrecy of the household shrine, where they are ritualized as part of the body-rites. Psychological shock results from the fact that body secrecy is suddenly lost upon entry into the latipso. A man, whose own wife has never seen him in an excretory act, suddenly finds himself naked and assisted by a vestal maiden while he performs his natural functions into a sacred vessel. This sort of ceremonial treatment is necessitated by the fact that the excreta are used by a diviner to ascertain the course and nature of the client's sickness. Female clients, on the other hand, find their naked bodies are subjected to the scrutiny, manipulation and prodding of the medicine men. 15

Few supplicants in the temple are well enough to do anything but lie on their hard beds. The daily ceremonies, like the rites of the holy-mouth-men, involve discomfort and torture. With ritual precision, the vestals awaken their miserable charges each dawn and roll them about on their beds of pain while performing ablutions, in the formal movements of which the maidens are highly trained. At other times they insert magic wands in the supplicant's mouth or force him to eat substances which are supposed to be healing. From time to time the medicine men come to their clients and jab magically treated needles into their flesh. The fact that these temple ceremonies may not cure, and may even kill the neophyte, in no way decreases the people's faith in the medicine men. 16

17   There remains one other kind of practitioner, known as a "listener." This witchdoctor has the power to exorcise the devils that lodge in the heads of people who have been bewitched. The Nacirema believe that parents bewitch their own children. Mothers are particularly suspected of putting a curse on children while teaching them the secret body rituals. The counter-magic of the witchdoctor is unusual in its lack of ritual. The patient simply tells the "listener" all his troubles and fears, beginning with the earliest difficulties he can remember. The memory displayed by the Nacirema in these exorcism sessions is truly remarkable. It is not uncommon for the patient to bemoan the rejection he felt upon being weaned as a babe, and a few individuals even see their troubles going back to the traumatic effects of their own birth.

18   In conclusion, mention must be made of certain practices which have their base in native esthetics but which depend upon the pervasive aversion to the natural body and its functions. There are ritual fasts to make fat people thin and ceremonial feasts to make thin people fat. Still other rites are used to make women's breasts larger if they are small, and smaller if they are large. General dissatisfaction with breast shape is symbolized in the fact that the ideal form is virtually outside the range of human variation. A few women afflicted with almost inhuman hyper-mammary development are so idolized that they make a handsome living by simply going from village to village and permitting the natives to stare at them for a fee.

19   Reference has already been made to the fact that excretory functions are ritualized, routinized, and relegated to secrecy. Natural reproductive functions are similarly distorted. Intercourse is taboo as a topic and scheduled as an act. Efforts are made to avoid pregnancy by the use of magical materials or by limiting intercourse to certain phases of the moon. Conception is actually very infrequent. When pregnant, women dress so as to hide their condition. Parturition takes place in secret, without friends or relatives to assist, and the majority of women do not nurse their infants.

20   Our review of the ritual life of the Nacirema has certainly shown them to be a magic-ridden people. It is hard to understand how they have managed to exist so long under the burdens which they have imposed upon themselves. But even such exotic customs as these take on real meaning when they are viewed with the insight provided by Malinowski when he wrote:

21   "Looking from far and above, from our high places of safety in the developed civilization, it is easy to see all the crudity and irrelevance of magic. But without its power and guidance early man could not have mastered his practical difficulties as he has done, nor could man have advanced to the higher stages of civilization."

1956

QUESTIONS FOR DISCUSSION

Content

a. What is Miner's purpose?

b. What is the essay's thesis? What is the author's opinion of the behavior of the Nacirema? What is his relationship to them?

c. At which point in the essay do you begin to realize who the Nacirema are? What clues to their identity does Miner provide?

d. What do you learn about the Nacirema that you never knew before?

e. In paragraph 4, Miner says that "the fundamental belief underlying the whole system appears to be that the human body is ugly." In paragraph 20, he comments that the Nacirema are "magic-ridden people." Do you agree with his assessment of his subject?

Strategy and Style

f. Comment on the sophistication of Miner's style. Is it appropriate to a parody? Explain why or why not.

g. To whom is the author writing? What reaction might his readers have to this essay?

h. Why did Miner use an analogy to write this piece? Was it fair to present his observations in this form?

i. Look up the words *parody* and *satire* in a dictionary or glossary of literary terms. In what ways is this essay a parody? In what ways is it a satire? Do you think it is effective as either? Why or why not?

j. What is the effect of Miner's including references to actual anthropologists and tribes?

k. Choose any paragraph and paraphrase it using ordinary language. What patterns does Miner use in transforming terms for bathroom activities into "body rituals"?

l. Discuss Miner's tone at different levels of meaning in this essay. How do the differences in tone reflect his attitude toward his subject?

ENGAGING THE TEXT

a. Describe one of the Nacirema based upon what you have learned about these people from Miner. You might discuss your subject's physical, emotional, behavioral, or intellectual characteristics. In what way is your subject different from you or from people you know well? In what way is he or she the same?

b. Using Miner's approach, write a humorous explanation of the activities in a particular room in a house, or in a garage, studio, workshop, or office.

SUGGESTIONS FOR SUSTAINED WRITING

a. Write a descriptive report of some aspect of contemporary society from the point of view of an animal who has been transformed into an anthropologist. For example, consider how a cat or dog might think of a human family's behavior if it were sent to study one as an anthropologist.

b. Compare Miner's essay to Brandon Griggs's "12 Most Annoying Types of Facebookers" (Chapter 5) or Philip Meyer's "If Hitler Asked You to Electrocute a Stranger, Would You? Probably" (Chapter 8). How do the writers of these essays define and describe their subjects? What similar kinds of conclusions do they reach about human behavior?

c. Closely observe a particular group of people or the people in a particular area and write an anthropological analysis of those people. You might study the "tribe" on your floor of the dorm, write about the character of the people in a club or group to which you belong, or observe the culture in a particular part of town, park, or neighborhood. Include outside sources to support or illustrate your analysis.

READ MORE

Miner and His Works

Miner, Horace Mitchell. *The Primitive City of Timbuctoo*. Garden City, NY: Anchor Books, 1965.

"The Nacirema" (http://www.beadsland.com/nacirema): *Links to many sites related to Miner's famous essay.*

Cultural Anthropology

Levinson, David, and Melvin Ember. *Encyclopedia of Cultural Anthropology*. New York: Henry Holt, 1996.

"Anthropology Resources on the Internet" (http://www.aaanet.org/resources): *Links to many sources provided by the American Anthropological Association.*

The Cosmic Prison

Loren Eiseley

An anthropologist, educator, and poet, Loren Eiseley (1907–1977) was one of the most highly respected and prolific scientific writers of this century. Born in Lincoln, Nebraska, Eiseley was educated at the University of Pennsylvania, where he later became professor of the history and of anthropology of science. His other teaching assignments included appointments to the faculties of the University of Kansas and of Oberlin College. The recipient of numerous honors and awards for public service, Eiseley is also known for his work as a conservationist and nature lover. He contributed scores of scientific studies and articles to scholarly journals but has also authored two books of poetry, a genre he found difficult to escape even when writing highly "technical" prose. Eiseley's major works include The Immense Journey *(1957),* Darwin's Century *(1959),* The Firmament of Time *(1960),* The Unexpected Universe *(1969), and* The Invisible Pyramid *(1970), from which this selection is taken.*

Eiseley will probably be best remembered for the unique, eloquent, and sometimes verselike style with which he treats subject matter that would otherwise seem cold, abstract, and esoteric. "The Cosmic Prison" is a good example of how Eiseley blends poetry and science: perceptiveness, accuracy, insight, and, above all, an ability to make profound contact with the reader.

"A name is a prison, God is free," once observed the Greek poet Nikos 1 Kazantzakis. He meant, I think, that valuable though language is to man, it is by very necessity limiting, and creates for man an invisible prison. Language implies boundaries. A word spoken creates a dog, a rabbit, a man. It fixes their nature before our eyes; henceforth their shapes are, in a sense, our own creation. They are no longer part of the unnamed shifting architecture of the universe. They have been transfixed as if by sorcery, frozen into a concept, a word. Powerful though the spell of human language has proven itself to be, it has laid boundaries upon the cosmos.

No matter how far-ranging some of the mental probes that man has 2 philosophically devised, by his own created nature he is forced to hold the specious and emerging present and transform it into words. The words are startling in their immediate effectiveness, but at the same time they are always finally imprisoning because man has constituted himself a prison keeper. He does so out of no conscious intention, but because for immediate purposes he has created an unnatural world of his own, which he calls the cultural world, and in which he feels at home. It defines his needs and allows him to lay a small immobilizing spell upon the nearer portions of his universe. Nevertheless, it transforms that universe into a cosmic prison house which is no sooner mapped than man feels its inadequacy and his own.

He seeks then to escape, and the theory of escape involves bodily 3 flight. Scarcely had the first moon landing been achieved before one U.S. senator boldly announced: "We are the masters of the universe. We can go anywhere we choose." This statement was widely and editorially acclaimed. It is a striking example of the comfort of words, also of the covert substitutions and mental projections to which they are subject. The cosmic prison is not made less so by a successful journey of some two hundred and forty thousand miles in a cramped and primitive vehicle.

4   To escape the cosmic prison man is poorly equipped. He has to drag portions of his environment with him, and his life span is that of a mayfly in terms of the distances he seeks to penetrate. There is no possible way to master such a universe by flight alone. Indeed such a dream is a dangerous illusion. This may seem a heretical statement, but its truth is self-evident if we try seriously to comprehend the nature of time and space that I sought to grasp when held up to view the fiery messenger that flared across the zenith in 1910. "Seventy-five years," my father had whispered in my ear, "seventy-five years and it will be racing homeward. Perhaps you will live to see it again. Try to remember."

5   And so I remembered. I had gained a faint glimpse of the size of our prison house. Somewhere out there beyond a billion miles in space, an entity known as a comet had rounded on its track in the black darkness of the void. It was surging homeward toward the sun because it was an eccentric satellite of this solar system. If I lived to see it, it would be but barely, and with the dimmed eyes of age. Yet it, too, in its long traverse, was but a flitting mayfly in terms of the universe the night sky revealed.

6   So relative is the cosmos we inhabit that, as we gaze upon the outer galaxies available to the reach of our telescopes, we are placed in about the position that a single white blood cell in our bodies would occupy, if it were intelligently capable of seeking to understand the nature of its own universe, the body it inhabits. The cell would encounter rivers ramifying into miles of distance seemingly leading nowhere. It would pass through gigantic structures whose meaning it could never grasp—the brain, for example. It could never know there was an outside, a vast being on a scale it could not conceive of and of which it formed an infinitesimal part. It would know only the pouring tumult of the creation it inhabited, but of the nature of that great beast, or even indeed that it was a beast, it could have no conception whatever. It might examine the liquid in which it floated and decide, as in the case of the fall of Lucretius's atoms, that the pouring of obscure torrents had created its world.

7   It might discover that creatures other than itself swam in the torrent. But that its universe was alive, had been born and was destined to perish, its own ephemeral existence would never allow it to perceive. It would never know the sun; it would explore only through dim tactile sensations and react to chemical stimuli that were borne to it along the mysterious conduits of the arteries and veins. Its universe would be centered upon a great arborescent tree of spouting blood. This, at best, generations of white blood cells by enormous labor and continuity might succeed, like astronomers, in charting.

8   They could never, by any conceivable stretch of the imagination, be aware that their so-called universe was, in actuality, the prowling body of a cat or the more time-enduring body of a philosopher, himself engaged upon the same quest in a more gigantic world and perhaps deceived

proportionately by greater vistas. What if, for example, the far galaxies man observes make up, across void spaces of which even we are atomically composed, some kind of enormous creature or cosmic snowflake whose exterior we will never see? We will know more than the phagocyte in our bodies, but no more than that limited creature can we climb out of our universe, or successfully enhance our size or longevity sufficiently to thrust our heads through the confines of the universe that terminates our vision.

Some further "outside" will hover elusively in our thought, but upon 9 its nature, or even its reality, we can do no more than speculate. The phagocyte might observe the salty turbulence of an eternal river system, Lucretius the fall of atoms creating momentary living shapes. We suspiciously sense, in the concept of the expanding universe derived from the primordial atom—the monobloc—some kind of oscillating universal heart. At the instant of its contraction we will vanish. It is not given us, nor can our science recapture, the state beyond the monobloc, nor whether we exist in the diastole of some inconceivable being. We know only a little more extended reality than the hypothetical creature below us. Above us may lie realms it is beyond our power to grasp.

1970

QUESTIONS FOR DISCUSSION

Content

a. What is Eiseley saying in the last two sentences of this essay, and how are they related to the analogy he has created? Would it be accurate to say that these ideas compose his thesis?
b. What is the "fiery messenger" to which Eiseley alludes in paragraph 4? How does it and the analogy of the human life span to that of a mayfly help him convey the immensity of time and space?
c. How would you explain the analogy between humans and the white blood cell that forms the basis of this essay? What makes the analogy logical and consistent?
d. Who was Lucretius, and what was his "atomic theory"? How does mentioning this theory help Eiseley develop the central analogy of his essay?
e. What does Eiseley mean when he says that "some further 'outside' will hover elusively in our thought" (paragraph 9)? Why can we only speculate on "its nature, or even its reality"?
f. In paragraph 4, the author tells us that the dream of escaping from the "cosmic prison" is a "dangerous illusion." What does he mean by

this curious statement, and why would someone like the U.S. senator quoted in paragraph 3 find it "heretical"?

g. What is "the oscillating universal heart" (paragraph 9) that we can only "suspiciously sense"? How would you define a "monobloc"?

Strategy and Style

h. How do the quote from Nikos Kazantzakis and the explanation that proceeds from it serve as an appropriate introduction to this selection?

i. Define "the cosmic prison" that Eiseley describes in this selection. Why does he call it a prison? How is his use of the term *prison* related to Plato's use of the word in *prison-house*?

j. How would you characterize Eiseley's tone in this piece? What image of Eiseley himself does the tone project?

ENGAGING THE TEXT

a. Find a passage (a sentence or a paragraph) that has meaning for your own life, and write about the connections you see between Eiseley's words and your life.

b. Eiseley writes of humankind's condition from an earthbound position; writing from a position outside the Earth, describe what you see as humankind's relation to the rest of the cosmos. You might try writing from the point of view of Halley's Comet.

SUGGESTIONS FOR SUSTAINED WRITING

a. Eiseley has created a startling comparison between the existence of a human being in the universe and the life of a white blood cell in the human body. Create your own analogy by comparing yourself or someone you know well to a fictional character, to a famous historical figure, or even, for that matter, to an animal whose habits would be easily recognized by your audience. Incidentally, the analogy you develop need not be complimentary.

b. Compare Eiseley's ideas with those of John (Fire) Lame Deer and Richard Erdoes in "Alone on the Hilltop" (Chapter 3) or to those of Annie Dillard in "Living Like Weasels" (this chapter). What does each writer say about humankind's limited perspective on the world?

c. Research the life and works of Loren Eiseley. (We list a few sources below to get you started.) Write an essay in which you make clear what Eiseley means by "the cosmic prison." Compare the essay "The Cosmic Prison" to one or more other essays by Eiseley. Discuss how his ideas about the cosmos are reflected in those other essays.

READ MORE

Eiseley and His Works

Angyal, Andrew J. *Loren Eiseley.* Boston: Twayne, 1983.

"Loren Eiseley" (http://www.eiseley.org): *The Friends of Loren Eiseley Society's website.*

"Cosmic Prison"

Furley, David J. *Cosmic Problems: Essays on Greek and Roman Philosophy of Nature.* Cambridge, UK: Cambridge UP, 1989.

"Great Books & Philosophy Forums" (http://westerncanon.com): *Offbeat approach to several world authors and philosophers, including discussion forums.*

Living Like Weasels

Annie Dillard

Born in Pittsburgh in 1945, Annie Dillard attended Hollins College, Roanoke, Virginia, where she studied literature, creative writing, and theology, earning a B.A. in 1967 and an M.A. in 1968. She began her career as a columnist for the publication of The Wilderness Society, The Living Wilderness, *from 1973 to 1975. She was also a contributing editor to Harper's magazine from 1973 to 1985. Meanwhile, she was at work on* Pilgrim at Tinker Creek *(1974), a collection of essays that sprung from the journals she kept while living in the Roanoke Valley. She won a Pulitzer Prize for* Pilgrim, *and the book became a best-seller. Uneasy with her sudden fame, she took a job as scholar-in-residence at Western Washington University, where she could devote herself to writing and teaching. In 1979, she took a position at Wesleyan University in Connecticut, where she is currently writer-in-residence. In 1982, Dillard was a member of the U.S.–Cultural Delegation to the People's Republic of China and served on the National Committee for United States–China Relations. From these experiences came* Encounters with Chinese Writers *(1984). She has published two anthologies of narrative essays:* Holy the Firm *(1977) and* Teaching a Stone to Talk *(1982). She also has published poetry, including* Tickets for a Prayer Wheel *(1974); novels, including* The Living *(1993) and* The Maytrees *(2007); and memoirs, including* An American Childhood *(1988) and* The Writing Life *(1992).*

"Living Like Weasels," from Pilgrim at Tinker Creek, *uses a brief encounter with a weasel to envision how humans ought to live in proximity to wild creatures. Behind its poetic description lies a critique of humans' isolation from nature.*

1   A weasel is wild. Who knows what he thinks? He sleeps in his underground den, his tail draped over his nose. Sometimes he lives in his den for two days without leaving. Outside, he stalks rabbits, mice, muskrats, and birds, killing more bodies that he can eat warm, and often dragging the

carcasses home. Obedient to instinct, he bites his prey at the neck, either splitting the jugular vein at the throat or crunching the brain at the base of the skull, and he does not let go. One naturalist refused to kill a weasel who was socketed into his hand deeply as a rattlesnake. The man could in no way pry the tiny weasel off, and he had to walk half a mile to water, the weasel dangling from his palm, and soak him off like a stubborn label.

2   And once, says Ernest Thompson Seton—once, a man shot an eagle out of the sky. He examined the eagle and found the dry skull of a weasel fixed by the jaws to his throat. The supposition is that the eagle had pounced on the weasel and the weasel swiveled and bit as instinct taught him, tooth to neck, and nearly won. I would like to have seen that eagle from the air a few weeks or months before he was shot: was the whole weasel still attached to his feathered throat, a fur pendant? Or did the eagle eat what he could reach, gutting the living weasel with his talons before his breast, bending his beak, cleaning the beautiful airborne bones?

3   I have been reading about weasels because I saw one last week. I startled a weasel who startled me, and we exchanged a long glance.

4   Twenty minutes from my house, through the woods by the quarry and across the highway, is Hollins Pond, a remarkable piece of shallowness, where I like to go at sunset and sit on a tree trunk. Hollins Pond is also called Murray's Pond; it covers two acres of bottomland near Tinker Creek with six inches of water and six thousand lily pads. In winter, brown-and-white steers stand in the middle of it, merely dampening their hooves; from the distant shore they look like miracle itself, complete with miracle's nonchalance. Now, in summer, the steers are gone. The water lilies have blossomed and spread to a green horizontal plane that is terra firma to plodding blackbirds, and tremulous ceiling to black leeches, crayfish, and carp.

5   This is, mind you, suburbia. It is a five-minute walk in three directions to rows of houses, though none is visible here. There's a 55 mph highway at one end of the pond, and a nesting pair of wood ducks at the other. Under every bush is a muskrat hole or a beer can. The far end is an alternating series of fields and woods, fields and woods, threaded everywhere with motorcycle tracks—in whose bare clay wild turtles lay eggs.

6   So. I had crossed the highway, stepped over two low barbed-wire fences, and traced the motorcycle path in all gratitude through the wild rose and poison ivy of the pond's shoreline up into high grassy fields. Then I cut down through the woods to the mossy fallen tree where I sit. This tree is excellent. It makes a dry, upholstered bench at the upper, marshy end of the pond, a plush jetty raised from the thorny shore between a shallow blue body of water and a deep blue body of sky.

       The sun had just set. I was relaxed on the tree trunk, ensconced in the 7 lap of lichen, watching the lily pads at my feet tremble and part dreamily over the thrusting path of a carp. A yellow bird appeared to my right and flew behind me. It caught my eye; I swiveled around—and the next instant, inexplicably, I was looking down at a weasel, who was looking up at me.

Weasel! I'd never seen one wild before. He was ten inches long, thin 8 as a curve, a muscled ribbon, brown as fruitwood, soft-furred, alert. His face was fierce, small and pointed as a lizard's; he would have made a good arrowhead. There was just a dot of chin, maybe two brown hairs' worth, and then the pure white fur began that spread down his underside. He had two black eyes I didn't see, any more than you see a window.

The weasel was stunned into stillness as he was emerging from 9 beneath an enormous shaggy wild rose bush four feet away. I was stunned into stillness twisted backward on the tree trunk. Our eyes locked, and someone threw away the key.

Our look was as if two lovers, or deadly enemies, met unexpectedly 10 on an overgrown path when each had been thinking of something else: a clearing blow to the gut. It was also a bright blow to the brain, or a sudden beating of brains, with all the charge and intimate grate of rubbed balloons. It emptied our lungs. It felled the forest, moved the fields, and drained the pond; the world dismantled and tumbled into that black hole of eyes. If you and I looked at each other that way, our skulls would split and drop to our shoulders. But we don't. We keep our skulls. So.

He disappeared. This was only last week, and already I don't remem- 11 ber what shattered the enchantment. I think I blinked, I think I retrieved my brain from the weasel's brain, and tried to memorize what I was seeing, and the weasel felt the yank of separation, the careening splash-down into real life and the urgent current of instinct. He vanished under the wild rose. I waited motionless, my mind suddenly full of data and my spirit with pleadings, but he didn't return.

Please do not tell me about "approach-avoidance conflicts." I tell you 12 I've been in that weasel's brain for sixty seconds, and he was in mine. Brains are private places, muttering through unique and secret tapes—but the weasel and I both plugged into another tape simultaneously, for a sweet and shocking time. Can I help it if it was a blank?

What goes on in his brain the rest of the time? What does a weasel 13 think about? He won't say. His journal is tracks in clay, a spray of feathers, mouse blood and bone: uncollected, unconnected, loose-leaf, and blown.

I would like to learn, or remember, how to live. I come to Hollins Pond not 14 so much to learn how to live as, frankly, to forget about it. That is, I don't think I can learn from a wild animal how to live in particular—shall I suck warm blood, hold my tail high, walk with my footprints precisely over the prints of my hands?—but I might learn something of mindlessness, something of the purity of living in the physical senses and the dignity of living without bias or motive. The weasel lives in necessity and we live in choice, hating necessity and dying at the last ignobly in its talons. I would like to live as I should, as the weasel lives as he should. And I suspect that for me the way is like the weasel's: open to time and death painlessly, noticing everything, remembering nothing, choosing the given with a fierce and pointed will.

15   I missed my chance. I should have gone for the throat. I should have lunged for that streak of white under the weasel's chin and held on, held on through mud and into the wild rose, held on for a dearer life. We could live under the wild rose wild as weasels, mute and uncomprehending. I could very calmly go wild. I could live two days in the den, curled, leaning on mouse fur, sniffing bird bones, blinking, licking, breathing musk, my hair tangled in the roots of grasses. Down is a good place to go, where the mind is single. Down is out, out of your ever-loving mind and back to your careless senses. I remember muteness as a prolonged and giddy fast, where every moment is a feast of utterance received. Time and events are merely poured, unremarked, and ingested directly, like blood pulsed into my gut through a jugular vein. Could two live that way? Could two live under the wild rose, and explore by the pond, so that the smooth mind of each is as everywhere present to the other, and as received and as unchallenged, as falling snow?

16   We could, you know. We can live any way we want. People take vows of poverty, chastity, and obedience—even of silence—by choice. The thing is to stalk your calling in a certain skilled and supple way, to locate the most tender and live spot and plug into that pulse. This is yielding, not fighting. A weasel doesn't "attack" anything; a weasel lives as he's meant to, yielding at every moment to the perfect freedom of single necessity.

17   I think it would be well, and proper, and obedient, and pure, to grasp your one necessity and not let it go, to dangle from it limp wherever it takes you. Then even death, where you're going no matter how you live, cannot you part. Seize it and let it seize you up aloft even, till your eyes burn out and drop; let your musky flesh fall off in shreds, and let your very bones unhinge and scatter, loosened over fields, over fields and woods, lightly, thoughtless, from any height at all, from as high as eagles.

1982

QUESTIONS FOR DISCUSSION

Content

a. What is Dillard's message to humans?
b. What makes weasels a good choice for this essay?
c. What might be a "dearer life" (paragraph 15)?

d. What might Dillard mean when she writes, "The weasel lives in necessity and we live in choice" (paragraph 14)? What do *necessity* and *choice* connote?

e. Why is it important to know that Hollins Pond is in suburbia (paragraph 5)?

Strategy and Style

f. If this essay was not easy to read, what in particular about Dillard's writing style made it difficult? Could she have said the same thing more simply? How?

g. What figurative language does Dillard use, and to what effect? For instance, what makes "soak him off like a stubborn label" (paragraph 1) effective?

h. Find a few phrases that strike you as particularly interesting. What makes these phrases interesting to you?

i. Dillard inserts the single word *So* in two places (paragraphs 6 and 10). What purpose does this word serve?

j. "The sun had just set," Dillard writes in paragraph 7. What does the time of day do to establish the mood?

ENGAGING THE TEXT

a. In paragraph 15, Dillard states that "[w]e could live under the wild rose wild as weasels, mute and uncomprehending." Write a short description of how this might be possible.

b. Dillard's writing is highly visual. Describe one of the images that runs through her mind as she watches the weasel.

SUGGESTIONS FOR SUSTAINED WRITING

a. Write an essay in which you make an analogy between living and something else. Fill in the blank: "Living Like _____." Examples might include "children," "ants" or "grasshoppers," "cats" or "dogs." Choose either a model for how we should live or a sample for how we do live. Your stance can be either serious or humorous.

b. Compare Dillard's essay to Louise Erdrich's in Chapter 2. Begin by considering what they have in common in their descriptions of place. Examine their style and organization. Discuss how they create mood.

c. Write a descriptive essay based on your own close observation of a natural setting, or at least a setting with minimal human activity. Take detailed notes on what you notice with all five senses. Shape your first draft around the one detail that strikes you as being important but something that most people would overlook.

READ MORE

Dillard and Her Works

"Annie Dillard" (http://www.anniedillard.com/): *Dillard's official website, with links to works by and about her.*

"The Ecotheology of Annie Dillard: A Study in Ambivalence" (http://www.crosscurrents.org/dillard.htm): *An article by Pamela A. Smith about Dillard's work.*

Smith, Linda L. *Annie Dillard.* New York: Twayne, 1991.

Writing about Nature

"Whole Terrain: Reflective Environmental Practice" (http://wholeterrain.com): *Website for this online journal about nature and writing.*

"Web Resources on Nature Writing" (http://www.vcu.edu/engweb/eng385/natweb.htm): *Links to many sources about nature writing, including works by nature writers and websites for environmental organizations.*

Extreme Reading

Rebecca Brown

Rebecca Brown (b. 1956) is a prolific writer of novels, short stories, and performance-related works. She has a BA in English from George Washington University and an MFA in Creative Writing from the University of Virginia. Brown is one of the Pacific Northwest's leading literary figures and should not be confused with the controversial religious writer or with the actress of the same name. Many of her books have been reprinted, translated and published in several countries, or transformed into performance pieces. Her first novel, The Haunted House *(1986), about alcoholism, was reprinted in 2007, and her novel* The Gifts of the Body *(1995) has been translated into several languages and is a bestseller in Japan. Some of her other books include the story collections* The Terrible Girls *(1992) and* What Keeps Me Here *(1996), the essay collections* The End of Youth *(2003) and* American Romances *(2009), and the memoir* Excerpts from a Family Medical Dictionary *(2003), about giving end-of-life care for her mother. Brown is also the co-editor, with Mary Jane Knecht of the Frye Art Museum, of* Looking Together: Writers on Art *(2009) and the co-writer, with painter Nancy Kiefer, of* Woman in Ill-Fitting Wig *(2005), a book of text and image. Her performance-related writing includes the libretto for the dance opera* The Onion Twins *(2005) and the play* The Toaster *(2005). At least two of her books have been adapted for performance—*The Terrible Girls *by About Face Theater in Chicago and four pieces from* The End of Youth *by The Los Angeles New Short Fiction Series. Brown's books have received numerous awards, and Brown herself received a Genius Award in 2005 from the Seattle-based newsweekly* The Stranger. *Brown has taught for more than twenty-five years at various colleges, including the University of Washington, Pacific Lutheran University, and Naropa University;*

she lectures, does readings, and organizes readings across the country. For four years she was Creative Director of Literary Programs at Centrum, an arts center in Port Townsend, Washington, and she has served on the selection panels for several arts colonies. She is currently a member of the MFA in writing faculty at Goddard College.

"Extreme Reading" is one of the pieces in American Romances, *a collection of essays on culture. Brown combines personal narrative with instructions of a sort to guide you in transforming the books you read into something more than books: art, healing tools, your own stories. As you read, consider your relationship to reading—how and why you read.*

You eat because you have to, it sustains you. But once you get past the basics of hydration and calories, what you eat and how you eat are determined by your own peculiar, and in the most literal sense, taste, by what can satisfy your sweet tooth or your sour tooth, your savory or unsavory desires. You eat some things because they're good for you, but there are only so many hours in a day, so may days in a life, so you also consume other things solely because you want to, because you have some craving or urge or longing that only this particular thing can fulfill. To be polite you'll eat whatever the people who invited you to dinner at their house have made for you, but when you go out you won't order something you don't like, and if something shows up on your plate in some brownish sauce or gelatinous pool or that gets in your craw or goes down wrong or doesn't appeal, you turn away from it, discreetly if you can, but if you can't if push comes to shove, if spit comes to fore, you hawk it or gag it or cough it out and you don't care who's watching. 1

I can't finish books I think are bad. I can't get through somebody's prose that reads to me like Sucaryl or some brownish lumpy sauce or is salt-and-peppered or soy-sauced beyond a shadow of its former self, that's watered down or stupid or pretentious. 2

Anthropologically speaking, we all recognize there are taboos regarding what we should not eat. 3

But no one agrees about everything. 4

We're taught to read because we need to navigate our culture, to read road signs and the names of stuff at the grocery story, to sign our names on documents when we marry or when we ought to be able to marry. This kind of reading is like hydration and calories. You need it to survive. If you don't get it you get rickets. If you are illiterate you are probably poor, you're missing something basic from your diet and you'll probably die sooner than you should. 5

But then after we've taken care of our basic needs, we're taught to read in ways that are "good for us," to provide us with a grounding in the humanities, to broaden our minds, etc., then finally to give us pleasure. At this level we decide what we like: chicken or fish, poached or grilled, comics or Rilke, the *New York Times*, the Bible, Barbara Cartland, tacos, cheese. 6

7　　　Extreme reading is like cannibalism. You take a book, like a piece of food, and eat it. For sustenance, for blood, if not to ritually ingest the soul or heart or power of your enemy or someone you loved. You take it in and chew and grind and tear it down to the smallish bits, to things that you can swallow. You rid yourself of some of it and keep some of the rest. Sometimes you keep what may not be the best for you. Your body knows what's good for you, but sometimes you don't listen, The things you eat and keep become a part of you. You re-create inside yourself, with caverns, juices, processes you can and can't control, a kind of meat.

8　　　A book is a thing that someone made from words you think you understand. You take it in and think you are sophisticated, a connoisseur, or at least someone with manners enough to wield a knife and fork, and not talk with your mouth full. You know that whatever it is, a ham and cheese on rye, or popcorn or *foie de* something, no matter how humble or fine, you'll break it into broken things that can be used by you and your voracious flesh.

9　　　When you read a book, you read what someone else wrote, but you also read your own book. You may read all the words or not, but the words you keep—those that stick to your ribs and keep you awake, dyspeptic, bilious, or that nourish you as if to health, become you muscle, bone or heart—are words you shape as you desire. The book you read is what you want; you will it to your own.

10　　Every time you read a book you read what you desire.

11　　Every time you read a book you make that book your own.

12　　One weekend when I was a teenager, I was sitting alone on a bus on my way to my first Bible Camp Youth Retreat. Most of the other kids on the bus—Texas natives or come-here from somewhere else in the Bible Belt—had been raised in Christian households, but a few of us were recent converts. Though I believed a lot of what Christians were supposed to, I had trouble with the heaven and hell thing. This may have been part of the reason I was sitting apart from the kids singing Christian songs or doing Bible study, but I was also alone because I was reading a book that was not the Bible, but something my sister had just finished reading in college, *A Portrait of the Artist as a Young Man.*[1] As our bus hurtled through the steamy,

[1]The *A Portrait of the Artist as a Young Man* I read these days is not my sister's copy, though I thank her for the loan and for a million others. (Lawrence Ferlinghetti's *A Coney Island of the Mind*, Aldous Huxley, Margaret Atwood, etc.; tons of music—the Beatles and the Rolling Stones, then Hendrix, Simon and Garfunkel, Jethro Tull.) My reading copy is, rather, included in *The Portable James Joyce* (Viking, 1966), edited and with an introduction and notes by Harry Levin, the same guy who did my Hawthorne Riverside anthology (that guy gets around!) which I purchased, used, for the pathetic sum of $6.60.

spice-scented night toward the East Texas piney woods, I read about Stephan Dedalus and his family and Ireland and food and I came to this:

> Now what is the meaning of this word retreat and why is it . . . a practice of all who desire to lead before God and in the eyes of men a truly Christian life? A retreat, my dear boys, signifies a withdrawal for a while from the cares of our life, the cares of this workaday world, in order to examine the state of our conscience, to reflect on the mysteries of holy religion and to understand better why we are here in this world. During these few days I intend to put before you some thoughts concerning the four last things . . . death, judgment, hell and heaven.

Was it a coincidence that I was reading these words about Stephen 13 Dedalus going on a Christian retreat to learn about heaven and hell at exactly the moment as I myself was going on a Christian retreat and worried about heaven and hell? Or had God arranged for me to read these words right here and now because He was trying to tell me something? A little later I read this: 14

> Now let us try for a moment to realize, as far as we can, the natures of that abode of the damned which the justice of an offended God has called into existence for the eternal punishment of sinners. Hell is a strait and dark and foul-smelling prison, an abode of demons and lost souls, filled with fire and smoke. The straitness of this prisonhouse is expressly designed by God to punish those who refused to be found by His laws.

I knew that God sometimes spoke to His children in signs. Was God 15 using these words in this book to say something to me? Or was I only hoping or fearing that He was? I don't remember much else about that weekend besides reading those passages over and over and over to myself.

I do not remember what I decided. 16

When I reread *A Portrait of the Artist as a Young Man* several years 17 later, I could hardly believe it was the same book. The words on the page hadn't changed of course, but I had. Having abandoned my Christian faith, I read a romantic, very male tale of the self and home and family, of nostalgia, growing up and art and God and loss.

Every book you read contains the story of your life. 18
Every book you read you make your own. 19

I left home, read a lot and lost my faith. I became a writer and hung 20 around with artists. One time, I went with a bunch of artist pals to the town dump. My visual artist friends had to pay the dump for the things they scavenged—bedsprings and auto parts, engines and tool handles and fence posts—whereas the dump was giving away the books. They were trying to get rid of them. Unlike the materials the artists wanted, the books did not have neat little hinges or squeaky things, they only had wilted, moldy, dirty or stuck-together pages. You couldn't make something cool out of books that you could stand up in your yard or hang your coat on or put flowers in. The books were taking up room and creating a fire hazard. No one had read them for years and probably no one was ever going to read them again. These books were utterly useless. I loved them for that. I think I also felt kind of sorry for them. I took some home.

21   I felt sorry for some and had contempt for others. For some books I felt both. I thought about how there are so many books out there and how my work would never measure up. But also how there were so many books that were just plain shitty, worse than anything I or anyone I knew would write on our very worst day, yet those shitty books got published and people even bought them, while some actually great books languished in libraries, unchecked-out for years, then got tossed into some twenty-five-cent sale bin or thrown out to the dump. Was this what I wanted my life to be about?

22   I got a bunch of these books and pens and glue and crayons and tape and invited friends over to my apartment to mess these books up. Some of us "illuminated" our own books, and some we made together. We gave them to each other or slipped them onto the shelves of used bookstores or libraries and fantasized what would happen when someone found them. These cut-and-paste books or illuminated manuscripts or what a librarian friend of mine calls defaced books and artists call "altered text" or "erasures" are all variations of the kinds of things Orton and Halliwell[2] did and the great Tom Phillips[3] is doing. The story about Orton and Halliwell is that their defacing was prompted by trying to check out some actual literature at the Islington library and being informed that their branch didn't stock whatever they were looking for although it did have all kinds of stupid tripe. Which the couple checked out, doctored and returned. Some of the extreme reading/book demolition my friends and I enjoyed had elements of lit crit or political commentary, like bringing forward the gay subtext in the novel of a closeted writer we knew or splicing a photography book about World War II with one about Japanese flower arranging, but mostly we were just having fun while we drank.

[2]The altered texts made by playwright Joe Orton and his lover Kenneth Halliwell are described in John Lahr's terrific biography *Prick Up Your Ears* (Knopf, 1978). Orton and Halliwell, before the one whacked the other to death with a hammer, lived in a tiny little flat in Islington, the same part of London where I lived in the '80s. I went to what had been their place and stood outside and looked at it. I went to the library too. Though the artful altering of shitty library books earned Orton time in the slammer, those same defaced books, once evidence of criminal destruction of property, are now the crown jewels of the Islington library.

[3]Tom Phillips's great and beautiful altered text, the daddy of them all, is *A Humument*, which you should look up at www.tomphillips.co.uk and humument.com.

One of those old books from the dump came to my rescue.   23

For a long time after my parents died I wasn't good for much. Some 24
days I didn't get out of bed. I lost my keys a lot. I watched a lot of videos and took a lot of walks. I'd walk downtown or to the water and
sometimes drive out of the city. One time I was at some pretty place—a
mountain view or by the sea—and there was one of those benches people
put up with a plaque on it that says, "In memory of so'n'so, who used to
love this place." I'd seen those benches and read those words a million
times, but this time, when I read the words, I lost it. It had never regis-
tered with me before that every one of those nice memorial benches was
for someone who was dead, someone whose dying had left behind other
people who were knocked out by that death. The words, the bench, the
pretty place where once I would have thought, "Oh, what a nice place to
sit," were all the same, but after my parents were dead, I wasn't. I just
keeled over and bawled my weepy eyes out.

For a long time after my parents died, I also couldn't read. I could 25
flip through magazines or stare at the backs of cereal boxes and even read
liner notes, but books were too much. They took concentration and an
ability to track and to remember, and if they had stories, the stories were
wrong. Or perhaps I should say what the words added up to was wrong,
although not every single word was wrong, because some words were
right. As I tried to read, the wrong words faded or disappeared, leaving
only the horrible right ones.

I picked up one of those twenty-five-cent books I had lying around 26
and, though I couldn't really read it, individual words jumped out at me.
Words like "dead" or "mother" or "no." Or "gone" or "father" or "dead."
I started going through the book and finding the words in it that made
sense to me. I discovered that the book was, unbeknownst to itself, telling
exactly the story of what I was feeling and not feeling and remembering. There were other words between, within the words that were telling
something useful to me. It started in the title, *The Mortal Storm*,[4] a novel
about heroic people fighting proto-Nazies in the '30s. But actually of
course, *The Mortal Storm* contained a book for me, *The MortalS*, less a narrative than a collection of fragments about the deaths of my parents.

---

[4]*The Mortal Storm* (Little, Brown, 1938) is probably the most well-known of the many, many
books by Phyllis Bottome, the British daughter of an American clergyman. Bottome's
output included novels, short fiction and a biography of the man with whom she studied
psychoanalysis in Vienna, Alfred Adler. In 1940, the unabashedly anti-Nazi *Mortal Storm*
was made into a film starring James Stewart as a good German who doesn't join the Nazis,
and Margaret Sullivan as the non-German (read Jewish) girl with whom he falls in love. The
movie pissed the Nazis off so much that they banned all MGM films from being shown in
Germany. *The Mortal Storm* isn't banned anywhere anymore but it might as well be, in the
sense that we can't find it readily because our tastes have changed and now it comes across
as just a toothless bit of cinematic junk food.

27   Here are my severe edits of the 1,000 or so words that make up the
first three pages:

> a long   illness
> She lay quite still
> What happened to   her
> mother
> would lie   remembering in   the bed
> mother   sick
> it's all over now   mother
> Nothing can be helped
> dead   dying   dead   dead
> her mother   her mother   her mother

> And so on.

28   It took me a few years to cut and paste (the term I prefer to "erasure"
or "altered text" because it sounds more like what you did in grade
school and less like something that you are going to call Art), through
the entirety of *The MortalS*, during which I got past much of my parents'
deaths. I believe that being able to, however thoughtlessly or subcon-
sciously, engage with others' words and find the words I needed in them
helped me obsess over or meditate my way through my sadness.

29   A few years later, though I had stopped having cut-and-paste parties, I still kept at it on my own. The next book I completed I'd bought
for a dollar at a used bookstore in Vermont. *I Want to Be a Lady* by
Maximilian Foster (J.B. Lippincott Company, 1926), is a comic western
romance that tells the story of an Eastern girl who, in late nineteenth-
century America, goes west where she encounters a group of lovable
cowboys and scrappy, "unladylike" frontier folk. Though our heroine
wants to be a lady (i.e., live a genteel, back-east-style life), she realizes
that the lovable cowboys and scrappy frontier fold are warm-hearted
and good and she is happier being the honest frontier wife of a lovable
cowboy than a proper back-east Lady. *I Want to Be a Lady*, however,
contains within it an entirely other book, which I discovered through
severe editing. I went through the book, page by page, for more than a
year, and painted or colored or collaged over most of the words, leaving
only the words that told the story I needed to tell. My book, the book
I desired, contained therein, is titled, *I Want a Lady* and it is a woeful
autobiography about a doomed lesbian romance I had with an older—
uh—lady, when I was young and still believed the words that books and
people said.

30   Every time you read a book you read what you desire.

31   Every book you read includes the story of your life.

2009

QUESTIONS FOR DISCUSSION

Content

a. What is extreme reading?
b. What are the three kinds of reading used to "navigate" culture, according to Brown in paragraphs 5 and 6? Must these kinds of reading be learned before one moves on to extreme reading?
c. What connections does Brown make between eating and reading?
d. In paragraph 7, Brown writes that extreme reading entails eating a book. In practical terms, what is she advocating that you do with a book?
e. In paragraph 9, Brown claims that you will "read your own book" as you read. What does this mean for you?
f. In your opinion, was the project that Brown and her friends did, described in paragraph 18, "art" or "vandalism"? What would Brown say?
g. Why might books be "too much" (paragraph 21) for a person to handle?

Strategy and Style

h. "Extreme reading" is a play on the phrase "extreme sport." How is extreme reading, as Brown defines it, analogous to extreme sports?
i. Why might Brown have divided her essay into short sections with extra space between sections?
j. Why does Brown repeat the two sentences, "Every book you read contains the story of your life. Every book you read you make your own"?
k. Brown addresses a "you" throughout this essay—to whom is she referring, you the student reader, herself, or some other person?
l. Are the notes included at the end of the essay necessary? How do they add to or detract from the main essay?

ENGAGING THE TEXT

a. As college students, you have all mastered the reading for "basic needs" (paragraph 5). Discuss to what extent you have mastered other levels of reading: reading that is good for you, reading for pleasure, and extreme reading. Use Brown's definitions to guide you.
b. If you had a reaction to a book similar to what Brown experienced during her Christian retreat, describe your experience. How did circumstances influence the way you read the book? If you did not have a similar experience, describe your reaction to "Extreme Reading."

SUGGESTIONS FOR SUSTAINED WRITING

a. Write a narrative about a time that a book, story, poem, or other text had a major impact on your life or that always reminds you of a particular event. Alternative assignment: Create your own altered text of a poem or page from a book, accompanying that altered text with a written explanation of what you did and why.
b. Compare Rebecca Brown's attitudes toward writing with that of Sherman Alexie's in "Superman and Me." Explain how reading "saves" each writer.
c. Research artists who have created altered texts. Look at the texts themselves—many online versions exist—as well as the artists' writing about them. In your essay, describe the works and discuss the philosophy behind them.

READ MORE

Brown and Her Works

"Rebecca Brown" (http://www.goddard.edu/rebeccabrown): *Faculty information page for Brown on the Goddard College website.*

"Two Pieces from P-I Writer in Residence Rebecca Brown" (http://www.seattlepi.com/books/336866_writerinresidence26.html): *Interview with and writing by Brown posted on the Seattle-based online newspaper,* The Post-Intelligencer.

"Literature: Rebecca Brown" (http://www.thestranger.com/seattle/Content?oid=23582): *2005 article by Charles Mudede for* The Stranger *explaining why the Stranger Genius Award was being given to Brown.*

Extreme Reading and Altered Texts

Several websites devoted to the art of altered texts:
"Altered Books"(http://www.logolalia.com/alteredbooks/)
"Altered Book Cam" (http://www.art-e-zine.co.uk/alteredbook.html)
"A Cyber Home for the Altered Book Artist" (http://www.altered-book.com/)

"A Humument" (http://www.humument.com/): *Slide show of the altered Victorian novel A Humument by Tom Phillips, with links to essays about the project.*

"Global Reading Challenge" (http://2011globalreadingchallenge.blogspot.com/): *Information about the 2011 Challenge, with lists of books, links to blogs, and instructions on how to get involved.*

"An Extreme Reading of Facebook" (http://openanthcoop.net/press/2010/10/22/an-extreme-reading-of-facebook/): *An academic article by Daniel Miller of University College, London, analyzing the influence of Facebook.*

[handwritten: Two Types of Argument!]
[handwritten: Inductive reasoning, on the other hand, proceeds from several specific occurrences to one general truth.]

Argument and
Persuasion

[handwritten: Deductive: proceeds from a general truth or principle to a more specific instance based on that principle.]

Strictly speaking, argument is a rhetorical technique used to support or deny a proposition by offering detailed evidence for or against it in a logically connected fashion. Classical argument relies on *[handwritten: 1]*deductive and *[handwritten: 2]*inductive thinking; it appeals to reason and reason alone. Deduction proceeds from a general truth or principle to a more specific instance based on that principle. You would be using deduction if you argued: All full-time students are permitted to use the college weight room free of charge; I am a full-time student; I am permitted to use the weight room free of charge.

[handwritten: 2.] Inductive reasoning, on the other hand, proceeds from several specific occurrences to one general truth. Let's say you come down with a bad case of food poisoning—fever, cramps, vomiting, the works! When you feel better, you call up the five people with whom you had dinner; each of them claims to have suffered the same symptoms. It is probably safe to infer that all six of you ate contaminated food.

Sometimes, of course, one's purpose may go beyond simply proving a point. The writer may feel a need to persuade (i.e., to convert the audience, or even to convey a sense of urgency that will convince readers to act and act quickly). In such cases, pure logic may not suffice. Thus, while grounding the paper in logic and well-developed evidence, a writer may also want to appeal to the emotions.

Both methods are legitimate forms studied under the general category of argumentation, and both are represented, to varying degrees, in the essays that follow. Indeed, it is often hard to draw a line. Jonathan Swift's "A Modest Proposal"—a model of deductive reasoning expressed in language that is cool, clear, and eminently logical—is couched in a bitter irony that expresses the author's rage over Britain's treatment of the Irish.

Argument lends itself naturally to debate on matters scientific, social, and political. Three sets of essays in this chapter take various sides on economics and social responsibility, free speech, and cloning. As you will see, Janet Kornblum and Michael Rubinkam give slightly different takes on the issue of texting by students. Nat Hentoff and Alan M. Dershowitz

363

discuss matters relevant to the First Amendment; and Andrew C. Revkin and Philip Stott present two views on global warming. It is important to note that, as reasoned and clear as these seven selections are, each remains unique, varying in tone and urgency according to the proximity from which its author views the subject.   *Persuasion - convice them to act*

The six selections listed under Persuasion illustrate techniques you might use when trying to move your readers or convince them to act. Make sure to read the classics "On Liberty" by John Stuart Mill and "I Have a Dream" by Martin Luther King, Jr. In addition, Naomi Shihab Nye's "To Any Would-Be Terrorists" and Jonathan Safran Foer's "Let Them Eat Dog" illustrate how effective emotional appeals are in changing readers' minds. Finally, the essays by Judy Brady and Medicine Grizzlybear Lake might help you see familiar subjects in a new light.

Even though the essays in this chapter are examples of well-written and well-reasoned arguments, you might want to take issue with the positions they advocate and write a rebuttal to one or two of them. Keep in mind, however, that the essential ingredient in building an effective argument is a thorough knowledge of your subject. Without it, your readers will remain unconvinced despite your ability to stir their emotions. Think of yourself as an attorney. You will have difficulty defending your client unless you know all the facts. Anything less will jeopardize your credibility with the jury. This idea also applies to your role as a writer. Good readers will approach your thesis with a healthy skepticism. They may be open to persuasion—some may even want to be convinced—but most will insist that you provide reasonable, well-developed, and convincing evidence before they give you their trust.

ARGUMENT

Texting

Tapping into Text Messaging

Janet Kornblum

Janet Kornblum (b. 1962) received a B.A. in Political Science from the University of California at Berkeley. After college, she reported for several San Francisco area newspapers, then worked as a reporter for USA Today *from 1999 to 2008. She is now a freelance writer, specializing in topics about social networking, the Internet, and private investigations, and she is also a founding writer of CNET News.*

"Tapping into Text Messaging" first appeared in USA Today *in 2003. Taking a neutral stance, Kornblum discusses some of the benefits and drawbacks of text messaging.*

It's 9:30 a.m., and Larry Blair hopes that his 16-year-old son doesn't forget 1
his orthodontist appointment after school.

So Blair, who is on a conference call in his office in Saratoga, Calif., 2
pulls out his cell phone and thumbs in a short message. "can u b @ sasaki
@ 330," he asks.

Seconds later, Aaron, sitting at his desk at Saratoga High School, feels 3
his cell phone vibrating in his pocket. He surreptitiously looks at the
screen and quietly pumps in a response: "can b there @ 320."

Welcome to the future, where the family that texts together stays 4
together.

Instant, fast, fun and cheap, texting—sending and receiving brief text 5
messages on cell phones and other portable devices—has been the rage in
Europe since the late 90s. Now it's making inroads in the USA. Early users
love it, but some people worry that it will add yet another distraction to
already overtasked lives.

Teens, techies and other early adopters leading the charge to text say 6
it's a great way to communicate when they are too busy to talk or when
making a call would be rude or impractical. Parents keep tabs on kids.
Business people silently check facts in meetings. Young professionals
text-flirt at concerts. And teens gossip with friends, anytime, anywhere.

Teens are especially ahead of the curve: 45% of Americans ages 7
12-19 have a cell phone, according to market research company Teenage
Research Unlimited of Northbrook, Ill. And 37% of teen cell users also use
text messaging, with numbers rising every year.

"Some people do it for eight hours at a time," says Lita Cho, 17, a 8
Youth Radio reporter in Alameda, Calif.

Teens aren't the only ones. Texting in the USA has grown from 33 mil- 9
lion messages sent in June 2001 to more than 1 billion in December 2002,
says the Cellular Telecommunications & Internet Association.

"When I go out, I hate to be called," says Steven Chan, 30, who owns 10
Cyber Hunt, a cyber cafe in San Francisco. "I hate people leaving voice-
mail. Just text me."

Though Yankee Group analysts estimate that only 12% of cell phone 11
users in the USA send or receive text messages, that soon could change:
144 million people—half of all U.S. residents—have cell phones, the telecommunications association says. And 90% of those phones are digital
and can at least accept text messages. About 60% also can send messages,
Jupiter Research says.

"Texting is a small indicator that cyberspace has now arrived—not 12
just at our desks, but in our pockets, in our hands and in our cars," says
Paul Saffo, director of the Institute for the Future in Menlo Park, Calif.

13   But is adding yet another communications tool to our already stuffed belts really a good idea?

14   Some worry that texting—also known as SMS, for Short Message Service—will make people even more distracted than they already are. Instead of watching the road, will drivers be typing into their cell phones? Instead of listening to the teacher, will kids be checking their messages? Will pedestrians watch where they're going when they walk down the street?

15   "I've seen a lot more people walking into parking meters," Saffo says. "No joke."

16   People may be "physically present," but they're increasingly "psychologically absent," says James Katz, a professor of communications at Rutgers University.

17   Katz says cell phones are largely responsible for the "ghosting of America," his phrase for "the hollowing-out of people. They're physical ghosts involved in their messaging and talking on the mobile phones."

18   But others say teens and twentysomethings who grew up multitasking might simply be able to handle more distractions.

19   "Aaron will be on the phone at home with music playing in the background and doing homework. You're time-sharing your brain," says Blair, 47, vice president of a software company. Plus, "it has made both of us more accessible at times when even a cell phone couldn't have gotten to us."

20   People have been concerned about the adverse effects of new communication tools since Plato worried that the alphabet would cause us to lose our memorization skills and cut down on our quality time together, says Howard Rheingold, a longtime technology watcher and author of *Smart Mobs: The Next Social Revolution.* And he was right. But there's always a reason you pay the price.

21   "Communications behavior is filling parts of our time that used to be idle or devoted to talking to strangers or noticing parts of the world that we're not going to notice as much anymore. That has an impact on individuals as well as on cities. More and more, people are walking down the street communicating with people who are somewhere else."

22   But, he adds, "I wouldn't be so quick to judge that (teens) are paying less attention than they were before. Maybe they're multiplying the amount of attention that they pay. We call it distracted. Our grandchildren will say, 'Oh, yeah, our grandparents couldn't think on more than one track at once.'"

23   Go to any high school and you're likely to see kids staring at tiny cell phone screens, picking at tiny keypads with their thumbs.

24   Most schools ban talking and texting in the classroom. But that doesn't stop everyone.

25   Though phone calls require talking, texting can be done on the sly. Some students don't even need to look at their phones as they type.

"You're not allowed, but they rarely notice if you have it under the 26
table," Aaron says. "Teachers aren't looking around for that sort of thing.
You can pass notes to people in other classes."

Some do more than that. 27

In January, students at the University of Maryland were caught cheat- 28
ing on a test by sending text messages to each other.

Rutgers' Katz says his informal surveys show that about half the 29
students with text-enabled phones have used them in class, and a substantial minority say they know of others who have used texting to cheat.
But it's no easier than other kinds of cheating, so few expect it to take off
in a big way.

Regardless of where teens text, debating whether they should use the 30
new technology "is somewhat futile," Rheingold says. "They're going to
do it."

And adults probably will continue to adopt texting as well as other 31
new forms of communication. Why? It fulfills a deep need.

"We've had speech," Rheingold says. "We've had writing. We've had 32
the alphabet. We've had the printing press. These are technologies for
extending the way we think and communicate.

"That's what humans do: We come up with new ways to communi- 33
cate and new ways to build civilizations."

2003

QUESTIONS FOR DISCUSSION

Content

a. According to Kornblum, what might be the benefits of tapping into text
   messaging?
b. In paragraph 4, Kornblum humorously suggests that "the family that
   texts together stays together." Do you agree with that claim?
c. When might sending a text be more polite than making a phone call?
   What other situations can you think of to add to Kornblum's list?
d. Why should people be worried about texting?
e. What is "the 'ghosting of America'"?

Strategy and Style

f. What might have been Kornblum's strategy for referring to Plato
   (paragraph 20)? What does Plato's concern about language and
   memory add to the debate about texting?
g. What is the effect of using short paragraphs throughout the essay?

h. How does Kornblum balance the pros and cons of texting? Does she provide an equal number of problems and benefits?

i. Is Kornblum successful in maintaining a neutral voice? What neutral phrases does she use? What biased phrasing, if any, does she use?

j. Even though the last two paragraphs are direct quotes from one of her sources, what point is Kornblum indirectly making in these concluding paragraphs? Why might she have made her point through someone else's speech?

ENGAGING THE TEXT

a. Reread the essay and make a list of the pros and cons of texting. Add to the list any other items that come to mind. Explain your own position in this debate.

b. Compare texting, as described in this essay, to using Twitter, which was not yet invented when this piece was written. Which of the items on your pros and cons list would also apply to Twitter?

SUGGESTIONS FOR SUSTAINED WRITING

a. If you text, monitor your texting over the course of a specified time—a day or a week. Keep a log and note the time of day, the length of the message, the recipient, and the reason for texting. Write an analysis of your activities and discuss anything you consider to be significant. You might also decide to include a defense of your texting habits.

   If you do not text, observe other students who do and write an essay in which you either defend the habit or persuade texters to stop.

b. Compare this essay to the one by Michael Rubinkam. Both writers attempt to be neutral toward the topic, but do either or both also betray a bias? Describe the writer's views about texting in particular and technology in general.

c. Research future trends for SMS or electronic communication in general. Begin by researching the organizations quoted in the essay to see whether they have updated their 2003 figures. Also research the market outlook for text messaging. Write an essay in which you predict the future of texting.

READ MORE

Kornblum and Her Works

"Janet Kornblum" (http://janetkornblum.com): *Kornblum's personal website.*

"CNET" (http://www.cnet.com): *Web page of the technology news site Kornblum helped found.*

Texting

"Texting" (http://www.insidehighered.com/content/search?searchText =texting): *Links to articles about texting in class published by* Inside Higher Ed.

"Digital Directions: Trends and Advice for K-12 Technology Leaders" (http://www.edweek.org/dd): *Links to articles about technology trends in education.*

"Generation Text" (http://www.thevlc.org/2011/02/generation-text .html): *Discussion forum for teachers, parents, and students about using digital communication in the schools.*

"Generation Text" (http://www.generationtextonline.com): *Website of a group attempting to stop cyberbullying, using texting as one of its tools.*

Texting in Class Is Rampant

Michael Rubinkam

Michael Rubinkam is an Associated Press reporter based in northeastern Pennsylvania.
"Texting in Class Is Rampant" was first posted in November 2010 on lehighvalleylive .com.

When his professors drone, Dan Kautz whips out his phone.   1

Kautz, a senior at Wilkes University, might send a text message to 2 someone across the room—"I can't wait to get out of here"—or make plans with his roommates. He's become so adept at texting during class that he can tap out a message without even looking at the screen, making it appear as if he's paying attention to the instructor when he's really chatting with his girlfriend.

"Every single person I know texts in class at least occasionally," said 3 Kautz, a communications studies major from Pelham, N.Y.

It's no surprise that high school and college students are obsessive 4 texters. What alarms Wilkes psychology professors Deborah Tindell and Robert Bohlander is how rampant the practice has become during class: Their recent study shows that texting at the school has surpassed doodling, daydreaming and note-passing to become the top classroom distraction.

The anonymous survey of 269 Wilkes students found that nine in 10 5 admit to sending text messages during class—and nearly half say it's easy to do so undetected. Even more troubling, 10 percent say that they have sent or received texts during exams, and that 3 percent admit to using their phones to cheat.

6   The phenomenon is part of a broader revolution in the way young adults communicate. Most prefer texting to e-mail and certainly to talking on the phone, Tindell said.

7   Indeed, most view texting as their right.

8   Almost all the students surveyed by Tindell and Bohlander said they should be allowed to have their phones in class. And a clear majority—62 percent—said they should be allowed to text in class as long as they're not disturbing those around them. About one in four said texting creates a distraction.

9   "Students these days are so used to multitasking . . . they believe they are able to process information just as effectively when they are texting as when they are not," Tindell said.

10   Tom Markley, 21, of Lehighton, Pa., is constantly trading texts with his friends and his girlfriend during class.

11   "If it's a really boring class, texting is a nice alternative to having to sit there and focus," said Markley, a senior computer science major at Wilkes.

12   But, he conceded, "there are definitely times when it takes away from your concentration. Suddenly you'll be at the end of the period and say, 'What did we do today?'"

13   Tindell instituted a no-texting policy as a result of the study, which has been presented at a pair of academic conferences. She tells students that if she even sees a cell phone during a test, its owner gets an automatic zero.

14   One Syracuse University professor has taken an even harsher stand.

15   Laurence Thomas, a popular philosophy professor whose courses have waiting lists, walked out on his class of nearly 400 students last week when he caught a couple of students fiddling with their phones instead of paying attention to him.

16   It wasn't the first time Thomas has cut a class short because a student broke his no-texting rule. To Thomas, texting saps the class of its intellectual energy.

17   "My job is to engage the class, to give them stuff to think about," he said. "They need to respect that."

18   While Thomas keeps his eyes peeled for illicit texters, Tindell said most professors are likely as clueless as she used to be about the ubiquity of in-class cell phone use. Many of the surveyed students said their professors would be shocked if they knew about their texting habits.

19   Kautz said most of his professors either don't notice or don't care if students text during class time. He doesn't believe a blanket prohibition is the right way to go.

20   "There are people who can text and still be focused on class," he said. "If my roommate is short on quarters for laundry and wants to borrow

some, of course I'm going to want to text him back right away and not hold him back for 40 minutes."

But he acknowledged that some students text excessively.   21

"I know some people will sit there for the entire class just typing 22 away," he said. "I don't even know why they bother coming."

Chelsea Uselding, 20, a Wilkes junior from Chicago, sends an aver- 23 age of 150 texts a day. But she's the rare student who doesn't text during class—viewing that hour or two as a "nice break" from the phone and its unceasing demands on her time and attention.

There's also a practical reason why Uselding, a dual major in psychol- 24 ogy and international studies, idles her thumbs.

"I'm paying all this money to listen to the person speak, and I figure 25 it's a waste of my time if I'm not going to be listening," she said.

Some high school and college teachers have sought to adapt text 26 messaging to classroom use, texting assignments; asking questions of the class and having students respond via text, with the results shown on a large screen; and allowing students to text questions or comments during class.

"Our experience has shown that positive results can be achieved by 27 encouraging students to bring their mobile phones out in the open and to use them to contribute to the class, and to their own learning—that is, by joining them instead of trying to beat them," New Zealand scholars wrote in a 2009 paper published in the journal Communications of the ACM.

Tindell and Bohlander advise professors to have clear, written poli- 28 cies on texting, to circulate around the classroom and make frequent eye contact, and to avoid focusing all their attention on their lecture notes or PowerPoint presentations.

Tindell does allow students to text before class starts—and almost all 29 of them do.

"If they are going to go through withdrawal," she quipped, "they 30 might as well get their fix."

2010

QUESTIONS FOR DISCUSSION

Content

a. In paragraph 4, Rubinkam tells us that texting "has surpassed doodling, daydreaming and note-passing" as the top classroom distraction. In your opinion, is texting in the same category as these other distractions? Is it more, or less, distracting than these other activities?

b. Why might students prefer texting to e-mailing and phone-calling? What advantages does texting have?

c. What are some of the effects, both positive and negative, of texting in class, according to the people Rubinkam interviewed?

d. To what extent do you agree with psychology professor Tindell that students "'believe they are able to process information just as effectively when they are texting as when they are not'" (paragraph 9)?

e. Do you agree with student Markley that texting is a "nice alternative" to sitting in a "really boring class" (paragraph 11)? What else might a student do to deal with boredom?

Strategy and Style

f. What are some of the ways that Rubinkam makes this article interesting?

g. What conventions of online publication and of feature writing does Rubinkam follow?

h. In what ways is the article itself like texting?

i. Although Rubinkam takes a fairly neutral path in reporting on texting in class, what attitude does he have toward texting? If he were a teacher, would he be inclined to allow students to text?

j. How does Rubinkam balance the pros and cons of texting on campus?

k. What facts does Rubinkam use to frame the argument for and against texting in class? What shared values does he draw on?

ENGAGING THE TEXT

a. With the permission of your teacher, purposefully text in class at a prearranged time and note what you remember from the time you were texting. If you do not have a cell phone, try purposefully doodling, daydreaming, or note-passing (paragraph 4). Besides describing what you recall of the class material, also discuss whether or not the "distracting" activity was actually distracting.

b. A Syracuse University professor (paragraphs 13-17) is described as walking out on classes when students text. In a short response, state whether you agree or disagree with his reaction. Is his reaction too extreme, or not extreme enough? What would you do in his position?

SUGGESTIONS FOR SUSTAINED WRITING

a. What makes texting a powerful form of communication? Discuss the benefits and drawbacks of texting from your own perspective.

Consider both texting in general and texting in specific situations, such as in class or while walking or driving.

b. Using "Tapping into Text Messaging" by Janet Kornblum, and the people who were quoted by Rubinkam as being in favor of texting, write a defense of texting in class.

c. Poll your classmates or other students on campus to find out how many of them text during class and why. Report on your findings, summarizing the reasons why students text and proposing some ways that teachers and students can deal with texting.

READ MORE

Rubinkam and His Works

"Michael Rubinkam" (http://ap-1403.newsvine.com): A list of recent articles by Rubinkam, with links, on Newsvine.com.

Texting in Class

"Wilkes News Archives" (http://www.wilkes.edu/pages/194.asp?item=61477): Press release from Wilkes University about the study done at Wilkes.

"Professor Encourages Texting in Class" (http://www.npr.org/templates/story/story.php?storyId=126299162): Audio file and transcript of an April 27, 2010 National Public Radio news story.

Free Speech

Should This Student Have Been Expelled?

Nat Hentoff

Nat Hentoff (b. 1925) writes a regular column for the Village Voice *and contributes frequently to the* Washington Post, *the* New Yorker, *and other major magazines, journals, and newspapers. Born in Boston, he took his B.A. at Northeastern University and attended Harvard University for postgraduate study. He also studied at the Sorbonne in Paris as a Fulbright fellow. He was associate editor at* Down Beat *magazine from 1953 to 1957. He has received a Guggenheim Fellowship in education and an American Bar Association Silver Gavel Award. In 1985, he was awarded an honorary doctorate by Northeastern*

University. Hentoff describes himself as an "advocacy writer," and his interests range from jazz to educational reform, subjects on which he has written several books and articles. He also has written several novels and biographies. However, Hentoff's reputation rests chiefly on his writings on the First Amendment to the U.S. Constitution. Indeed, he is among America's staunchest defenders of free speech and its most outspoken opponent of censorship. His book on this subject is The First Freedom: The Tumultuous History of Free Speech in America *(1989). His other books on this subject include* Living the Bill of Rights: How to Be an Authentic American *(1998),* The War on the Bill of Rights and the Gathering Resistance *(2003), and* At the Jazz Band Ball: Sixty Years on the Jazz Scene *(2010).*

"Should This Student Have Been Expelled?" which first appeared in the Village Voice *in 1991, responds to a letter to the* New York Times *by Vartan Gregorian, president of Brown University, and to a* Times *editorial supporting Brown's expulsion of Douglas Hann. Both the letter and the editorial appear after Hentoff's essay.*

> *The day that Brown denies any student freedom of speech is the day I give up my presidency of the university.*
> —Vartan Gregorian, president of Brown University,
> February 20, 1991

1   Doug Hann, a varsity football player at Brown, was also concentrating on organizational behavior and management and business economics. On the night of October 18, 1990, Hann, a junior, was celebrating his twenty-first birthday, and in the process had imbibed a considerable amount of spirits.

2   At one point, Hann shouted into the air, "Fuck you, niggers!" It was aimed at no one in particular but apparently at all black students at Brown. Or in the world. A freshman leaned out a dormitory window and asked him to stop being so loud and offensive.

3   Hann, according to reporters on the *Brown Daily Herald,* looked up and yelled, "What are you, a faggot?" Hann then noticed an Israeli flag in the dorm. "What are you, a Jew?" he shouted. "Fucking Jew!"

4   Hann had achieved the hat trick of bigotry. (In hockey, the hat trick is scoring three goals in a game.) In less than a minute, Hann had engaged in racist, anti-Semitic, and homophobic insults.

5   He wasn't through. As reported by Smita Nerula in the *Brown Daily Herald,* the freshman who had asked Hann to cool it recruited a few people from his dorm "and followed Hann and his friends."

6   "This resulted in a verbal confrontation outside of Wayland Arch. At this time, [Hann] was said to have turned to one of the freshman's friends, a black woman, and shouted, 'My parents own your people.'"

7   To the Jewish student, or the student he thought was Jewish, Hann said, "Happy Hanukkah."

8   There are reports that at this juncture Hann tried to fight some of the students who had been following him. But, the *Brown Daily Herald* reports, he "was held back by one of his friends, while [another] friend

stretched his arm across the Wayland Gates to keep the students from following Hann."

John Howard Crouch—a student and Brown chapter secretary of the   9 American Civil Liberties Union there—tells me that because Hann had friends restraining him, "nobody seriously expected fighting, regardless of anyone's words."

Anyway, there was no physical combat. Just words. Awful words, but   10 nothing more than speech. (Nor were there any threats.)

This was not the first time Hann's disgraceful drunken language had   11 surfaced at Brown. Two years before, in an argument with a black student at a fraternity bar, Hann had called the student a "nigger." Thereupon he had been ordered to attend a race relations workshop and to get counseling for possible alcohol abuse. Obviously, he has not been rehabilitated.

Months went by after Hann's notorious birthday celebration as   12 Brown's internal disciplinary procedures cranked away. (To steal a phrase from Robert Sherrill, Brown's way of reaching decisions in these matters is to due process as military music is to music. But that's true of any college or university I know anything about.)

At last, the Undergraduate Disciplinary Council (five faculty or   13 administration members and five students) ruled that Doug Hann was to leave the university forevermore. Until two years ago, it was possible for a Brown student to be dismissed, which meant that he or she could reapply after a decent period of penance. But now, Brown has enshrined the sentence of expulsion. You may go on to assist Mother Teresa in caring for the dying or you may teach a course in feminism to 2 Live Crew, but no accomplishments, no matter how noble, will get you back into Brown once you have been expelled.

Doug Hann will wander the Earth without a Brown degree for the   14 rest of his days.

The president of Brown, Vartan Gregorian—formerly the genial head   15 of the New York Public Library—had the power to commute or even reverse the sentence. But the speech code under which Hann was thrown out had been proposed by Gregorian himself shortly after he was inaugurated in 1989, so he was hardly a detached magistrate.

On January 25, 1991, Vartan Gregorian affirmed, with vigor, the   16 expulsion decision by the Undergraduate Disciplinary Council.

Hann became a historic figure. Under all the "hate speech" codes   17 enacted around the country in recent years, he is the first student to actually be expelled for violating one of the codes.

The *New York Times* (February 12) reported that "Howard Ehrlich, the   18 research director of the National Institute Against Prejudice and Violence, said that he did not know of any other such expulsions, but that he was familiar with cases in which students who had harassed others were moved to other dormitories or ordered to undergo counseling."

19   But that takes place in *educational* institutions, whose presidents recognize that there are students who need help, not exile.

20   At first, there didn't seem to be much protest among the student body at Brown on free speech grounds—except for members of the Brown chapter of the ACLU and some free thinkers on the student paper, as well as some unaffiliated objectors to expelling students for what they say, not for what they do. The number of these dissenters is increasing, as we shall see.

21   At the student paper, however, the official tone has changed from the libertarian approach of Vernon Silver, who was editor-in-chief last semester. A February 13 *Brown Daily Herald* editorial was headed: "*Good Riddance.*"

22   It began: "Doug Hann is gone, and the university is well to be rid of him."

23   But President Gregorian has been getting a certain amount of flack and so, smiting his critics hip and thigh, he wrote a letter to the *New York Times*. Well, that letter (printed on February 21) was actually a press release, distributed by the Brown University News Bureau to all sorts of people, including me, on February 12. There were a few changes—and that *Brown Daily Herald* editorial was attached to it—but Gregorian's declaration was clearly not written exclusively for the *Times*.

24   Is this a new policy at the *Times*—taking public relations handouts for the letters page?

25   Next week I shall include a relentlessly accurate analysis of President Gregorian's letter by the executive director of the Rhode Island ACLU. But first, an account of what Gregorian said in that letter to the *Times*.

26   President Gregorian indignantly denies that Brown has ever expelled "anyone for the exercise of free speech, nor will it ever do so." Cross his heart.

27   He then goes into self-celebration: "My commitment to free speech and condemnation of racism and homophobia are well known. . . .

28   "The university's code of conduct does not prohibit speech; it prohibits *actions*."

29   Now watch this pitiable curve ball:

30   "Offense III [of the Brown code]—which deals with harassment—prohibits inappropriate, abusive, threatening, or demeaning actions based on race, religion, gender, handicap, ethnicity, national origin, or sexual orientation."

31   In the original press release, Gregorian underlined the word *actions*. There, and in the letter to the *Times*—lest a dozing reader miss the point—Gregorian emphasizes that "The rules do not proscribe words, epithets, or slanders, they proscribe behavior." Behavior that "shows flagrant disrespect for the well-being of others or is unreasonably disruptive of the University community."

Consider the overbreadth and vagueness of these penalty-bearing 32
provisions. What are the definitions of "harassment," "inappropriate,"
"demeaning," "flagrant," "disrespect," "wellbeing," "unreasonably"?

Furthermore, with regard to Brown's termination of Doug Hann with 33
extreme prejudice, Gregorian is engaging in the crudest form of Orwellian
newspeak. Hann was kicked out for *speech,* and only speech—not for
actions, as Gregorian huffily insists. As for behavior, the prickly folks
whose burning of the American flag was upheld by the Supreme Court
were indeed engaged in behavior, but that behavior was based entirely on
symbolic speech. So was Hann's. He didn't punch anybody or vandalize
any property. He brayed.

Art Spitzer, legal director of the ACLU's National Capital Area affili- 34
ate, wrote a personal letter to Gregorian:

"There is a very simple test for determining whether a person is being 35
punished for his actions or his speech. You just ask whether he would
have received the same punishment if he had spoken different words
while engaging in the same conduct."

"Thus, would your student have been expelled if he had gotten drunk 36
and stood in the same courtyard at the same hour of the night, shouting at
the same decibel level, 'Black is Beautiful!' 'Gay is Good!' or 'Go Brown!
Beat Yale!' or even 'Nuke Baghdad! Kill Saddam!'?

"I am confident," Spitzer said, that "he would not have been expelled 37
for such 'actions.' If that is correct, it follows that *he was expelled for the
unsavory content of his speech,* and not for his actions. I have no doubt that
you can understand this distinction. (Emphasis added.)

"Now, you are certainly entitled to believe that it is appropriate to 38
expel a student for the content of his speech when that content is sufficiently offensive to the 'university community.' . . .

"If that is your position, why can't you deliver it forthrightly? Then 39
the university community can have an open debate about which opinions
it finds offensive, and ban them. Perhaps this can be done once a year, so
that the university's rules can keep pace with the tenor of the times—after
all, it wouldn't do to have outmoded rules banning procommunist or
blasphemous speech still on the books, now that it's 1991. Then students
and teachers applying for admission or employment at Brown will know
what they are getting into.

"Your recent statements, denying the obvious, are just hypocritical. . . ." 40

And what did the *New York Times*—in a stunningly fatuous February 41
21 editorial—say of Vartan Gregorian's sending Doug Hann into permanent exile? "A noble attempt both to govern and teach."

The *Times* editorials should really be signed, so that the rest of the 42
editorial board isn't blamed for such embarrassments.

1991

How Much Hate to Tolerate

New York Times editorial (February 21, 1991)

1 Free speech and human relations seemed to collide last month at Brown University when it expelled a student for racial and religious harassment. In fact, however, to judge by all that is publicly known, the school walked a fine line with sensitivity toward its complex mission.

2   One mission of a university is to send into the world graduates who are tolerant of many races, faiths and cultures. Another mission is to teach the value of free expression and tolerance even for hateful ideas. But should such tolerance cover racist, sexist or homophobic speech that makes the learning environment intolerable for racial and religious minorities, women and other targets of abuse? Brown found a reasonable basis for saying, clearly, no.

3   Douglas Hann, white, a junior and a varsity football player, had previously been disciplined for alcohol abuse and for racial insults against a black fellow student. Then, one evening last fall, he shouted racial insults in a university courtyard. A Jewish student who opened a dormitory window and called for quiet was answered with a religious insult. Later that evening Mr. Hann directed a racial insult at a black undergraduate.

4   The student-faculty discipline committee found him guilty of three violations of student rules, including another count of alcohol abuse. Vartan Gregorian, the university's president, upheld the student's expulsion last month. He had a sound basis for doing so. If the facts are reported correctly, Mr. Hann crossed the line between merely hateful speech and hateful speech that directly confronted and insulted other undergraduates.

5   Some courts have found that public universities are bound by the First Amendment's ban on state censorship and thus may not punish students for expressing politically incorrect or socially distasteful ideas. Brown, like other private schools, is less directly bound by the Constitution but committed to its precepts. It is trying to avoid censorship but draws a line between strong language and what the courts often call "fighting words."

6   In the adjacent Letters column today, Mr. Gregorian insists that Brown does not punish unruly speech as such but will decide case-by-case whether a student has passed "the point at which speech becomes behavior" that flagrantly disregards the well-being of others or "subjects someone to abusive or demeaning actions."

7   That formula is a noble attempt both to govern and teach. It offers a principled basis for disciplinary action against Mr. Hann for his direct, confrontational conduct.

8   The lines may not be so clearly drawn in other cases. There may also be more of them in the present climate of evidently increasing student

intolerance. But when bigots attack other students with ugly invective, universities, whether public or private, need not remain silent. Their presidents, like Mr. Gregorian, may denounce indecency and, in so doing, protect tolerance.

Brown Expulsion Not About Free Speech

New York Times letter to the editor (February 21, 1991)

To the Editor:

"Student at Brown Is Expelled Under a Rule Barring 'Hate Speech'" 1 (news article, Feb. 12) suggests I have instituted "hate-speech" prohibitions at Brown University and that the expulsion of a student who shouted racial and homophobic epithets on campus last October is the first such in the nation based on restrictions of free speech. Brown University has never expelled anyone for free speech, nor will it ever do so.

My commitment to free speech and condemnation of racism and 2 homophobia are well known. In April 1989, several students were subjected to a cowardly attack of racial and homophobic graffiti. The words and slogans scrawled anonymously on doors in one of our dormitories were vicious attacks threatening the well-being and security of Brown students.

I condemned that anonymous poisoning of our community and 3 said I would prosecute vigorously and seek the expulsion of those who incite hatred or perpetuate such acts of vandalism. Nothing I said then or have done since should be construed as limiting anyone's freedom of speech, nor have I revised the university's code of conduct to that effect.

The university's code of conduct does not prohibit speech; it prohibits 4 actions, and these include behavior that "shows flagrant disrespect for the well-being of others or is unreasonably disruptive of the university community."

Offense III, which deals with harassment, prohibits inappropriate, 5 abusive, threatening or demeaning actions based on race, religion, gender, handicap, ethnicity, national origin or sexual orientation.

"The Tenets of Community Behavior," which outline community 6 standards for acceptable behavior at Brown, have been read for more than 10 years by entering students, who agree in writing to abide by them.

The rules do not proscribe words, epithets or slanders; they proscribe 7 behavior. The point at which speech becomes behavior and the degree to which that behavior shows flagrant disrespect for the well-being of others (Offense II), subjects someone to abusive or demeaning actions (Offense III) or is related to drug or alcohol use (Offense IV) is determined by a hearing to consider the circumstances of each case. The student is entitled to an appeal, which includes review by a senior officer and a decision by the president.

8   I cannot and will not comment about any specific case. I regret the release of any student's name in connection with a disciplinary hearing and the exposure any case may receive in *The Brown Herald*.

9   Freedom-of-speech questions lie at the heart of any academic community. The very nature of the academic enterprise necessitates that universities remain partisans of heterodoxy, of a rich and full range of opinions, ideas and expression. Imposed orthodoxies of all sorts, including what is called "politically correct" speech, are anathema to our enterprise.

10   The university's most compelling challenge is to achieve a balance between the right of its individual members to operate and speak freely, and fostering respect for and adherence to community values and standards of conduct.

VARTAN GREGORIAN
President, Brown University
Providence, R.I., Feb. 21, 1991

QUESTIONS FOR DISCUSSION

Content

a. In a sentence or two, summarize Hentoff's argument against Hann's expulsion.

b. Explain the analogy the author uses in paragraph 12.

c. Why, according to Hentoff, wouldn't Vartan Gregorian "commute or even reverse" Hann's sentence (paragraph 15)?

d. What does Hentoff imply about Brown's president in paragraph 19?

e. What is "Orwellian newspeak" (paragraph 33)? According to Hentoff, in what way is Gregorian engaging in "newspeak"?

f. Explain the test "for determining whether a person is being punished for his actions or his speech" as articulated by Art Spitzer in paragraphs 35–37.

g. Explain the advice Spitzer gave Gregorian as quoted from his letter in paragraph 39.

h. What purpose does Hentoff's conclusion serve? What is his point in the essay's very last paragraph?

Strategy and Style

i. Why does Hentoff include paragraph 10? Is it really necessary?

j. Why does he characterize Gregorian's letter to the *Times* as a "public relations" handout (paragraph 24)? How would you describe Hentoff's attitude toward the newspaper's editorial board?

k. Analyze the structure of the essay. If necessary, write a brief outline that includes its key points and reveals its organization.
l. Where in this selection does Hentoff appeal to authority by quoting expert testimony? Who are those experts? Is their testimony convincing?
m. What advantage does Hentoff achieve by quoting directly from Gregorian's letter to the *Times*? Other than directly attacking the letter's contents, how does he refute Gregorian?

ENGAGING THE TEXT

a. Summarize the arguments made by the writer of the *New York Times* editorial "How Much Hate to Tolerate." Then, do the same for Vartan Gregorian's letter to the editor.
b. Are you in favor of unlimited freedom of expression? If so, explain why. In an attempt to anticipate opposing arguments, explain how you would defend the right of others to express themselves in ways you consider immoral, abhorrent, or even dangerous. If you don't support that right, explain why freedom of expression should be limited in certain instances. Refer to Hentoff's essay in your response.

SUGGESTIONS FOR SUSTAINED WRITING

a. In your own letter to the editor, attack or defend Hentoff's position on the expulsion of Doug Hann and on its implications vis-à-vis the exercise of free speech on college campuses. Whichever position you take, make reference to or quote from Hentoff's essay, the *New York Times* editorial, and/or Gregorian's letter. On the other hand, remember that this is *your* letter, so rely heavily on your own arguments and ideas.
b. Compare Hentoff's ideas with those in the essays by Gloria Naylor (Chapter 4) and William Lutz (Chapter 5). Write an essay in which you discuss how language is used to cover or to expose a person's "true" feelings. What does one's choice of words reveal about one's worldview?
c. The American college is a place where open and free debate should be encouraged. You probably know of several important issues—academic, political, cultural, scientific, theological, economic, and so on—being discussed by students and faculty at your college. Take a clear position on an issue that affects you as a student, that you have studied or read about, or that you have debated with others at your school. You need not choose an issue of universal significance.

Interesting and effective arguments can be written on increasing scholarship aid, providing more parking spaces for college commuters, keeping the library open late at night and on Sundays, or giving students access to computer labs free of charge. Research your topic as thoroughly as you can through secondary and primary sources.

READ MORE

Hentoff and His Works

Hentoff, Nat. *The Nat Hentoff Reader.* Cambridge, MA: Da Capo, 2001.

"Nat Says" (http://www.mouthmag.com/says/natsays.htm): *An online interview with Hentoff at* Mouthmag.

Campus Issues

For information about campus speech codes and other related free-speech issues, go to the "Civil Liberties" website at http://civilliberty.about.com/od/freespeech. *To find a range of campus issues, use the search phrase "campus issues," "campus controversies," or similar terms to find print and online sources.*

Shouting "Fire!"

Alan M. Dershowitz

A graduate of Brooklyn College and Yale Law School, Alan M. Dershowitz (b. 1938) was appointed to the law faculty at Harvard University in 1963, where he has taught courses on a variety of subjects, including criminal law, legal ethics, and civil liberties. He has written several books for the lay reader, some of which are discussions of criminal law, such as Psychoanalysis, Psychiatry, and the Law *(coauthored with others, 1967). Other books discuss some of the controversial cases on which he has worked, such as* The Best Defense *(1982) and* Reversal of Fortune *(1982), on the Claus von Bulow case. In 1997, Dershowitz published* The Abuse Excuse, *a series of essays on personal responsibility and the law. From his experience as a member of the team that defended O. J. Simpson, Dershowitz wrote* Reasonable Doubts: The O. J. Simpson Case and the Criminal Justice System *(1996). Recent books include* The Case for Peace: How the Arab-Israeli Conflict Can Be Resolved *(2005),* Preemption: A Knife That Cuts Both Ways *(2006),* Blasphemy: How the Religious Right Is Hijacking the Declaration of Independence *(2007), and* The Case for Moral Clarity: Israel, Hamas and Gaza *(2009).*

"Shouting 'Fire!'" was first published in The Atlantic Monthly *in 1989. Some critics of Dershowitz have called him an apologist for racism, pornography, and torture—topics about which Dershowitz holds strong, often controversial, views. As you read "Shouting 'Fire!'" consider to what extent Dershowitz is being controversial.*

When the Reverend Jerry Falwell learned that the Supreme Court had   1
reversed his $200,000 judgment against *Hustler* magazine for the emotional
distress that he had suffered from an outrageous parody, his response was
typical of those who seek to censor speech: "Just as no person may scream
'Fire!' in a crowded theater when there is no fire, and find cover under the
First Amendment, likewise, no sleazy merchant like Larry Flynt should be
able to use the First Amendment as an excuse for maliciously and dishon-
estly attacking public figures, as he has so often done."

Justice Oliver Wendell Holmes's classic example of unprotected   2
speech—falsely shouting "Fire!" in a crowded theater—has been invoked
so often, by so many people, in such diverse contexts, that it has become
part of our national folk language. It has even appeared—most appropriately—in the theater: In Tom Stoppard's play *Rosecrantz and Guildenstern
Are Dead* a character shouts at the audience, "Fire!" He then quickly
explains: "It's all right—I'm demonstrating the misuse of free speech."
Shouting "Fire!" in the theater may well be the only jurisprudential analogy that has assumed the status of a folk argument. A prominent historian
recently characterized it as "the most brilliantly persuasive expression
that ever came from Holmes's pen." But in spite of its hallowed position in both the jurisprudence of the First Amendment and the arsenal
of political discourse, it is and was an inapt analogy, even in the context
in which it was originally offered. It has lately become—despite, perhaps
even because of, the frequency and promiscuousness of its invocation—
little more than a caricature of logical argumentation.

The case that gave rise to the "Fire!"-in-a-crowded-theater analogy,   3
Schenck v. United States, involved the prosecution of Charles Schenck,
who was the general secretary of the Socialist Party in Philadelphia, and
Elizabeth Baer, who was its recording secretary. In 1917 a jury found
Schenck and Baer guilty of attempting to cause insubordination among
soldiers who had been drafted to fight in the First World War. They and
other party members had circulated leaflets urging draftees not to "submit to intimidation" by fighting in a war being conducted on behalf of
"Wall Street's chosen few."

Schenck admitted, and the Court found, that the intent of the pam-   4
phlet's "impassioned language" was to "influence" drafters to resist the
draft. Interestingly, however, Justice Holmes noted that nothing in the
pamphlet suggested that the draftees should use unlawful or violent means
to oppose conscription: "In form at least [the pamphlet] confined itself to
peaceful measures, such as petition for the repeal of the act" and an exhortation to exercise "your right to assert your opposition to the draft." Many
of its most impassioned words were quoted directly from the Constitution.

Justice Holmes acknowledged that "in many places and in ordinary   5
times the defendants, in saying all that was said in the circular, would
have been within their constitutional rights." "But," he added, "the

character of every act depends upon the circumstances in which it is done." And to illustrate that truism he went on to say:

> The most stringent protection of free speech would not protect a man in falsely shouting fire in a theater, and causing panic. It does not even protect a man from an injunction against uttering words that may have all the effect of force.

6   Justice Holmes then upheld the convictions in the context of a wartime draft, holding that the pamphlet created "a clear and present danger" of hindering the war effort while our soldiers were fighting for their lives and our liberty.

7   The example of shouting "Fire!" obviously bore little relationship to the facts of the *Schenck* case. The Schenck pamphlet contained a substantive political message. It urged its draftee readers to *think* about the message and then—if they so chose—to act on it in a lawful and nonviolent way. The man who shouts "Fire!" in a crowded theater is neither sending a political message nor inviting his listener to think about what he has said and decide what to do in a rational, calculated manner. On the contrary, the message is designed to force action *without* contemplation. The message "Fire!" is directed not to the mind and the conscience of the listener but, rather, to his adrenaline and his feet. It is a stimulus to immediate *action*, not thoughtful reflection. It is—as Justice Holmes recognized in his follow-up sentence—the functional equivalent of "uttering words that may have all the effect of force."

8   Indeed, in that respect the shout of "Fire!" is not even speech, in any meaningful sense of the term. It is a *clang* sound, the equivalent of setting off a nonverbal alarm. Had Justice Holmes been more honest about his example, he would have said that freedom of speech does not protect a kid who pulls a fire alarm in the absence of a fire. But that obviously would have been irrelevant to the case at hand. The proposition that pulling an alarm is not protected speech certainly leads to the conclusion that shouting the word "fire" is also not protected. But the core analogy is the nonverbal alarm, and the derivative example is the verbal shout. By cleverly substituting the derivative shout for the core alarm, Holmes made it possible to analogize one set of words to another—as he could not have done if he had begun with the self-evident proposition that setting off an alarm bell is not free speech.

9   The analogy is thus not only inapt but also insulting. Most Americans do not respond to political rhetoric with the same kind of automatic acceptance expected of schoolchildren responding to a fire drill. Not a single recipient of the Schenck pamphlet is known to have changed his mind after reading it. Indeed, one draftee, who appeared as a prosecution witness, was asked whether reading a pamphlet asserting that the draft law was unjust would make him "immediately decide that you must

erase that law." Not surprisingly, he replied, "I do my own thinking." A theatergoer would probably not respond similarly if asked how he would react to a shout of "Fire!"

Another important reason why the analogy is inapt is that Holmes emphasizes the factual falsity of the shout "Fire!" The Schenck pamphlet, however, was not factually false. It contained political opinions and ideas about the causes of the war and about appropriate and lawful responses to the draft. As the Supreme Court recently reaffirmed (in *Falwell v. Hustler*), "The First Amendment recognizes no such thing as a 'false' idea." Nor does it recognize false opinions about the causes of or cures for war.

A closer analogy to the facts of the *Schenck* case might have been provided by a person's standing outside a theater, offering the patrons a leaflet advising them that in his opinion the theater was structurally unsafe, and urging them not to enter but to complain to the building inspectors. That analogy, however, would not have served Holmes's argument for punishing Schenck. Holmes needed an analogy that would appear relevant to Schenck's political speech but that would invite the conclusion that censorship was appropriate.

Unsurprisingly, a war-weary nation—in the throes of a know-nothing hysteria over immigrant anarchists and socialists—welcomed the comparison between what was regarded as a seditious political pamphlet and a malicious shout of "Fire!" Ironically, the "Fire!" analogy is nearly all that survives from the *Schenck* case; the ruling itself is almost certainly not good law. Pamphlets of the kind that resulted in Schenck's imprisonment have been circulated with impunity during subsequent wars.

Over the past several years I have assembled a collection of instances—cases, speeches, arguments—in which proponents of censorship have maintained that the expression at issue is "just like" or "equivalent to" falsely shouting "Fire!" in a crowded theater and ought to be banned, "just as" shouting "Fire!" ought to be banned. The analogy is generally invoked, often with self-satisfaction, as an absolute argument-stopper. It does, after all, claim the high authority of the great Justice Oliver Wendell Holmes. I have rarely heard it invoked in a convincing, or even particularly relevant, way. But that, too, can claim lineage from the great Holmes.

Not unlike Falwell, with his silly comparison between shouting "Fire!" and publishing an offensive parody, courts and commentators have frequently invoked "Fire!" as an analogy to expression that is not an automatic stimulus to panic. A state supreme court held that "Holmes's aphorism . . . applies with equal force to pornography"—in particular to the exhibition of the movie *Carmen Baby* in a drive-in theater in close proximity to highways of a secondary boycott" to shouting

"Fire!" because in both instances "speech and conduct are brigaded." In the famous Skokie case one of the judges argued that allowing Nazis to march through a city where a large number of Holocaust survivors live "just might fall into the same category as one's 'right' to cry fire in a crowded theater."

15   Outside court the analogies become even more badly stretched. A spokesperson for the New Jersey Sports and Exposition Authority complained that newspaper reports to the effect that a large number of football players had contracted cancer after playing in the Meadowlands—a stadium atop a landfill—were the "journalistic equivalent of shouting fire in a crowded theater." An insect researcher acknowledged that his prediction that a certain amusement park might become roach-infested "may be tantamount to shouting fire in a crowded theater." The philosopher Sidney Hook, in a letter to the *New York Times* bemoaning a Supreme Court decision that required a plaintiff in a defamation action to prove that the offending statement was actually false, argued that the First Amendment does not give the press carte blanche to accuse innocent persons "any more than the First Amendment protects the right of someone falsely to shout fire in a crowded theater."

16   Some close analogies to shouting "Fire!" or setting off an alarm are, of course, available: Calling in a false bomb threat; dialing 911 and falsely describing an emergency; making a loud, gun-like sound in the presence of the President; setting off a voice-activated sprinkler system by falsely shouting "Fire!" In one case in which the "Fire!" analogy was directly to the point, a creative defendant tried to get around it. The case involved a man who calmly advised an airline clerk that he was "only here to hijack the plane." He was charged, in effect, with shouting "Fire!" in a crowded theater, and his rejected defense—as quoted by the court—was as follows: "If we built fire-proof theaters and let people know about this, then the shouting of 'Fire!' would not cause panic."

17   Here are some more-distant but still related examples: The recent incident of the police slaying in which some members of an onlooking crowd urged a mentally ill vagrant who had taken an officer's gun to shoot the officer; the screaming of racial epithets during a tense confrontation; shouting down a speaker and preventing him from continuing his speech.

18   Analogies are, by their nature, matters of degree. Some are closer to the core example than others. But any attempt to analogize political ideas in a pamphlet, ugly parody in a magazine, offensive movies in a theater, controversial newspaper articles, or any of the other expressions and actions catalogued above to the very different act of shouting "Fire!" in a crowded theater is either self-deceptive or self-serving.

19   The government does, of course, have some arguably legitimate bases for suppressing speech which bear no relationship to shouting "Fire!" It

may ban the publication of nuclear-weapon codes, of information about troop movements, and of the identity of undercover agents. It may criminalize extortion threats and conspiratorial agreements. These expressions may lead directly to serious harm, but the mechanisms of causation are very different from those at work when an alarm is sounded. One may also argue—less persuasively, in my view—against protecting certain forms of public obscenity and defamatory statements. Here, too, the mechanisms of causation are very different. None of these exceptions to the First Amendment's exhortation that the government "shall make no law . . . abridging the freedom of speech, or of the press" is anything like falsely shouting "Fire!" in a crowded theater; they all must be justified on other grounds.

A comedian once told his audience, during a stand-up routine, 20 about the time he was standing around a fire with a crowd of people and got in trouble for yelling "Theater, theater!" That, I think, is about as clever and productive a use as anyone has ever made of Holmes's flawed analogy.

1989

QUESTIONS FOR DISCUSSION

Content

a. Explain the connection between shouting "Fire!" and censorship.
b. What is the false connection (analogy) with which Dershowitz finds fault? Why does he find fault with it?
c. What is the valid analogy?
d. Why is it important for us to see the difference between the false analogy and the valid one? What impact does this distinction have on your life?
e. Reread paragraph 8 and paraphrase it. What are the "core analogy" and the "derivative example"? How did Holmes make it "possible to analogize one set of words to another"?
f. Why is it necessary for Dershowitz to explain the concept of shouting "Fire!" so thoroughly?

Strategy and Style

g. What is a "folk argument" (paragraph 2)? What is the author's attitude toward folk arguments?

h. Why does the author end with the humorous example of shouting "Theater!"?

i. Dershowitz relies heavily on quotations from the people and cases with which he finds fault. How does he use these quotations? Is it appropriate to use such material in an argumentative essay? Does this practice work here?

j. Dershowitz constructs sentences so that the quotations he uses sound as if they were his own prose. What techniques does he use to accomplish this?

ENGAGING THE TEXT

a. Write definitions of *free speech* and *censorship* as you understand them. Then, write definitions of these terms as you believe Dershowitz understands them. Are there differences between your definitions and his? Explain these differences.

b. With two or three classmates, brainstorm a list of other examples of how the shouting "Fire!" analogy would apply to your lives.

SUGGESTIONS FOR SUSTAINED WRITING

a. What does Dershowitz's essay have to do with you and your world? Write an essay in which you first explain Dershowitz's thesis, main points, and purpose. Then, with examples drawn from your own experiences, observations, or reading, argue that Dershowitz's thesis has or does not have relevance to you or to the people with whom you associate.

b. Read or reread the essay by Nat Hentoff. Consider how Hentoff might have approached Dershowitz's topic in "Shouting 'Fire!'" Would he have engaged the topic by using analogy as Dershowitz did, or would he have used a different technique? In an essay, explain how this topic might be treated by Hentoff.

c. Should there be laws limiting free speech? If you believe that speech should be limited, write an essay in which you argue for such laws. What are the limitations you would impose and why? Explain your proposal in detail and defend it by citing real or hypothetical cases in which your laws would be beneficial. If you believe that speech should not be limited in any way, write an argument in which you show that limitations would have a detrimental effect on society. Again, be detailed and use real or hypothetical cases to illustrate your points. Whichever position you take, consider doing some additional reading on this subject via print or electronic sources. (We list a few to get you started.)

READ MORE

Dershowitz and His Works

"Alan M. Dershowitz" (http://www.alandershowitz.com): *Dershowitz's personal web page.*

"Alan Dershowitz" (http://dmoz.org/Society/Law/Legal_Information/ Legal_History/Dershowitz,_Alan): *A page with several links to articles by and about Dershowitz, compiled and maintained by The Open Directory Project.*

Free Speech

"The Freedom Forum" (http://www.freedomforum.org): *The website of The Freedom Forum, a nonpartisan center for information about free press and free speech.*

Hargreaves, Robert. *The First Freedom: A History of Free Speech.* Herndon, VA: 2003.

Global Warming

Global Warming Is Eroding Glacial Ice
Andrew C. Revkin

Andrew C. Revkin (b. 1956) has been an environmental reporter for the New York Times *since 1995. He earned a degree in biology in 1978 from Brown University and a Master's degree in journalism from Columbia University, where he has taught environmental reporting as an adjunct professor at Columbia's Graduate School of Journalism. Before joining the* Times, *Revkin was a senior editor of* Discover, *a staff writer for the* Los Angeles Times, *and a senior writer at* Science Digest. *He still publishes articles in these magazines, as well as in the* New Yorker *and* Condé Nast Traveler. *He has won several awards for his writing, including two Science Journalism Awards, an Investigative Reporters and Editors Award, a Guggenheim Fellowship, the John Chancellor Award, and a National Academies Communication Award for his coverage of climate change. Revkin's books include* The Burning Season *(1990), which is about a rain forest activist and won the Sidney Hillman Foundation Book Prize, received a Robert F. Kennedy Book Award, and was a New York Times Notable Book of the Year;* Global Warming: Understanding the Forecast *(1992); and* The North Pole Was Here: One Man's Exploration at the Top of the World *(2006), written for young adult readers. He is also a songwriter who often performs in his folk band, Uncle Wade.*

"Global Warming Is Eroding Glacial Ice" is from At Issue: Is Global Warming a Threat? *edited by Mary E. Williams. As you read, take note of how Revkin builds his case by citing authorities and statistics.*

1   The recent melting of mountain glaciers indicates that contemporary global warming is largely the result of human activity. Although natural climatic changes are partly responsible for the rise in average temperatures over the past century, the current rate of glacial erosion suggests that higher levels of greenhouse gases—resulting from pollution—are contributing significantly to global warming. Glacial melting could lead to damaging flash floods in some locales. Other regions that depend on melting snow for hydroelectric power could run low on water after glaciers have disappeared, requiring more communities to use pollution-creating oil or coal for energy—which in turn would produce more greenhouse gases and more global warming.

2   The icecap atop Mount Kilimanjaro, which for thousands of years has floated like a cool beacon over the shimmering plain of Tanzania, is retreating at such a pace that it will disappear in less than 15 years, according to new studies.

3   The vanishing of the seemingly perpetual snows of Kilimanjaro that inspired Ernest Hemingway, echoed by similar trends on ice-capped peaks from Peru to Tibet, is one of the clearest signs that a global warming trend in the last 50 years may have exceeded typical climate shifts and is at least partly caused by gases released by human activities, a variety of scientists say.

4   Measurements taken over a year-long period on Kilimanjaro show that its glaciers are not only retreating but also rapidly thinning, with one spot having lost a yard of thickness between February 2000 and February 2001, said Dr. Lonnie G. Thompson, a senior research scientist at the Byrd Polar Research Center of Ohio State University.

5   Altogether, he said, the mountain has lost 82 percent of the icecap it had when it was first carefully surveyed, in 1912.

6   Given that the retreat started a century ago, Dr. Thompson said, it is likely that some natural changes were affecting the glacier before it felt any effect from the large, recent rise in carbon dioxide and other heat-trapping greenhouse gases from smokestacks and tailpipes. And, he noted, glaciers have grown and retreated in pulses for tens of thousands of years.

7   But the pace of change measured now goes beyond anything in recent centuries.

8   "There may be a natural part of it, but there's something else being superimposed on top of it," Dr. Thompson said. "And it matches so many other lines of evidence of warming. Whether you're talking about

bore-hole temperatures, shrinking Arctic sea ice, or glaciers, they're tell-ing the same story."

GLACIAL EROSION

Dr. Thompson presented the fresh data in February 2001 at the annual 9
meeting of the American Association for the Advancement of Science in
San Francisco.

Other recent reports of changes under way in the natural world, like 10
gaps in sea ice at the North Pole or shifts in animal populations, can still
be ascribed to other factors, many scientists say, but many add that having
such a rapid erosion of glaciers in so many places is harder to explain
except by global warming.

The retreat of mountain glaciers has been seen from Montana to 11
Mount Everest to the Swiss Alps. In the Alps, scientists have estimated
that by 2025 glaciers will have lost 90 percent of the volume of ice that was
there a century ago. (Only Scandinavia seems to be bucking the trend,
apparently because shifting storm tracks in Europe are dumping more
snow there.)

But the melting is generally quickest in and near the tropics, Dr. 12
Thompson said, with some ancient glaciers in the Andes—and the ice on
Kilimanjaro—melting fastest of all.

Separate studies of air temperature in the tropics, made using 13
high-flying balloons, have shown a steady rise of about 15 feet a year
in the altitude at which air routinely stays below the freezing point.
Dr. Thompson said that other changes could also be contributing to
the glacial shrinkage, but the rising warm zone is probably the biggest
influence.

Trying to stay ahead of the widespread melting, Dr. Thompson and 14
a team of scientists have been hurriedly traveling around the tropics
to extract cores of ice from a variety of glaciers containing a record of
thousands of years of climate shifts. The data may help predict future
trends.

The four-inch-thick ice cylinders are being stored in a deep-frozen 15
archive at Ohio State, he said, so that as new technologies are developed
for reading chemical clues in bubbles and water in ancient ice, there will
still be something to examine.

The sad fact, he said, is that in a matter of years, anyone wanting 16
to study the glaciers of Africa or Peru will probably have to travel to
Columbus, Ohio, to do so.

Dr. Richard B. Alley, a professor of geosciences at Pennsylvania 17
State University, said the melting trend and the link—at least partly—to

human influence is "depressing," not only because of the loss of data but also because of the remarkable changes under way to such familiar landscapes.

18   "What is a snowcap worth to us?" he said. "I don't know about you, but I like the snows of Kilimanjaro."

THREATENED WATER SUPPLIES

19   The accelerating loss of mountain glaciers is also described in a scientific report on the impact of global warming, which [was] released in February 2001 in Geneva by the Intergovernmental Panel on Climate Change, an influential network of scientists advising world governments under the auspices of the United Nations. The melting is likely to threaten water supplies in places like Peru and Nepal, the report says, and could also lead to devastating flash floods.

20   Kilimanjaro, the highest point in Africa, may provide the most vivid image of the change in glaciers, but, Dr. Thompson said, the rate of retreat is far faster along the spine of the Andes, and the consequences more significant. For 25 years, he has been tracking a particular Peruvian glacier, Qori Kalis, where the pace of shrinkage has accelerated enormously just since 1998.

21   From 1998 to 2000, the glacier pulled back 508 feet a year, he said. "That's 33 times faster than the rate in the first measurement period," he said, referring to a study from 1963 to 1978.

22   In the short run, this means the hydroelectric dams and reservoirs downstream will be flush with water, he said, but in the long run the source will run dry.

23   "The whole country right now, for its hydropower, is cashing in on a bank account that was built up over thousands of years but isn't being replenished," he said.

24   Once that is gone, he added, chances are that the communities will have to turn to oil or coal for power, adding even more greenhouse gases to the air.

25   The changes in the character of Kilimanjaro are registering beyond the ranks of climate scientists. People in the tourism business around the mountain and surrounding national park are worried that visitors will no longer be drawn to the peak once it has lost its glimmering cap.

26   Dr. Douglas R. Hardy, a geologist at the University of Massachusetts, returned from Kilimanjaro in February 2001 with the first yearlong record of weather data collected by a probe placed near the summit.

27   Just before he left, he had a long conversation with the chief ranger of Kilimanjaro National Park, who expressed deep concern about the trend. "That mountain is the most mystical, magical draw to people's

imagination," Dr. Hardy said. "Once the ice disappears, it's going to be a very different place."

And the melting continues. When Dr. Hardy climbed the mountain 28 to retrieve the data, he discovered that the weather instruments, erected on a tall pole, had fallen over because the ice around the base was gone.

2001

QUESTIONS FOR DISCUSSION

Content

a. According to Revkin, how have humans hastened the melting of glaciers?
b. What has happened already and what will happen as a result of the glaciers melting?
c. What reasons does Revkin offer to explain why glaciers started to melt even before the twentieth century?
d. Who is Dr. Lonnie G. Thompson, and why is he a useful source for Revkin?
e. What other environmental changes are occurring along with melting glaciers, and what is implied by this?

Strategy and Style

f. How does Revkin support the claim made in the first sentence?
g. What is the ideal audience for this essay? Is Revkin writing more to people who would agree with him or to people who would disagree?
h. What statistics does Revkin use? How convincing are they?
i. Despite his reasonable tone, a reader can tell that Revkin is passionate about his topic. What phrases reveal his feelings?
j. Revkin twice refers to Hemingway's story "The Snows of Kilimanjaro" (paragraphs 3 and 18). What do these references add to the argument?

ENGAGING THE TEXT

a. Outline the arguments made by Revkin and by Philip Stott; compare the structures of the arguments. Use this prompt as a start for item *a* in Suggestions for Sustained Writing.
b. Find out what you can do personally about climate change, and write up a list of actions that you and classmates could follow. Meet with classmates to swap or critique ideas.

SUGGESTIONS FOR SUSTAINED WRITING

a. Begin with item *a* under Engaging the Text. Then write an analytical essay in which you explain why either Revkin's or Stott's essay is the stronger argument. Base your analysis on how well the argument is written, rather than on whether you agree with the author.
b. Write an essay in which you take a neutral stance and try to find a compromise solution that both Revkin and Stott would accept.
c. Look up the sources cited in Revkin's and Stott's essays, and write an essay in response to the two authors.

READ MORE

Revkin and His Works

"Andrew C. Revkin" (http://topics.nytimes.com/top/reference/timestopics/people/r/andrew_c_revkin/index.html): *Biography and links to his articles on the* New York Times *website.*

"Dot Earth" (http://dotearth.blogs.nytimes.com): *Revkin's* New York Times–*based blog on environmental issues.*

Global Warming from Revkin's Perspective

"Exploring Earth and Space with Supercomputers" (http://ct.gsfc.nasa.gov): *Website of the National Aeronautics and Space Administration's Computational Technologies Project.*

"Global Warming" (http://topics.nytimes.com/top/news/science/topics/globalwarming/index.html#): *The* New York Times *Science page on the topic of global warming, with links to articles and interactive maps.*

Cold Comfort for 'Global Warming'

Philip Stott

Philip Stott (b. 1943) is professor emeritus of biogeography at the University of London. A native of England, he studied civil engineering at Manchester University, earning B.S. and Master's degrees. He taught in Nigeria and South Africa for six years before returning to England. At the University of London, he was head of the department and dean of student admissions. An expert on ecology and biogeography, particularly of Thailand, Stott has published articles in many academic journals and was editor-in-chief of the Journal of Biogeography *from 1987 to 2004. He has lectured in numerous countries and is often a guest on television and radio talk shows, discussing his views on environmental issues such as global warming, energy policy, and biotechnology; he also hosts a blog,* EnvironSpin Watch. *He is featured in a 2007 BBC documentary,* The Great Global Warming Swindle. *Stott's books reflect his varied interests. He has published a textbook,* Historical Plant Geography; *books on the environment, including* Global Environmental Change *(with Peter D. Moore and Bill Chaloner, 1996) and* Political Ecology: Science, Myth and Power *(edited with Dr. Sian Sullivan, 2000); and books on Thailand, including* Royal Siamese Maps: War and Trade in Nineteenth Century Thailand *(with Santanee Phasuk, 2004). He has also written books of recorder music for children.*

"Cold Comfort for 'Global Warming'" was first published in The Wall Street Journal. *As you read, take note of how Stott builds his case by negating the opposing theories.*

Last week's dramatic demise of the Larsen B ice shelf in Antarctica 1 has been embraced by environmentalists and commentators who warn of human-induced "global warming." After all, the ice shelf was 200 meters thick, with a surface area three times the size of Hong Kong. Around 500 billion tons of ice collapsed in less than a month. How could President Bush ignore such evidence of our guilt with regard to climate change?

An ice shelf is a floating extension of the continental ice that covers 2 the landmass of Antarctica. Larsen B was one of five shelves that have been monitored by scientists. The U.S.-based National Snow and Ice Data Center described its break-up as "the largest single event in a series of retreats by ice shelves in the peninsula over the last 30 years."

One worry can be dismissed immediately: Having been a shelf—a 3 floating part of an ice sheet, rather than over land—it does not raise sea levels upon melting. Yet the collapse has proved to be a perfect natural disaster for the "Apocalypse Now" school of journalism. It is now perfectly clear that we are all doomed and that this is the wake-up call for urgent action on greenhouse gas emissions, automobiles, industry, and virtually everything else to do with economic growth.

Unfortunately, the story isn't quite so straightforward. Antarctica 4 illustrates the complexities behind understanding climate change, and it provides little support for a simplistic myth of human-induced "global warming." In fact this scare is reminiscent of a much-hyped New York Times story last year that "leads" of open water in ice fields near the North Pole filled cruise passengers with a "sense of alarm" about impending climate disasters. But icebreakers are always searching for "leads" to make their way through the ice, and after a long summer of 24-hour days it is not unusual to find them all over the place, especially after strong winds break up the winter ice. Sorry, the North Pole isn't disappearing—and neither is the South Pole.

5   Research on the West Antarctic Ice Sheet has shown precisely the opposite trend seen at Larsen B, namely that this ice sheet may be getting thicker, not thinner. Most scientists think that the sheet has probably been retreating, spasmodically, for around the last 10,000 years, but instead of the rate accelerating in recent years, it now appears to have halted its retreat. There is evidence that the ice sheet in the Ross Sea area is growing by as much as 26.8 gigatons per year, particularly on a part of the ice sheet known as Stream C.

6   This demonstrates the innate complexity of Antarctica as a continent. In reality, it has many "climates," and many geomorphological and glaciological regimes. It does not respond to change, whatever the direction, in a single, unitary fashion. Geomorphological and ecological trends are thus very difficult to interpret in a linear way.

7   One trend has been toward a colder climate. Over the last 50 years, the temperatures in the interior appear to have been falling. University of Illinois researchers have reported, in Nature, on temperature records covering a broad area of Antarctica. Their measurements show "a net cooling on the Antarctic continent between 1966 and 2000." Indeed, some regions, like the McMurdo Dry Valleys, the largest ice-free area, appear to have cooled between 1986 and 1999 by as much as two degrees centigrade per decade. As the researchers wryly comment, "Continental Antarctic cooling, especially the seasonality of cooling, poses challenges to models of climate and ecosystem change."

8   At the same time that parts of the continent are cooling, it's hardly surprising to see some ice melting. We are currently emerging—granted in a somewhat jerky fashion—out of the Little Ice Age that ended around 1880. It's to be expected that some parts of Antarctica like Larsen B are retreating. Yet we seem to be shocked at this perfectly natural event. When will we recognize the basic truth that change, both evolutionary and catastrophic, is the norm on our ever-restless planet?

9   Extreme environmentalists and sensationalist journalists pretend that every environmental event is of our own making. If only. We don't have that much control over Mother Nature. While we've been busy gabbing about global warming, the planet may be moving in the opposite direction.

10   Our current interglacial period is already 10,000 years old. No interglacial period during the last half-million years has persisted for more than 12,000 years. Most have had life spans of only 10,000 years or less. Statistically, therefore, we are due to slither into the next glacial period.

11   Despite a short-term rise in temperature of around 0.6 degrees centigrade over the last 150 years, the long-term temperature trend remains, overall, one of cooling. It may not be too long, therefore, before we see the ice spreading again. At worst, the emission of greenhouse gases is only

likely to produce a super interglacial period; at worst, withdrawing gases might help to speed the descent into the next glacial period. And what would you prefer, a warmer or a colder world?

2002

QUESTIONS FOR DISCUSSION

Content

a. What is Stott's basic argument?
b. What are the trends that support Stott's argument?
c. Stott claims that Earth's climate is too complex for simple theories to explain adequately. Where does he make this claim explicitly or implicitly?
d. According to Stott, why should we not worry about what we read in the news about climate change?
e. In your opinion, should decisions about climate change be made by politicians? What would Stott and Revkin say?

Strategy and Style

f. Stott's stand is in the minority on this issue, so how does he create a strong voice and convincing tone?
g. How does Stott use sources to discredit the theories that oppose his?
h. Where does Stott use definition as a way to strengthen his argument and deflect criticism?
i. What would you say is the reading level of this essay, and who is the target audience?
j. When Stott writes, "Sorry, the North Pole isn't disappearing" (paragraph 4), to whom is he saying "sorry"?

ENGAGING THE TEXT

a. Reread the essay and write a question in the margin or in a notebook for each paragraph. You can later use these questions in a class discussion or as the basis for a research paper by tracking down possible answers.
b. Take the side of Stott and make a case for why you personally should not worry about climate change.

SUGGESTIONS FOR SUSTAINED WRITING

a. Using an interactive map of the earth (many can be found with the Internet search term "interactive maps of the earth"), check out images of Mount Kilimanjaro, the North Pole, and Antarctica. Write a descriptive essay about what you notice. In addition, critique the websites you use to determine their bias.

b. With a classmate, research any controversial issue and write your essays in the point/counterpoint style of Revkin and Stott. As in researching any "hot" issue, be sure to avoid generalizing, by choosing a specific angle from which to argue and finding specific examples to illustrate your argument.

c. Look up one or more of the sources mentioned by Stott, and do some research to find out whether they are supported by others in the scientific and academic communities. Write an analytical report to your classmates to convince them that Stott's sources are, or are not, supported by independent studies.

READ MORE

Stott and His Works

"Parliament of Things" (http://parliamentofthings.info/index.html): *Philip Stott's personal website.*

"Simple Truth about Global Warming" (http://wordpress.com/tag/philip-stott): *A blog about Stott's message.*

Global Warming from Stott's Perspective

"Discuss Global Warming" (http://www.discussglobalwarming.com): *Website with links to articles and blogs.*

"The Great Global Warming Swindle" (http://www.greatglobalwarming swindle.com): *Website about the 2007 BBC documentary that featured Stott.*

PERSUASION

A Modest Proposal
Jonathan Swift

Jonathan Swift (1667–1745) was born in Dublin, Ireland; he studied at Trinity College, Dublin, and took an M.A. at Oxford. Ordained an Anglican priest, he was eventually made dean of St. Patrick's Cathedral in Dublin. He is remembered chiefly for his satires, the most famous of which are A Tale of a Tub *(1704), a vicious satire on government abuses in education and religion, and* Gulliver's Travels *(1726). From 1710 to 1714, Swift lived in London and edited* The Examiner, *a Tory publication. However, the political mood changed when Queen Anne died in 1714, and Swift returned to Ireland, where he became the dean of St. Patrick's Cathedral in Dublin, a post he held to the end of his life.*

"A Modest Proposal" is one of a series of satirical essays that exposed English cruelties in Ireland. It demonstrates Swift's keen sensitivity to the problems of the poor in his native country, as well as his ability to create satire that is both ironic and incisive.

It is a melancholy object to those who walk through this great town or travel in the country, when they see the streets, the roads, and cabin doors, crowded with beggars of the female sex, followed by three, four, or six children, all in rags and importuning every passenger for an alms. These mothers, instead of being able to work for their honest livelihood, are forced to employ all their time in strolling to beg sustenance for their helpless infants: Who as they grow up either turn thieves for want of work, or leave their dear native country to fight for the Pretender in Spain, or sell themselves to the Barbadoes. 1

I think it is agreed by all parties that this prodigious number of children in the arms, or on the backs, or at the heels of their mothers, and frequently of their fathers, is in the present deplorable state of the kingdom a very great additional grievance; and, therefore, whoever could find out a fair, cheap, and easy method of making these children sound, useful members of the commonwealth, would deserve so well of the public as to have his statue set up for a preserver of the nation. 2

But my intention is very far from being confined to provide only for the children of professed beggars; it is of a much greater extent, and shall take in the whole number of infants at a certain age who are born of parents in effect as little able to support them as those who demand our charity in the streets. 3

As to my own part, having turned my thoughts for many years upon this important subject, and maturely weighed the several schemes of our projectors, I have always found them grossly mistaken in their computation. It is true, a child just dropped from its dam may be supported by her milk for a solar year, with little other nourishment; at most not above the value of 2s., which the mother may certainly get, or the value in scraps, by her lawful occupation of begging; and it is exactly at one year old that I propose to provide for them in such a manner as instead of being a charge upon their parents or the parish, or wanting food and raiment for the rest of their lives, they shall on the contrary contribute to the feeding, and partly to the clothing, of many thousands. 4

There is likewise another great advantage in my scheme, that it will prevent those voluntary abortions, and that horrid practice of women 5 murdering their bastard children, alas! too frequent among us! sacrificing the poor innocent babes I doubt more to avoid the expense than the shame, which would move tears and pity in the most savage and inhuman breast.

6   The number of souls in this kingdom being usually reckoned one million and a half, of these I calculate there may be about 200,000 couples whose wives are breeders; from which number I subtract 30,000 couples who are able to maintain their own children (although I apprehend there cannot be so many, under the present distress of the kingdom); but this being granted, there will remain 170,000 breeders. I again subtract 50,000 for those women who miscarry, or whose children die by accident or disease within the year. There only remain 120,000 children of poor parents annually born. The question therefore is, how this number shall be reared and provided for? which, as I have already said, under the present situation of affairs, is utterly impossible by all the methods hitherto proposed. For we can neither employ them in handicraft or agriculture; we neither build houses (I mean live in the country) nor cultivate land; they can very seldom pick up a livelihood by stealing, till they arrive at six years old, except where they are of towardly parts; although I confess they learn the rudiments much earlier; during which time they can, however, be properly looked upon only as probationers; as I have been informed by a principal gentleman in the county of Cavan, who protested to me that he never knew above one or two instances under the age of six, even in a part of the kingdom so renowned for the quickest proficiency in that art.

7   I am assured by our merchants, that a boy or a girl before twelve years old is no saleable commodity; and even when they come to this age they will not yield above 3l. or 3l.2s. 6d. at most on the exchange; which cannot turn to account either to the parents or kingdom, the charge of nutriment and rags having been at least four times that value.

8   I shall now therefore humbly propose my own thoughts, which I hope will not be liable to the least objection.

9   I have been assured by a very knowing American of my acquaintance in London, that a young healthy child well nursed is at a year old a most delicious, nourishing, and wholesome food, whether stewed, roasted, baked, or broiled; and I make no doubt that it will equally serve in a fricassee or a ragout.

10   I do therefore humbly offer it to public consideration that of the 120,000 children already computed, 20,000 may be reserved for breed, whereof only one-fourth part to be males; which is more than we allow to sheep, black cattle, or swine; and my reason is, that these children are seldom the fruits of marriage, a circumstance not much regarded by our savages; therefore one male will be sufficient to serve four females. That the remaining 100,000 may, at a year old, be offered in sale to the persons

of quality and fortune through the kingdom; always advising the mother to let them suck plentifully in the last month, so as to render them plump and fat for a good table. A child will make two dishes at an entertainment for friends; and when the family dines alone, the fore or hind quarter will make a reasonable dish, and seasoned with a little pepper or salt will be very good boiled on the fourth day, especially in winter.

I have reckoned upon a medium that a child just born will weigh 12 pounds, and in a solar year, if tolerably nursed, will increase to 28 pounds. 11

I grant this food will be somewhat dear, and therefore very proper for landlords, who, as they have already devoured most of the parents, seem to have the best title to the children. 12

Infant's flesh will be in season throughout the year, but more plentiful in March, and a little before and after; for we are told by a grave author, an eminent French physician, that fish being a prolific diet, there are more children born in Roman Catholic countries about nine months after Lent than at any other season; therefore, reckoning a year after Lent, the markets will be more glutted than usual, because the number of popish infants is at least three to one in this kingdom: and therefore it will have one other collateral advantage, by lessening the number of papists among us. 13

I have already computed the charge of nursing a beggar's child (in which list I reckon all cottagers, laborers, and four-fifths of the farmers) to be about 2s. per annum, rags included; and I believe no gentleman would repine to give 10s. for the carcass of a good fat child, which, as I have said, will make four dishes of excellent nutritive meat, when he has only some particular friend or his own family to dine with him. Thus the squire will learn to be a good landlord, and grow popular among the tenants; the mother will have 8s. net profit, and be fit for work till she produces another child. 14

Those who are more thrifty (as I must confess the times require) may flay the carcass; the skin of which artificially dressed will make admirable gloves for ladies, and summer boots for fine gentlemen. 15

As to our city of Dublin, shambles may be appointed for this purpose in the most convenient parts of it, and butchers we may be assured will not be wanting: although I rather recommend buying the children alive, and dressing them hot from the knife as we do roasting pigs. 16

A very worthy person, a true lover of his country, and whose virtues I highly esteem, was lately pleased in discoursing on this matter to offer a refinement upon my scheme. He said that many gentlemen of this kingdom, having of late destroyed their deer, he conceived that the want of venison might be well supplied by the bodies of young lads and maidens, not exceeding fourteen years of age nor under twelve; so great a number of both sexes in every country being now ready to starve for want of work and service; and these to be disposed of by their parents, if 17 alive, or otherwise by their nearest relations. But with due deference to so excellent a friend and so deserving a patriot, I cannot be altogether in his sentiments; for as to the males, my American acquaintance assured me from frequent experience that their flesh was generally tough and lean, like that of our schoolboys by continual exercise, and their taste disagreeable; and to fatten them would not answer the charge. Then as to the females, it would, I think, with humble submission be a loss to the public, because they soon would become breeders themselves; and besides, it is not improbable that some scrupulous people might be apt to censure such a practice (although indeed very unjustly), as a little bordering upon cruelty; which, I confess, has always been with me the strongest objection against any project, how well so-ever intended.

18   But in order to justify my friend, he confessed that this expedient was put into his head by the famous Psalmanazar, a native of the island Formosa, who came from thence to London about twenty years ago: And in conversation told my friend, that in his country when any young person happened to be put to death, the executioner sold the carcass to persons of quality as a prime dainty; and that in his time the body of a plump girl of fifteen, who was crucified for an attempt to poison the emperor, was sold to his imperial majesty's prime minister of state, and other great mandarins of the court, in joints from the gibbet, at 400 crowns. Neither indeed can I deny, that if the same use were made of several plump young girls in this town, who without one single groat to their fortunes cannot stir without a chair, and appear at the playhouse and assemblies in foreign fineries which they never will pay for, the kingdom would not be the worse.

19   Some persons of a desponding spirit are in great concern about that vast number of poor people, who are aged, diseased, or maimed, and I have been desired to employ my thoughts what course may be taken to ease the nation of so grievous an encumbrance. But I am not in the least pain upon that matter, because it is very well known that they are every day dying and rotting by cold and famine, and filth and vermin, as fast as can be reasonably expected. And as to the young laborers, they are now in as hopeful a condition: they cannot get work, and consequently pine away for want of nourishment, to a degree that if at any time they are accidentally hired to common labor, they have not strength to perform it; and thus the country and themselves are happily delivered from the evils to come.

20   I have too long digressed, and therefore shall return to my subject. I think the advantages by the proposal which I have made are obvious and many, as well as of the highest importance.

21   For first, as I have already observed, it would greatly lessen the number of papists, with whom we are yearly overrun, being the principal breeders of the nation as well as our most dangerous enemies; and who stay at home on purpose to deliver the kingdom to the Pretender, hoping

to take their advantage by the absence of so many good Protestants, who have chosen rather to leave their country than stay at home and pay tithes against their conscience to an Episcopal curate.

Secondly, the poor tenants will have something valuable of their own, which by law may be made liable to distress and help to pay their landlord's rent, their corn and cattle being already seized, and money a thing unknown. 22

Thirdly, whereas the maintenance of 100,000 children from two years old and upward, cannot be computed at less than 10s. apiece per annum, the nation's stock will be thereby increased £50,000 per annum, beside the profit of a new dish introduced to the tables of all gentlemen of fortune in the kingdom who have any refinement in taste. And the money will circulate among ourselves, the goods being entirely of our own growth and manufacture. 23

Fourthly, the constant breeders beside the gain of 8s. sterling per annum by the sale of their children, will be rid of the charge of maintaining them after the first year. 24

Fifthly, this food would likewise bring great custom to taverns, where the vintners will certainly be so prudent as to procure the best recipes for dressing it to perfection, and consequently have their houses frequented by all the fine gentlemen, who justly value themselves upon their knowledge in good eating; and a skilful cook who understands how to oblige his guests, will contrive to make it as expensive as they please. 25

Sixthly, this would be a great inducement to marriage, which all wise nations have either encouraged by rewards or enforced by laws and penalties. It would increase the care and tenderness of mothers toward their children, when they were sure of a settlement for life to the poor babes, provided in some sort by the public, to their annual profit instead of expense. We should see an honest emulation among the married women, which of them would bring the fattest child to the market. Men would become as fond of their wives during the time of their pregnancy as they are now of their mares in foal, their cows in calf, their sows when they are ready to farrow; nor offer to beat or kick them (as is too frequent a practice) for fear of a miscarriage. 26

Many other advantages might be enumerated. For instance, the addition of some thousand carcasses in our exportation of barreled beef, the propagation of swine's flesh, and improvement in the art of making good bacon, so much wanted among us by the great destruction of pigs, too frequent at our table; which are no way comparable in taste or magnificence to a well-grown, fat, yearling child, which roasted whole will make a considerable figure at a lord mayor's feast or any other public entertainment. But this and many others I omit, being studious of brevity. 27

Supposing that 1,000 families in this city would be constant customers for infants' flesh, besides others who might have it at merry-meetings, 28 particularly at weddings and christenings, I compute that Dublin would take off annually about 20,000 carcasses; and the rest of the kingdom (where probably they will be sold somewhat cheaper) the remaining 80,000.

29   I can think of no one objection that will possibly be raised against this proposal, unless it should be urged that the number of people will be thereby much lessened in the kingdom. This I freely own, and it was indeed one principal design in offering it to the world. I desire the reader will observe, that I calculate my remedy for this one individual kingdom of Ireland and for no other than ever was, is, or I think ever can be upon Earth. Therefore let no man talk to me of other expedients: Of taxing our absentees at 5s. a pound: Of using neither clothes nor household furniture except what is of our own growth and manufacture: Of utterly rejecting the materials and instruments that promote foreign luxury: Of curing the expensiveness of pride, vanity, idleness, and gaming in our women: Of introducing a vein of parsimony, prudence, and temperance: Of learning to love our country, in the want of which we differ even from Laplander and the inhabitants of Topinamboo: Of quitting our animosities and factions, nor acting any longer like the Jews, who were murdering one another at the very moment their city was taken: Of being a little cautious not to sell our country and conscience for nothing: Of teaching landlords to have at least one degree of mercy toward their tenants: Lastly, of putting a spirit of honesty, industry, and skill into our shopkeepers; who, if a resolution could now be taken to buy only our native goods, would immediately unite to cheat and exact upon us in the price, the measure, and the goodness, nor could ever yet be brought to make one fair proposal of just dealing, though often and earnestly invited to it.

30   Therefore I repeat, let no man talk to me of these and the like expedients, till he has at least some glimpse of hope that there will be ever some hearty and sincere attempt to put them in practice.

31   But as to myself, having been wearied out for many years with offering vain, idle, visionary thoughts, and at length utterly despairing of success, I fortunately fell upon this proposal; which, as it is wholly new, so it has something solid and real, of no expense and little trouble, full in our own power, and whereby we can incur no danger in disobliging England. For this kind of commodity will not bear exportation, the flesh being of too tender a consistence to admit a long continuance in salt, although perhaps I could name a country which would be glad to eat up our whole nation without it.

32   After all, I am not so violently bent upon my own opinion as to reject any offer proposed by wise men, which shall be found equally innocent, cheap, easy, and effectual. But before something of that kind shall be advanced in contradiction to my scheme, and offering a better, I desire the author or authors will be pleased maturely to consider two points. First, as things now stand, how they will be able to find food and raiment for 100,000 useless mouths and backs. And secondly, there being a round

million of creatures in human figure throughout this kingdom, whose subsistence put into a common stock would leave them in debt 2,000,000*l.* sterling, adding those who are beggars by profession to the bulk of farmers, cottagers, and laborers, with the wives and children who are beggars in effect; I desire those politicians who dislike my overture, and may perhaps be so bold as to attempt an answer, that they will first ask the parents of these mortals, whether they would not at this day think it a great happiness to have been sold for food at a year old in the manner I prescribe, and thereby have avoided such a perpetual scene of misfortunes as they have since gone through by the oppression of landlords, the impossibility of paying rent without money or trade, the want of common sustenance, with neither house nor clothes to cover them from the inclemencies of the weather, and the most inevitable prospect of entailing the like or greater miseries upon their breed for ever.

I profess, in the sincerity of my heart, that I have not the least personal interest in endeavoring to promote this necessary work, having no other motive than the public good of my country, by advancing our trade, providing for infants, relieving the poor, and giving some pleasure to the rich. I have no children by which I can propose to get a single penny; the youngest being nine years old, and my wife past childbearing.

1714

QUESTIONS FOR DISCUSSION

Content

a. Just what is Swift proposing? What is his purpose in making this seemingly absurd proposal?
b. At which point in the essay do you begin to suspect that Swift is being satirical?
c. Indirectly, "A Modest Proposal" provides a clear indication of Swift's attitudes toward the poor and the ruling classes. Recalling information from the text, explain his attitude toward each of these segments of society.
d. Swift makes a number of allusions to the politics and history of his time. Consult an encyclopedia or other appropriate reference work in your college library to learn a bit about the history of Ireland during the early 1700s. In particular, make sure you understand the following:

The Pretender	Episcopal curate
Papists	Psalmanazar
Roman Catholic countries	Mandarins
cottagers	tenants

e. Near the end of the essay, we come upon a list of "expedients." Although the speaker claims otherwise, they represent the kinds of solutions to Ireland's problems in which Swift actually believes. What are these solutions? Why does Swift wait until late in his essay to mention them? Why does he mention them at all?

Strategy and Style

f. Swift the speaker in "A Modest Proposal" is quite different from Swift the author. Describe the speaker. What function does Swift's use of a persona serve?

g. Swift's mention of Psalmanazar serves a particularly ironic purpose. What is it?

h. Swift's solutions to Ireland's problems, though ironic, are explained in a no-nonsense, businesslike tone. Point to specific passages in which this tone is most apparent.

i. Swift's irony is especially biting when he says, "I grant this food will be somewhat dear, and therefore very proper for landlords, who, as they have already devoured most of the parents, seem to have the best title to the children" (paragraph 12). What other passages reveal his anger toward the ruling class?

ENGAGING THE TEXT

a. How did you respond on an emotional level when you read this essay? Write a response in which you describe your "gut reaction" to "A Modest Proposal."

b. Write a paragraph response to this essay from the point of view of one of the poor of Ireland; then write a paragraph from the point of view of a member of the ruling class. Compare the two responses.

SUGGESTIONS FOR SUSTAINED WRITING

a. One of Swift's real solutions to Ireland's problems is that its inhabitants use "neither clothes nor household furniture except what is of [their] own growth and manufacture" (paragraph 29). This seems to be the same idea behind the "Buy American" movement. Do you believe that buying only goods manufactured at home would improve our economy? Explain.

b. Like Swift, approach a serious subject in tongue-in-cheek fashion and write your own "modest proposal." For instance, discuss a controversial government policy and, while pretending to defend it, describe those aspects of it that you find most offensive. Or you might simply try to convince your classmates that there really are "advantages" to becoming a chain smoker, to walking into class unprepared day after day, or to cramming for exams rather than studying for them systematically. You can also use one of the societal problems described in any of the following essays: Jo Goodwin Parker's "What Is Poverty?" (Chapter 4), Bailey White's "Forbidden Things" (Chapter 7), Barbara Dafoe Whitehead's "Where Have All the Parents Gone?" (Chapter 8), Lars Eighner's "On Dumpster Diving" (Chapter 11), or any of the essays in Chapter 10. Write a proposal, either "modest" or realistic, to solve the problem.

c. One aspect of Swift's proposal focuses on the relationship between tenants and landlords. This is still an important issue. Using information you find in the library or on the Internet, write an essay that argues for the enactment of

- Laws that keep rents at reasonable levels and protect tenants from unscrupulous landlords.

- Laws that help landlords make a fair profit and protect their properties from irresponsible tenants.

READ MORE

Swift and His Works

Hunting, Robert. *Jonathan Swift.* New York: Twayne, 1967.

"Jonathan Swift" (http://dmoz.org/Arts/Literature/Authors/S/Swift, _Jonathan): *Information about Swift at The Open Directory.*

Tenant Rights

Shore, Cris, and Susan Wright. *Anthropology of Policy: Critical Perspectives on Governance and Power.* London: Routledge, 1997.

Donnelly, James S. *The Great Irish Potato Famine.* Phoenix Mill, UK: Sutton Publishing, 2001.

"The National Landlord Tenant Guides" (http://www.rentlaw.com): *Information about laws and current issues.*

I Have a Dream

Martin Luther King, Jr.

Martin Luther King, Jr. (1929–1968) had at first planned to become a doctor or a lawyer, but when he graduated from Morehouse College in Atlanta at the age of 19, he abandoned these ambitions and went into the seminary. After seminary, he went to Boston University, where he received his Ph.D. in 1955. He was ordained as a Baptist minister in his father's church, the Ebenezer Baptist Church in Atlanta, a church he co-pastored with his father from 1960 to 1968. He was also founder and director of the Southern Christian Leadership

Conference from 1957 to 1968 and a member of the Montgomery Improvement Association, an activist group protesting racial segregation. Inspired by Mahatma Gandhi's principles of nonviolent protest, King led this group in several demonstrations. In May of 1963, he was arrested and imprisoned in Birmingham for demonstrating against segregation in hotels and restaurants. In jail, he wrote his famous "Letter from Birmingham Jail," a work that was published in 1963 and expanded and republished in 1968. King received numerous awards for his work for human rights, including the Nobel Prize for Peace in 1964.

The speech "I Have a Dream" was given to more than 200,000 people at the 1963 March on Washington. A little more than a year later, King said in his Nobel Prize acceptance speech, "Sooner or later all the people of the world will have to discover a way to live together in peace, and thereby transform this pending cosmic elegy into a creative psalm of brotherhood. If this is to be achieved, man must evolve for all human conflict a method which rejects revenge, aggression and retaliation. The foundation of such a method is love." On April 4, 1968, while talking with other human rights activists on a motel balcony in Memphis, King was assassinated.

1 Five score years ago, a great American, in whose symbolic shadow we stand, signed the Emancipation Proclamation. This momentous decree came as a great beacon light of hope to millions of Negro slaves who had been seared in the flames of withering injustice. It came as a joyous daybreak to end the long night of captivity.

2 But one hundred years later, we must face the tragic fact that the Negro is still not free. One hundred years later, the life of the Negro is still sadly crippled by the manacles of segregation and the chains of discrimination. One hundred years later, the Negro lives on a lonely island of poverty in the midst of a vast ocean of material prosperity. One hundred years later, the Negro is still languishing in the corners of American society and finds himself an exile in his own land. So we have come here today to dramatize an appalling condition.

3 In a sense we have come to our nation's capital to cash a check. When the architects of our republic wrote the magnificent words of the Constitution and the Declaration of Independence, they were signing a promissory note to which every American was to fall heir. This note was a promise that all men would be guaranteed the unalienable rights of life, liberty, and the pursuit of happiness.

4 It is obvious today that America has defaulted on this promissory note insofar as her citizens of color are concerned. Instead of honoring this sacred obligation, America has given the Negro people a bad check; a check which has come back marked "insufficient funds." But we refuse to believe that the bank of justice is bankrupt. We refuse to believe that there are insufficient funds in the great vaults of opportunity of this nation. So we have come to cash this check—a check that will give us upon demand the riches of freedom and the security of justice. We have also come to this hallowed spot to remind America of the fierce urgency of *now*. This is no time to engage in the luxury of cooling off or to take the tranquilizing drugs of gradualism. *Now* is the time to make real the promises of Democracy.

Now is the time to rise from the dark and desolate valley of segregation to the sunlit path of racial justice. *Now* is the time to open the doors of opportunity to all of God's children. *Now* is the time to lift our nation from the quicksands of racial injustice to the solid rock of brotherhood.

It would be fatal for the nation to overlook the urgency of the moment 5 and to underestimate the determination of the Negro. This sweltering summer of the Negro's legitimate discontent will not pass until there is an invigorating autumn of freedom and equality. 1963 is not an end, but a beginning. Those who hope that the Negro needed to blow off steam and will now be content will have a rude awakening if the nation returns to business as usual. There will be neither rest nor tranquility in America until the Negro is granted his citizenship rights. The whirlwinds of revolt will continue to shake the foundations of our nation until the bright day of justice emerges.

But there is something that I must say to my people who stand on the 6 warm threshold which leads into the palace of justice. In the process of gaining our rightful place we must not be guilty of wrongful deeds. Let us not seek to satisfy our thirst for freedom by drinking from the cup of bitterness and hatred. We must forever conduct our struggle on the high plane of dignity and discipline. We must not allow our creative protest to degenerate into physical violence. Again and again we must rise to the majestic heights of meeting physical force with soul force. The marvelous new militancy which has engulfed the Negro community must not lead us to a distrust of all white people, for many of our white brothers, as evidenced by their presence here today, have come to realize that their destiny is tied up with our destiny and their freedom is inextricably bound to our freedom. We cannot walk alone.

And as we walk, we must make the pledge that we shall march ahead. 7 We cannot turn back. There are those who are asking the devotees of civil rights, "When will you be satisfied?" We can never be satisfied as long as the Negro is the victim of the unspeakable horrors of police brutality. We can never be satisfied as long as our bodies, heavy with the fatigue of travel, cannot gain lodging in the motels of the highways and the hotels of the cities. We cannot be satisfied as long as the Negro's basic mobility is from a smaller ghetto to a larger one. We can never be satisfied as long as a Negro in Mississippi cannot vote and a Negro in New York believes he has nothing for which to vote. No, no, we are not satisfied, and we will not be satisfied until justice rolls down like waters and righteousness like a mighty stream.

I am not unmindful that some of you have come here out of great tri- 8 als and tribulations. Some of you have come fresh from narrow jail cells. Some of you have come from areas where your quest for freedom left you battered by the storms of persecution and staggered by the winds of police brutality. You have been the veterans of creative suffering. Continue to work with the faith that unearned suffering is redemptive.

Go back to Mississippi, go back to Alabama, go back to South 9 Carolina, go back to Georgia, go back to Louisiana, go back to the slums and ghettos of our northern cities, knowing that somehow this situation can and will be changed. Let us not wallow in the valley of despair.

10   I say to you today, my friends, that in spite of the difficulties and frustrations of the moment I still have a dream. It is a dream deeply rooted in the American dream.

11   I have a dream that one day this nation will rise up and live out the true meaning of its creed: "We hold these truths to be self-evident; that all men are created equal."

12   I have a dream that one day on the red hills of Georgia the sons of former slaves and the sons of former slaveowners will be able to sit down together at the table of brotherhood.

13   I have a dream that one day even the state of Mississippi, a desert state sweltering with the heat of injustice and oppression, will be transformed into an oasis of freedom and justice.

14   I have a dream that my four little children will one day live in a nation where they will not be judged by the color of their skin but by the content of their character.

15   I have a dream today.

16   I have a dream that one day the state of Alabama, whose governor's lips are presently dripping with the words of interposition and nullification, will be transformed into a situation where little black boys and black girls will be able to join hands with little white boys and white girls and walk together as sisters and brothers.

17   I have a dream today.

18   I have a dream that one day every valley shall be exalted, every hill and mountain shall be made low, the rough places will be made plain, and the crooked places will be made straight, and the glory of the Lord shall be revealed, and all flesh shall see it together.

19   This is our hope. This is the faith with which I return to the South. With this faith we will be able to hew out of the mountain of despair a stone of hope. With this faith we will be able to transform the jangling discords of our nation into a beautiful symphony of brotherhood. With this faith we will be able to work together, to pray together, to struggle together, to go to jail together, to stand up for freedom together, knowing that we will be free one day.

20   This will be the day when all of God's children will be able to sing with new meaning

> My country, 'tis of thee,
> Sweet land of liberty,
> Of thee I sing:
> Land where my fathers died,
> Land of the pilgrims' pride,
> From every mountain-side
> Let freedom ring.

And if America is to be a great nation this must become true. So let   21
freedom ring from the prodigious hilltops of New Hampshire. Let freedom ring from the mighty mountains of New York. Let freedom ring from
the heightening Alleghenies of Pennsylvania!

Let freedom ring from the snowcapped Rockies of Colorado!   22
Let freedom ring from the curvaceous peaks of California!   23
But not only that; let freedom ring from Stone Mountain of Georgia!   24
Let freedom ring from Lookout Mountain of Tennessee!   25
Let freedom ring from every hill and molehill of Mississippi.   26
    From every mountainside, let freedom ring.

When we let freedom ring, when we let it ring from every village and   27
every hamlet, from every state and every city, we will be able to speed up
that day when all of God's children, black men and white men, Jews and
Gentiles, Protestants and Catholics, will be able to join hands and sing in
the words of the old Negro spiritual, "Free at last! free at last! thank God
almighty, we are free at last!"

1963

QUESTIONS FOR DISCUSSION

Content

a. What does King hope to evoke in his audience by mentioning various
historical documents (the Emancipation Proclamation, the Declaration
of Independence, the Constitution)?

b. King makes it a point to address issues that are of particular interest
to white listeners and readers. What might have been his reasons for
doing this?

c. Why might King have decided to quote all of the first seven lines of
"My Country 'Tis of Thee"? Why did he not stop at "Of thee I sing"?

d. What effect does King create when he makes reference to specific
places, events, and public figures?

e. King makes reference to the Bible and to the faith that has sustained
him throughout his struggle for civil rights. What effect is created with
such references?

Strategy and Style

f. King's speech is especially moving because he succeeds in creating
emphasis through parallelism. Find a few examples of this technique.

g. What does King mean when he says, "America has given the Negro
people a bad check" (paragraph 4)? Identify other metaphors that he
uses and explain why they are effective.

h. Why does King use the term *marvelous* to describe the "new militancy which has engulfed the Negro community" (paragraph 6)?
i. How would you describe King's tone? Controlled? Angry? Impassioned?

ENGAGING THE TEXT

a. Choose one of the metaphors that King uses in this essay, the metaphor that strikes you as most or least effective. Explain why you chose the metaphor and what makes it effective or ineffective.
b. What is King's dream? Summarize it in a paragraph.

SUGGESTIONS FOR SUSTAINED WRITING

a. Do you have a "dream" that in the future some social or political injustice will be eliminated, that a cure will be found for a disease, that war and famine will cease? Describe your "dream" and propose ways in which to make it a reality.
b. Has King's dream of equality and opportunity for African-Americans been fulfilled in the decades since he spoke at the Lincoln Memorial? Has the situation of black Americans changed, or not changed, since King gave this speech? Explain by using as much specific detail as possible. Bring in comments from Maya Angelou's "Grandmother's Victory" (Chapter 1), Malcolm X's "Coming to an Awareness of Language" (Chapter 1), Gloria Naylor's "Meanings of a Word" (Chapter 4), or Brent Staples's "Black Men and Public Space" (Chapter 7).
c. In your college library, read several newspaper or magazine articles that chronicle the events leading up to King's address at the Lincoln Memorial. Summarize these events, and try to comment on their significance to the Civil Rights movement of the 1960s. Be certain to footnote or in some way cite the authorship of material you quote or paraphrase.

READ MORE

King, Jr. and His Works

"The Martin Luther King, Jr. Papers Project" (http://mlk-kpp01.stanford.edu/): *One of many dependable sites about Martin Luther King, Jr., with biographical information and texts of his writings and speeches.*

Oates, Stephen B. *Let the Trumpet Sound: The Life of Martin Luther King, Jr.* New York: Harper & Row, 1982.

The Civil Rights Movement

"National Civil Rights Museum" (http://www.civilrightsmuseum.org/home.htm): *Website of this museum, housed at the Lorraine Motel in Memphis, Tennessee.*

Young, Andrew. *An Easy Burden: The Civil Rights Movement and the Transformation of America.* New York: HarperCollins, 1996.

To Any Would-Be Terrorists

Naomi Shihab Nye

Naomi Shihab Nye (b. 1952) was born in St. Louis, Missouri, to an American mother and a Palestinian father. She received a B.A. from Trinity College, Texas. She is primarily known as a poet and has traveled to several states in the United States, teaching writing and poetry in schools. She also has traveled to the Middle East and Asia promoting cultural understanding. Her several volumes of poetry include Hugging the Jukebox *(1982),* Red Suitcase *(1994),* 19 Varieties of Gazelle: Poems of the Middle East *(2002), and* Honeybee: Poems and Short Prose *(2008). She has also written for children, including fiction such as* Habibi *(1997) and poetry such as* Come with Me *(2000) and* There Is No Long Distance Now *(2012). A nonfiction book,* I'll Ask You Three Times, Are You OK?: Tales of Driving and Being Driven *(2007), recounts anecdotes of short trips in vehicles. Nye has won several awards for her writing, including three Pushcart Prizes and an Arab American Book Award, for* Honeybee; *in 2009, she was named a peace hero by PeaceByPeace. An outstanding performer, she has produced recordings of her original songs and poems, as well as performing her work throughout the country.*

Nye wrote the following piece as a response to the September 11 attacks, and it has been circulated on the Internet since then. Of her work in general, Nye says, "For me, the primary source of poetry has always been local life, random characters met on the streets, our own ancestry sifting down to us through small essential daily tasks."

I am sorry I have to call you that, but I don't know how else to get your attention. I hate that word. Do you know how hard some of us have worked to get rid of that word, to deny its instant connection to the Middle East? And now look. Look what extra work we have. Not only did your colleagues kill thousands of innocent, international people in those buildings and scar their families forever, they wounded a huge community of people in the Middle East, in the United States, and all over the world. If that's what they wanted to do, please know the mission was a terrible success, and you can stop now.

Because I feel a little closer to you than many Americans could possibly feel, or ever want to feel, I insist that you listen to me. Sit down and listen. I know what kinds of foods you like. I would feed them to you if you were right here, because it is very very important that you listen. I am humble in my country's pain and I am furious.

3   My Palestinian father became a refugee in 1948. He came to the United States as a college student. He is 74 years old now and still homesick. He has planted fig trees. He has invited all the Ethiopians in his neighborhood to fill their little paper sacks with his figs. He has written columns and stories saying the Arabs are not terrorists, he has worked all his life to defy that word. Arabs are businessmen and students and kind neighbors. There is no one like him and there are thousands like him—gentle Arab daddies who make everyone laugh around the dinner table, who have a hard time with headlines, who stand outside in the evenings with their hands in their pockets staring toward the far horizon.

4   I am sorry if you did not have a father like that. I wish everyone could have a father like that.

5   My hard-working American mother has spent 50 years trying to convince her fellow teachers and choir mates not to believe stereotypes about the Middle East. She always told them, there is a much larger story. If you knew the story, you would not jump to conclusions from what you see in the news. But now look at the news. What a mess has been made. Sometimes I wish everyone could have parents from different countries or ethnic groups so they would be forced to cross boundaries, to believe in mixtures, every day of their lives. Because this is what the world calls us to do. WAKE UP!

6   The Palestinian grocer in my Mexican-American neighborhood paints pictures of the Palestinian flag on his empty cartons. He paints trees and rivers. He gives his paintings away. He says, "Don't insult me" when I try to pay him for a lemonade. Arabs have always been famous for their generosity. Remember? My half-Arab brother with an Arabic name looks more like an Arab than many full-blooded Arabs do and he has to fly every week.

7   My Palestinian cousins in Texas have beautiful brown little boys. Many of them haven't gone to school yet. And now they have this heavy word to carry in their backpacks along with the weight of their papers and books. I repeat, the mission was a terrible success. But it was also a complete, total tragedy and I want you to think about a few things.

8   **1.** Many people, thousands of people, perhaps even millions of people, in the United States are very aware of the long unfairness of our country's policies regarding Israel and Palestine. We talk about this all the time. It exhausts us and we keep talking. We write letters to newspapers, to politicians, to each other. We speak out in public even when it is uncomfortable to do so, because that is our responsibility. Many of these people aren't even Arabs. Many happen to be Jews who are equally troubled by the inequity. I promise you this is true. Because I am Arab-American, people always express these views to me and I am

amazed how many understand the intricate situation and have strong, caring feelings for Arabs and Palestinians even when they don't have to. Think of them, please: All those people who have been standing up for Arabs when they didn't have to. But as ordinary citizens we don't run the government and don't get to make all our government's policies, which makes us sad sometimes. We believe in the power of the word and we keep using it, even when it seems no one large enough is listening. That is one of the best things about this country: the free power of free words. Maybe we take it for granted too much. Many of the people killed in the World Trade Center probably believed in a free Palestine and were probably talking about it all the time.

But this tragedy could never help the Palestinians. Somehow, miracu- 9 lously, if other people won't help them more, they are going to have to help themselves. And it will be peace, not violence, that fixes things. You could ask any one of the kids in the Seeds of Peace organization and they would tell you that. Do you ever talk to kids? Please, please, talk to more kids.

2. Have you noticed how many roads there are? Sure you have. You 10 must check out maps and highways and small alternate routes just like anyone else. There is no way everyone on earth could travel on the same road, or believe in exactly the same religion. It would be too crowded, it would be dumb. I don't believe you want us all to be Muslims. My Palestinian grandmother lived to be 106 years old, and did not read or write, but even she was much smarter than that. The only place she ever went beyond Palestine and Jordan was to Mecca, by bus, and she was very proud to be called a Hajji and to wear white clothes afterward. She worked very hard to get stains out of everyone's dresses—scrubbing them with a stone. I think she would consider the recent tragedies a terrible stain on her religion and her whole part of the world. She would weep. She was scared of airplanes anyway. She wanted people to worship God in whatever ways they felt comfortable. Just worship. Just remember God in every single day and doing. It didn't matter what they called it. When people asked her how she felt about the peace talks that were happening right before she died, she puffed up like a proud little bird and said, in Arabic, "I never lost my peace inside." To her, Islam was a welcoming religion. After her home in Jerusalem was stolen from her, she lived in a small village that contained a Christian shrine. She felt very tender toward the people who would visit it. A Jewish professor tracked me down a few years ago in Jerusalem to tell me she changed his life after he went to her village to do an oral history project on Arabs. "Don't think she only mattered to you!" he said. "She gave me a whole different reality to imagine—yet it was amazing how close we became. Arabs could never be just a 'project' after that."

Did you have a grandmother or two? Mine never wanted people 11 to be pushed around. What did yours want? Reading about Islam since my grandmother died, I note the "tolerance" that was "typical of Islam" even in the old days. The Muslim leader Khalid ibn al-Walid signed a Jerusalem treaty which declared, "In the name of God, you have complete security for your churches which shall not be occupied by the Muslims or destroyed." It is the new millennium in which we should be even smarter than we used to be, right? But I think we have fallen behind.

12   **3. Many Americans do not want to kill any more innocent people** anywhere in the world. We are extremely worried about military actions killing innocent people. We didn't like this in Iraq, we never liked it anywhere. We would like no more violence, from us as well as from you. HEAR US! We would like to stop the terrifying wheel of violence, just stop it, right on the road, and find something more creative to do to fix these huge problems we have. Violence is not creative, it is stupid and scary and many of us hate all those terrible movies and TV shows made in our own country that try to pretend otherwise. Don't watch them. Everyone should stop watching them. An appetite for explosive sounds and toppling buildings is not a healthy thing for anyone in any country. The USA should apologize to the whole world for sending this trash out into the air and for paying people to make it.

13   But here's something good you may not know—one of the bestselling books of poetry in the United States in recent years is the Coleman Barks translation of Rumi, a mystical Sufi poet of the 13th century, and Sufism is Islam and doesn't that make you glad?

14   Everyone is talking about the suffering that ethnic Americans are going through. Many will no doubt go through more of it, but I would like to thank everyone who has sent me a consolation card. Americans are usually very kind people. Didn't your colleagues find that out during their time living here? It is hard to imagine they missed it. How could they do what they did, knowing that?

15   **4. We will all die soon enough.** Why not take the short time we have on this delicate planet and figure out some really interesting things we might do together? I promise you, God would be happier. So many people are always trying to speak for God—I know it is a very dangerous thing to do. I tried my whole life not to do it. But this one time is an exception. Because there are so many people crying and scarred and confused and complicated and exhausted right now—it is as if we have all had a giant simultaneous breakdown. I beg you, as your distant Arab cousin, as your American neighbor, listen to me. Our hearts are broken, as yours may also feel broken in some ways we can't understand, unless you tell us in words. Killing people won't tell us. We can't read that message. Find another way to live. Don't expect others to be like you. Read Rumi. Read Arabic poetry. Poetry humanizes us in a way that news, or even religion, has a harder time doing. A great Arab scholar, Dr. Salma Jayyusi, said, "If we read one another, we won't kill one another." Read American poetry. Plant mint. Find

a friend who is so different from you, you can't believe how much you have in common. Love them. Let them love you. Surprise people in gentle ways, as friends do. The rest of us will try harder too. Make our family proud.

2001

QUESTIONS FOR DISCUSSION

Content

a. What is Nye trying to persuade you to do, say, or feel? How successful is she?
b. "And it will be peace, not violence, that fixes things," Nye writes in paragraph 9. Do you agree? Or do you think that Nye is naïve—that some situations can be fixed only with violence?
c. What does Nye dislike about American movies and television? Why might she have singled out American movies and television and not focused on European or Asian films?
d. What is the image of her grandmother that Nye creates? Is her grandmother meant to represent all grandmothers? If so, at what point in one's life does a person take on a grandmother's view toward the world?
e. In paragraph 14, Nye asks about the terrorists who planned the attacks: "It is hard to imagine they missed [that Americans are kind people]. How could they do what they did, knowing that?" Although this is a rhetorical question, how might it be answered?

Strategy and Style

f. What makes this a persuasion rather than an argument?
g. Nye addresses this letter to "you," and we assume that the "you" is "would-be terrorists." However, are would-be terrorists Nye's real audience? Whom else is she addressing?
h. How persuasive would this essay be to actual would-be terrorists?
i. Is numbering her points an effective technique? Why or why not?
j. Nye will often drop in a surprising image in one sentence, then explain it in the following sentence, using the image to create a metaphor for a broader concept. For example, she mentions that her father plants fig trees in the fourth sentence of paragraph 3 and then elaborates on it in the fifth sentence; the fig tree is a metaphor for cultural understanding. Find other uses of this technique in the essay. How effective is this poetic technique?

k. Nye implies a cause/effect relationship between violent entertainment and violent behavior (paragraph 12). What other implicit cause/effect relationships can you find in the essay? Do you agree with her?

ENGAGING THE TEXT

a. Describe your first, "gut" reactions to this essay. How did it affect you as you read it?
b. Imagine Nye wrote this letter as an argument. Summarize her implicit argument, and point out flaws in her reasoning. What would she have to do to make this an airtight argument?

SUGGESTIONS FOR SUSTAINED WRITING

a. Write your own narrative of September 11, 2001. What was your story of that day?
b. Compare Nye's essay to Malcolm X's "Coming to an Awareness of Language" (Chapter 1), Martin Luther King, Jr.'s "I Have a Dream" (Chapter 10), or John Stuart Mill's "On Liberty" (Chapter 10). Write an essay in which you compare or contrast the authors' attitudes about peace and freedom.
c. Become more informed about the situation in the Middle East and write a report to explain one cause of one problem. Depending on your prior knowledge or the time available to do this assignment, extend your report to propose a solution. Alternatively, look up the Seeds of Peace organization, and report to your classmates about its history and one of its programs.

READ MORE

Nye and Her Works

"Naomi Shihab Nye" (http://www.poets.org): *Biographical information and links to Nye's poetry.*

"Naomi Shihab Nye: Poet and Author" (http://imeu.net/news/article 005786.shtml): *Profile of Nye on the Institute for Middle East Understanding website.*

"Peace Hero Naomi Shihab Nye" (http://www.peacebypeace.com/ heroes/view/id/89): *Bio of Nye and links to related sites.*

Middle East Issues

Hasan, Asma Gull. *American Muslims: The New Generation.* New York: Continuum, 2000.

"Islam and Islamic Studies Resources" (http://www.uga.edu/islam): *An Islamic studies website created and maintained by the University of Georgia.*

Why I Want a Wife

Judy Brady

Born in San Francisco, Judy Brady (b. 1937) took her B.F.A. in 1962 at the University of Iowa. She is a freelance writer, publishing articles on abortion, education, and women's issues. Brady has worked to support the principles of feminism and of the other contemporary political and social movements to which she is committed, including Greenaction, an organization that fights for environmental justice, and the Women's Cancer Resource Center.

This essay, which has been anthologized many times, was first published in Ms. *magazine's inaugural issue in 1971. A follow-up essay, "Why I Still Want a Wife," was published in* Ms. *in the July/August 1990 issue.*

I belong to that classification of people known as wives. I am A Wife. And, 1
not altogether incidentally, I am a mother.

Not too long ago a male friend of mine appeared on the scene fresh 2
from a recent divorce. He had one child, who is, of course, with his ex-
wife. He is looking for another wife. As I thought about him while I was
ironing one evening, it suddenly occurred to me that I, too, would like to
have a wife. Why do I want a wife?

I would like to go back to school so that I can become economically 3
independent, support myself, and, if need be, support those dependent
upon me. I want a wife who will work and send me to school. And while
I am going to school I want a wife to take care of my children. I want a
wife to keep track of the children's doctor and dentist appointments. And
to keep track of mine, too. I want a wife to make sure my children eat
properly and are kept clean. I want a wife who will wash the children's
clothes and keep them mended. I want a wife who is a good nurturant
attendant to my children, who arranges for their school, makes sure that
they have an adequate social life with their peers, takes them to the park,
the zoo, etc. I want a wife who takes care of the children when they are
sick, a wife who arranges to be around when the children need special
care, because, of course, I cannot miss classes at school. My wife must
arrange to lose time at work and not lose the job. It may mean a small
cut in my wife's income from time to time, but I guess I can tolerate that.
Needless to say, my wife will arrange and pay for the care of the children
while my wife is working.

I want a wife who will take care of *my* physical needs. I want a wife 4
who will keep my house clean. A wife who will pick up after my children,

a wife who will pick up after me. I want a wife who will keep my clothes clean, ironed, mended, replaced when need be, and who will see to it that my personal things are kept in their proper place so that I can find what I need the minute I need it. I want a wife who cooks the meals, a wife who is a *good* cook. I want a wife who will plan the menus, do the necessary grocery shopping, prepare the meals, serve them pleasantly, and then do the cleaning up while I do my studying. I want a wife who will care for me when I am sick and sympathize with my pain and loss of time from school. I want a wife to go along when our family takes a vacation so that someone can continue to care for me and my children when I need a rest and change of scene.

5   I want a wife who will not bother me with rambling complaints about a wife's duties. But I want a wife who will listen to me when I feel the need to explain a rather difficult point I have come across in my course of studies. And I want a wife who will type my papers for me when I have written them.

6   I want a wife who will take care of the details of my social life. When my wife and I are invited out by my friends, I want a wife who will take care of the babysitting arrangements. When I meet people at school that I like and want to entertain, I want a wife who will have the house clean, will prepare a special meal, serve it to me and my friends, and not interrupt when I talk about things that interest me and my friends. I want a wife who will have arranged that the children do not bother us. I want a wife who takes care of the needs of my guests so that they feel comfortable, who makes sure that they have an ashtray, that they are passed the hors d'oeuvres, that they are offered a second helping of the food, that their wine glasses are replenished when necessary, that the coffee is served to them as they like it. And I want a wife who knows that sometimes I need a night out by myself.

7   I want a wife who is sensitive to my sexual needs, a wife who makes love passionately and eagerly when I feel like it, a wife who makes sure that I am satisfied. And, of course, I want a wife who will not demand sexual attention when I am not in the mood for it. I want a wife who assumes the complete responsibility for birth control, because I do not want more children. I want a wife who will remain sexually faithful to me so that I do not have to clutter up my intellectual life with jealousies. And I want a wife who understands that *my* sexual needs may entail more than strict adherence to monogamy. I must, after all, be able to relate to people as fully as possible.

8   If, by chance, I find another person more suitable as a wife than the wife I already have, I want the liberty to replace my present wife with another one. Naturally, I will expect a fresh, new life; my wife will take the children and be solely responsible for them so that I am left free.

When I am through with school and have a job, I want my wife to 9 quit working and remain at home so that my wife can more fully and completely take care of a wife's duties.

My God, who *wouldn't* want a wife?   10

1970

QUESTIONS FOR DISCUSSION

Content

a. List the reasons Brady offers for wanting a wife.
b. Define the word *wife* as portrayed in this essay. Do you agree with this definition?
c. What does Brady imply in the first paragraph when she says, "And, not altogether incidentally, I am a mother"? How does this statement predict the contents and/or organization of the rest of the essay?
d. In what ways is the role that Brady assigned to wives in 1971 similar to the role you think wives play today? In what ways is it different?
e. Might husbands also look for their mothers when they choose wives? What examples of motherly behavior do you find in this essay?

Strategy and Style

f. What technique(s) does Brady use to introduce her essay? Comment on their effectiveness.
g. How does Brady conclude? Is her conclusion long enough for this essay?
h. *Ms.* is a popular publication, in contrast to a scholarly journal. In light of this, describe Brady's style and explain why she uses the level of vocabulary and sentence structure she does.
i. How would you describe Brady's tone? Does it change, or evolve, as we get nearer to her conclusion?
j. To what audience is Brady writing? How do you know?
k. Is the length of the essay appropriate? Should Brady have extended it? Why or why not?
l. What role does illustration play in this persuasive essay? What other methods does Brady use to develop her argument?

ENGAGING THE TEXT

a. If you are female, list a few additional reasons why you might want a "wife." If you are male, list a few reasons why you might want a "husband."

b. What to you is an ideal wife? What is an ideal husband? What is an ideal mother? What is an ideal father? Write a short definition of one or more of these people, using a serious or an ironic approach.

SUGGESTIONS FOR SUSTAINED WRITING

a. Is Brady attacking marriage itself? Write an essay in which you explain why marriage is right or wrong for you now or at any time. Or is Brady simply trying to expose the double standard applied to husbands and wives? Write an essay in which you argue that the double standard for husbands and wives still exists, is disappearing, or has disappeared since Brady's essay was first published.
b. Compare Brady's view of gender tensions with the views depicted in Joan Didion's "Marrying Absurd" (Chapter 2) or Sandra Cisneros's "Only Daughter" (Chapter 11).
c. Write an essay in which you expand upon the notes you made when responding to item *b* under Engaging the Text.

Main idea : a father informing his son's teacher on how his son different browse the way he grew up and and prove that son "isn't slow"

READ MORE

Feminist Issues

"Feminist Majority Foundation" (http://www.feminist.org): *Sources for practical use, including job postings, ways to get involved, and information about global initiatives.*

Gender Stereotypes

"Gender Stereotypes and Sexual Archetypes" (http://www.friesian.com/gender.htm): *Theories, definitions, and links to related sites about gender stereotypes.*

Gilman, Sander L. *Difference and Pathology: Stereotypes of Sexuality, Race, and Madness.* Ithaca: Cornell UP, 1985.

Topic Main idea Vocab Telli

Topic: He is not disadvantage, but is culturally different.

An Indian Father's Plea

Medicine Grizzlybear Lake

Medicine Grizzlybear Lake, also known as Bobby Lake-Thom, is a Native healer and a member of the Seneca and Cherokee Indian tribes. He is half Karuk and part Seneca, Cherokee, and Anglo. Throughout childhood and as a young man, Lake studied with numerous Native healers. He taught Native American Studies at Humboldt State University and Eastern Montana College, and he is currently an associate professor at Gonzaga University's School of Education in Spokane, Washington. He is also a consultant for reservation programs, tribes, and government agencies, advising on health, education, and other issues. His books include Native Healer: Initiation into an Ancient Art *(1991),* Spirits of the Earth: A Guide to Native American Nature Symbols, Stories, and Ceremonies *(1997), and* Call of the Great Spirit: The Shamanic Life and Teachings of Medicine Grizzly Bear *(2001). His articles have appeared in* The Indian Historian, The Shaman's Drum, Teacher's Magazine, Herbs Magazine, *and other publications.*

(Written in the form of a letter, Lake's essay makes a passionate plea for cultural sensitivity and implicitly for educational reform.) A few years after this article was published, Lake reported that Wind-Wolf was doing better in school but that he was still struggling for cultural identity.

Dear teacher:

I would like to introduce you to my son, Wind-Wolf. (He is probably   1
what you would consider a typical Indian kid.) He was born and raised
on the reservation. He has black hair, dark brown eyes, and an olive complexion. And like so many Indian children his age, he is shy and quiet in
the classroom. He is five years old, in kindergarten, and I cannot understand why you have already labeled him a ("slow learner.")

At the age of five, he has already had quite an education compared   2
with his peers in Western society. As his first introduction into this world,
he was bonded to his mother and to the Mother Earth in a traditional
native childbirth ceremony. And he has been continuously cared for
by his mother, father, sisters, cousins, aunts, uncles, grandparents, and
extended tribal family since this ceremony.

From his mother's loving arms, Wind-Wolf was placed in a secure and   3
specially designed Indian baby basket. His father and the medicine elders
conducted another ceremony to bond him with the essence of his genetic
father, the Great Spirit, the Grandfather Sun, and the Grandmother Moon.
This was all done in order to introduce him into the natural world, and to
protect his soul. It is our people's way of showing the newborn respect,
ensuring that he starts life on the path of spirituality.

The traditional Indian baby basket became his "turtle's shell" and   4
served as the first seat for this classroom. He was strapped in for safety,
protected from injury by the willow roots and hazelwood construction.
The basket was made by a tribal elder who had gathered her materials
with prayer. It is specially designed to provide the child with the knowledge and experience he will need in order to survive in his culture and
environment.

Wind-Wolf was strapped in snuggly with a deliberate restriction   5
upon his arms and legs. Although you in Western society may argue that
such a method serves to hinder motor-skills development and abstract

Argument is

His son is not slow but different →

reasoning, we believe it forces the child to first develop his intuitive faculties, rational intellect, symbolic thinking, and five senses. Wind-Wolf was
with his mother constantly, closely bonded, as she carried him on her back
or held him in front while breast feeding. She carried him everywhere
she went, and every night he slept with both parents. Because of this,
Wind-Wolf's educational setting was not only "secure," but also colorful, complicated, and diverse. He has been with his mother at the ocean
at daybreak when she made her prayers and gathered fresh seaweed
from the rocks, he has sat with his uncles in a rowboat on the river while
they fished with gill nets, and he has watched and listened to elders as
they told creation stories and animal legends and sang songs around the
campfires.

With family growing up

6   He has attended the sacred and ancient White Deerskin Dance of
his people and is well acquainted with the cultures and languages of
other tribes. He has been with his mother when she gathered herbs for
healing and watched his tribal aunts and grandmothers gather and
prepare traditional foods such as acorn, smoked salmon, eel, and deer
meat. He has played with abalone shells, pine nuts, iris grass string,
and leather while watching the women make beaded jewelry and
traditional native regalia. He has had many opportunities to watch
his father, uncles, and ceremonial leaders use different kinds of colorful feathers and sing different kinds of songs while preparing for the
sacred dances and rituals.

7   As he grew older, Wind-Wolf began to crawl out of the baby basket
and explore the world around him. When frightened or sleepy, he could
always return to the basket, as a turtle withdraws into its shell. Such an
inward journey allows one to reflect in privacy on what he has learned
and to carry the new knowledge deeply into the unconscious and the
soul. Shapes, sizes, colors, texture, sound, smell, feeling, taste, and the
learning process are therefore integrated—the physical and spiritual, matter and energy, conscious and unconscious, individual and social.

8   Wind-Wolf was with his mother in South Dakota while she danced
for seven days straight in the hot sun, in the sacred Sun Dance Ceremony
of a distant tribe. He has been doctored in a number of different healing ceremonies by medicine men and women from places ranging from
Alaska and Arizona to New York and California. He has been in more
than twenty different sacred sweat lodge rituals—used by native tribes
to purify mind, body, and soul—since he was three years old, and he has
already been exposed to many different religions of his racial brothers:
Protestant, Catholic, Asian Buddhist, and Tibetan Lamaist.

9   It takes a long time to absorb and reflect on these kinds of experiences, so maybe that is why you think my Indian child is a slow learner."
His aunts and grandmothers taught him to count while they sorted out
the materials used to make the abstract designs in native baskets. He

learned his basic numbers by helping his father count and sort the rocks to be used in the sweat lodge—seven rocks for a medicine sweat, say, or thirteen for the summer solstice ceremony. And he was taught mathematics by counting the sticks we use in our traditional native hand game. So I realize he may be slow in grasping the methods that you are now using in your classroom but I hope you will be patient with him. It takes time to adjust to a new cultural system.

He is not culturally "disadvantaged," but he is culturally "different." 10 If you ask him how many months there are in a year, he will probably tell you thirteen. He will respond this way not because he doesn't know how to count properly, but because he has been taught by our traditional people that there are thirteen full moons in a year according to the native tribal calendar and thirteen tail feathers on a perfectly balanced eagle.

But he also knows that some eagles may only have twelve tail feath- 11 ers, or seven. He knows that the flicker has exactly ten tail feathers; that they are red and black, representing east and west, life and death, and that this bird is a "fire" bird, a power used in native healing. He can probably count more than forty different kinds of birds, tell you what kind of bird each is and where it lives, the seasons in which it appears, and how it is used in a sacred ceremony. He may have trouble writing his name on a piece of paper, but he knows how to say it and many other things in several different Indian languages. He is not fluent yet because he is only five years old and required by law to attend your educational system, learn your language, your values, your ways of thinking, and your methods of teaching.

So you see, all of these influences together make him somewhat 12 shy and quiet—and perhaps "slow" according to your standards. But if Wind-Wolf was not prepared for his first tentative foray into your world, neither were you appreciative of his culture. On the first day of class, you had difficulty with his name. You wanted to call him "Wind"—insisting that Wolf somehow must be his middle name. The students in the class laughed at him, causing him embarrassment.

While you are trying to teach him your new methods, he may be look- 13 ing out the window as if daydreaming. Why? Because he has been taught to watch and study the changes in nature. It is hard for him to switch from the right to the left hemisphere of the brain when he sees the leaves turning bright colors, the geese heading south, and the squirrels scurrying to get ready for winter. In his heart, in his young mind, and almost by instinct, he knows that this is the time of year he is supposed to be with his people gathering and preparing fish, deer meat, and plants and herbs, and learning his assigned tasks in this role. He is caught between two worlds.

Yesterday, for the third time in two weeks, he came home crying 14 and said he wanted to have his hair cut. He said he doesn't have any *making fun of his hair*

friends at school because they make fun of his long hair. I tried to explain to him that in our culture, long hair is a sign of masculinity and balance and is a source of power. But he remained adamant in his position.

15   To make matters worse, he recently encountered his first harsh case of racism. Wind-Wolf had managed to adopt at least one good school friend. On the way home from school one day, he asked his new pal if he wanted to come home to play with him until supper. That was okay with Wind-Wolf's mother, who was walking with them. When they got to the friend's house, the two boys ran inside to ask permission while Wind-Wolf's mother waited. But the other boy's mother lashed out: "It is okay if you have to play with him at school, but we don't allow that kind of people in our house!" When my wife asked why not, the other boy's mother answered, "Because you are Indians and we are white, and I don't want my kids growing up with your kind of people."

16   So now my young Indian child does not want to go to school anymore (even though his hair is cut). He feels that he does not belong. He is the only Indian child in your class, and instead of being proud of his race, heritage, and culture, he now feels ashamed. When he watches television, he asks why white people hate us so much and always kill our people in the movies and why they take everything from us. He asks why the other kids in school are not taught about the power, beauty, and essence of nature. Now he refuses to sing his native songs, play with his Indian artifacts, learn his language, or participate in his sacred ceremonies. When I ask him to go to an urban pow-wow or help me with a sacred sweat lodge ritual, he says no because "that's weird."

17   So, dear teacher, I want to introduce you to my son, Wind-Wolf. He stems from a long line of hereditary chiefs, medicine men and women, and ceremonial leaders whose knowledge is still being studied and recorded in contemporary books. He has seven different tribal systems flowing through his blood; he is even part white. I want my child to succeed in school and in life. I don't want him to be a dropout or to end up on drugs and alcohol because he is made to feel inferior or because of discrimination. I want him to be proud of his rich culture, and I would like him to succeed in both cultures. But I need your help.

18   What you say and what you do in the classroom has a significant effect on my child. All I ask is that you work with me to help educate my child in the best way. If you don't have the knowledge and experience to deal with culturally different children, I am willing to help you with the few resources I have or direct you to other resources.

19   Millions of dollars have been appropriated by Congress each year for "Indian Education." All you have to do is encourage your school to use these resources. My Indian child has a constitutional right to learn and maintain his culture. By the same token, I believe that non-Indian

children have a constitutional right to learn about our Native American heritage and culture, because Indians play a significant part in the history of Western society.

My son, Wind-Wolf, is not an "empty glass" coming into your class to be filled. He is a "full basket" coming into a different society with something special to share. Please let him share his knowledge, heritage, and culture with you and his peers.

[handwritten: ne knowledge]

20

[handwritten: main idea: Wind-wolf had a differ]
[handwritten: Culturally different]
[handwritten: Topic: Cultural education]

[handwritten: test 487: Day]

1995

QUESTIONS FOR DISCUSSION

Content

[handwritten: His education is based off experience]

a. How would you characterize Wind-Wolf's non-Western education?
b. What are the main differences between Wind-Wolf's Western and non-Western educations?

[handwritten: Harder for me to learn.]

c. Why might Wind-Wolf have been labeled a "slow learner" (paragraph 1)?
d. What are the negative effects on Wind-Wolf of his Western education?
e. In paragraph 18, Lake urges Wind-Wolf's teacher to help him educate his son. What might be some ways in which Wind-Wolf's teacher could work with Lake?

[handwritten: is Culturally different from the way he grew up]

Strategy and Style

f. Because it was written for *Teacher's Magazine*, you would expect this piece to have elicited responses from teachers across the country. What might these responses have been? How does Lake counter these potential responses?

g. What is the effect of writing this piece as a letter rather than as an expository essay? *[handwritten: This piece of writing is meant for the teacher/explaining the]*

h. What is the argument embedded in this persuasive piece? *[handwritten: cultal differene]*

i. What metaphorical language does Lake use to describe his son?

[handwritten: take his not slow yet different]

ENGAGING THE TEXT

a. Write a brief response to Lake's letter in the form of a letter from the teacher. Respond to one of the examples provided by Lake.

b. Summarize the main conflicts between Wind-Wolf's Western and Indian educations, and speculate about how one of the conflicts could be resolved.

SUGGESTIONS FOR SUSTAINED WRITING

a. Write an essay in the form of a letter to a former teacher (or even a current one) in which you make a plea for a different form of education. Include details and examples.
b. Write an essay in which you compare Lake's vision of education with the visions presented in "Coming to an Awareness of Language" by Malcolm X (Chapter 1) and/or "Superman and Me" by Sherman Alexie (Chapter 11).
c. Research the current issues in Native American education. Choose one issue and report on it to your classmates.

READ MORE

Lake and His Works

"Medicine Grizzlybear: Traditional Native Healer" (http://www .nativehealer.net): *Lake's personal website.*

Native American Education

"American Indian Education" (http://jan.ucc.nau.edu/~jar/AIE/index .html): *Links to organizations, programs, policies, and language websites.*

"Index of Native American Education Resources on the Internet" (http:// www.hanksville.org/NAresources/indices/NAschools.html): *Links to teacher resources and curriculum information. Note: This URL is case-sensitive.*

Let Them Eat Dog

Jonathan Safran Foer

Jonathan Safran Foer (b. 1977) is a novelist living in Brooklyn, New York. He studied philosophy at Princeton University, receiving a degree in 1999. He had then planned to study medicine, but quickly discovered that his fainting at the sight of blood would possibly be an obstacle to that profession. While at Princeton, he had taken a creative writing course with Joyce Carol Oates, who had encouraged him to write, and his senior thesis, a work about his grandfather, a Holocaust survivor, had received the university's Senior Creative Writing Thesis Prize. After graduating, Foer traveled to the Ukraine to explore his grandfather's life in more detail; his experiences there eventually became the novel Everything Is Illuminated *(2002), a book that won the National Jewish Book Award and was made into a feature film in 2005. With this book, his path as a writer was determined. Foer went on to write the novel* Extremely Loud and Incredibly Close *(2005); a libretto for the*

Berlin State Opera's Seven Attempted Escapes from Silence *(2005); the nonfiction work* Eating Animals *(2009); and a die-cut book,* Tree of Codes *(2010), created out of the novel* The Street of Crocodiles *by Bruno Schultz. He has also written numerous articles and edited anthologies. He was a visiting professor at Yale University in 2008 and is currently a professor in the Graduate Creating Writing Program at New York University.*

"Let Them Eat Dog" was published in The Wall Street Journal *in October 2009. His sarcastic voice is similar to that in his book* Eating Animals, *and his approach to the topic is resonant of Jonathan Swift's "A Modest Proposal," in Chapter 10.*

Despite the fact that it's perfectly legal in 44 states, eating "man's best 1 friend" is as taboo as a man eating his best friend. Even the most enthusiastic carnivores won't eat dogs. TV guy and sometimes cooker Gordon Ramsay can get pretty macho with lambs and piglets when doing publicity for something he's selling, but you'll never see a puppy peeking out of one of his pots. And though he once said he'd electrocute his children if they became vegetarian, one can't help but wonder what his response would be if they poached the family pooch.

Dogs are wonderful, and in many ways unique. But they are remark- 2 ably unremarkable in their intellectual and experiential capacities. Pigs are every bit as intelligent and feeling, by any sensible definition of the words. They can't hop into the back of a Volvo, but they can fetch, run and play, be mischievous and reciprocate affection. So why don't they get to curl up by the fire? Why can't they at least be spared being tossed on the fire? Our taboo against dog eating says something about dogs and a great deal about us.

The French, who love their dogs, sometimes eat their horses.
The Spanish, who love their horses, sometimes eat their cows.
The Indians, who love their cows, sometimes eat their dogs.

While written in a much different context, George Orwell's words 3 (from "Animal Farm") apply here: "All animals are equal, but some animals are more equal than others."

So who's right? What might be the reasons to exclude canine from the 4 menu? The selective carnivore suggests:

Don't eat companion animals. But dogs aren't kept as companions in 5 all of the places they are eaten. And what about our petless neighbors? Would we have any right to object if they had dog for dinner?

OK, then: Don't eat animals with significant mental capacities. If by 6 "significant mental capacities" we mean what a dog has, then good for the dog. But such a definition would also include the pig, cow and chicken. And it would exclude severely impaired humans.

Then: It's for good reason that the eternal taboos—don't fiddle 7 with your crap, kiss your sister, or eat your companions—are taboo.

Evolutionarily speaking, those things are bad for us. But dog eating isn't a taboo in many places, and it isn't in any way bad for us. Properly cooked, dog meat poses no greater health risks than any other meat.

8   Dog meat has been described as "gamey" "complex," "buttery" and "floral." And there is a proud pedigree of eating it. Fourth-century tombs contain depictions of dogs being slaughtered along with other food animals. It was a fundamental enough habit to have informed language itself: the Sino-Korean character for "fair and proper" (yeon) literally translates into "as cooked dog meat is delicious." Hippocrates praised dog meat as a source of strength. Dakota Indians enjoyed dog liver, and not so long ago Hawaiians ate dog brains and blood. Captain Cook ate dog. Roald Amundsen famously ate his sled dogs. (Granted, he was really hungry.) And dogs are still eaten to overcome bad luck in the Philippines; as medicine in China and Korea; to enhance libido in Nigeria and in numerous places, on every continent, because they taste good. For centuries, the Chinese have raised special breeds of dogs, like the black-tongued chow, for chow, and many European countries still have laws on the books regarding postmortem examination of dogs intended for human consumption.

9   Of course, something having been done just about everywhere is no kind of justification for doing it now. But unlike all farmed meat, which requires the creation and maintenance of animals, dogs are practically begging to be eaten. Three to four million dogs and cats are euthanized annually. The simple disposal of these euthanized dogs is an enormous ecological and economic problem. But eating those strays, those run-aways, those not-quite-cute-enough-to-take and not-quite-well-behaved-enough-to-keep dogs would be killing a flock of birds with one stone and eating it, too.

10   In a sense it's what we're doing already. Rendering—the conversion of animal protein unfit for human consumption into food for livestock and pets—allows processing plants to transform useless dead dogs into productive members of the food chain. In America, millions of dogs and cats euthanized in animal shelters every year become the food for our food. So let's just eliminate this inefficient and bizarre middle step.

11   This need not challenge our civility. We won't make them suffer any more than necessary. While it's widely believed that adrenaline makes dog meat taste better—hence the traditional methods of slaughter: hang-ing, boiling alive, beating to death—we can all agree that if we're going to eat them, we should kill them quickly and painlessly, right? For example, the traditional Hawaiian means of holding the dog's nose shut—in order to conserve blood—must be regarded (socially if not legally) as a no-no. Perhaps we could include dogs under the Humane Methods of Slaughter Act. That doesn't say anything about how they're treated during their lives, and isn't subject to any meaningful oversight or enforcement, but

surely we can rely on the industry to "self-regulate," as we do with other eaten animals.

Few people sufficiently appreciate the colossal task of feeding a world 12 of billions of omnivores who demand meat with their potatoes. The inefficient use of dogs—conveniently already in areas of high human population (take note, local-food advocates)—should make any good ecologist blush. One could argue that various "humane" groups are the worst hypocrites, spending enormous amounts of money and energy in a futile attempt to reduce the number of unwanted dogs while at the very same time propagating the irresponsible no-dog-for-dinner taboo. If we let dogs be dogs, and breed without interference, we would create a sustainable, local meat supply with low energy inputs that would put even the most efficient grass-based farming to shame. For the ecologically-minded it's time to admit that dog is realistic food for realistic environmentalists.

For those already convinced, here's a classic Filipino recipe I recently 13 came across. I haven't tried it myself, but sometimes you can read a recipe and just know.

Stewed Dog, Wedding Style
First, kill a medium-sized dog, then burn off the fur over a hot fire. Carefully remove the skin while still warm and set aside for later (may be used in other recipes). Cut meat into 1" cubes. Marinate meat in mixture of vinegar, peppercorn, salt, and garlic for 2 hours. Fry meat in oil using a large wok over an open fire, then add onions and chopped pineapple and sauté until tender. Pour in tomato sauce and boiling water, add green pepper, bay leaf, and Tabasco. Cover and simmer over warm coals until meat is tender. Blend in purée of dog's liver and cook for additional 5–7 minutes.

There is an overabundance of rational reasons to say no to factory- 14 farmed meat: It is the No. 1 cause of global warming, it systematically forces tens of billions of animals to suffer in ways that would be illegal if they were dogs, it is a decisive factor in the development of swine and avian flus, and so on. And yet even most people who know these things still aren't inspired to order something else on the menu. Why?

Food is not rational. Food is culture, habit, craving and identity. 15 Responding to factory farming calls for a capacity to care that dwells beyond information. We know what we see on undercover videos of factory farms and slaughterhouses is wrong. (There are those who will defend a system that allows for occasional animal cruelty, but no one defends the cruelty, itself.) And despite it being entirely reasonable, the case for eating dogs is likely repulsive to just about every reader of this paper. The instinct comes before our reason, and is more important.

2009

QUESTIONS FOR DISCUSSION

Content

a. What is Foer's focus—his primary subject—in this essay? Is "eating dogs" his real topic?

b. What is Foer's thesis, and where does it come in the essay? Do you agree with Foer's take on the topic?

c. In paragraph 2, Foer writes that "[o]ur taboo against dog eating says something about dogs and a great deal about us." What does "our taboo" say about us?

d. What points does Foer make about the meat industry and about laws regulating that industry?

e. What reasons does Foer put forth to eat dog? What reasons does he proffer for not eating dog? Which set of reasons seem more convincing, and why?

Strategy and Style

f. What evidence does Foer use to critique the dog-eating taboo? What evidence might he have purposely overlooked?

g. Who might be the proponents and opponents of a proposal to eat dog? How does Foer address each side?

h. Foer uses humorous alliteration, such as "puppy peeking . . . pots" and "poached the family pooch," to introduce the essay. Where else does he use alliteration for humorous effect? What does this joking style tell you about Foer's approach to the topic?

i. In paragraph 15, Foer refers to "inefficient use of dogs" as a key problem. Is he really saying that this is the problem? If not, what *is* he saying is the problem?

j. How does the concluding paragraph sum up the points made in the essay? Why might Foer have placed them at the end of the essay rather than making these points right at the beginning?

k. In the concluding paragraph, Foer refers to the readers of "this paper," meaning *The Wall Street Journal*. From what you know about the paper, why are these readers likely to react negatively to Foer's semi-serious proposal to eat dogs?

ENGAGING THE TEXT

a. In paragraph 12, Foer suggests that using stray dogs for food would solve ecological and economic problems. Take his suggestion further to consider what might happen if "farming" stray dogs were made into a formal industry. Speculate on ways this industry might succeed or fail.

b. Reread the recipe for "Stewed Dog, Wedding Style" and pay attention to your emotional reaction to it. Then replace the word "dog" and "fur" in the recipe for with the word "chicken" and "feathers." What differences do you notice in how you react? Are there still words in the recipe that generate an uneasy emotion for you?

SUGGESTIONS FOR SUSTAINED WRITING

a. Write a defense of your personal eating and nutrition habits, using examples from your own experience. Address the arguments that might be made against your defense.
b. Read this essay alongside Jonathan Swift's "A Modest Proposal." As you read, take notes, comparing argument technique, organization, and voice. Write an essay in which you compare the choices made by each author.
c. Research methods of meat production in the United States. Begin by reading the Humane Methods of Slaughter Act, mentioned in paragraph 14 and then discuss this Act in a report that focuses on a particular animal, company, or process.

READ MORE

Foer and His Works

"Jonathan Safran Foer Page" (http://www.authortrek.com/jonathan_safran_foer_page.html): *Links to works by Foer and websites about Foer on Authortrek, an informal database of information about new authors.*

"The Project Museum (http://www.theprojectmuseum.com): *Foer's creative project site.*

"Author Podcast: Jonathan Safran Foer" (http://www.bookbuffet.com/index.cfm/fuseaction/news.article/type/home/article_ID/96E2863D-1064-4A00-AFB9EE21038CBDC6/index.cfm): *Transcript and podcast link to an interview with Foer by BookBuffet.*

Factory Farming

"Humane Methods of Livestock Slaughter Act" (http://www.fsis.usda.gov/regulations_&_policies/Humane_Methods_of_Livestock_Slaughter_Act/index.asp): *The text of the entire Act on the United State Department of Agriculture's website.*

"Topic: Factory Farming Pros and Cons" (http://www.reference.com/topic/Factory-Farming-Pros-and-Cons): *Links to many websites on both sides of the issue.*

"If This Is Kosher" (http://www.spike.com/video-clips/xs24ml/-if-this-is-kosher--a-video-narrated-by-jonathan-safran-foer (five-minute version) and http://video.google.com/videoplay?do cid=-7330038074290819722# (full version): *Short film about factory farming, with particular attention to kosher practices, narrated by Foer.*

On Liberty

John Stuart Mill

John Stuart Mill (1806–1873) was a British philosopher, most usually connected with Utilitarianism. His father, James Mill, was a historian and economist, who taught his son at home, adhering to a strict regimen of reading the classics—in their original Latin and Greek, of course—and of studying the sciences, mathematics, languages, and political economy. Besides his father, Mill's informal teachers included the philosopher Jeremy Bentham and economist David Ricardo. By the time Mill was ten, he had mastered Greek and Latin and was well on his way to mastering the other subjects as well. From 1820 to 1821, he lived in France with the family of Samuel Bentham, Jeremy's brother, and studied chemistry, botany, mathematics, and French. Back in England, he added psychology and law to the mix. The intense and unrelenting intellectual work, however, led to a nervous breakdown at the age of twenty. As relief, he turned to poetry and to Wordsworth in particular. Although he could have attended Oxford or Cambridge University, he opted not to because he would have had to take Anglican orders. Instead, he took a post at the East India Company, where his father worked, and stayed there until the Company was dissolved in 1858. He balanced his Company job with writing and editing, publishing articles in the political magazines of the day, editing The London and Westminster Review *from 1835 to 1840, and publishing books such as* A System of Logic *in 1843 and* The Principles of Political Economy *in 1848. His wife, Harriet Taylor, was a major influence on his work, but when she died in 1858, the same year that the Company was dissolved, Mill immersed himself in writing and politics, even serving as a Member of Parliament from 1865–1868. His main books of this time are* On Liberty *(1859),* Utilitarianism *(1863), and* The Subjection of Women *(1869). Two other books of note are his* Autobiography *(1873) and the posthumously published* Three Essays on Religion *(1874). Mill was seen as a progressive thinker, arguing for the rights of workers and women, fighting against slavery, and contending that the environment should not be destroyed for the sake of economic growth.*

"On Liberty" is an excerpt from the opening chapter of the book by the same name. Mill sets out to describe the limits that society should have over individuals, limits that should be minimal. A key concept is the "harm principle," which Mill defines as that which individuals are allowed to do as long as their actions harm no one, either directly or indirectly. This concept, however clear Mill thought it was, has been used by both sides in debates about political process, individual freedom, education, and the use of political force.

1 The subject of this Essay is not the so-called Liberty of the Will, so unfortunately opposed to the misnamed doctrine of Philosophical Necessity;

but Civil, or Social Liberty: the nature and limits of the power which can be legitimately exercised by society over the individual. A question seldom stated, and hardly ever discussed, in general terms, but which profoundly influences the practical controversies of the age by its latent presence, and is likely soon to make itself recognised as the vital question of the future. It is so far from being new, that, in a certain sense, it has divided mankind, almost from the remotest ages; but in the stage of progress into which the more civilized portions of the species have now entered, it presents itself under new conditions, and requires a different and more fundamental treatment.

The struggle between Liberty and Authority is the most conspicuous feature in the portions of history with which we are earliest familiar, particularly in that of Greece, Rome, and England. But in old times this contest was between subjects, or some classes of subjects, and the Government. By liberty, was meant protection against the tyranny of the political rulers. The rulers were conceived (except in some of the popular governments of Greece) as in a necessarily antagonistic position to the people whom they ruled. They consisted of a governing One, or a governing tribe or caste, who derived their authority from inheritance or conquest, who, at all events, did not hold it at the pleasure of the governed, and whose supremacy men did not venture, perhaps did not desire, to contest, whatever precautions might be taken against its oppressive exercise. Their power was regarded as necessary, but also as highly dangerous; as a weapon which they would attempt to use against their subjects, no less than against external enemies. To prevent the weaker members of the community from being preyed on by innumerable vultures, it was needful that there should be an animal of prey stronger than the rest, commissioned to keep them down. But as the king of the vultures would be no less bent upon preying upon the flock than any of the minor harpies, it was indispensable to be in a perpetual attitude of defence against his beak and claws. The aim, therefore, of patriots was to set limits to the power which the ruler should be suffered to exercise over the community; and this limitation was what they meant by liberty. It was attempted in two ways. First, by obtaining a recognition of certain immunities, called political liberties or rights, which it was to be regarded as a breach of duty in the ruler to infringe, and which, if he did infringe, specific resistance, or general rebellion, was held to be justifiable. A second, and generally a later expedient, was the establishment of constitutional checks, by which the consent of the community, or of a body of some sort, supposed to represent its interests, was made a necessary condition to some of the more important acts of the governing power. To the first of these modes of limitation, the ruling power, in most European countries, was compelled, more or less, to submit. It was not so with the second; and, to attain this, or when already in some degree possessed, to attain it more completely, became everywhere the principal object of the lovers of liberty. And so long as mankind were content to combat one enemy by another, and to be ruled by a master, on condition of being guaranteed more or less efficaciously against his tyranny, they did not carry their aspirations beyond this point.

3   A time, however, came, in the progress of human affairs, when men ceased to think it a necessity of nature that their governors should be an independent power, opposed in interest to themselves. It appeared to them much better that the various magistrates of the State should be their tenants or delegates, revocable at their pleasure. In that way alone, it seemed, could they have complete security that the powers of government would never be abused to their disadvantage. By degrees this new demand for elective and temporary rulers became the prominent object of the exertions of the popular party, wherever any such party existed; and superseded, to a considerable extent, the previous efforts to limit the power of rulers. As the struggle proceeded for making the ruling power emanate from the periodical choice of the ruled, some persons began to think that too much importance had been attached to the limitation of the power itself. *That* (it might seem) was a resource against rulers whose interests were habitually opposed to those of the people. What was now wanted was, that the rulers should be identified with the people; that their interest and will should be the interest and will of the nation. The nation did not need to be protected against its own will. There was no fear of its tyrannizing over itself. Let the rulers be effectually responsible to it, promptly removable by it, and it could afford to trust them with power of which it could itself dictate the use to be made. Their power was but the nation's own power, concentrated, and in a form convenient for exercise. This mode of thought, or rather perhaps of feeling, was common among the last generation of European liberalism, in the Continental section of which it still apparently predominates. Those who admit any limit to what a government may do, except in the case of such governments as they think ought not to exist, stand out as brilliant exceptions among the political thinkers of the Continent. A similar tone of sentiment might by this time have been prevalent in our own country, if the circumstances which for a time encouraged it, had continued unaltered.

4   But, in political and philosophical theories, as well as in persons, success discloses faults and infirmities which failure might have concealed from observation. The notion, that the people have no need to limit their power over themselves, might seem axiomatic, when popular government was a thing only dreamed about, or read of as having existed at some distant period of the past. Neither was that notion necessarily disturbed by such temporary aberrations as those of the French Revolution, the worst of which were the work of an usurping few, and which, in any case, belonged, not to the permanent working of popular institutions,

but to a sudden and convulsive outbreak against monarchical and aristocratic despotism. In time, however, a democratic republic came to occupy
a large portion of the earth's surface, and made itself felt as one of the
most powerful members of the community of nations; and elective and
responsible government became subject to the observations and criti-
cisms which wait upon a great existing fact. It was now perceived that
such phrases as "self-government," and "the power of the people over
themselves," do not express the true state of the case. The "people" who
exercise the power are not always the same people with those over whom
it is exercised; and the "self-government" spoken of is not the government of each by himself, but of each by all the rest. The will of the people,
moreover, practically means the will of the most numerous or the most
active *part* of the people; the majority, or those who succeed in making
themselves accepted as the majority; the people, consequently, *may* desire
to oppress a part of their number; and precautions are as much needed
against this as against any other abuse of power. The limitation, therefore,
of the power of government over individuals loses none of its importance
when the holders of power are regularly accountable to the community,
that is, to the strongest party therein. This view of things, recommend-
ing itself equally to the intelligence of thinkers and to the inclination of
those important classes in European society to whose real or supposed
interests democracy is adverse, has had no difficulty in establishing itself;
and in political speculations "the tyranny of the majority" is now generally included among the evils against which society requires to be on its
guard.

    Like other tyrannies, the tyranny of the majority was at first, and is 5
still vulgarly, held in dread, chiefly as operating through the acts of the
public authorities. But reflecting persons perceived that when society is
itself the tyrant—society collectively, over the separate individuals who
compose it—its means of tyrannizing are not restricted to the acts which
it may do by the hands of its political functionaries. Society can and does
execute its own mandates: and if it issues wrong mandates instead of
right, or any mandates at all in things with which it ought not to meddle,
it practises a social tyranny more formidable than many kinds of political
oppression, since, though not usually upheld by such extreme penalties,
it leaves fewer means of escape, penetrating much more deeply into the
details of life, and enslaving the soul itself. Protection, therefore, against
the tyranny of the magistrate is not enough: there needs protection also
against the tyranny of the prevailing opinion and feeling; against the tendency of society to impose, by other means than civil penalties, its own
ideas and practices as rules of conduct on those who dissent from them;
to fetter the development, and, if possible, prevent the formation, of any
individuality not in harmony with its ways, and compel all characters
to fashion themselves upon the model of its own. There is a limit to the

legitimate interference of collective opinion with individual independence: and to find that limit, and maintain it against encroachment, is as
indispensable to a good condition of human affairs, as protection against
political despotism.

6   But though this proposition is not likely to be contested in general
terms, the practical question, where to place the limit—how to make the
fitting adjustment between individual independence and social control—
is a subject on which nearly everything remains to be done. All that makes
existence valuable to any one, depends on the enforcement of restraints
upon the actions of other people. Some rules of conduct, therefore, must
be imposed, by law in the first place, and by opinion on many things
which are not fit subjects for the operation of law. What these rules should
be, is the principal question in human affairs; but if we except a few of the
most obvious cases, it is one of those which least progress has been made
in resolving. No two ages, and scarcely any two countries, have decided
it alike; and the decision of one age or country is a wonder to another. Yet
the people of any given age and country no more suspect any difficulty
in it, than if it were a subject on which mankind had always been agreed.
The rules which obtain among themselves appear to them self-evident
and self-justifying. This all but universal illusion is one of the examples
of the magical influence of custom, which is not only, as the proverb
says, a second nature, but is continually mistaken for the first. The effect
of custom, in preventing any misgiving respecting the rules of conduct
which mankind impose on one another, is all the more complete because
the subject is one on which it is not generally considered necessary that
reasons should be given, either by one person to others, or by each to himself. People are accustomed to believe, and have been encouraged in the
belief by some who aspire to the character of philosophers, that their feelings, on subjects of this nature, are better than reasons, and render reasons
unnecessary. The practical principle which guides them to their opinions
on the regulation of human conduct, is the feeling in each person's mind
that everybody should be required to act as he, and those with whom he
sympathizes, would like them to act. No one, indeed, acknowledges to
himself that his standard of judgment is his own liking; but an opinion
on a point of conduct, not supported by reasons, can only count as one
person's preference; and if the reasons, when given, are a mere appeal
to a similar preference felt by other people, it is still only many people's
liking instead of one. To an ordinary man, however, his own preference,
thus supported, is not only a perfectly satisfactory reason, but the only
one he generally has for any of his notions of morality, taste, or propriety,
which are not expressly written in his religious creed; and his chief guide
in the interpretation even of that. Men's opinions, accordingly, on what is
laudable or blameable, are affected by all the multifarious causes which
influence their wishes in regard to the conduct of others, and which are

as numerous as those which determine their wishes on any other subject. Sometimes their reason—at other times their prejudices or superstitions: often their social affections, not seldom their antisocial ones, their envy or jealousy, their arrogance or contemptuousness: but most commonly, their desires or fears for themselves—their legitimate or illegitimate self-interest. Wherever there is an ascendant class, a large portion of the morality of the country emanates from its class interests, and its feelings of class superiority. The morality between Spartans and Helots, between planters and negroes, between princes and subjects, between nobles and roturiers, between men and women, has been for the most part the creation of these class interests and feelings: and the sentiments thus generated, react in turn upon the moral feelings of the members of the ascendant class, in their relations among themselves. Where, on the other hand, a class, formerly ascendant, has lost its ascendancy, or where its ascendancy is unpopular, the prevailing moral sentiments frequently bear the impress of an impatient dislike of superiority. Another grand determining principle of the rules of conduct, both in act and forbearance, which have been enforced by law or opinion, has been the servility of mankind towards the supposed preferences or aversions of their temporal masters, or of their gods. This servility, though essentially selfish, is not hypocrisy; it gives rise to perfectly genuine sentiments of abhorrence; it made men burn magicians and heretics. Among so many baser influences, the general and obvious interests of society have of course had a share, and a large one, in the direction of the moral sentiments: less, however, as a matter of reason, and on their own account, than as a consequence of the sympathies and antipathies which grew out of them: and sympathies and antipathies which had little or nothing to do with the interests of society, have made themselves felt in the establishment of moralities with quite as great force.

The likings and dislikings of society, or of some powerful portion of it, are thus the main thing which has practically determined the rules laid down for general observance, under the penalties of law or opinion. And in general, those who have been in advance of society in thought and feeling, have left this condition of things unassailed in principle, however they may have come into conflict with it in some of its details. They have occupied themselves rather in inquiring what things society ought to like or dislike, than in questioning whether its likings or dislikings should be a law to individuals. They preferred endeavouring to alter the feelings of mankind on the particular points on which they were themselves heretical, rather than make common cause in defence of freedom, with heretics generally. The only case in which the higher ground has been taken on principle and maintained with consistency, by any but an individual here and there, is that of religious belief: a case instructive in many ways, and not least so as forming a most striking instance of the fallibility of what is called the moral sense: for the *odium theologicum*, in a sincere bigot, is one of the most unequivocal cases of moral feeling. Those who first broke the yoke of what called itself the Universal Church, were in general as little willing to permit difference of religious opinion as that church itself. But when the heat of the conflict was over, without giving a complete victory to any party, and each church or sect was reduced to limit its hopes to retaining possession of the ground it already occupied; minorities, seeing that they had no chance of becoming majorities, were under the necessity of pleading to those whom they could not convert, for permission to differ. It is accordingly on this battle field, almost solely, that the rights of the individual against society have been asserted on broad grounds of principle, and the claim of society to exercise authority over dissentients, openly controverted. The great writers to whom the world owes what religious liberty it possesses, have mostly asserted freedom of conscience as an indefeasible right, and denied absolutely that a human being is accountable to others for his religious belief. Yet so natural to mankind is intolerance in whatever they really care about, that religious freedom has hardly anywhere been practically realized, except where religious indifference, which dislikes to have its peace disturbed by theological quarrels, has added its weight to the scale. In the minds of almost all religious persons, even in the most tolerant countries, the duty of toleration is admitted with tacit reserves. One person will bear with dissent in matters of church government, but not of dogma; another can tolerate everybody, short of a Papist or an Unitarian; another, every one who believes in revealed religion; a few extend their charity a little further, but stop at the belief in a God and in a future state. Wherever the sentiment of the majority is still genuine and intense, it is found to have abated little of its claim to be obeyed.

8   In England, from the peculiar circumstances of our political history, though the yoke of opinion is perhaps heavier, that of law is lighter, than in most other countries of Europe; and there is considerable jealousy of direct interference, by the legislative or the executive power, with private conduct; not so much from any just regard for the independence of the individual, as from the still subsisting habit of looking on the government as representing an opposite interest to the public. The majority have not yet learnt to feel the power of the government their power, or its opinions their opinions. When they do so, individual liberty will probably be as much exposed to invasion from the government, as it already is from public opinion. But, as yet, there is a considerable amount of feeling ready to be called forth against any attempt of the law to control individuals in things in which they have not hitherto been accustomed to be controlled by it; and this with very little discrimination as to whether the matter is, or is not, within the legitimate sphere of legal control; insomuch that the feeling, highly salutary on the whole, is perhaps quite as often misplaced as well grounded in the particular instances of its application. There is,

in fact, no recognised principle by which the propriety or impropriety of government interference is customarily tested. People decide according to their personal preferences. Some, whenever they see any good to be done, or evil to be remedied, would willingly instigate the government to undertake the business; while others prefer to bear almost any amount of social evil, rather than add one to the departments of human interests amenable to governmental control. And men range themselves on one or the other side in any particular case, according to this general direction of their sentiments; or according to the degree of interest which they feel in the particular thing which it is proposed that the government should do, or according to the belief they entertain that the government would, or would not, do it in the manner they prefer; but very rarely on account of any opinion to which they consistently adhere, as to what things are fit to be done by a government. And it seems to me that in consequence of this absence of rule or principle, one side is at present as often wrong as the other; the interference of government is, with about equal frequency, improperly invoked and improperly condemned.

The object of this Essay is to assert one very simple principle, as 9 entitled to govern absolutely the dealings of society with the individual in the way of compulsion and control, whether the means used be physical force in the form of legal penalties, or the moral coercion of public opinion. That principle is, that the sole end for which mankind are warranted, individually or collectively, in interfering with the liberty of action of any of their number, is self-protection. That the only purpose for which power can be rightfully exercised over any member of a civilized community, against his will, is to prevent harm to others. His own good, either physical or moral, is not a sufficient warrant. He cannot rightfully be compelled to do or forbear because it will be better for him to do so, because it will make him happier, because, in the opinions of others, to do so would be wise, or even right. These are good reasons for remonstrating with him, or reasoning with him, or persuading him, or entreating him, but not for compelling him, or visiting him with any evil in case he do otherwise. To justify that, the conduct from which it is desired to deter him, must be calculated to produce evil to some one else. The only part of the conduct of any one, for which he is amenable to society, is that which concerns others. In the part which merely concerns himself, his independence is, of right, absolute. Over himself, over his own body and mind, the individual is sovereign.

It is, perhaps, hardly necessary to say that this doctrine is meant to 10 apply only to human beings in the maturity of their faculties. We are not speaking of children, or of young persons below the age which the law may fix as that of manhood or womanhood. Those who are still in a state to require being taken care of by others, must be protected against their own actions as well as against external injury. For the same reason, we may leave out of consideration those backward states of society in which the race itself may be considered as in its nonage. The early difficulties in the way of spontaneous progress are so great, that there is seldom any choice of means for overcoming them; and a ruler full of the spirit of improvement is warranted in the use of any expedients that will attain an end, perhaps otherwise unattainable. Despotism is a legitimate mode of government in dealing with barbarians, provided the end be their improvement, and the means justified by actually effecting that end. Liberty, as a principle, has no application to any state of things anterior to the time when mankind have become capable of being improved by free and equal discussion. Until then, there is nothing for them but implicit obedience to an Akbar or a Charlemagne, if they are so fortunate as to find one. But as soon as mankind have attained the capacity of being guided to their own improvement by conviction or persuasion (a period long since reached in all nations with whom we need here concern ourselves), compulsion, either in the direct form or in that of pains and penalties for non-compliance, is no longer admissible as a means to their own good, and justifiable only for the security of others.

11   It is proper to state that I forego any advantage which could be derived to my argument from the idea of abstract right, as a thing independent of utility. I regard utility as the ultimate appeal on all ethical questions; but it must be utility in the largest sense, grounded on the permanent interests of man as a progressive being. Those interests, I contend, authorize the subjection of individual spontaneity to external control, only in respect to those actions of each, which concern the interest of other people. If any one does an act hurtful to others, there is a *primâ facie* case for punishing him, by law, or, where legal penalties are not safely applicable, by general disapprobation. There are also many positive acts for the benefit of others, which he may rightfully be compelled to perform; such as, to give evidence in a court of justice; to bear his fair share in the common defence, or in any other joint work necessary to the interest of the society of which he enjoys the protection; and to perform certain acts of individual beneficence, such as saving a fellow-creature's life, or interposing to protect the defenceless against ill-usage, things which whenever it is obviously a man's duty to do, he may rightfully be made responsible to society for not doing. A person may cause evil to others not only by his actions but by his inaction, and in either case he is justly accountable to them for the injury. The latter case, it is true, requires a much more cautious exercise of compulsion than the former. To make any one answerable for doing evil to others, is the rule; to make him answerable for not preventing evil, is, comparatively speaking, the exception. Yet there are many cases clear enough and grave enough to justify that exception. In all things which regard the external relations of the individual, he is *de jure* amenable to those whose interests are concerned, and if need be, to society as their

protector. There are often good reasons for not holding him to the responsibility; but these reasons must arise from the special expediencies of the case: either because it is a kind of case in which he is on the whole likely to act better, when left to his own discretion, than when controlled in any way in which society have it in their power to control him; or because the attempt to exercise control would produce other evils, greater than those which it would prevent. When such reasons as these preclude the enforcement of responsibility, the conscience of the agent himself should step into the vacant judgment seat, and protect those interests of others which have no external protection; judging himself all the more rigidly, because the case does not admit of his being made accountable to the judgment of his fellow-creatures.

But there is a sphere of action in which society, as distinguished from the individual, has, if any, only an indirect interest; comprehending all that portion of a person's life and conduct which affects only himself, or if it also affects others, only with their free, voluntary, and undeceived consent and participation. When I say only himself, I mean directly, and in the first instance: for whatever affects himself, may affect others through himself; and the objection which may be grounded on this contingency, will receive consideration in the sequel. This, then, is the appropriate region of human liberty. It comprises, first, the inward domain of consciousness; demanding liberty of conscience, in the most comprehensive sense; liberty of thought and feeling; absolute freedom of opinion and sentiment on all subjects, practical or speculative, scientific, moral, or theological. The liberty of expressing and publishing opinions may seem to fall under a different principle, since it belongs to that part of the conduct of an individual which concerns other people; but, being almost of as much importance as the liberty of thought itself, and resting in great part on the same reasons, is practically inseparable from it. Secondly, the principle requires liberty of tastes and pursuits; of framing the plan of our life to suit our own character; of doing as we like, subject to such consequences as may follow: without impediment from our fellow-creatures, so long as what we do does not harm them, even though they should think our conduct foolish, perverse, or wrong. Thirdly, from this liberty of each individual, follows the liberty, within the same limits, of combination among individuals; freedom to unite, for any purpose not involving harm to others: the persons combining being supposed to be of full age, and not forced or deceived. 12

No society in which these liberties are not, on the whole, respected, is free, whatever may be its form of government; and none is completely free in which they do not exist absolute and unqualified. The only freedom which deserves the name, is that of pursuing our own good in our own way, so long as we do not attempt to deprive others of theirs, or impede their efforts to obtain it. Each is the proper guardian of his own 13 health, whether bodily, or mental and spiritual. Mankind are greater gainers by suffering each other to live as seems good to themselves, than by compelling each to live as seems good to the rest.

1859

QUESTIONS FOR DISCUSSION

Content

a. Mill begins the essay by distinguishing between two types of liberty—what does he see as the difference between "Liberty of the Will" and "Civil, or Social Liberty"?

b. Historically, what are the two ways that the populace can limit the power of their rulers? Why do "lovers of liberty" (paragraph 2) value the second way over the first way?

c. How and where does Mill define his key terms "liberty" and "authority"? How closely do his definitions mesh with how you might define them?

d. In paragraph 6, Mill writes that the most pressing question is "where to place the limit . . . between individual independence and social control." Where does Mill believe that the limit should be placed?

e. Also in paragraph 6, Mill points out that social rules always seem "self-evident" to the people in that society. To what extent do you agree that social rules are a "universal illusion"? How might the "magical influence of custom" account for abuse of power, hypocrisy, and greed?

f. What problems arise when specific likes or dislikes are focused on and the general rules ignored?

g. The famous harm principle is introduced in paragraph 9. Do you agree that "[t]he only purpose for which power can rightfully be exercised over any member of a civilised community, against his will, is to prevent harm to others"?

h. What are some of the responsibilities that individuals must take on when they are given social liberties?

Strategy and Style

i. How does Mill build his argument? What does he do in each paragraph that leads readers from one point to the next?

j. Where does Mill use definition and process as techniques to build his case?

k. To whom does Mill appear to be writing? What background knowledge must readers have to follow him easily?

l. How does Mill's sentence style compare to what you are familiar with? What assumptions does this style make about Mill's original readers?

m. To what extent does Mill's organization match what you are taught for writing arguments? What advice would you give him for revising? What advice might he give you for making a strong argument?

ENGAGING THE TEXT

a. Mill's sentences are complex and paragraphs are long, and students often find they need to "unpack" them to understand them. Reread Mill's essay in short sections, treating each paragraph as a mini-essay. Choosing one or more of the paragraphs, annotate the paragraph as you read and then write a summary statement of it.

b. Find one sentence that seems significant. Write it on the top of a new page, then write a paragraph focusing just on that sentence. Write everything that comes to mind to help you explain that sentence to yourself. Consider word choice, sentence structure, allusions. Repeat this process with other sentences, as needed.

SUGGESTIONS FOR SUSTAINED WRITING

a. Mill bases his essay on events in Europe and particularly in England. Write an essay in which you reflect on how his ideas might apply to twenty-first century United States.

b. Write an essay in which you discuss Mill's ideas with those of Nat Hentoff and Alan M. Dershowitz (Chapter 10). Discuss to what extent individuals have the right to do as they wish in the situations described by Hentoff and Dershowitz.

c. Read more about John Stuart Mill, Jeremy Bentham, and utilitarianism. With a current issue in mind, discuss how this issue might be addressed from a utilitarian perspective. Also research Kantian or deontological ethics as a counterpoint to utilitarianism, and discuss how the issue would be addressed from that perspective.

READ MORE

John Stuart Mill and His Works

"On Liberty" (http://www.bartleby.com/130): *The entire text of* On Liberty.

"John Stuart Mill" (http://www.victorianweb.org/philosophy/mill/millov.html): *Thematically grouped links to many resources on Mill.*

Reeves, Richard. *John Stuart Mill: Victorian Firebrand*. London: *Atlantic Books, 2007*.

Utilitarianism

"Utilitarianism Resources" (http://www.utilitarianism.com): *A long selection of link to resources about utilitarianism, including a page on John Stuart Mill, with further links.*

"Utilitarian Philosophers" (http://www.utilitarian.net/): *A site similar to the above, organized around a few key philosophers.*

Mixed Strategies

Chapter

As the title of this chapter indicates, the essays contained in it do not rely on a predominant method of development, technique, or strategy to make their points; instead, they are models of the kind of writing that draws widely and freely on various approaches and that blends them naturally and seamlessly. They have been collected in this chapter to provide you with additional readings on a variety of subjects. Each of them is a model of effective writing. Moreover, although they differ in terms of the subjects they address and the methods they use to develop those topics, each selection makes a clear statement in a strong voice. Like the other essays in this text, they were written by people highly committed to the art of communication and to the subjects they chose to write about.

Steven Jay Gould's "Sex, Drugs, Disasters, and the Extinction of Dinosaurs" is an example of clear, accurate, and interesting scientific writing intended for an audience of nonspecialists. Gould's essay is essentially an argument, but it makes good use of techniques ordinarily associated with narrative, definition, process analysis, and cause/effect essays. Ian Frazier's "Coyote vs. Acme" relies heavily on examples and illustrations; nonetheless, its purpose is to argue a point, albeit humorously, and it does so by making use of all the other strategies illustrated in this book.

Amy Tan's "Mother Tongue" aims at definition, but she also makes excellent use of direct quotations. In addition, her writing relies on narration and illustration. Narration is the most obvious strategy in "Test Day" by Frank Bures, but this essay also relies heavily on description, on examples, and even on some comparison and contrast.

Lars Eighner's "On Dumpster Diving" appears to be a narrative on first inspection, but this is a far more complex piece. Eighner's purpose is to defend a distinctive—if not odd—lifestyle choice. But first he must define this lifestyle, establish his authority on the subject through the narration of personal experience, provide specific details of his observations through concrete and vivid description, explain the process of "diving," and, when appropriate, apply a pinch of irony and sardonic humor.

In "Only Daughter," Sandra Cisneros explains what it is like to be female with career aspirations in a male-dominated culture. She uses

447

definition and examples in a narrative framework. Sherman Alexie uses narration, process, and cause and effect to explain the power of reading.

Pay especially close attention to the items under Engaging the Text and Suggestions for Sustained Writing, which follow each selection in this chapter. They provide guidance and inspiration on writing essays enriched by the use of varied strategies and approaches. In addition, consider making your own connections between these essays and those appearing earlier in the text. Doing so will help you exercise skills important to the analysis of language and the synthesis of ideas. In fact, it might also lead you to design unique approaches to discussing the subjects you find most interesting and important.

Sex, Drugs, Disasters, and the Extinction of Dinosaurs

Stephen Jay Gould

Stephen Jay Gould (1941–2002) was professor of Geology and Zoology at Harvard University, where he taught since 1967. He was born in New York City, attended Antioch College (A.B., 1963) and Columbia University (Ph.D., 1967). He was an advisor to the Children's Television Workshop from 1978 to 1987 and an advisor to Nova *from 1980 to 1992. At Harvard University, his research specialties were paleontology, evolutionary biology, and the history of science. He was also the curator of Harvard's Museum of Comparative Zoology. A prolific writer, he published a monthly column in* Natural History *magazine and contributed more than 100 articles to scientific journals across the United States. Among numerous full-length works are several collections of essays first published in* Natural History. *They include* Ever Since Darwin *(1978),* The Panda's Thumb *(1980),* Hen's Teeth and Horses' Toes *(1983),* The Flamingo's Smile *(1985), and* Bully for Brontosaurus *(1991). He is also the author of* The Mismeasure of Man *(1980),* Wonderful Life *(1990), and* Full House: The Spread of Excellence from Plato to Darwin *(1996), which argue against the theory of biological determinism and explain the notion of chance in evolution. Shortly before his death, Gould published his comprehensive scientific book,* The Structure of Evolutionary Theory.

Like K. C. Cole in Chapter 8, Gould makes scientific fact and theory appetizing even to the reader with no scientific training. John Noble Wilford, science editor of the New York Times, *has called him "one of the most spirited essayists of our time." Indeed, his common sense and delightful wit make it seem as if we are reading an article in a popular magazine rather than a reasoned and thoroughly researched scientific study.*

1   Science, in its most fundamental definition, is a fruitful mode of inquiry, not a list of enticing conclusions. The conclusions are the consequence, not the essence.

My greatest unhappiness with most popular presentations of science 2 concerns their failure to separate fascinating claims from the methods that scientists use to establish the facts of nature. Journalists, and the public, thrive on controversial and stunning statements. But science is, basically, a way of knowing—in P. B. Medawar's apt words, "the art of the soluble." If the growing corps of popular science writers would focus on *how* scientists develop and defend those fascinating claims, they would make their greatest possible contribution to public understanding.

Consider three ideas, proposed in perfect seriousness to explain that 3 greatest of all titillating puzzles—the extinction of dinosaurs. Since these three notions invoke the primally fascinating themes of our culture—sex, drugs, and violence—they surely reside in the category of fascinating claims. I want to show why two of them rank as silly speculation, while the other represents science at its grandest and most useful.

Science works with testable proposals. If, after much compilation and 4 scrutiny of data, new information continues to affirm a hypothesis, we may accept it provisionally and gain confidence as further evidence mounts. We can never be completely sure that a hypothesis is right, though we may be able to show with confidence that it is wrong. The best scientific hypotheses are also generous and expansive: They suggest extensions and implications that enlighten related, and even far distant, subjects. Simply consider how the idea of evolution has influenced virtually every intellectual field.

Useless speculation, on the other hand, is restrictive. It generates 5 no testable hypothesis, and offers no way to obtain potentially refuting evidence. Please note that I am not speaking of truth or falsity. The speculation may well be true; still, if it provides, in principle, no material for affirmation or rejection, we can make nothing of it. It must simply stand forever as an intriguing idea. Useless speculation turns in on itself and leads nowhere; good science, containing both seeds for its potential refutation and implications for more and different testable knowledge, reaches out. But, enough preaching. Let's move on to dinosaurs, and the three proposals for their extinction.

1. **Sex:** Testes function only in a narrow range of temperature (those of mammals hang externally in a scrotal sac because internal body temperatures are too high for their proper function). A worldwide rise in temperature at the close of the Cretaceous period caused the testes of dinosaurs to stop functioning and led to their extinction by sterilization of males.

2. **Drugs:** Angiosperms (flowering plants) first evolved toward the end of the dinosaurs' reign. Many of these plants contain psychoactive agents, avoided by mammals today as a result of their bitter taste. Dinosaurs had neither means to taste the bitterness nor livers effective enough to detoxify the substances. They died of massive overdoses.

3. **Disasters:** A large comet or asteroid struck the Earth some 65 million years ago, lofting a cloud of dust into the sky and blocking sunlight, thereby suppressing photosynthesis and so drastically lowering world temperatures that dinosaurs and hosts of other creatures became extinct.

6   Before analyzing these three tantalizing statements, we must establish a basic ground rule often violated in proposals for the dinosaurs' demise. *There is no separate problem of the extinction of dinosaurs.* Too often we divorce specific events from their wider contexts and systems of cause and effect. The fundamental fact of dinosaur extinction is its synchrony with the demise of so many other groups across a wide range of habitats, from terrestrial to marine.

7   The history of life has been punctuated by brief episodes of mass extinction. A recent analysis by University of Chicago paleontologists Jack Sepkoski and Dave Raup, based on the best and most exhaustive tabulation of data ever assembled, shows clearly that five episodes of mass dying stand well above the "background" extinctions of normal times (when we consider all mass extinctions, large and small, they seem to fall in a regular 26-million-year cycle). The Cretaceous debacle, occurring 65 million years ago and separating the Mesozoic and Cenozoic eras of our geological time scale, ranks prominently among the five. Nearly all the marine plankton (single-celled floating creatures) died with geological suddenness; among marine invertebrates, nearly 15 percent of all families perished, including many previously dominant groups, especially the ammonites (relatives of squids in coiled shells). On land, the dinosaurs disappeared after more than 100 million years of unchallenged domination.

8   In this context, speculations limited to dinosaurs alone ignore the larger phenomenon. We need a coordinated explanation for a system of events that includes the extinction of dinosaurs as one component. Thus it makes little sense, though it may fuel our desire to view mammals as inevitable inheritors of the Earth, to guess that dinosaurs died because small mammals ate their eggs (a perennial favorite among untestable speculations). It seems most unlikely that some disaster peculiar to dinosaurs befell these massive beasts—and that the debacle happened to strike just when one of history's five great dyings had enveloped the Earth for completely different reasons.

9   The testicular theory, an old favorite from the 1940s, had its root in an interesting and thoroughly respectable study of temperature tolerances in the American alligator, published in the staid *Bulletin of the American Museum of Natural History* in 1946 by three experts on living and fossil reptiles—E. H. Colbert, my own first teacher in paleontology; R. B. Cowles; and C. M. Bogert.

The first sentence of their summary reveals a purpose beyond alliga- 10 tors: "This report describes an attempt to infer the reactions of extinct reptiles, especially the dinosaurs, to high temperatures as based upon reactions observed in the modern alligator." They studied, by rectal thermometry, the body temperatures of alligators under changing conditions of heating and cooling. (Well, let's face it, you wouldn't want to try sticking a thermometer under a 'gator's tongue.) The predictions under test go way back to an old theory first stated by Galileo in the 1630s—the unequal scaling of surfaces and volumes. As an animal, or any object, grows (provided its shape doesn't change), surface areas must increase more slowly than volumes—since surfaces get larger as length squared, while volumes increase much more rapidly, as length cubed. Therefore, small animals have high ratios of surface to volume, while large animals cover themselves with relatively little surface.

Among cold-blooded animals lacking any physiological mechanism 11 for keeping their temperatures constant, small creatures have a hell of a time keeping warm—because they lose so much heat through their relatively large surfaces. On the other hand, large animals, with their relatively small surfaces, may lose heat so slowly that, once warm, they may maintain effectively constant temperatures against ordinary fluctuations of climate. (In fact, the resolution of the "hot-blooded dinosaur" controversy that burned so brightly a few years back may simply be that, while large dinosaurs possessed no physiological mechanism for constant temperature, and were not therefore warm-blooded in the technical sense, their large size and relatively small surface area kept them warm.)

Colbert, Cowles, and Bogert compared the warming rates of small 12 and large alligators. As predicted, the small fellows heated up (and cooled down) more quickly. When exposed to a warm sun, a tiny 50-gram (1.76-ounce) alligator heated up one degree Celsius every minute and a half, while a large alligator, 260 times bigger at 13,000 grams (28.7 pounds), took seven and a half minutes to gain a degree. Extrapolating up to an adult 10-ton dinosaur, they concluded that a one-degree rise in body temperature would take eighty-six hours. If large animals absorb heat so slowly (through their relatively small surfaces), they will also be unable to shed any excess heat gained when temperatures rise above a favorable level.

The authors then guessed that large dinosaurs lived at or near their 13 optimum temperatures; Cowles suggested that a rise in global temperatures just before the Cretaceous extinction caused the dinosaurs to heat up beyond their optimal tolerance—and, being so large, they couldn't shed the unwanted heat. (In a most unusual statement within a scientific paper, Colbert and Bogert then explicitly disavowed this speculative extension of their empirical work on alligators.) Cowles conceded that this excess heat probably wasn't enough to kill or even to enervate the great beasts, but since testes often function only within a narrow range of temperature, he proposed that this global rise might have sterilized all the males, causing extinction by natural contraception.

14   The overdose theory has recently been supported by UCLA psychiatrist Ronald K. Siegel. Siegel has gathered, he claims, more than 2,000 records of animals who, when given access, administer various drugs to themselves—from a mere swig of alcohol to massive doses of the big H. Elephants will swill the equivalent of twenty beers at a time, but do not like alcohol in concentrations greater than seven percent. In a silly bit of anthropocentric speculation, Siegel states that "elephants drink, perhaps, to forget . . . the anxiety produced by shrinking rangeland and the competition for food."

15   Since fertile imaginations can apply almost any hot idea to the extinction of dinosaurs, Siegel found a way. Flowering plants did not evolve until late in the dinosaurs' reign. These plants also produced an array of aromatic, amino-acid-based alkaloids—the major group of psychoactive agents. Most mammals are "smart" enough to avoid these potential poisons. The alkaloids simply don't taste good (they are bitter); in any case, we mammals have livers happily supplied with the capacity to detoxify them. But, Siegel speculates, perhaps dinosaurs could neither taste the bitterness nor detoxify the substances once ingested. He recently told members of the American Psychological Association: "I'm not suggesting that all dinosaurs OD'd on plant drugs, but it certainly was a factor." He also argued that death by overdose may help explain why so many dinosaur fossils are found in contorted positions. (Do not go gentle into that good night.)

16   Extraterrestrial catastrophes have long pedigrees in the popular literature of extinction, but the subject exploded again in 1979, after a long lull, when the father-son, physicist-geologist team of Luis and Walter Alvarez proposed that an asteroid, some 10 km in diameter, struck the Earth 65 million years ago. (Comets, rather than asteroids, have since gained favor. Good science is self-corrective.)

17   The force of such a collision would be immense, greater by far than the megatonnage of all the world's nuclear weapons. In trying to reconstruct a scenario that would explain the simultaneous dying of dinosaurs on land and so many creatures in the sea, the Alvarezes proposed that a gigantic dust cloud, generated by particles blown aloft in the impact, would so darken the Earth that photosynthesis would cease and temperatures drop precipitously. (Rage, rage against the dying of the light.) The single-celled photosynthetic oceanic plankton, with life cycles measured in weeks, would perish outright, but land plants might survive through the dormancy of their seeds. (Land plants were not much affected by the Cretaceous extinction, and any adequate theory must account for the curious pattern of differential survival.) Dinosaurs would die by starvation and freezing; small, warm-blooded mammals, with more modest

requirements for food and better regulation of body temperature, would squeak through. "Let the bastards freeze in the dark," as bumper stickers of our chauvinistic neighbors in sunbelt states proclaimed several years ago during the Northeast's winter oil crisis.

All three theories, testicular malfunction, psychoactive overdosing, [18] and asteroidal zapping, grab our attention mightily. As pure phenomenology, they rank about equally high on any hit parade of primal fascination. Yet one represents expansive science, the others restrictive and untestable speculation. The proper criterion lies in evidence and methodology; we must probe behind the superficial fascination of particular claims.

How could we possibly decide whether the hypothesis of testicular [19] frying is right or wrong? We would have to know things that the fossil record cannot provide. What temperatures were optimal for dinosaurs? Could they avoid the absorption of excess heat by staying in the shade, or in caves? At what temperatures did their testicles cease to function? Were late Cretaceous climates ever warm enough to drive the internal temperatures of dinosaurs close to this ceiling? Testicles simply don't fossilize, and how could we infer their temperature tolerances even if they did? In short, Cowles's hypothesis is only an intriguing speculation leading nowhere. The most damning statement against it appeared right in the conclusion of Colbert, Cowles, and Bogert's paper, when they admitted: "It is difficult to advance any definite arguments against the hypothesis." My statement may seem paradoxical—isn't a hypothesis really good if you can't devise any arguments against it? Quite the contrary. It is simply untestable and unusable.

Siegel's overdosing has even less going for it. At least Cowles extrapo- [20] lated his conclusion from some good data on alligators. And he didn't completely violate the primary guideline of siting dinosaur extinction in the context of a general mass dying—for rise in temperature could be the root cause of a general catastrophe, zapping dinosaurs by testicular malfunction and different groups for other reasons. But Siegel's speculation cannot touch the extinction of ammonites or oceanic plankton. (Diatoms make their own food with good sweet sunlight; they don't OD on the chemicals of terrestrial plants.) It is simply a gratuitous, attention-grabbing guess. It cannot be tested, for how can we know what dinosaurs tasted and what their livers could do? Livers don't fossilize any better than testicles.

The hypothesis doesn't even make any sense in its own context. [21] Angiosperms were in full flower ten million years before dinosaurs went the way of all flesh. Why did it take so long? As for the pains of a chemical death recorded in contortions of fossils, I regret to say (or rather I'm pleased to note for the dinosaurs' sake) that Siegel's knowledge of geology must be a bit deficient: Muscles contract after death and geological strata rise and fall with motions of the Earth's crust after burial—more than enough reason to distort a fossil's pristine appearance.

22   The impact story, on the other hand, has a sound basis in evidence. It can be tested, extended, refined, and, if wrong, disproved. The Alvarezes did not just construct an arresting guess for public consumption. They proposed their hypothesis after laborious geochemical studies with Frank Asaro and Helen Michael had revealed a massive increase of iridium in rocks deposited right at the time of extinction. Iridium, a rare metal of the platinum group, is virtually absent from indigenous rocks of the Earth's crust; most of our iridium arrives on extraterrestrial objects that strike the Earth.

23   The Alvarez hypothesis bore immediate fruit. Based originally on evidence from two European localities, it led geochemists throughout the world to examine other sediments of the same age. They found abnormally high amounts of iridium everywhere—from continental rocks of the western United States to deep sea cores from the South Atlantic.

24   Cowles proposed his testicular hypothesis in the mid-1940s. Where has it gone since then? Absolutely nowhere, because scientists can do nothing with it. The hypothesis must stand as a curious appendage to a solid study of alligators. Siegel's overdose scenario will also win a few press notices and fade into oblivion. The Alvarezes' asteroid falls into a different category altogether, and much of the popular commentary has missed this essential distinction by focusing on the impact and its attendant results, and forgetting what really matters to a scientist—the iridium. If you talk just about asteroids, dust, and darkness, you tell stories no better and no more entertaining than fried testicles or terminal trips. It is the iridium—the source of testable evidence—that counts and forges the crucial distinction between speculation and science.

25   The proof, to twist a phrase, lies in the doing. Cowles's hypothesis has generated nothing in thirty-five years. Since its proposal in 1979, the Alvarez hypothesis has spawned hundreds of studies, a major conference, and attendant publications. Geologists are fired up. They are looking for iridium at all other extinction boundaries. Every week exposes a new wrinkle in the scientific press. Further evidence that the Cretaceous iridium represents extraterrestrial impact and not indigenous volcanism continues to accumulate. As I revise this essay in November 1984 (this paragraph will be out of date when the book is published), new data include chemical "signatures" of other isotopes indicating unearthly provenance, glass spherules of a size and sort produced by impact and not by volcanic eruptions, and high-pressure varieties of silica formed (so far as we know) only under the tremendous shock of impact.

26   My point is simply this: Whatever the eventual outcome (I suspect it will be positive), the Alvarez hypothesis is exciting, fruitful science because it generates tests, provides us with things to do, and expands outward. We are having fun, battling back and forth, moving toward a resolution, and extending the hypothesis beyond its original scope.

As just one example of the unexpected, distant cross-fertilization that 27 good science engenders, the Alvarez hypothesis made a major contribution to a theme that has riveted public attention in the past few months— so-called nuclear winter. In a speech delivered in April 1982, Luis Alvarez calculated the energy that a ten-kilometer asteroid would release on impact. He compared such an explosion with a full nuclear exchange and implied that all out atomic war might unleash similar consequences.

This theme of impact leading to massive dust clouds and falling 28 temperatures formed an important input to the decision of Carl Sagan and a group of colleagues to model the climatic consequences of nuclear holocaust. Full nuclear exchange would probably generate the same kind of dust cloud and darkening that may have wiped out the dinosaurs. Temperatures would drop precipitously and agriculture might become impossible. Avoidance of nuclear war is fundamentally an ethical and political imperative, but we must know the factual consequences to make firm judgments. I am heartened by a final link across disciplines and deep concerns—another criterion, by the way, of science at its best. A recognition of the very phenomenon that made our evolution possible by exterminating the previously dominant dinosaurs and clearing a way for the evolution of large mammals, including us, might actually help to save us from joining those magnificent beasts in contorted poses among the strata of the Earth.

1984

QUESTIONS FOR DISCUSSION

Content

a. In paragraph 1, Gould claims that science is a "fruitful mode of inquiry," not a list of "conclusions." What does he mean, and how does this assertion help explain his argument? Where is this assertion illustrated in his essay?
b. Why can we "never be completely sure" that a hypothesis is correct (paragraph 4)?
c. Summarize the three hypotheses on the extinction of dinosaurs. What is the main element in each that makes it testable or untestable?
d. What distinctions does the author make between scientific hypothesis and speculation? Explain his assertion that the "proper criterion lies in evidence and methodology" (paragraph 18).
e. Why, according to Gould, is a hypothesis suspect if one cannot mount arguments against it?

f. What does he mean when he implies that science should be fun (paragraph 26)? In what way does the Alvarez hypothesis meet this criterion? Why are the other two theories not fun?

Strategy and Style

g. In paragraph 9, Gould reports that the "testicular theory" had its origins in a respectable scientific study. Why does he say this if he wants to discredit that theory?
h. What are his views of the various scientists whose studies he cites? Compare his opinions of the team of Colbert, Cowles, and Bogert (paragraphs 9–13); of Siegel (paragraphs 14 and 15); and of the Alvarezes (paragraphs 16 and 17). What words does he use to describe each? How do these words provide foreshadowing?
i. In paragraph 6, Gould writes, "Too often we divorce specific events." Who is "we"?
j. Is Gould's intended audience limited to scientists or people interested in science? How do you know?
k. What is the effect of quoting poet Dylan Thomas in paragraph 17 ("Rage, rage, against the dying of the light")?
l. What rhetorical strategies does Gould use, and where are they most apparent in the essay? What might be his reasons for choosing these strategies?

ENGAGING THE TEXT

a. Read through the essay once more, writing in the margins questions that you would ask the author if you had the chance to meet with him. For example, you might inquire why he believes it is "silly" to think that elephants might experience anxiety (paragraph 14).
b. Look around your town or college. Briefly "speculate" about what it or the land it sits on might have looked like 50, 100, or even 1,000 years ago. Use Gould's style of speculation as a guide.

SUGGESTIONS FOR SUSTAINED WRITING

a. In paragraphs 15 and 17, Gould quotes from "Do Not Go Gentle into That Good Night" by Dylan Thomas. Find a copy of the poem in your library and read it. Then, write an essay in which you explain the significance of the lines that Gould takes from it.
b. Compare Gould's essay to Diane Ackerman's "Why Leaves Turn Color in the Fall" (Chapter 3) or to K. C. Cole's "The Arrow of Time" (Chapter 8). Comment on the style of these three science writers. How do they make, or attempt to make, science seem exciting?

c. When he brings in the idea of nuclear war in his concluding paragraphs, Gould suggests that the Alvarezes's theory has implications
   beyond the scope of paleontology. What other implications might their
   theory have? Do research to write an essay in which you speculate on
   these implications.

READ MORE

Gould and His Works

Sterelny, Kim. *Dawkins vs. Gould: Survival of the Fittest.* Cambridge, UK:
Icon, 2001.

"The Official Stephen Jay Gould Archive" (http://www.sjgarchive.org/):
An archive still under development.

"The Unofficial Stephen Jay Gould Archive" (http://www.stephenjaygould
.org): *Gould's former personal website, which now provides links to his biography, interviews, articles, and more.*

Theories of Dinosaur Extinction

Bakker, Robert T. *The Dinosaur Heresies: New Theories Unlocking the Mystery
of the Dinosaurs and Their Extinction.* New York: Citadel, 2001.

"Blast from the Past!" (http://paleobiology.si.edu/blastPast): *A page about
dinosaur extinction at the Smithsonian National Museum of Natural History.*

Mother Tongue

Amy Tan

*Amy Tan (b. 1952) studied at San Jose State University, earning a B.A. in 1973 and
an M.A. in 1974, and did postgraduate work at the University of California–Berkeley
from 1974 to 1976. From 1976 to 1987 she worked in San Francisco in various jobs:
as a language consultant to programs for children with disabilities from 1976 to 1981;
as the project director for the MORE Project in 1980 and 1981; as a reporter, managing editor, and associate publisher for* Emergency Room Reports *from 1981 to 1983;
and as a freelance technical writer from 1983 to 1987. Realizing that she had become a
"workaholic," Tan began therapy to deal with the problem. Unfortunately (or perhaps
fortunately), her therapist tended to fall asleep during their sessions, so Tan turned to
herself for therapy, taking jazz piano lessons and beginning to write fiction as a way
to slow down. Her enormously successful novel* The Joy Luck Club *(1989) was the
result of this "therapy" and the start of a literary career. Since then, Tan has published
novels—*The Kitchen God's Wife *(1991),* The Hundred Secret Senses *(1995), The*

Year of the Flood *(1995),* The Bonesetter's Daughter *(2001), and* Saving Fish from Drowning *(2005)—and children's books:* The Moon Lady *(1992) and* The Chinese Siamese Cat *(1994). In addition, she has written short stories and essays for various magazines, some of which have been collected in books such as* The Opposite of Fate *(2003), and she wrote the libretto for the San Francisco Opera's 2008 production of* The Bonesetter's Daughter. *Tan is also a member of the Rock Bottom Remainders, a garage band comprised of famous authors who perform to raise money for literacy programs.*

Tan and her mother were often in conflict—Tan failed at piano lessons as a child, she dropped out of the college that her mother had selected for her, and she chose to become a writer rather than a doctor. However, in 1987, after her mother recovered from a serious illness, Tan took her to China, a trip that brought the two of them closer. Both irritation and sympathy toward her mother come through in the tone of the following essay.

1   I am not a scholar of English or literature. I cannot give you much more than personal opinions on the English language and its variations in this country or others.

2   I am a writer. And by that definition, I am someone who has always loved language. I am fascinated by language in daily life. I spend a great deal of my time thinking about the power of language—the way it can evoke an emotion, a visual image, a complex idea, or a simple truth. Language is the tool of my trade. And I use them all—all the Englishes I grew up with.

3   Recently, I was made keenly aware of the different Englishes I do use. I was giving a talk to a large group of people, the same talk I had already given to half a dozen other groups. The nature of the talk was about my writing, my life, and my book *The Joy Luck Club.* The talk was going along well enough, until I remembered one major difference that made the whole talk sound wrong. My mother was in the room. And it was perhaps the first time she had heard me give a lengthy speech, using the kind of English I have never used with her. I was saying things like, "The intersection of memory upon imagination" and "There is an aspect of my fiction that relates to thus-and-thus"—a speech filled with carefully wrought grammatical phrases, burdened, it suddenly seemed to me, with nominalized forms, past perfect tenses, conditional phrases, all the forms of standard English that I had learned in school and through books, the forms of English I did not use at home with my mother.

4   Just last week, I was walking down the street with my mother, and I again found myself conscious of the English I was using, the English I do use with her. We were talking about the price of new and used furniture and I heard myself saying this: "Not waste money that way." My husband was with us as well, and he didn't notice any switch in my English. And then I realized why. It's because over the twenty years we've been together I've often used that same kind of English with him, and

sometimes he even uses it with me. It has become our language of intimacy, a different sort of English that relates to family talk, the language I grew up with.

So you'll have some idea of what this family talk I heard sounds 5 like, I'll quote what my mother said during a recent conversation which I videotaped and then transcribed. During this conversation, my mother was talking about a political gangster in Shanghai who had the same last name as her family's, Du, and how the gangster in his early years wanted to be adopted by her family, which was rich by comparison. Later, the gangster became more powerful, far richer than my mother's family, and one day showed up at my mother's wedding to pay his respects. Here's what she said in part:

"Du Yusong having business like fruit stand. Like off the street kind. He 6 is Du like Du Zong—but not Tsung-ming Island people. The local people call putong, the river east side, he belong to that side local people. That man want to ask Du Zong father take him in like become own family. Du Zong father wasn't look down on him, but didn't take seriously, until that man big like become a mafia. Now important person, very hard to inviting him. Chinese way, came only to show respect, don't stay for dinner. Respect for making big celebration, he shows up. Mean gives lots of respect. Chinese custom. Chinese social life that way. If too important won't have to stay too long. He come to my wedding. I didn't see, I heard it. I gone to boy's side, they have YMCA dinner. Chinese age I was nineteen."

You should know that my mother's expressive command of English 7 belies how much she actually understands. She reads the *Forbes* report, listens to *Wall Street Week,* converses daily with her stockbroker, reads all of Shirley MacLaine's books with ease—all kinds of things I can't begin to understand. Yet some of my friends tell me they understand 50 percent of what my mother says. Some say they understand 80 to 90 percent. Some say they understand none of it, as if she was speaking pure Chinese. But to me, my mother's English is perfectly clear, perfectly natural. It's my mother tongue. Her language, as I hear it, is vivid, direct, full of observation and imagery. That was the language that helped shape the way I saw things, expressed things, made sense of the world.

Lately, I've been giving more thought to the kind of English my 8 mother speaks. Like others, I have described it to people as "broken" or "fractured" English. But I wince when I say that. It has always bothered me that I can think of no way to describe it other than "broken," as if it were damaged and needed to be fixed, as if it lacked a certain wholeness and soundness. I've heard other terms used, "limited English," for example. But they seem just as bad, as if everything is limited, including people's perceptions of the limited English speaker.

I know this for a fact, because when I was growing up, my mother's 9 "limited" English limited *my* perception of her. I was ashamed of her

English. I believed that her English reflected the quality of what she had to say. That is, because she expressed them imperfectly her thoughts were imperfect. And I had plenty of empirical evidence to support me: the fact that people in department stores, at banks, and at restaurants did not take her seriously, did not give her good service, pretended not to understand her, or even acted as if they did not hear her.

10   My mother has long realized the limitations of her English as well. When I was fifteen, she used to have me call people on the phone to pretend I was she. In this guise, I was forced to ask for information or even to complain and yell at people who had been rude to her. One time it was a call to her stockbroker in New York. She had cashed out her small portfolio and it just so happened we were going to go to New York the next week, our very first trip outside California. I had to get on the phone and say in an adolescent voice that was not very convincing, "This is Mrs. Tan."

11   And my mother was standing in the back whispering loudly, "Why he don't send me check, already two weeks late. So mad he lie to me, losing me money."

12   And then I said in perfect English, "Yes, I'm getting rather concerned. You had agreed to send the check two weeks ago, but it hasn't arrived."

13   Then she began to talk more loudly. "What he want, I come to New York tell him front of his boss, you cheating me?" And I was trying to calm her down, make her be quiet, while telling the stockbroker, "I can't tolerate any more excuses. If I don't receive the check immediately, I am going to have to speak to your manager when I'm in New York next week." And sure enough, the following week there we were in front of this astonished stockbroker, and I was sitting there red-faced and quiet, and my mother, the real Mrs. Tan, was shouting at his boss in her impeccable broken English.

14   We used a similar routine just five days ago, for a situation that was far less humorous. My mother had gone to the hospital for an appointment, to find out about a benign brain tumor a CAT scan had revealed a month ago. She said she had spoken very good English, her best English, no mistakes. Still, she said, the hospital did not apologize when they said they had lost the CAT scan and she had come for nothing. She said they did not seem to have any sympathy when she told them she was anxious to know the exact diagnosis, since her husband and son had both died of brain tumors. She said they would not give her any more information until the next time and she would have to make another appointment for that. So she said she would not leave until the doctor called her daughter. She wouldn't budge. And when the doctor finally called her daughter, me, who spoke in perfect English—lo and behold—we had assurances the CAT scan would be found, promises that a conference call on Monday

would be held, and apologies for any suffering my mother had gone through for a most regrettable mistake.

I think my mother's English almost had an effect on limiting my possibilities in life as well. Sociologists and linguists probably will tell you that a person's developing language skills are more influenced by peers. But I do think that the language spoken in the family, especially in immigrant families which are more insular, plays a large role in shaping the language of the child. And I believe that it affected my results on achievements tests, IQ tests, and the SAT. While my English skills were never judged as poor, compared to math, English could not be considered my strong suit. In grade school I did moderately well, getting perhaps Bs, sometimes B-pluses, in English and scoring perhaps in the sixtieth or seventieth percentile on achievement tests. But those scores were not good enough to override the opinion that my true abilities lay in math and science, because in those areas I achieved As and scored in the ninetieth percentile or higher.

This was understandable. Math is precise; there is only one correct answer. Whereas, for me at least, the answers on English tests were always a judgment call, a matter of opinion and personal experience. Those tests were constructed around items like fill-in-the-blank sentence completion, such as: "Even though Tom was _____, Mary thought he was _____." And the correct answer always seemed to be the most bland combinations of thoughts, for example, "Even though Tom was shy, Mary thought he was charming," with the grammatical structure "even though" limiting the correct answer to some sort of semantic opposites, so you wouldn't get answers like, "Even though Tom was foolish, Mary thought he was ridiculous." Well, according to my mother, there were very few limitations as to what Tom could have been and what Mary might have thought of him. So I never did well on tests like that.

The same was true with word analogies, pairs of words in which you were supposed to find some sort of logical, semantic relationship—for example, "*Sunset* is to *nightfall* as _____ is to _____." And here you would be presented with a list of our possible pairs, one of which showed the same kind of relationship: *red* is to *stoplight*, *bus* is to *arrival*, *chills* is to *fever*, *yawn* is to *boring*. Well, I could never think that way. I knew what the tests were asking, but I could not block out of my mind the images already created by the first pair, "*sunset* is to *nightfall*"—and I would see a burst of colors against a darkening sky, the moon rising, the lowering of a curtain of stars. And all the other pairs of words—red, bus, stoplight, boring— just threw up a mass of confusing images, making it impossible for me to sort out something as logical as saying: "A sunset precedes nightfall" is the same as "a chill precedes a fever." The only way I would have gotten that answer right would have been to imagine an associative situation, for example, my being disobedient and staying out past sunset, catching a chill at night, which turns into feverish pneumonia as punishment, which indeed did happen to me.

18   I have been thinking about all this lately, about my mother's English, about achievement tests. Because lately I've been asked, as a writer, why there are not more Asian Americans represented in American literature. Why are there few Asian Americans enrolled in creative writing programs? Why do so many Chinese students go into engineering? Well, these are broad sociological questions I can't begin to answer. But I have noticed in surveys—in fact, just last week—that Asian students, as a whole, always do significantly better on math achievement tests than in English. And this makes me think that there are other Asian-American students whose English spoken in the home might also be described as "broken" or "limited." And perhaps they also have teachers who are steering them away from writing and into math and science, which is what happened to me.

19   Fortunately, I happen to be rebellious in nature and enjoy the challenge of disproving assumptions made about me. I became an English major my first year in college, after being enrolled as premed. I started writing nonfiction as a freelancer the week after I was told by my former boss that writing was my worst skill and I should hone my talents toward account management.

20   But it wasn't until 1985 that I finally began to write fiction. And at first I wrote using what I thought to be wittily crafted sentences, sentences that would finally prove I had mastery over the English language. Here's an example from the first draft of a story that later made its way into *The Joy Luck Club*, but without this line: "That was my mental quandary in its nascent state." A terrible line, which I can barely pronounce.

21   Fortunately, for reasons I won't get into today, I later decided I should envision a reader for the stories I would write. And the reader I decided upon was my mother, because these were stories about mothers. So with this reader in mind—and in fact she did read my early drafts—I began to write stories using all the Englishes I grew up with: the English I spoke to my mother, which for lack of a better term might be described as "simple"; the English she used with me, which for lack of a better term might be described as "broken"; my translation of her Chinese, which could certainly be described as "watered down"; and what I imagined to be her translation of her Chinese if she could speak in perfect English, her internal language, and for that I sought to preserve the essence, but neither an English nor a Chinese structure. I wanted to capture what language ability tests can never reveal: her intent, her passion, her imagery, the rhythms of her speech and the nature of her thoughts.

Apart from what any critic had to say about my writing, I knew I had   22
succeeded where it counted when my mother finished reading my book
and gave me her verdict: "So easy to read."

1990

QUESTIONS FOR DISCUSSION

Content

a. How does Tan define the term *writer* (paragraph 2)? How does this
   definition compare with other definitions you have heard?
b. What are "the different Englishes" (paragraph 3) that Tan and her
   mother use in their public and private lives? What differentiates each
   type of English from the others?
c. In what ways does Tan's public English contrast with her mother's
   public English? Why would two women so closely related have such
   different public "Englishes"?
d. What influence has her mother had on Tan's writing? Describe Tan's
   mother's type of English. Why does calling it "broken" (paragraph 8)
   make Tan wince?
e. Why did Tan not do well on language tests? How did her "mother
   tongue" contribute to her not doing well?
f. How did Tan train herself to write literary English?

Strategy and Style

g. What rhetorical strategies does Tan use, and where are they most
   apparent in the essay? What might be her reason for choosing these
   strategies? How effectively does she use them?
h. How would you describe the style of this essay? What type of English
   is it? What terms or phrases illustrate the type of English it is?
i. Are the examples of her mother's Englishes effective ones? Why or
   why not?
j. "Mother Tongue" was first published in *Threepenny Review*, a literary
   journal. How does Tan craft her essay for the type of people who read
   literary journals? How would they respond to her essay? How might
   Tan's mother react to it?

ENGAGING THE TEXT

a. Describe the Englishes (or other languages) that you grew up speaking
   or now use. How does the way you speak with your family differ from

the way you speak with your teachers, co-workers, and friends? Refer to Tan's essay in your response.

b. Write your definition of *writer*. You can begin with Tan's definition and expand it, making it more specific, adding examples, and so forth.

SUGGESTIONS FOR SUSTAINED WRITING

a. Write an essay combining the strategies of narrative and example or narrative and definition. Possible topics are stories about your family or friends, especially a difference between you and a family member or between you and a friend.

b. Compare Tan's essay to John McPhee's "Silk Parachute" (Chapter 7) or Sandra Cisneros's "Only Daughter" in this chapter. Discuss the relationship that the younger person has with her or his elders and the attitudes they have toward the culture of their ancestors. Or read Tan's novel *The Joy Luck Club*, or a part of it, and identify the Englishes used in the book that Tan describes in paragraph 21. Write an essay discussing how these Englishes help or hinder those who speak or write with those Englishes.

c. Do research into another version or dialect of English, such as ebonics, Gullah, or Creole. Write an essay tracing the history of this other type of English and explaining its current status. Explore the historical and political relationship of the dialect to standard English.

READ MORE

Tan and Her Works

"Amy Tan" (http://www.amytan.net/): *Tan's personal website.*

"Anniina's Amy Tan Page" (http://www.luminarium.org/contemporary/amytan): *One of many online sources created by fans of Amy Tan, with links to many interviews.*

Huntley, E. D. *Amy Tan: A Critical Companion*. Westport, CT: Greenwood, 1998.

"The Rock Bottom Remainders" (http://www.rockbottomremainders .com/): *Website for the literary rock band in which Tan is a member.*

English Dialects

"American Dialect Society" (http://www.americandialect.org): *Information about the English language in North America.*

Cassidy, Frederic Gomes, and Joan Houston Hall. *Dictionary of American Regional English*. Cambridge, MA: Belknap Press of Harvard UP, 1985.

On Dumpster Diving

Lars Eighner

A freelance writer living in Austin, Lars Eighner (b. 1948) was born in Corpus Christi, Texas, and attended the University of Texas from 1966 to 1969. He was an attendant and ward worker at the Austin State Hospital from 1980 to 1987 and worked off and on for a drug crisis program and as a freelance writer. Eighner lived on the streets for several years, and his homeless experiences are recalled in Travels with Lizbeth *(1993), which became a best-seller and from which "Dumpster Diving" is excerpted. "Dumpster Diving" was first anthologized in* The Pushcart Prize Best of the Small Presses *in 1992. Among Eighner's other works are* Elements of Arousal *(1994), advice to would-be authors of gay erotica; a novel,* Pawn to Queen Four *(1995); and a collection of essays,* Gay Cosmos *(1995).*

Travels started as a series of letters to his friends describing life on the street. His sentence style has been compared to the style of the nineteenth-century English novel.

Long before I began Dumpster diving I was impressed with Dumpsters, 1 enough so that I wrote the Merriam-Webster research service to discover what I could about the word *Dumpster*. I learned from them that it is a proprietary word belonging to the Dempster Dumpster company. Since then I have dutifully capitalized the word, although it was lowercased in almost all the citations Merriam-Webster photocopied for me. Dempster's word is too apt. I have never heard these things called anything but Dumpsters. I do not know anyone who knows the generic name for these objects. From time to time I have heard a wino or hobo give some corrupted credit to the original and call them Dipsy Dumpsters.

I began Dumpster diving about a year before I became homeless.   2

I prefer the word *scavenging* and use the word *scrounging* when I 3 mean to be obscure. I have heard people, evidently meaning to be polite, use the word *foraging*, but I prefer to reserve that word for gathering nuts and berries and such, which I do also according to the season and the opportunity. *Dumpster diving* seems to me to be a little too cute and, in my case, inaccurate because I lack the athletic ability to lower myself into the Dumpsters as the true divers do, much to their increased profit.

I like the frankness of the word *scavenging*, which I can hardly think 4 of without picturing a big black snail on an aquarium wall. I live from the refuse of others. I am a scavenger. I think it a sound and honorable niche, although if I could I would naturally prefer to live the comfortable consumer life, perhaps—and only perhaps—as a slightly less wasteful consumer, owing to what I have learned as a scavenger.

While Lizbeth [Eighner's dog] and I were still living in the shack on 5 Avenue B as my savings ran out, I put almost all my sporadic income into rent. The necessities of daily life I began to extract from Dumpsters. Yes, we ate from them. Except for jeans, all my clothes came from Dumpsters. Boom boxes, candles, bedding, toilet paper, a virgin male love doll, medicine, books, a typewriter, dishes, furnishing, and change, sometimes amounting to many dollars—I acquired many things from the Dumpsters.

6   I have learned much as a scavenger. I mean to put some of what I have learned down here, beginning with the practical art of Dumpster diving and proceeding to the abstract.

7   What is safe to eat?

8   After all, the finding of objects is becoming something of an urban art. Even respectable employed people will sometimes find something tempting sticking out of a Dumpster or standing beside one. Quite a number of people, not all of them of the bohemian type, are willing to brag that they found this or that piece in the trash. But eating from Dumpsters is what separates the dilettanti from the professionals. Eating safely from the Dumpsters involves three principles: using the senses and common sense to evaluate the condition of the found materials, knowing the Dumpsters of a given area and checking them regularly, and seeking always to answer the question "Why was this discarded?"

9   Perhaps everyone who has a kitchen and a regular supply of groceries has, at one time or another, made a sandwich and eaten half of it before discovering mold on the bread or got a mouthful of milk before realizing the milk had turned. Nothing of the sort is likely to happen to a Dumpster diver because he is constantly reminded that most food is discarded for a reason. Yet a lot of perfectly good food can be found in Dumpsters.

10   Canned goods, for example, turn up fairly often in the Dumpsters I frequent. All except the most phobic people would be willing to eat from a can, even if it came from a Dumpster. Canned goods are among the safest of foods to be found in Dumpsters but are not utterly foolproof.

11   Although very rare with modern canning methods, botulism is a possibility. Most other forms of food poisoning seldom do lasting harm to a healthy person, but botulism is almost certainly fatal and often the first symptom is death. Except for carbonated beverages, all canned goods should contain a slight vacuum and suck air when first punctured. Bulging, rusty, and dented cans and cans that spew when punctured should be avoided, especially when the contents are not very acidic or syrupy.

12   Heat can break down the botulin, but this requires much more cooking than most people do to canned goods. To the extent that botulism occurs at all, of course, it can occur in cans on pantry shelves as well as in cans from Dumpsters. Need I say that home-canned goods are simply too risky to be recommended.

13   From time to time one of my companions, aware of the source of my provisions, will ask, "Do you think these crackers are really safe to eat?" For some reason it is most often the crackers they ask about.

14   This question has always made me angry. Of course I would not offer my companion anything I had doubts about. But more than that, I wonder

why he cannot evaluate the condition of the crackers for himself. I have no special knowledge and I have been wrong before. Since he knows where the food comes from, it seems to me he ought to assume some of the responsibility for deciding what he will put in his mouth. For myself I have few qualms about dry foods such as crackers, cookies, cereal, chips, and pasta if they are free of visible contaminates and still dry and crisp. Most often such things are found in the original packaging, which is not so much a positive sign as it is the absence of a negative one.

Raw fruits and vegetables with intact skins seem perfectly safe to me, excluding of course the obviously rotten. Many are discarded for minor imperfections that can be pared away. Leafy vegetables, grapes, cauliflower, broccoli, and similar things may be contaminated by liquids and may be impractical to wash. 15

Candy, especially hard candy, is usually safe if it has not drawn ants. Chocolate is often discarded only because it has become discolored as the cocoa butter de-emulsified. Candying, after all, is one method of food preservation because pathogens do not like very sugary substances. 16

All of these foods might be found in any Dumpster and can be evaluated with some confidence largely on the basis of appearance. Beyond these are foods that cannot be correctly evaluated without additional information. 17

I began scavenging by pulling pizzas out of the Dumpster behind a pizza delivery shop. In general, prepared food requires caution, but in this case I knew when the shop closed and went to the Dumpster as soon as the last of the help left. 18

Such shops often get prank orders; both the orders and the products made to fill them are called *bogus*. Because help seldom stays long at these places, pizzas are often made with the wrong topping, refused on delivery for being cold, or baked incorrectly. The products to be discarded are boxed up because inventory is kept by counting boxes: A boxed pizza can be written off; an unboxed pizza does not exist. 19

I never placed a bogus order to increase the supply of pizzas and I believe no one else was scavenging in this Dumpster. But the people in the shop became suspicious and began to retain their garbage in the shop overnight. While it lasted I had a steady supply of fresh, sometimes warm pizza. Because I knew the Dumpster I knew the source of the pizza, and because I visited the Dumpster regularly I knew what was fresh and what was yesterday's. 20

The area I frequent is inhabited by many affluent college students. I am not here by chance; the Dumpsters in this area are very rich. Students throw out many good things, including food. In particular they tend to throw everything out when they move at the end of a semester, before and after breaks, and around midterm, when many of them despair of college. So I find it advantageous to keep an eye on the academic calendar. 21

22   Students throw food away around breaks because they do not know whether it has spoiled or will spoil before they return. A typical discard is a half jar of peanut butter. In fact, nonorganic peanut butter does not require refrigeration and is unlikely to spoil in any reasonable time. The student does not know that, and since it is Daddy's money, the student decides not to take a chance. Opened containers require caution and some attention to the question, "Why was this discarded?" But in the case of discards from student apartments, the answer may be that the item was thrown out through carelessness, ignorance, or wastefulness. This can sometimes be deduced when the item is found with many others, including some that are obviously perfectly good.

23   Some students, and others, approach defrosting a freezer by chucking out the whole lot. Not only do the circumstances of such a find tell the story, but also the mass of frozen goods stays cold for a long time and items may be found still frozen or freshly thawed.

24   Yogurt, cheese, and sour cream are items that are often thrown out while they are still good. Occasionally I find a cheese with a spot of mold, which of course I just pare off, and because it is obvious why such a cheese was discarded, I treat it with less suspicion than an apparently perfect cheese found in similar circumstances. Yogurt is often discarded, still sealed, only because the expiration date on the carton had passed. This is one of my favorite finds because yogurt will keep for several days, even in warm weather.

25   Students throw out canned goods and staples at the end of semesters and when they give up college at midterm. Drugs, pornography, spirits, and the like are often discarded when parents are expected—Dad's Day, for example. And spirits also turn up after big party weekends, presumably discarded by the newly reformed. Wine and spirits, of course, keep perfectly well even once opened, but the same cannot be said of beer.

26   My test for carbonated soft drinks is whether they still fizz vigorously. Many juices or other beverages are too acidic or too syrupy to cause much concern, provided they are not visibly contaminated. I have discovered nasty molds in vegetable juices, even when the product was found under its original seal; I recommend that such products be decanted slowly into a clear glass. Liquids always require some care. One hot day I found a large jug of Pat O'Brien's Hurricane mix. The jug had been opened but was still ice cold. I drank three large glasses before it became apparent to me that someone had added the rum to the mix, and not a little rum. I never tasted the rum, and by the time I began to feel the effects I had already ingested a very large quantity of the beverage. Some divers would have considered this a boon, but being suddenly intoxicated in a public place in the early afternoon is not my idea of a good time.

27   I have heard of people maliciously contaminating discarded food and even handouts, but mostly I have heard of this from people with

vivid imaginations who have had no experience with the Dumpsters themselves. Just before the pizza shop stopped discarding its garbage at night, jalapeños began showing up on most of the thrown-out pizzas. If indeed this was meant to discourage me, it was a wasted effort because I am a native Texan.

For myself, I avoid game, poultry, pork, and egg-based foods, 28 whether I find them raw or cooked. I seldom have the means to cook what I find, but when I do I avail myself of plentiful supplies of beef, which is often in very good condition. I suppose fish becomes disagreeable before it becomes dangerous. Lizbeth is happy to have any such thing that is past its prime and, in fact, does not recognize fish as food until it is quite strong.

Home leftovers, as opposed to surpluses from restaurants, are very 29 often bad. Evidently, especially among students, there is a common type of personality that carefully wraps up even the smallest leftover and shoves it into the back of the refrigerator for six months or so before discarding it. Characteristic of this type are the reused jars and margarine tubs to which the remains are committed. I avoid ethnic foods I am unfamiliar with. If I do not know what it is supposed to look like when it is good, I cannot be certain I will be able to tell if it is bad.

No matter how careful I am I still get dysentery at least once a month, 30 oftener in warm weather. I do not want to paint too romantic a picture. Dumpster diving has serious drawbacks as a way of life.

I learned to scavenge gradually, on my own. Since then I have initi- 31 ated several companions into the trade. I have learned that there is a predictable series of stages a person goes through in learning to scavenge.

At first the new scavenger is filled with disgust and self-loathing. He 32 is ashamed of being seen and may lurk around, trying to duck behind things, or he may try to dive at night. (In fact, most people instinctively look away from a scavenger. By skulking around, the novice calls attention to himself and arouses suspicion. Diving at night is ineffective and needlessly messy.)

Every grain of rice seems to be a maggot. Everything seems to stink. 33 He can wipe the egg yolk off the found can, but he cannot erase from his mind the stigma of eating garbage.

That stage passes with experience. The scavenger finds a pair of run- 34 ning shoes that fit and look and smell brand-new. He finds a pocket calculator in perfect working order. He finds pristine ice cream, still frozen, more than he can eat or keep. He begins to understand: People throw away perfectly good stuff, a lot of perfectly good stuff.

At this stage, Dumpster shyness begins to dissipate. The diver, after 35 all, has the last laugh. He is finding all manner of good things that are his for the taking. Those who disparage his profession are the fools, not he.

36   He may begin to hang on to some perfectly good things for which he has neither a use nor a market. Then he begins to take note of the things that are not perfectly good but are nearly so. He mates a Walkman with broken earphones and one that is missing a battery cover. He picks up things that he can repair.

37   At this stage he may become lost and never recover. Dumpsters are full of things of some potential value to someone and also of things that never have much intrinsic value but are interesting. All the Dumpster divers I have known come to the point of trying to acquire everything they touch. Why not take it, they reason, since it is all free? This is, of course, hopeless. Most divers come to realize that they must restrict themselves to items of relatively immediate utility. But in some cases the diver simply cannot control himself. I have met several of these pack-rat types. Their ideas of the values of various pieces of junk verge on the psychotic. Every bit of glass may be a diamond, they think, and all that glistens, gold.

38   I tend to gain weight when I am scavenging. Partly this is because I always find far more pizza and doughnuts than water-packed tuna, nonfat yogurt, and fresh vegetables. Also I have not developed much faith in the reliability of Dumpsters as a food source, although it has been proven to me many times. I tend to eat as if I have no idea where my next meal is coming from. But mostly I just hate to see food go to waste and so I eat much more than I should. Something like this drives the obsession to collect junk.

39   As for collecting objects, I usually restrict myself to collecting one kind of small object at a time, such as pocket calculators, sunglasses, or campaign buttons. To live on the street I must anticipate my needs to a certain extent: I must pick up and save warm bedding I find in August because it will not be found in Dumpsters in November. As I have no access to health care, I often hoard essential drugs, such as antibiotics and antihistamines. (This course can be recommended only to those with some grounding in pharmacology. Antibiotics, for example, even when indicated are worse than useless if taken in insufficient amounts.) But even if I had a home with extensive storage space, I could not save everything that might be valuable in some contingency.

40   I have proprietary feelings about my Dumpsters. As I have mentioned, it is no accident that I scavenge from ones where good finds are common. But my limited experience with Dumpsters in other areas suggests to me that even in poorer areas, Dumpsters, if attended with sufficient diligence, can be made to yield a livelihood. The rich students discard perfectly good kiwifruit; poorer people discard perfectly good apples. Slacks and Polo shirts are found in the one place; jeans and T-shirts in the other. The population of competitors rather than the affluence of the dumpers most affects the feasibility of survival by scavenging. The large number of competitors is what puts me off the idea of trying to scavenge in places like Los Angeles.

Curiously, I do not mind my direct competition, other scavengers, so 41
much as I hate the can scroungers.

People scrounge cans because they have to have a little cash. I have 42
tried scrounging cans with an able-bodied companion. Afoot a can
scrounger simply cannot make more than a few dollars a day. One can
extract the necessities of life from the Dumpsters directly with far less effort
than would be required to accumulate the equivalent value in cans. (These
observations may not hold in places with container redemption laws.)

Can scroungers, then, are people who must have small amounts of 43
cash. These are drug addicts and winos, mostly the latter because the
amounts are so small. Spirits and drugs do, like all other commodities,
turn up in Dumpsters and the scavenger will from time to time have a half
bottle of a rather good wine with his dinner. But the wino cannot survive
on these occasional finds; he must have his daily dose to stave off the DTs.
All the cans he can carry will buy about three bottles of Wild Irish Rose.

I do not begrudge them the cans, but can scroungers tend to tear up 44
the Dumpsters, mixing the contents and littering the area. They become
so specialized that they can see only cans. They earn my contempt by
passing up change, canned goods, and readily hockable items.

There are precious few courtesies among scavengers. But it is com- 45
mon practice to set aside surplus items: pairs of shoes, clothing, canned
goods, and such. A true scavenger hates to see good stuff go to waste, and
what he cannot use he leaves in good condition in plain sight.

Can scroungers lay waste to everything in their path and will stir one 46
of a pair of good shoes to the bottom of a Dumpster, to be lost or ruined in
the muck. Can scroungers will even go through individual garbage cans,
something I have never seen a scavenger do.

Individual garbage cans are set out on the public easement only on 47
garbage days. On other days going through them requires trespassing
close to a dwelling. Going through individual garbage cans without scattering litter is almost impossible. Litter is likely to reduce the public's
tolerance of scavenging. Individual cans are simply not as productive as
Dumpsters; people in houses and duplexes do not move so often and for
some reason do not tend to discard as much useful material. Moreover,
the time required to go through one garbage can that serves one household is not much less than the time required to go through a Dumpster
that contains the refuse of twenty apartments.

But my strongest reservation about going through individual gar- 48
bage cans is that this seems to me a very personal kind of invasion to
which I would object if I were a householder. Although many things in
Dumpsters are obviously meant never to come to light, a Dumpster is
somehow less personal.

I avoid trying to draw conclusions about the people who dump in 49
the Dumpsters I frequent. I think it would be unethical to do so, although

I know many people will find the idea of scavenger ethics too funny for words.

50   Dumpsters contain bank statements, correspondence, and other documents, just as anyone might expect. But there are less obvious sources of information. Pill bottles, for example. The labels bear the name of the patient, the name of the doctor, and the name of the drug. AIDS drugs and antipsychotic medicines, to name but two groups, are specific and are seldom prescribed for any other disorders. The plastic compacts for birth-control pills usually have complete label information.

51   Despite all of this sensitive information, I have had only one apartment resident object to my going through the Dumpster. In that case it turned out the resident was a university athlete who was taking bets and who was afraid I would turn up his wager slips.

52   Occasionally a find tells a story. I once found a small paper bag containing some unused condoms, several partial tubes of flavored sexual lubricants, a partially used compact of birth-control pills, and the torn pieces of a picture of a young man. Clearly she was through with him and planning to give up sex altogether.

53   Dumpster things are often sad—abandoned teddy bears, shredded wedding books, despaired-of sales kits. I find many pets lying in state in Dumpsters. Although I hope to get off the streets so that Lizbeth can have a long and comfortable old age, I know this hope is not very realistic. So I suppose when her time comes she too will go into a Dumpster. I will have no better place for her. And after all, it is fitting, since for most of her life her livelihood has come from the Dumpster. When she finds something I think is safe that has been spilled from a Dumpster, I let her have it. She already knows the route around the best ones. I like to think that if she survives me she will have a chance of evading the dog catcher and of finding her sustenance on the route.

54   Silly vanities also come to rest in the Dumpsters. I am a rather accomplished needleworker. I get a lot of material from the Dumpsters. Evidently sorority girls, hoping to impress someone, perhaps themselves, with their mastery of a womanly art, buy a lot of embroider-by-number kits, work a few stitches horribly, and eventually discard the whole mess. I pull out their stitches, turn the canvas over, and work an original design. Do not think I refrain from chuckling as I make gifts from these kits.

55   I find diaries and journals. I have often thought of compiling a book of literary found objects. And perhaps I will one day. But what I find is hopelessly commonplace and bad without being, even unconsciously, camp. College students also discard their papers. I am horrified to discover the kind of paper that now merits an A in an undergraduate course. I am grateful, however, for the number of good books and magazines the students throw out.

In the area I know best I have never discovered vermin in the 56 Dumpsters, but there are two kinds of kitty surprise. One is alley cats whom I meet as they leap, claws first, out of Dumpsters. This is especially thrilling when I have Lizbeth in tow. The other kind of kitty surprise is a plastic garbage bag filled with some ponderous, amorphous mass. This always proves to be used cat litter.

City bees harvest doughnut glaze and this makes the Dumpster at 57 the doughnut shop more interesting. My faith in the instinctive wisdom of animals is always shaken whenever I see Lizbeth attempt to catch a bee in her mouth, which she does wherever bees are present. Evidently some birds find Dumpsters profitable, for birdie surprise is almost as common as kitty surprise of the first kind. In hunting season all kinds of small game turn up in Dumpsters, some of it, sadly, not entirely dead. Curiously, summer and winter, maggots are uncommon.

The worst of the living and near-living hazards of the Dumpsters 58 are the fire ants. The food they claim is not much of a loss, but they are vicious and aggressive. It is very easy to brush against some surface of the Dumpster and pick up half a dozen or more fire ants, usually in some sensitive area such as the underarm. One advantage of bringing Lizbeth along as I make Dumpster rounds is that, for obvious reasons, she is very alert to ground-based fire ants. When Lizbeth recognizes a fire-ant infestation around our feet, she does the Dance of the Zillion Fire Ants. I have learned not to ignore this warning from Lizbeth, whether I perceive the tiny ants or not, but to remove ourselves at Lizbeth's first pas de bourée. All the more so because the ants are the worst in the summer months when I wear flip-flops if I have them. (Perhaps someone will misunderstand this. Lizbeth does the Dance of the Zillion Fire Ants when she recognizes more fire ants than she cares to eat, not when she is being bitten. Since I have learned to react promptly, she does not get bitten at all. It is the isolated patrol of fire ants that falls in Lizbeth's range that deserves pity. She finds them quite tasty.)

By far the best way to go through a Dumpster is to lower yourself 59 into it. Most of the good stuff tends to settle at the bottom because it is usually weightier than the rubbish. My more athletic companions have often demonstrated to me that they can extract much good material from a Dumpster I have already been over.

To those psychologically or physically unprepared to enter a Dumpster, 60 I recommend a stout stick, preferable with some barb or hook at one end. The hook can be used to grab plastic garbage bags. When I find canned goods or other objects loose at the bottom of a Dumpster, I lower a bag into it, roll the desired object into the bag, and then hoist the bag out—a procedure more easily described than executed. Much Dumpster diving is a matter of experience for which nothing will do except practice.

Dumpster diving is outdoor work, often surprisingly pleasant. It is 61 not entirely predictable; things of interest turn up every day and some days there are finds of great value. I am always very pleased when I can turn up exactly the thing I most wanted to find. Yet in spite of the element of chance, scavenging more than most other pursuits tends to yield returns in some proportion to the effort and intelligence brought to bear. It is very sweet to turn up a few dollars in change from a Dumpster that has just been gone over by a wino.

62   The land is now covered with cities. The cities are full of Dumpsters. If a member of the canine race is ever able to know what it is doing, then Lizbeth knows that when we go around to the Dumpsters, we are hunting. I think of scavenging as a modern form of self-reliance. In any event, after having survived nearly ten years of government service, where everything is geared to the lowest common denominator, I find it refreshing to have work that rewards initiative and effort. Certainly I would be happy to have a sinecure again, but I am no longer heartbroken that I left one.

63   I find from the experience of scavenging two rather deep lessons. The first is to take what you can use and let the rest go by. I have come to think that there is no value in the abstract. A thing I cannot use or make useful, perhaps by trading, has no value however rare or fine it may be. I mean useful in a broad sense—some art I would find useful and some otherwise.

64   I was shocked to realize that some things are not worth acquiring, but now I think it is so. Some material things are white elephants that eat up the possessor's substance. The second lesson is the transience of material being. This has not quite converted me to a dualist, but it has made some headway in that direction. I do not suppose that ideas are immortal, but certainly mental things are longer lived than other material things.

65   Once I was the sort of person who invests objects with sentimental value. Now I no longer have those objects, but I have the sentiments yet.

66   Many times in our travels I have lost everything but the clothes I was wearing and Lizbeth. The things I find in Dumpsters, the love letters and rag dolls of so many lives, remind me of this lesson. Now I hardly pick up a thing without envisioning the time I will cast it aside. This I think is a healthy state of mind. Almost everything I have now has already been cast out at least once, proving that what I own is valueless to someone.

67   Anyway, I find my desire to grab for the gaudy bauble has been largely sated. I think this is an attitude I share with the very wealthy—we both know there is plenty more where what we have came from. Between us are the rat-race millions who nightly scavenge the cable channels looking for they know not what.

68   I am sorry for them.

1993

QUESTIONS FOR DISCUSSION

Content

a. What is Eighner's thesis?

b. What is the purpose of this essay? Is it simply a guide to finding food while living on the streets? Or is there more involved? Explain.

c. What differences do you see in connotations of the words "scavenging," "scrounging," and "foraging" (paragraph 3)? Why does Eighner prefer to call what he does "scavenging"? How does this distinction affect the content and presentation of what is to come in this essay?

d. Other than how to spot edible food, what has Eighner learned from Dumpster diving?

e. What are the emotional drawbacks to Dumpster diving? What pleasures does the author take in this activity?

f. Why won't he scavenge in places like Los Angeles (paragraph 40)?

g. What does the author have against "can scroungers," and why does he bother to discuss them in such detail (paragraphs 42–47)?

h. Why does Eighner restrict his diving to Dumpsters and not search through individual garbage cans?

i. Who is Lizbeth, and why does the author mention her so often?

Strategy and Style

j. In what ways is this essay an argument?

k. In what ways is it a process analysis? Where in the essay do you find classification and description?

l. How would you describe the author's tone, his attitude toward his subject? Toward his audience?

m. What is the author's attitude toward the people who discard things in Dumpsters? Why is it important for him to reveal this attitude?

n. Why does the author bother to tell us about the derivation of the word *Dumpster?*

o. Comment on Eighner's introduction and conclusion. Do you find them effective? Why or why not?

ENGAGING THE TEXT

a. The author reveals a great deal about himself in this essay. Reread "On Dumpster Diving" and make marginal notes in places that contain such detail. Then, write a paragraph or two that comment on Eighner's character.

b. In one or two well-developed paragraphs, explain Eighner's attitude toward college students. Make direct reference to his text and use direct quotations whenever appropriate.

SUGGESTIONS FOR SUSTAINED WRITING

a. Explain what the contents of your garbage might reveal about you to anyone who cared to go through it.

b. Compare Eigher's descriptions of poverty to those of Angelou in Chapter 1, Parker in Chapter 4, or Salopek in Chapter 8. Discuss the similarities and differences in how poverty and the poor are depicted by the writers.

c. Do you agree with Eighner's vision of college students? Are they as spoiled and wasteful as he says? Write an essay in which you address this issue by agreeing with Eighner, rebutting him, or defending a third point of view. Find statistical as well as anecdotal evidence to support your opinion.

READ MORE

Eighner and His Works

Eighner, Lars. *Travels with Lizbeth*. New York: St. Martin's P, 1993.

"Lars Eighner" (http://larseighner.com): *Eighner's personal web page.*

College Student Life

Levine, Arthur, Jeanette S. Cureton, and Arthur Levine. *When Hope and Fear Collide: A Portrait of Today's College Student*. San Francisco: Jossey-Bass, 1998.

Homelessness

Jencks, Christopher. *The Homeless*. Cambridge, MA: Harvard UP, 1994.

Only Daughter

Sandra Cisneros

Sandra Cisneros (b. 1954) grew up in the United States and Mexico. As Cisneros mentions in "Only Daughter," her family was poor and moved frequently between Mexico City and Chicago, never giving her time to make friends. Her six brothers were no substitute for childhood friends, and her resulting loneliness forced Cisneros to turn to reading and writing as a means of creating a community for herself. In high school, she wrote poetry and was the literary magazine editor; in college, she studied creative writing. After earning a B.A. in English from Loyola University in Chicago in 1976 and an M.F.A. from the University of Iowa Writers' Workshop in 1978, she worked first in the Chicano barrio in Chicago, teaching high school dropouts, and then at Loyola University as an administrative assistant. Her first book, the novel The House on Mango Street *(1983), received the Before Columbus American Book Award. Cisneros's work explores love, religion, and Mexican-American culture. Her publications include books of poems, such as* My Wicked Wicked Ways *(1987) and* Loose Woman *(1994); short stories, such as* Woman Hollering Creek and Other Stories *(1991); novels such as* Caramelo *(2002); and articles for* Americas Review *and other publications. Among other awards over the years, Cisneros has received two National Endowment for the Arts fellowships and a MacArthur Foundation fellowship.*

In trying to find her own voice as a writer in the 1970s, Cisneros realized that the Latina experience in America had not been written about much. She thus decided to write about her own experiences, particularly about the conflicts in her own family, including divided cultural loyalties and feelings of alienation. "Only Daughter" explains more about how she found her niche.

Once, several years ago, when I was just starting out my writing career, I 1 was asked to write my own contributor's note for an anthology I was part of. I wrote: "I am the only daughter in a family of six sons. *That* explains everything."

Well, I've thought about that ever since, and yes, it explains a lot to 2 me, but for the reader's sake I should have written: "I am the only daughter in a *Mexican* family of six sons." Or even: "I am the only daughter of a Mexican father and a Mexican-American mother." Or: "I am the only daughter of a working-class family of nine." All of these had everything to do with who I am today.

I was/am the only daughter and *only* a daughter. Being an only 3 daughter in a family of six sons forced me by circumstance to spend a lot of time by myself because my brothers felt it beneath them to play with a *girl* in public. But that aloneness, that loneliness, was good for a would-be writer—it allowed me time to think and think, to imagine, to read and prepare myself.

Being only a daughter for my father meant my destiny would lead 4 me to become someone's wife. That's what he believed. But when I was in the fifth grade and shared my plans for college with him, I was sure he understood. I remember my father saying, "*Que bueno, mi'ja,* that's good." That meant a lot to me, especially since my brothers thought the idea hilarious. What I didn't realize was that my father thought college was good for girls—good for finding a husband. After four years in college and two more in graduate school, and still no husband, my father shakes his head even now and says I wasted all that education.

In retrospect, I'm lucky my father believed daughters were meant 5 for husbands. It meant it didn't matter if I majored in something silly like English. After all, I'd find a nice professional eventually, right? This allowed me the liberty to putter about embroidering my little poems and stories without my father interrupting with so much as a "What's that you're writing?"

6   But the truth is, I wanted him to interrupt. I wanted my father to understand what it was I was scribbling, to introduce me as "My only daughter, the writer." Not as "This is only my daughter. She teaches." *Es maestra*—teacher. Not even *professora*.

7   In a sense, everything I have ever written has been for him, to win his approval even though I know my father can't read English words, even though my father's only reading includes the brown-ink *Esto* sports magazine from Mexico City and the bloody ¡*Alarma!* magazines that feature yet another sighting of *La Virgen de Guadalupe* on a tortilla or a wife's revenge on her philandering husband by bashing his skull in with a *molcajete* (a kitchen mortar made of volcanic rock). Or the *fotonovelas*, the little picture paperbacks with tragedy and trauma erupting from the characters' mouths in bubbles.

8   My father represents, then, the public majority. A public who is disinterested in reading, and yet one whom I am writing about and for, and privately trying to woo.

9   When we were growing up in Chicago, we moved a lot because of my father. He suffered bouts of nostalgia. Then we'd have to let go our flat, store the furniture with mother's relatives, load the station wagon with baggage and bologna sandwiches and head south. To Mexico City:

10   We came back, of course. To yet another Chicago flat, another Chicago neighborhood, another Catholic school. Each time, my father would seek out the parish priest in order to get a tuition break, and complain or boast: "I have seven sons."

11   He meant *siete hijos*, seven children, but he translated it as "sons." "I have seven sons." To anyone who would listen. The Sears Roebuck employee who sold us the washing machine. The short-order cook where my father ate his ham-and-eggs breakfasts. "I have seven sons." As if he deserved a medal from the state.

12   My papa. He didn't mean anything by that mistranslation, I'm sure. But somehow I could feel myself being erased. I'd tug my father's sleeve and whisper: "Not seven sons. Six! and *one daughter*."

13   When my oldest brother graduated from medical school, he fulfilled my father's dream that we study hard and use this—our heads, instead of this—our hands. Even now my father's hands are thick and yellow, stubbed by a history of hammer and nails and twine and coils and springs. "Use this," my father said, tapping his head, "and not this," showing us those hands. He always looked tired when he said it.

14   Wasn't college an investment? And hadn't I spent all those years in college? And if I didn't marry, what was it all for? Why would anyone go to college and then choose to be poor? Especially someone who had always been poor.

15   Last year, after ten years of writing professionally, the financial rewards started to trickle in. My second National Endowment for the

Arts Fellowship. A guest professorship at the University of California, Berkeley. My book, which sold to a major New York publishing house.

At Christmas, I flew home to Chicago. The house was throbbing, 16 same as always; hot *tamales* and sweet *tamales* hissing in my mother's pressure cooker, and everybody—my mother, six brothers, wives, babies, aunts, cousins—talking too loud and at the same time, like in a Fellini film, because that's just how we are.

I went upstairs to my father's room. One of my stories had just been 17 translated into Spanish and published in an anthology of Chicano writing, and I wanted to show it to him. Ever since he recovered from a stroke two years ago, my father likes to spend his leisure hours horizontally. And that's how I found him, watching a Pedro Infante movie on Galavisión and eating rice pudding.

There was a glass filmed with milk on the bedside table. There 18 were several vials of pills and balled Kleenex. And on the floor, one black sock and a plastic urinal that I didn't want to look at but looked at anyway. Pedro Infante was about to burst into song, and my father was laughing.

I'm not sure if it was because my story was translated into Spanish, 19 or because it was published in Mexico, or perhaps because the story dealt with Topeyac, the *colonia* my father was raised in and the house he grew up in, but at any rate, my father punched the mute button on his remote control and read my story.

I sat on the bed next to my father and waited. He read it very slowly. 20 As if he were reading each line over and over. He laughed at all the right places and read lines he liked out loud. He pointed and asked questions: "Is this So-and-so?" "Yes," I said. He kept reading.

When he was finally finished, after what seemed like hours, my father 21 looked up and asked: "Where can we get more copies of this for the relatives?"

Of all the wonderful things that happened to me last year, that was 22 the most wonderful.

1990

QUESTIONS FOR DISCUSSION

Content

a. In paragraph 7, Cisneros says that "everything I have ever written has been for him" (for her father). What does she mean by this?

b. Cisneros considers her father to represent the "public majority" of readers (paragraph 8). Who are these readers? How does Cisneros define them? Why is she trying to woo them?

c. How does Cisneros differ from her father? Why does she go to such lengths to set herself apart from him?

d. What type of Mexican-American is Cisneros's father, as she describes him? What is Cisneros's attitude toward that type? Does she see herself as part of that group?

e. Why does Cisneros need her father's approval?

f. Why does her father lump Cisneros in with the sons, as described in paragraphs 11 and 12? What might have been his reasons for saying he has "seven sons"?

Strategy and Style

g. Where does Cisneros use comparison and contrast? What is being compared and contrasted?

h. What other strategies are at work in this essay?

i. Why might Cisneros have included the dialogue that she includes? What might she have left out?

j. How would you describe the tone of this piece? How does the tone create negative images of the father?

k. Cisneros frequently uses sentence fragments. Where does she use them, and to what effect?

l. Because this essay was originally written for *Glamour* magazine, what can you speculate about the audience? How do the content and style suit that audience?

ENGAGING THE TEXT

a. Do you feel yourself to be an insider or an outsider to your own family? Explain, comparing yourself to Cisneros's story.

b. Summarize Cisneros's father's rationale for sending her to college and his disappointment in her "failure." Compare his reasoning to your own parents' reasons for encouraging you to go to college. Do your own parents, the parents of your friends, or even you, yourself, think of college as a place for women to find husbands?

SUGGESTIONS FOR SUSTAINED WRITING

a. Write a narrative in which you relate what you have done (or are doing) to prove yourself to your parents or other authority. Explain the effects you hope your actions will cause, and if possible, try to articulate why you need to gain that person's approval.

b. Reflect on the relationship between parents and children in immigrant families, discussing the relationships described elsewhere in the book, such as Judith Ortiz Cofer's "A Partial Remembrance of a Puerto Rican Childhood" in Chapter 2, Richard Rodriguez's "Blaxicans" in Chapter 4, Kesaya E. Noda's "Growing Up Asian in America" in Chapter 5, Bharati Mukherjee's "Two Ways to Belong in America" and Gary Soto's "Like Mexicans" in Chapter 6, Naomi Shihab Nye's "To Any Would-Be Terrorists" in Chapter 10, or Amy Tan's "Mother Tongue" in this chapter.

c. Through library and Internet research, find out more about Chicana/Latina writers, and report to your classmates about one particular writer or piece of writing. Discuss whether there is a particular style or typical choice of topics for these writers, and whether there is a growing Chicana/Latina literary movement in the United States.

READ MORE

Cisneros and Her Works

"The Authorized Sandra Cisneros Website" (http://www.sandracisneros .com): *Cisneros's personal website, with photos, biographical information, interviews, study guides, and links to her works.*

Madsen, Deborah L. *Understanding Contemporary Chicana Literature.* Columbia, SC: U of South Carolina P, 2000.

"Voices from the Gaps" (http://voices.cla.umn.edu/vg/Bios/entries/ cisneros_sandra.html): *Biographical information about Cisneros on the University of Minnesota website.*

Chicana and Latina Writers

"Chicana and Chicano Studies" (http://www.ku.edu/~asags/chica-nastudies.html): *Clearinghouse of Internet resources for Chicana and Latina history and the arts.*

Horno Delgado, Asunción. *Breaking Boundaries: Latina Writing and Critical Readings.* Amherst: U of Massachusetts P, 1989.

Coyote v. Acme

Ian Frazier

Born in Cleveland in 1951, Ian Frazier earned a B.A. from Harvard University, where he wrote for the Harvard Lampoon. *He worked briefly at* Playboy *and then became a staff writer for the* New Yorker *in 1974, writing "Talk of the Town" pieces. He left in 1982 to become a freelance writer, although he has continued to contribute articles to the magazine. Frazier is now a regular contributor to the* Atlantic Monthly, Outside, *the* New Republic, *and* Mother Jones. *He is well known for his humorous nonfiction books such as* Dating Your Mom *(1986) and the collection of essays* Coyote v. Acme *(1996), which won the Thurber Prize for American Humor. But he also writes on serious topics, as in his memoir* Family *(1994);* The Great Plains *(1989);* On the Rez *(2000), an examination of life on the Oglala Sioux Pine Ridge reservation; and* Travels in Siberia *(2010). Some of his essays are collected in* The Fish's Eye: Essays about Angling and the Outdoors *(2002),* Gone to New York: Adventures in the City *(2005), and* Lamentations of the Father: Essays *(2008).*

One reviewer of Coyote v. Acme *said that Frazier "may not be the funniest writer alive, as a jacket blurb proclaims, but he may well have the weirdest imagination." We think you will agree.*

In the United States District Court,
Southwestern District,
Tempe, Arizona
Case No. B19294,
Judge Joan Kujava, Presiding
Wile E. Coyote, Plaintiff
—v.—
Acme Company, Defendant

1 Opening Statement of Mr. Harold Schoff, attorney for Mr. Coyote: My client, Mr. Wile E. Coyote, a resident of Arizona and contiguous states, does hereby bring suit for damages against the Acme Company, manufacturer and retail distributor of assorted merchandise, incorporated in Delaware and doing business in every state, district, and territory. Mr. Coyote seeks compensation for personal injuries, loss of business income, and mental suffering caused as a direct result of the actions and/or gross negligence of said company, under Title 15 of the United States Code, Chapter 47, section 2072, subsection (a), relating to product liability.

2 Mr. Coyote states that on eighty-five separate occasions he has purchased of the Acme Company (hereinafter, "Defendant"), through that company's mail-order department, certain products which did cause him bodily injury due to defects in manufacture or improper cautionary labelling. Sales slips made out to Mr. Coyote as proof of purchase are at present in the possession of the Court, marked Exhibit A. Such injuries sustained by Mr. Coyote have temporarily restricted his ability to make a living in his profession of predator. Mr. Coyote is self-employed and thus not eligible for Workmen's Compensation.

3 Mr. Coyote states that on December 13th he received of Defendant via parcel post one Acme Rocket Sled. The intention of Mr. Coyote was to use the Rocket Sled to aid him in pursuit of his prey. Upon receipt of the Rocket Sled Mr. Coyote removed it from its wooden shipping crate and, sighting his prey in the distance, activated the ignition. As Mr. Coyote gripped the handlebars, the Rocket Sled accelerated with such sudden

and precipitate force as to stretch Mr. Coyote's forelimbs to a length of fifty feet. Subsequently, the rest of Mr. Coyote's body shot forward with a violent jolt, causing severe strain to his back and neck and placing him unexpectedly astride the Rocket Sled. Disappearing over the horizon at such speed as to leave a diminishing jet trail along its path, the Rocket Sled soon brought Mr. Coyote abreast of his prey. At that moment the animal he was pursuing veered sharply to the right. Mr. Coyote vigorously attempted to follow this maneuver but was unable to, due to poorly designed steering on the Rocket Sled and a faulty or nonexistent braking system. Shortly thereafter, the unchecked progress of the Rocket Sled brought it and Mr. Coyote into collision with the side of a mesa.

Paragraph One of the Report of Attending Physician (Exhibit B), prepared by Dr. Ernest Grosscup, M.D., D.O., details the multiple fractures, contusions, and tissue damage suffered by Mr. Coyote as a result of this collision. Repair of the injuries required a full bandage around the head (excluding the ears), a neck brace, and full or partial casts on all four legs. 4

Hampered by these injuries, Mr. Coyote was nevertheless obliged to support himself. With this in mind, he purchased of Defendant as an aid to mobility one pair of Acme Rocket Skates. When he attempted to use this product, however, he became involved in an accident remarkably similar to that which occurred with the Rocket Sled. Again, Defendant sold over the counter, without caveat, a product which attached powerful jet engines (in this case, two) to inadequate vehicles, with little or no provision for passenger safety. Encumbered by his heavy casts, Mr. Coyote lost control of the Rocket Skates soon after strapping them on, and collided with a roadside billboard so violently as to leave a hole in the shape of his full silhouette. 5

Mr. Coyote states that on occasions too numerous to list in this document he has suffered mishaps with explosives purchased of Defendant: the Acme "Little Giant" Firecracker, the Acme Self-Guided Aerial Bomb, etc. (For a full listing, see the Acme Mail Order Explosives Catalogue and attached deposition, entered in evidence as Exhibit C.) Indeed, it is safe to say that not once has an explosive purchased of Defendant by Mr. Coyote performed in an expected manner. To cite just one example: At the expense of much time and personal effort, Mr. Coyote constructed around the outer rim of a butte a wooden trough beginning at the top of the butte and spiralling downward around it to some few feet above a black X painted on the desert floor. The trough was designed in such a way that a spherical explosive of the type sold by Defendant would roll easily and swiftly down to the point of detonation indicated by the X. Mr. Coyote placed a generous pile of birdseed directly on the X, and then, carrying the spherical Acme Bomb (Catalogue #78–832), climbed to the top of the butte. Mr. Coyote's prey, seeing the birdseed, approached, and Mr. Coyote proceeded to light the fuse. In an instant, the fuse burned down to the stem, causing the bomb to detonate. 6

7   In addition to reducing all Mr. Coyote's careful preparations to naught, the premature detonation of Defendant's product resulted in the following disfigurements to Mr. Coyote:

1. Severe singeing of the hair on the head, neck, and muzzle.
2. Sooty discoloration.
3. Fracture of the left ear at the stem, causing the ear to dangle in the aftershock with a creaking noise.
4. Full or partial combustion of whiskers, producing kinking, frazzling, and ashy disintegration.
5. Radical widening of the eyes, due to brow and lid charring.

8   We come now to the Acme Spring-Powered Shoes. The remains of a pair of these purchased by Mr. Coyote on June 23rd are Plaintiff's Exhibit D. Selected fragments have been shipped to the metallurgical laboratories of the University of California at Santa Barbara for analysis, but to date no explanation has been found for this product's sudden and extreme malfunction. As advertised by Defendant, this product is simplicity itself: two wood-and-metal sandals, each attached to milled-steel springs of high tensile strength and compressed in a tightly coiled position by a cocking device with a lanyard release. Mr. Coyote believed that this product would enable him to pounce upon his prey in the initial moments of the chase, when swift reflexes are at a premium.

9   To increase the shoes' thrusting power still further, Mr. Coyote affixed them by their bottoms to the side of a large boulder. Adjacent to the boulder was a path which Mr. Coyote's prey was known to frequent. Mr. Coyote put his hind feet in the wood-and-metal sandals and crouched in readiness, his right forepaw holding firmly to the lanyard release. Within a short time Mr. Coyote's prey did indeed appear on the path coming toward him. Unsuspecting, the prey stopped near Mr. Coyote, well within range of the springs at full extension. Mr. Coyote gauged the distance with care and proceeded to pull the lanyard release.

10   At this point, Defendant's product should have thrust Mr. Coyote forward and away from the boulder. Instead, for reasons yet unknown, the Acme Spring-Powered Shoes thrust the boulder away from Mr. Coyote. As the intended prey looked on unharmed, Mr. Coyote hung suspended in air. Then the twin springs recoiled, bringing Mr. Coyote to a violent feet-first collision with the boulder, the full weight of his head and forequarters falling upon his lower extremities.

11   The force of this impact then caused the springs to rebound, whereupon Mr. Coyote was thrust skyward. A second recoil and collision followed. The boulder, meanwhile, which was roughly ovoid in shape, had begun to bounce down a hillside, the coiling and recoiling of the springs adding to its velocity. At each bounce, Mr. Coyote came into contact with

the boulder, or the boulder came into contact with Mr. Coyote, or both came into contact with the ground. As the grade was a long one, this process continued for some time.

The sequence of collisions resulted in systemic physical damage to 12 Mr. Coyote, viz., flattening of the cranium, sideways displacement of the tongue, reduction of length of legs and upper body, and compression of vertebrae from base of tail to head. Repetition of blows along a vertical axis produced a series of regular horizontal folds in Mr. Coyote's body tissues—a rare and painful condition which caused Mr. Coyote to expand upward and contract downward alternately as he walked, and to emit an off-key accordionlike wheezing with every step. The distracting and embarrassing nature of this symptom has been a major impediment to Mr. Coyote's pursuit of a normal social life.

As the Court is no doubt aware, Defendant has a virtual monopoly of 13 manufacture and sale of goods required by Mr. Coyote's work. It is our contention that Defendant has used its market advantage to the detriment of the consumer of such specialized products as itching powder, giant kites, Burmese tiger traps, anvils, and two-hundred-foot-long rubber bands. Much as he has come to mistrust Defendant's products, Mr. Coyote has no other domestic source of supply to which to turn. One can only wonder what our trading partners in Western Europe and Japan would make of such a situation, where a giant company is allowed to victimize the consumer in the most reckless and wrongful manner over and over again.

Mr. Coyote respectfully requests that the Court regard these larger 14 economic implications and assess punitive damages in the amount of seventeen million dollars. In addition, Mr. Coyote seeks actual damages (missed meals, medical expenses, days lost from professional occupation) of one million dollars; general damages (mental suffering, injury to reputation) of twenty million dollars; and attorney's fees of seven hundred and fifty thousand dollars. Total damages: thirty-eight million seven hundred and fifty thousand dollars. By awarding Mr. Coyote the full amount, this Court will censure Defendant, its directors, officers, shareholders, successors, and assigns, in the only language they understand, and reaffirm the right of the individual predator to equal protection under the law.

1996

QUESTIONS FOR DISCUSSION

Content

a. Does Acme have a responsibility toward Coyote? What is Acme's corporate responsibility toward its customers?

b. What in recent news about corporate scandals is mirrored in this essay?
c. Does Wile E. Coyote have a case? Why or why not?
d. What point does this essay make about the *Roadrunner* cartoon or about the people who watch it?
e. What is the common denominator in all the Acme product malfunctions?

Strategy and Style

f. What makes this essay so funny?
g. What does the choice of wording add to the humor of the piece?
h. This essay draws on every other type of strategy discussed in this book. Where does Frazier use narration, description, and so forth?
i. Find examples of legal language. What does this language add to the overall tone?
j. Why is the Roadrunner never mentioned by name?

ENGAGING THE TEXT

a. Imitate the language and style of a section of this essay as you describe another of Coyote's mishaps due to a malfunction of an Acme product.
b. Write a response as if you were a lawyer on Acme's law team. Respond to specific points in Schoff's statement.

SUGGESTIONS FOR SUSTAINED WRITING

a. Write a complaint letter, real or imaginary, about a defective product. Consider where you will use argument, narrative, and description.
b. Compare this essay to the selections in the argument section of Chapter 10. What argumentative rules does "Harold Schoff" follow? Explain whether you think Schoff's argument is a convincing one or not.
c. Analyze a popular cartoon or other corny television comedy. Use the perspective and voice of a serious field of study such as psychology, law, or criminal justice. For instance, analyze the *Brady Bunch* from the point of view of a family psychologist, analyze the newly discovered archeological site of Bedrock from the point of view of a cultural anthropologist, or write a police report for an episode of *Scooby-Doo*.

READ MORE

Frazier and His Works

"Coyote v. Acme Products Corp." (http://www.legalnews.net/quotes/wilee.htm): *A parody reply from Acme's lawyer.*

an engish teacher telling his experience teaching in a non motivat School with bad learning conditions.

"Ian Frazier" (http://www.believermag.com/issues/200409/?read=interview_frazier): *An interview posted on Believermag.com.*

"Ian Frazier's Heroes" (http://www.powells.com/authors/frazier.html): *An interview posted on Powells.com.*

Parodies and Legal Humor

Macdonald, Dwight. *Parodies: An Anthology from Chaucer to Beerbohm—and After.* New York: Da Capo, 1985.

"McClurg's Legal Humor Headquarters" (http://www.lawhaha.com): *A site devoted to legal humor and parodies, with links to serious as well as humorous legal web pages.*

Test Day

Frank Bures

Frank Bures was born in Wisconsin and has lived in Italy, New Zealand, Thailand, and Tanzania, the African country in which this essay is set. Now living in Minneapolis, Bures, a one-time teacher of English, is a contributing editor for the online magazine World Hum *and for* Poets & Writers. *His work has also appeared in* Wired, Audubon, Outside, Outpost, The Atlantic Online, *and* Mother Jones, *among other magazines and newspapers. His interests are science/ecology, cross-cultural influences, world politics, and travel. In 2007 Bures won a Lowell Thomas Travel Journalism Award for his* World Hum *article "How to Use a Squat Toilet." "Test Day" was selected for inclusion in* The Best American Travel Writing 2004.*

This selection uses a variety of methods to reveal the frustration, the irony, and the love felt by all teachers who are dedicated to their students and to their profession.

From the doorway, I can see the last of my students walking up the dirt 1 road into the school grounds. They're late as usual, but Mr. Ndyogi isn't here to beat them, so no one is running. Their crisp blue and white uniforms move slowly beneath the outline of Mt. Meru. I can see they're even less eager for class to begin than normal, less enthused about English grammar than ever.

They know, as they drag their feet through the dust, that today is test 2 day.

The last students straggle into class as I write the final questions on 3 the blackboard. When the talking and the scraping of wooden chairs dies down, I tell them to put their notebooks away and begin.

Testing is a futile exercise in so many ways. For most of these stu- 4 dents, all 47 of them on a good day, English is their third language, after

Does? ← → Reason why

Swahili and Maasai. My own Swahili is very bad and even though we've been working on prepositions for some time, I still have no idea what the Swahili word for preposition is, or if there is one.

5   Instead, I'm reduced to crude hand gestures and bad drawings on the board. Walking around the room, glancing at the papers, I can see this hasn't worked as well as I thought it would. Instead, judging from their writing, preposition roulette is the favorite strategy once again.

6   "Go apologize to your brother *by* punching him in the nose."

7   "Where should I get *inward* the bus?"

8   "What sort of things are you interested *nothing*?"

9   Our school is a small one, not far from Arusha, the semi-cosmopolitan urban center of northern Tanzania. We have eight classrooms, which are staggered at intervals down a hill. The students begin at the top and after a four-year downhill slide, they end up with their "certificate." My students are about mid-slide, in Form III. I'm here for the year on a mostly self-funded teaching program, the idea being that, as an English speaker I should have enough grasp of it to pass it along. This, in other words, is test day for me too. *See if keep*

10   The walls of our classroom are whitewashed and the room is packed tight with desks and stools. The blackboard at the front is badly chipped and overhead are corrugated iron sheets, with one plastic panel to allow the sunshine through. Our school is called "Ekenywa," which in Maasai means "Sunrise," because (as our headmaster told us) with education, the area around the school is waking up. *Word*

11   If some of my students would wake up, they might do better on this test.

12   My only real ambition here has been to leave them with a few practical English skills—how to write a letter, for example, or what the plot of "No Longer at Ease" is. Something to help them get a job in town, or at least to pass their national exam.

13   On test day, walking between the desks, I see how far we are from such lofty goals. Take, for example, their "Letter to a friend." I don't know how many times I told them—how many times I made them write in their notebooks—to end a letter, any letter, with, "Yours sincerely."

Not listening 14   Around the room, there are many interpretations of this: "Your thinthially," "you thinkfully," "Yours sincefully," "Your sincilier," "your sceneially," "Senceally," "Your friendly," "Yours be love friend." A few students do get the basics. John signs his, "Yours in the Building of the Nation," which I'm quite happy with. But mostly test day is the day I wonder why I'm here.

15   My students wonder this too. Imani even writes in his letter: "The aim of sending this letter to you is to tell you about my exam I do. The test I taking was very hard. I try to think, but I am not understand anything in this test. The teacher who make this test was not like the Form III to go in the Form IV."

A good effort, and not a bad letter, as they go. Rukia takes a more 16
flattering tack.

"I study in Ekenywa Secondary School, and the teacher is the very 17
good and the teacher of English is come from America so they teach very
well." Or, "Frank was teach me English very well. I like it because I trie
to speak English and I want to go some o my town to teach a young girl
and boy, like Frenck teach me." Or, "I will get 18 points on this test are
very big points."

Her points, I'm afraid, will be the same size as everyone else's. But 18
they try so hard, in spite of everything working against them. At primary
school everything is taught in Swahili. Then they hit secondary school
and suddenly all their classes are taught in English. In this kind of immer-
sion, most students drown. The school provides no life rafts either, such
as dictionaries or grammar books or workbooks. Never mind school supplies. Some days there aren't even any teachers.   *Schools are not providing*

Nonetheless, the Ministry of Education sets a huge task before them. 19
Form III students, it says, should "develop the habit of reading for pleasure and for information," as well as to increase reading speed. It says
they should complete 13 books during the third year.

But our school only has five of the books on the syllabus, and enough 20
copies of only three to actually use.

Of the two we finally read—"Things Fall Apart" and "No Longer 21
at Ease," both by Chinua Achebe—we had 14 and 23 copies, and only
a handful in good condition. These were shared by groups of three and
four students. But actually reading them would be like me reading "Don
Quixote" in Spanish. Impossible.

Of course, this shows on test day. We spent several weeks going over 22
these books, and I wrote explicit outlines of everything that happened on
the board, which I watched them copy down.

But on test day, students who once seemed to have mastered the plot, 23
or at least memorized the characters, answer question about Obi and his
grandfather, Okonkwo, like this:

"Okonkwo Obi is falling apart."   24

"Obi is republic."   25

"Clara was very dislike because Obi's parents they don't want Clara 26
to be wife of Obi. So Clara want to kill himself for that. THIS IS NOT GOD TO
WANT TO KILL YOURSELF. EVEN YOU MR. FRANK."

Hmm. The thought hadn't crossed my mind. But with many more 27
days like this, it just might.

On the other hand, sometimes on test day, a previously illiterate stu- 28
dent mysteriously becomes a brilliant literary critic.   ← *Cheating*

"Okonkwo," writes Godson, "through his fears, becomes exiled from 29
his tribe and returns only to be forced in the ignominy of suicide to escape
the results of his rash courage against the white man."

30   Godson is the class Rastafarian and knows the words to every Bob Marley song. I know he doesn't know anything about Okonkwo.

31   "Obi Okonkwo," writes Tumaini in suspiciously good English, "returns from his studies in England to try to live up to the expectations of his family and his tribe and at the same time to breathe the heady atmosphere of Lagos."

32   Such is the heady atmosphere of test day. Martin writes in his letter, "Just a quick note to let you know that I've had a rather serious accident in my holiday, and my leg is now in plaster. The doctor said that I've fractured it, and that I'll be laid up for about six weeks. After that I should be right as rain. I will tell you more in another letter. For now, let me end here. Yours ever, Martin Paul."

33   There are about three students in the class who might be able to write something like this. Martin is not one of them. He is one of the other 44 who come to school, sit, talk, use cheat sheets I can never find, and don't pay attention, except on days when I give up on grammar and answer questions about America. *Bond to Martian*

34   "Is it true," they would ask, "that the government gives every American a gun at age 18?" "Is it true that even the poorest Americans have 12 cars?" "What's up, man?" they would ask. "Hey," I'd say. "Not much."

35   Those days were the best of all, the days when I felt that I really had something to offer, something they wanted to know. These were the days we connected. These were the days when they sat rapt, as I unlocked the secrets of America, and they, in turn, unlocked their own country, giving me all the street lingo I could use.

more english?

36   But there was no slang on the national syllabus, and it didn't help them on test day.

37   "So," I ask again as we go over the test (we've been over the material before), "Obi and Christopher went out with some Irish girls. Does anyone know what Irish means?"

38   "Irish potatoes!" someone shouts.

39   "Yes," I say, "like Irish potatoes. But what does Irish mean?"

40   "Beautiful!" someone else shouts.

41   Next question: "So, the girl tried to bribe Obi with sex. What . . . "

42   Suddenly they are all fluent. "Explain! Explain!" they yell.

43   "No!" says Seuri, "don't explain in words. Give demonstration so we can see."

44   The students hand in the tests, and the scores are abysmal again. I'm not even sure how to grade them. If I make it on a curve, it will be a very small bump. The hardest part is that I know they could do it if they had the chance, if they had some hope. But there are too many obstacles and too few incentives. Most of my students will be married off or end up putting their certificate to work in the fields.

45   Yet as with so many things in Tanzania, we move on. Life is hard here, but giving up is even harder, and it's not really an option. So we go forward,

to the next test, the next lesson. Along the way, we look for hope and laughter and comfort where there is little, and make our own where there is none.

As class finishes, wooden chairs scrape across the floor again as the 46
students stand up to leave with their tests. I too move to the door, but accidentally step on Matthew's foot.

"Oh, sorry," I say.   47
"It's cool," he says.   48
"Where did you learn that?" I ask.   49
He looks at me and smiles.   50
"You."   51

Loyal to teacher

Strong Bond.

It's frustrating to teach them.   2003

QUESTIONS FOR DISCUSSION

Content

a. What is the author's purpose?
b. What is his thesis? In what way does his frustration over the test results contribute to developing that thesis?
c. According to Bures, what will happen to most of his students once they leave school? Will they ever complete their educations?
d. What conflict does Bures mention in paragraphs 35 and 36? How is this conflict related to his thesis?
e. Which days "were the best days of all" for Bures? Why were they so good?
f. Why is this a "test day" for both the students and the teacher?

Strategy and Style

g. Where in this essay does Bures use description? Where does he use illustration?
h. What other methods of development does he use?
i. How would you describe the author's tone?
j. Where does Bures use figurative language?
k. What is the effect of the author's quoting directly from the students? Should he have corrected their spelling, grammar, and word choice before telling us what they wrote?

ENGAGING THE TEXT

a. Write a short paragraph in which you explain Bures's attitude toward his students.

b. Summarize some of the obstacles the students are faced with as they attempt to meet the requirements for Form III as set by the Ministry of Education.

SUGGESTIONS FOR SUSTAINED WRITING

a. Have you ever held a job in which you felt both the frustration and the satisfaction that Bures discusses in this essay about his teaching English in Tanzania? Write an essay that uses a variety of methods of development—perhaps narration, description, illustration, and cause/effect—to explain what you went through and to evaluate the experience.

b. Read Malcolm X's essay "Coming to an Awareness of Language" (Chapter 1). It, too, is about learning about language, but it is very different from "Test Day." Contrast Bures's essay with Malcolm X's in terms of purpose, thesis, and tone. Then explain what you have learned about education from each essay.

c. Using the Internet or print sources, write an essay in which you discuss education, medical care, nutrition, housing, or human rights in any third-world country. Like Bures, you may wish to write about Tanzania, but Brazil, Haiti, Guatemala, Sudan, Rawanda, the Dominican Republic, Afghanistan, and Somalia—among many others—might make good choices as well.

READ MORE

Bures and His Works

Bures, Frank. "From Civil War to the Drug War: East African Immigrants Are Risking Prison for a Taste of Home" (http://www.motherjones .com/news/outfront/2001/11/khat.html): *Article written for* Mother Jones Online.

Bures, Frank. "Making Bombs in Zanzibar" (http://www.salon.com/travel/ feature/1999/12/08/zanzibar/index.html): *An article on* Salon.com.

"Frank Bures" (http://www.frankbures.com): *Bures's personal web page, with links to samples of his writing.*

Education in the "Third World"

Chaudhry, Lakshmi. "First-Rate Ed for Third World" (http://wired-vig .wired.com/news/culture/0,1284,21434,00.html): *Article written for* Wired.

Nestvogel, Renate. "School Education in "Third-World" Countries: Dream or Trauma?" (http://www.waxmann.com/fileadmin/media/zusatztexte/postlethwaite/nestvoge.pdf).

Superman and Me

Sherman Alexie

The writer, filmmaker, and occasional stand-up comic Sherman Alexie (b. 1966) grew up on the Spokane Indian Reservation in Washington State. From the moment he could hold a book, he was a reader and as he progressed through the reservation school, he soon realized that he needed to go off the reservation for further education. He chose to go to nearby Reardan High School, where, according to his website, he "was the only Indian, except for the school mascot." After graduating from high school, he studied at Gonzaga University and then at Washington State University, where he earned a BA in American Studies. While still in college, Alexie began writing and quickly made writing his career. A prolific writer in several genres, Alexie has published several collections of poetry and stories, as well as novels. His most well known books are the short story collection The Lone Ranger and Tonto Fistfight in Heaven *(1993), the novel* Reservation Blues *(1995), and the young-adult novel* The Absolutely True Diary of a Part-time Indian *(2007). Many readers might know of Alexie via his films* Smoke Signals *(1998), which was based on a story from* The Lone Ranger *and for which Alexie co-wrote the screenplay, or* The Business of Fancydancing *(2002), based on his 1991 poetry collection of the same title and which Alexie wrote and directed. From 2003 to 2009, he wrote essays for a Seattle-based alternative newspaper,* The Stranger, *and he has taught creative writing, notably as Artist in Residence at the University of Washington in 2004, 2006, and 2008.*

"Superman and Me" first appeared in the Los Angeles Times *in 1998 as part of a series on reading that also included articles from J.D. McClatchy, Robert Pinsky, Mona Simpson, and Ted Kooser. The essay shows how reading has the power to change the direction of readers' lives and makes a personal appeal for encouraging children to read.*

I learned to read with a Superman comic book. Simple enough, I suppose. I cannot recall which particular Superman comic book I read, nor can I remember which villain he fought in that issue. I cannot remember the plot, nor the means by which I obtained the comic book. What I can remember is this: I was 3 years old, a Spokane Indian boy living with his family on the Spokane Indian Reservation in eastern Washington state. We were poor by most standards, but one of my parents usually managed to find some minimum-wage job or another, which made us middleclass by reservation standards. I had a brother and three sisters. We lived on a combination of irregular paychecks, hope, fear and government surplus food.

My father, who is one of the few Indians who went to Catholic school on purpose, was an avid reader of westerns, spy thrillers, murder mysteries, gangster epics, basketball player biographies and anything else he could find. He bought his books by the pound at Dutch's Pawn Shop, Goodwill, Salvation Army and Value Village. When he had extra money, he bought new novels at supermarkets, convenience stores and hospital gift shops. Our house was filled with books. They were stacked in crazy piles in the bathroom, bedrooms and living room. In a fit of unemployment-inspired creative energy, my father built a set of book-shelves and soon filled them with a random assortment of books about the Kennedy assassination, Watergate, the Vietnam War and the entire 23-book series of the Apache westerns. My father loved books, and since I loved my father with an aching devotion, I decided to love books as well.

3   I can remember picking up my father's books before I could read. The words themselves were mostly foreign, but I still remember the exact moment when I first understood, with a sudden clarity, the purpose of a paragraph. I didn't have the vocabulary to say "paragraph," but I realized that a paragraph was a fence that held words. The words inside a para-graph worked together for a common purpose. They had some specific rea-son for being inside the same fence. This knowledge delighted me. I began to think of everything in terms of paragraphs. Our reservation was a small paragraph within the United States. My family's house was a paragraph, distinct from the other paragraphs of the LeBrets to the north, the Fords to our south and the Tribal School to the west. Inside our house, each family member existed as a separate paragraph but still had genetics and common experiences to link us. Now, using this logic, I can see my changed family as an essay of seven paragraphs: mother, father, older brother, the deceased sister, my younger twin sisters and our adopted little brother.

4   At the same time I was seeing the world in paragraphs, I also picked up that Superman comic book. Each panel, complete with picture, dialogue and narrative was a three-dimensional paragraph. In one panel, Superman breaks through a door. His suit is red, blue and yellow. The brown door shatters into many pieces. I look at the narrative above the picture. I cannot read the words, but I assume it tells me that "Superman is breaking down the door." Aloud, I pretend to read the words and say, "Superman is break-ing down the door." Words, dialogue, also float out of Superman's mouth. Because he is breaking down the door, I assume he says, "I am breaking down the door." Once again, I pretend to read the words and say aloud, "I am breaking down the door" In this way, I learned to read.

5   This might be an interesting story all by itself. A little Indian boy teaches himself to read at an early age and advances quickly. He reads "Grapes of Wrath" in kindergarten when other children are struggling through "Dick and Jane." If he'd been anything but an Indian boy liv-ing on the reservation, he might have been called a prodigy. But he is an Indian boy living on the reservation and is simply an oddity. He grows into a man who often speaks of his childhood in the third person, as if it

will somehow dull the pain and make him sound more modest about his talents.

A smart Indian is a dangerous person, widely feared and ridiculed 6 by Indians and non-Indians alike. I fought with my classmates on a daily basis. They wanted me to stay quiet when the non-Indian teacher asked for answers, for volunteers, for help. We were Indian children who were expected to be stupid. Most lived up to those expectations inside the classroom but subverted them on the outside. They struggled with basic reading in school but could remember how to sing a few dozen powwow songs. They were monosyllabic in front of their non-Indian teachers but could tell complicated stories and jokes at the dinner table. They submissively ducked their heads when confronted by a non-Indian adult but would slug it out with the Indian bully who was 10 years older. As Indian children, we were expected to fail in the non-Indian world. Those who failed were ceremonially accepted by other Indians and appropriately pitied by non-Indians.

I refused to fail. I was smart. I was arrogant. I was lucky. I read books 7 late into the night, until I could barely keep my eyes open. I read books at recess, then during lunch, and in the few minutes left after I had finished my classroom assignments. I read books in the car when my family traveled to powwows or basketball games. In shopping malls, I ran to the bookstores and read bits and pieces of as many books as I could. I read the books my father brought home from the pawnshops and secondhand. I read the books I borrowed from the library. I read the backs of cereal boxes. I read the newspaper. I read the bulletins posted on the walls of the school, the clinic, the tribal offices, the post office. I read junk mail. I read auto-repair manuals. I read magazines. I read anything that had words and paragraphs. I read with equal parts joy and desperation. I loved those books, but I also knew that love had only one purpose. I was trying to save my life.

Despite all the books I read, I am still surprised I became a writer. I 8 was going to be a pediatrician. These days, I write novels, short stories, and poems. I visit schools and teach creative writing to Indian kids. In all my years in the reservation school system, I was never taught how to write poetry, short stories or novels. I was certainly never taught that Indians wrote poetry, short stories and novels. Writing was something beyond Indians. I cannot recall a single time that a guest teacher visited the reservation. There must have been visiting teachers. Who were they? Where are they now? Do they exist? I visit the schools as often as possible. The Indian kids crowd the classroom. Many are writing their own poems, short stories and novels. They have read my books. They have read many other books. They look at me with bright eyes and arrogant wonder. They are trying to save their lives. Then there are the sullen and already defeated Indian kids who sit in the back rows and ignore me with theatrical precision. The pages of their notebooks are empty. They carry neither pencil nor pen. They stare out the window. They refuse and resist. "Books," I say to them. "Books," I say. I throw my weight against their locked doors. The door holds. I am smart. I am arrogant. I am lucky. I am trying to save our lives.

1998

QUESTIONS FOR DISCUSSION

Content

a. How does Alexie define "paragraph"? What analogies does he make between paragraphs and things in his life?
b. According to Alexie, why did he read so much as a child?
c. What is Alexie's relationship to reading? What does reading do for him, and why does he want to pass on his love of reading to the children at reservation schools?
d. "A smart Indian is a dangerous person" Alexie writes in paragraph 6. What might Alexie mean here?
e. Why would Alexie's classmates not want him to show his intelligence?
f. How does Alexie see himself as partnered with Superman?

Strategy and Style

g. What rhetorical strategies are used in this essay?
h. How is a paragraph analogous to a fence, a house, a reservation?
i. Why might Alexie have contrasted the words "prodigy" and "oddity" (paragraph 5)? What does context have to do with the meaning of words?
j. What is the effect of the short sentences and staccato style in some paragraphs, such as paragraph 7?
k. As a narrative, Alexie is telling the story of his childhood, "saved" by Superman. Where will Alexie's story go next? What is needed for a "happy ending"?

ENGAGING THE TEXT

a. As you reread Alexie's essay, respond in writing to each paragraph by relating something in that paragraph to your own life.
b. In short narrative, recall how you learned how to read. What is your first memory of reading? What were the first books you read? Were your experiences negative or positive, and why?

SUGGESTIONS FOR SUSTAINED WRITING

a. Find a series of images, from your own photos, from the Internet, or from magazines and arrange them into a story strip that reflects your life, more or less. Create a narrative based on the images.
b. Write an essay in which you compare Sherman Alexie's essay to Rebecca Brown's "Extreme Reading" (Chapter 8). Discuss the connections both writers make between reading and life, particularly how reading helped them transform their lives as children and heal their lives as adults.
c. Research reading programs in the United States. Choosing one program, write a report about the program's history and discuss its success.

READ MORE

Alexie and His Works

"ShermanAlexie.com" (http://www.fallsapart.com/): *Alexie's official website, with links to every one of his books and to events in which he is featured.*

"Sherman Alexie" (http://www.poets.org/poet.php/prmPID/395): *Selected poems on the Academy of American Poets website.*

"Sherman Alexie" (http://www.poetryfoundation.org/bio/sherman-alexie): *Selected poems on the Poetry Foundation website.*

"Author Archive: Sherman Alexie" (http://www.thestranger.com/seattle/Author?oid=14116): *Links to articles written between 2003 and 2009 by Alexie for the Seattle-based newspaper* The Stranger.

Reading and Reservation Schools

"Reservation Schools Preserve Cultures, Boost Academics" (http://www.educationworld.com/a_issues/schools/schools010.shtml): *Article on the Education World website discussing the positive features of reservation schools.*

"On the Reservation and Off, Schools See a Changing Tide" (http://www.nytimes.com/2008/05/25/education/25hardin.html): *New York Times article discussing problems facing Indian Reservation Schools.*

"U.S. Department of the Interior: Bureau of Indian Affairs" (http://www.bia.gov/) and "U.S. Department of the Interior: Bureau of Indian Education" (http://www.bie.edu/): *United States government websites with links to many related sources.*

Permissions Acknowledgments

Ackerman, Diane. "Where Fall Color Comes From" from *A Natural History of the Senses* by Diane Ackerman, copyright © 1990 by Diane Ackerman. Used by permission of Random House, Inc.

Alexie, Sherman. "Superman and Me" originally published in the *Los Angeles Times,* April 19, 1998, as part of a series called "The Joy of Reading and Writing."

Angelou, Maya. "Grandmother's Victory," copyright © 1969 and renewed 1997 by Maya Angelou, from *I Know Why the Caged Bird Sings* by Maya Angelou. Used by permission of Random House, Inc.

Baldwin, James. "Fifth Avenue, Uptown: A Letter from Harlem" by James Baldwin. Originally published in *Esquire*. Copyright © 1960 by James Baldwin. Copyright renewed. Collected in *Nobody Knows My Name*, published by Vintage Books. Reprinted by arrangement with the James Baldwin Estate.

Blodget, Henry. "China's Biggest Gamble: Can It Have Capitalism without Democracy? A Prediction." Copyright © 2008 by *The Washington Post*.

Brady, Judith. "Why I Want a Wife." Copyright © 1970 by Judith Brady. Reprinted by permission of the author.

Britt, Suzanne. "Neat People vs. Sloppy People" from *Show and Tell* by Suzanne Britt. Copyright © 1982 by Suzanne Britt. Reprinted by permission of the author.

Brown, Rebecca. "Extreme Reading" from *American Romances: Essays by Rebecca Brown* by Rebecca Brown. San Francisco: City Lights Books, 2009.

Bures, Frank. "Test Day" by Frank Bures as appeared in *World Hum,* September 10, 2003. Reprinted by permission of Frank Bures.

Byers, Michael. "Monuments to Our Better Nature" by Michael Byers. Originally appeared in *Preservation,* January/February 2003. Reprinted by permission of Michael Byers.

Casey, Susan. "Our Oceans Are Turning into Plastic . . . Are We?" Copyright © 2007 by *Best Life Magazine*.

Catton, Bruce. "Grant and Lee: A Study in Contrasts" from *The American Story* by Bruce Catton. Copyright U.S. Capitol Historical Society; all rights reserved. Reprinted by permission.

Cisneros, Sandra. "Only Daughter," copyright © 1990 by Sandra Cisneros. First published in *Glamour*, November 1990. Reprinted by permission of Susan Bergholz Literary Services, New York. All rights reserved.

Cofer, Judith Ortiz. "A Partial Remembrance of a Puerto Rican Childhood" by Judith Ortiz Cofer is reprinted with permission from the publisher of *Silent Dancing: A Partial Remembrance of a Puerto Rican Childhood* (Houston: Arte Publico Press—University of Houston, 1990).

Index